Across the Empty Sky

ACROSS THE EMPTY SKY

*A Biography of Patrick Hawk,
Catholic Priest and Zen Master*

Helen Amerongen

ISBN: 979-8-9866014-2-7

Only in silence the word,
only in dark the light,
only in dying life;
bright the hawk's flight
on the empty sky.

Ursula K. LeGuin
The Wizard of Earthsea

To Julia and Dave

Contents

Preface

"Of course, it'll all be fiction," Pat Hawk said when we first discussed documenting his life story. The initial idea was that I would record the details of his life as an oral history, to be a resource for whoever would write the larger history of Zen and Christianity, or the trajectory of Zen in America, or the sometimes rocky relationship of Zen in the West with its Japanese forebears. But the project that began as a series of recorded interviews with Pat focusing on his recollections and vital statistics broadened to a much wider enterprise including examining extensive correspondence, listening to dozens of Pat's talks, sifting through file folders of his personal papers, traveling to places of significance, exploring contemporary sociopolitical contexts, interviewing Pat's family members, classmates, colleagues, students and friends… in short, all the stock-in-trade of biography.

In declaring that the story would be fiction, Pat was not suggesting it would be cut from the whole cloth of imagination. Rather he was expressing a fundamental truth of language, that what is put in words is not the thing itself. In the star-filled sky we identify constellations. The naming — of Orion, of Centaurus — predisposes the eye to see these familiar forms, which in turn orient a person in time and space, even as they introduce limits. Pat understood both the utility and the limitation of language and ideas, and fruit of his many years of Zen and contemplative* practice, saw beyond them to undescribable reality.

Pat Hawk was a Catholic priest and Zen Master whose example and guidance positively altered the lives of a few hundred students and through them, that of countless others. I worked with him from 1997 until his death in 2012. As with so many people, from my first one-on-one encounter, which lasted all of about ten minutes, I saw that this ordinary, unassuming man offered something vital. His absolute presence, his spare words, delivered a clarity I had never encountered. As I left that first meeting, grateful tears welled up, that such a person existed and that he made himself accessible. Thereafter I took every opportunity, within the limits of family and full-time job, to work with him.

In a recollection included in a Festschrift scrapbook assembled for Pat's 65th birthday, Stephen Slottow wrote, "It was Robert Todd who told me about Pat

---

* Contemplative practice will be used throughout to refer to the practice of wordless prayer or meditation as seen for example among the medieval mystics. Zen is a movement within Buddhism that emphasizes meditation practice including *zazen*: sitting in silence, usually on a cushion or chair, often for extended periods.

Hawk. He said that Pat hardly said anything, had no charisma, was minimal, dry, and understated. In fact, much like myself, he said." It's a good snapshot. In any gathering, Pat tended to be on the outskirts, keeping to himself, perhaps smoking a cigarette. He was of slight build and unremarkable looks. In person he exuded neither compassion nor kindness, yet in his presence there was the sense that no sin was alien, none unabsolved. He was an alcoholic, though with long periods in recovery including the last fifteen years of his life. In *dokusan** he neither praised nor criticized. The absence of evaluation in Pat's feedback could be disconcerting for many raised on praise and criticism, and whose orientation in the world was to aim for one and away from the other. Yet the disorientation of Pat's non-judgment could be life-giving. It made the world bigger and kinder. It was not: "Good job, you're doing well." There was simply the unspoken, palpable "Here" of complete attention.

At the same time, Pat was master of the terse, pointed instruction. So penetrating and so apt were his offerings in dokusan that I, though skeptical by nature as well as by profession, looked at him earnestly one day and asked in all seriousness if he could read my mind. He didn't laugh at the question — perhaps he'd been asked it by others — but he shook his head gently, "No."

By nature both taciturn and private, Pat rarely said anything about himself in any setting. One could experience a deep connection in dokusan yet know practically nothing about the man personally. His impact on individual lives was profound. Naturally, people wanted to know "how the roshi† ties his shoes."

In December 2006, having recently read *Crooked Cucumber,* David Chadwick's biography of Shunryu Suzuki,[1] I suggested to Pat that it might be good to have someone gather the many intersecting stories of people and events to which his work had been an important contributor. I was surprised when instead of shrugging dismissively, he said, "Well, there's a project!" In a follow-up conversation, I pointed out that if such a project were undertaken, he would have to be interviewed about his life. Confident that this would turn him against the whole idea, I was stunned when he said, "Well, you could interview me." I hurried to purchase a digital voice recorder before he got cold feet.

In January 2007, we began meeting about twice monthly in his office. Over the course of six months he recounted his life from the beginning, providing scant facts and little commentary. To add flesh to the skeletal story I found ways to spiral back over the territory, looking at his photo albums together, talking about books he'd read at various stages, extracting questions from listening to tapes of

---

* Private meeting between Zen student and teacher.

† Roshi: (Japanese) venerable teacher; an honorific often given to a Zen master.

his talks. At some point a few years into our work together he mentioned "this biography of me that you're doing," and I began to look back on the stories that had accumulated with an eye to filling gaps and better understanding events. At times during the early interviews he was in obvious pain from a ureteral stent, placed because of a large kidney stone that had been resistant to various treatments. He sometimes stopped mid-sentence to catch his breath and grip his side. More than once I suggested we quit and he shook his head, no, and said he appreciated the distraction.

In our conversations Pat could be open or not, unpredictably. Over time he became more confiding, but I never knew when a question would suddenly cause a shadow to cross his face and his reticence to return. Even with something he himself brought up, he might abruptly seem to think he was getting into deep water and clam up. It made me cautious with questions, seeking to draw him out without probing anything too private. And what constituted too private was not always predictable — some days almost anything. Other days he would spontaneously share something I wouldn't have dared ask about. Ever-present alongside my interest in learning as much as I could of Pat's life story was the relationship, which I wouldn't risk jeopardizing for any prize outside of it.

With Pat's acquiescence, I expanded the scope of information-gathering and sought opportunities to interview as many people as I could who knew him. Over the many years of this project, I spoke with more than 100 people including students, colleagues, friends and family. About half of these conversations were recorded interviews. Where conversations were not recorded, I hurried to write down whatever was said as near verbatim as I could as soon as possible after the encounter.

Pat's personal history interweaves significantly with a period in the history of the Diamond Sangha and therefore of Zen in the West. My main sources for this aspect include Pat's recollections and personal papers — mainly his notes from teachers' meetings and related correspondence — as well as correspondence obtained from the Robert Baker Aitken Papers at the University of Hawaii Manoa. In selecting from these materials, I have focused on Pat's perspective and involvement — the larger history of which this is a part remains to be told. My inclusion of some conversations and events from within the Diamond Sangha Teachers' Circle, mainly informed by Pat's personal records, has centered on providing context relevant to Pat's life.

From the outset I was aware of occasional conflicts revolving around Pat, and as I interviewed people, I became aware of others. It is evident to anyone paying attention in Zen circles or Catholic congregations of religious* that hot-house environments of spiritual practice are no refuge from difficult people. There is the Zen aphorism: "Before enlightenment: chop wood, carry water. After enlightenment: chop wood, carry water." In a Q&A once, when Pat was asked about misbehaving Zen teachers — all that diligent practice and still these people — he paraphrased the aphorism to something like, "If before enlightenment, a jackass, after enlightenment, a jackass."

In his conversations with Brother David Steindl-Rast, published as *The Ground We Share,* Robert Aitken said, "My most promising students have felt an imperative to power."[2] No doubt, when there are promising students together, that imperative can lead to conflict. There was plenty of conflict in Pat's Zen world and in his Catholic world. Some of this he observed from a safe distance, in which case he might even be wryly amused. Other times he himself was involved, in which case he tended to be tight-lipped.

A few of Pat's longtime students cautioned me that I should leave out the difficult stories, not risk opening old wounds. "You're not going to talk about X are you!?" Others encouraged reporting "warts and all." Early in our work on this project, I said to Pat that I was not interested in doing a whitewash. He seemed to agree. My sense is that drawing a heavy curtain over difficult facts creates darkness. Although I've necessarily sifted data based on what I felt would best give a flavor of personalities and events, I have not used a moral axis as a yardstick in selecting what to include. As Pat would say, every person is alright down to the very bottom.

There are no villains in this story and also no saints, unless we recognize that among the saints — consider Augustine of Hippo, Teresa of Avila, Alphonsus of Liguori, to name a few — none were without fault, nor would any claim such. Far from it. And as Stuart Lachs has amply pointed out,[3] hagiography serves no one and may in fact sow seeds of pathology in teacher-student relationships. The idealization of authority in Zen, and I would add in the Catholic Church, is destructive to its participants. Witness the many sex scandals born of exploitation of the power dynamic within the intense, intimate student-teacher encounter. As Zen students we want to worship the master — that return to childhood to which Sam Harris has referred[4] — but it does not allow us to grow up.

This is a love story, not in the sense of love as perfect and unfaltering devotion, but rather in the messy, human sense of love as action, intention, injury,

---

* Religious in this context refers to a person who has taken religious vows, i.e. of poverty, chastity and obedience. A co-religious is a person in the same congregation or order. A religious congregation is a type of Catholic institute of priests or nuns.

forgiveness — challenge. The practice environment around Pat was vital. It saved lives, not necessarily in the direct sense of averting suicide, though there could be that too, but in the sense of providing the soil in which life could become authentic and free. That very vitality could bring forth conflict: something akin to a mother bear protecting her cubs, a terrible energy sometimes appears, and it too is grist for practice.

Pat Hawk was a man living in a private, sometimes tortured, inner world who was the midwife of redemption for many lives. In Pat's one-on-one meetings, whether dokusan with his Zen students or interviews with his contemplative students — often the same people doing both — he gave complete, unconditional attention. It was not friendly, and it was not not friendly. It was not sexual, and it was not not sexual. It was a boundless intimacy, opening a window to unmediated reality. That Pat was fallible, sometimes depressed, sometimes maddening — in so many respects an ordinary man — is part of the inspiration that is his life.

I undertook this project because Pat had a profound effect on my life, yet I knew almost nothing about him. I saw myself looking up to him as to an archetypal giant and felt a need to see him on the ground, so to speak. I wanted to know this person. As I said to him one day, I'm tired of the Wizard of Oz, I want to see the man behind the curtain. (He said, "Good luck.") From conversations with others who worked with him, I know that my interest was widely shared.

Ramón Y Cajal, pioneer of neuroscience, once said, "Reality overflows every concise phrase as liquid poured into a tiny cup."[5] No doubt the image applies to any biography. The story presented here, though distilled from a bewildering amount of information gathered from widely diverse sources, can give only an incomplete and inevitably slanted view of the life itself. Yet I hope that those who knew Pat will recognize him in these pages, and that others can meet him here. This is a man I would like you to know.

PATRICK HAWK
SHIN'UN SEISHŌ DAI ŌSHO

1

Early Years

In late April 2012, as the plane swung out over the Mississippi River, tilting into a descent toward Lambert International Airport, Granite City appeared below, uncannily familiar. Where the Mississippi curves around St. Louis, Missouri, the city's great steel arch visible from the air, Granite City, population under 30,000, lies on the Illinois side of the river, on the delta-like shelf formed from thousands of years of Mississippi highs and lows depositing silt. This flood plain is the great American Bottom, about ten miles wide in the north, narrowing toward the south, bounded on the east by the limestone bluffs that rise 200 to 300 feet to the prairie that covers most of Illinois.

Here is some of the most fertile soil on the planet. It is ironic that most of this rich land has been put to industrial rather than agricultural use since the late 1800s. Granite City began as a planned community, established on 3,500 acres of farmland to support a steel mill stamping works for the production of speckled enameled kitchen utensils, called graniteware, the company town being named after the ware — there is no actual granite in the area. The success of the graniteware industry in the late 1800s and early 1900s attracted related industries bringing jobs and tall stacks belching dirty smoke, still in 2012 inspiring the nickname Gritty Granite. When Edwin Patrick Hawk was born there in 1942 the town's factories were putting out smoke for the war effort, emerging from being one of the American towns hardest hit by the Great Depression.

Looking down from the plane, I orient myself to landmarks. There is the improbably shaped Horseshoe Lake, its deep curve carved by the circular currents of the depositing river that formed the Bottom. Seeing the familiar layout of Granite City streets is like "coming home to a place I've never been before." The actual landscape is exactly the one I have studied with Pat time and again in his Tucson office as Google Maps helped locate the significant places of his childhood. Wilson Park stands out, and from there I easily locate Sacred Heart School and Church, the streets of Pat's childhood home, his maternal grandparents' place — all within a few blocks of each other. About a mile away there is the conspicuous industrial area, the railroad yard, the small downtown, and Gateway Regional Hospital, formerly St. Elizabeth's, where Pat was born and where both his parents and his only sister died.

By the time we land and I have my luggage and a rental car it's mid-afternoon, too late to make it through St. Louis traffic and down to Liguori in time to visit Pat at St. Clement Health Care Center, where he has been in hospice for a week. They eat supper early, and the nurse I'd spoken to on the phone didn't sound keen about evening visitors. Instead, I head to the St. Louis Public Library to spend some time with their microfiche archive of the *St. Louis Post Dispatch*, looking up headlines and news stories on important dates for the Hawk family, to take in the atmosphere that would have come in with the news. I look up Pat's parents' wedding day, the bombing of Pearl Harbor, headlines on Pat's birth date, and on the day Pat left home at 13 to enter the seminary. The family subscribed to the *St. Louis Post Dispatch*. "Of course," Pat said, "the Democratic paper." They also got the Granite City *Press Record*. "Everyone in Granite City got the *Press Record*."

Parents

Ed Hawk and Elnora Delmar were married in Granite City on June 7, 1941. The war overseas was ominously threatening to become America's war, and Illinois communities were organizing for civilian defense with block captains, air raid wardens and first aid facilities. A reserve militia was being developed in anticipation of the National Guard being called away.[6] Less than two weeks before the wedding, President Roosevelt escalated what had been a limited national emergency to an unlimited national emergency, declaring that Hitler was after world domination and would come after the Western Hemisphere if not checked in Europe. The Nazis were in possession of the greater part of Europe and had made inroads into North Africa. FDR argued against the isolationism by which many Americans disowned the conflict and hoped to stay out of the war.

That very week of the wedding, the *Granite City Press Record* confirmed that local manufacturers would be turned toward munitions production, the news a double-edged sword, cutting unemployment while increasing unease. Ed and all his brothers had registered for the draft the previous autumn following the Selective Service Act of 1940, the first peacetime conscription in United States history. They were signed up for a year and could be called up for training at any time determined by lottery.

The same issue of the *Press Record* carried a double column and photo on the Societies page reporting Ed and Elnora's wedding. They were married at Sacred Heart Church by Father Mike Costello. A longtime friend of the family, Costello would be a steady presence in Pat's life until he went into the seminary. The wedding breakfast for about 50 guests, mostly family on Elnora's side, was at the Iowa Street home of her parents a few blocks from the church, after which the newlyweds left for a week-long honeymoon in the Ozarks. With America stepping up production of materiel to ship to the allies, Ed got a job with General Steel Castings Company. Elnora worked at the foundry as a billing clerk. Between the two of them, they were able to put a down payment on a small house on Ralph Street in the Sacred Heart neighborhood. They happily set up housekeeping there.

They were a study in opposites attracting. Ed was taciturn, his usual silence belying a sentimentality that showed in a teary eye when an event or story moved him. He enjoyed woodworking and was often to be found in his basement workshop while Elnora did the cooking and cleaning. He would listen in wordless amusement to Elnora's cheerful stories and if he found something very funny, shake with silent laughter. Elnora was chatty to a fault, quick to laugh and given to light mockery, including at her own foibles. She was dyed-in-the-wool Catholic, faithful to the core, though as in so many cradle Catholics, not conspicuously pious. Bright and capable, she accomplished tasks with ease, readily juggling work outside the home, which she usually had, with the homemaking that she understood as her wifely role.

As their first summer together deepened, they were hopeful that Ed's year of being on the draft rolls would pass without him being taken away for training. Then in August, the period of conscription was increased to two years. Inevitably, Ed's number was called and he headed to a training camp in Arkansas. Suddenly the war news was deeply personal.

On December 19, 1941, in the wake of Pearl Harbor, the Selective Service extended the term of conscription to six months after the war ended and age limits up to 64, with those 18-45 immediately liable for induction. It meant that even Elnora's father, Archie Delmar, was drafted. With Ed, his brothers and his brothers-in-law all called away, Elnora rented out the Ralph Street house and moved back to her parents' place. There was a shortage of accommodation in Granite City because of the influx of workers to support war manufacturing, so finding renters was easy.

Elnora was the third of five daughters born to Archie and Elnora Delmar. Archie worked for years as a train switchman and helped his sons-in-law, spouses of Elnora's older sisters, through the '30s by getting them jobs on the railroad. They were a sociable family, Catholic, and closely involved with Sacred Heart

Parish. The girls had lots of fun together growing up. During the war, with their men away, not only Elnora but also her sister Patsy moved home with their parents and youngest sister Mona, still a teenager. Both women and their mother worked war jobs, Elnora in one of the Granite City factories inspecting tanks for sand holes needing to be patched.

Ed was given a weekend leave the following February, which he and Elnora spent in accommodations near where he was stationed. His sergeant, looking for him one morning, knocked and poked his head into their room, finding the two of them still in bed. Indoctrinated by then into army protocol, Ed sat up abruptly and saluted. They laughed about it for years. Nine months from that weekend, on November 18, 1942, Pat was born.

Pat saw his father only twice during his first three years. The first time was when Elnora traveled with him by train to spend a weekend leave with Ed near the base. She remembered all her life the experience of being on the south side of the Mason-Dixon Line, because of an incident at the train station in Arkansas. She and Ed had had their visit and she was at the station to catch a train back to Illinois. A woman, noticing her struggling with baggage and baby, offered assistance. Elnora handed Pat over to her and they walked along together until they arrived at the station building. Elnora indicated that she was going into a waiting room — not noticing or not caring that it was occupied by blacks. The woman handed Pat back hastily, saying, "I can't go in there!" The personal encounter with Jim Crow left Elnora appalled.

Pat and his father met a second time when Ed was allowed home for a few days' leave before he was sent overseas late in the war. After a short visit, he headed to New York to catch a boat for France. While in New York, he recorded a greeting cut onto a vinyl record that he mailed to Elnora and Pat. There were booths for making the recordings down near the docks and all the soldiers were doing it. He boarded a ship to Europe, likely not long after Normandy. A cousin was among those who stormed the beaches and was killed on June 6, 1944. Ed's age and slight build may have saved him from being sent earlier. As it was he did not see active combat, his platoon landing in France after the German occupation had been pushed back. Pat's understanding was that his father was assigned to rail-car maintenance and other mechanical jobs similar to his work in Granite City.

During those war years, Pat was looked after during the day by his Aunt Mona while his mother, his Aunt Patsy and his grandmother went to work, going on foot and staying close to home on weekends because of gas and rubber rationing. They learned creative ways to put meals on the table with what ingredients they could get. They were energetic and hopeful even while they listened to the news and worried.

In the evenings and on days off, all the women attended to Pat. When he was almost a year old, Nora was born to his Aunt Patsy, and the women looked after both infants in adjacent cribs. For Pat, it meant another adoring female in his entourage. Once he'd learned to talk, he would wake up from his nap and call out, "Mommy, Mona… or whoever's there…" He amused them all. One day he asked his Aunt Mona, "Is my mommy at work?" "Yes." "Is my Daddy in France?" "Yes." "Well, I'm in a heck of a fix!" He sometimes — whether out of boredom or jealousy — threw his bottle at Nora. Notwithstanding, the two became each other's closest friend until Pat went to the seminary.

When Pat was wakeful at night, his mother took him to bed with her — a comfort for her as much as for him. It was an all-loving world that cradled Pat in those early years. For the remainder of the war and for several months beyond until Ed was discharged from the army, he was the crown prince in this very female home front.

After the war

Following V-E Day, Elnora had high hopes of Ed returning by the end of summer, but V-J Day came and went, leaves turned from green to gold and they began to wonder if he would be home for Christmas. Around the time Pat turned three, in November 1945, Ed came back. Even before he was sent overseas, the *St. Louis Post Dispatch* began to carry stories of the returning soldier — what to expect, what to do, what not to ask. Re-integration would be a challenge, perhaps most of all for Pat.

The family moved back into the Ralph Street house, father and son beginning to take stock of each other. By this time, Pat was used to clambering into his mother's bed any night he felt like it. Now here was this stranger. "Who's this?" he would say. "That's your Daddy!" "Oh… Hi Daddy." Having lived for three years in a blissful world in which his mother had eyes only for him, like thousands of other war babies, he had to face the Oedipal struggle without the mitigating influence of a loving bond with his father. It was the first deep wound. It felt like a betrayal, and betrayal became a lens through which Pat would perceive loss thereafter. In time he and his father developed a mutual respect, but the relationship never grew beyond the superficial and distant.

Still adjusting to being in his own room, Pat was soon moved back in with his parents so that his bedroom could be given to his grandmother. His father's mother, née Nora Quinn, long-suffering and never very strong, was diagnosed with stomach cancer. Nora's husband, Pat's grandfather, James Elbert Hawk, was born the first of six children on a farm near Winchester, Illinois, 40 miles north of Granite City. In a photograph of his family taken when James was in his late teens he is dressed in jacket, vest and tie neatly put together with a pin on his lapel, full hair combed straight back with a bit of a wave, sensitive and pleasant looking. The women are all attractive in lacy, high-collared dresses, each with their hair up and tied with large ribbons. There's a photo of James alone taken at the same time, chiseled features framing a neutral gaze as he poses seated, the open book in his hands adding to an impression of sensitive intelligence. He was perhaps unsuited to the rough and heavy work of farm life. For whatever reason, he left the farm at 17, working at various town jobs, his choice interrupting the succession of Hawks that generation after generation had farmed in Illinois since before statehood. In his early twenties, James courted Nora Quinn, daughter of devout Irish Catholic immigrants living in Winchester, and they married in 1906. They had five sons, the third of which, Edwin, would be Pat's father.

James worked variously as a house painter, a sawmill hand, a cotton gin manager. The family moved around from Illinois to Missouri to Colorado, where their youngest son Leo died when he was four years old. Moving back to Illinois, they settled in Granite City and managed to buy a house on Hodges Street in the blue-collar neighborhood around Sacred Heart Church. James drank heavily, often heading off across the railway tracks to a rundown shack where lived a buddy with whom he would drink the night away until, stumbling home one dark night in late November 1941, he was struck and killed by a truck.

Two of Pat's three uncles also drank. Pat's Uncle Bob and his family lived with their mother Nora in the Hodges Street house after James was killed. Strangely, Bob had taken to drinking with the same buddy his father had hung out with. What with Bob's deepening alcohol dependence and failing marriage, when Pat's grandmother, Nora, became ill with stomach cancer she was not well cared for, so Ed and Elnora took her in. Pat's room became the sick room. His cousins Dave and Barb, children of Bob, were at the Ralph Street place a few times while Nora was bedridden there, and their one memory of those visits is that they had to be very quiet because their grandmother couldn't stand any noise in the house. Father Costello came around regularly from Sacred Heart to bring her communion. She died in December 1946, when Pat was four.

That same year Pat entered kindergarten at Sacred Heart. He was not keen on formal education, and there were days when Elnora would walk him to school and return home only to find him sitting on the front step. Church and school were under the same roof, with classrooms flanking the large chapel in the center. His family walked to Mass every Sunday, to fish frys on Friday evenings, and to various other parish social events. So Pat knew the route and the building well, including the shortcuts home. An indulged child, his parents were amused rather than stern. Pat had a confidence that delighted his mother and that his father tolerated. To his mother, Pat was the dauphin, often as not, she his devoted servant. And in varying degrees, he related to women that way all his life.

Pat's boldness in those early years, especially vis-à-vis the family religion, became legend in the Hawk family such that his sister Mary Ellen, not born until Pat was almost seven and knowing of the stories through lore rather than experience, recounted them easily decades later.

There was the one about walking home from Mass one day. Pat took a rosary out of his pocket and was swinging the crucifix around. His mother chided him. He paused, then started up again. She gave him a look. Uncowed, he called out, "Hang on Jesus! You're going for a ride!" Costello, in his sermons, was apt to go on at length between strategic pauses so that the weight of his words could sink in. He would become rapt with his exposition, rocking back and forth on his heels as he held forth from behind the communion rail. As impatient as any boy, Pat one Sunday took the opportunity of a pause to step into the breach, calling out loudly, "Aaaaaamen!" The good Father took it in stride and wrapped up quickly. The sermons did not get shorter, however, and another time the drone of Father Costello's voice reminded Pat of the auctioneer in the Lucky Strike commercial then airing on the radio. This time at one of Costello's pauses, Pat called out, "SOOOOLD American!"[7] It seems that even from this early age, he felt an authority to speak to the Church in his own authentic voice. His irreverence would appear alongside his sometimes deep reverence throughout most of his life. The irreverent streak left him for a time in elementary school, but he found it again in the seminary.

Though he settled into the school routine, he disliked it. In the early years his teachers found him unpromising. He ignored much of what went on in the classroom, instead staring out the window, a dreamer. It was not until about fifth grade that a school nurse realized he was having difficulty with his eyes and recommended glasses. The difference that made meant he finished eighth grade with an American Legion Award for scholastic achievement.

One day when Pat was in kindergarten, his maternal grandfather, Archie Delmar, still a switchman on the railway, found a stray puppy running along the tracks. He gave him to Pat to have as his own dog, a small white terrier-type. Pat named him Rip after Rip van Winkle because he slept so much. Rip knew he was Pat's dog. He followed him wherever he could and slept on his bed at night. One day he disappeared. As weeks then months went by, they gave up looking for him. Then one afternoon as Pat was playing in the street with some neighbor kids, he saw him at a distance come bounding into view. "Rip!" Dog and boy joyfully reunited. Sixty years later, Pat still remembered details of the street, the angle of the light, and where he was standing when Rip came back.

Pat's grandfather Archie was a fulcrum for the Delmar family. It was he who encouraged gatherings at every holiday — Thanksgiving at one house, Christmas at another, Easter at another. Or sometimes the main course at one house and dessert at another. All five Delmar sisters married and had children, and all those small cousins including Pat sat at their own table. After supper the card tables came out and everyone old enough played canasta. The conviviality of these gatherings is captured in many family photos.

After school, on weekends and all summer long, Pat and his cousin Nora played together. Nora was afraid of her father, an aggressive, unpredictable man. She spent as much time as she could at their grandparents, the Delmars', place on Iowa Street. While still very young, she moved in with them, making it easy to spend liberal amounts of time with Pat, living a few blocks away.

Pat's father Ed was still working for Commonwealth Steel (formerly General Steel Castings Company), now in quality control. They were making steel frames for railroad boxcars, and when the frames were cast, they came out with little test bars on the sides. Ed's job was to cut off the test bars. It was dull, repetitive work. His overseers, recognizing an intelligent man, put Ed into training as a machinist, but he disliked the mental work of slide rules and calculations. He had a different dream, which was to go back to the life of his father's roots. Pat's paternal grandfather, so much in the throes of drink, had made little effort to keep in touch with the Hawk clan up in Winchester, but Ed as an adult had a nostalgia for the farming life that he knew was in his history. Ed wanted that life for his own family, and they were saving up for it.

Rural life, briefly

The death from stomach cancer of Pat's grandmother Nora Hawk restored a certain measure of freedom to Ed and Elnora. At Christmas, Elnora would take Pat into St. Louis to shop and enjoy the Christmas dioramas in department store windows. On Sunday afternoons in the summer, Ed, Elnora and Pat would pile into the old Ford for long drives and a picnic. They sometimes drove up to Winchester to the old Hawk farmstead. Pat remembered visiting his Aunt Nell there, a warm, tough farm woman who seemed to him to be old as the landscape. Back in Granite City, with his grandmother gone, Pat was moved back into his own room, and by the fall of 1948, Elnora was pregnant again.

They sold the Ralph Street house and bought a small farm near Collinsville, about 15 miles east of Granite City. In the spring of 1949, with Elnora nearly eight months pregnant and Pat not quite finished first grade, they moved to the country. Ed kept his job with the steel company and commuted during the week, taking Pat with him to school. In May, Pat had his First Communion at Sacred Heart Church. Toward the end of June, as the school year was finishing, he got appendicitis. A Dr. Phillips diagnosed and referred him to St. Elizabeth's Hospital in Granite City. Dr. Phillips' office recorded Pat's age incorrectly as four years old — he was so small for his six years. But when the nurses, many of them nuns, were dressing him for surgery, they noticed he was wearing a scapular, only given after First Communion, so they knew he had to be older. He was in the hospital for a miserable two weeks, the unairconditioned building humid and sweltering. "God, it was hot. All plastered up. And when they came in to remove the stitches, they just held you down and pulled them out."

While Pat was in the hospital, Elnora was also admitted. His father came to Pat in the children's ward one day and said, "Did they tell you?" "Tell me what?" "You have a baby sister." They named her Mary Ellen.

Recovered from appendicitis, Pat took to farm life heart and soul. Besides the small, unplumbed farmhouse, there was a rundown cabin on the land, which they rented to a family who supported themselves by making moonshine and selling it on the backroads. They had a boy and a girl Pat's age. Pat was given very few chores and mostly spent the time amusing himself either alone or with these two children. They explored creeks, climbed trees, built forts, watched the cows and pigs (two of each), saw kittens born, rode along on the farm trucks. They passed their days full of fresh air, physical activity and the natural world.

In the fall, Pat went to the local school, where one teacher oversaw first through seventh grades. Besides the one-room school building, there was an outhouse and a storm shelter. Since it was a public school with no religious education, his parents took Pat to the Catholic Church in Collinsville for catechism class on Saturdays. "I was in school all week and I wanted Saturday morning off. And the Sunday school was full of kids, and it was hard for the nuns to keep order and it was chaos. So I told them I didn't want to go to that anymore." With great faith in Pat and his decisions, even from this very young age, Ed and Elnora let him give it up, leaving him to a blissful, mostly heathen life.

"But we went to church, and one of the great things were these great chicken frys that they had — the church outside in the summertime, and all the people from the rural areas came. I used to love those things, fish frys, chicken frys, big church dos." He reveled in life on the farm, winter and summer, looking back on it as perhaps his happiest year.

Alas, it did not work as well for Pat's father, Ed. The dirt road leading to the farmhouse got muddy when it rained and the car would get stuck, making it hard to get to his job in Granite City. He was essentially holding down two full-time jobs and it wore him down. And although Elnora's sisters and their children would sometimes make the trip out to Collinsville for a visit, she missed the easy proximity of her family. Toward the end of the second summer they decided to move back to town.

Back in Granite City — piety and vocation

They moved into the Hodges Street house that Pat's grandfather, James Hawk, had purchased before the Thirties and that he somehow managed to hang onto through the Great Depression despite alcohol and scarce employment. Pat's father had lived there from the age of about 15, moving out when he got married. Pat's Uncle Bob and family had lived there since Pat's grandfather died. Neither Bob nor his father before him had done anything much by way of upkeep or repairs, and the place was derelict. There were holes in the walls, bare floors, no central heating, no electricity, an icebox for a fridge.

Ed enjoyed working with his hands and had some skill as a woodworker. He installed central heating and electricity. He removed the rotting front porch. He set up a workshop in the basement with a lathe and other tools and built some beautiful furniture. There was a half-floor upstairs with dormer windows — an open storage space that Pat and his cousins played in and found spooky. Ed built a bedroom for Pat up there, livable but never quite finished, although he worked on it for years.

Ed was an avid baseball fan and tried unsuccessfully to get Pat to play. In retrospect, they realized that Pat couldn't see the ball — his poor eyesight was not discovered until he was in fifth grade — although once his vision was corrected with glasses, Pat still took little interest in sports. Ed and his brother, Pat's Uncle Paul, on the other hand, played baseball for the Sacred Heart team, competing with other city teams. Paul was eventually inducted into the Granite City Sports Hall of Fame.

Elnora took Pat to watch the games. Sitting on the sidelines one day, Pat was playing with a toy pistol and causing a disturbance. Ed took the pistol from him. Just then, the umpire made what Ed, who was team manager by then, thought was a bad call. They argued, Ed shaking the toy pistol. The whole bench shouted, "Shoot him, Arky! Shoot him!" Arky, short for Arkansas, was Ed's nickname, likely from the war years when he was training in the army. There's a group photo of the team with the pastor on one side and Ed as manager on the other. Pat is there, crouched down with the men in the front row.

Elnora, and to a lesser extent Ed, were much involved in parish life. They belonged to the Confraternity of Christian Doctrine, a lay organization that put on discussion groups and taught catechism classes for children attending secular schools. Elnora was following in the footsteps of her mother, who was also very active and did some of the major fundraising to build Holy Family Church, mainly by organizing card parties and other social events. The new church eventually opened in 1988,[8] across the street from the combined Sacred Heart Church and School Pat attended as a boy. The pastor, Michael Costello, and his assistants relied on Elnora for all sorts of things, including writing and assembling articles for the parish bulletin, helping to organize parish functions, and not least, plain common sense. Costello not infrequently visited the family in the house on Hodges. He was down to earth and at home in their kitchen, where he would always make his own coffee, not trusting that critical function to Elnora since she and Ed were tea drinkers. He sometimes gave Pat a dime.

The Hawks were equally at home at church and at school, integrated as they were into a single building. Wide steps led up from Jerden Street into a foyer opening to the chapel in front and a corridor on either side, each giving access to three classrooms. Two additional classrooms upstairs in a partial second story made a total of eight — one for each grade. A chalkboard stretched across the front of each classroom and was flanked by doors opening to a wide cloakroom where, in cold weather, students would hang and retrieve coats, hats, scarves and mitts to begin and end the day and also at recess. The classrooms were large and bright with big windows. The chapel, in contrast, was dimly lit with wood pews and a tall, ornate white altar — Pat described it as a wedding cake affair. Along the length of the nave on either side were remarkable life-sized statues depicting Stations of the Cross, later moved to the Shrine of Our Lady of the Snows in Belleville, Illinois.

The physical integration of church and school gave direct access to the chapel for students, and pious observances permeated school life. They were lined up several times a day, shortest to tallest, to walk in procession into and out of the chapel. Pat was always first in line.

Besides the Sunday Masses, there was weekday Mass at 8 AM for the students and anyone else who wanted to attend. On Friday evenings there was Benediction, a rite dating to the early days of the Church, the focus of which is kneeling adoration of the Blessed Sacrament placed in a gold monstrance on the altar. It includes incense, many lit candles, singing of the "Tantum Ergo" and reciting or singing the "Litany of Loreto." At one such Benediction, Pat, at seven years old, had an epiphany that set the course of his life.

> From very early in life I was attracted to Catholic ritual, the bright vestment colors, the sounds of bells and music, the smell of beeswax candles and incense. Something present inside me called to me through these things, and

> I followed that Something through the path of regular Catholic discipline right into a religious congregation of priests and brothers and ordination to the priesthood.[9]

The common practice from the earliest grades in Catholic schools is to encourage students to consider whether they have a vocation to the religious life. It was a point of pride in Catholic families when a child with an aptitude stepped forward in that direction. For most Catholic schoolchildren, it was a cause for mild consideration, some guilt, some squirming discomfort and casual dismissal of the idea. Not so for Pat. He knew from that time forward that he wanted to be a priest. Late in life, his recollection was that he never wavered.

Pat was memorable in his unobtrusiveness. Time and again, his classmates looking back on those elementary school years, remembered how quiet he was. It was the first thing that came to anyone's mind. His small physical stature and quiet nature stood out all the more against the antics of others. There were the usual pranks involving mostly boys, often the same boys: a hose aimed at an open window, a frog put in the teacher's desk, spiders let loose in the classroom. Enraged nuns would sometimes keep control with a heavy hand: yanked hair, the strap, humiliation — things frowned on and even illegal in schools a few decades later. There was a record 59 students in Pat's graduating eighth-grade class, most of whom had been there for all eight years, moving up together.

They rehearsed catechism, preparing for visits from the bishop when they would be expected to recite rote answers. Years later, Dottie, a classmate, remembered, "One time, I didn't know my catechism. Sister came in to check our catechism; all the other girls knew theirs and they got to go home. Sister told me that my parents did not love me because if they loved me, I would know my catechism. So I cried all the way home. Pat came, and I can remember he was riding his bike slowly, and he was trying to make me feel better all the way home." Dottie lived on Sheridan on the other side of the cemetery from the Hawks, in a housing project. "I remember being up in his room one time. I don't know if we were playing a game or what; I kind of had a bit of a crush on him." He was good-looking in a boyish way.

Although students had to attend Mass daily, they didn't have to go to communion except on first Fridays. Communion required fasting from midnight on, including no water. "And on first Fridays, we would all have to bring a sack breakfast [to eat after Mass]." After his epiphany, Pat never missed. At the end of eighth grade, he and Kitty Reither were voted the most pious boy and girl in the school.

Ursuline nuns taught the students until Pat and his classmates were in about fourth grade, at which time Dominican sisters took over. The Ursulines were strict with themselves — they could not go out in public alone, for example, and they lived in the basement. The Dominicans were a little looser, although it was a Dominican seventh-grade teacher, Sister Mary Ackland, who was referred to among the students as the nun from hell.

The nuns subsisted on a tight budget which drew the attention of some of the women in the parish, none of whom had much money, but who complained to Costello — comfortable in the rectory while the nuns scraped by — and brought them baked goods and other treats. One boy delivering a fish dinner was shocked by a nun who answered the door without her veil. "She had a crew cut; you could have knocked me downstairs. But she would have a glass of wine, smoke a cigarette." Such surprises became the grist for raised eyebrows and whispered conversations whose novelty would never completely wane.

Outside of school, Pat still played most often with his cousin Nora. Following Pat's epiphany, they played pious games, Pat being the priest and Nora the congregation. They dodged Pat's sister, Mary Ellen, sometimes cruelly, and kept to themselves. Their close friendship ended abruptly when Pat left for the seminary.

Toward the end of eighth grade at Sacred Heart, there was strong encouragement from the nuns for students to continue their schooling at the Catholic high school in Belleville, although many, for convenience, went to the public school in Granite City. There was a lot of talk that spring leading up to eighth-grade graduation about who was going where. His parents knew that Pat wanted to be a priest, and they assumed he would go to the Catholic high school, then to the diocesan seminary. But he found out that his friend, Ed Ruder, was going straight into the seminary for ninth grade. Pat recalled, "Immediately I became envious and wanted to know how, when and where. He told me he was going to the same place Dan Betinec was going who had a brother there."

Dan Betinec's mother brought Pat for his first look at the Redemptorist seminary high school in Kirkwood, Missouri. In her youth, Mrs. Betinec had felt a strong vocation for the convent. But finding herself falling in love with a man, instead she married, promising the Lord that her children would be given to the Church. She had two sons and a daughter. Joe, the oldest, had entered seminary training at Kirkwood seven years earlier. Janet, the middle child, became a nun. Dan dutifully did the expected. Pat once commented, "There's a saying that for some people, it's their mother that had the vocation, not them."

It was from Dan's mother, Gabrielle Betinec, that Pat first heard the name Redemptorist and learned that there were differences between diocesan and so-called religious priests. Diocesan priests are ordained into a particular diocese. They generally do parish work and are answerable to the bishop. They do not take vows, although in the Western Church they pledge a life of celibacy. Religious priests (and nuns) belong to a community — a congregation or order (those are not the same thing), — take vows of poverty, chastity and obedience, and are responsible to a religious Superior within the community. Their lives are informed by a particular charism or gift, such as, in the case of Redemptorists, to lead a missionary life preaching to "the most abandoned." Gabrielle Betinec's view — later also Pat's — was that life in a congregation was better than life as a diocesan priest.

She arranged for Pat to meet her personal spiritual advisor, John Treinen, the Redemptorist who had been instrumental in her older son Joe getting into the seminary. One could not be admitted without someone to vouch for you from within. Pat liked what he heard about Redemptorist life and mission from Treinen and was glad to be included when Mrs. Betinec took the three boys — her son Dan, along with Pat and Ed Ruder — to check out St. Joseph's Preparatory College in Kirkwood, Missouri.

They drove over from Granite City one day in the spring of eighth grade. Years later, Pat hardly remembered his impressions of the place on that day — just that as they turned from Geyer Road onto the grounds of St. Joseph's, drove up the tree-lined avenue to the entrance and entered the building, he knew. He went home and told his parents, "Sign me up." They took him for another visit in April, then he went back in June to register. He entered that fall at the age of thirteen.

2

Seminary Years

Minor Seminary

Arrival at Kirkwood

On Monday, September 3, 1956, a sunny, warm day, Pat and his family drove out of Granite City over the Eads Bridge and through St. Louis traffic to Kirkwood and St. Joseph's College, a world away but only about 25 miles from home. At the time, Kirkwood, Missouri — now part of greater St. Louis — was a small town with a rural feel. The school property shared borders with a few farms and a nearby forest that separated the 80-acre college grounds from the Meramec River a few miles away.

They drove up to the imposing, dark brick building — four stories counting an unfinished attic under a steeply pitched roof, a bell tower rising above the entrance. The front doors opened to a vestibule and parlor area directly beyond which was the large Gothic chapel. On either side, corridors led away from the main foyer to cloistered areas from which families were excluded.

Built in 1887 to house about 200 seminarians plus Redemptorist faculty and administrators,[10] by the 1940s the structure was unsound, with large metal bolts and a metal frame installed on the outside of the building to keep it from collapsing. There were cracks right through the walls in places, letting drafts of icy air into the gym and some classrooms during the winter. A new structure was needed, and beginning in the '40s, the Redemptorists had been actively fundraising and looking for the property that would eventually become St. Joseph's College in Edgerton, Wisconsin.

The Kirkwood building housed the minor seminary, comprising four years of high school and the first two years of college. College was interrupted by a year of novitiate, a period of intense religious formation. Then would follow six years in major seminary, including graduation from the last two years of college with a degree in philosophy and four years of post-graduate training in dogmatic and moral theology, yielding Master of Divinity and Master of Religious Education degrees. One year before the end of major seminary came ordination, the Holy

Grail for these boys. This long trajectory was an adaptation of the European seminary model, and in the mid-20th century it was the norm among Catholic seminaries.

As an introverted boy accustomed to a doting mother, now thrown among several hundred boisterous strangers to live a new and rigid routine in the decrepit, crowded-feeling building, Pat's time at Kirkwood began with deep loneliness. Looking back a handful of years after ordination, he said he would never want to do it again.[11] He was one of an entering class of 54 boys 13 or 14 years old. For those like Pat entering at 13 on the 13-year program of study, they would have spent half their lives in the seminary by the time they finished.

Pat said goodbye to his family, and without turning to wave nor to watch them drive away, he allowed himself to be led into the cloistered area. He and his new classmates began to find their way around. There were dark corridors and sunlit rooms. There was the large high-ceilinged Gothic chapel, the refectory, classrooms, library, auditorium, gymnasium, sports fields, recreation room, lavatories and dormitory. The latter was a huge open room that slept all the boys in ninth through eleventh grades. Each boy's personal space consisted of a locker and a cot. The beds were lined up in rows like desks in a classroom and not much farther apart. Like the building, they were old and sagging. Any extra belongings — not many — Pat could store in his trunk, which he lugged up to the attic, sweltering and stuffy in that late summer season. He had a few minutes to look out the dormer windows across the grounds of St. Joseph's to the water tower, the estates and farms of Kirkwood and the woods along the Meramec River before the bell rang for dinner. The boys hurried downstairs and trooped into the refectory.

Incoming students scrambled to know where to sit. Eventually, with some help from the waiters — boys in classes ahead of them — they figured out their assigned places and the room settled. All said prayers in Latin, sat down and dug into rather uninteresting food. After dinner, there were prayers in the chapel, then more orientation. They received a copy of the Student Rule: 50 pages of instruction and guidance describing the purpose of the minor seminary, the program for spiritual growth and character formation, the academic program, and rules governing conduct in every place, for every activity, and during every moment of the day. It was a daunting booklet. Students would be continually stumbling on and supported by these rules as they embarked on intensive academic study and adapted to seminary life.

A smorgasbord of recollections in *The Mirror*, newsletter of the minor seminary, provides a snapshot of their first impressions: "Thursday morning at 5:35 a very horrible thing happens — the rising bell rings. You don't want to get up, but you figure you have to, so you drag yourself out of bed," "You line up in the morning waiting for a turn at the sinks to wash and brush teeth. When you get to Chapel and Holy Mass, you hit the kneelers and feel that there isn't any padding, and halfway through the Mass you know it. The rest of the day you find your thoughts wandering away towards home. You might get active and then for an instant you're not doing anything and soon you find yourself homesick, lonesome, and not a little bit dejected. Sometimes you really have to work hard to shake it..." "After Mass, breakfast and prayers, there's time to unpack properly, read, explore, begin to get to know your classmates, with whom you realize you are to spend the next 13 years learning, living, praying." "It all seems a big mass of confusion, with the 'Follow yous' and the 'On Conditions' but finally you find yourself taking a nice hot shower — well, it was hot a minute ago. Ouch! It's too hot again." "Friday morning it's up and at 'em at 5:20. It turns out that rising at 5:35 the day before was sleeping in. The extra 15 minutes is allowed on Thursdays and Sundays." "St. Joseph's College is the minor seminary for the St. Louis province, which includes the midwest, the south, the southwest, so they come from New Orleans, Baton Rouge, St. Louis, Omaha, Chicago, Grand Rapids, Detroit... there's a big variety of accents and backgrounds."[12]

They were introduced to Separation. This policy recognized that maturity level changes greatly over the six years of minor seminary, and to avoid conflict and perhaps corrupting influence, juniors and seniors were not allowed to speak to each other. Students in the high school years were referred to as "first academic," "second academic," "third academic" and "fourth academic." The first three grades comprised the juniors. The seniors were students in their last year of high school — fourth academic — plus the college freshmen and sophomores. According to the Student Rule: "To preserve a prudent division of the student body according to age, size and maturity, both seniors and juniors will use only those areas and facilities appointed to them, unless permission to do otherwise is given by the Superiors, and this will not be given lightly."[13] Juniors and seniors had separate sports fields, tennis courts, baseball fields, lounge rooms and dormitories. They sat in different sections of the dining room. Within juniors and seniors, upper classes waited tables and lower classes did the dishes. They were together in chapel but sat on opposite sides, in ranks according to year. Likewise in Study Hall.

"During the day you receive your first taste of *sum, es, est*, and *rosa, rosae*. After each class when you receive your study hall work, you wonder, 'When am I ever going to get it done?' " There was Mass, breakfast, classes in the morning, lunch, classes again in the afternoon, a recreation period with organized sports, a half-hour remission [recess], then supper, study hall, bed at 9:00. Prayers were interspersed throughout, in and out of the chapel all day long. "You have been busy all day and have never been able to think of home and at night you think that you would go to sleep right away, but homeward bound thoughts keep coming in. You try to get rid of them, but they keep coming back. Eventually you succeed in cleansing your mind of them." "Saturday morning came fast after you took care of the homeward bound thoughts. It seems strange to have to go to class."[14]

Saturday afternoon was work order. Pat remembered, "We cleaned the lavatories, the showers, waxed floors, mopped, everything. All the students were assigned a job, and we all worked Saturdays. Most of it was janitorial kinds of things. Although there were specialized kinds of work. Some boys knew how to do some plumbing, some did farm work. We had cornfields. We had cows. There were milkers — [who] had to go out every morning and milk."[15]

There was hazing. A newcomer might be wrestled to the floor and slapped on the bare belly or made to do errands for older juniors. Boys had to weather "not only our homesickness and the heat, but also the second academic."[16] Pat fended off this added harassment with his natural gravitas, well-developed even at that age, and a cold stare that froze would-be harassers.

A classmate wrote, "Leaving home for the first time was for many of us, an ordeal that was as unpleasant as it was adventurous and we usually don't discuss it. It was sad, it was painful. It is all over now and we don't twinge so much when the subject is broached." Inevitably that wrenching wound is given spiritual purpose: "We all know what that first sorrow meant. It was our first test to see if your desire to follow Christ was genuine. We who are here now have all passed that first test. What seemed so unsurmountable then, is something we wistfully recall now."[17]

Arriving that first day, saying goodbye to his family, Pat knew almost nothing of what he was getting into beyond what he had understood at the age of seven, that he wanted to be a priest and that this was the way to accomplish that goal. His mother expected him to be back home within a month or two, and bet him a steak that he wouldn't last. Recalling those days years later Pat said, "It was a good steak."

Seminary life was intense, full, and very different from Pat's first 13 years. One of his classmates reflected: "Like Lot's wife in the Bible, some have stopped and looked back. They were not turned to salt as she — they simply made themselves more difficulties by distracting their minds from our supreme goal…"[18]

If a boy's family lived close enough or had the resources, they could visit their son once a month. While he was at Kirkwood, Pat's family never missed. They visited in the old parlors at Kirkwood, or with permission of the Director, they could go out for lunch and occasionally to a movie. Pat's sister, Mary Ellen, remembered the decrepit old building looking like it was about to fall down, external beams and scaffolding supporting the walls, and worn, dated furniture in the parlor. Often, she and Elnora would visit with Pat. Ed would say a quick hello, then sit in the car and listen to the ballgame. All of them had little in common with Pat in his new life. Pat: "It was kind of artificial, visiting like that, but it was okay."

Students were allowed to go home for a day at Christmas and Thanksgiving, but only if home was close by, since they couldn't stay overnight and they had to be at the seminary through lunch on the day of the holiday. There's a photo of Pat on one of these visits, Elnora beside him on the couch with a tentative smile while Pat sits erect in white shirt and tie, arms crossed tightly, looking every bit the annoyed and disapproving teenager. He was part of a new culture. For his family, home was still there on Hodges Street, but for Pat it was at Kirkwood.

He went back to Granite City for the summers of the first through fifth years of minor seminary. The first summer, he babysat Mary Ellen, age seven to Pat's fourteen. Later he got summer jobs, his first working at St. Elizabeth's Hospital printing menus, other things the Sisters needed to have done. He wrote in advance and said he was a seminarian and wanted to work for the summer. They hired him. One year he worked at Mercantile Mortgage Company, stuffing envelopes and running errands. His mother worked there at that time as well. After those hot months of mundane employment, he welcomed the return of fall and Kirkwood, the joys and rigors of seminary life.

Spiritual life, Redemptorist culture

Besides being a vehicle whereby daily life was ordered and maintained, practice of the Student Rule was an acculturation to Redemptorist life. First and foremost, it included a detailed guide to spiritual formation, to be practiced "faithfully, in spite of weariness at times, and with the sole intention of giving glory to God."[19] Prayers were scheduled throughout the day, the virtues of charity, truthfulness, humility, obedience, purity and piety,[20] set as objects for meditation and touchstones for self-examination.

First thing at the sound of the bell, each boy dropped to his knees beside his bed for morning prayer. At this time, and during meditation a short while later in the chapel, each was to set himself a conscious practice for the day, generally aligned with a virtue assigned for that month. Mass followed, then after breakfast there was spiritual reading, each boy from his own book, or at times, communal reading of the Student Rule. Particular Examen was performed at moments during the day with conscious self-assessment vis-á-vis the day's intention, noting inevitable shortfalls and renewing determination to do better. They recited the Angelus in common before breakfast and lunch. After supper there was the rosary — on free days said individually, most days communally — followed by private devotions, again in the chapel. Students would often pray the Stations of the Cross at this time though it was optional, and they could go to confession, something they were required to do at least once a week. On all days in the evening, there was a visit to the Blessed Sacrament. Lastly, after Study Hall, students returned to the chapel for Night Prayer, including an examination of conscience in which each student "should review the events of the entire day, beg God for forgiveness of his faults, and thank Him for the countless graces and blessings of the day."[21]

In addition to these prayers throughout the day and the individual guidance of one's faculty advisor, the Rector, the Director of Students or the Sub-directors gave conferences on the meaning of the virtues, to point out applications in seminary life, "and to exhort and inspire the students to form themselves in the imitation of Christ."[22] The Director of Students was available for individual counseling, and there was an expectation that he would meet with each boy from time to time during the year. Besides these opportunities, each student could choose anyone among the faculty to be his spiritual advisor and confessor — the grist for confession coming from shortcomings identified during Particular Examen in relation to the specific virtue for each day as well as any other transgressions. Meeting at least weekly with the student, the confessor would learn the challenges a boy faced and monitor his progress. Twice during the year — once in the fall and once in the spring — there was a three-day retreat for the entire student body. These were times away from studying and other activities, devoted mainly to silence and prayer with the express object that each one "examine himself thoroughly regarding his God-given vocation."

Students were encouraged to conduct all activities, academic and recreational, prayerfully. Supporting this was the Rule of Silence "to preserve recollection of mind, to promote study and reflection, and to foster union with God." Students were to maintain silence at all times — in study halls, in dormitories, in lavatories, in the library and in the refectory — except on free days and when dispensation was given by the Superior.

From the beginning, it was deemed a privilege for students to be at St. Joseph's College seminary, receiving a first rate education and spiritual formation, heading toward the holiest of life work. Faculty and students alike held this view. Students for the most part engaged sincerely and wholeheartedly in the program offered them. Besides the obvious and immediate spiritual and academic opportunities, which they valued, the possibility of dismissal was ever understood and served as a strong encouragement to adhere to every aspect of the program.

In the early years, Pat exulted in the shared rigor of study, the sometimes wild high spirits, the constant call to prayer. This was his in-group. These were his people. "When I was 14 years old this was terrific, yeah. I was on my way to what I wanted, my life's goal. Just wasn't in high school looking for a future, I had it. I was all set!"[23] He embraced the life, heart and soul.

Program of study

The Reverend Dean of Studies — effectively the Principal — oversaw the academic program, including selecting professors, choosing curriculum, and conferring with the Directors about student progress. The program included all the regular high school courses, with a heavy emphasis on language: Latin, English, German, Spanish and Greek; also History and of course, Religious Studies. Composition and oral presentation were important as preparation for being preachers. It was lighter on mathematics, general science and biology but fulfilled the requirements.

In Pat's day, all the teaching was done by Redemptorists, many of them skilled educators. Years later, he reminisced with mixed fondness.

> George Liesveld was the first academic Latin teacher, fairly young man in those times, a powerful athlete kind of person. Geometry teacher was an old priest. Corrigan was his name. He was a great old man. Science teacher was named Schmidt. He left later on. He just lectured and wrote on the board, didn't ask any questions, didn't even look at us. And he wrote backwards. He'd look in his book and write on the board like this [over the shoulder]. English teacher was Jim Gleason. Tall, powerful man. He was very influential on that whole group. Second-year biology was Joe Armshaw, who always talked about himself. We called him Ego. Very seldom taught biology, just talked about what was going on, rumors, shake-ups, his life.[24]

Pat laughed and continued,

> And the biology was straight out of a book. Corrigan taught Latin the second year. Al Babbin taught Latin third year; he was very straitlaced, phlegmatic kind of person. Marty Coyne taught us trigonometry. I didn't learn anything. He just winged it off the top of his head. He'd put up a problem and we'd work on it. Nobody could solve it, and he'd say, "Oh yeah, it's unsolvable." Gerry Pecht taught German. Small little man — he taught for years and years and years there. Pat Kaler was a wonderful man. He taught biology and

> chemistry later on. Bill Broker taught public speaking. We had public speaking all six years. That was one of the big emphases for Redemptorists to be preachers. There was a big emphasis on public speaking. And they encouraged theatrics because it helped in that kind of thing.[25]

Whether in the classroom, the refectory or the chapel, the faculty wore the Redemptorist habit, always standing out from the boys as example and authority.[26]

The Student Rule and the schedule supported strong academic development, the idea being that "a priest without learning is as helpless as a soldier without weapons." Academic ability was weighed alongside spiritual aptitude in screening boys for the seminary, and all were expected to thrive in the intense learning environment. As with all things, the stated primary motive of the student was to please God. "God judges success in studies by how well a student uses the talents he possesses, not by his standing in the class, for not all have been given equal ability. Therefore, a student who works diligently at his classwork, but whose performance is *only* average, is more pleasing to God than one who works lazily but attains a higher level of performance because he has greater God-given ability."[27]

Dramatics, clubs

Students were expected to take an interest in extracurricular activities. "...they provide a relief from ordinary studies and give the student an opportunity to use and develop creative talents. Each student can find some activity which helps him to develop his personality and work with others in a common effort." Always, the emphasis was on community. Opportunities included drama, choir, band, forum — focused on discussion and debating current events — and publications, especially the student newsletter, *The Mirror*.

Prominent among the choices was drama, as another aspect of formation for the preaching life that was the charism of all Redemptorists. "Students are required to provide dramatic entertainment in the form of plays, skits, and musicals. ... The priest must continually appear before others and assume the role of a leader, and his participation in student drama will be a valuable preparation as an aid in overcoming self-consciousness and in developing poise and confidence." They put on plays several times a year, including musicals and lots of one-act plays. Pat remembered them doing *Solitaire*, *Cox and Box*, *Ghost Hunters*. Also longer productions: *Brigadoon*, *My Fair Lady*, *Harvey*, *Mr. Roberts*, *Inherit the Wind*.[28] They were the players and sometimes a large part of the audience, or they played for the Vocation Directors and the Sisters, or there were special occasions when families could come and watch. Students would usher them in past the parlor area through the cloistered halls to the auditorium on the second floor.

They rewrote plays to edit out the female parts — "My Fair Lady" was Freddy Doolittle instead of Eliza — or males played female roles dressed in drag. Lots of time was spent making elaborate sets and costumes, doing make-up, producing playbills, the works. Talented vocalists played the leads in productions like *My Fair Lady*, and the music was often outstanding.

Pat got heavily involved in theatrics, both acting and directing. He loved it. In his class's minor seminary yearbook, he is "Granite City's answer to Barrymore." He directed a successful production of *Harvey* to rave reviews. Likewise, *The Sound of Hunting*, written up in *The Mirror*: "To supply what was lacking in the play itself, Pat Hawk gathered together a cast that could have put this play over with the enthusiasm alone. This genuine interest is always seen in a production. But enthusiasm was far from the only noticeable quality. The stage was actually crowded with talent. I believe the players will agree with me when I say that most of the potential in each of them was developed mainly through the efforts of Pat Hawk."[29]

Besides dramatics, Pat participated most years in production of *The Mirror*, at least as typist, and not infrequently as a contributor. He wrote reviews of books, in-house plays and debates, and from time to time a short story, the latter published under Pat's byline, *Hawk's Hawkings*. A couple of stories, one a mystery set in the time of Caesar, the other a Christmas story, were published when Pat was in 10th grade. They show a student capable of smooth if somewhat purple prose. The Christmas story is set in Bethlehem, and even a half dozen years after it was written, would have made Pat cringe from its naive racism and earnest embrace of pre-Vatican II orthodoxies. Some excerpts:

> The sharp wind cut through the dark night like a razor with a newly sharpened edge. One lone star shone dimly through the overcast sky from which snow was being poured like meal into the great bowl of the earth. Off into the distance there was a small cave. It was used as a stable, and once it was used as a shelter so that a King might be born, but now it was being used by the sacrilegious Mohammedans, who had overrun the Holy Land. … Not too far from the camp there was a group of tall pine trees, standing as if they were guarding the small camp of soldiers; but really they were guarding, sheltering and hiding a man. … Long ago, the man had been an ardent sinner and a hater of the Church. … As the priest was praying over him, he was suddenly cured. In thanksgiving he was baptized and made a vow to walk from England to Bethlehem to make a visit on Christmas Eve. … He entered the cave and knelt in a secluded corner of the stable not more than four feet from the holy spot. … The light of morning sun crept into the little cavern like something fearful of waking the Babe who was once sleeping in a manger there. The rays soon reached the humbly bent figure and circled

> the body like a vine. ... it unveiled the radiance of his face and the joyous smile which it bore. The light did not disturb him, but the broad bleak figure, which suddenly blotted out the light did. ... "Prepare to die, Christian," ... The saintly one looked up, extended his arms in the form of a cross and said in a low unfaltering tone, "I am ready." ... With one mighty thrust the Mohammedan transfixed the cold iron into the Christian's breast. The prayerful man slowly slumped to the frozen earth and with his last ounce of life crawled to the manger in which God had once lay sleeping. He grasped one of the legs with a smile on his face and his life slipped away. ... This is not a sad ending. By all means it is the most happy ending that the story could have. For, when our Christian drew his last breath, he exchanged gifts with Christ![30]

In the reviews filling pages in each issue of *The Mirror,* criticism of classmates was blunt and constructive. Reviewing the play *The Devil and Daniel Webster*, Pat wrote:

> I think it is agreed that Steve Palmer was excellent in his portrayal of Daniel Webster. Mike Kane certainly put in all he had into the part of the devil, but it seemed that many of the fine points of the art were lacking. Joe Blair did well enough, indeed. He wasn't extraordinary but he was acting all the time. Tom Hakel looked like Steve Palmer in a dress. But then a woman's part is very difficult to portray. Tom did his best. The damned souls seemed pretty well damned. The judge and his recorder did the job they were supposed to do. All in all it was, in Father Mulligan's own words, "One of the finest things we have seen around in a long time!!"

A lengthy Hawk review of a debate pulls no punches but is again well within the range and tone of the boys' writings overall.[31] They were sincere about honing their critical and presenting skills.

Work order

Jobs assigned to each boy were to be taken seriously. "The work program of the seminary is intended not only to maintain our home in neat and orderly condition, but also to develop in the student a sense of responsibility to duty, trustworthiness in an assigned task, and a concern for material things which are not privately owned but shared by all."[32] "A student lives at the college nine and a half months a year. This is truly, then, his home. Let him be as a member of the family — take pride and care in keeping his home beautiful."

The Sisters did the cooking and the laundry, but the students did almost everything else. Saturday afternoons were for work order. Students were assigned as secretaries to type office business and to sort the mail; store managers; masters of ceremony for liturgical events to appoint and train servers; sacristans to attend to the chapel, altars and linens; dormitory light-and-windows men — no one else was allowed to operate light switches or windows; librarians to distribute books and collect them before and at the end of Study Hall; barbers — older students taught the younger ones how to cut hair; infirmaries, to bring communion to the sick and keep track of medical expenditures; prefects of laundry to collect dirty laundry and sort and distribute clean laundry; garage men to service cars, sport secretaries to select teams and referees, "put up a sign immediately after breakfast of all the games to be played that day," and oversee care of sports equipment; printing men to run the multilith; movie men to pick up and return the selected films — they watched a movie about once a month — from the Fathers' side and run the projector; book binders; life guards; shoe men to organize repair of shoes; photographers to document sports, plays, debates and other events for *The Mirror*; stage crew including Dramatics Director; holy water person to see to it that the fonts were cleaned and filled; waiters at table; sweepers to care for outdoor walks, and crews for cleaning recreation room, refectory, gymnasium, chapel, stairways, hallways, lavatory fixtures, locker rooms, windows, drinking fountains — every corner of every part of the seminary was cleaned at least once a week.

The Directors of Students assigned the jobs, and a person could have the same job for a few months or for longer periods at the discretion of the Directors. Pat's assignments included various cleaning tasks as well as supervising cleaning; office boy, librarian, and for three years — Dramatics Director. Librarian was his favorite job, though in minor seminary he had it for only a semester.

Sports & recreation

Physical activity was an important and required outlet for burgeoning adolescent energy and hormones. "The priest must possess not only holiness and knowledge but also good health."[33] A recreation period following afternoon classes usually involved organized sports of one kind or another, depending on season and weather.

A lot of lively seminary spirit revolved around the sports scene. Pat could have been marginalized by this but for the inclusive structure of a league system with teams at all levels. The top division was majors or pro, then the semis, then the minors or beer league, where Pat was placed if he couldn't escape altogether and curl up somewhere with a book. Tom Schiltz, Pat's classmate through minor seminary and most of the novitiate, remembers him as never a great athlete but spunky. He was captain of his softball team in third academic. Greg Mayers, two years behind Pat in the seminary, later close friend and colleague, later still, estranged, met him for the first time at the start of a minor league practice:

> He was a junior in high school, I was a freshman, and we all had to play sports. I'd never played any organized sports and I was scared stiff. It was softball and I walked out onto the field. They had given Pat — maybe as a consolation prize — they made Pat the captain of a minor league. I'm sure that was no consolation to Pat because he didn't like sports either. So he comes out rather disgusted about the whole thing. And we were all running around, freshmen, I wanna play this and I wanna play this, and the first words I ever heard come out of Pat Hawk's mouth were, "Give me your name, rank and serial number." I said, "I want to play right field," because I figured no one would hit anything to right field, and he looked at me with this withering look and said, "That's my position."[34]

If Pat's name appeared in the sports reporting that featured in every issue of *The Mirror*, most often it was at the low end of scoring tallies. A rare triumph came after the minor seminary moved to new quarters at Edgerton, Wisconsin at the beginning of Pat's twelfth grade. There they had hockey, something Pat was decent at. At one point he found himself captain of a minor league team that did well. "Hawk's team and Romero's team were battling for first place. This game was a do or die struggle. The starting whistle blew at 1:15 and there was never a dull moment. With pounding sticks and flying skates both teams fought for possession of the puck and that all-important goal. Pat Hawk's squad dominated the play in the final periods.... When the final whistle blew Pat was the proud possessor of an 8-4 win and the league championship."[35] He grinned about that one — victory in a realm he at best tolerated.

While sports were mainly intramural, they sometimes played teams from local high schools, including some Kirkwood home games over the winter holiday. This despite cracks in the wall of the gym making it impossible to heat adequately. "Christmas week saw a group of eight or nine basketball players of the Kirkwood area come to our frigid gym in search of a few friendly contests.[36] ..." Some played, others cheered. Loudly, lustily from the bleachers would come, "Three cheers for CSsR,* God bless the gang wherever they are!" sung to the tune of the Notre Dame fight song.[37]

Besides organized sports played on class days, on free days they could get a few others together and play handball, tennis, volleyball. There was also track, which included a field day once or twice a year, boxing, and later at Edgerton, ping pong, billiards and swimming. Or they could read, or play cards, or chess, or

---

* "Congregation of the Most Holy Redeemer" is the official name of the Redemptorist congregation of priests. Latin: *<u>C</u>ongregatio <u>S</u>anctis<u>s</u>imi <u>R</u>edemptoris.*

other board games. They were not allowed to remain indoors the whole day unless the weather was inclement. Even for the daily afternoon remissions on class days, they could not stay in to study without special permission. Pat was an ace at ping pong and fiercely competitive. Likewise with chess. There's a photo of him from those days wearing a wicked grin as he reaches over the board to move his queen.

Books for recreational reading — mostly novels — would be requested from the library the day before a free day, then brought to the common room by the student whose job it was to do this. They could read their novels on Thursdays and Sundays, then they were returned to the library for the rest of the week. All books had to be approved by the Director of Students or Sub-directors. Pat chose mainly adventure stories. A favorite author at that time was Kenneth Roberts who authored a series of novels about the American Revolution: *Northwest Passage*, *Arundel*, *Lively Lady*, various other titles, all of which Pat read and reread.

During extended free time they could go off the property —at least six boys together, with permission. There was an old quarry nearby and they would fool around there. In fair weather, they could take a picnic lunch. Especially in the spring with everything growing and blooming, Pat loved to walk the few miles through the woods to the Meramac River, explore along the embankment, follow creeks, breathe in the wild outdoors.

Supervision

The Very Reverend Father Rector was the head of St. Joseph's College. He was ultimate Superior, and students were encouraged to regard him as their father. He would give a conference every month, meant to encourage students in their vocation and spiritual development. Though they were not yet bound to him by a vow of obedience, they understood well the importance of his approval. He was responsible for all matters related to running the seminary, however, his administrative duties made it so that he had little to do with the students. The distance amplified his gravitas, especially in the minds of younger students.

The Director of Students and his two Sub-directors were in charge of the young men. In Pat's day, the Director was Father Bernie Mulligan, from Detroit, a serious man of gentle disposition, aged by the time Pat knew him. He walked with a limp. Sub-directors, Fathers Al Babbin and Jim Gleason, had an office in the student area just outside the study hall and were available most of the time. They ate with the students, keeping order by their presence. There was usually one of them walking around keeping an eye on things — in the refectory at mealtimes, in the corridors, in the dormitory following lights out. They could enforce the silence with a glance.

Student prefects selected from upper classes were appointed by the directors and assisted them in supervising observance of the student rule. For the youngest boys, the prefects carried almost the same authority as the directors themselves. In the classroom, this meant seeing to it that students kept silence, that they rose when the professor entered, that they kept their desk tidy and free of all but permitted items, and if the Reverend Professor had not arrived by eight minutes after the bell, ushering everyone to Study Hall in silence. They were appointed to supervise work crews, and if lax in exacting a high standard, were under threat of redoing the job themselves. In the dormitories, they made sure beds were made, the cover turned down on rising so the bed could air, then made after breakfast such that the surface was like glass. It meant making sure that all articles were stowed properly, that modesty was practiced at all times, and that nobody entered the dormitory during the day except to mend clothing on recreation days or to use the showers after sports because the showers off the locker rooms were full. Taking a nap was out of the question.

During meals for which conversation was not permitted — most meals — there was a reader appointed from among the students. Directors or Sub-directors selected the content, not necessarily religious. Sometimes there was reading from the Student Rule, sometimes a secular topic. Besides keeping minds busy, it was another opportunity to practice delivery. "Reading aloud is excellent practice for public speaking, and it can be said truly that one who learns to read well to others will have no difficulty in preaching well in later life."[38] The student was expected to prepare beforehand using a dictionary to learn correct pronunciation of unfamiliar words, and to be engaging: "The use of a microphone and public address system are not to be regarded as substitutes for personal effort, for they have no magic which makes a dull and listless reading lively and interesting."[39]

Manners

Emily Post would have felt at home with the long section of the Student Rule devoted to manners, both for its level of detail and its relatedness to her era, except perhaps where the details went beyond standard mores into the spiritual. All is done as the will of God, in support of the vows, and for their success as priests. Having taken these boys from their homes as young teenagers, it fell to the seminary to educate them not only in academics and spiritual matters but also in the proper use of a knife and fork.

> The Code of Canon Law places the obligation on rectors and directors of seminarians of teaching the students the precepts of true Christian politeness. The Church wants the candidates for the priesthood to observe faithfully the laws of hygiene, cleanliness of dress and person, and propriety in

> conversation and manners. Any seminarian who would deliberately disregard the essentials of good manners would manifest a spirit wholly opposed to the example of Christ, the mind of the Church, and the decencies of normal social living.[40]

Much of the detail is prosaic. There are lengthy instructions on how to sit, including: "do not loll back, do not rock your chair, do not shuffle your feet, do not drum the table with your fingers;" and how to stand: "straight, do not lean indolently against the wall or furniture; dignity of carriage is to be preserved at all times." There is specific and lengthy instruction on conversation, "…politeness condemns excessive loudness as well as effeminacy; it is generally better not to contradict at all, unless it should be a matter of conscience, and that rarely happens; others will not be interested in hearing you expatiate on your family and relatives, your health and infirmities, your dreams, your method of study, etc.; as you should not speak of yourself, neither should you be curious about the affairs of others." These latter exhortations would only have reinforced Pat's natural tendency to be unforthcoming about himself and uncurious about others.

The seminarians were expected to write letters home regularly and they were given advice on doing so: "Write with care, for carelessness and haste in letter writing show that you hold your correspondent in slight regard. The letter should be well-thought-out beforehand and neatly folded when finished. Never fold a letter until you have read it again. Do not read the letters that you receive while in the company of others. It would be a very serious breach of politeness to look into anything being read in private by another. No one should read a letter, sealed or unsealed, not addressed to himself. The secret of letters is sacred." Somehow this sentiment was reconciled with the fact that students' letters were to be turned in to the directors unsealed, and incoming letters were delivered to the students already opened.

Dress and hygiene were not to be neglected nor overemphasized. "…never allow dress to exhibit either vanity or ostentation." "Cleanliness of person renders us agreeable to others; it promotes cheerfulness, and is an excellent preservative of health. It also bears an analogy to godliness. Do not be afraid of soap and water. But it should be remembered that too much care of the hair, or excessive precision in its adjustment, is inconsistent with Christian and religious modesty." And so on to care and use of handkerchiefs and other practical niceties. Of course, manners when eating were given full attention.

Certainly, a great deal of this became second nature to Pat as was intended, but of the formal instruction he remembered only two things: "There was one we always quoted, which was a section on table manners and eating. There are two lines in it that are classics that everybody remembers. One was, 'Be sure that your soup is cooled enough to eat, otherwise you will be driven to the unpardonable alternative of returning it to the bowl.' The other one was, 'Do not fall upon your food as if it were a fumbled football.' Can't remember anything else!"[41]

Through all, they were exhorted to be cheerful. This can't have failed to irritate Pat. "Two qualities prejudicial to Christian Politeness should be combated — selfishness and moroseness. ... Moroseness of temper kills politeness. A cheerful disposition is one of the greatest blessings; it imparts sunshine and diffuses joy and happiness. How gloomy the house from which, through the angry, vehement and dissatisfied disposition of some of its members, cheerfulness is banished! Peace, union, and good feeling cannot be inmates of such a house." That requirement, taken seriously by superiors, was to haunt Pat in the major seminary and would nearly derail him from his chosen path.

Antics

Students were required to observe the regulations with fidelity: "Let the student always remember that no rule is trivial or unimportant, because it is the will of God," and with good intention. "All the rules and regulations of the seminary have been judged necessary by the authorities, either for the training of the students or for the good order of the house. When the seminary authorities discover that a student is not observing the Rule as he should, they will correct him." If all else fails, the student is dismissed from the seminary. Of course, there were infractions, confessions of which became subjects for creative writing in *The Mirror*. One student wrote:

> Then the glorious day came when prefects were changed and luck was with me??????? How I was ever picked is beyond my imagination. Naturally all former prefects have many stories to relate. I must admit I didn't mind the job at all, especially since I had the easiest position of all. It's good for your training not to get mad just because 'young men' pull your jacket to threads and call you 'father' all the time. And how about the time when I could hardly stand up and retired about 11:30 at night [prefects had duties after curfew]. I got undressed and was about to settle down for a long winter nap, only to discover that I had been short-sheeted. They say these are the things that make saints.

Another student remembered:

> While the moon played peek-a-boo behind the clouds, the wind shifted from a quiet lull to a minor gale. The air whistled through the broken garret windows. The light poured in the skylight above the creaky stairwell. And the floor let out a groan every now and then. I had just finished cleaning the

> jakes and was headed toward bed when a thought or rather a temptation popped into my head. Quickly yielding to it, I woke up Charley and ransacked his locker for something to eat. After shooing away the mice, we came up with a can of mixed nuts. … In the meantime, unknown to us, a lamp was flicked off and the office door closed. … Then the reprimanding voice spoke out, "Better get to bed!!" As the black-robed watchman escorted us downstairs, I quickly scrambled off to bed. The incident was forgotten until about a week later Father gave us a sermon in chapel and sure enough, I then began to appreciate his policy of not mentioning names in his sermons.[42]

The priests' side of the seminary was mostly forbidden to the students and therefore held special attraction, as a student entry in the *Mirror* illustrates:

> One day during the Easter work order of my third year at Kirkwood, Kenny Couvillion and I were appointed to a special job. We were to go over on the Priests' side of the house and sand the finish off of some old chairs. We assembled our gear and set to working like Trojans so that we could get out for some handball in that fresh Missouri spring air. We worked diligently for at least ten minutes, then, getting tired of such an arduous task, we decided to have a look around the mysterious Priests' side, which no one except a few icebox-robbing seniors knew anything about.
>
> I began to go through one stack of cartons, and Kenny another. Now these were not cartons of canned tuna or Spam, they were the cartons that the altar wine had been shipped in. We both contributed our little witticisms as to the quantity of wine we would consume after ordination. Kenny said, "I think I will send the altar boy back for more." And I, of course not to be outdone, was so clever as to say, "My altar boy will need two hands to pour my sized cruet." The next carton my meandering eyes met was an empty one. The label on the side declared the contents to have been "Wartime Mixer." Unthinking I blurted out, "Hey Kenny, look at this! Must have been some party, huh?" "Yes," he says, "look at that, a whole case."
>
> Suddenly from behind came the unmistakable jingle of a Redemptorist rosary. We turned to see no one else but Fr. Liesveld standing there as big as life. Apparently he had heard everything, for with a big grin on his face he merely hailed us a good day, and left us there wrapped in our own thoughts, spellbound with anxiety. From that time on we both waited to be summoned to the office, but fortunately the call never came.[43]

"Keep the rule and the rule will keep you," was a common saying. The shared culture of strict regulation and discipline, besides keeping order, fostered strong bonds. There was nothing to think about, all was decided in advance. But if some aspect went against the grain it would chafe, though this would not come to a head until several years later, in major seminary.

In the meantime, in May of Pat's second year of high school, Mulligan announced that final exams would be moved up, and they'd be going home two weeks early. This was so they could do some further shoring up of the disintegrating structure, a temporary measure while a new seminary was at last being built. They came back in the fall to one more year at Kirkwood. The summer after Pat's third year, St. Joseph's College at Edgerton, Wisconsin, was finally ready for occupancy and they left Kirkwood for the last time.

Edgerton — the transition

The new St. Joseph's College was on a large property in rural Wisconsin, just outside the town of Edgerton on the shores of Lake Koshkonong. At the end of the summer of 1959, instead of the short trip to Kirkwood, his parents made the long drive up to Edgerton. For Pat and his cohort, the change coincided with the transition from junior to senior. They arrived to a brand new, yellow brick building. Casing the place thoroughly they located the chapel: modern, with light-filled bright stained-glass windows in contrast to the old dark Gothic chapel of Kirkwood; the refectory: it was huge. There was bright paint on the walls, cheerful colors, everything spacious. The dorms were vast, the beds comfortable — none of the old "canoes" with slumping mattresses. Each student had a locker and a set of drawers close to his bed. Years later, Pat remembered:

> The new building in Wisconsin was… Of course, we'd complained about everything at Kirkwood. There weren't enough sinks. You had to stand in line to get to a sink to wash in the morning. And there were showers down in the basement. I think there were eight of them, for — I think there were about 200 boys trying to get in a shower after an hour's recreation. Locker rooms were old and the floor was cracked linoleum. The gymnasium had cracks in the walls, they could never keep it heated. So the new building… There were plenty of sinks, plenty of showers, plenty of toilets. Two locker rooms, one for the juniors, one for the seniors. Two big common rooms. Two big gymnasiums. Two floors of dormitories, four big study halls instead of one big study hall. Two very wonderful labs; physics labs and chemistry, biology labs. Classrooms, super beautiful refectory. We had a big auditorium, brand new stage with lighting. Stuff like that. For the thespians it was paradise. Big chapel, but all modern, marble. It was a big modern building. In the old place, we had to wear blazers and ties. But you could pick your own. There was a variety. There wasn't any uniform. Except on Saturday nights and Sundays we had to wear black suits, white shirts and a black tie. In the new place they instituted uniforms, which were just kind of windbreaker jackets, Izod pullover shirts. Juniors wore brown, seniors wore grey. I never liked that. It was more informal. Still on Saturdays and Sundays we wore suits and ties.

> So it was a big change. And I was kind of sorry for it because it was really kind of a nice old… "This is our home. It's old but we love it," kind of thing. Then everything changed in this new place. And of course, the traditions changed. We couldn't teach the newcomers the old traditions.[44]

Pat was not alone in resisting the change. The strong reaction, the hesitancy about Edgerton, the deep nostalgia for Kirkwood, were a measure of the degree to which he and the others had become attached to their seminary home. They poured out their feelings in *The Mirror:*

> A happy bunch of boys with a cheery, live spirit were the ingredients of the old St. Joe's. … When we contrast brick for brick between the two colleges, Kirkwood is left far behind. But if we balance finished products yielded from Kirkwood, Edgerton looks rather shady so far. In Kirkwood rules were set down, order was present which gave way to harmony, a peaceful routine resulted throughout the years. That's one thing Edgerton hasn't acquired yet. The atmosphere has changed too. At Kirkwood you always looked out the window to view the huge water tower, Mr. Nepos' house, then the grove, the fields, the pond, the barns, and these became a part of us. Kirkwood contained so many memorable events that now we sometimes wish the good old days back. … In spite of all imperfections, it held a spot in our hearts.

One student waxed poetic:

> Kirkwood's profession has ever been the same — the formation of the true Redemptorist. For Kirkwood still exists. It does not lie buried under tons of brick, wood and steel; it is very much alive! For Kirkwood is a spirit. This spirit is not merely one of loyalty to the old alma mater — it spells a loyalty to the Redeemer. It is the very font of our seminary life, the soil in which our future apostolic labors take root. It is vital to each and every one of us. Without it our environment becomes harsh, the atmosphere grows noxious, we wither and die. What is the identity of this spirit? You may call it Edgerton; but to me it's still "Kirkwood."[45]

They understood it was up to them to make the new place home.

> …There's one thing that the contractors couldn't plan and the workmen couldn't build and that's the spirit of the place. Without spirit it could be the most beautiful or the most comfortable place in the world but it wouldn't be the happiest. Putting the spirit into this frame is our job.[46]

The shift in morale was sufficiently concerning that the directors worked with the students to try to restore equanimity. A student wrote:

> If you look at this question in a material way, the contrast is too glaring even to be shown … Maybe the reason for the lack of Kirkwood warmth and quiet happiness here at Edgerton is the fact, as Father Director mentioned, that there was a slow start in the regularity to which we were accustomed. I like to think that the fault lies partly in the building itself. It just isn't hallowed yet. Please don't get me wrong. I'm not saying that the spirit here isn't good, just that it is inferior to the spirit enjoyed at Kirkwood, and I'm certainly not saying that a building is the whole cause of this "spirit," rather a building can invigorate this spirit and deplete this spirit. I'm sure that in three or four years Edgerton will surpass Kirkwood in every regard, as soon as it becomes a true *home*, which is deeply loved by the students. Then these new walls will enclose a group of souls as happy as those living anywhere.[47]

Teachers from Kirkwood moved with the students to Edgerton. Teaching was still very good and still done entirely by Redemptorists — lay teachers for the minor seminary would not come until later. The same activities went on according to the same schedule. Whether the loss of spirit was because of the move to Edgerton or simply coincident with it is hard to say. It was 1959, and the Church stood at the brink of an exodus from seminaries and the priesthood that began before Vatican II and would see more than half of seminaries closing over the next 20 years.

Students rebounded from the disorienting change of building, grounds and climate — it was much colder in the winter in Wisconsin — and the ebullient spirit returned, but not with the same intensity. There had been a push when the new St. Joseph's College at Edgerton opened to encourage additional vocations so they could fill the place. Pat felt that entrance requirements, not just as regards academic ability but also character, had been loosened. "They really beat the bushes," he said. There were new faces in all years. At the same time, there was attrition. When Pat's class entered in September 1956, Mulligan, the Director of Students, predicted to them that 99% would go on to be ordained priests. He was speaking looking backward on the cusp of a seismic shift in recruitment to the priesthood. Had he been able to look forward, he would have known that only seven would be ordained of Pat's entering class of 54 boys. The high morale of the Kirkwood years never fully returned.

Students pushed for greater integration across years — always within the structure of Separation, which is to say juniors with juniors and seniors with seniors. Father Mulligan gave a talk to the seniors on interclass mingling and how it could be improved, the gist summarized in *The Mirror*:

> Some of the sources of improvement are: table, sports and short remissions. At *table*, the conversation should be shared by all the members at the table. It shouldn't be monopolized by one person. And *sports*; Sports should be a community matter. There shouldn't be any "private" games. And finally, *short remissions*: During short remissions, students from different classes should mingle. I'm sure they'd have something in common to talk about. *No Cliques.*[48]

Other students chimed in:

> I think it could and *would* be improved if the second academic put a little more effort into breaking down the wall between themselves and the first academic.* I think that this in itself would be a big step toward more perfect unity and understanding among the Juniors. Again, I'm not saying this as a 'cut-up' to the second academic, because I know that this is the natural second-year spirit of the college. But I am saying that with the little effort that we'd have to put into this project, they could do an awful lot for Junior spirit, and thus, for the spirit of the college. … Just a little effort, and we'll be able to make St. Joe's one big community; not an institution made up of six separate classes, each containing several little inseparable 'groups'.[49]

It was part of the Student Rule that no one would have "particular friendships." Yet inevitably, close friendships developed, and it became a problem for some. This too was written about in *The Mirror*:

> What follows is something a little out of the ordinary for this page. Usually it contains a few news items and an occasional cut-up. This is not a cut-up and is not to be taken as such. It might seem funny to the people concerned, but it is said in all seriousness. The subject is particular friendship. It seems that no matter how much is said against it, certain people are drawn into it. Particular friendship does have its own righteousness, but only in certain circumstances. Take, for example, a man who is ready to get married. He must go with a girl until he finds if she is the right one for him or not. No one would expect him to marry some girl he hardly knew. If you were to take a look at some of the friendships here, all you would have to do is put a dress on the sweet little one, and they'd be all set to get married! No matter where you go, there they are. And if they're not together, they're continually looking for each other. When found, a warm smile passes between them that virtually turns the stomach. But what can you do about it? Since everything

---

* First academic is ninth grade; second academic is tenth grade. These are the first two years of minor seminary. See Glossary, Minor Seminary, for a more complete summary.

> else has failed, the only thing left is to leave the "men" alone, and just hope it will peter out. Because if it doesn't, they will meet with disastrous ends.[50]

Pat may have been one of those guilty of particular friendship. He was very close friends with Ed Crotty. They shared an interest in Dramatics, an appreciation for the same books, for walks and other quiet pursuits. Ed had been Dramatics Director for several years, and Pat took over the job from him. Sports were very much peripheral to their interests, and that shared attitude made sports more palatable. There's a color photo of the soccer team grouped around their banner. Ed is leaned up against Pat and draped comfortably over his shoulder as they squat together near the banner, both of them smiling. Mostly they spent a lot of time together selecting plays, discussing casting, direction, sets, everything. It was a tight bond for Pat. There were others he loved, including Harry Grile; also Ed Ruder, with whom he had been friends since first grade. And Dan Betinec was always a comfortable presence. Pat had broad affections for many of his classmates, but his close friends mattered to him most. Especially with Ed Crotty, the seminary's ideal of "general friendships only" did not fit for him.

Bequests

The final issue of *The Mirror* each year served as a yearbook for the college sophomores, now leaving minor seminary for the novitiate. Each graduating senior had standard contributions, including a full-page professional photo and with much tongue-in-cheek, some vital statistics, a list of favorite things in different categories, a list of bequests to students coming after them, and an essay with a theme specific to the year.

Pat had made an impression on minor seminarians in years ahead of him. Larry Aniol left "to P Hawk: my ability to choose different definite topics for conversation — your scope is entirely too braud [*sic*]." Dick Mevisen: "to Pat Hawk: ...my love of fine music." Joe Fritz: "to Pat Hawk — my love for any kind of music." Terry McCloskey: "To Pat Hawk... I leave the fate of always being in the Minors whether you're good or not." James Whalen "to Pat 'ax-handle' Hawk I leave patience. You will need this virtue when you start ringing those bells." John McDermott: "to Pat Hawk I leave my battered hockey stick so he will have a spare ready when he breaks his own over an opponent's head." Gary Clifford: "to Pat Hawk: I leave *woops censored*!" Jaime aka The Glee Man: "to Pat Hawk, a bit of glee." On the Laughs page: "Confucius says (maybe you can correct me on this if you've read him) that Humor is infectious. So if you find you've worked up more than a smile reading this page, see Pat Hawk; we don't want to start another epidemic."[51] When Pat's turn came in spring 1962, he left variously,

> …my soccer uniform, a stack of 50 unfinished short stories for *The Mirror*, my dislike of asinine jokes, a whole room of mutilated plays, one 'Houla' honey, my one and only but most effective judo punch, my office as papal secretary of state to impious Ron I, one free ticket to HMS Pinafore so you can see how it's supposed to be done, my tapeworm to add to your collection, and my collection of 'picture' calendars, my assorted forbidden novels, address books, art slides they wouldn't let us show, and ten easy lessons on how to look cheerful by me.

After nothing but silliness in their bequests to classmates, most of the boys finish with sincere, even sentimental, thank yous and blessings. "To all the other friends I have I leave you my sincerest wishes that Our Lady of Perpetual Help will shower you with many graces so that all of you may persevere with your God-given vocation." "To all I leave the perseverance to continue toward the goal of the priesthood, and the knowledge that I will be behind you all with my prayers. Goodbye and God love you." "To all I leave a sincere 'thanks' for making these years as pleasant as possible. Please forgive me for faults that are so evident in my makeup. Pray for us." Not so, Pat. He bequeaths to all, "Love and kisses and a few scattered half said prayers between my scourgings at the Novitiate."[52]

Vital statistics for Pat at graduation are age 19, weight 125 pounds, height five foot seven. He writes for the yearbook:

> Pet peeve: people who are insincere. Favorite hobby: none. Secret ambition: To be able to talk to John Ott for five minutes straight. Frustrated ambition: To be junior prefect. Favorite sports: Tennis and Hockey. Favorite food: Hotdog. Favorite books: Many — Gone with the Wind, Quo Vadis, Hatter's Castle, Agony and Ecstasy, among others. Favorite class: Lab class. Favorite job: Library while I had it. Favorite room: Fr. Feit's office. Favorite liquid refreshment: Tea. Favorite bodybuilder: What's this??? Favorite song: Zombie Jamboree. Favorite Professor: Fr. Collins.[53]

In Pat's year, the requisite parting essay was an obituary written by the student about himself. Pat's offering reveals a very different person from the pious boy who entered the seminary at 13:

> After five short years of teaching, Fr. Pat was sent to labor in Africa among a mau-mau tribe for ten years. Fr. Pat loved his work there immensely. Following this "choice" assignment Fr. Prov., decided to give him a break and send him to Brazil. While in Brazil he started several programs which were to his credit. One of which was that he raised money to help his missions by selling yo-yos with the picture of Mother of Perpetual Help on them. This

> went over very well, matter of fact it was a sell-out. The money poured in. Another endeavor of Fr. Pat's was his club for young people. He formed the "Heckle and Jeckle" Club. It consisted of the Heckle Club of Mary and the Jeckle Club of Joseph. The goal of both was to be a crow [*sic*] of Jesus 'in Aeternum'. The club spread like wildfire and was still quite active when Fr. Prov. received that telegram from Brazil conveying the joyful news of Fr. Pat's death.[54]

In his obituary he predicted 2015 as the date of his own death — as it turned out, off by three years. The casual, cynical references, the yo-yos with pictures of the Mother of Perpetual Help, are in stark contrast to the pious short stories he wrote in high school. Somewhere between his early years at Kirkwood and his departure from Edgerton, he lost the simple devotion of his childhood. And in his imagining of a standard Redemptorist trajectory for his life and work, he did not fathom the turn his personal charism would take.

Novitiate

Mount St. Clement's College was another aged, creaking building by the time Pat and his class arrived in June 1962 for their year of novitiate. It was situated in the foothills of the Ozark Plateau overlooking the town of De Soto, Missouri, about an hour's drive southeast of Kirkwood. Coming from the well-appointed facilities at Edgerton, its venerable worn halls were reminiscent of Kirkwood, although the plain, four-story brick building was smaller than the seminaries at Kirkwood or Edgerton.

During their six years of minor seminary, the men graduated from high school and completed two years of a four-year college degree in liberal arts. College was interrupted by the novitiate year, to be resumed as the first two years of major seminary. The focus of the novitiate was on deepening the spiritual life of the seminarian. There was the same tightly regulated schedule with bells waking the men early and ringing periodically throughout the day to signal each activity, but academic studies were set aside in favor of devotional exercises.

Pat and his group from Edgerton were joined by a few men whose vocation to the priesthood manifested at a later age and who therefore had finished high school and in some cases college, as well as some who were on a path to become Redemptorist Brothers rather than priests. All arrived at De Soto in late June and for the first approximately six weeks, overlapped with the preceding novitiate class. The newcomers were postulants for those six weeks, traditionally a period of probation in which the candidate seeks to be admitted to the novitiate, but in Pat's day essentially a formality. The outgoing novices oriented them to the new place and new expectations. It was July, hot and humid, and there was a lot of time off during that first period to go on walks and picnics.

As in the minor seminary, the novices did a substantial part of the work of running the place, with work order on Saturday afternoons or as needed, each with assigned jobs. They cultivated grapes and made their own wine, on special occasions having a glass with dinner. They kept rabbits, sheep and a few pigs for meat. They made Redemptorist habits and rosaries, ran a printer, kept the building clean. They also looked after aging priests and monks, the place serving as a care facility for those no longer able to care for themselves. The schedule of prayer and work was relieved with recreation periods for sports, long walks — always still in groups of six or more — picnics, reading.

Pat's job for much of the time was to look after Brother Hank — a difficult man who needed supervision as well as physical care. He had a lifetime pass on the railroad, having worked there before he joined the Redemptorists, and while he was still fully mobile, he'd hop on a train and send a message saying something like, "I'm in Seattle, see you in a couple of weeks." While in residence Hank found various ways to be irritating, such as when he had a window-cleaning job he would clean a small circle in the middle and say, "Good enough!" He trapped mice then took the live mice and asphyxiated them. He would loosen the screws on the doorknob so it would fall off when someone tried to open it. Or he would try to lock himself in his room. Everyone heard about "Hank's pranks."[55] Among other chores, Pat had to bathe him, something Hank hated and would fight. Pat did not grow to like the job, though his sense of duty kept him from shirking.

At the end of the postulancy period, on August 1 each year, there was Investiture, in which the men donned the Redemptorist habit for the first time, a simple black robe with white clerical collar. There is a wide cincture for the waist around which is carried a long rosary, said to be arranged like the letter M for Mary. The rosary's large crucifix, inserted in the cincture, is recycled — when a Redemptorist dies, his crucifix goes to a novice. Once invested with the habit, the novices wore it every day thereafter through the novitiate and major seminary, and in some cases, depending on their apostolate,* also in their professional lives. The day after the incoming novices put on the habit, the outgoing novices professed vows and left, whereupon the novitiate year began in earnest for the new class.

The novice master was in charge of all aspects of life and spiritual development of the men. He could have a huge impact on the overall experience. When Pat's class arrived, the novice master was Father Peter Forbes. He was generally

---

* The assigned ministry of each priest.

easygoing as far as requiring the regular order, at least for the first month, but for some reason he was hard on Pat. How much this had to do with Pat's sometimes surliness or irreverence and how much was par for the course, Pat couldn't say. There was an explicit expectation that candidates unsuited for the priesthood would be weeded out during their seminary years, and severe treatment was sometimes encouraged. In *Practice of the Vows*, an important text during the novitiate, there is the admonition to the novice master, "Be severe. These are hard words, it is true, but they are full of love."[56] Pat said, "While Forbes was alive, he was testing me. He was giving me hard jobs and criticizing me almost daily. I don't know if I would have lasted."

He didn't have to find out. During the night before Labor Day, Forbes had a heart attack in his bed and died. For a month, they had Forbes's assistant, a young and inexperienced man who left them mostly to their own devices. In October, there was a radical change when Father Joe Powers, who had been novice master from 1953 to 1955, was recruited back to the job. The tendency toward obsessive-compulsive disorder can express itself in religious men and women as scrupulosity, something with which St. Alphonsus himself, founder of the Redemptorists, was said to be afflicted.[57] It manifests in an obsessive concern about what is or is not sinful and in compulsion toward performance of religious devotions. Powers was scrupulous.

Canon Law required that, to be valid, the novitiate — not just for Redemptorists but for any religious* — must be "an entire and uninterrupted year, under the direction of a Master, specially appointed for the training of novices."[58] Pat said, "As far as Joe Powers was concerned, this group was *ruined*, and he told us so." Powers was appalled by the lack of discipline among the novices. From the time he took over, he held them to a strict regimen with very little levity. The outgoing class had talked about how wonderful their novitiate had been and how they'd gladly do another year. Pat's class only hoped to survive.

Besides being strict and by the book, Powers had a somewhat depressed affect, but Pat did not feel singled out by him as he had by Forbes and found his severity easier to take. He respected Powers's even-handedness and was at ease with his somber manner. Perhaps Pat also took a dim view of some of his fellow novices. For whatever reason, "We got along fine, Joe and I. I liked Joe a lot. He was a fine man, just a fine man. One of those people who had integrity. ... I remember when he received a letter from Rome approving us for taking vows. He came up to our common room where he gives these talks, and he read off the

---

* Religious (priests and nuns) belong to a community, take vows of poverty, chastity and obedience, and are responsible to a Superior within the community.

list. And I never heard anybody so disgusted — that these people had been approved."

They settled into the regular order. It was still life in community but with a greater emphasis on solitude. A major change was that each man now had his own room, and there was more time scheduled for solitary devotions. As in the minor seminary, to provide a framework for spiritual practice, there were assigned virtues, expanded from six to twelve, one for each month: Faith, Hope, Love toward God, Love of Neighbor, Poverty, Purity, Obedience, Humility, Mortification, Recollection and Silence, Prayer, and Love of the Cross.

After rising and dressing, the men assembled in chapel for half an hour of spiritual reading and meditation, during which each man was to set an intention — how he would practice the monthly virtue that day — similar to what they had begun in minor seminary but with more focus on the virtue of the month. There was Particular Examen around midday to review how you were doing with the intention, notice any lapse and recommit, then at the end of the day, review how you did. At regular individual meetings the novice master would evaluate and give feedback to the novice regarding how he was doing with the virtue of the month — how strong was his faith, how much hope he manifested, whether he was practicing love of God and love of neighbor, and so on.

Mass followed meditation, then came a period of thanksgiving, then the novices went back to their rooms for an hour. During that time they were to read from the Constitutions and Statutes, a fuller and more stringent document than the Student Rule from minor seminary, but like the Student Rule, governing life in minute detail. It specified such things as the allowable size of the bed — not more than 24 inches wide, and what articles are permissible in a person's room — very few. Benedict* himself required "that before a novice be admitted to Profession, the Rule should be read to him on three occasions, 'that he may know unto what he cometh,' and that it should be said to him, 'Behold the law, under which thou desirest to fight. If thou canst observe it, enter in, if thou canst not, freely depart'."[59] Novitiate was the time for this reckoning.

Following this period of solitary reading, by then several hours after rising, the men went down to the refectory for breakfast in silence. Everyone ate in the same room, but they were segregated — the priests from the Brothers and both from the novices. As with silent meals in the minor seminary, there was reading at table — usually spiritual biographies or memoirs, or if there was an important political book out they might read that. Rachel Carson's *Silent Spring* was one Pat

* Benedict of Nursia (480-548 CE), founder of the monastic Order of St. Benedict.

remembered was read at table. The novice master chose the reading. The men took turns. Often it was translations from the works of Alphonsus or the French Redemptorist Louis Colin, prolific author in the 1950s and '60s of guidance for life in the Congregation.

Talking was only allowed on Sundays and special days designated by the novice master. He could grant levels of free days: on a one-quarter-star day you could talk, on a half-star day there were additional freedoms, and on a full-star day there was nothing scheduled. After breakfast, the men gathered again, for spiritual reading and a conference given by the novice master, or on Saturdays by his Socius.[60] That was Ray Stewart — they called him Stewy. Unlike Powers, he was lighthearted. Powers could have a sense of humor but he didn't show it much around the novices, so Stewy was a welcome change of pace.

Pat and his fellow seminarians learned about the novitiate as they lived it. The importance of this phase of formation was emphasized in the writings of Colin: "Every candidate must appear before the authorities and agree to undergo a period of probation, which is the novitiate."[61] Parents, directors and recruiters are responsible only for discovering true vocations, cultivating them and bringing them to a successful issue, without ever presuming to invent them, still less to impose them. In the long run, it is up to the candidate to convince himself personally of the reality of the divine call, and to respond with complete freedom; to this end, let him pray, ask advice and reflect."[62] "The profession [of vows], which crowns the novitiate, is an act which is too holy in itself, too grave in its consequences, to be made lightly, without knowing exactly what one is doing, what one wants, what one is undertaking, forever. He must live apart from the world, from its foolish pleasures, its pomps and vanities, its frivolity and its business; above all he must eschew its outlook, its desires and its morals."[63] "The religious state is a holocaust, which consists in the first place, in the total gift of oneself to God."[64] Pat said, "I remember they talked about it as being a white martyrdom instead of a red martyrdom."

According to Canon Law at the time, "The formation of novices shall be entrusted to a Master, who shall be at least 35 years old, have been professed for at least ten years (dating from the first profession), and conspicuous for his prudence, charity, piety and religious observance." "The year of novitiate, under the guidance of the Master of Novices, is intended to form the character of the novice by the study of the Rule and Constitutions, by pious meditations and assiduous prayer, by instruction in all matters pertaining to the vows and the cultivation of virtue, and by pious exercise conducive to the complete eradication of faulty habits, the control of the passions, and the acquisition of virtues."[65] Besides the deepening of spirituality and preparation for the vows that was the objective of novitiates Church-wide, the Redemptorist novitiate sought to more intimately acquaint the men with the life and spirituality of Alphonsus of Liguori, revered founder of the Congregation.

Assigned readings, and the novice master in his talks, presented each of the vows the men would profess at the end of the novitiate year. The Vow of Poverty, Colin explains, is a vow of non-attachment. The poor can betray the vow if they are attached to their few possessions. The rich can honor the vow if they are unattached. "…the spirit of poverty is not irreconcilable with riches and magnificence."[66] Pat said: "The emphasis to us was always really the common life. Everything is held in common. That's the point. You're to be detached but not necessarily indigent." "Thus, in a Community, the aggregate of property belongs to all the religious in general and nothing to each one in particular. No one is an owner, all are merely users."[67]

The Vow of Chastity is to remain faithful to one's state in life as far as sexuality is concerned. The married person may be called chaste if he or she is faithful to the marriage. For the Catholic religious, since marriage is not permitted, the vow of chastity means a commitment to celibacy. It includes "…the province of modesty: immodest looks, readings, conversations, touches, recollections, imaginings, too tender affections, these, like the others, involve a double sin: mortal or venial according to their gravity and the more or less proximate danger they create."[68] It is expressly not considered sterile. "When we gave up the idea of founding a family, we adopted as our children all the souls redeemed by Jesus. 'My little children of whom I am in labor again until Christ be formed in you!' (Galatians 4:19)"[69] The dualism and negativity toward the body are prominent in Colin's florid counsels:

> As for gross and impure pleasures, how can they have any weight, when compared to the divine joy of loving God? What man would choose to drink from a stagnant, slimy pool rather than a limpid spring? God ever suffices, for those who love Him ardently. … Without despising the prescriptions of hygiene, we must not overlook the laws of modesty, and must beware of rousing passion, that sleeping wild beast! … Let us play the hedgehog toward those whose manner would be too familiar, or who offer a friendship that is too human.[70]

Pat said, "We had sex talks in every retreat every year, of course. And then again when the virtue of the month came around to chastity — but counseling, I don't think so, unless there was individual counseling. Wear your habit. Don't go to movies. Turn your eyes away from lascivious displays, that kind of thing. I suppose it just presumed you were well enough formed by the time you got out. That was a ridiculous presumption. … We got the same rigamarole all the time. Beware, beware. … Put up the barriers. Keep the barriers intact and you'll be all right. Keep the Rule and the Rule will keep you. Pray. Pray. Say three Hail Marys." He shook his head.

The challenge and discipline of celibacy were understood to be helped by practices of physical mortification — taming the flesh. Colin wrote, "Mortification is not a fashionable word, and might with advantage be found more often in the mouths of preachers, and in the writings of spiritual authors. The age we live in has no use for it and readily treats it as a 'luxury' virtue. Yet without its help, no chastity can preserve its virginal freshness."[71]

Practices included, at prescribed times, wearing a cilicium around the arm, a chain-like device made of metal with spokes that pointed inward at the flesh so as to prick it. They were made to fit each man snugly but not too snugly. One was not allowed to wear it so tight as to break the skin. The cilicium given to Pat's classmate, later confrere, Father Harry Grile, was initially too tight for him. The first time he wore it, at 5:30 in the morning in the hot chapel, he keeled over. Picking him up, they had to be careful not to make things worse by pushing on it. You could tell who was wearing the cilicium under his shirt if you saw a man holding his arm out so as not to let it rest against his body. Occasionally someone would deliberately bump into a classmate or give a friendly squeeze in the right place.

The Discipline was another prescribed practice. Every novice was issued a scourge made of seven or eight ropes, each a few feet long and attached to a central handle. The ends of the rope were knotted and dipped in wax to make them hard. Standing with their pants dropped, they would swing the whip over their shoulders to one side and then the other, hitting bare buttocks. This was while reciting the *Miserere* in Latin — they all knew it by heart — and swinging to the rhythm of the psalm.[72] It was usually done privately, each in his own room. Occasionally it was done together, doors open along the corridor with each man standing just outside his own room.

Greg Mayers remembered: Their rooms had transoms above the door to allow air circulation. One of his best friends had put a bar across the transom so he could do chin-ups. One night after prayers, Greg was using the bar just outside the closed door of his friend's room and thought it would be funny to knock on the door so when his friend opened, he would just see his legs. He knocked, then quickly pulled himself up. In full view through the transom window was his friend, drawers dropped, doing the Discipline. The guy swatted at him with the whip. Never mind mortification of the flesh, both were just plain mortified.[73]

On days when the cilicium was worn, it was from the time of morning prayer until after breakfast. The Discipline was done at night, after night prayer. And there were other penances. You could be assigned "soup on your knees" for lunch. Pat said, "The idea was that you mortify the flesh so it will go away. To keep it in control. Make it back off. Like you punish your child to keep it from bad behavior." None of this was continued after the novitiate year, and after Vatican II it was dropped completely. Commenting years later on whether physical mortification practices had any spiritual value, Pat said he thought not. But he pointed out that so many of the medieval mystics, including the contemplatives — John of the Cross, Teresa of Avila, many others — are known to have practiced mortification, sometimes extreme, and that it seemed at least for some to support deep religious experience.

Obedience was presented as the greatest of the vows in that it includes the other two. In *Practice of the Vows*, Colin says: "The virtue of obedience, which, that it may be perfect, according to Saint Thomas, must be adorned with seven qualities: spontaneity, simplicity, joy, promptness, virility, humility, perseverance.[74] … It is good to give up one's possessions to follow Christ, it is better to dedicate one's body as an inviolable sanctuary of purity; it is best to renounce what man clings to most closely, what constitutes the core of his personality, i.e., the independent use of his liberty."[75] Colin rises to great flowery heights: "In praise of obedience: raising the rampart of a Rule and sacred authority against the assaults of egotism and the passions, I have but defended my liberty against its worst enemies. By making a sacred and eternal promise to never stray from the will of God, expressed to me by His representatives I have merely shored up my buckling will and so made good the deficiencies of my liberty." It was suggested to Pat years later that in choosing the Vow of Obedience, one has chosen to yield and that this might paradoxically make the yielding easier in that it has become a personal choice, once and for all. He nodded equivocally.

There is also the matter of freedom from responsibility. Colin writes: "For those who subject themselves, in all simplicity and loyalty, there can be no fear of error, no motive for discouragement, no possibility of failure. Are they under obedience? Then all is well and could not be better.[76] … One of the most striking characteristics of the perfectly obedient is serenity. Why should he be troubled, since he incurs no moral responsibility? Obedience is a completely safe situation."[77] Pat said, "You can use that argument to justify what the Nazis did under obedience. But they presume since you're in a religious organization, it's got to be moral. Maybe not."

Colin goes on, "There are always inconveniences and risks in the religious state, and they too, are part of the 'job'. There is a risk of receiving annoying, difficult, or painful commands. The risk of being put under the jurisdiction of uncongenial superiors, or in the company of disagreeable colleagues. ... And when the risk becomes a reality what are we to say? Nothing! What are we to do? Obey."[78] Pat said, "We took that with a grain of salt. And in any event, you always have ultimate responsibility for yourself and your own conscience, even under a vow of obedience. Because if you think you've been given an order to do something against your conscience, you don't have to obey. You have to follow your conscience."

In the seminary, and especially in the novitiate, there was little room for choice. Pat recalled, "In a place like that, the whole thing is geared to following the Rule, following the schedule of the day, following instructions of the novice master and the rector. The whole year. Submitting to being in a group. Doing everything together. We didn't do anything alone practically. Everything was done as a whole group or in breakdown groups. It's hard to think of something that you did alone, except go to your room and meditate or read or whatever." There's also the purely practical. Preposterous to require permission for all the minutiae of life, and in most situations one simply presumes permission. "Presume, consume, forget," Pat quoted. But the ideal is there.

Besides the vows of poverty, chastity and obedience, Redemptorists profess a vow of perseverance. When Alphonsus founded the first group of Redemptorists, most of the men abandoned him. At the second try, in addition to the religious vows, he had his recruits take a Vow of Perseverance. This is not part of temporary vows made at the end of the novitiate year; rather, it is added three years later at profession of perpetual vows. However, the spirit of the oath is part of the instruction during the novitiate.

The novices were exhorted to repay their debt to the Church with fidelity.

> ...religious receive from their Order great graces and innumerable gifts. After being educated for long years with maternal solicitude, freely, would it not be strange, even shocking, if, when they were in a position to repay their debts by their work, they were to leave the Institute, without reason or regret?[79] How could one abandon a mother, though she be infirm and sick — and the Congregation in which one was born to the religious life is a Mother — if one loves her dearly? How could one give the slip to brethren with whom one forms one heart and one soul, in the service of the same Lord, and for the conquest of one same ideal?[80] ... Indeed, is not assurance of Heaven the supreme grace granted to fidelity? To die as a religious is one of the surest pledges of predestination: founders, theologians, and ascetics have

> never wearied of recalling and commenting the promise of Our Lord: *et vitam aeternam possidebit.*[81]

Even at the time, Pat and his classmates raised eyebrows at this sort of thing. Once when it was Pat's turn to read after breakfast, he held up the book and said, "Well, and here we have another dandy from Colin." Nonetheless, the lessons of Colin were the lessons of the novitiate. There was great emphasis on sanctification, becoming saints, the core of which meant the very future-oriented goal of gaining heaven after death. Pat said, "To die a happy death and be rewarded forever with a high position in celestial hierarchy. And if there was any recognition of a present holiness or sanctity it should be hidden because to display it is to be proud." As a young boy going into the seminary and still in the novitiate, his goals were for the afterlife. "Yeah. It was all quite literal in those days. A great deal of spiritual materialism, piling up merits, indulgences, graces. ... You see all these pictures of saints with the *memento mori.* The skull on their desk. All comes down to your last breath."[82]

In all of the spiritual exercises and instruction, there was nothing to encourage the novices to follow the path taken by the Christian mystics, to seek direct insight such as had John of the Cross, Teresa of Avila, Meister Eckhart, Tauler, and many others recognized by the Church as saints. In fact, they were discouraged from reading the works of these seekers.

Years later, in Amarillo, while watching Arnold Schwarzenegger as Conan the Barbarian harnessed to a wheel and pushing, pushing, pushing, Pat said, "That was my novitiate!"[83] There was that sense, looking back, of having been harnessed to something oppressive.

Several people left, including Dan Betinec, with whom Pat had been in elementary school and whose mother had first introduced Pat to the Redemptorists. Pat stuck it out. Somehow whatever seemed missing or not right didn't matter. "It was just the way things were." Toward the end of the novitiate year, each novice was to prepare a *curriculum vitae* of their vocation thus far. Pat's resolve was strong as ever:

> My vocation is one of those that I can say about it, as far as I can remember I have been attracted to the priesthood. I've always wanted to be a priest. I am unable to say exactly when God gave me the first notion, although it must have been at Mass about the end of the first grade. That is what I think because I distinctly remember coming home and mimicking the motions of the priest using one of the back steps for an altar. From then on I was "playing priest" quite often. After I became a server at the beginning of the sixth grade the attraction became more and more an ambition, a goal. I always

> loved serving Mass and can recall having missed an appointment only once and found myself in tears over the matter.
>
> Toward the end of my eighth grade, thoughts of what kind of priest I should be and of how to get into a seminary began filling my mind. It was more or less agreed upon between my parents and me that I should go to a Catholic high school and after that try for the diocesan priesthood. This was too uncertain for me and I was still hoping for a better chance. Then I asked my best friend Edward Ruder where he was going to high school and he announced that he was going to the seminary. Immediately I became envious and wanted to know how, when and where. He told me he was going to the same place that Dan Betinec was going who had a brother there.
>
> It was from Mrs. Betinec that I first heard the name Redemptorist and of how much better the religious life was compared to the secular priesthood. She arranged for us to have a talk with Fr. John Treinen at her home. He was the first Redemptorist I ever met and I was very much impressed by what he said about the Redemptorist apostolate and of Kirkwood. I made two visits to Kirkwood that April and in June I was accepted.
>
> My next three years were then spent at Kirkwood. There was nothing unusual about them nor the next three spent at Edgerton. I did my best to learn what was being taught and grew to know and like the Redemptorists. During all this time I can say that I have had no serious temptations directly against my vocation. I've always wanted to be a priest and after I found out about the religious life, a religious priest.* And I desire it even more strongly now, after six years of training in the Redemptorist way. That is the story of my vocation thus far.[84]

The profession at the end of the year of novitiate was temporary, so that life under the vows could be tried before final vows and a permanent commitment made three years later. Besides the pressure on the novices to discern whether theirs was a true vocation, there was pressure on the novice master to identify those who were unsuited and to discourage them from continuing. "If the suitability of a novice is in doubt, the novitiate can be prolonged for six months, and the first vows, for three years. After this lapse of time, the religious must make his vows or return to secular life. But — let us repeat it once more — the Superiors must take care to reject, not only candidates who are unfit, but also the mediocre and useless."[85] Pat said, "You get examined all the time, all the way through. The religious part — you're always examined by the dean of men first [at minor seminary] then the novice master, then the prefect of students [at major seminary]. He picks up from the novice master."

---

* A religious priest is a member of a religious congregation or order; as opposed to a diocesan priest.

In the spring of the novitiate year, each novice's application to be admitted to temporary vows was sent to Rome, approvals came back in due course, then the new postulants arrived in June. After the year at Mount St. Clement's, it was Pat and his classmates showing the ropes. August 1, the new crop of postulants had investiture, donning robes and officially becoming novices. On August 2, 1963, Pat and his class professed temporary vows. Families came from all over, and marquees were put up over tables to feed everyone. It was a big day. The title of Frater is bestowed on the newly professed and stays with them until ordination. Frater Patrick Hawk, CSsR, left Mount St. Clement's College, De Soto, headed to the major seminary, Immaculate Conception College at Oconomowoc, Wisconsin.

Major Seminary

Oconomowoc

Of the many austerities of seminary life, austerity of place was not among them. Perhaps surpassing the minor seminaries and the novitiate, Immaculate Conception College was in an exquisite setting on the shores of Lac La Belle in southeastern Wisconsin, about an hour's drive northeast of Edgerton and about 30 miles from Milwaukee.

The Redemptorists purchased a 20-acre property in 1911 from the Eckels family and adapted the mansion and outbuildings to use as classrooms, common rooms, refectory, library and chapel. Existing guest rooms were bared to monastic simplicity to serve as sleeping rooms. In the 1940s, the property was expanded to 80 acres. It was flanked by a golf course and the homes of the very wealthy along the lake. At various times through the years the buildings were remodeled, rebuilt and added onto. The faculty quarters were on one end. The refectory was at the opposite end on the lower floor. In between, the lower two floors were common areas and classrooms, the top floors were sleeping rooms. Some of the decoration, both external and internal, retained the patrician character of the original mansion. The front doors led into a vestibule that opened directly to the chapel, with an elaborate marble altar. Grand old trees grew around the buildings and grounds. A cloister walk made of arcades of red brick to match the building was added on the lake side; it extended from the chapel in both directions along most of the length of the building. Years later, looking at photographs of the long, graceful walkway Pat's confrere, Bob Halter, reflected, "Thousands of rosaries were said in there." [86]

By now, their eighth year in seminary, the routine was second nature for Pat and his fellow fraters, and they entered upon it without resistance. They had their various devotions. One of the long-standing customs at Oconomowoc was to kneel and say an Ave Maria at the foot of her statue. The marble floor was worn where generation after generation of seminarians had paused in prayer. There was the same regulated schedule, up early, morning prayer, meditation, breakfast, prayers, classes, and so on. The various sports in season. They had sailboats and canoes and could go out on the lake on free days when the weather allowed. Or they would take the canoes on what they called "flits" — exploring one of the many nearby lakes for the day. Lac la Belle would freeze over in winter, and years earlier the men would watch eagerly for the first solid ice to skate on, but a tragedy in which a man fell through and drowned put a stop to that. So they flooded an area of the grounds, put up boards and made a rink. Some of the priests golfed at the nearby course. The fraters could watch from a bluff, and when the priests came back from their game they would heckle them. They'd collect any golf balls hit onto the property.

As always, work order was on Saturday afternoons and during the week as needed. They worked as cleaners, plumbers, carpenters, mechanics, electricians. They fiberglassed canoes and hockey sticks. They tended the flower gardens that kept the chapel in flowers year-round. They operated the Multilith for the many printing jobs. They kept bees and had a rich honey harvest. They bound and repaired books. As before, they had silent meals with reading at table except on Thursdays, Sundays and special days.

They continued training in public speaking. They put on plays and other entertainments, Pat and Ed Crotty as involved as ever. Although they had a television set, watching TV was regulated. They could watch all the ball games on Thanksgiving. Every once in a while, they'd have a cultural Sunday and watch something like Nureyev and Joan Fontaine on the Ed Sullivan show. Later they got addicted to watching Batman — the old campy version, the original Batman with Adam West. It was on about 6:30 PM. The refectory was a single very large room with the priests at one end and the students' tables extending to the other end. From their end, the priests couldn't see when the students were finished eating so they had a signal. On a pillar at the student end was a picture of Our Lady of Perpetual Help, blank on the other side, and when the students were finished eating, they were to turn the picture face to the pillar and show the blank side. Then the Rector or whoever was presiding would ring the bell to signal the end of the meal. They'd say grace and go out. On Batman night the students put the Batman signal on the blank side of the picture. When the meal was over they could go and watch Batman.

There was no longer the rigid Separation of minor seminary, but in the refectory the class just out of the novitiate was kept separate at table from the upperclassmen, perhaps so as not to have their fervor wear off too soon. Harry Grile remembered, "Just out of novitiate we called everybody Frater. We were addressing each other as Frater this and Frater that. Piety. Eventually wears off."[87]

Pat shared the end of a table with Harry Grile and George Bredeman — the latter a strange and difficult man who had almost been dismissed during the novitiate but had somehow persuaded Joe Powers to let him stay. At the end of the novitiate, when there was overlap between the outgoing class and the new postulants, Pat, Harry and George shared sleeping quarters incompletely divided by partitions. George irritated the other two in various ways. One time he was counting rosary beads, tossing each one into a can, making a lot of noise. Pat yelled out, "Shut up, you son of a bitch!" Earlier at Edgerton, sometimes the men would swim from end to end of the pool without coming up for breath. George was doing this one day and wasn't coming up at all. Two others dove in and rescued him. Pat said, "Should have let the son of a bitch drown." George was dismissed from Oconomowoc before he professed perpetual vows, but he managed to get ordained into the diocesan priesthood. He was convicted on several counts of pedophilia over several years, put on parole, violated the terms of his parole, was caught and jailed. He died in prison in 2012.

Harry Grile was good company for Pat. Harry tells the story: There's a line in the writings of St. Alphonsus where a hawk is capturing a songbird and the songbird calls, "Ave Maria, Ave Maria," and the hawk drops dead. So Harry would walk past Pat's door saying, "Ave Maria, Ave Maria." Pat would give him the finger. They got along well and were friends for the rest of Pat's life, more remarkable for Pat, the great loner, than for Harry who was loved by most.

Pat's family would come up a few times a year for the allowed visits and stay at an old hotel in Madison, spend the day, then drive back to Granite City. Where in his adolescent years he had needed their visits more and enjoyed them less, he was now so thoroughly removed to another world that he could relax with them and be social.

After their year away from studies, the fraters settled down once again to academic work. Minor seminary had given them high school and the first two years of a college degree in liberal arts. Life had been within a setting of strong spiritual practice, but the topics taught were mainly secular. Then came the year of novitiate with intense spiritual formation. Now in the major seminary, they were to undertake the study of disciplines that would prepare them specifically for their lives as priests. The first two years were to complete their college degrees. They focused on philosophy. The remaining four years were devoted to the study of theology and would give them dual master's degrees in theology and religious studies.

Vatican II and the New Theology

In October 1962, while Pat and his fellow seminarians had been ensconced in the novitiate, Pope John XXIII convened the Second Vatican Council, a major goal of which was to bring about a reconciliation of Christian strands separated at the Reformation. The Council was to "provoke a new attitude of the Church to the world, one of dialogue based on goodwill with other religious traditions and with agnostics."[88]

A major obstacle was the understanding within the Church that the articles of faith could only be determined by interpreting tradition largely as articulated in the works of Thomas Aquinas. There was the assumption that Christian revelation had ended with the death of the last apostle. In fact, in 1907 Pope Pius X had condemned as heresy the belief that revelation continued up to the present,[89] and that condemnation was still in effect when Pat was in the major seminary. The task was only to understand what had been revealed, with the pope having ultimate authority, that authority having been declared infallible as regards Church teaching. Within the Church, Scripture was to be studied only by the anointed, which is to say the ordained — the faithful were allowed no direct access to their own faith. And direct experience of the divine was not to be sought by anyone, anointed or not. Among some seminarians, this rankled.

As a follow-up to his declaration of heresy, Pius X instituted an Oath Against Modernism, which all clergy, including all professors in seminaries, were required to swear. This was in place until 1967. Pat's class encountered articles of the Oath via their professors at Oconomowoc. In practical terms, it meant that the study of philosophy in the major seminary focused almost exclusively on neo-scholasticism and the philosophy and theology of Aquinas, ignoring other voices, for example, Immanuel Kant, who steered a middle path between dogmatic rationalism and skeptical modern empiricism.[90] A standard text was Jacques Maritain's *An Introduction to Philosophy*.[91]

There were strong dissenting voices within the Church to the orthodoxy in Catholic thought and the chokehold of the Church hierarchy. A "new theology" was emerging from, among others, Karl Rahner, Hans Küng, Yves Congar, Marie-Dominique Chenu, Pierre Teilhard de Chardin (published posthumously — his writings were banned from publication during his lifetime). Joseph Ratzinger, later Pope Benedict XVI, rose to prominence in opposition to some of the tenets of the Oath Against Modernism.

Through these Catholic priests came many of the roots of reform in the Church — including a call for decentralization of authority, an understanding of revelation that allowed for its evolution, and a reconciliation of Christian faiths — all of which required a return to direct interpretation of the Gospel. Related to this came an appreciation for the truths of other faiths, and from Rahner especially, the notion — *contra* Church teaching since the third century — that people who had never heard of Christ might nonetheless be eligible for eternal life. A revived appreciation for direct spiritual experience — unmediated "knowledge of" rather than explicated "knowledge about" ultimate reality, came to be expressed by people like Teilhard de Chardin, whose ideas were controversial but whose books, along with others warned against by the Vatican, were available in the library at Immaculate Conception if you knew where to look.

Given the resistance in the Church hierarchy to the new theology, it came as somewhat of a surprise, when Pope John XXIII announced the Second Vatican Council. The announcement, apparently made without much consultation with the curia, created a new atmosphere of optimism among bishops who wanted change.[92] John XXIII's express goal for the Council was working toward *aggiornamento* or updating of the manner in which the Church presented itself to its own faithful and to the world. The new vision for the Church was to be developed at least in part by a *ressourcement*, literally "re-sourcing," return to the sources, i.e., scripture and the Church fathers, especially Augustine. In other words, it was very much influenced by the agenda of the "new theologians."

By the time Pat entered major seminary, the council had already had the first of its four major sessions and the second was about to begin. There were pitched battles between the reformists and the conservatives. Yves Congar kept a daily journal, a few excerpts[93] from which give a flavor of some of the more human interactions. These attitudes could trickle into the major seminary and fuel dissent rather than blind acceptance among the fraters — Pat and his classmates. From Congar's journal:

> Bishop Bandeira of Brazil publicly asserted that the council must not touch the Roman rite, which, he explained, was instituted by St. Peter himself.
> Cardinal Pizzardo is an idiot and known to be such by all.
> Rahner once again monopolised the conversation.
> Cardinal Ottaviani went over his allotted time to speak, and the moderator, Cardinal Alfrink, turned off his microphone....

Various limericks circulated, among which was:

There was Rahner, and Congar and Küng,
Whose praises were everywhere sung,
But one fine domani
Ottaviani
Will have the three buggers hung.[94]

The ferment of ideas and controversy spilled into the seminary, in the communications back to the United States of the participants and in the published works of the leading thinkers. These were procured for Immaculate Conception College by Father George Rassley, trained librarian, an intellectual in the best sense, and for many years in charge of the library at Oconomowoc.

Access to these books was restricted, indeed some were on the Index of Prohibited Books. The Index was doing precisely the unintended by giving a lively boost to advertisement of the very books from which the Church wished to protect the faithful. Far from serving as an effective deterrent, authors sought to have their works put on the Index so they would get a wider readership and more sales. (Pope Paul VI would finally abolish the Index in 1966 because it was apparent that banning a book was the surest way to provoke interest in it.) Rassley's acquisitions for the library included prohibited books, ostensibly for research by those judged sufficiently orthodox to be safe with them. Pat was the assistant librarian. Had they noticed that that had been his favorite job at Edgerton and chosen it for him for that reason? There was that kind of thoughtfulness and individual attention. In any case, he could browse any book in the library including those on the Index, sequestered in an area they called Hell. In fact, anyone who could persuade George Rassley that they had a legitimate interest in a book could usually borrow it, and he wasn't hard to persuade.

Pat remembered, "We had pretty good access to good books, especially new theological stuff coming in. Everybody wanted to read them, so it was hard to get a hold of some of these things. But there was a room full of what were called forbidden books. Books on the Catholic Index that you weren't allowed to read. But if you could get on the good side of this librarian, he'd get them for you and you could read them." Bob Halter had a similar recollection. "Students would read the radical books that Rassley brought in, then form study groups and discuss. Some faculty thought this was a good thing. The ones who disapproved were mostly faculty who had learned their stuff, then never kept up. They were behind the times and couldn't answer students' questions arising out of their study of the French and German theologians: Teilhard de Chardin, Rahner, …"[95]

The young seminarians were almost universally in sympathy with the Council reformers,[96] which put them in direct opposition to many of their professors, entrenched in the old ways and the old texts partly out of conviction, partly out of habit, perhaps mostly out of a perceived necessity. What with the Oath Against Modernism that they had all sworn, their vows of obedience, the culture of censorship, and perhaps a large dose of "it worked for me," many of the faculty were uninterested in rocking the boat. It meant that alongside the optimism and energy of renewal brought in with the Council, there was the stagnation of status quo in seminary course work. "Certainly, most of the Scholastic manuals, written in Latin, which we studied in philosophy in the 1960s, were arid, out of date, impersonal, and mechanistic."[97] The students were interested in the new inclusivity, the ecumenism, the collegiality, the historical study of scripture, and — most relevant to Pat's future journey — in personal religious experience.

The possibility of a married clergy was entertained. This was a question of vital importance at Oconomowoc and seminaries everywhere, as already, before the Council had begun, they had seen scores of their friends — dedicated young men — leave the seminary, many of them because they wanted to marry and have families.

The March on Washington and Martin Luther King's *I Have a Dream* speech called many of these bright young men to the cause of civil rights. They were committed, after all, to the teachings of Alphonsus, founder of the Redemptorists, and preaching to the most abandoned. Students wanted to get out into the community and do ministry, they wanted to begin to practice their profession as part of their training. George Rassley was sympathetic to the men asking to get African American publications: *Ebony* magazine, *Jet* magazine; so they had some access. They wanted to be involved, and they met with resistance except from a few of the more progressive faculty.

Instead they were isolated, stuck studying the dry and abstract fundamental theses of Catholic Thomistic philosophy. They wanted a subscription to *Time* and were told it was too full of radical ideas and pictures of nudes, too liberal. Students offered to read a conservative magazine for balance. Still no go. Their professors expected them to learn what was put before them, not to question. Looking back years later Pat said, "This is where the old notions of obedience would come in. 'You guys don't read that stuff.' Of course, it's like throwing gas on a fire. We weren't very obedient as far as that went. We fought over books!"

The Council ferment came close to home when the American bishops brought some of the leading figures of Vatican II over for a conference. Pat remembered, "One of the professors of dogmatic theology invited some of the smarter people in his classes who were advocating advanced ideas to go with him — this was really unusual — to go with him down to Chicago for this conference. And they all went. The professor went in and talked with Rahner and came out and said, 'Rahner agrees with me.' So the student went and knocked on Rahner's door and talked to him, came out and said to the professor, 'Rahner agrees with *me*.' So that — a Mexican standoff kind of thing…" That student was dismissed, one of the casualties of what Pat referred to later as the dark days at Oconomowoc.

There was a fundamental loss of trust in the program. Pat's class was part of a generation of war babies, growing up with "duck and cover" drills, coming of age realizing that their parents' generation had developed the potential to destroy the world with the push of a button. Adolph Eichmann had stood trial for Nazi war crimes, pleading innocence using a defense based on obedience. He gave obedience a bad name. The failure of confidence extended into all aspects of seminary life. Pat recalled:

> In the minor seminary, yeah, there was a lot of trust. That this was the way to go. Then we hit the '60s, and there was a lot of back and forth between authority and the spirit of youth and freedom that was going on in the '60s. New theology versus old theology. New liturgy versus old liturgy. New scripture studies versus old scripture studies. There was that clash. And some people felt they had to go underground to survive and hide what they really thought. So as not to be expelled.[98]

Pat crisis

For Pat, there came a personal crisis. He saw no connection between the propositions of scholastic philosophy and the lived spiritual experience of his childhood that had propelled him toward the priesthood. At the age of seven, he had found a deep faith to which he had responded heart and soul, directing himself toward it in every way he could. In elementary school and still in the minor seminary, the daily round of devotions was to some degree a conduit to that experience and a support to that faith, but the elaborate reasoning of neo-scholasticism and its 24 propositions was anything but. A curtain fell between his childhood experience and his learned beliefs. His heart fell with it. He lost access to the primal faith that had carried him. The weather deepened his inner darkness, delivering a long, dark, cold Wisconsin winter.

Besides bringing in as many as possible of the significant books of the day, Rassley obtained movies for the seminary. He would get in excellent foreign films — Ingmar Bergman, Akira Kurosawa, Federico Fellini, French new wave films. Pat remembered a big controversy about showing *La Dolce Vita.* Many faculty judged it inappropriate on its face, but they themselves previewed the film. Some students, including Pat, managed to sneak into the preview to see the film anyway.

Around that time, as Pat was floundering, Rassley brought in Bergman's *Through a Glass Darkly.*

> It's about people isolated on an island in Scandinavia, and the woman in it is mentally ill. She's expecting a visitation from God. She's in this upper room. Kind of a barn-like place. They sent for a helicopter to take her away to an institution, and the sound of this helicopter coming is, to her, God

> arriving. But God appears as a gigantic spider and attacks her. This was a big crisis of faith for me. After the movie I went to say the rosary and I couldn't even get the first words 'I believe' out of my mouth. Is God a spider? That kind of thing.

Years later, writing about his spiritual path he said:

> One of the huge rocks in that path was that the regular way of devotion and piety eventually comes to a dead end, and the path begins to take a turn that is dark and difficult. Then one cannot practice as one did before. It is a bewildering time. There is no more consolation; all is dry and seemingly unprofitable.[99]

Pat needed something beyond the literal given wisdom at that time. Rather than learn propositions and recite rote prayers, he was searching for experience, direct experience of what centuries of spiritual seeking had been all about. "As far as the regular devotions, they were just that — they were devotions. Rosary, the Stations of the Cross, Masses, saying the breviary. They weren't even teaching us … spiritual practice." Many, perhaps most, of his contemporaries would disagree with this observation. After all, what is spiritual practice if not the rosary, the Stations of the Cross, Masses, saying the breviary — the prayers that punctuated the days and filled its interstices. But for Pat looking back, spiritual practice centered on contemplative practice, and in the seminary of his day, this was frowned upon.

Pat wondered about the depth of spirituality in the priests who were teaching. He considered that they must be holy men, and surely they were asking questions themselves. "But no one talked about it, it seems no one wanted to touch it with a ten-foot pole." Pat had to find his own way.

> They told us to keep away from [the writings of the mystics]. And years later, when I was studying with Willigis Jäger, he was talking about the same kind of experience. When he was in his seminary training, he came across a copy of *The Cloud of Unknowing*, but he was put on the list of suspicious persons because he was reading a mystic. I mean, he was planning to be a Benedictine monk and they were afraid of *The Cloud of Unknowing*! Those of us who were really looking for a genuine depth experience, spirituality, they stiffed on, they didn't give us proper training! Just: learn your dogma; learn your moral theology. That's not for you. That mystical experience is for God's chosen, don't have the pride to think you have been chosen. It's for special people, not you.

The loss of heart in devotion, the meaninglessness for Pat at that time, was not unusual for someone deeply engaged in spiritual practice. Great saints before — John of the Cross's *Dark Night of the Soul* is a prime example — wrote at length about this spiritual dryness. Had Pat had access to *The Dark Night of the Soul* at that time, it could have provided real guidance. Even Louis Colin, whose writings had been important in the novitiate, touched on this, though at that time the warnings held no meaning for Pat:

> ...God has for these people called novices, the tenderness and indulgence of a father. Nonetheless, it does happen that these sensible graces of fervor and joy come to a sudden end, and give way to spiritual darkness, aridity and interior desolation. ... The Rule, with its thousand and one regulations, silence and solitude, endless pious exercises, the monotony of a life free from highlights and events, can all combine to engender sadness and disgust for the vocation.[100]

But this was not emphasized nor recognized as a potentially fruitful, though difficult, stage in spiritual maturation. Still, despite the darkness, as far as Pat could remember years later, at no point did he waver in his determination to become a priest. He stuck with the daily schedule along with the others — morning prayer, Mass, in and out of chapel all day. But he stopped speaking the words.

At some point, he was drawn to a new book Rassley had brought into the library — *Christian Yoga* by Jean Déchanet.[101] It became for Pat a formative work of the sort one looks back on years later as a turning point. He began sitting in his room in the lotus position and doing breath counting. He kept this up on his own for years. It was a way of facing the darkness without seeking a solution for it. It was a way to ride a growing tide of depression that would otherwise have swamped him.

All this was happening for Pat as the larger drama of new versus old played out among his classmates and the faculty.

Oconomowoc crisis

In the spring of 1964, Father Francis Evans was appointed Prefect of Students. Hearing about it, at first the men thought it must be a bad joke. Evans taught logic and Canon Law. They felt he was clueless. He wanted things to go along as they were, couldn't understand the fuss. "Why do you guys want to go out and do ministry and read those books. What's all the talk about spirituality. Just follow the Rule and you'll be fine.[102]"

Among the theological questions, there was the challenge of celibacy. Very little attention was given to psychosexual development. There were men who felt strong commitment to the priesthood but questioned the need for celibacy and felt a greater need for a life partner. The internal conflict was huge. Rumors surfaced, then facts — some men had snuck out for trysts. There was scandal. The ineffectual response was a stern lecture on the dangers of forming relationships with women, and clamping down on opportunity. Tension mounted. Morale was low. It wasn't only Pat's personal darkness, though that was perhaps deeper than the more intellectually-based dispiritedness of some of the other students. Regardless, many were struggling. Faculty struggled to respond. They brought in Father Kevin O'Shea, an Australian Redemptorist theologian, then on the faculty of Fordham University. O'Shea was on the side of reform in the Church but sympathetic to and understanding of both sides, able to be a bridge across the widening gulf.

The spring term ended, and students went off to camp for the summer. As was traditional, they went to a place called Snyder's Pasture on Okauchee Lake, put up tents, and lived in the great outdoors. There were wooden tent platforms and cots to sleep on. They drew water from a well. There was a kitchen tent with a refrigerator and propane stove, a mess tent, a clapboard chapel. They had electric lights in the common spaces and Coleman lanterns for the sleeping quarters. Many days they'd go on longer "flits" than were possible during the term, exploring local lakes in canoes, portaging, hiking, fighting mosquitoes. Some of the time Pat was camp cook. "We ate a lot of hotdogs." It was tradition that every summer they would make a pilgrimage to Holy Hill,[103] a monastery of Discalced Carmelites, traveling on foot or by bike a distance of about 13 miles. Once up at the Hill a pilgrimage Mass was sung at the shrine, followed by a meal and a visit with the Carmelites. Then a bus would carry them back to camp. Another annual summer event was an exchange of visits with seminarians at nearby St. Francis Seminary.

Many of the men loved going to camp. Pat barely tolerated it. At the end of the summer, they returned to Oconomowoc for their second year of major seminary and final year of college. Tensions between students and faculty still simmered.

At the end of that school year, in June 1965, with his college degree completed, Pat's closest friend, Ed Crotty, left major seminary to pursue a career in the theater. He settled in New York and acted in plays on and off Broadway: *The King and I* starring Yul Brynner, and *Anything Goes* with Ginger Rogers were among his credits. It was piercingly difficult for Pat to see Ed go. The steady attrition through the latter years of minor seminary, then during the novitiate, was demoralizing. Every departure was difficult. Such strong bonds formed out of the shared experience of seminary life, it could feel almost like a death, yet it had become so commonplace people would say, "Guess who's leaving?" or, "Now who?" But Ed's departure was the hardest of all for Pat. He had never been so close to anyone. He felt betrayed and brokenhearted. Even toward the end of his life, reflecting on the friends who left the seminary, Pat felt the old wound of betrayal open up again. He soldiered on at Oconomowoc, but thereafter there was a sense in which he felt himself always alone.

Summer of 1965, they again went to Snyder's Pasture for camp. Pat — inoculated against any inclination to live outdoors the previous summer, now bereft of his closest friend besides — brought a footlocker of books and buried himself in them. Always somewhat apart even from the beginning, he fit in less and less with the group. Back for their third year at Oconomowoc, they began their first year of post-graduate work in theology. Of that fall and winter Pat said, "It was like being in solitary confinement except you were in a group. It was Wisconsin, and most of the day was darkness and cold. We were just in this building, and there was nothing but study and prayer. It could get psychologically oppressive."

In late fall of 1965, the festering conflict came to a head. Faculty woke to find a manifesto tacked to the refectory bulletin board. Taking a page from Luther, a group of students had signed an itemized list of demands that included getting rid of the Prefect of Students. There was a boycott — students refused to go to Canon Law class. They wanted more breadth in what they were studying, more freedoms, more access to television, more engagement with the world outside the seminary. The group who signed the manifesto included some who were sincerely seeking and some who were just malcontents, simply in the wrong place. Evans gave a talk trying to calm things down and made the mistake of asking if there were any comments. The students tore into him.

Faculty responded by drawing the line. Instigators of the uprising were identified and dismissed or put on probation, in which case they were threatened with being denied ordination if they didn't toe the line. The decision as to what to do with people depended partly on where they were with respect to their vows. At the end of their novitiate year, all had professed temporary vows to last three years, after which the candidate on the one hand and the Superiors on the other decided whether that person would go on to perpetual vows. Once in perpetual vows, one could not be dismissed. It was a two-way, lifelong commitment; the individual to the Church and the Church to the individual. It meant that some they tried to expel refused to leave because they were in final vows. According to Pat, one person was sent to the novitiate where he lived for years until finally they relented and ordained him. Another, HD as he was called, became a diocesan priest. He and Pat remained lifelong friends.

As heads rolled at Oconomowoc, Pat kept a low profile. He was sympathetic to the protesters but not greatly involved with them; their political demands were peripheral to him. He was not one of the signers of the manifesto, however, he was sufficiently withdrawn and uncollegial that the powers that be were considering whether he should be allowed to stay.

That winter, the faculty began sending students to lay psychologists. They were given the Minnesota Multiphasic Personality Inventory to help decide if they needed psychological intervention. This was not only in the major seminary. Sophomores in the minor seminary at Edgerton were also tested, with the hope of nipping rebellious tendencies in the bud. Some students were asked to leave, and some were selected for ongoing counseling. Pat was assigned to Dr. John Liccione and hit it off very well with him. "Married, kids. Some of his kids went to the Catholic schools in Milwaukee. I've heard from the grapevine that they were very unruly. So they didn't think much of Liccione. But he was a very down-to-earth, great guy. He did psychic evaluations for the court. Milwaukee County. One year he was asked to evaluate Jeffrey Dahmer. They asked Dr. Liccione, 'Do you think he's crazy?' Dr. Liccione said, 'So this guy seduces young boys, has sex with their dead bodies then eats them. Do *you* think he's nuts?' " Pat laughed. "That was his approach."[104]

One of the first things Liccione had Pat do was write an autobiography. Pat did as he was told, Liccione read it, handed it back to him and said, "What's missing?" Pat searched his mind for details he'd left out and began to elaborate. Liccione interrupted him: "Family." Pat had said not a word about his parents, sister, cousins, aunts, uncles, grandparents. Although the observation gave him a start, he was aware of no regrets. He was 22 and had thoroughly left home.

Pat remembered, "I liked Liccione very much. There was a handful of us who kind of became his disciples, friends. After we got ordained, we used to go and have lunch with him when we got together in the summer. And I invited him to come to Edgerton to take part in psychological testing of our seniors. He encouraged me in my vocation. Gave a lot of encouragement. … All we did was talk. He was somebody outside the religious part of it who seemed to understand. He said, 'These guys are fucked up.' " Though sympathetic to what the seminarians were going through, he supported Pat in his will to persevere.

Vatican II closed on December 8, 1965. Kevin O'Shea summarized:

> The practical result was that on Sunday, a good Catholic could come to a different, and more participative Eucharist (*Sacrosanctum Concilium and Lumen Gentium*), and on weekdays could go to the workplace with a new and more positive appreciation of "the world" (*Gaudium et Spes*), and occasionally, but genuinely, get into an adult education program in biblical sources and the

> dynamics of the present world (*Dei Verbum*).[105] And attitudes to other religions, Eastern Christians, laity, priests, bishops, etc., would correspondingly be open to renegotiation.[106]

That the light and promise of the Council was in many ways snuffed out by a conservative curia reasserting its influence with the cooperation, and even assistance, of a succession of popes, at least through Benedict XVI, is a continuation of that story.

Change was slow to come in the seminary curriculum, and trust was fragile at best. In the spring of 1966, Father Francis Bockwinkel replaced Evans as Prefect of Students. Pat said the first thing he did was call him into his office. Bockwinkel said to him, "We're kicking you out. You'll be gone by tonight." It was like a mule kick in the gut, the shock turning quickly to outrage. Pat went door to door with the faculty, saying he wouldn't stand for it, "Nobody's talked to me, they're just springing it on me."[107] He never saw the complaints against him, and he never knew the exact reason. Apparently, they thought he was unhappy. They may also have thought he was stirring up trouble with the others, and they were aware of his sitting in lotus posture and breath counting, suspect behavior for someone intending to become a Catholic priest.

By the end of the day, he had persuaded them to reinstate him, but on probation. He was due to take final vows that spring. They had him renew temporary vows, delaying final vows for another year. He knuckled under. Asked years later if the doubting by his Superiors instilled any doubt about his vocation, Pat replied with a firm "No." Was he just sure they were mistaken? "Yup."[108]

That summer was the first year major seminary students did not go to camp. Their demand that they be allowed to participate in community work took root widely in American seminaries, and not just Catholic ones. Immaculate Conception students were sent to Redemptorist communities all over the midwest, assigned to work in parishes to get involved in active ministry as a part of their formation. Pat was given census work to do, which he found uninspiring. He'd go door to door to addresses in the parish register, talk to people and make sure that the register was up to date. "They had a youth program, we worked in the youth program. And I can't even remember what we did with those damn things. I remember they had a slide show for the kids one time, and it was absolutely boring. I really felt for the kids having to sit through that. Or else we'd go on expeditions to the zoo, and I don't know what else… Took them swimming at the YMCA. Things like that."

After a short visit home at the end of the summer, Pat was back in September for his fourth year in major seminary, his second year in theology. Mostly indifferent to his coursework, he still hung on. Bockwinkel lasted a year, after which they brought in Father Joe Bilsley as the new Prefect of Students. Here was a lifeline. Kevin O'Shea had helped tremendously with student morale, but Bilsley more than anyone was able to pull the situation out of the fire and set them once again on an even course. He and Pat began getting to know each other that spring.

> One of the most important people in my life was named Joe Bilsley. He became the Dean of Men when we were still in Oconomowoc. This man knew reality. He was clear-sighted and honest as the day is long. And he'd been trained in Rogerian psychology. One of the things he did was establish a group, completely voluntary, where you could talk. There was a facilitator, but in a Rogerian manner. He wouldn't direct, he would simply reflect what you were saying. We could share really personal issues. And the guidance he gave was really solid. He's probably the greatest influence of a Redemptorist on my life. We became great friends through the years. He was one of my best friends. I was close to him all his life until he died. He would call a spade a spade. He would not brook *any* dishonesty or hypocrisy or shillyshally. "This is the way it is."
>
> One of his great talks to a whole group was, "If you join the Redemptorists, you join a ship of *fools*. Make no mistake!" Then he'd tell one horrifying story after another about scandals. Just to make sure you were clear-eyed about what you were joining. Wonderful man. He had all kinds of little sayings. At the time we were going to make a little book — *The Sayings of Chairman Bilsley,* we were gonna call it. He was from Chicago. He'd been pastor in a couple of parishes, a parish priest. And in that dark hour when things were really bad in Oconomowoc, and guys were getting kicked out, he was brought in to set things straight. He did a good job because everybody trusted him. He'd call you on your faults. But he was also encouraging.[109]

Years later, George Rassley said, "Joe Bilsley was a strong man, good at psychology. Not a very big man physically, but a strong man."[110]

The steady attrition in seminarians that had begun at Edgerton continued at De Soto and at Oconomowoc. It meant that by 1967 there weren't enough students to justify keeping Immaculate Conception College as a major seminary. The Redemptorists addressed the problem with a decision to combine the Theology programs of the St. Louis and Baltimore Provinces at the latter's seminary in Esopus, New York. Just before they left Immaculate Conception to move to Esopus, Joe Bilsley walked by as Pat was washing dishes. He said, "You've been approved for final vows." It was one more hurdle crossed, and for Pat it marked the end of the dark days at Oconomowoc.

Esopus

In August, 39 students, dispersed across the four years of theology, plus Joe Bilsley as Prefect of Students, George Rassley as librarian, and six other faculty moved from Oconomowoc to Mount St. Alphonsus College near Esopus, New York. They rented a bus and drove east, stopping overnight in North East, Pennsylvania, at St. Mary's College, the Redemptorist minor seminary of the Baltimore Province. The students joined 59 already at Esopus from the Baltimore province to make a student body of 98.

Mount St. Alphonsus, built by the Redemptorists and opened in 1907, was a fortress-like building of grey granite in a large clearing on 235 acres overlooking the Hudson River. Rooms were spacious, hallways wide, the refectory marble-walled, common rooms high-ceilinged and elegant. The library was four floors around a central atrium. The Romanesque chapel had elaborately trimmed arches, stained glass windows illustrating the life of St. Alphonsus, and over the main altar, a massive dome of stained glass depicting Alphonsus's coronation in heaven. The floor, the altars, the communion railing, the statuary, all were marble. At the doors were two large angels holding holy water fonts. Life-sized angels made in colorful mosaic, representing the monthly virtues, stood each in their own arch high above the main altar. Outdoors, the view from the building roof over the ramparts looked a long way up and down the Hudson River, north toward Albany and south past Poughkeepsie. There were four large bells in two towers. "A half-hour before Mass or Benediction, four strong students pulled the four ropes near the chapel door to toll the bells for five to ten minutes, a joyous sound ringing out over the glorious Hudson Valley."[111]

A commemorative book produced on the 100th anniversary of Esopus describes the student rooms: "...severely simple: a deal table instead of a desk, a washstand with a pitcher and basin, a bed with a thin white spread, several army-issue blankets, a standing desk for those who preferred to study on their feet, four monochrome, cardboard religious pictures on the walls; nothing more was permitted by Rule."[112] But a student sitting at his typewriter could look up through two arched windows to lawns extending to the wide river valley below.

The daily schedule was essentially the same for Pat and his cohort as it had been since minor seminary in 1956. Drama was still a major extracurricular focus. They put on large professional productions in the auditorium and invited the surrounding community. In 1970 — this was the year after Pat and his class left — they put on five performances of the musical *1776* to a collective audience of over 2,000.[113] They had pigs, cows, chickens, bees, a greenhouse for flowers, and fields planted in vegetables. They had the usual sports. When he could be excused,

Pat took long walks along the river or down backroads and into the foothills of the Marlboro Mountains.

The shared recreation of men from very diverse backgrounds brought together by the merger was itself an important addition to their formation in the emerging global village, of which they were gradually being allowed to be a part. The very experience of argument and change to which they were witness was in itself a powerful lesson in the reformability— the non-immutability — of the Church.[114] About a half dozen times a year, the men were allowed to go into New York City, take in a Broadway play or other entertainment, and visit the museums and other cultural riches of the metropolis. Pat told of one of these trips:

> I'm going to tell you a great story about Joe Bilsley. We were going to take a trip down to the city, and he needed money to give to the students to spend. It wasn't much, maybe five bucks apiece to spend. That's why we went to any free thing we could. At any rate, the one who was handling the money wouldn't give him the money for us. What his motivation was I don't know, but he wouldn't give the money. So Joe Bilsley started shouting in the corridor where priests and faculty lived — the rector was right there. And the rector came out and said, 'Joe, Joe, what's the matter, what's the matter?' Joe shouts at the top of his voice, 'All I want is 500 fuckin' bucks!' Everyone scattered all over the place...got him his money! That was one of the stories. We'd always repeat it. 'All I want is...' He'd stand up when that kind of crap was going on. He was an advocate for the students. He did a great job.[115]

Things settled down, and the men focused on their studies in the new post-Conciliar world. The main courses in both years at Esopus were in moral theology. Prior to Vatican II, theology textbooks had been in Latin according to the Rule. Now they had some texts in English translation, and reading from a variety of sources began to be encouraged. The emphasis in theology was changed. "Vatican II accepted 'with respect and affection as brothers' those whom it had previously regarded as heretics and schismatics and as adversaries to be refuted in theological manuals."[116] "The historical, evolutionary consciousness legitimated by the Council allowed a shift in theological education from preoccupation with immutable essences to a consciousness which recognized the historical location of Scripture, discipline and doctrine."[117] There was a new emphasis on pluralism and diversity and an interest in understanding differences in liturgy and governance within the Church and in other Christian communities. The changes occurred gradually as faculty acquired the necessary new training. Pat's class saw only the beginnings of change. He continued to self-educate, and haunting the library as before, he discovered the works of Joseph Campbell and Carl Jung, both of whom contributed profoundly to his evolving outlook.

In the normal course of seminary training at the time, ordination took place at the end of the 12th year of seminary, after the men had had three of the four years of theology and had earned a Master's Degree in Divinity. Pat was awarded the degree but was held back from ordination, again for reasons he was not told. His classmates thought it might have been his own choice, that he himself thought he was not ready.[118] It was not his choice. Whether because they had concerns about his continued yoga and breath-counting practice, whether because he stood out as a loner in an organization whose fundaments centered around community life, whether they sensed his growing skepticism about literal Catholic dogma, whether because they were aware of his interest in mythology and other religions — for whatever reason, he was held in limbo.

The rites of ordination began with tonsure, in which a few locks of hair are ceremonially cut. Then followed the minor orders of porter, lector, exorcist and acolyte. Finally, there are the major orders of subdeacon, deacon and priest. All the orders up to the last occur essentially as formalities and in quick succession, with rites conducted during Mass. The last — ordination to the priesthood — took place in June each year and was suitably momentous. Families came. All the priests of the Province who were able came from far and wide to participate in the great solemnity. Along with his classmates, Pat had watched the ordinations of the fifth-year fraters at the end of each year of major seminary — he and his fellow seminarians looking ahead to their turn. Now he watched his classmates go through this great initiation, the goal of his life thus far, not knowing if his turn would come.

"I was four years in temporary vows and didn't get ordained until my final year. So you didn't know when the sword would fall, you know, it was the sword of Damocles the whole time. Especially for those who were honest enough to say what they actually thought about the way things were going. It's interesting that those who made it through, who actually were in peril but made it through, persevere today. But many of the ones who knuckled under and mouthed the party line eventually left the priesthood." Years later, one of his former professors said, "You know Pat, in those days we put pressure on this person and that person, and now you guys are the lights of the Province." Looking back toward the end of his life, did the holding back still sting? "No," Pat said. "Kind of a badge of honor. I never completely fit in with the ideal Redemptorist. Even today — I'm a Zen Master, and do contemplative retreats in the Christian tradition, nobody else does. There's only one other priest I know, he's a Jesuit in the United States, who's a Zen Master. So it's sort of an anomaly."

Then it was the summer of 1968. With one more year to go in their training, the men emerged for a few months from the seminary hothouse into a world in chaos. The number of American planes lost in Vietnam would pass 10,000 over the next five years. The massive Tet Offensive begun in January had shocked Americans into a realization of the strength of North Vietnamese forces and had fanned the flames of resistance to the War. Martin Luther King Jr. was assassinated. Racial tensions were erupting into riots. Robert Kennedy was assassinated.

The students who had come to Esopus from the St. Louis Province went back to a new seminary at Waterford, Wisconsin, for the ordinations and stayed on to be assigned for the summer to community work in various parishes. Even as they themselves had weathered their own uprising at Oconomowoc, they felt their ignorance and unpreparedness as they entered a world in protest. Pat was again assigned to parish census work, and he muddled through. They returned to Esopus for their last year of training. During that last year, Pat's classmates, the newly ordained of the previous June, were pressed into service saying Masses on weekends in neighboring parishes. Pat watched from the sidelines.

In that last year of major seminary, they studied moral theology, the field of St Alphonsus' greatest contribution to Catholic understanding as a whole, for which he had been made a Doctor of the Church. Pat's classmates, though ordained, were not permitted to hear confession until after this critical final year. They studied the *Medulla theologiae moralis* of Busenbaum,[119] and *Praxis Confessarii*[120] written by Alphonsus, both in English translation. The latter was an important book for Pat for two reasons:

The approach to confession that Alphonsus espoused suited Pat's temperament.

> ...the confessor must have charity. He must show this love first of all by receiving everyone who comes to him in confusion with kindness. ...He remembers the words of Christ: "It is my mission to call sinners, and not saints. (Mk 2/17)" ... God will surely forgive you all your sins. ... You've got every reason in the world to be at peace now. ... The confessor ... must be careful to show no impatience or weariness. ... God's mercy is bigger than your sins.[121]

It was apparent to anyone who knew Pat for the rest of his life that he resonated with and deeply internalized this Alphonsian approach to the penitent. All who came to Pat in distress were received with this mercy, whether they came for confession in the Catholic way, or brought their vulnerabilities into Zen *dokusan*. It was his great gift — full attention and full acceptance.

Secondly and at least as important, Pat recognized his practice of silence in the words of Alphonsus:

> Contemplation is very different from meditation. In meditation, a person goes out in search of God through the effort of reasoning. In contemplation, he gazes upon God Who has been found without effort. In meditation a person acts through the operation of his own faculties. In contemplation, on the other hand, God acts and the soul is only acted upon and receives the gifts which are infused into it by grace without any contribution of its own.[122]

It was an affirmation that whatever dubious glances he might get from classmates and faculty, his silent practice was something Alphonsus would have understood and approved.

Ordination

Not long after Easter in 1969, Pat left Esopus for the last time, traveling to Holy Redeemer seminary at Waterford, Wisconsin, to be ordained with the class behind him. By then he was untroubled about having been held back, just so the thing happened. Over the course of about two months, the men were tonsured, went through the minor, sub-diaconate and diaconate orders. On June 27, 1969, Pat's parents, Ed and Elnora, and his sister Mary Ellen joined the other families and younger seminarians filling the pews of Holy Redeemer's chapel. Families arrived dressed as for a wedding.

Archbishop William Cousins presided. As the ordinands donned the alb, they recited, "Purify me, O Lord, and cleanse my heart; that, being made white in the Blood of the Lamb, I may come to eternal joy," then as they put on the stole, "Restore unto me, O Lord, the stole of immortality, which was lost through the guilt of our first parents: and, although I am unworthy to approach Your sacred Mysteries, nevertheless grant unto me eternal joy." As the organ began and the choir sang, a long procession moved from the vestibule up the center aisle to the chancel. A thuriber led, clouds of incense rising as he waved the censer. Acolytes carrying tall candles followed. Then Redemptorists from all over the province processed two by two, row on row, all vested in white, up the aisle, around the altar to their places in rows of chairs filling the back of the chancel. Last came the mitered archbishop with his attendants. Following the regular order of Mass up through the readings, each ordinand was then called by name, and replying, "Present," stepped forward. Joe Bilsley gave testimony that each of the candidates was prepared for and worthy of ordination. As during a wedding, the congregation was asked if there were objections.

In a series of questions, the response to each of which was, "I do," the archbishop asked the ordinands if each was willing to serve Christ as a faithful priest. The litany of the saints was sung antiphonally as the ordinands lay fully prostrate, belly to the ground, in a line down the center aisle. Each ordinand in turn then knelt before the bishop, who placed his hands silently on each head. This is considered the essential act, the moment of apostolic succession when the archbishop is transmitting to the ordinand what was transmitted to him from bishops in an unbroken line going back to the first apostles and through them to Christ. Following this laying on of hands, the ordinands knelt in a single row across the front of the chancel, and as the choir intoned *Veni Sancti Spiritu*, each of the Redemptorist confreres — including Pat's classmates ordained the year before — walked by and laid hands on the head of each of the newly ordained priests. This took time, as the long line of confreres filed past the kneeling men.

Once the confreres had regained their places, Pat and all the new priests removed their deacon's stole, replacing it with the priestly stole and chasuble. The archbishop anointed the palms of each man with the oil of chrism, and the hands were bound together with linen cloth, leaving the fingers free to receive the paten and chalice briefly handed to each. At consecration, the new priests and all the assembled confreres together extended their right hands in concelebration. As Pat lifted his hands, Mary Ellen glanced over at her parents and saw Ed dabbing away tears.

After communion, the bishop knelt to receive the first blessing of each new priest, then the newly ordained faced the congregation and offered a blessing to families and friends together. The Mass ended, and the Redemptorists processed out to the choir singing *Ecce Quam Bonum* (Psalm 133) in glorious arrangement.[123] Years later, Pat said that of all the liturgical music it is the piece he remembered and loved most: "*Ecce quam bonum et quam jucundum habitare fratres in unum.*" ("Behold how good and how pleasant it is for brethren to dwell together in unity…") He had heard it every year of major seminary at the ordinations of those who preceded him, and it cannot have failed to move him deeply at this moment when he arrived at last — amidst the incense, vestments and candles that had first called to him — to the beginning of the life he had chosen when he was seven.

By tradition, the new priest says his first Mass in his home parish. Ed proudly designed the Mass card and had it printed. On June 29, 1969, which happened also to be Mary Ellen's 20th birthday, Pat, his relatives, and some elementary school classmates and friends, gathered with the parish faithful at Sacred Heart Church in Granite City for the event. Redemptorists from the Mission House at Liguori and the Rock Church in St. Louis came over, as they would come again years later in support of their confrere each time he commemorated a major loss — burying first his father, then his mother just six months apart in 1995, then his only sister Mary Ellen in 2009.

The dates of Pat's ordination and first Mass are entered in the Delmar family bible on a page included especially to register vocations in the family, headed in print with, "We, like all Catholic parents, hoped to have a son a priest. God calls, by a divine vocation, certain men to be His special ministers in the priesthood. The Christian home is greatly blessed when one of its sons ascends the Christian altar as a priest." The photo of Pat with his family taken after his first Mass leaves no doubt as to his parents' — especially his mother's — pride and joy in the event.

Tirocinium

The year after ordination is an internship year, the tirocinium, for which period the new ordinands were often assigned to St. Alphonsus Liguori "The Rock" Catholic Church, built in 1867, a soaring Gothic limestone building towering above Grand Boulevard in central St. Louis. It gave the men the opportunity to build pastoral skills under the direction of an experienced pastor, and time to write their first mission talks. A few years before, the then pastor, Rev. Joe Campbell, had begun an active outreach to the impoverished neighborhoods — Pat described it as a black ghetto — that surrounded the church. Campbell was in charge of the tirocinium, and his big priority was to Christianize the area.

Pat and Harry Grile were assigned to the recently opened Blumeyer Village public housing complex built for the elderly a few blocks away from The Rock. Pat had one high-rise and Harry had the other. There was little structure to their work. They went knocking on doors to identify the Catholics. They said one Mass a week at the complex. They worked with kids from the area, organized volleyball teams, other activities. Pat remembered:

> There weren't any white people living within miles... People who came into the rectory were black. We worked with black kids, with volleyball teams and stuff like that. And we visited homes, high rises, and of course, we being liberal bleeding hearts, we wanted to do something. But our background just didn't prepare us for that kind of poverty, difficulty in life and everything. The guys who went in and worked their hearts out burned out fast because it was so difficult. One wanted to be of use, to be successful as a minister and missionary, but often couldn't tell if actions were a help or a hindrance.[124]

It was the real world of jobs and bills and needy children, bewildering to these men who had spent half their lives in a cloister.

And still, there was attrition. There came the news of classmates who, even though they'd made it through ordination, were giving up the vocation, leaving, getting married. Now delivered to the world, exploring life outside the constraints and repressions of the seminary, they were finding themselves called to something different. For Pat this loss brought once again to the surface the familiar, unspoken, undermining sense of betrayal, perhaps first encountered as a toddler when his mother allowed his father to intrude into their happy twosome after the War.

During nine months of work at The Rock, neither Harry nor Pat had any idea where they would be assigned next nor what they would be expected to do. At last, in April 1970, they were called to Waterford, Wisconsin, learning on arrival that it was for an education formation meeting with the intention that they would become teachers. Still with no idea where or of what. Finally, at the end of the workshop, Pat learned he was to go back to Edgerton and teach English at the high school seminary. First, he had to get a formal teaching qualification.

Appointment to Edgerton

For the four years of postgraduate work that Pat and his classmates had begun at Oconomowoc and completed at Esopus, they were granted two Master's degrees, one in Divinity and one in Religious Education, neither of which qualified Pat to teach English. So that summer confreres taught Pat to drive, he got his license, then spent the better part of the next two years commuting from Edgerton to the University of Wisconsin, Whitewater, to earn a Master of Art in Teaching.

For those two years, he lived between the worlds of Catholic seminary and secular academia in Protestant rural Wisconsin. He enjoyed the half-hour drive along back roads to his classes and the contact with secular professors. The feeling was mutual. Most students in the program had come from Bachelor's degrees. Here was Pat with his Master's degrees and a strong background in Aristotelian logic, writing, and public presentation. Students had to write a proposal for a dissertation (not the dissertation itself). Father Al Weinert, a confrere who was two years behind Pat in the seminary and followed him to Whitewater, was told while he was there that Pat's proposal was the best they'd ever seen.[125] Professors appreciated this reserved, unassuming, dedicated young man who could write clearly and speak clearly. They treated him as an equal.

The last semester he did practice teaching at the public high school in the nearby town of Jefferson, "...and this was a delightful thing," he remembered years later. Most students were Protestant, mainly Lutheran. Pat showed up every day in his clerical collar and black suit. From the beginning, some school authorities feared that parents would hit the roof, but the principal was supportive. He assigned Pat a supervising teacher, Mr. Fliegel, who was also Catholic and had been in the seminary. Even though Fliegel had left and gotten married, the shared seminary experience gave them an instant mutual understanding. They hit it off well, Pat went often to his house, and they had an easy working relationship.

The anticipated fuss from parents never materialized. One day between classes, Pat was greeted by a group of students with a Polaroid camera, clearly on a mission. It was highly unusual to have a Catholic priest in the school, and some parents doubted their children's reports of this. The students crowded around Pat in his clerical garb to have a picture taken as proof.

He did no proselytizing, but sometimes a teacher or student would ask him religious questions. One of the seniors, perhaps put up to it by his parents, challenged Pat on the question of Catholics' prohibition of birth control in the face of overpopulation. Pat said, "What do you mean we don't allow birth control? I'm doing my part!" A few teachers overheard. From this and other incidents, all soon knew that this very quiet man had a sense of humor. Smoking was allowed in the teachers' lounge, and that was another bond.

Pat fit in, but by his own choice, never completely. He kept hearing about a regular Friday after-school meeting of teachers called the Poet's Society, eventually prying out of a librarian that it stood for Piss On Everything Tomorrow's Saturday. They were at first shy about inviting him to join. When the invitation did come, he declined. At the end of the day he was glad to head back to Edgerton and his confreres. Blossoming professional development at Whitewater and Jefferson notwithstanding, his life still centered on his community. Even while he was making the Monday to Friday commute working full time, grading in his off-hours, he took his turn saying Mass, hearing confessions and offering spiritual guidance to the young seminarians.

After he graduated from Whitewater it was an easy transition to teaching at St. Joseph's College in Edgerton. He taught freshman, sophomore and senior English, which he loved despite challenges. Some of the freshmen had a thin grasp of English — not that it wasn't their native language, they just hadn't learned it well. It meant he had to teach basic grammar, which he found tedious, but writing and literature engaged him. Pat instituted a filmmaking session for the sophomores. He had everybody write a story for a film, then they chose the story that the class wanted to do, and everybody had to write a screenplay for the thing. They reviewed them all and picked the best one. The class was then divided into crews, actors, photographers, the prop people, everything. They filmed with a 16 mm camera, edited and spliced, and finally showed the finished product. Pat loved it, students loved it. And they loved him.

His classroom was quiet and productive. He had no need ever to raise his voice — the wayward student could be redirected with a single, steely, Hawk glance. Yet he respected them as autonomous. A student at the time, Greg Wiest, prone to insomnia and walking the halls long after lights out, was occasionally discovered by Pat, up late himself, reading. With just about anyone else this would have brought a strong reprimand. Pat saw him and said nothing, a fact Greg remembered years later with appreciation.[126] Pat attended not only to academics. So that students could discuss their concerns, he instituted class meetings with the Rector and Deans of Men, somewhat reminiscent of Bilsley's Rogerian talk groups.

While Pat was on the faculty, they introduced things that would, as he put it, "open up the place." They got horses and students rode them and took care of them. Some of the boys captured and kept wild animals — raccoons, ferrets — that would get loose in the halls. There was a lot of tobacco-growing in the area, and in the fall they allowed students to pick tobacco and make some money for themselves. They could keep the money — a big change from Pat's high school days — and spend it on trips into town about once a week. As always, they put on plays. They often showed movies. And of course, there continued to be sports. As the student population shrunk, there was a gradual shift from sports that required lots of people on teams and in leagues, to sports like tennis that didn't need so many.

Early on, to distinguish himself from the students (he was very youthful looking), Pat grew a mustache, wide and tipped up at the ends. In keeping with the times he also grew his hair almost to his shoulders. It was dark, thick and belled out below the ears, making him look like a young Shakespeare in Redemptorist habit. After a few years, he grew a full beard and cut his hair, still thick and wavy, to collar level.

Very soon, Pat's superiors saw leadership potential and signed him up for summer school to earn administration credits at Marquette, Wisconsin, a Jesuit University on the western shore of Lake Michigan, about an hour's drive from Edgerton. In 1976 he was made Principal of the seminary high school.[127] Besides teaching — now it was English to seniors and Religion to freshmen — Pat arranged curriculum for the whole school, hired teachers, made out class schedules, maintained a sizable Redemptorist staff, kept records and test scores for all students, sent out transcripts, wrote reports, ran faculty meetings, arranged study time, graduation and awards, and made out report cards.[128] Even before Pat came back to Edgerton as faculty, lay teachers had been hired for Biology and Physical Sciences. There just weren't enough Redemptorists anymore to train as teachers. Eventually, there was a lay librarian and laypersons teaching Mathematics and English. A few were women. This was not only a cultural shift. Redemptorists had a vow of poverty and worked essentially for room and board. Now Pat had to worry about money for salaries.

The Redemptorist faculty were with the students all day — in chapel, in class, for meals. Then in the evenings until about nine o'clock, most were in their offices preparing, grading, advising any student who would drop in to talk. On weekends they preached in the neighboring parishes. During the school year, there was very little break from the schedule or from work or from each other. With the students gone home during the summers, Pat was given time off while others organized vocation camps for seminary high school students. Some of the more senior seminarians from Esopus came to help as part of their summer experience. Pat kept an eye out among them, and among students at the college seminary at Waterford for potential faculty recruits. As the time for ordination of a new crop drew near, he would approach someone he thought promising. There wasn't the announcement out of the blue that was the practice when Pat was first assigned to teach. He inquired if the person was interested and if yes, what they'd like to teach. From there, they could make arrangements to go for training in whatever it was. He expected the men to take charge of their own lives. If someone had a particular direction they wanted to go, Pat encouraged it, largely by staying out of the way. "Sure, go ahead," he would say. As he put it years later, "There was no power trip, no arbitrary decision."

One of Pat's later recruits was Father Pete Schavitz, who was ordained in 1976. Pete had an interest in communications and persuaded Pat that public speaking was not the same discipline as English and should split off as a separate class (which it had been when Pat was in minor seminary). Schavitz then got trained and taught the class. Early on, he came to Pat and said, "What would really help me is to have a video camera." It was a substantial request, not without risk that the thing might end up gathering dust. Pat told Pete to find out the cost, Pete came back with the details and an explanation of how he would use the camera, and Pat, both practical and open-minded, said fine.[129]

At the first faculty meeting after he had been appointed principal, Pat announced that from now on the library would be open during remission periods, after classes, in the evenings, on free days and on weekends. It was one of his first decisions as the new principal. The librarian who had been there for some time said, "Oh, we can't do that — they'll just mess it up!" There was a silence, and Pat looked at the man with his steely-eyed gaze. Then in a low, firm voice he said, "This is not an item on the agenda for discussion. It will be so." A dropped pin would have been audible. After a pause, Pat looked at the priest and said more conversationally, "Larry, what good are all those books if they're never opened?"[130]

Caught up in his various duties, Pat had little time for the contemplative practices he had taken up while at Oconomowoc and Esopus, but he still did breath-counting during morning meditation, and he still held — albeit by a thin thread — to the notion of the contemplative direction as a lifeline. When school let out for the summer and he had time off, the Bilsley talk groups continued.

Some of Pat's teachers from high school days were still at Edgerton — Gerry Pecht, for example; they became colleagues and Pecht reported to Pat as Principal. Joe Bilsley, beloved and admired father figure of Pat's seminary years, became a colleague. Bob Halter, ordained two years behind Pat, came in as Dean of Students. Bob had entered the seminary after college, so he had not known Kirkwood and the wrench from home at 13, nor had he been to Edgerton as a student. He was down-to-earth, resilient, forthright — very different from Pat in personality and very much appreciated by him. There were confreres that felt distanced, even offended by Pat's sometimes dark aloofness, but Bob took it in stride. They worked well together as colleagues and became lifelong friends.

There was camaraderie among faculty in the common room along with ashtrays, cigarette smoke, and the perpetual smell of coffee. In all the gatherings — common room chatter, evening socials — in the various opportunities to talk, Pat was comfortable saying nothing. He showed no inclination to make conversation with anyone and no compunction about snubbing anyone trying to strike up a conversation with him. He was especially taciturn in the early hours. A cheerful, "Good morning, did you rest well?" or anything along those lines was guaranteed to get a scowl, possibly a low snarl.

Bob Halter remembered a day in late March, with bare trees and cold wet snow under cloudy skies still greying the landscape toward the tail end of the always long Wisconsin winter. Pat came into the staff lounge, made his coffee, walked over and stood staring out the window, his back to the room. Redemptorist faculty were sitting around talking, having coffee after morning prayer. Pat, facing the window, addressed the frozen landscape in a voice that cut through the chatter, saying, "May God come down from heaven, open the earth, and swallow this whole goddam state into hell." Chatter abruptly stopped. Pat took another thoughtful sip of his coffee, then looking neither to left nor right, as if leaving an empty room, he shuffled out.

Redemptorist faculty gathered after supper for drinks, chatting, smoking. Everybody loosened up. Pat mostly just smoked. One time, Joe Bilsley asked him why he wasn't drinking. Pat said he didn't like beer. Bilsley said, "*I'll* make you a drink that you'll like." He came back with a Brandy Manhattan. Pat told this story years later, intoning "Brandy Manhattan" as if it were ambrosia. Gradually he came to look forward to the cocktail hour, showing up regularly, then avidly. He began enjoying wine on his own. It wasn't that difficult to help oneself to the altar stock, plus he had cash and could buy it by the box. It was an occupational hazard.

In those days, if someone got expelled or defrocked — still decades before the sex abuse scandal rocked the priesthood — they used to say it was for one of two reasons: Punch or Judy.

The same attrition that had contributed to Pat's despair during the '60s continued at Edgerton through the '70s. The sprawling building constructed in the early '60s for hundreds was emptier year by year. Some students whom Pat had nurtured and loved left. In the fall of 1976, Pat's Aunt Mona died of breast cancer. She had cared for him as an infant during the war and had kept in touch with him in the seminary. His Aunt Patsy died the following April. Perhaps even because of Pat's having distanced himself from family so ruthlessly when he left home at 13, these losses penetrated. The memories of the early, cocooned family life bubbled up around the irreversibility of these deaths. And the long Wisconsin winters wore heavily — dark, snowy and cold. Pat settled into drinking heavily.

There were two Redemptorist brothers on the staff who worked on the physical plant. Their jobs included keeping the driveway area outside the garage clear of snow. The plow was on a tractor with no shield from the weather, and it could be bitter cold out, so necessarily they would come into the common room to warm up, leaving the tractor running in case it would be hard to start again. The faculty would drop into the common room between classes and find them lost in conversation about the inner child or other popular explorations of the '70s. Hours later, with the tractor still standing alone in the drive, there'd be banter: "Did Stan ever get out there again or did the tractor just run out of gas?" The Brothers' sensibilities were ruffled by Pat's sometimes scowling taciturnity, and the more they chaffed, "Geez, he isn't even kind enough to say good morning," the less patience he had with them. One night in the common room — they were not present — a dam of sorts broke. Beginning with the Brothers and their various foibles, Pat held forth.

There was Pat's language — fuck this, fuck that, those goddamn sonofabitch fuckers. There was the clever turn of phrase, the pithy put down. Confreres dropping by the common room were drawn in by the performance and stuck around. Far from anyone reining him in, they fed into it. Other topics surfaced. Pat was the entertainment for a long evening. A few people tore themselves away at 2:00 AM. It went on until about 3:00. No one who was there managed to show up for morning prayer. One person dragged himself out of bed in time to teach his class at 8:00. He had a break at 9:30 and went to get coffee in the common room. It was still dark and empty. Classes were canceled left and right. Students loved it, though none knew the cause.

In February 1978, Pat wrote a note to Edmund "Jeff" Langton, then Provincial Superior* of the St. Louis Province, thanking him for his support. It is clear that Pat was struggling:

> Dear Jeff,
>
> Thank you so much for your note. It is very consoling for me. When I received it this morning I felt it was unnecessary, because I already know you and the rest are appreciative people. On the other hand I was not surprised, because it is the kind of support you are always so ready to give. I thank you.
>
> I also hope you are not overly concerned. You've got enough to worry about without me adding to any burdens. I am tenacious, and also very readable when down. But don't read too much into my dour expressions. They're infamous.
>
> I can't deny that I'm depressed by many recent happenings and especially the uncertainty concerning our work and home. But I'm functioning quite well and have not given up.
>
> I've always wondered what I'd say if I ever wrote a personal letter to a Provincial. I had decided that if I ever did, it should be one that would bring some light and happiness to his day.
>
> I'm really at a loss now, however, as to how to allay your suffering because of me. Just thanks from the heart. May all our sufferings be in Christ and lead to His Resurrection.
>
> Pat Hawk, CSsR[131]

Not long afterward, the triennial appointments† had Joe Bilsley assigned away from Edgerton. Pat somehow took it personally, and he sent in a letter resigning as principal. Perhaps, deep in depression and an alcoholic fog, he was feeling a lack of confidence in his own performance and decided to step aside before he could be fired. No doubt there was also distress at the loss of Bilsley as mentor and colleague. The letter reveals deep anger and frustration. After the personal tone of the letter to Jeff Langton in February, which was handwritten and addressed simply to Jeff, this one in June is typed and addressed to V. Rev. Langton:

> I herewith submit my resignation as Principal of St. Joseph's Preparatory College High School. In your capacity as President of the Board of Directors

---

* Redemptorist administration is organized by Provinces. The Province is administered by an elected Provincial Council consisting of the Provincial or Provincial Superior, the Consultor, the Vicar and four at-large members.
https://redemptoristsdenver.org/administration/ accessed August 2020.

† Redemptorists are reassigned every three years. They may or may not be reassigned to the same position.

of the above-mentioned high school and Provincial Superior, I also request to be relieved of any teaching duties and continued residence in the above-mentioned institution.

In support of this request, I cite irretrievable breakdown of confidence between the board and myself as principal. I cite regulation 2.96 of the North Central Association standards: "The working relationships between the board and principal shall be such as to insure the effective administration and operation of the school."

The recent actions of the board in regard to St. Joseph's indicates that the board no longer has confidence in this administration and renders it increasingly difficult for me to continue effective administration. Therefore, I request you to meet with the newly constituted board and appoint a principal you can work with to carry out your policies in good conscience.

Sincerely yours,
E. Patrick Hawk, CSsR[132]

He sent the letter and left for a vacation at his parents' place in Granite City. Perhaps to his surprise, the Province leadership rejected his resignation, instead writing back sympathetically about the challenges Pat faced, and surmising that the precipitating factor was anger at the loss of Bilsley: "Your letter arrived yesterday and was matter for consultation this morning. It renewed the concern felt both by me and the two consultors for the tension and frustration you have endured during recent months. ... We approached the matter as confreres concerned about a fellow Redemptorist, before deliberating as a board in relation to a principal." Referring to the re-assignment of Bilsley, the letter went on, "...it is important for you to know that no lack of confidence in the administration, and particularly in you, was implied by the change. While we are aware of the great difficulty you have in accepting the Chapter decisions, we respect your right to your own judgments and do not see the lack of agreement as necessitating your resignation." It was on the heels of this turmoil, with Pat back in the saddle at St. Joseph's College, that he got a call from his confrere, Greg Mayers, opening the door to a new direction.

Over several summers of Joe Bilsley's talk groups, Pat and Greg had become friends, sharing a deepening interest in meditation. Greg introduced him to *Zen Mind, Beginner's Mind* by Shunryu Suzuki, a seminal figure in bringing Zen Buddhism to the United States, founder of the San Francisco Zen Center and Tassajara. The book remains a classic among American Zen offerings. In the midst of the hustle and bustle of life at St. Joe's, the book resonated strongly for Pat, although it was to be several years more before he would turn resolutely in that direction. Pat and Greg had developed a practice of sitting for 30 minutes then reading a short section from *Zen Mind, Beginner's Mind.* While they were thus exploring, several threads were coming together in the larger world, in a web of convergence that would affect Pat's life profoundly.

3

Zen and Contemplative Training

Bangor Summer, 1977

One of the nodes in this convergence was *Pacem in Terris*, the Catholic Workers community in Seattle, Washington. The Catholic Worker Movement was started by Dorothy Day and Peter Maurin in Dirty-Thirties New York, with the goal of feeding the hungry. It evolved into a worldwide network of activist communities committed to living with the poor: "The poor are our teachers." The group engaged in non-violent direct action against threats to the poor, including against American militarism, with the observation that militarism massively diverts resources away from serving people's basic needs. *Pacem in Terris*, founded by Alice Ray and Larry Keil in the mid-1970s, was a group of bright, energetic, socially engaged faith practitioners doing their best to live out the grassroots message of the gospels in a house on 17th Street East in central Seattle.

They were also part of Pacific Life Community, an activist group founded in early 1975 by Canadians Jim and Shelley Douglass, spurred on by Robert Aldridge, who had been a missile designer for Lockheed but resigned when he realized the missiles were being constructed as first-strike rather than as defensive weapons.[133] The Douglasses and the 14 others who were at the inaugural meeting of Pacific Life Community had been active in the civil rights movement and in protesting the Vietnam War. Now with nearby Bangor, Washington on the Kitsap Peninsula having been designated as the home for Trident nuclear-missile-carrying submarines, they were uniting for direct, non-violent action against this foothold of nuclear armament.

The spiritual and political were intimately linked in Pacific Life Community, as its members acknowledged the need "to find the 'Trident within' and the myriad ways in which violence manifests in each individual's daily life." Though not all identified as Christian, they were motivated by spiritual/moral underpinnings rooted in the Sermon on the Mount in Matthew's Gospel. Alongside the dedication to direct action there was a thoughtful and dynamic spiritual practice that went beyond the catechisms they had been raised on. This included exploring the contemplative dimension of Christian practice that had percolated out from the writings of Thomas Keating and other Catholic monastics and a parallel interest in the Zen Buddhist practice that was increasingly visible and accessible in America. In this spiritual aspect, some, including Alice Ray, Larry Keil, Dan Mintie and others among the Catholic Workers, were in contact with the Trappists of Our Lady of Guadalupe Abbey near Lafayette, Oregon.

The Abbot at Our Lady of Guadalupe was Reverend Bernard McVeigh, raised a blue-blooded New York Episcopalian. He grew up with an original Matisse over his bed. When he told his parents he was going to join the Trappists, they wondered if they should have him deprogrammed. He was tall, slim, sturdy, articulate, affable, and spoke with an aristocratic, stentorian voice — when he said something, everyone heard.[134] Spiritual advisees, men and women, clerics and laypeople, came to him from all over. The spiritual and the quotidian were not separate for him — he took an interest in the details of who was doing what, who said what to whom, how it was all going. If you ever wanted to know what was going on, you could ask Bernard.

Bernard McVeigh was interested in Contemplation and in Zen. He would go to the Trappist monastery at Snowmass, Colorado, to work with his co-religious, Thomas Keating, and had also done Zen retreats with Joshu Sasaki in Massachusetts and at Mount Baldy Zen Center in California.[135] He and a small group of his monks were sitting in the early mornings in the library at Guadalupe, and Bernard was encouraging his advisees to do contemplative practice. Laymen visiting Guadalupe on personal retreats — women were not allowed to be at the monastery overnight at that point — could join the monks for sitting.

Still in the mid-1970s, Alice Ray had gone to Hawaii and met Robert Aitken, also a peace activist, who was one of the central figures in the history of American Zen. Aitken grew up in Hawaii and was a civilian working on Guam when the US declared war on Japan after the bombing of Pearl Harbor in 1941.[136] He was captured by the invading Japanese forces on Guam and imprisoned for the duration of World War II. While Aitken was interned, one of his guards showed him a book, *Zen Buddhism in English Literature and Oriental Classics*, by an Englishman living in Japan, R.H. Blyth.[137] He took such an interest the guard bought him a copy so he could have his own back.[138] Aitken read the book cover to cover again and again. By chance, Blyth himself turned up as a prisoner at the same camp. He became Aitken's first Zen teacher. After the war, Aitken worked with Japanese Zen masters in America and in Japan. When Aitken returned to live in Hawaii with his wife, Anne, they bought a place in Honolulu with a view to starting their own Zen group. This they did in 1959, the beginning of the Honolulu Diamond Sangha. Among other teachers, Aitken worked intensively with Yamada Ko'un Zenshin, Abbot of the Sanbo Kyodan* Zen lineage[139] based in Kamakura, Japan, and in 1974 Yamada Ko'un gave Aitken permission to teach Zen.

Aitken was friends with Jim and Shelley Douglass and although not identifying as Christian himself, drew inspiration from their work as well as that of the Catholic religious Left, including the Berrigan brothers, Dorothy Day and the Catholic Worker Movement. In the summer of 1976, Aitken had joined the Continental Walk for Disarmament and Social Justice partway into its march from the west coast to Washington, D.C. He was in close touch with Pacific Life Community's dozens of actions at the base in Bangor during the mid-'70s, mainly consisting of penetrating the fence (sometimes referred to as transcending the fence),[140] once managing to stay long enough to plant a vegetable garden before being arrested. These various actions built up to what came to be called Bangor Summer, the summer of 1977, in which people were invited "... to come to Kitsap County for a week or two and to take part in workshops designed to explore personal violence while simultaneously taking action at the Trident base."[141]

Robert Aitken was among the thousands that came from all over to participate. He was giving mindfulness training to groups doing civil disobedience at the base, and at the request of Alice Ray and others, he led a *zazenkai* (a one-day Zen retreat) for interested activists. It was a big hit. Afterwards, Alice ran into Casey Bailey, then a Jesuit, later a Trappist at Guadalupe Abbey. Casey knew Bernard McVeigh and thought he might be interested in collaborating on something with Zen in mind. With this encouragement, Alice brought Aitken down from Bangor, Washington, to the monastery at Lafayette, Oregon, to meet Bernard.

Greg Mayers was stationed at Palisades Retreat Center, a Redemptorist facility in the town of Federal Way on Puget Sound just north of Tacoma, Washington. Alice Ray and Robert Aitken would have passed near Federal Way on the drive down to see McVeigh. Sometime before, Greg had heard about the Trappists at LaFayette and gone down for a private retreat, during which Bernard McVeigh would come and talk to him every day. After a while, Greg started going regularly. McVeigh encouraged him to join the monks who were doing silent sit-

---

* Variously written as Sanbo Kyodan, Sanbokyodan and Sambokyodan (English: Order of the Three Treasures, or Three Treasures Religious Organization): The Harada-Yasutani Zen lineage of which the Diamond Sangha, founded by Robert and Anne Aitken, is an offshoot. In 2014 the Sanbo Kyodan was renamed Sanbo Zen International.

ting several times a day. Greg resisted, but eventually, partly based on his observation that Bernard seemed like a pretty sane person, Greg decided to give it a try and pretty quickly he was hooked. He happened to be on one of his Abbey visits when Ray brought Aitken down to meet Bernard.[142]

Bernard told Greg, "There's a Zen master, an American Zen master, here and we're going to have a meeting with him after supper, why don't you come." So Greg attended this crowded meeting in a small room at the Abbey, and Aitken taught a little Zen sitting to some of the monks. As a plan began to take shape to have Aitken lead a Zen *sesshin*,* they asked Greg if it could be held at Palisades. It took until the early summer of 1978 for the date to be fixed to October of that year. As soon as he knew, Greg called Pat in Wisconsin and said, "We've got a real Zen master coming." Pat knew the timing was bad — it was going to be over Parents' Weekend at the seminary, and besides that, the friction with his Redemptorist superiors, though resolved, was still recent. Nonetheless, he told Greg, "I'll *be* there." Not a moment's hesitation.

First sesshin — October 1978

Design of the sesshin was worked out in correspondence among Robert Aitken, Alice Ray, Bernard McVeigh, Jim Douglass and Bob Baird. Aitken outlined a format very much like that of sesshin he was offering regularly in Hawaii and California, with no pulling of punches as to rigor but some concessions of liturgy to the Christian leanings of the group.[143]

Aitken insisted that each participant do *shoken* — an initial interview that includes a token offering of "incense money," to be three dollars per student and individually presented. "No additional honorarium is necessary, though if the group would like to make a small gift of a book, say, it might give people the feeling that they have responded suitably." He gave detailed instructions about meal preparation, what and how food was to be served, clothing, comportment and schedule, conceding that if the organizers would like to do some things differently, he'd go along with it. He was even willing to forego having each participant do *samu*, or work practice, considered an important part of Zen training, if it seemed inappropriate at Palisades. "I attended a sesshin held at San Juan Bautista near San Jose, California, where the resident priests did all the cooking and cleanup. A rather lazy sesshin, I thought. However, if that is the arrangement at Palisades, okay." He reluctantly decided they could eat in the dining room rather

---

* Sesshin: Japanese: To touch the mind; a multi-day Zen retreat.

than have each participant bring the formal bowls for *oryoki** and eat in the room where they would do *zazen* (seated meditation). He accepted that the morning sutra service would be tailored to the Christian participants, with Western spiritual readings introduced in place of some of the Japanese chants. He suggested that the usual Buddhist icons on the altar be replaced with an image of St. Francis or one of the other principal Christian saints, then added, "I can bring a Buddhist figure from here in the event we have a more conventional sesshin or in addition."

A letter of invitation sent out by Alice Ray on behalf of the organizers captures the spirit of this unconventional sesshin.

> Dear Friends,
>
> It is with a real sense of excitement and hope that I invite you to share in a unique collective spiritual experience. Robert Aitken, Roshi of the Maui and Koko An Zendos,† has agreed to return to the Northwest this fall to conduct a special sesshin for Christians and other interested travelers. The sesshin will be held from October 13 to 18.
>
> During his visit this past spring, it became apparent to several of us that there are many "closet sitters" within the worshipping Christian community. In addition, there seem to be quite a few "closet Christians" sitting regularly with Zen Buddhist groups. Our idea was a simple one: To set up an intense, disciplined experience of spiritual practice that does not force us to choose between our Zen and our Christian "sides."
>
> With this idea in mind we approached Aitken Roshi about the possibility of conducting a special *sesshin* — one in which Christian images, scripture and worship forms might be the "jumping off point" for deepening in Zen practice; one in which rigorous *zazen* (sitting), *dokusan* (formal interviews) and *teisho* (formal talks) might be the means for deepening in the mysteries of Christian life. Aitken Roshi has agreed to conduct such a sesshin. To guard against a reverse of the kind of sectarianism that has sometimes been a stumbling block for Christians attempting to practice with Zen Buddhist groups, he has especially asked that this *sesshin* be open to all "interested travelers." Buddhists and/or humanists who are open to the use of Christian symbols as a means toward deepening in their own practice are thus also invited. There will be no pressure for anyone to alter the shape of his or her personal belief.
>
> There are two requirements for anyone wishing to make this sesshin. The first is that each person listen to a taped set of eight introductory talks

---

* Oryoki: (Sino-Japanese, just the right amount): a highly choreographed Zen meal service ritual that includes chanting at various stages.

† Zendo: (Japanese) Meditation hall; the term may be used to refer to the building in which the meditation hall is a room or to the room itself, also called dojo.

given by Aitken Roshi and available in Seattle and Olympia, WA, and Lafayette, OR. The second is that each person make a commitment to work with Aitken Roshi as teacher during the sesshin. He is not asking for a permanent commitment from anyone, but each person must be willing to follow his way for the five days. This sesshin is not set up to provide an atmosphere for people to do their own thing. It is a highly structured experience composed of a rigorous schedule of *zazen*, *teisho* and *dokusan*. There will also be periods for *samu* (mindful work) and for eating and sleeping.

Since we do not have our own zendo in the Northwest, we have to rent facilities for the sesshin. The best price we can get for a place that will accommodate us is $10 per person per day, plus food (which we will supply and prepare ourselves), plus travel expenses for Robert Aitken and a helper, plus $3 "incense money" for the Roshi from each participant. For some of us, this price is prohibitively steep, representing about half a month's wages. We would not like anyone to miss the sesshin for purely financial reasons, thus, for now, it would be good to consider $75 the norm. Hopefully, those who have greater resources will contribute more so that those with fewer resources can still attend.

We are excited about the possibilities of this sesshin and about developing a *Sangha* (Zen community) in the Northwest. If you would like to participate, please let us know as soon as possible. Since space is limited, participants will be selected on a first-come, first-served basis. To register, please send your name, address, to Fr. Gregory Mayers, Palisades Retreat, PO Box 2214, Tacoma, WA, 98401. Also please tell us if you have a *zafu* (cushion) and *zabuton* (pad) which you can bring for zazen. We will send you a copy of the "Sesshin Cautions" developed by Aitken Roshi for the Diamond Sangha in Hawaii and try to arrange a time and place for you to hear the tapes. Meanwhile, we urge you to maintain a disciplined personal schedule of zazen in preparation for the sesshin.

In peace and hope,
Alice Ray-Keil
For the Coordinators[144]

Participants were to be up at 4:00 AM with light exercise at 4:15 before settling on their cushions in the zendo by 4:30, then they would spend about 11 hours of the day in successive rounds of zazen, for periods of 25 minutes followed by *kinhin* (meditative walking) for five minutes, until bedtime at 9:00 PM. Each morning would begin with tea ceremony followed by *kentan* (formal inspection of the zendo by the teacher) toward the end of the first zazen period, teisho (oral presentation by the teacher) during the late morning period, sutras in the afternoon, and dokusan (one-on-one encounter with the teacher) offered during the early morning, afternoon and evening blocks of sitting. The daily rhythm included meals and a short break after each meal. During the break after breakfast, participants would do *samu* — "people not chopping vegetables and fruit are assigned cleanup jobs in the *dojo*,* in the garden, in the bathroom, etc."

They worked Christian elements into this time-honored sesshin frame. In addition to the "Great Vows" recited three times a day and the "Heart Sutra" recited once a day, they chanted a prayer during the early morning block. They replaced the usual "On Opening the Dharma" recitation before teisho with the Beatitudes. They filled out the sutra service with psalms and spiritual poetry. And there was Mass offered during the break after supper. For the closing ceremony at the end of each full day, they read Angelus Silesius[145] instead of Hakuin Zenji.[146] Dan Mintie recalled, "They came up with a beautiful liturgy that spoke to the heart of the matter in Japanese and English, Christian and Buddhist.[147]"

In the weeks leading up to the sesshin the Catholic Workers put together booklets with the liturgy, integrating Christian with Buddhist and editing the Christian texts to remove sexist and violent language. They organized food and cooking. They sewed *zafus* and *zabutons* (sitting cushions and under-mats respectively) for those who couldn't bring their own, using the stuffing from stuffed animals when they didn't have kapok.[148]

Pat arrived for the sesshin in time to explore the Palisades Retreat Center briefly — enough time to fall in love with the place. The Center is built on a 39-acre wooded property named for the high bluffs on which it sits, overlooking the waters of Puget Sound in the Pacific Northwest. Pat stood at the top of the bluff looking out across the water to Vashon Island and the Olympic Mountains, the smoke from his cigarette carried by a mild sea breeze. He strolled along wooded paths, breathing in the northwest rainforest scent of hemlock, fir and cedar. He made the first of many trips down the steep flights of wooden stairs zigzagging through trees and brush to the beach.

About 40 people came for the sesshin. Besides Pat Hawk, there were four Catholic Workers from *Pacem in Terris*, others from the anti-nuclear activist community, Aitken's seasoned Zen assistant Stephen Mitchell who hitchhiked up from California, four Trappists including Bernard McVeigh, as well as various spiritual directees of McVeigh from all over including Greg Mayers.

The first evening they gathered for an informal supper (informal meaning they could talk to each other) in the dining room with picture windows looking west to the sun setting behind the Olympic Mountains. Then as smoke curled up from the first stick of incense on the altar, people drifted into the zendo, finding

---

* Dojo: Meditation or practice hall.

their places on the black cushions or low meditation benches. They settled in to listen to detailed Sesshin Cautions beginning with the three essentials: "First, don't talk or whisper. Second, don't look around. Third, don't indulge in social greetings." They learned about the sesshin leaders seated at the four corners of the room: the *jikijtsu* (aka *jiki*) or timekeeper, the *jisha*, or teacher's attendant, the *ino* or chant leader, and the *tanto*, or head of practice — responsible for all the others. They learned about clappers, bells and other sound makers that announced zazen, *kinhin*,* *teisho*,† meals — everything — without the need for words. They learned about conducting themselves quietly, the silence not only of no words but also of no body language, no social gestures. They learned how to bow, how to walk in *kinhin*, how to hold their hands while walking. When committed to, the minute details of sesshin discipline establish a setting for mindful attention without the mental distractions of personality and choice — the paradox of strict discipline within which is the childlike freedom of not having to think.

The struggle with sore knees and aching back began almost immediately for many participants, but Pat's body folded easily into full lotus, accustomed by more than a decade of solitary practice at Oconomowoc, Esopus and Edgerton. It seemed his whole life had prepared him for this silence and this discipline. He was in his element. The next morning, not very bright but very early, the daily routine began, most of the day spent sitting on cushions in silence, facing the wall both literally and figuratively.

As is traditional for the first teisho of sesshin, Aitken's was based on Joshu's Mu, first case in the koan‡ collection, *Mumonkan*,[149] a compilation put together in the 13th century by the Chinese Zen master Mumon (Wumen). Aitken began by reading the case, his voice deep and congested with one of his frequent respiratory ailments.

> A monk asks: Does a dog have Buddha nature?
> Joshu replies: Mu.

Aitken spoke the Mu with a long Muuuuuu. He went on to Mumon's commentary, then began his presentation.[150] "Over the years, over the decades, over the

---

* Kinhin: Walking meditation.
† Teisho: Literally, "presentation of the shout." Presentation of dharma insight by a Zen master.
‡ Koan: A story, question or statement, engagement with which can help a student break through the bounds of conventional thought to a deeper perception of reality. Many koans in current use are stories of master – student interactions from Tang dynasty Chinese Buddhism (Ch'an).

centuries, this case has proved the most efficacious of all koans for students starting out in Zen practice." At a few points, Aitken incorporated the Christian background of many of his listeners: "It is interesting, the anonymous text on Christian practice, *Cloud of Unknowing*, a 14th-century text, suggests that one pick a single word of a single syllable that sums up all religious concern for the student. A word such as 'love' or 'God' is suggested, but any word may do. So long as it has the context, the background. A word like chair won't do. But a word with no association is even better, and for that, mu is perfect." Indeed, as he spoke with each person in dokusan, Aitken found that even the priests and nuns preferred not to use "God" or "love," finding these words too heavy with associations.

Aitken continued, "All beings have Buddha Nature, the sutras tell us. That mountain, that stream, all Buddha Nature itself. What is Buddha Nature really, that monk is asking. Joshu says, 'muuuu'… Key that mu to your breath in the same way you key the count to your breathing when you are counting your breath." He returned to the *Mumonkan* text, quoting: " 'For realization* it is of the utmost importance that you cut off the mind road,' " then he elaborated, "This does not mean that you block your thoughts. Yasutani Roshi says there are many people, even really advanced students of meditation, who think that the purpose of zazen is to cut off all thoughts. It is not."

There was a silence, then: "The purpose of zazen is to forget yourself in the act of uniting with something. Quite a different matter. On your cushions uniting with mu. In your daily life, uniting with your task, or if you're walking down the trail, uniting with the act of walking down the trail, doing mu." He punctuated periodically with a rhetorical, "hmm?" or a low chuckle. "Forgetting everything else. Thoughts die down in this process… a byproduct — you have a quiet mind as a result of your practice of mu. … So we become absorbed in mu, only mu, muuu, muuuu. Muuu. Nothing else! Totally absorbing ourselves in one thing! Body and mind truly fall away. … We call this the gateless barrier of the Zen sect." Aitken continued at length, adding his own comments to Mumon's. When he came to Mumon's: "You enjoy a *Samadhi*† of frolic and play," he said, "Where? Doing God's will." A very un-Aitken-like allusion offered for the benefit of his Christian audience.

In his individual meetings with participants, Aitken started many of them on the koan Mu. The student is to sit with the koan, and presenting their understanding in dokusan, must convince the teacher of that understanding. The teacher

---

* Realization, also referred to as enlightenment or awakening; an experience that includes breaking through ordinary conceptual constraints to a wider experience of reality. Japanese: kensho, satori.
† Samadhi: A state of intense, sometimes blissful, concentration.

asks a series of checking questions. When satisfied that the student has penetrated this "gateless barrier", they are cleared to embark on the long koan curriculum. Students wrestle — some for months, some for years — to penetrate Mu until it dissolves into nothing and everything. Years later, Aitken remembered that Pat passed Mu at that first sesshin.[151]

Three of the priests took turns saying Mass in the evenings, their different styles evident. Bernard was forthright and urbane. Greg wore vestments decorated with butterflies symbolizing death and resurrection. Pat was unobtrusive, always the invisible vehicle.

The strict discipline imposed by the sesshin cautions is variegated inevitably by the jostling of individual personalities against each other. This both irritates and instructs. The liturgy was too Christian for some, not Christian enough for others. Some were uncomfortable with all the bowing. Some skipped whole blocks of zazen. Greg Mayers and Redemptorist confrere Mike Ortega gave up early on and disappeared to their usual occupations. Pat had to get a chair about halfway through but stuck it out more or less. Here and there, people broke the silence with side conversations. At some point, Bernard stumbled on Pat and Greg off somewhere having a beer.[152] Most people hardly noticed Pat and would not have remembered that he was there, but for the major role he later came to play.

Regardless, in the end the silence had done its work, and as they gathered for the last meal — informal like the first — the dining room bubbled with joyful conversation. Pat met Aitken's wife Anne at that closing meal. She had not sat sesshin but was with Bob and took care of him. As anyone who met her, Pat loved and trusted her right away. Robert Aitken commented to Alice that of all the people there, he thought Pat Hawk was someone who really got it. She would not have noticed him but for the fact that both he and she were smokers and ducked out for a cigarette between blocks of sitting. The principals chatted about the success of the enterprise and decided they would do it again the next year.

In the meantime, Aitken took on a number of the participants as students, including Pat. This began a correspondence — one of dozens that Aitken kept up — centered on koan study and whatever was coming up in his practice. Pat wrote of this years later:

> Here, at last, was a teacher who could spur and guide my practice. From the beginning my Christian foundation was deepened, broadened and heightened by Zen practice. I began to discover the depth of riches not only in Zen, but also in the Christian Scriptures, early Christian writers, and mystics down to our own time. The encounter with Zen opened a capacity to realize

> in experience the Words that were so intimate to me, yet were, for an adult, immature in expression.[153]

Edgerton to Guest House

Pat went back to the darkening Wisconsin winter, resuming his duties and his drinking, until at the winter break his confreres Bob Halter and Joe Bilsley intervened. They sent Pat for treatment without discussion or notice, arranging for someone else to take over as principal. Pat was distraught. As he was leaving, he turned to Bob with pure rage saying, "You *Judas*!" Bob thought he'd lost a friend, but within a few months, he received from Pat the best letter he'd ever gotten. It was an apology and sincere thank you.

They sent Pat to Guest House, an addiction treatment facility for Catholic clergy in Lake Orion, Michigan, founded in 1956 by Austin Ripley, a popular mystery fiction writer, himself a recovering alcoholic. He knew Catholic priests who were struggling unsuccessfully with addiction and saw the need for a treatment program that respected the vocation of the religious as well as their dignity as human beings. "Ripley's profound belief was that his program should 'save the individual; save the vocation,' and in precisely that order."[154] It meant discarding the punitive, guilt-ridden language of sin and spiritual failure and welcoming the addict into beautiful surroundings where they could be treated with respect and receive appropriate therapy.

Guest House was in the Scripps mansion, a grand old house remodeled for the purpose and surrounded by parklike grounds. Pat remembered:

> The beauty of it is that the staff is all lay. There are no priests giving therapy. They're all laypeople, and they're all dedicated to getting priests back on their feet. The whole setup is to really treat the priests respectfully. It's first-class service. You've got maids that clean your room, make your bed. The food was — they had chefs for food. It was a beautiful house, old, beautiful grounds. Then of course they had the counselors for the alcoholism. There was a big emphasis on 12-step, AA [Alcoholics Anonymous]. They had psychologists there. They had a tiptop medical thing. You went through a huge medical examination. A lot of times, when you're in the midst of alcoholism, you neglect your health. Teeth go bad, you just don't go to the doctor. Your teeth, your eyes, the whole bit is taken care of. There were two nurses on staff. They had chauffeurs to take you for recreations once or twice a week, into shopping centers and whatnot. The whole course is about three months. It's not quick. They have classes every day, and they have art things for you to do, ceramics and painting. It's an amazing thing.[155]

Toward the end of his stay at Guest House, Pat, an apparently different person than the one who had written with so much anger the year before, wrote a long letter to Jeff Langton, still Provincial Superior of the Redemptorists' St. Louis Province:

Dear Jeff,

Hope all is well with you. At least that Christ's peace is with your soul. Thanks for the visit you and Jack paid to Ray and me. It was good seeing you.

Life continues to grow brighter for me. Compared to my arrival here, life is brilliant. I wasn't happy about the state of affairs when I heard the news and made matters pretty heavy for my confreres at Edgerton. But I am grateful to you and them for this opportunity. It was a relief to get away and now it seems long ago and far away. I know that many matters remain, but this oasis has given my soul, mind, and body time and space to gain perspective and freedom from alcohol.

This is a wonderful community to live in. The priests and brothers here have shared themselves generously and taught me how good and comparatively easy it can be. The staff is caring and generous and most especially, gentle.

Besides the priests and brothers, my counselor, Jo Holladay, and the psychologist, Jack Gregory, have enabled me to become comfortable with myself in many ways, to come out of myself on a more realistic basis, to make my own insights become operable in my life. Of course I cannot express adequately how much broader and more enjoyable these people have made the world, nor will I be able adequately to thank them, especially Jo. My best thanks will be to live fully and ask God to give them all they deserve.

I've certainly learned much from the lectures and other information given here about my disease. It has helped me personally and, I pray, is going to add a significant dimension to my future ministry.

I have always sought God. Yet in subtle, and not so subtle, ways cut myself off from Him. The way to Him seems more possible to me now. I've found my prayer becoming more simple and direct. Even more basically, I've found I could still pray, which was a relief. I look forward to a renewed spiritual life. There is so much to grow into — the infinite.

This has been a vacation I have denied myself for many years. Truly free from worry and able to enjoy completely and without guilt the beauty of nature here and doing simple things like eating, exercising, sightseeing, relaxing at the movies and in the sun. Even the mosquitoes can't destroy the good times I've had.

One of the most enjoyable, helpful, and enlightening aspects of the program is AA. I've met and learned from such a wide variety of people. It's hard for me to describe this. It's like meeting the world for the first time and discovering that people are good, that there is certainly evil in the world, but

God is there. In our weakness we are made strong by finally surrendering to Him. I've seen it, really experienced this in a wild variety. I see the priesthood in a new light because of this. I am not, nor is the priesthood humiliated by God's strange and mysterious ways, but I am certainly humbled and awed. I will always hold to and bless this fellowship. I accept more fully God's plan, role, and state for me and I can share it with so many different people as they share with me.

This letter has become windy. I hadn't intended that, but I'll let it all stand. It seems I enjoy my own spontaneity now and I hope you do too.

Take care. Enjoy your walks in the woods and get them when you can. I'll be seeing you on the 16th of July. God bless and Mary keep you.

In the Redeemer,
Pat Hawk, CSsR[156]

Pat left Guest House, stopping in at Villa Redeemer in Glenview to see Langton as promised before going on to visit his family. They discussed Pat's next assignment. Pat was firm about not returning to work at Edgerton, instead asking to be stationed at Palisades Retreat Center. Already, confreres Greg Mayers and Mike Ortega had been angling to have Pat come, and Ortega had written to Langton independently to propose it.

As soon as Pat left Glenview, Langton met with his Provincial Council, then wrote three letters in quick succession. The first was to the Provincial Superior of the Oakland Province — under whose jurisdiction the Palisades Retreat Center fell — asking permission for Pat to spend a year at Palisades. In his letter, Langton commented, "Pat has done exceptionally well at Guest House and is in top condition emotionally and physically, as well as spiritually. He has sound reasons for being attracted to the Palisades on a temporary basis."[157]

Although the Redemptorist superiors gave him permission to go to Palisades, they wished that Pat not be lost to the St. Louis Province, therefore the transfer would be temporary. Whatever they felt about Pat's rough edges and his drinking problem, they saw him as a valuable asset. As with his attempt to resign from the principal's job the year before, far from wanting to give up on him, they were at pains to keep him among them.

Langton then wrote to Pat himself, thanking him for having spent the night at Glenview instead of just passing through for the meeting. "I want to say how happy I am that you spent a full day with us and stayed overnight. It made a real visit out of what might have been merely a business appointment. I appreciate your giving us such a generous portion of your limited time." He again congratulated him on having so well taken advantage of the opportunity of Guest House and gave him permission to discuss the proposed move with the community at Palisades.

Langton's third letter was to Jo Holladay, Pat's counselor at Guest House. He wrote, "Father Pat Hawk is now visiting with his parents, having left here before noon today. He was generous with his limited time, staying with us here overnight and for a full day. That in itself says something positive about his attitudes. More explicitly, I had several good conversations with him and can only report positively." He thanks her for the help she has given to Pat and for having sent an interim report on Pat's progress.[158]

An implication of these letters in which Langton is so pleased simply that Pat would stop overnight to visit at Glenview is that Pat's behavior in the latter period at Edgerton before he went to Guest House had been decidedly anti-social.

By September, Pat was able to move to Palisades.

Palisades Retreat Center, Washington 1979-80

Pat's working life at Palisades included leading retreats at the center — many weekend men's retreats, a few women's retreats, several 8-day retreats. These were not contemplative events dedicated to sitting in silence. They were structured retreats with guided reflection, times for prayer, light socializing at meals. He led Days of Recollection and Prayer at various times. He and the others helped out with saying Masses at local parishes in Seattle, Olympia and Tacoma. Immediately north along the coast from Palisades was the Sisters of the Visitation Monastery, and the Redemptorist confreres at Palisades took turns going over to offer daily Mass and sometimes to lead retreats for the Sisters, so those duties too appeared on Pat's calendar regularly. He preached 3-day missions for nearby Catholic parishes — Poulsbo, Ferndale, St. Anne, Bainbridge. A few of these involved a ferry ride across Puget Sound, which he enjoyed. Toward the end of Pat's time in the Northwest, Progoff journaling sessions* — something Greg Mayers got trained in and began practicing and teaching — appeared on his calendar.

Throughout the time at Palisades, Pat and Greg led a small group, sometimes just themselves, in regular silent sitting. Occasionally they incorporated contemplative practice into some of the retreats they offered at the Center. In his letters to Aitken, Pat called it Zen sitting, although there were no Buddhist icons, no "Great Vows," no other chanting, nothing that would identify it specifically as Zen. His calling it Zen may have been sensitivity to Aitken's mild squeamishness about Christianity and its articles of belief. In any case, it was all the same silence.

---

* A psychotherapeutic method developed by Ira Progoff (1921-1998) involving intensive, integrative writing exercises led by trained guides.

When Pat had free time, he read books, and on many days he took long walks. If he felt agitated, he could trek along trails in the woods at a strong pace and cover a lot of ground. Other times he would meander aimlessly, pause to watch a squirrel or sit on a mossy log and have a smoke, watch a thrush deliver its call and chatter, or tune in to the liquid churring of a white-crowned sparrow. He took a casual interest in these fellow creatures, not caring particularly about learning their identifications but appreciating their different personalities. Sometimes he would just sit and be in the moist forest.

Often he would take the steep stairs down the palisade to the water. If the tide was in when he got to the beach, he would sit on a driftwood log a little way above the waterline and let himself be mesmerized by the steadily breaking waves. Where the stairs opened to the beach, there was an old, wrecked wooden barge that was partially submerged. He would watch the water pull away from its various crevices then flood back, or he would look up over the waters of the Sound at the massive boats going to and from Tacoma, or have a silent conversation with a nearby gull. Someone heading down the stairs from the top could tell if he was below by the smoke of his cigarette wafting up from the shore. If the tide was out, he could walk along the beach in either direction. A few times, he was so absorbed in the moment that he was nearly trapped against the palisade by the incoming tide.

He made two trips of two days each back to Guest House as part of their standard follow-up, combining these with visits to his family and to the St. Louis Province. He and Greg made several trips to Guadalupe Abbey in Oregon to sit with the monks and work with Abbot Bernard McVeigh. While at the Abbey, Pat discovered Thomas Merton[159] through the monks' extensive collection of Merton recordings, mostly his talks to the novices at Gethsemani Abbey from the days he was novice master there. For several years Pat spent a lot of time with Merton's voice, having acquired a collection of his taped talks and books. Merton was a good bridge for him between West and East, Christian and Buddhist.

While living at Palisades, Pat was able to attend the second and third sesshins led by Robert Aitken for the Pacific Northwest group. It is evident from his letters that there was great trust on Pat's side in this man that he was only beginning to know. In the fall of 1979, after the second sesshin, Pat wrote to Aitken:

> Dear Aitken Roshi,
>
> I hope your stay on the mainland accomplished much. It was most good to be with you once more.
>
> I am continuing to sit; much more consistently than after the 1978 sesshin here. Greg Mayers sits with me almost every day and George Whalen,

who made this year's sesshin, and his wife, will begin to sit with us on Monday evenings. So we have a small nucleus here that may grow, God willing.

There are two things that I wish to share with you at this writing. One is a theme that has to do with "door-gate." It began at the 1978 sesshin when during one dokusan you said, "Through that gate." This struck me strongly for some reason, but began to bear fruit for me only this past summer while meditating on John 8:9, "I am the gate." Since then, everything that has to do with gates-doors and the spiritual life has demanded my attention. For instance, while reading a book on Merton, I found that he determined to predispose himself for union with God by going through the door of self. A Redemptorist confrere of mine, in a series of lectures, refers to entering deeply into pain and doubt as the door to true conversion — Mumon says, "Make your whole body a mass of doubt." These and others have confirmed me further in practice and helped integrate it with my Christianity.

The other thing is that after sitting one evening I sat watching a fire in a fireplace. The logs which grew from earth and energy from the sun were returning energy and being reduced to ash by combining with oxygen. It occurred to me that the human body does the very same thing. The log went back to what it was or became what it is. From Merton: ...become someone that one already (potentially) is, the person one is truly meant to be. I had no experience of the logs or fire and myself as one or Mu. I did feel death was no longer fearful but a natural stage of growth.

My own comment on both matters: intellectual. I appreciated your comment on the difficulty of the Way for the intellectual. So, I am not surprised nor discouraged.

I hope the photographs of the sesshin and the *Christ Abandoned* turned out.

Peace to you and all who sit with you,
Patrick Hawk, CSsR[160]

The *Christ Abandoned* sculpture belonged to Palisades and had been on the altar during the sesshins for Christians. It showed Christ dead on the cross, a shroud draped over his body including his face. The fact of Christ dead on the cross — something Aitken had never seen imaged before — struck him as profound. He had asked Pat the provenance of the sculpture, apparently with an eye to getting one for himself. That turned out not to be possible, so he settled for a photograph. Pat made several attempts to get him a photo he felt would be good enough.

Aitken replied to Pat's letter with encouragement of his practice.

Dear Pat,

Thanks very much for your interesting letter. I am very pleased that the nucleus of a Zen group is being established at the Palisades. ... Yes, the gate is an important image and metaphor. I resonate to the words of your confrere and to the words of Merton, "The self is the agent of realization."

The analogy of fire is found throughout Buddhism. The Lotus Sutra contains a parable which likens the body to a burning house. Dogen Zenji* in his essay "Genjo Koan" points out that the fire was once wood and will become ashes, and that as it burns its action is complete in itself and also contains both past and future.

I don't think your two experiences were excessively intellectual. … It may be difficult for the true blue intellectual to do zazen because he is used to working at an entirely conceptual level. However, it is not possible for a mentally handicapped person to do zazen at all. The intellect, integrated with body, will and spirit is an important element of the practice.

Debra sent me copies of the sesshin photograph and of *Christ Abandoned.* They came out pretty well. I hope that you have received your copies by now.[161]

With *gassho*,†

Pat's reply to Aitken's letter is full of frank revelation. It seems from the tone of this letter that the depression that dogged Pat at Oconomowoc and returned during the latter years teaching at Edgerton has re-surfaced at Palisades:

Dear Bob,

Thank you for your letter with its words of encouragement. I received the pictures from the sesshin. To say "they came out pretty well" is far too kind. They were quite unsatisfactory. There is nothing to be done about the group picture, but I did some more of the crucifix and have sent you some of the results under a separate cover. Please accept them with my gassho.

Since I wrote last, I spent three days with the Trappists and was privileged to sit with them while there. It was quite a good experience. I experienced deeply the poverty of my ego and the abyss of the Void, but none of its fullness.

I find it most difficult to do zazen. I read Alan Watts' "*The Way of Zen.*" I found it to be most interesting, especially on what he says concerning Western thought and spontaneity of living by grasping experience directly. Now, I find myself frustrated, and Zen and everyday happenings are beating my head against a wall.

Recently I wrote in my journal, "I acted and watched myself acting and watched myself watching." I am quite aware of my thought process and the futility of its ever giving meaning to what just is — And that's about where I am. There is much I can say about everything, but it sticks in my throat. I

---

* Dogen Zenji, aka Dogen Kigen, Eihei Dogen (1200-1253 CE). Japanese Buddhist priest, credited with bringing Ch'an (Japanese: Zen) to Japan in the 13th century.

† Gassho: A simple bow with hands held in front, palms together.

> don't want to say anything, because it is ignorance, better to be silent, thus be ignorant. This letter then means nothing. Just a reaching to touch you.[162]

This coming to the limit of words, so necessary, particularly for someone of Pat's intellectual bent, was not yet total for him. He was still doing a lot of thinking, and still very much trying to interrelate Zen and Christian aspects of his understanding.

The third sesshin for Christians led by Aitken, again at Palisades, continued to have strong participation, including as before, Trappists from Guadalupe Abbey and Catholic Workers from Seattle. Among newcomers was Bob Walker, at the time considering joining the Trappists, later a significant figure in Pat's life, though they hardly noticed each other at this first encounter.

The time in sesshin deepened Pat's bond with Aitken as his teacher and strengthened Aitken's conviction that Pat was exceptionally promising. Aitken was impressed with the quality of Pat's attention, palpable in dokusan. It gave him patience with Pat's attempts to integrate his unfolding discovery of Zen with the language of Catholicism so long familiar to him. Pat wrote to Aitken:

> Dear Bob,
>
> Thank you for leading the sesshin for us in Tacoma. It was a marvelous, deepening experience. I find the Bible to be ever more the Living Word through the practice.
>
> You asked in one of our dokusan if something happened. I was somewhat at a loss to say exactly what and replied yes, at a teisho. That is true, but it was a series of happenings. Your words at teisho about outside and inside being not different struck me. At the next zazen I experienced this to be so. Then walking in the woods after dinner I found, as Wallace Stevens said, green has "its own implacable sting," and the color of MU.
>
> I was reminded by the story of the master calling "O Shin"* of the call of the prophet Samuel in Samuel 3:1-10. And your words on obedience resonated in me as they do now.
>
> I found you are more aware of and speak more clearly of Christian teaching in your teisho. I appreciate your study. You made no comment at the sharing session however, on the request for more explicit presentation of Christian teaching. I hope this request will be given some consideration in the planning for the next sesshin. It would not have to be much, perhaps

---

* This is a reference to *Mumonkan* Case 12: Every day Master Zuigan [O Shin] called to himself, "Master!" and would answer, "Yes!" And again he would call, "Thoroughly awake! thoroughly awake!" and he would answer, "Yes! Yes!" "Don't be deceived by others, any day or any time!" "No! No!" From Robert Aitken, *The Gateless Barrier*, North Point Press, 1991.

five minutes at the Eucharist,* some words of explanation of the Eucharistic images, Lamb of God, memorial, or such like.

I have enclosed the negatives [of the *Christ Abandoned* photo] you asked for. No. 15 on this band is the one you liked better. No. 14 is very similar. You may wish to have 15 & 14 printed to see which is better in definition and color. Also enclosed is the letter in our files with information on the artist's name. I am under the impression she is dead.

My greetings to your wife and all at the centers.

With gassho,

Pat Hawk[163]

Aitken replied in a postcard, thanking Pat for the second attempt at photographing the *Christ Abandoned* sculpture and expressing reservations about mixing religions:

> Thank you very much for your letter, and for the enclosed statement of provenance and negative of the photo of the crucifix. I will return the letter to you soon. I know in my bones that the sculpture was a most exceptional work, and I'm glad to have the details. Please do bring it next time, and the next! I am consulting with Father Bernard about your suggestion to include explicit Christian teachings at sesshin. If we continue to have Mass, it would fit there. However, I want to avoid too much mixing. My preference is for a "sesshin for Catholics."
>
> Warmest regards, Bob[164]

Aitken's reservations about mixing would later become conspicuous in Pat's own approach. As a teacher, Pat would keep the Zen and Christian forms clearly distinct, although his experience of the interpenetration of the two streams would add a sophistication and breadth to his understanding that enriched his teaching for the rest of his life.

Pat wrote back to Aitken that summer, still from Palisades. His letter is in beautiful calligraphy, something he began practicing while still at Oconomowoc. Pat's earnestness of practice is apparent:

> Dear Bob,
>
> Thanks for your card of last May. It was good to hear from you. I hope sesshin went well.
>
> I ran across something while listening to a tape by Thomas Merton. I

---

* Eucharist is the ritual commemorating the Last Supper of Jesus of Nazareth with his disciples. The term is often used interchangeably with Mass.

immediately connected it with my koan — the sound of one hand.* Merton quotes the medieval monk Guigo (+1137), a Carthusian, as saying in "Scale of Cloisters & Meditations":[165]

All creatures are syllables, a song sung by God. Everything that is, is a note of His song which He continually sings, passing from note to note. Our happiness consists in following Him and listening to his singing. Our suffering comes from clinging to one syllable while God does not pause but constantly moves on. We must let go just experience each note as it is sung then follow along with the rest.

As often happens with me I began connecting many things I have heard or read. The above quote reminded me of Basho's poem:

The old pond;
A frog jumps in-
The sound of water.

I myself wrote the following after sitting one evening two months ago:

Seeing the sound of the tree,
Smelling the smoke move,
I hear the grain of the wood.

And another quote from Merton: "Who am I? I am myself a word spoken by God."

Sekishu no oto

Father Jäger was in the area recently, but unfortunately I was unable to be at his meeting with the others in Seattle. I did receive a copy of his homily on the Eucharist.

Greg Mayers is away this summer so I am sitting all by myself, but not alone.

Although I use Mu in my sitting and work still on the sound of one hand, I find that many of the daily circumstances of my life working with people bring to mind the story of Kyogen's person up a tree† and your comment on Jesus on the tree. I find it has great connection with my life and

---

* "Two hands clap and there is a sound. What is the sound of one hand?" Japanese: *Sekishu no oto.* A koan from Hakuin Ekaku (1686-1769), often given early in a student's koan study. Note that the common phrasing, "What is the sound of one hand clapping?" is a misstatement of the koan.

† "Kyogen said, 'It's like a man up a tree, hanging from a branch by his mouth; his hand cannot grasp a bough, his feet won't reach one. Suppose there is another man under the tree who asks him, "What is the meaning of Bodhidharma's coming from the West?" If he does not respond he

those who speak with me. I find that I sense there is no answer in words and as a result live and sit with more faith, it is the only thing that can be done.

May all be well with you. I enjoyed writing this letter to you. It seems that sometimes in writing in this style I can forget myself in uniting with the letters.

In these and with gassho.

P.H.[166]

For all his confidence in Pat's genuine promise, Aitken could see that Pat was still a novice tending toward abstraction, a barrier to direct experience. Once again, he responded with encouragement, still keeping Pat's feet to the fire on the koan:

Dear Pat,

Thank you very much for your wonderful letter of August 11 and please pardon this long silence.

I was interested in your response to your koan, but I feel the matter is not settled yet. I should like to have you present something much more simple and personal.

I liked your poem and resonated with Merton's words, "Who am I? I am myself a word spoken by God." This reminds me of the koan I occasionally use with Christians, "In the beginning was the word — show me that word." I think you can probably do this.

Father Jäger was a big hit at both Koko An and the Maui Zendo, and he has now returned to his home in Kamakura. After our zazenkai ended last Saturday noon, members took him for a drive to the top of Haleakala (our 10,000-foot volcano here on Maui) and he did a Mass for everybody on the top at sunset. His words about liturgy for Catholic sesshins were very useful to me, as I am sure they must have been for Father Bernard.

Your experiences of connecting things you have heard or read symptomize movement in your practice. I am sure they must be very encouraging for you. I look forward so much to seeing you once again next year. Enclosed is the strip of negatives you so graciously loaned me. I have the big picture on the wall of my office at Koko An and have distributed many copies made from your negative to friends.

Steadfastly,

Bob[167]

This exchange marks the appearance on Pat's radar of Willigis Jäger, a Benedictine monk from Würzburg, Germany, who was to become an important teacher for Pat. Jäger was a dharma brother of Aitken, both of them being students of

---

goes against the wish of the questioner. If he answers, he will lose his life. At such a time, how should he respond?" Case 5, *Mumonkan.*

Yamada Ko'un Roshi. At this time, he was on leave from his community, living in Kamakura to be near Yamada Ko'un. Jäger had come across writings of the Christian mystics during his seminary training, including the anonymous *Cloud of Unknowing*, offering that its simple instructions, if diligently practiced, could lead anyone to mystical experience. This was a proposition anathema to the Church hierarchy who, as Pat knew only too well, held that direct encounter with the divine was a rare grace not to be aspired to. Jäger followed the instructions and came to the promised realization, confirmed retrospectively by Yamada Ko'un as *kenshō**. Some years later, he attended two Zen sesshins in Germany with Brigitte D'Ortschy.[168] This encounter with Zen through D'Ortschy motivated Willigis to study in Japan with her teacher, Yamada Ko'un, and hence he connected with Aitken.

While working with Yamada Ko'un, Jäger had had a further, deeper experience, which (as was encouraged in the Sanbo Kyodan) he wrote out for their newsletter, *Kyosho*. The description of Jäger's kensho having caught Aitken's eye, he encouraged Willigis to present at the second *East West Religions Encounter,* a conference to be held at the University of Hawaii. Aitken thought Jäger's perspective could contribute to the ongoing Christian Buddhist dialogue in academic circles, which he felt was in danger of being overly intellectual. Jäger accepted, but then Yamada forbade him to go since he had not finished his koan work and therefore Yamada felt it would be inappropriate. At the time, Jäger was working through the *Shoyoroku*, third of the four major koan collections in the curriculum. He noticed that for koan work with English-speaking students, Yamada was relying heavily on notes that he and Robert Aitken had developed together.[169] This gave Jäger an interest in working directly with Aitken on some of the koans, and to this Yamada did agree. Accordingly, Jäger asked Aitken if he could visit him for a few weeks in Honolulu to be tacked onto a trip he was making to some of his Benedictine confreres in the United States. Aitken agreed, suggesting he might also be interested in visiting the Zen Christian group in the Northwest, including Abbot McVeigh at Guadalupe Abbey and the Catholic Workers in Seattle. It was based on this trip that Aitken wrote to Pat about Jäger having been a big hit in Hawaii.

At this time, the prospect of a Catholic monk who was also a Zen teacher held little interest for Pat. He had found Aitken, and his emphasis was to follow the Zen path that Aitken's teaching opened up to him. His Redemptorist superiors had little inkling of this, and it's not clear that greater awareness would have

---

* Kensho: Japanese, ken = seeing; sho = essence or nature; the experience of seeing into essential nature.

made any difference at this point anyway. They had loaned him to Palisades and the Oakland Province for 14 months, that time was up, and they wanted him back. On December 1, 1980, Pat flew back to Chicago and the St. Louis Province.

Back in the Midwest, 1981

Among the first things Pat did when he got back was to write for permission to avoid alcohol when saying Mass. Presumably, he had also had this permission from the Oakland Province while he was at Palisades. Becoming fluent now in the language of two religions, he naturally shifted back from closing with the more Buddhist, "Gassho," in his letters to Aitken, to the Christian formulations he learned in the seminary. He signed off with, "Mary keep you" and "In the Redeemer."

He was assigned to the Redemptorist Mission Team stationed at St. Alphonsus Rectory in central Chicago. The easy shift from Zen to Christian references notwithstanding, it was a culture shock to go from the quiet community and beautiful surroundings of Palisades Retreat Center to the multistoried rectory in a bustling downtown. Assignment to the Mission Team meant lots of travel — going to various parishes to preach week-long missions, then back to Chicago for a few days to do laundry, then off again. At the rectory, there were about 20 priests around the table for supper every night, some doing the work of the parish, a few coming in and out from mission trips, some doing doctorates or other higher studies. There were the very young to the very old, a big variety, and since most were unconnected to the work of the Mission Team, for Pat there was a sense of isolation.[170]

"It was good work and kind of gratifying to a certain extent. I was a pretty good preacher." This view offered matter-of-factly is affirmed by laypeople who attended his missions at the time, including his young niece, Tina Pope. "He had a retreat here once, at St. Elizabeth's, a mission, and it was for five nights in a row, and that place was packed every night I went. I was probably about 12 at the time and I just was fascinated." But Pat disliked all the travel, disliked living in Chicago, and just didn't take to the work. Looking back years later he said, "Being on the road, I didn't... I was wanting to do something different."

That summer, he made another of the follow-up visits to Guest House. On top of Pat's strong desire to be living and working a contemplative life, his Guest House counselor advised that the Mission Team work was not good for him. Pat made a radical decision and wrote a formal letter — typed, instead of written in what had become his usual calligraphy — to then Provincial Reverend John [Jack] Dowd. In his letter he focused on contemplative practice, avoiding whatever resistance an allusion to Zen might have raised, recognizing that silent sitting was the kernel in any case. Besides his request to leave mission work and possibly the Redemptorists altogether, it contained a contemplative manifesto of sorts, placing his aspirations within the Redemptorist charism of preaching to the most abandoned, and providing by implication, an incompletely veiled criticism of contemporary Redemptorist life:

> Dear Father Provincial,
>
> Saturday morning, August 9, I made a decision about my vocation. This decision was in some way quite sudden in that it was clear to me in an instant what I wished to do. In another way the decision had a long history and preparation.
>
> For some time now I have been drawn to a way of praying that might be called "contemplative." I have done much reading on this way of prayer and have actively pursued it in my living, but never to the point of being content with my efforts.
>
> For the past two years I have hoped and worked a little to fulfill this development with the Redemptorists. The way I read our history, the contemporary Constitutions, and other documents on our spirituality, contemplation is an essential element of our vocation. Indeed, I find that now I cannot get along without it.
>
> The pain I found myself feeling since my return from the Palisades is that I find no support for contemplative prayer in this province. My hope was that I could hang on and promote and encourage change in Redemptorist living situations and even get some kind of "house of prayer" going. I find, however, that I can no longer hang on. This is in no way due to the Redemptorists. It flows from my own weakness.
>
> This past May I visited Guest House for a few days as part of the aftercare program. While there I talked to my counselor Ms. Jo Holladay. She told me she thought I was in a bad condition. That working as a missionary was not a healthy lifestyle for me in the light of my disease. She suggested that I stay at Guest House for a few weeks and offered to write a letter suggesting I be given different work. I rejected both courses of action. The first because I would be spending the summer at Edgerton and the novitiate giving retreats and I thought that would accomplish the same thing as staying at Guest House. The second because I thought I could still hack the life and really ought to handle the situation myself without using her by waving a letter and saying this is what someone else thinks. Saturday I realized she was right. I simply cannot go on in this work and have a good prospect of remaining sober.
>
> But it is more than that. The negative condition is not all that important. It is the positive indicators that I wish to emphasize. I judge at this time that I am called to a simpler way of living, to silence and solitude, to a purification that both elates and frightens me. I have found this call within my vocation

as a Redemptorist. But now I see that I can go to a new stage of call. I would like to go forward in it.

It seems that I have reached a plateau in being a priest in an active apostolic congregation. In order to progress now I must go to a contemplative order. I need their structure and solitude. I believe the contemplative dimension can fruitfully be pursued by Redemptorists, and I pray it will be. But for me this is not so. My weakness has told me beyond doubt that I require what the monastery offers when one reaches this point.

I am mindful that there are dangers and difficulties in transferring, I have few if any illusions about life in a monastery. It is not a panacea nor is contemplative life a joy ride.

I know Abbot Bernard McVeigh, OCSO of Our Lady of Guadalupe Trappist Abbey and some of the monks there. I have lived at their monastery. I find them a most congenial group.

I therefore request two things of you:

1. To be relieved of my assignment as a parish missionary,
2. Permission to spend 70 days with the monks of Our Lady of Guadalupe in Lafayette, Oregon as an "observer" to the end of making a further determination in regard to my vocation.

I demand nothing. I make no ultimatum. I subject myself to obedience in all matters. I ask only that you help me.

In Christ Redeemer,
Patrick Hawk, CSsR[171]

The Provincial Council met to discuss the letter. Father Jack Dowd reported on the meeting in a long phone call with Pat, summarized in a short follow-up letter:

To put in writing the gist of our phone conversation; OPC[172] met and discussed your letter and the request it contained. Obviously your decision was not made in haste, but only after much prayer, thought and pain. We want to compliment you for the courage you have shown in trying to discern and follow the Lord's direction for your life.

We are giving permission to both items you requested:

1. As of today you are relieved of your assignment as a parish missionary.
2. You have permission to spend 70 days with the Trappists of Our Lady of Guadalupe in Lafayette, Oregon as an "observer" for the purpose of making a further determination concerning a move to a contemplative order.

...I hope that the quiet time and experience of the life at Our Lady of Guadalupe will aid you to see the direction in which the Lord is leading you.

Sincerely in Him,
John Dowd CSsR
Provincial Superior[173]

There followed an exchange of letters between Pat, Bernard McVeigh and Jack Dowd working out the details. Bernard wrote to Pat, "In regard to your request: Our normal procedure for vocational prospects is to have 3 or 4 short visits with some notable space between them and then offer the observership if the candidate really looks promising. In other words, the observership is the *last* step in the process." This was not practical for Pat, so Bernard suggested as an alternative that Pat "take advantage of our long-term residence [LTR] program which allows one to live within the community for one to 3 months living the full life with a mentor as a guide (or "guardian angel"). Normally this program is not for those with vocational aspirations. But we have used it as such and often with LTRers it turns into such."[174]

Pat wrote to Jack Dowd, in calligraphy again with the letter addressed to Dear Jack, finishing with:

> I will be leaving for Oregon on October 12 and expect to return here around Christmas. Perhaps we can then discuss what were the results of my stay and what I will do next. Enclosed are Abbot Bernard's letters to me so you may have a full picture of what is going on. I wish to express my thanks to you for your help. There is no adequate way to discharge my debt. I shall be praying for you and the province.[175]

Residency with the Trappists, Fall 1981

Pat arrived at Guadalupe, spent a week in the guest house then moved into one of the tiny monk's cells. He recalled, "The beds are slabs of wood. The mattresses are about three inches thick cotton batting. You have a little desk, some pegs to hang your clothes and that's it. The showers, lavatories are in the basement. And in the middle there is the dining room, kitchen, bakery."

In addition to the vows of poverty, chastity and obedience, the Trappists take a vow of stability, committing themselves for the rest of their lives to the monastery they enter. A line of plain white wooden crosses in the cloistered area marks the graves of the monks who have lived out their lives there.

Each Trappist monastery tries to be self-sufficient, the monks doing some kind of work to support themselves. At Guadalupe during the time Pat was there, the work included farming and forestry, binding periodicals for colleges in Oregon, and making fruitcakes for sale. Like every monk, Pat had work to do, most often in the bakery. He wrote to Harry Grile saying, "I'm making fruitcake. I never want to look at another fruitcake in my life." Years later he recalled, "I dipped their fruitcake, in, if you can believe it, 100 proof brandy, or it was maybe 140 proof. At any rate, you could get high just on the fumes!" Was Bernard McVeigh aware of Pat's history? "Yes, he was aware."[176]

The property is extensive, partly wooded, partly farmland, with a large pond behind the main buildings, and paths along the pond and through the woods. Pat followed the monks' schedule faithfully and took long walks when he could. Toward the end of the 70 days, he sent a letter describing his frame of mind to the Provincial Superior, done in slightly sloppy calligraphy on a simple Christmas card:

> Dear Jack,
>
> I thought I would send early Christmas greeting and let you know how things are progressing with me. I had intended to write much sooner than this. But time has gone very quickly and gotten away on me. First of all, thanks for the letter you sent to the Abbot. He was very impressed with the promptness with which you sent it. I guess his previous experiences were quite the contrary.
>
> Secondly, things are going quite well for me. It is hard to describe accurately in a few words. It is not easy, yet not impossible. I'm not having the time of my life, yet I'm content to find a quiet kind of peace with all of this when I look at the past two months as a whole. So at this point I am going to go on with the process of transferring to the Trappists, most likely here. The Abbot & his advisors have not yet given me *their* opinion so that could change matters. But they have indicated that I probably could start phase two in May.
>
> My concern right now is to be of productive service to the province in the meantime. I will be returning to Chicago on December 19. Perhaps you would let me know if you wish to see me before or after Christmas about where I might be and what I may be doing so I could make plans. I think my mother wants to see whether I have turned green or something.
>
> Take care. May God be with you and Mary keep you.
>
> Yours in the Coming of the Savior,
>
> Pat Hawk, CSsR[177]

When Bernard McVeigh did weigh in, it was to advise Pat against joining the Trappists. He may have been uneasy on behalf of the community, knowing Pat's tendency to dark taciturnity and resistance to life in the collective. And Pat, though it didn't strike him at the time, realized in retrospect that the life of solitude he sought was not offered among the Trappists. There is a lot of silence, but they are not hermits. A great deal of the time is spent doing things together. Whatever it was, Bernard told Pat to go out and find his niche and if he didn't find it, to come back to Guadalupe. Pat couldn't remember being disappointed about this. He said that he'd told Bernard some years later, no doubt tongue in cheek, "Thank you for saving me from a fate worse than death." He returned to the St. Louis Province Redemptorists and was assigned to be a Retreat Master at Villa Redeemer Retreat House in Glenview, Illinois.

Glenview, Illinois 1982-84

The work at Glenview was similar to that at Palisades, minus the air and landscape Pat loved and the support of like-minded companions. Not that the retreat center wasn't beautiful. Villa Redeemer had extensive wooded grounds where Pat could take the long strolls he loved, but it was part of greater Chicago, on the edge of the big city. And not that there weren't confreres for company, but none of them understood him. They regarded his sitting practice dubiously, with suspicion even.

Pat conducted mostly weekend retreats, some for men, some for women, some for both. Like most of the events he had offered in and around Palisades, these were standard Catholic talking retreats that included three conferences a day by Pat, daily Mass, opportunities to receive personal counsel from Pat, and time for reflection and prayer. They lacked the long periods of silence that were the substance of contemplative and Zen retreats. Participants could nonetheless benefit from Pat's personal contemplative practice, the radical acceptance that the practice fosters, his economy of words, his occasional flashes of dry humor, and his utterly attentive presence. He became a known and well-loved retreat leader there.

Pat's first contemplative student, Sister Shirley Morrissey, appeared in his life at this time.[178] A Franciscan Sister of Perpetual Adoration (FSPA), Shirley worked in Freeport, Illinois at a residential school for the mentally (and behaviorally) challenged. She was struggling with burnout from her demanding job, with unresolved issues from a difficult childhood, and with a nagging uncertainty about her vocation as a Catholic and a nun. Looking for places within range of Freeport that she might go for a rest, she found Glenview and arranged to do an individual retreat there.

Upon arrival, she was told that her retreat director would be a Father Patrick Hawk and that he would be contacting her. By the next morning, she still hadn't seen anyone, but somebody pointed out to her "this very petite guy, over at a distance, walking along with a staff and smoking. 'That's Father Hawk.' " At lunch, she looked over and noticed the same person sitting alone having lunch at another table. Not long after, a quiet, low voice behind her said, "Hello." She turned, he introduced himself, instructed her to come to his office after lunch and disappeared.

Upon meeting her he asked about her prayer life. She explained she was at a loss with her prayers, just sitting in the chapel saying nothing. To her surprise, he approved and encouraged her to continue. She spent most of her time in chapel or walking on the wooded paths. She saw him periodically and told him what was happening in her life, what was happening as she rested and sat in silence. At one point he told her simply, "I think you just need to go and cry." Mostly he listened and said very little. It was exactly what she needed. At the end of her stay, she asked him if he would be her spiritual director. He said, "No. But I will be your spiritual companion."

She got permission from her Superior to go to Glenview on weekends. Three out of four weekends, she helped with Pat's retreats, setting up for Mass, copying materials, doing odd jobs. One out of four she spent on her own, in silence except for brief conversations with Pat. At one point, she went to confession and for her penance, he asked her to sit in on his conference for the retreatants and give him feedback. Another time, no one had signed up to do the reading at Mass, so just moments beforehand Pat asked Shirley to do it. She was terrified of reading in public. She did it anyway. "The words were coming out of my mouth and all I was thinking was, I'm reading, people! I'm reading! I'm reading!" "Afterwards, I went to Pat in his office and said, 'Pat! What the hell did you do that for! You know I don't read in public.' He said, 'I know that. But I knew you could.' "

She injured her back at work — one of her charges got violent — and before she had surgery to help correct the injury, she was in enormous pain. She called Pat about it. He said, "Breathe with it." "Be with it." Back at work after the surgery, she found that for the first time, she was afraid of the children. She asked to be transferred from that job, and Father Vic Karls, then director of the retreat center, gave her a position on the staff at Glenview. It meant she could see Pat daily. They set up a regular schedule, the two of them sitting in silence in the chapel.

Robert Aitken handoff to Willigis Jäger 1982

Meanwhile, since the first Zen sesshin for Christians in 1978, Robert Aitken had led an annual sesshin for the Pacific Northwest group three more times. Attendance was strong and growing stronger. Pat had attended three of the four sesshin. Many of the same people — the Trappists from Guadalupe Abbey, the Catholic Workers, the directees of Abbot Bernard McVeigh — came back year after year and new people joined.

While holding a great affection for the group and many individuals in it, Aitken felt increasingly that he was not the right teacher for them. For one thing, when he compared this fledgling group to others that had crystallized around him, he was frustrated with the fact that they had not become a more cohesive entity. By contrast, a group in Sydney, Australia, for which he was then leading sesshin yearly, had come together as the Sydney Zen Centre. They had rented space and maintained a regular practice schedule in between Aitken's visits, including hosting zazenkais and sesshin. Likewise, Gary Snyder's Ring of Bone Zen group near Nevada City, California, who had invited Aitken to come and teach annually, was keeping a regular practice schedule and building a new zendo. Aitken wrote to Willigis Jäger, "Very little is happening in Seattle. Two or three meet here or there once a week or so. I think the diversity in attitudes on the subject of ritual plays some role in this disorganization, and I feel sorry the practice itself is not given the chance to develop"[179] Besides this, he was simply very busy. But perhaps these things would not have been obstacles were it not for the fact that fundamentally, Aitken was uncomfortable leading this group of Christians in Zen practice. He looked to Willigis Jäger as a possible better option for them.

Jäger's study with Yamada Ko'un overlapped at times with Aitken's, the two had attended sesshin together at Kamakura, and Jäger had worked with Aitken briefly in Hawaii, so they knew each other more than casually. Recently, Jäger had finished his koan study with Yamada, who had then given him permission to teach Zen. Aitken encouraged some of the Christian Zen group leaders to approach Willigis Jäger about potentially leading a sesshin for them. They had had an exploratory meeting with him during a visit he made to Guadalupe Abbey in the summer of 1980. On that same trip, Willigis stopped in for a several-day visit at Koko An during which he was reassured that Aitken would be happy to have him teach the Northwest group. In time the thing was arranged and the first sesshin with Jäger took place in July 1982 at Loyola Retreat House in Portland, Oregon. Before the sesshin, Aitken wrote to thank him and explain more clearly his own withdrawal:

> For one thing, I am overburdened with responsibility here in Hawaii and also with the satellite centers in Sydney and Nevada City, California [Ring of Bone Zendo]. I cannot do them all justice as it is. More important, however, is my feeling that I am not the right person for the Christian Sangha. My knowledge of Christianity is quite impressionistic, and I do not feel that I am really meeting the needs. Moreover, I sense that there is something quite malignant festering at the heart of modern Christian practice. I understand this sickness a little, but I feel that you would be a better doctor.[180]

As became customary among Diamond Sangha teachers later, Aitken then went into some detail about where individual students were in their practice, whether they were working on a koan and if so which one, and how they were doing with it — in general, what his sense was of whether a student was "getting it", so that Jäger could provide continuity. Aitken cautioned Willigis that he found the Sisters in the group rather doubtful of their own potential but otherwise unremarkable. "The priests and monks, however, tend to be very intellectual in their approach to the practice and to be analytical regarding the differences in their condition which they find from day to day. As a group I find them rather difficult as they seem to bring many preconceptions into the dojo." He did not single out Pat for special comment, and in any case, Pat was unable to attend that first sesshin with Willigis Jäger.

Many years later, looking back on this handoff to Jäger, Aitken said bluntly:

> I was tired of the insistence on Catholic ritual during my visit. This *mea culpa* business just drove me up the wall because *mea culpa* means it's my fault, you know. And we're taught in zazen to forget about the self, so there was a clash there in my mind. And I realized that it was not possible for me to continue trying to teach a bunch of Catholic priests and nuns and laypeople stuff that I didn't believe in. They were insisting on doing the psalms before meals and so on, and I couldn't handle it. So I knew Father Jäger — Willigis — from our work in Japan together. We had sat with Yamada Ko'un Roshi together. And so when he was given dharma transmission* by Yamada Roshi, I told the folks, well why don't you invite him. He's a better teacher than I am anyway. His heart is in it, but mine isn't. So that's how it stopped, thank goodness."

Aitken chuckled at the recollection.[181]

As for the Christian Zen people themselves, there was a lot of excitement about having this Benedictine monk with extensive Zen training come over and lead sesshin. Here was someone who would guide them in Zen practice, interpret the path in Christian terms, and, they hoped, relate it to the activism that motivated many in the group:

> If we realize we are the Body of Christ, then the Chinese, the Vietnamese, the Americans, the Japanese, the Filipinos are all one body. So, let us not slacken in our sitting but press on toward an ever deeper realization … "Love your enemies, do good to those who hate you," can be understood only on this level. As long as we think this is only a command, our understanding is indeed shallow. Only if we realize there is no difference between

---

* Zen dharma transmission originated with Ch'an Buddhism in China, as a formal acknowledgement from a Zen Master to a disciple of a "mind to mind" recognition of essential nature. Transmission goes beyond a simple permission to teach, and makes the recipient an independent Master, authorized to give transmission in turn. Although Willigis Jäger had been given permission to teach Zen, he had not, in fact, been given dharma transmission at this point.

you and the other, will you love the other in the right way. God is in him and in you, and you and the other and God are one.[182]

Although not able to attend the first sesshin with Jäger, Pat signed up for the second one, to be held in late October 1983. Even as he planned his trip west for this retreat, his mind was still on practice with Robert Aitken. Pat wrote to Aitken from Glenview:

> Dear Bob,
>
> Greetings! It has been some time since I have made a presentation. The last time was at the Tacoma sesshin [May 1980]. I have been working on the sound of one hand.[183] This summer during a meditation period the following scene happened to me. It was like sitting in the center of a hologram, a vivid waking dream:
>
> > I'm sitting at the edge of a pond. The water is stagnant and covered with algae. A fountain spurts up in the middle of the pond and freshens the water dispersing the scum. I hear the splashing water, colors are bright. A gold ring is thrust above the surface held in a child's hand. I wade into the water feeling its coolness. As I grasp the hand, I am frightened by its strength. I feel I might be pulled under, but simultaneously realize I can pull the child out and do so. The child is dressed in a white tunic. I carry it to the bank and sit down. I find the ring on my finger and the child gone.
>
> Such was the scene. The following is a record of my response written in my journal immediately afterward:
>
> > This is it. All present now. The sound of one hand. I have the ring. Ring! I ring the roshi's bell and bow. The ring rings myself. This given image is not separate in some "mind space." It is Mind Itself. The sound of one hand, my original face. This is the freedom of the children of God; to choose, no compulsion. The beginning place. "God is not silence, nor is He speaking, speakingly silent." What did they experience when they said, God is…? Nothing between.
>
> I hope you and Anne are well. I heard from Greg Mayers that you had moved and he gave me your new address. I will be seeing him and the Guadalupe monks at sesshin this month. Remember us as we sit, as we remember and revere you.
>
> With gassho
> Pat Hawk, CSsR[184]

In early November — after Pat returned to Glenview from the retreat with Willigis Jäger— he received from Aitken a newsy boilerplate letter addressed to "Dear Friends." Aitken began: "With the appearance of my new starship, I mean computer I have hopes of catching up on my correspondence. Please pardon the impersonal nature of this letter — It was composed with a lot of personal energy, anyway!" The letter went on for several typed pages, on the flip side of the last of which was a short handwritten note responding to Pat's letter sent the previous month:

> Dear Pat,
> An interesting vision. Where did the child go?
> Hope you had a good sesshin. Be careful not to intellectualize. Trust your dreams.
> Yours, Bob[185]

In the interim between Pat's letter to Aitken and Aitken's response, Pat met Willigis Jäger for the first time at the October 1983 sesshin in Portland, Oregon. Greg Mayers was also at that sesshin. For Greg, there was an immediate recognition, "This is my teacher." Although deeply drawn to Zen practice, he had found the language and culture of the Zen koans foreign, and he found it a huge relief when Willigis came along. "He was a guy who went through the same training, the same mentality. Took up with koans where I'd left off with Aitken, and made great progress very quickly. He could speak in a language I already understood: Catholic. Make it make sense. Oh, that's what that means. That makes sense to me."[186]

For Pat, Willigis's appearance on the scene was less of a revelation. He had been viewing Christian language and doctrine through a jaded lens for a long time. He found that seeing with Aitken's Zen lens opened up his experience in a way that expanded his world and ironically, helped him cultivate a new and deeper appreciation of scripture as metaphor and archetype. For Greg, Catholicism gave him a window on Zen. For Pat, it was the reverse — his jaded lens was wiped clearer by the stripping away of concepts, including Catholic dogma, that Zen accomplished. This new, spare language of Zen gave Pat a clearer understanding of the one he'd grown up with.

Nonetheless, when Willigis invited him to come and spend a year working with him at Haus St. Benedikt, his recently established practice center in Germany, Pat saw an irresistible opportunity.

Germany 1984-85

In April of 1984, Pat submitted a two-and-a-half-page proposal to the Redemptorist Provincial Council structured as Who, What, Why, When, and How much. Although he was working diligently on koans, first with Aitken, now also with Jäger, there is not a word about Zen in his proposal. The "Who" was obviously

Pat himself, The "When" was flexible, but he suggested September 1984 to August 1985, and the "How much" was $6,000 — figuring ten dollars plus four hours work per day for his keep, and travel expenses. It was not exorbitant, and Villa Redeemer had already provisionally offered to cover the cost. The "What" and the "Why" provide a snapshot of Pat's view of his vocation at that time:

> *In regard to the What:* I wish to spend a year of training under a spiritual teacher, Rev. Willigis Jager, OSB, at St. Benedict Abbey, Würzburg, West Germany. This year would not be academic nor result in a degree or certificate. In the spiritual life intellectual knowledge has a limited, circumscribed value; personal experience is invaluable.
>
> 1. The heart of the year of training would be the practice of prayer and meditation, at least four hours a day, plus other times of more intensive practice.
> 2. There would also be a conceptual background provided through selected reading so that what is experienced could be adequately communicated. This would cover the ascetical/mystical tradition of the Church explained by the great spiritual masters and the insights of scripture and theology.
> 3. There would be an assimilation of the mysteries of faith nourished by prayer, liturgy, and work.
> 4. The training would be arranged and personally directed by Willigis Jäger.
>
> *In regard to the why:* I have been moved in recent years by many documents to pursue the spiritual dimension of apostolic religious living.

Pat cites three recent articles, all from Redemptorist sources, then elaborates:

> Spiritual direction is one of the traditional hallmarks of Redemptorists. "St. Alphonsus was highly distinguished by his charism for spiritual direction, and our tradition has always held it in high esteem. It is exceptionally important in our times when people are given to such continual self-questioning. This ministry must be given new forms suitable to the mentality of the people of today." <Statute 024>[187]
>
> It is widely reported, and I have found from personal experience of working five years in the retreat movement, that laypeople and religious find it difficult to find good spiritual directors. Young people are seeking spiritual wisdom outside the Church. Twenty or thirty years ago these might have entered seminaries or novitiates. Not today. Eastern religions, by sharing their ancient spiritual disciplines, are attracting these sincere seekers. I personally have attended spiritual training sessions by Buddhists where over half the participants were Catholics. The hunger for spiritual instruction is there, but the persons who can give this teaching, for the most part, are missing.

> The post-Vatican II Church has seen a burst of renewed interest in spirituality, evidenced by concern for prayer, directed retreats, and spiritual direction. Simultaneously, concern for Christian analysis of unjust social structures and need for action against injustice has been very visible. One of the tasks facing the contemporary Church is the bridging of the gap between spirituality and social justice. I see more experts in the social justice area and priority given to it than the spiritual. We need more balance.
>
> There comes a time in the spiritual direction of individuals when the directee has equal or superior attainment than the director. Another time comes when a directee may seek more systematic and rigorous direction and the director needs to know how to proceed and what to expect through his own experience. Spiritual teachers are not the same as theologians. Spiritual teachers might be described as those who are able to teach the contemplative dimension of the Gospel out of their own experience. As Father Pfab[188] says in *Communicanda* #51,* "If we are to preach the word of God, or for that matter to exercise effectively any pastoral or social function, it is essential that we be able to transmit to others our own experience of God… Obviously our zeal for evangelization must spring from an authentic and deep spirituality which really permeates our life."[189]

In additional background, Pat explained briefly that he had taken as a spiritual teacher "…a man who was working out of Hawaii. His spiritual lineage goes back to ancient times and he received his training from impeccable teachers."[190] One imagines the careful thought that went into omitting mention of the fact that Aitken was a Zen teacher. Obviously, Pat's closer confreres were aware of his Zen involvement, but he avoided putting it in writing. Pat goes on:

> Two years ago this man could no longer come to the mainland as had been his custom and recommended we contact another teacher who had been trained in the same tradition and by the same teachers, namely Father Willigis Jäger, OSB. Father Jäger has come to the United States twice to continue the leading of retreats for our group. This past August, however, he thought it was important for people in the U.S. to develop their own teachers. … At the last retreat he invited me to come and spend a year in Germany where he runs a continuing training program for those who wish to have a thoroughgoing training in the contemplative/mystical traditions of the Church. I believe in the benefits of spending a sabbatical year in this training both for myself and for the retreat apostolate of our province. I began this formally five years ago and I believe I am at a point where an intensive year would be a marvelous opportunity to advance personally and increase my directive/teaching skills.[191]

---

* *Communicanda* are official communications of the Redemptorist General.

The proposal was examined and approved by the Redemptorist Province's Continuing Education Committee and sent on to the Provincial Superior with the recommendation that it be allowed, "…for the following reasons: spiritual direction is one of the works specifically mentioned in our C&S [Constitutions and Statutes]; it will help our retreat work; and finally, he looks to using his acquired skills in working with youth. Also, it would seem to me that Pat might do some writing in this field for the *Liguorian*."[192]

Pat attended another retreat with Willigis at Loyola Retreat House in Portland, then followed him to Germany, arriving at Haus St. Benedikt in Würzburg at the end of August 1984. It was a chilly, wet fall in Germany that year, but Pat's spirits were undampened. After being there a month, he sent a cheerful letter back to his confreres in Illinois, including birthday greetings for Harry Grile (Pat entered the birthdays of his parents, his sister, and Harry Grile into his day planner every year):

> Dear Steve,[193]
>
> Hello. The peace of Christ be with you and greetings from Germany. It is almost a month now since I arrived. On one hand it seems only a short time yet on the other I feel like I've always been here. I guess it is a sign that I have adjusted quickly. And indeed all is going smoothly. The language is not as big a barrier as I imagined. There are several living here who speak English excellently. The house community are taking turns teaching me German, some of them are pretty cute, better to learn with.
>
> I've taken two courses so far, begin another next week. Have had time to do some sightseeing and shopping. I had to go see the town officials the first week and had a couple of minor adventures with money but it all worked out. They are very forgiving, especially if you try to speak German.
>
> Please tell Henry Novak[194] that Haus St. Benedikt will send a statement every two months. So the first bill should arrive at the beginning of November. My present funds are holding up. You're right, the Marlboros here are different — better, but only 19 in a pack and damn expensive. Luckily I'm down to 10 or 12 a day.
>
> I did not bring my address list for the Redemptorist house so I can't write Harry Grile to wish him a happy birthday. Would you convey my best wishes when you see him? Thanks. Also greetings to Vic and the others there.
>
> I hope you are enjoying the retreats and that your other duties are not too burdensome. Be well and prosper.
>
> In the Redeemer
>
> Pat[195]

Pat was one of the 15 or so *Hausgemeinschaft* (house community) living at Haus St. Benedikt as long-term students of Zen and/or contemplation. The building was the largest of several on grounds belonging to the Benedictine monks of Willigis Jäger's order. They had completely remodeled it to accommodate his Zen-contemplative program.[196] The monks lived in other buildings on the property — Haus St. Benedikt was entirely devoted to Jäger's Zen-contemplative enterprise, a lucrative thing for the monks. During retreats, the number of overnight guests swelled to about a hundred, mostly Germans but also people from Spain, Italy, Czechoslovakia, Denmark, Sweden, India, and the United States. On non-retreat days there was a regular but less extensive sitting schedule, except on Sundays when there was free time. Lots of people from town came to the regular sits and to see Willigis. He would spend many hours daily in the dokusan room for individual meetings with students.

Contemplative and Zen retreats happened often, and especially for people like Pat, who spoke little German, they weren't that different from each other. The altar held neither Zen nor Christian images. It was a simple low table with ikebana* on one end and the lamp and incense pot on the other. Behind the altar hung a long cloth banner with abstract design. There was daily Mass whether the retreats were Zen or Christian, but for the latter, the Mass took place as part of the retreat schedule, whereas for sesshin, Mass was separate.

Various kinds of classes were offered. Pat took tai chi while he was there. Ikebana was taught in special retreats that also included sitting, and the beautiful simple flower arrangements were everywhere. The zendo/contemplation room had rows of light-colored *zabutons* under black *zafus* or low sitting benches, the rows separated by partitions so all could sit facing a wall. The gardens outside were gorgeous and peaceful with inviting paths through trees, beautiful rock gardens, lots of flowers in season, a gazebo, a small arched wooden bridge over a stream bed. Extending out from the back of the building was a sheltered area where the smokers congregated. A lot of the *samu* was done in the garden, and over the years, each new group added something of their own.

At Easter that year in Würzburg, the European senior students of Yamada Ko'un, some of them clergy, all of them already trained as Christian spiritual leaders,[197] had the first of what became an annual meeting. Willigis was the host for this meeting, and although Pat had not worked with Yamada Ko'un — in fact, he never met him — Willigis asked the group if Pat could attend the meeting. They

---

* Ikebana: The Japanese art of flower arranging; also the arrangements themselves.

voted among themselves with the result in the affirmative. He found himself witness to discussions that both amused and shocked him.

> Let's see if I can remember who was there. It was Willigis leading it, and they had it at Lassalle House. Hugo Lassalle was there also. He was a Jesuit priest who was the very first Zen practitioner from the Catholic Church. He was actually Yasutani's student, but after Yasutani died, he was friends with Yamada, I think, and a student also, because Yamada gave him a cloud name, although he never gave him transmission, formal transmission. At any rate, Hugo Lassalle was there, and he was a very old man at the time and deaf as a post, and all he did was sit there and smile. Willigis, Pia [Gyger], Joan Rieck, AMA Samy* from India, Niklaus Brantschen from Switzerland, and Ana Maria Schlüter from Spain. Ana Maria gave a talk where she really mixed things together. How Vatican II was completely a Zen thing. Just infuriated Willigis. That she was mixing things together. He did a tirade against her. Ana Maria was crying. AMA Samy was trying to make peace. Joan Rieck said, "All you people should have settled this a long time ago." Niklaus Brantschen translated for me. [Pat chuckled.] It was my first revelation of what enlightened teachers are like.[198]

Pat's first job at Haus St. Benedikt was setting the table for meals. Then as Willigis knew him better, he shifted him to things like reading English books and reporting to him on their contents, as well as doing a little translation. The latter Pat did with an American woman who knew German well. The idea was that Pat understood the contemplative dimension in Willigis's writing and could make sure the language approached it as closely as possible.

The food was vegetarian and macrobiotic. Pat said, "I thought I was gonna *die*. Really some strange stuff. Even Willigis, every once in a while, would ask the cook, 'Was ist *das*?' But I survived. Luckily there was a McDonald's in town which I patronized every once in a while. That was the first German I learned: *Ein Big Mac, eine groß Pommes Frîtes und ein Schokoladeshake*."[199] Plus, there was a bakery right across the street where he often went to get cheesecake. Occasionally, they had a fast over several days — nothing but water and juice. Pat left and ate with the monks in the monastery.

A photo of Pat taken that fall shows him in a warm jacket and wool cap, flanked by three smiling women, one with her arm linked through his, everyone looking relaxed and happy. The group that comprised the *Hausgemeinschaft* had meals together at a table that included people who remained in Pat's life for years

---

* Arul Maria Arokiasamy, called AMA Samy.

afterward: Cäcilia von Schöning, who became a student of Pat's when he was at Amarillo, later a teacher in her own right;[200] Rolf Drosten who later worked with Aitken and was given transmission by him; and Christa Reier who adored Pat and paid him a few visits when he was in Amarillo. There was Klaus Kopitek, of whom Pat said, "You might call him Willigis's tanto. Very interesting person. Big man, red face, very earthy. He had been in the French Foreign Legion. And I don't know exactly what his difficulty was, but I think he was in a mental institution when he met Willigis. And Willigis said, 'You're not crazy. You've had a mystical experience. Come and live with me.' And it changed his life completely. Wonderful man."[201]

There was a break in the middle of the morning, which for Pat was a coffee break: "There was a little what they called Teeküche — tea kitchen — a little closet, and there were makings for tea in there. So we went out and bought a coffee maker. And in the middle of the morning, we'd take our break and have our coffee. After a while, more and more people were crowding into this closet, and it became known as the American Coffee Break." As always, Pat kept to himself a lot. Dan Mintie, one of the Catholic Workers in Seattle and a participant in all the Zen retreats for Christians in the Pacific Northwest, was there the year after Pat. Dan remembered, "The stories they told about him amounted to: 'We never saw him. He was always up in his room or out smoking with Klaus'."[202]

Feeling no need to add anything to the conversation at meals (or anywhere), Pat was as if invisible until he'd slip in a pithy comment, then disappear again. Rolf Drosten told this story: "One member of the *Hausgemeinschaft* was Father Guido. He loved to instruct the other members of the *Hausgemeinschaft*, especially women. One day at the end of lunch Guido was talking and talking — and then there came a quiet voice from the end of the table, 'Guido for president.' End of Guido."[203]

Pat walked and walked all over Würzburg. He discovered wonderful coffee shops with bakeries. The magnificent and palatial Würzburg Residenz, former home of the Prince-Bishop, was nearby, the huge grounds practically across the street from Haus St. Benedikt. One could walk through the park down to the Main River, then along the banks to the edge of town. Once Pat and a few others took a trip to Rome and spent several days exploring the Holy City. Another time he went to Saarburg with Guido Joos, whose religious order, the White Fathers, was there. On these trips, they stopped to go into churches and castles.

Years later Pat said, "You get tired of castles and medieval torture instruments after a while. A lot of these churches we visited were very baroque. It was nice to find a more Romanesque church, more plain, I liked those better." At times, Pat and some of the others would get into cars to go out in the countryside and tramp trails. Willigis was a great walker and a fast walker. Pat said, "One time during the winter, it was snowing like the devil … we were taking a walk together, and I was wondering how I was doing so I asked Willigis, 'How am I doing?' He said, 'Oh, you're a very stable person.' And then he said, 'I will finish you.' We were doing koans, and he planned on finishing me. Well, during that walk I thought he was gonna finish me for good! He was very German. '*Muss sein*!' What they call a walk in the woods was a forced march!"

As Christmas approached, Pat sent another upbeat letter to his confreres.

> Dear Chuck,[204]
>
> Hello and thanks a million for your card and newsy letter. It was good to hear from you, and I appreciate your sending on my mail.
>
> I can really appreciate your memories of Christmas in Germany. Although it is not here yet, the public squares are all decorated, their open-air stalls selling handmade wares. This is a very Catholic area in Germany and there are churches every few steps. But there are more bakeries than churches, and this time of year they outdo themselves. The whole city smells of baking. It almost drives a person crazy. I can imagine what the day itself is going to be like.
>
> I will be spending Christmas in a monastery called St. Georgenberg near Innsbruck, Austria. I've seen a picture of it, perched on the side of a mountain. I will be making a four-day retreat there, then spending Christmas Day there. Should be very interesting.
>
> Things continue to go smoothly here. I'm very deep into the training now and have taken some leadership roles in the courses here. The language has been no great barrier, although it would help if I knew more of it.
>
> Merry Christmas to you and the whole community and staff. May the celebration of the appearance of the Light of the world illumine all your hearts and make us one in Him.
>
> In the Redeemer
>
> Pat Hawk, CSsR[205]

When he mentions leadership roles and courses Pat is partly thinking of the fact that he was frequently the timekeeper for retreats. In addition, Willigis often asked him to say Mass. He would give a short homily in English, somebody interpreting as he went along. People enjoyed them so much that Willigis encouraged Pat to collect his homilies into a book, a work he began but did not complete.[206]

St. Georgenberg Abbey is about a two-and-a-half-hour drive from Würzburg, southeast past Munich and just over the border into Austria and the Tyrolian Alps. The monastery dates to 1138, the current buildings to the 18th century. The switchbacking road that brought them up the mountain arrived at a footbridge* that spans the deep Wolfsklamm Gorge. On the far side is St. Georgenberg, its plain white buildings rising directly, steeply, almost continuous with the sheer wall of the rocky prominence that plunges to the Stans River far below.

Everything in this beautiful, isolated place lent to stillness — the simple routine, the spartan monastery, the long midwinter nights, the deep, close silence of snow. Pat and the others settled strongly into practice. One of their night readings during the Christmas retreat at Georgenberg, Merton's poem, *Advent*, fit perfectly this silent world, and years later was among the readings Pat selected for his contemplative program.† They broke the four-day silence in an exuberant Midnight Mass, the lovely antiphons of Christmas intoned in candlelight, rising to a crescendo of joyful hymns welcoming the Child.

Then back to Würzburg and the daily round of sitting, dokusan, Eucharist, long walks, and frequent retreats. Pat began thinking ahead to what he would do when the year in Germany was over. He wanted to go the whole nine yards with Zen, including doing *Jukai* — a public ceremony in which someone professes commitment to the Buddhist way. The student presents personal responses to the Buddhist precepts and the teacher bestows a dharma name inscribed on a *rakusu*.‡ Since, as with most of the Christian European Zen teachers, Willigis had not done Jukai himself, he could not offer Jukai to his students. It meant Pat would do it with Aitken. He read Aitken's, *The Mind of Clover*[207] to help him think about his own responses, and as winter was turning to spring in Germany, he wrote to reconnect:

> Dear Bob,
>
> Hello from Germany. I have been thinking of writing my yearly letter to you, but have remembered that it has been a year and a half since I last wrote. I have just finished reading your new book, *The Mind of Clover* and your words about communication added an extra sting to propel my pen.
>
> Thanks for writing your books. I enjoy and profit from them. Some of the chapters in *The Mind of Clover* recalled the Tacoma sesshins to mind. The words are as fresh now as then. I hear the sound and rhythm of your voice as I read.
>
> Germany is a long way from Tacoma. In a way it is amazing that what began there has led me here. Yet, I feel very natural about it and that it was

---

* Tyrol's oldest footbridge — some parts are over 500 years old.

† Full text of the poem is available online, e.g., Poeticous.com: https://www.poeticous.com/thomas-merton/advent-charm-with-your-stainlessness-these-winter-nights

‡ A bib-like garment sewed with pieces of cloth in a rice-field pattern, symbol of the fecundity of the dharma.

somehow destined.

I have been here six months. The group here sits 4½ hours a day and sesshins are quite frequent. Willigis is a ball of energy. He has many Zen students and I'm really fortunate to be allowed to stay a year. I plan to return to the States at the end of August. After that I don't know what will happen. I will have to talk with my religious superiors, of course, but one question is with whom to finish my study.

Willigis has suggested that it would be good to do the precepts with you. I have no idea now when or how that would take place. In any event, I want to keep in contact with you. Events have developed well for me so far. We will see how it stands in September.

I participated in a sesshin with Joan Rieck last October. I hope to visit her in Switzerland soon. I also spent a couple of enjoyable days with AMA Samy, who is here raising funds to build a zendo in Madras.

My best to you and Anne. May your work and the sangha prosper.

—with gassho—

Pat Hawk CSsR[208]

The *Hausgemeinschaft* went back to St. Georgenberg at Easter. The days were warming up. There were crocuses blooming, bright sunshine and melting snow. The retreat ended with the Easter Vigil. Pat remembered:

> ...the first thing is the lighting of the new fire. Well, you know, in ordinary churches they've got this little bowl with a few sticks in it. *Not* for Willigis! It's spring. The snow is melting, the river is *roaring* down below. We'd go across the footbridge and go down, down, down. We had this *enormous* bonfire! And part of the ceremony is blessing the new Easter water. Well, what he does is bless the river. This was at midnight, the dead of night. And this *huge* bonfire! Then there are the different readings from the Old Testament ... everybody would light torches, we'd march a little way up the path, stop and have a reading, then we'd march up until we finally got way up at the top. They'd finish off with the Eucharist, in a little chapel a little bit away from the main building. It was kind of like a vault, like a little tomb, and the chanting in there was really beautiful. After it was over we came out. We stood on a crag and we sang songs until the sunrise.

Pat made one more trip to St. Georgenberg that summer. There, as in Würzburg, he went on solitary walks, and in the summer with the snow gone he wandered far through woods and alpine meadows, exploring the slopes and valleys. One day he got out farther than he realized on a narrow ledge and found himself stuck, his back to the rock wall with the vast landscape below him. He sat there alone with no idea of time, no impulse to go anywhere, "body and mind dropped away," as Dogen says. "The destination, the journey and the path itself disappeared into that intimate Something I had sensed so long ago in the candles, incense and songs of worship."[209] He found himself nowhere and everywhere. He managed to inch back to the path, then back to the monastery, and thence to Würzburg.

Greg Mayers came over for a month at the end of Pat's year in Germany and was there for that last trip to St. Georgenberg. Back in Würzburg, Greg and Pat went sightseeing, including a side trip to visit Joan Rieck. Joan had lived in Japan for 18 years, having gone there as a Maryknoll nun. During a dark period spiritually she left her order, and casting about, attended a sesshin with Yasutani Roshi, co-founder with Harada Roshi of the Sanbo Kyodan lineage and one of Yamada Ko'un's teachers. He was known for being rigorous, and the sesshin was harsh. It was the old story — she wondered if she should leave but somehow stuck it out. At the end, everyone was invited to share something from their experience. Trying to speak, she found herself in tears of joy. She began studying Zen with Yamada Ko'un Roshi and got to know both Willigis Jäger and Robert Aitken, also students of Yamada Ko'un. Yamada Ko'un gave Joan permission to teach Zen in 1983. She went on to study at the Jung Institute in Zurich, then was asked to be the teacher for a Zen group in Lucerne.

Willigis Jäger had led the Zen sesshin for Christians in the Pacific Northwest in 1982 and '83, then the following year asked Joan to come and help him. For one thing, he was insecure about his English and wanted her to help with interpreting. Besides, he recognized that among the participants, there were some who wanted to do a very Christian-oriented contemplative practice and others who were comfortable with Zen. He thought the group should split, that he would take the Christians and Joan take the Zennies, as Pat called them. So the next retreat was Willigis and Joan together, and that is where Pat and Greg met her.

At the time of their visit to her in Europe, Joan was living in a lovely place on the edge of a small town on the outskirts of Lucerne. The trip is documented in one of Pat's photo albums. In one photo taken in Joan's apartment, there are various scrolls spread out on the carpet and Pat is sitting next to a framed black and white image of a nude propped up beside him. Joan had collected a lot of different art while she was in Japan, and Willigis had suggested she give something to Greg and Pat, so she had things out. Greg picked up the nude, set it down beside Pat, and snapped the photo. Looking at it wryly decades later, Pat said Greg wanted to have a picture of him with a naked woman. Other photos show Pat relaxing, reading in Joan's pleasant living room or walking out among farms in the pastoral countryside.

They returned to Würzburg to say goodbye to Willigis and the *Hausgemeinschaft*. Pat gave a final homily:

> Grace is a gift. When we look at the Greek word for grace, we can get the feeling of what grace signifies. The Greek word is *charis*. *Charis* means innocence and beauty, charm of form, movement, and expression. In English, we find *charis* is a part of other important religious words, for example: charity, charism, eucharist.
>
> This beauty, innocence, and pleasing form is attractive. It invites love, protection, and other gifts, just as an innocent child attracts love, protection and gifts. All that is asked in return is gratitude. What makes the grace of a person attractive is life. The grace, the gift is life. A corpse is not attractive — only life.
>
> With God, it is he who gives life to begin with. He is attracted by that life and loves it, gives more life, his own life. Grace is simply the dynamic divine life giving itself, attracting itself, loving itself. All that is asked is gratitude. Thanks.
>
> When I look back on this year I have spent with you, I see grace and I can only be thankful. There is no other way to return the gift of life, beauty of form and movement, the dignity and innocence I see here and given to all who come here. It is so attractive. All the love, the conflicts, the practice, work, sorrows, laughter, and patience with an ignorant foreigner. It is all life, all grace, all the dynamic divine dance. Thanks. May this life be lived to the full in all of us.[210]

For Pat, the year in Germany had been "another encounter with traveling with no fixed plans — not intent on arriving, but steadily pressing on."[211] As a parting gift, Willigis gave Pat a brass handbell with the intention that it serve as a teacher's bell. It stayed with Pat for the rest of his life, over many years ringing in and ringing out hundreds of students from his dokusan and contemplation room.

He returned to Glenview, Illinois, at the end of August 1985 and took up retreat work again. It was a difficult re-entry.

Back at Glenview, Fall 1985

Returning from Germany to Villa Redeemer, Pat felt he was returning with a gift to share, but no one was interested. He and Shirley would do their silent sitting in the chapel, and the Provincial Superior, Jack Dowd, would complain about stumbling on them there. The administrative offices were directly across from the chapel, and Pat would complain that people were always talking, there was no time during the day when the chapel was quiet. Father Henry Novak was there — a man with the reputation of being very harsh, so much so that when in old age he ended up at the Redemptorist care facility at Liguori, Missouri, he feared being mistreated by those he himself had mistreated. He was one of a few people who were very hard on Pat, sometimes scathing, although looking back years later, with Henry and Pat both at St. Clement Health Care Center for the brief period before Pat died, he spoke of Pat with deep appreciation.[212]

The year in Germany had been life-giving for Pat, spiritually for sure, but also socially — living in a community of fellow wayfarers dedicated to the contemplative path, people he respected and related to and with whom he felt a deep connection. Returning to Glenview, he hit hard against the indifference and sometimes scorn of his Redemptorist community. To Pat, it felt like another betrayal.

He resumed offering retreats and working with spiritual directees. Shirley Morrissey remembered, "People loved him. They would say he was named Father Hawk because he was a hawk for truth." But the retreats were still the standard Catholic format, not contemplative retreats, and Pat wanted to be sharing what he had learned. The gift from Willigis of the brass bell came with an understanding — a sort of covenant — that Pat would teach. Robert Aitken was given transmission by Yamada Ko'un in 1985, which meant he could himself authorize Zen teachers. Willigis was not thus empowered. He wrote to Aitken to tell him that Pat was Zen teacher material[213] — something Aitken already knew. While Pat was still in Germany, Aitken had written encouraging him to come to Hawaii when he got back to the States. Finally, several months after he returned, Pat pulled himself together enough to write back to Aitken.

> Dear Bob,
>
> Thank you for your letter to me in August while I was in Germany. I am back in the States now and finally feel like I am getting into the swing of things. My year in Germany studying with Willigis affected me much more deeply than I was conscious of on my return. I think now I was in culture shock.
>
> It now looks like I will have some time this summer to come to Hawaii if you are going to be there. I would like to know the dates of any training sessions you will be holding. If I cannot make those perhaps I can make some other arrangements.
>
> I am also interested in receiving the "*Blind Donkey*" and any other newsletters, etc. I remember some years ago that one could join the Diamond Sangha as a corresponding member. If you would have your secretary send me information about these things, I will appreciate it.
>
> I talked with Joan Rieck a couple of times while she was in Seattle. Sounds as if the old group there is getting along. She wants Greg Mayers or myself to come there and take care of those who want to practice contemplation. It is not so easy to arrange, however.
>
> Studying with Willigis for a year has been quite a transforming experience, greater than my novitiate with my religious order. I'm looking forward to the time I can discuss some of this with you.

Hope you and Anne are well. Best regards –
Pat Hawk[214]

Aitken wrote back immediately to begin planning for Pat to come and work with him,[215] suggesting that he attend sesshin that summer at Ring of Bone Zendo in California and providing registration information.

Meanwhile, Greg Mayers had moved from Palisades Retreat to Coeur d'Alene, Idaho. He was preaching parish missions, giving Progoff Intensive Journaling workshops, serving as a spiritual director for Immaculate Heart Retreat Center, sitting on his own, and working with Willigis Jäger when he could. After about three years, he got a call from Father Bob Curry, the superior at Bishop DeFalco Retreat Center (BDRC) in Amarillo, Texas, asking if Greg would come there. "I did a particular exercise called a discernment to see whether that was the thing to do. In religious terminology, whether that was the will of God. It turned out positive that that's what I should do."[216]

Greg moved to Amarillo in 1983. As at Coeur D'Alene, in addition to doing his share of Retreat Center work, he continued sitting on his own and visiting Germany whenever he could get the time off. A young Amarillo man, Kevin Mahoney, was at BDRC for some event, and while speaking with one of the other priests, found out that Greg was practicing Zen. Greg remembered, "So Kevin got in contact with me and introduced himself, said I hear you're interested in Zen. I said yeah. He said would you teach me. I said well, I'm not a teacher but I'll show you what I do and here's my schedule. So he joined me. That's how the sangha [Zen community] got started. Word got out to other people and others started coming."[217]

Bob Curry was also interested in meditation. He and Greg got the idea of having Pat move from Glenview to join them in Amarillo so they could run contemplative retreats. The first step was to invite Pat down to lead a retreat for some of the Redemptorist priests, just to see how it went. It was arranged, and Pat came down with Shirley Morrissey that January 1986 to give a three-day "Contemplative Course for Spiritual Directors." It included an introduction to contemplation with practical advice about sitting, a talk on John of the Cross, another talk on attachment and non-attachment, and lots of silent sitting. Pat and Greg offered the same course at the Redemptorists' Villa Christi Retreat Center in Wichita, Kansas, in October of that year, in conjunction with a major meeting of the Redemptorist retreat houses (they had several) to discuss their retreat program in general and the contemplative path in particular.

Greg and Bob then proceeded to ask the St. Louis Province to transfer Pat to Amarillo. This began a long deliberation. Greg recalled, "There was a big thing going on about Pat being invited to Amarillo. And there was this big, big meeting of Redemptorists, and some vocal opposition to him coming down. Who knows why. We're just like a big family, and everybody has their hidden agendas… All of our issues were coming out against Pat going to Amarillo. It was all very complex. But it got passed anyway."[218]

While this intrigue was going on with the Redemptorists, Pat made arrangements to continue his Zen training. He managed to get away to the sesshin with Aitken at Ring of Bone Zendo that summer. Thereafter when prompted, he would tell a story accompanied with much eye-rolling of the primitive conditions at Ring of Bone — open-air showers, peeing in the bushes, etc. Some years later, when asked by one of his students if he would like to participate in one of the Mountains and Rivers sesshins — backpacking sesshins that Gary Snyder had initiated, later continued by others including Nelson Foster— he said dryly that the only way he would do that would be if he could sit in a palanquin and be carried by others. He said his idea of being out in nature was to watch a National Geographic program on TV. This was not entirely true. He loved long walks — through the beautiful parks of Würzburg, through the woods at Guadalupe, along the beach at Palisades — but he was not into roughing it.

Pat found the Ring of Bone sesshin to be a good one despite physical discomforts, and it re-established his relationship with Aitken as his teacher. Having spotted Pat's potential from the beginning and seeing his spiritual development after the year in Germany, Aitken determined that it was time Pat be given permission to teach Zen. He encouraged him to come and spend time in Hawaii.

Move to Amarillo, Texas

In late December 1986, Pat packed his bags at Glenview and flew southwest from St. Louis, reading and dozing until he found himself looking out over miles and miles of flat, windswept fields as his plane began its descent into Amarillo International Airport. A confrere picked him up, and they drove past the snow-dusted fields to pull up at Bishop DeFalco Retreat Center on the city's northeast outskirts. From the front drive, which opened onto Spring Street, the chapel stood out, the curved roof suggesting a bishop's miter, with a large cross standing at the peak. A biting gust swirled around them as they hurried from the car to the warmth of the retreat center, entering through double glass doors, then to the right through a curving hallway at the back of the circular chapel leading to the rectory beyond. Having deposited his bags, Pat went back past the front entrance to the office area thence to the cafeteria to pour himself a cup of retreat-center coffee. He stepped out for a smoke, huddling slit-eyed with his cigarette in a barely sheltered corner of the building, looking out over the sparse grasses and bare-branched winter trees swaying in the perpetual wind. This would be home for the next eleven and a half years.

The priests' quarters included a comfortable common room with a television, wet bar and small kitchen, and for each priest, a suite of two rooms and a bathroom. Greg and Bob Curry were at one end, Pat was at the other, nearest the chapel, with rooms for a few other confreres and special guests in between. The contemplation room was also on this floor. Upstairs were retreatant rooms and Meeting Room 4 — a common area with kitchenette that became the social hub of the contemplative program. This wing of the building formed one long arm of the retreat center, which was built around a central courtyard. The contemplative (and eventually Zen) program space was accessible from indoors only through a corridor behind the chapel. It was therefore nicely sequestered from the main retreat center, including the office area, the cafeteria, most guest rooms, and the meeting rooms that housed the more conventional programming.

Outside the retreat center buildings, the 12-acre property included Chancery Offices,[219] the residence of Amarillo's bishop, and a small Catholic college, on landscaped grounds with young trees, walking paths, and a pond.

The retreat center bordered a neighborhood of small, often run-down houses with barking dogs and pickup trucks in yards marked off by chain-link fences and barbed wire. Pat was a great walker in Amarillo as he had been at Palisades, at Glenview, at Guadalupe and in Germany. He walked everywhere on the property — through the courtyard, around the retreat center, toward the bishop's residence, around the pond — but seldom off it, although he sometimes filled in to offer services at the local parishes. He would occasionally drive into town for movies, to sample the fare at hamburger joints, or to attend performances of the Amarillo Symphony Orchestra. The latter was for Pat a small haven of culture in a world dominated by conservative, pro-military politics and Bible-Belt Protestant churches.

Pantex, the final assembly site for all nuclear warheads manufactured in the United States, was a major employer for the town, with the locals mostly fiercely supportive of its presence and its mission. A.G. Mojtabai, author and educator, came to Amarillo in the mid-'80s asking how this very religious town could coexist alongside both the danger and the purpose of nuclear warhead assembly. She published her findings from interviews of the townspeople in *Blessed Assurance: At home with the bomb in Amarillo, Texas.*[220]

Mojtabai quotes a Pantex worker who expressed the feeling of many, "I really think there's nothing much us human beings can do."[221] Another observed, "There's a possibility of nuclear war, but if it comes, it's because God allowed it. I believe as a Christian I'm ready to go home at any time — the world stinks."

For some that Mojtabai spoke with, there was the rapture to look forward to. Expected in 2012, it was going to lift the righteous into heaven, therefore the nuclear risk was moot: "The Christians — that's the saved of all ages, all denominations, any believer — they are raptured. They are caught up in the air before Armageddon. They avoid this terrible time that's coming. Christians look forward to this time and call it the 'blessed hope'."[222] They didn't know how the rapture was to be brought about. Perhaps the very missiles they were producing would be the instruments of the end of the world, which they welcomed because they were to be lifted up, to watch from above the fray the punishment of the damned.

Coincidentally the missiles assembled at Pantex in Amarillo were being transported to Bangor, Washington, where the Catholic Workers had protested in the late 1970s, thereby meeting Robert Aitken who was doing the same. Aitken met Abbot Bernard McVeigh through the Catholic Workers, and the Zen for Christians sesshin was conceived. Thus had arisen the spring that fed the whole Zen stream embraced by Pat and so many others.

Mojtabai's take on the Amarilloan's relationship with Pantex was criticized by some locals who themselves rejected the fundamentalist stance and saw the city's tolerance of the plant as purely economical. At that time, it accounted for about 25% of the local economy. These critics felt that for the average Amarilloan it was all about jobs, and there was certainly that element. For some, it was about protecting America from evil powers. For virtually all, it was a positive thing for the town. There was the morality of defending the righteous country; no thought to the immorality of killing millions regardless of what side they were on, no thought of the immorality of mutual assured destruction. Regardless, the dominant feeling for Pat encountering Amarillo was of a politically conservative, insular, fundamentalist Protestant populace whose genuine faith could draw his sympathy but that he mostly found alien.

The Redemptorists at Bishop DeFalco Retreat Center had an excellent working relationship with the Bishop, the Reverend Leroy Matthiesen, a broad-minded, farm-raised man with a heart for tolerance of people and intolerance of warmongering, including a strong anti-nuclear stance. He had dogs, kept bees, liked to work with his hands. He dug the pond himself with a tractor, then populated it with ducks, swans and fish. He was down to earth, but at the same time a ladies' man, very social and impeccably dressed when the occasion warranted. Matthiesen wrote a column for the *West Texas Catholic*, official publication of the Diocese of Amarillo, called "Wise and Otherwise," which later became a book: *Wise and Otherwise: The Life and Times of a Cottonpicking Texas Bishop.*[223] He gave work in the Diocese to several priests who were removed from elsewhere because of allegations of sexual impropriety. He spoke out against the Pantex missile plant from the pulpit, said that to work there was an immoral way to earn a living, and urged his parishioners to seek other employment.[224] From this, one man, Eloy Ramos, left his job at Pantex and came to work as a maintenance man at the retreat center. For his work, the Bishop received several social justice awards, the Teacher of Peace Award from Pax Christi, and a great deal of animosity from the people of Amarillo. Matthiesen supported the Redemptorists and presented no barrier to them developing the contemplative program — controversial for many Catholics, including many in the Catholic hierarchy — and eventually a Zen program.

Pat and Greg lost no time offering the first contemplative retreat at Bishop DeFalco Retreat Center (BDRC) in January 1987. They led it together, with the format based on that from Haus St. Benedikt. At the previous annual retreat in the Northwest, Greg had announced that BDRC was beginning a contemplative program. He announced the dates of their first contemplative retreat. This recruited Bob Walker, who years later would become one of Pat's dharma heirs.

Bob had connected with the Northwest group via the Trappists, having for a time considered becoming a Trappist himself. With that in mind, he spent six months at Our Lady of Guadalupe Abbey in 1982. It meant he was on hand to go with Bernard McVeigh and the others from Guadalupe to the first Zen for Christians retreat led by Willigis Jäger in Portland. He returned to his home in Ohio after the Trappist stay but continued the connection. Attending the retreats with Willigis in subsequent years, he knew Greg a little. He was only vaguely aware of Pat as a fellow participant at some of those retreats — Pat had made no particular impression. With Greg Mayers announcing the start of the program at BDRC, Bob, looking for additional retreats in between the visits of Willigis to the Pacific Northwest from Germany, signed up. It was in the one-on-one encounters at that first retreat at BDRC that Bob really saw Pat. He remembered, "By the end of that first day, I was aware that I had met my teacher."[225]

Bob was one of four who attended that first retreat. The others were Sister Shirley Morrissey, who came down from Glenview, Kevin Mahoney, the man who had been sitting with Greg, and a local townswoman — eventually student and close friend of Greg — Denise Fuller. With this quiet start, Pat and Greg began the program.

The activity and turmoil of the Amarillo move, both the negotiations and the transition, preoccupied Pat to the extent that he was out of touch with Aitken until spring when he was finally settled in at BDRC and the contemplative program was underway.

Dear Bob,

My apology for waiting so long to get in touch with you again. I had a letter written and ready to send to you last fall but circumstances have changed quickly and considerably. I hope you and Anne are well. I often recall our days at Ring of Bone with warmth and gratitude.

Our talk last summer about community and silence was very helpful. I have also found some confirming writings by Thomas Merton on sharing the fruits of contemplation. He puts things quite well. I have also pondered your suggestion about finding a simpler, more nature/close community. I have, in fact, changed communities. While not exactly of the type we talked of, I feel more suited to it and content without taking the drastic step of leaving my religious order.

At present I am living at a retreat center in Amarillo, Texas and working with Greg Mayers developing contemplative practice along the line of Willigis Jäger's Haus St. Benedikt. Matters have been moving quickly. I am surprised at how widespread word of our endeavor has spread. Besides our daily hours of contemplation, we are also doing two 5-day and one 7-day retreat. Next January we intend to begin operation of a resident training program.

So, my circumstances have changed quite a bit. In our planning we are blocking out times for our own continuing training. Greg is now in Würzburg doing a one-hundred-days training with Willigis. This summer I will be accompanying Willigis as his assistant on his American travels to give seven-day contemplation retreats in St. Louis, Tacoma and Portland. Then Greg and I are giving our own seven-day retreat here in Amarillo in early August.

This brings up the point of this letter. I am free from August 9 to September 30 to come to Hawaii. Would you let me know if this time is feasible for you and what sort of arrangements I need to make.

Willigis wrote to me this month saying he will try to meet with you this summer at Ring of Bone. He spent a couple of months in a hermitage this past fall and it seems to have done him a world of good.

This area of Texas is an interesting place to establish a center for contemplative practice. As you may know, Pantex, the final assembly plant of all US nuclear weapons is located here. At our contemplation retreat last January one of the participants was a member of the Peace Farm which pickets the plant every Friday. Across from him sat an engineer who works at Pantex. We just sat together — and very powerfully, too. I am looking to see something "quietly outrageous" to come of this.

May compassion, peace, and love be yours in every possible way —

Pat Hawk[226]

Years later Pat said that after the Trappist decision, he did not seriously consider leaving the Redemptorists again. Regarding the suggestion in his letter to Aitken that he might have been considering it, he said, "You know, you say things to people…"[227] Likewise with the comment on Pantex — Pat was never an activist himself, but he knew Aitken's interest.

Willigis Jäger handoff to Pat Hawk, July 1987

With the move to Amarillo, Pat was at last brought to what was for him the most authentic expression thus far of his vocation. He had taught in the seminary high school, a revered educator who regularly won teaching awards and who rose to the position of principal. He had been a retreat director at Palisades, offering traditional Catholic prayer and reflection-type retreats. He had served as a mission preacher and displayed a talent for that role though his heart was not in it. And he had served as a spiritual director at Glenview — his contemplative vision informing his work there such that he drew people in ever greater numbers. But it wasn't until he got to Amarillo that he began the work to which he felt most called. That work rapidly expanded.

By the time Willigis Jäger had given Pat the brass dokusan/interview bell at the end of his year in Germany, he was sure he wanted Pat to take over the Northwest group. Early on, Willigis had asked Joan Rieck to assist, which she did for the 1984 retreat. It had become clear to both of them at that time that there were two streams in the Northwest group, and at Willigis's behest, they split into Zen and Christian in 1985, with Joan taking the Zen group and Willigis leading the now smaller Christian group on his own. Pat was at neither of these events. In 1985 he was still in Germany, and in 1986, unable to get enough time off from Glenview for both the Willigis retreat and the Ring of Bone sesshin with Aitken, he chose to do the latter.

By 1987, Willigis persuaded Pat to take over the retreats for the Pacific Northwest contemplative group, as he himself was keen to give up the traveling. They arranged to do joint retreats that summer by way of introducing Willigis's American students to Pat. Of course, many knew who Pat was from hearing him say Mass at the earlier retreats he had attended, but up until July 1987, he was a fellow student. Willigis was charismatic and well-loved, some would say adored. Pat was almost invisible. There was a lot of concern about the handoff.

Leonard Marcel, who would become the first of six Hawk dharma heirs, noticed Pat for the first time at the 1987 retreat, though they had sat sesshin together at least once before. Unlike Pat, Leonard, a psychiatrist in Portland, with his close-cropped dark hair and upright bearing, had a commanding presence. Raised Catholic and with a strong spiritual bent, he had begun doing short private retreats with the Trappists around 1980. Abbot Bernard McVeigh invited him to join the handful of monks who were getting up at 2:30 AM so they could do a round of silent sitting together in the Chapter room before Vigils in the chapel.

At McVeigh's suggestion, Leonard signed up for one of the long retreats, the one co-led by Willigis Jäger and Joan Rieck.

Regarding his first Zen for Christians retreat, Leonard recalled:

> I had never sat more than one 25-minute sitting period and here was a 7-day sesshin. I had no idea what a 7-day sesshin was. There were about 60 people, including a number of the Seattle people who were part of the Catholic Worker movement. It was amazing. We had partitions up in the middle of the room and all sorts of rows of people, very convoluted *kinhin*. For me, it was all very confusing. I wasn't sure what was going on, and my main concern was just surviving. By the third day, I was in so much pain I was sure I was going to die there and I wasn't going to go on with the rest of my life.[228]

A sort of death — to the endless machinations of the ego-mind — can happen in a silent retreat, and this "death" can be so liberating, people come back for more despite the physical challenges which in any case decrease as the body adapts. Leonard stuck it out. He came regularly thereafter, and he was there for the Willigis to Pat hand-off. Leonard recalled:

> I didn't hear much from other people. But Bernard was quite anxious about it. And I think that some other people were also. Because Willigis is very charismatic, and of course you know how Pat was, so it was quite an adjustment. Personally, I didn't feel any kind of apprehension, in fact I remember saying to Bernard that things would be all right, and however this new fellow worked out, all of us, meaning the community that was forming, would be fine. It wasn't clear at all to me that we would stay with Pat or that he would work out for us. It may have just been my naiveté, but I had a sense that the group itself was going to be okay.[229]

The following year, when Pat led the Northwest retreat for the first time by himself, Leonard took him as his teacher.

Sister Joan Saalfeld, a spiritual directee of Abbot McVeigh since the mid-'70s, had attended the Zen retreats for Christians, initially with Aitken, then with Willigis. She was monitor at all the retreats with Willigis for the Pacific Northwest group and had spent an extended period with him in Würzburg the year before Pat was there. She said that when Pat gave his first talk at the Pacific Northwest retreat with Willigis, they were all sitting there with their arms crossed, figuratively. Just you try to do this. It felt like a betrayal, Willigis letting them go. Bernard McVeigh came up to Joan afterward, clearly skeptical, asking how she thought it had gone. Pat had come across as somewhat stiff, perhaps nervous. But, Joan said, when it was over, they all looked at each other, and most at least realized that he *saw*. He could do it. They didn't need Willigis.

Thinking back to Bernard McVeigh's response, Joan remembered that after any of the retreats, you could ask Bernard how it was and he would say — Booorrring! Bernard heard about wonderful things happening to everybody else, but they weren't happening to him. He did not have the consolation of that kind of encouragement. In all the years of sitting, nothing remarkable happened to him. At some point, he talked to Zen teacher Bernie Glassman about it. Bernie said, have you ever walked in the fog? You get saturated. You are saturated with it. That was a consolation to Bernard.[230] Given the absence of "aha" moments for him, his doubts about Pat may have related more to his need for the kind of charisma and personal warmth that Willigis Jäger provided than to any deficiency in Pat's insight or skill as a teacher.

Dan Mintie recalled Pat's taking over the retreats from Willigis:

> I remember saying to Pat afterwards, thank you for that. That was really very good. ... I had studied with Aitken — started with Aitken then picked up with Willigis — so I was one of Pat's confreres [so to speak; not a Redemptorist confrere], and now Pat was in this new status and I didn't know what he'd be like as a teacher. I knew a little bit what he was like as a student but didn't have any sense of how that would go. And I thought right out of the box that he was very good. I was doing koans with him. And again, I could see the family resemblances because I'd studied with *his* teachers.
>
> Over time he became a lot more comfortable in his own skin as a teacher. Initially he'd have his book that Willigis gave him or Aitken gave him that had all the [koan] answers and you'd say something, he'd look in his book. ... Then over time he did that less and less, then not at all. So I too at that retreat accepted Pat as a teacher of mine. I continued to study with Willigis and Aitken. Joan Rieck is also one of my teachers. So I've had this consortium of teachers. ... And yeah, he entered the pantheon for me in his own little dry way.[231]

After the Willigis Jäger handoff, Pat became the main teacher for the Northwest contemplatives and began offering retreats three times a year in Washington or Oregon.

Resident training in Hawaii, late summer 1987

In the midst of a rapidly filling retreat schedule, Pat was able to carve out time for a practice period with Aitken from early August to the end of September. His stay in Hawaii overlapped with two training periods devoted to building the new Diamond Sangha center in Palolo Valley and also with two sesshins. His accommodation for the *samu*/training period was the furnished studio apartment in a cottage on the Honolulu Diamond Sangha's Koko An Zendo property that also housed an office, a library and the dokusan room. It was comfortable and allowed welcome alone time. While they were planning the visit, Aitken wrote, "If you prefer, you can stay elsewhere in Honolulu, possibly with other priests, and commute to Koko An, taking part in as much or as little of the program as you choose." Pat opted for the cottage.

At that visit, Pat met Augusto Alcalde, a student of Aitken from Cordoba, Argentina, where he was leading his own Zen group. The two of them lost no time introducing coffee to the daily routine and got to know each other while spending time in the driveway in front of the house at Koko An having a smoke, steaming mugs in hand.

The first sesshin while Pat was in Hawaii was to be on the Big Island at Wood Valley. A photo taken during a social gathering beforehand shows Pat in a dark T-shirt smiling, standing next to Aitken. Both men have large white flowers tucked behind their right ears which, Pat explained, was a sign they were available. "...but no one took us up on it."

For both the Wood Valley sesshin and the one at Koko An, Pat was tanto. This was quite a leap. Except for the Ring of Bone sesshin the previous summer, his experience thus far of Zen retreat forms was unorthodox. The sesshin for Christians and other travelers in the Pacific Northwest was heavily overlaid with Christian elements. Willigis's sesshins in Germany had confessional elements more or less neutralized so that neither Christian nor Buddhist was prominent. Pat had often been timekeeper in Germany but otherwise had no experience as a sesshin leader.

It happened by surprise, with Aitken saying casually to Pat the day before, "Oh, and you'll be tanto." There were many more experienced Zen practitioners than he in attendance, yet Aitken had Pat take this central leadership role. The demonstration of confidence, the fact that people knew Pat was a Catholic priest, and Pat's personal presentation — calm, centered, unbuffeted by social interactions — meant that participants readily approached him for help with life and practice. As a Redemptorist, Pat was trained and perfectly accustomed to giving pastoral help, so even in this unfamiliar Zen setting, he fell naturally into the role of guide.

But he was not set apart. Although he could stay in the cottage during the resident training period,* for sesshin he was in the main house — upstairs, first on the right, with three other men — while others stayed in the cottage. Every morning, Pat piled into the van with everyone else to spend the days at the Palolo

---

* Variously called resident practice period, resident training period, resident training program, residential program.

building site. Aitken was there too, at least some of the time, and everyone helped with the necessary — carrying beams, hammering nails.[232] There's a photo of Pat at the site, relaxing on a newly built lanai, skinny in blue jeans and a T-shirt with calligraphed logo, "The pen is mightier than the sword," looking impossibly young except for a beard showing early streaks of grey.[233]

The fact of a Catholic clergyman training in Zen, well-known to Aitken through his association with Yamada Ko'un, was unfamiliar and unwelcome to some of Aitken's students. Pat's presence at Koko An, and especially his decision to do Jukai, met with resistance, perhaps fueled in part by Aitken's evident favor toward Pat. This did not come as a complete surprise to Pat — Aitken had told him before he arrived that Augusto "… is interested in the subject of Zen for Catholics (a bit dubious about it so far). We should have some good discussions."[234] The understanding that developed between Pat and Augusto over cigarettes and coffee could transcend Augusto's doubts, but there was also Manfred Steger, a senior student of Aitken at the time, arguing against Pat's participation. Pat remembered, "Manfred Steger opposed it quite strongly…Manfred thought if I was going to take Jukai and become a Buddhist, then I should stop being a Catholic and disrobe, as he put it, as far as being a priest goes…. I didn't think so. And Aitken Roshi said what does it mean to take Jukai and say you're a Buddhist? All it means is you're a follower of the teacher Shakyamuni. It doesn't mean that you're not something else."[235]

There were some people not necessarily opposed but curious. In the space of a few days, being introduced to people as a Catholic priest, Pat was asked the question by various of Aitken's students and even by a gas station attendant, "How can you be a Catholic priest and practice Zen?" This led Aitken to suggest that Pat give a Tuesday night class on the subject. He titled it "Interdisciplinary Practice: Christian and Buddhist" and framed the topic based on a series of questions that Yamada Ko'un asked his Christian students. In his preamble, Pat told them, "…It was said that this question was asked of Father AMA Samy when he was here and he replied, 'Try it!' My thought was somewhat the same, shoot first and ask questions later."

In answer to the question, "Why Zen?" he recalled for them his "dark night" in the seminary and the absence in that setting of teachers to guide him, that through books he discovered silent sitting, then he met Aitken. "Finally, I had a teacher in the Way." He said, "Most Catholics and Christians generally are stuck with a child's understanding of the practice of prayer … They were never taught an adult practice, a maturing way." In response to the question Yamada had raised, "What is the source of God?" Pat offered passages from the Christian mystics, Meister Eckhart and Angelus Silesius, then said, "He is what I or you, or any other creature has never come to know before we were created." To the question of life and death, he went to the central tenet, "Christ rose from the dead. … The mystical reading … must refer to what is neither past nor future, neither in this place nor in that, but everywhere, in all, now and forever … in this very body is our eternal life — not "to come," in any heavenly place, but here and now, on this earth, in the aspect of time. That is what the historical Jesus of Nazareth realized and taught."

Recalling the film *Through a Glass Darkly* and his own question in despair, "Is God a spider, a devouring monster, a product of my own imagination" Pat told a story:

> These past few weeks I have been privileged to live in the cottage. My first morning I walked into the kitchen and was surprised by a large, hairy, brown spider. I jumped, it jumped. I ran, it ran. But after that first surprise meeting we became fast companions. She used the place at night and I during the day and we met every morning and evening. She ate the bugs and I made coffee. I came to appreciate her dark beady eyes, the white stripe across her head, the marvelous articulated limbs. She displayed her miraculous powers of walking up walls. I displayed mine, boiling water. Is God a spider?
>
> Grasping in actual experience, not just intellectually, the reality that everything in the entire universe, including myself, is totally empty. … Practice helps us realize that the language of religion is a language of parable, ritual, symbol, and myth. … Anyone sincerely following these ways will in fact discover what they refer to in oneself here and now. … Thus I find my home in the Catholic mystical tradition. Thus I find my home in the Zen Buddhist tradition. No hindrance in the mind, thus no fear. It is like being ambidextrous. How is it done? Just do it.[236]

Pat and Loren Rivers, another Aitken student, were going to do Jukai together toward the end of Pat's stay. "So we bought all the materials to make rakusus. And one evening, we sat on the floor at Koko An and tried to decipher the pattern and make the cuts and everything, and we both decided that we were hopelessly beyond our depth!" Time ran out and the ceremony was postponed to the following summer. Notwithstanding, Pat left Hawaii with permission to teach Zen students and lead them in koan work under Aitken's supervision from a distance.[237] That fall, back in Amarillo, Pat sent Aitken a card with a beautifully calligraphed excerpt from the *Tao Te Ching*:

It gives them life and rears them.
It gives them life yet claims no possession.
It benefits them yet exacts no gratitude;
It is the steward yet exercises no authority.
Such is called the mysterious virtue.

With deep gratitude,
Pat Hawk[238]

Amarillo people

Pat returned to Amarillo and the growing contemplative program. He and Greg planned a resident practice period for January 1988. Three of the original four participants — Bob Walker, Shirley Morrissey and Denise Fuller — were able to extract themselves from obligations of work and family to attend. Shirley persuaded her superiors not only to let her attend the practice period but actually to spend a sabbatical year in Amarillo. Pat said, "Bring your sewing machine."

Pat and Greg set up a schedule similar to what they'd known in Germany, with silent sitting, work practice and time off. Bob Walker made shelves and cupboards. Shirley sewed *zafus*, *zabutons* and support cushions. Pat wrote to Aitken in mid-February saying it was all going rather well. He let Aitken know that his rakusu was ready at last: "I'm sure I must have taken it apart more times than I put it together." Indeed. Making a rakusu is a notoriously exacting sewing task, and in the end, it was Shirley who made it, not Pat. It was a challenge even for her, experienced seamstress though she was. In the midst of struggling with it, she went to Pat in frustration saying it just wasn't coming together properly. He was unconcerned. "In and out, in and out, one stitch at a time." Easy for him to say.

During the practice period, which continued into March, Pat took time out to visit Willigis in Germany for a few weeks. While in Europe, he traveled around to various places with Willigis, who was looking to establish his own center independent of the Benedictine Abbey. Joan Rieck had already built a place at Sonnenhof in Germany's Black Forest, and in the end Willigis decided to join forces with her there for a time. Pat reconnected, slipping into easy companionship with the *Hausgemeinshaft*, some of whom were beginning to feel like old friends. Here were others like him following a Zen path within a Christian background. Although most did not take the precepts in a formal Jukai ceremony, they understood and embodied Zen and Christian streams. The controversy Pat had encountered the previous summer at Koko An still on his mind, he found the conversations with this group about Zen, Christians and Jukai relevant.

Bob Curry had accompanied Pat to Europe and stayed on for seven weeks of training after Pat left. He returned from his stay with Willigis having had a marvelous practice experience, which prompted him to go to Hawaii with Pat the following summer to work with Aitken. Pat wrote to Aitken, "It is Greg's third time there and from the tone of his letters he seems to have become thoroughly European."[239] Even as the three Redemptorists developed this mutual support, practicing alone and together, covering the home front while they were thus each engaged in intense training, there appeared among them hints of small rifts that would resurface later.

Despite having permission from Aitken to teach Zen and lead sesshin since the previous summer in Hawaii, Pat continued to lead only contemplative retreats in Amarillo. He did, however, offer koan study in the interview room to interested students with Bob Walker being his first. When Aitken gave Pat permission to teach Zen, he also gave him a "key" to standard koan responses that he himself had received from Yamada Ko'un. As a very green Zen teacher, Pat kept the key to hand in case he needed help checking a student's koan presentation.

During Shirley Morrissey's sabbatical year at Bishop DeFalco Retreat Center, she established herself as indispensable, welcoming retreatants, helping with paperwork and whatever tasks she saw needed doing, befriending all and sundry with her easy chattiness and open grin. She was helpful not just for the contemplative program but for the more conventional retreats that filled the BDRC schedule. These included talk and prayer-based retreats for specific groups, including women's retreats, priests' retreats, Engaged Encounter and Marriage Encounter weekends, Intensive Journaling workshops, Cursillo, Catholic Teacher's Day of Recollection, Magellan Ladies Day (St. Gerard Magellan was an early Redemptorist saint), things of that sort. The offerings were not only for Catholics. Among others, there were retreats organized by the United Way, by Presbyterians for Presbyterians, and a Methodist group that met regularly and in which Shirley became involved — lots of variety.

The result was that soon after Shirley returned to Glenview at the end of her sabbatical, Greg Mayers asked if she would join the staff at BDRC. With the necessary permissions from her Superior she moved to Amarillo, becoming the first Head Resident for the vigorously growing contemplative program. Charged with managing everything except finances, she was the mother hen, welcoming everyone, managing the library and bookstore, managing registrations, receiving visitors, looking after them during their stay, and if needed, changing sheets and mending.

Some who attended retreats with Pat in the Northwest sought to spend more time working with him and followed him back to BDRC. Among them was Bill

Lawder. He had joined the Trappists at a young age and was among the monks who came with Bernard McVeigh to Zen and contemplative retreats, his first being with Willigis Jäger in the Fall of '83.[240] While contemplative practice drew Bill strongly, the Trappist life was somehow not a good fit. As the BDRC contemplative program was gaining ground, Bill was in his mid-20s and just out of the Trappists, getting his sea legs for secular life. Handsome, funny, young and vulnerable, Bill began to work with Pat once Pat took over from Willigis in the Northwest, then he followed Pat to Amarillo. He spent several years there, eventually taking over from Shirley as Head Resident.

Steve Daney became a strong participant in the Amarillo program in the early days. Like Bill Lawder, Steve had had an interest in joining the Trappists, but unlike Bill, he was refused. Raised Baptist but unconvinced, Steve had visited the Trappist community of Assumption Abbey in the Ozarks as part of a college religion class. There he had a significant meeting with a Brother Tobias. "I was 19 and this guy was just amazing to me. So I decided then and there I wanted to be a monk, which — I wasn't even a Catholic, I wasn't even a Christian. I just loved the life. And the fact that I had a lot of problems with Christianity was irrelevant. I called them up. They said, are you a Catholic? I said I didn't even know if I was a Christian, but I just wanted to live this life. And they said no."

Steve then connected with the North American East-West Dialogue based at Osage Monastery in Oklahoma and Sister Pascaline Coff, a Benedictine nun who felt called by Vatican II to "go back to the sources." Steve recalled: "Sister Pascaline — that whole group had some connection with Willigis, mostly through Bede Griffiths. They had started this little community there where they sat on cushions and were doing Hindu rituals. They invited people from all over the world. It was really a nice place. So I went there."

The Sisters pointed Steve toward Shantivanam in Kansas. In the early '70s Father Edward Hays, a priest from Kansas City, had been sent by his Archbishop on a pilgrimage to various places of prayer around the world with the idea that he would then establish a house of prayer locally. The result was Shantivanam, a beautiful, rustic retreat center on 120 acres near Easton, Kansas. Steve and his girlfriend (later wife), Sheila Morrow, lived at Shantivanam until Steve left, torn over whether he wanted to be a monk or get married and live in the world. Steve made forays to the Trappist monastery at Snowmass and to Jiyu Kennett's Shasta Abbey, a Buddhist monastery incorporating Anglican high church forms and music into its rituals along with a rigorous schedule.

He then decided, "to heck with the Christians, to heck with the Buddhists, I'm gonna do my own thing," and met with a rancher who allowed him to build a cabin near a creek on a remote corner of her 10,000-acre property in the Flint

Hills of Kansas. He lived there for two years, still in touch with Sheila at Shantivanam. Willigis Jäger's name had come up at Osage and at Shantivanam. When Steve heard about a retreat that Willigis would be offering in St. Louis they decided Sheila would go, in hopes that it would help her understand Steve's difficulty deciding what to do. It was one of the retreats Pat Hawk co-led with Willigis. Sheila came back with tapes of the talks, to which Steve listened over and over. He began working with Pat, initially by sending tapes back and forth.

Steve attended a retreat that was to be led by Pat and Greg in Wichita. It turned out Pat couldn't make it, and Greg led the retreat alone. "I had a wonderful retreat with Greg and, well, you know how Greg is. 'You should come to Amarillo, we're starting a sangha. You should come to Amarillo.' I had just left my hermitage. Decided I was going to get married. I'd made my decision. I wasn't gonna be a monk, I was gonna do this in the world. And a lot of it was the Sanbo Kyodan. It was that sort of influence."

Finally — as became something of a pattern for people choosing to work with Pat — when he met Pat in person, Steve knew this was his teacher. "Immediately. That's my recollection. The minute I sat with him face to face."[241] I went back and told Sheila, I think we should move to Amarillo. She's a therapist and was able to get a job in a really nice place, and we got an apartment in a really bad part of town, but it was really close to DeFalco so we could walk. So we sat morning and evenings and we did all the retreats. And our life was really building a community. Building the sangha."

Steve and Bill Lawder decided they should have a community-based business, something along the lines of Green Gulch for San Francisco Zen Center. "We wanted some way to support Pat. Our teacher. And Greg [Mayers] was instrumental in all that. I don't remember talking to Pat about it, but we all figured he'd go along for the ride if we had a way to support him." They began a company called Edge City that made silent meditation timers. There was a need for silent timers in the growing national movement toward meditation since commercial timers had beepers — undesirable for ending a period of silent sitting. Edge City's timers ended with a flashing light instead of a beep. They sold some for a while, including to Honolulu Diamond Sangha. Bill also developed a "Jisha" computer program to help teachers keep track of students. Set up as a beta tester, Aitken commented to Pat that he thought it would be addictive.

Thinking of his time with Pat in Amarillo, Steve said, "I remember his asking me at one point, 'Tell me what you've read.' I went through this whole list of stuff. And he said, 'Okay, now forget it all.' … Early on I was asking, and he said it's not even One. Not even One. Another time he said about kensho, 'This can be life-changing. Transformative. Or you can just go back and turn on the TV.' " Steve remembered:

> One of my favorite Pat remarks — I was struggling with an infatuation and I was married. Met this woman at the library. I was there a lot doing a lot of study. And then I found out by total accident that she was interested in me. So it became possible. And I was really, really struggling with this and was talking to Pat about it. And he just looked at me. I said I don't know what to do about it. He said, "Well don't do anything. But don't despise yourself for it either." And it helped. And I didn't do anything, and it slowly drifted away.

Steve went on:

> I never had any personal relationship with Pat. In terms of the social part of it — he would sit in the corner and just sit. He didn't interact. It's a relatively boisterous group. I mean Lawder is a clown. And you know Greg Mayers is pretty loud. And others. All pretty dynamic. And Pat would just be in the corner. I was invited over for dinner one night with all the priests. And I remember Pat was a little more... You know they got used to him being quiet and making these sort of asides. These sardonic remarks. And you waited for them because he was very funny. But he seemed fine with everybody else carrying on conversations around him. I don't remember having much interaction with him at all. And I didn't really try. I didn't really need it.
>
> I think people can assume that the priesthood was an old suit of Pat's, but I think his priesthood was very important to him. Like Merton — everybody assumed because he was off exploring all this other stuff that he was going to leave the Church, and I don't think he had a thought of leaving the Church.[242]

When it came to people, Pat held his cards close to his chest, and it could be difficult to discern his affections. He seemed sometimes to be critical of those he was fond of, especially women, as if to throw up a smokescreen. But it was obvious that he loved Steve and Bill — young, bright, good-looking, earnest men, trusting and sincere in their practice. Barbara Wooten, an administrator at BDRC and sometime participant in retreats, noticed Pat's face would brighten when either of them came into a room.[243] Bill with his light-hearted hilarity, Steve with his intense, buoyant energy. Barbara said that Pat once interrupted a sesshin to give Steve a birthday party.

Glenna Pittock, in time probably Pat's closest friend, came to Bishop DeFalco Retreat Center in the late '80s and remained a strong presence during all the years there. One of Glenna's earliest encounters with Pat outside formal practice happened when she was at BDRC for the first time. Figuring retreat centers generally have horrible coffee, she brought some with her, along with cone and filters for her personal use. Glenna and a few others were sitting around in Meeting Room 4 after the retreat, the coffee apparatus out on the counter. Pat walked in, spotted the coffee fixings and in a demanding voice said, "Whose is that?!" Shirley said, "It's Glenna's." Glenna figured she was in trouble. Pat turned to her and said, "Did you find that around here somewhere?" Glenna said, "I immediately realized that he coveted it, so of course I left it with him."[244]

Glenna and her husband Henry worked at Oregon State University's School of Oceanography where their friends Jane Huyer and Bob Smith were faculty. Glenna, Jane and Bob became committed to contemplative practice through encounter with Willigis Jäger. When Pat came along, they took him as their teacher. The encounter motivated Glenna and others in Oregon to begin regular sitting together. They attended monthly sits — first at Leonard Marcel's home in Portland, later at Guadalupe Abbey — and weekly sits in Corvallis begun by Connie Allen, Jane and Glenna.

Glenna arranged to take a sabbatical year from job and family in Corvallis to live at BDRC. She was a wonderful positive presence there — buoyant, witty, down to earth. She embodied Pat's frequent injunction to "take yourself lightly" and was practical besides, but with an all-pervasive sense of fun. You knew she was around from the soft voice and light laughter that rippled around her. She added an infectious levity to the dedicated practice of the growing group. She "got" Pat, and he was at ease with her. Not only did they have a shared smoking habit — a bond in itself, as anyone who has smoked can attest — but her easy humor buffered his dourness even for himself.

Shirley Morrissey, Bob Walker, Steve Daney, Bill Lawder, Glenna Pittock — these people were anchors for the early contemplative program in Amarillo.

Resident training Hawaii 1988 — Jukai

Pat was able to carve only two weeks from his increasingly heavy retreat schedule to go to Hawaii during the summer of 1988. By that time, Manfred Steger had changed his opinion about Catholic priests, or at least about Pat, doing Jukai. He said, "If anybody can do it, you can."

Pat's confrere, Bob Curry, who had traveled to Hawaii with him, was present for the Jukai ceremony and reported on the event for the Redemptorists:

> Several years ago, Pope John Paul II astounded the world by meeting the religious leader of Buddhism during his pilgrimage in Thailand and Southeast Asia. The press reported that they sat in silence for a full twenty minutes.
>
> On August 5, 1988, that respectful silence between two great religious traditions was punctuated when Rev. Patrick Hawk, CSsR, professed Jukai at Koko An Zendo in Honolulu, Hawaii, at the conclusion of a four-day Sesshin or Zen retreat. The sesshin was conducted by Robert Aiken Roshi for 28 participants including Fr. Hawk and Fr. Robert Curry, CSsR.
>
> In the Zen tradition, Jukai is a ceremony much like a Christian's religious profession. One vows to oneself before and with the community, to live with integrity and clear understanding. During the Jukai ceremony one vows to daily and continually return home and find refuge in one's true and deepest self, to follow and find refuge in the wisdom life teaches, and to respect, value and find refuge in the kinship and support of community.
>
> Fr. Hawk, vested in his habit, expressed in the traditional formulae and in his own words his experience and commitment to the 16 precepts of Zen. These precepts summarize the way of life that is a fruit of meditation and of the fundamental conversion of enlightenment to which it leads.
>
> In a departure from the usual ceremony, Fr. Pat renewed his three vows of Poverty, Celibacy, and Obedience with his oath of perseverance to commemorate his silver anniversary as a Redemptorist. … Fr. Bob Curry, the superior of Pat's community, officially represented the Redemptorist Congregation and the Church, while making the sesshin.[245]

The central element of Jukai is a presentation by the candidate of their personalized understanding of the precepts. With some, the responses are lengthy. Characteristically, Pat's were unembellished and to the point:

> I take refuge in the Buddha…
>
> I vow to return to integrity, my home.
>
> I take refuge in the Dharma…
>
> I vow to never leave the voices of all people and things, my home.
>
> I take refuge in the Sangha…
>
> I vow to enhance the experience of being alive for all, my home.
>
> I vow to keep all precepts…
>
> I vow to cut off willfulness.
>
> I vow to practice all good Dharmas…
>
> I vow to be willing to follow and encourage the Path of Life.
>
> I vow to save the many beings…
>
> I vow to use means at my disposal to free myself and lend strength to my confreres and students.
>
> I take up the way of not killing…
>
> Protecting and encouraging harmony, gentleness and peace in community and city.

> I take up the way of not stealing…
> Being content in few needs and giving care to those I am with.
> I take up the way of not misusing sex…
> Not indulging in power over others, striving to bring forth one heart and one mind.
> I take up the way of not speaking falsely…
> But guiding and supporting all in peace or turmoil.
> I take up the way of not handling drink or drugs…
> To be fully aware in the moment of clarity or confusion
> I take up the way of not discussing the faults of others…
> Giving concern and help for others maturing and receiving gladly their concern and help to me.
> I take up the way of not praising myself while abusing others…
> Acknowledging the fact of humanity and its fullness bright and dark in myself and all.
> I take up the way of not indulging in anger…
> Using this energy appropriately and compassionately.
> I take up the way of not defaming the three treasures…
> Realizing standing and sitting, respecting the gifts of Buddha, the Dharma, the Sangha.

Pat's decision to include a renewal of his vows as a Redemptorist in his Jukai ceremony was perhaps in part to make clear that in taking this step, he was not relinquishing any former commitment. Perhaps it was also to reaffirm the vows he had professed as a young seminarian so many years before in light of his developing Zen understanding. He paused briefly following the recitation and personalization of Buddhist precepts, then went on:

> Twenty-five years ago this week I made vows as a member of my religious order. In keeping with this day of vow I now renew my vow of obedience — whereby I vow to listen attentively to the sounds of the universe.
>
> I renew my vow of celibacy whereby I vow to dwell singleheartedly among women, men, children and all beings.
>
> I renew my vow of poverty whereby I vow to dwell in gentle reconciling compassion, attaching myself to no one and no thing.
>
> I renew my vow and oath of perseverance to travel the beginningless, endless path from beginning to end.[246]

The teacher chooses a dharma name for the student that both relates to that person's presentation in the world and expresses an aspiration. The chosen name is inscribed on a white cloth panel sewn into the back of the rakusu. Aitken gave Pat the name *Seisho*, Western Bell. *Sei* — Western — carries a strong Christian overtone, which Aitken undoubtedly intended. For example, the dictionary translation of *seikyo*, literally "Western teaching," is simply "Christianity."[247]

Besides bestowing the dharma name, standard for any Jukai, Aitken also gave Pat a "cloud" name: *Shin'un Ken* (House of the Spreading Cloud). This was unusual because typically not done except in the case of dharma transmission. It seems Aitken had made up his mind by this time that he would be naming Pat as one of his successors.

Dharma Transmission

Zen Buddhism claims an authentic lineage of deep realization that has been transmitted from master to disciple going back to the historical Buddha, Shakyamuni.* The story is that Shakyamuni one day addressed his disciples wordlessly, simply holding up a lotus flower. One among his audience, Mahakasyapa, signaled his understanding of this presentation with a smile. Seeing this, Shakyamuni named him as his successor, saying, "I possess the true Dharma eye, the marvelous mind of Nirvana, the true form of the formless, the subtle Dharma Gate that does not rest on words or letters but is a special transmission outside the scriptures. This I entrust to Mahakasyapa."[248] From Mahakasyapa, so the story goes, there has been an unbroken chain of "mind to mind" transmission from master to student, down to the Zen masters of the present day. An expression of this recognition is in the oft-quoted poem attributed to Bodhidharma, considered the founder of Ch'an, which is the forerunner in China of Zen Buddhism:

A special transmission outside the scriptures;
No dependence on words and letters;
Direct pointing to the mind;
Seeing into one's nature and becoming Buddha.

The Zen stories that comprise the koan curriculum include many transmission accounts. In these, there is no obligate connection between transmission and becoming a teacher, although the transmission, if public, can certainly serve as a signal to others that the recipient is deemed by the master to have seen reality clearly. In contemporary Zen in the West, there remains the sense that transmission acknowledges insight. In practical terms, it has also come to serve as an authentication of the person in the status of independent teacher within a particular lineage.

---

* Siddhartha Gautama: The historical Buddha, circa 5th to 4th century BCE, also called Shakyamuni, sage of the Shakya clan.

Aitken took it as an obligation in his role as a teacher to groom worthy successors.[249] For him, as for his Japanese Sanbo Kyodan predecessors, a critical factor in deciding to give transmission was not only that the teacher be convinced of the disciple's clear dharma eye but also that potential students recognize the person as someone from whom they could fruitfully receive instruction.

Aitken had recognized promising insight in Pat from the time of their first encounter at Palisades. Since then, he had watched this insight mature and deepen. In Hawaii, he saw firsthand Pat's talent as a teacher, hearing from his own students of Pat's spare style that pointed frugally and directly to the heart of the matter. Aitken himself had received transmission from Yamada Ko'un in 1985. Following that summer of 1988 when Pat did Jukai, the stars aligned, and Aitken was ready to act. Besides Pat, three others had emerged in Aitken's mind as teachers, and in November of 1988, he announced that he would give transmission to Pat Hawk, John Tarrant, Nelson Foster and Augusto Alcalde.

A busy exchange of letters between Aitken and Pat ensued that fall and winter, sorting out details. This included designing the *kechimyaku** (bloodline) or lineage chart. Aitken had given Pat and the others the complex family tree, with 72 generations from Shakyamuni Buddha to Hakuin† counted and spread out over seven pages. From that beginning, selecting only the names of ancestors whose descendants were in the direct line to Aitken and thence to the transmittees, Pat designed a layout. No matter that each individual in the line cannot be verified. As Nelson Foster has pointed out: "By strict standards of scholarship, none of us can trace our personal genealogies back to the beginning, and in a very real sense, it doesn't matter: no one questions the existence of their neolithic antecedents. Even though the elders' names and origins are utterly forgotten... They lived. We're proof."[250] Out of a discussion with John Tarrant came the decision to have each of the four prepare his own bloodline document based on Pat's design. Pat was to research what paper to use and other technical details, and figure out a slightly different design for a document to be given to any student doing Jukai, the latter to be titled "Transmission of the Precepts."

While these things were being worked out, word came from Japan that Yamada Ko'un Roshi, Aitken's direct ancestor in the lineage, had taken a fall and was in the hospital doing poorly. Coming as Yamada Ko'un's name was duly included in the written lineage Pat labored over, this news must have added a measure of vivid present tense to the long vista extending back to Shakyamuni Buddha.

---

* Kechimyaku: Literally blood vein, it lists names in the line of succession back to Shakyamuni Buddha.

† Hakuin Ekaku (1685-1769)

Dharma transmission implied granting of independence to the dharma heir, including authorization to evaluate the insight of others, give others permission to teach, and give dharma transmission. In this connection, in a letter to the four teachers, Aitken wrote: "John [Tarrant] suggested, and Nelson [Foster] and I agreed that newly established teachers should not name successors of their own for at least 10 years. I ask the concurrence of Augusto [Alcalde] and Pat regarding this agreement."[251] Pat wrote back, "Of course, I concur with all points readily. I think not naming successors for 10 years is wise. Such an agreed-upon policy is helpful and defuses any pressure that might arise." He had seen that some people coveted transmission, and he understood that pressure would indeed arise.

The ceremonies were conducted separately and at times that fit the schedules of Aitken, each teacher, and their sangha. John Tarrant's was the first, in December 1988. Augusto was next, in January 1989. Aitken traveled to Cordoba, Argentina, for Augusto's ceremony. He had gone there the previous year and reported back on what a wonderful mature group of mostly young people he found there. This time he sent an account of the event and said, "We had a very nice transmission ceremony for Augusto in Cordoba. I'm learning how to do it."

By February, Pat had a final version of the "Transmission of the Precepts" document that would be used for people doing Jukai, and he was ready to begin his own "Transmission of the Bloodline" document. All Pat's years of doing calligraphy were brought to bear in the preparation of these papers. He put everything he had into making them perfect, and inevitably he was frustrated. When he sent the Jukai document to Aitken, Pat wrote, "I think this is about as good as I am going to do with it. There are a couple of mistakes that have been corrected with Liquid Paper. I've decided I will never be satisfied and will have to be content with amateur results."

Aitken wrote back, "Do you know the story of Sen no Rikyu and his son? He asked his son to rake the leaves one autumn day. The son raked every leaf, and then called his father to inspect. His father said, 'Not good enough,' and he shook a tree and a few leaves came down. 'Now it's perfect,' he said."[252] Pat's actual transmission document, not completed until early May, was exquisite. The title "Transmission of the Bloodline" was in blood-red ink. The calligraphy was flawless, the lines and proportions perfect.

While he was preparing the documents, Pat kept up a full schedule of retreats at BDRC in Amarillo and in the Northwest. Some of the Northwest retreats were at a center in Indianola, on the Kitsap Peninsula near Seattle. For one of these, the Zen branch of the "Zen for Christians" group happened to be at Indianola at the same time. Seeing those familiar faces recalled for Pat the beginnings of his journey with Aitken back in 1978: "At the last contemplative retreat I gave at the end of January, Joan Rieck was leading sesshin at the same camp and we had a couple of real good talks together. I met with the Seattle sesshin members for their concluding lunch. It was wonderful seeing many of the people and recalling the first sesshin at the Palisades Retreat over 11 years ago."

The Zen/Christian conversation at Haus St. Benedikt, Koko An and other places was still in Pat's mind as the date of his transmission approached. He considered what the implications might be of his taking this major step in Buddhism. Pat wrote to Aitken in April:

> I found your article in *The Pacific World*, "The Lay Zen Buddhist Sangha in the West,"[253] fascinating. Bob Curry and I have discussed it a couple of times, focusing on 'anarchy in organization'. In our small circle of contemplatives, this seems to be working. But it is indeed small. The larger organization and its levels of the Roman Catholic Church touch us not at all except as a specter that deems us unworthy of notice, as yet. I have no idea of how the future will develop. Even when we discuss possibilities, I do not find them striking anything within me. I look into a formless void. The Spirit may be hovering over it, but it is no less formless.[254]

Though Aitken's idea was to have the transmission ceremonies at the home sangha of each teacher, Pat's was held at Koko An in Honolulu, perhaps to avoid raising red flags unnecessarily in Amarillo. Greg Mayers, Bob Curry and Joan Rieck attended. Aitken was pleased and impressed that Bob Curry — then Pat's religious Superior — would come. About 30 from the local sangha in Hawaii attended the event. It took place the evening of Wednesday, May 24, 1989.

Pat had no Zen robe. Not long after the transmission, Shirley sewed one for him, but for the transmission ceremony, he wore an old Redemptorist habit that Shirley altered to look like a Buddhist robe.[255] Pat and Aitken and almost everyone else were barefoot. They all crowded into the zendo at Koko An, finding places on double rows of cushions in the room or overflowing out the doorway.

Aitken opened the solemn ceremony with some words of introduction. There was chanting, then a talk by Pat that, like any teisho, was a presentation of dharma insight. It was based on the *Mumonkan* case, "Seijo and her soul are separated" — perhaps a recollection of Pat's long journey, his encounter with alienation in the seminary, and paradoxically, reunification with his own spiritual center by his discovery and embrace of Zen.

*Shosan** followed. Aitken explained that *Shosan* is an opportunity for anyone present to challenge the candidate on any point in their understanding. It can be

* Shosan: A public dharma exchange between student and teacher.

compared in a certain sense to the dissertation defense of a doctoral candidate — the pressure is high. Aitken did nothing to diminish this pressure in his opening remarks when, speaking of *shosan*, he said, "If all goes well, we will proceed to Jukai renewal and to confirmation of [Pat's] place in the Diamond Sangha lineage." Space was cleared for two cushions placed opposite each other, one for Pat and the other for anyone who wished to come up and challenge him. Loren Rivers, serving as tanto, stood behind Pat, *kyosaku** held upright.

Inevitably, the Zen-Catholic angle was probed.

> First questioner: Pat, the Catholic priest, Pat the Zen Buddhist roshi…which one is the true Pat?
> Pat: It's good to see you again, been well?
> Second questioner: Is Buddha Jesus Christ?
> P: No.
> Q: Is Jesus Christ Buddha?
> P: Hmmm. No.
> Q: They're totally different?
> P: "The clouds and the moon are the same, the mountains and valleys are different. All are blessed, all are blessed. Ten thousand things, ten thousand blessings. Is this one? Is this two?"[256]
> Q: You tell me.
> P: Well, from one point of view, it can't be told. There's this way and there's that way. When you walk both of them to the end, come back and we'll have a good laugh about it.[257]

And so on. The ceremony proceeded to renewal of Jukai and Aitken's words of confirmation:

> Transmission comes from two directions: from the old teacher and from the sangha. Your acceptance as a teacher by the many students who come to the Bishop DeFalco Retreat Center and by the many others who invite you to meet them in their practice in centers about the country, clearly indicates your acceptance by your sangha. Your presence here at Koko An over the past few years has been instructive and convincing for everyone and I sense clearly that with your words this evening your acceptance is confirmed by this sangha. For my part I recall that when we first met, I thought to myself, now *there* is a promising one. You verified my hunch at each step of our work together, to the final ones this evening. I confirm you as worthy to teach as a confirmed Master in the Diamond Sangha lineage which extends

---

* The 'stick of encouragement,' a flat wooden stick used to remedy sleepiness or inattention during long periods of sitting; also used ceremonially, as in this setting.

back through the Sanbo Kyodan and the Soto Zen stream, through the Chinese and Indian Buddhist traditions to Shakyamuni Buddha. So, a new beginning. Let me read my Cautions to the New Teacher:

1. Our practice begins now. You will probably mature as a teacher after ten years.
2. Remember that guidance is a matter of encouragement.
3. Respect transference from your students and turn it back with support of their practice.
4. Let the word go forth that your Sangha and you yourself are open and friendly.
5. Countless Buddhas have sweat blood for this transmission. Be faithful. Be faithful.

Aitken presented the handwritten cautions inscribed to Patrick Hawk, *Seisho Shin'un Ken*.[258] The document was dated, signed, "Robert Aitken The Old Layman," and stamped with his seal. He then led Pat in speaking the Vow of the New Master, a *gatha*[*] he had written for these transmissions: "Accepting my place in the lineage, I vow with all beings to maintain the Dharma faithfully which the Buddha handed down." This too was handwritten by Aitken. Pat signed and stamped it with his seal.

Aitken then presented the beautiful scrolled *kechimyaku* that Pat had prepared, now bearing Aitken's signature. These documents were not exactly the *Sanmotsu*,[†] the three documents traditional in Japanese transmission, such as had been given to Aitken by Yamada Ko'un. Aitken's documents were in Sino-Japanese, which Yamada was going to translate for him but never did. Realizing he might not get to it, Yamada Ko'un suggested that one of his Japanese heirs, Taizan Maezumi, do it. Aitken visited Maezumi for that purpose, but it was never done. It meant Aitken had to come up with his own three documents. These were the *kechimyaku*, the teacher's cautions, and the *gatha* of the new Master.

Aitken gave Pat a formal rakusu with Pat's given name, his dharma and cloud names, Aitken's name and the date, May 24, 1989, inscribed on the back. Pat took off his black cotton rakusu, not quite a year old, and swapped it for the ceremonial one of embroidered silk. Lastly, Aitken gave Pat the *kotsu*, a small curved stick

---

[*] Gatha: Sanskrit term meaning verse or poem.

[†] The three documents certifying transmission are the *shisho* (inheritance certificate), *odaiji* (the great matter), and the *kechimyaku* (bloodline of the authentic transmission). Only those with this certification are considered capable of certifying the kensho of others. Sharf, Robert H. "Sanbokyodan: Zen and the Way of the New Religions." *Japanese Journal of Religious Studies* 22, no. 3/4 (1995): 417-58. http://www.jstor.org/stable/30234461 Accessed September 2020.

shaped like a human spine, symbol of the master. It is carried on formal occasions, laid down in front of the master's cushion during teisho or dokusan, sometimes rapped on the lectern to make a point, sometimes brandished at a student.

As he handed over these items, he said to Pat: "As a master of the Diamond Sangha and Bishop DeFalco Retreat Center, you have the special responsibility of maintaining the perennial stream of no name and no sect where the Buddha and the Christ bathe together."

Pat, visibly moved, addressed Aitken: "One time when I was a teacher of high school students one of them was in great trouble. [Later] he asked, 'What can I do for you, for giving me my life back.' And I told him, 'Go, live it.' There are many who have done the same for me. I bow in great gratitude to you, for giving me life, transmitting life to me. And I vow to live it fully and to transmit in turn."[259] He presented Aitken a gift of a large crystal bowl, known as a singing bell. An accompanying stick, run around the lip of the bowl, caused it to sound. Western Bell. Pat gifted an identical bell to the sangha in Amarillo as a remembrance of the transmission.[260]

Refreshments, photo ops and much congratulating followed. Pat said he dodged the hugging except for Anne Aitken. Looking at the photo proof of this years later he said, "She's the only one who got a hug."[261]

Those among Haus St. Benedikt's *Hausgemeinshaft* who knew Pat sent congratulations from Würzburg:

> Dear Pat
>
> Last week we all had to think of you, knowing you were in Hawaii receiving Dharma transmission from Aitken Roshi. Many of us would have liked to have been there, but we are happy that there is now another teacher in our Zen school.
>
> We heard that Joan [Rieck] took a special trip to Hawaii to be present at the ceremony — perhaps you managed a few relaxing days in that beautiful Hawaiian weather. For that we envy you!
>
> Despite the fact that you do not "need" so much anymore to come to Würzburg, and despite the fact that you can now accept your own students, we hope to see you and Greg and Bob here with us again. The coffeemaker you presented the long-term guests is getting a bit of use, but it would be nice to have you all here to initiate those wonderful "American coffee breaks!"
>
> Please accept congratulations and best wishes from us here at Haus St. Benedikt.
>
> Liebe grü*ß*e.[262]

The note was signed by ten of the residents.

A four-page article in the July issue of the Diamond Sangha newsletter, *Blind Donkey,* announced the transmission to the larger Zen community. It included Aitken's introductory remarks, a brief biography, excerpts from the *shosan*, and a copy of the handwritten Teacher's Cautions signed by Aitken.

Whatever uneasiness Pat had about the Church and her response to his Zen path and transmission, and notwithstanding occasional mild derision (for example, once a visiting confrere, having looked into the zendo in Amarillo, commented, "My God they're in there staring at the wall thinking of nothing!"), no trouble reached him. In fact, a write-up of several paragraphs appeared in the Redemptorists' newsletter that autumn, proudly announcing the event and describing Pat's trajectory from the time he first met Aitken. News of the transmission spread in the Catholic community also because that year, Pat accepted an invitation to write an article on his experience as a Catholic priest and Zen teacher for the magazine, *Catholic World.* It was a timely opportunity to reflect on his trajectory from the time he was a boy attracted to the vestments and incense of Catholic ritual to his becoming a Zen teacher. He wrote:

> There is a need for someone ... to help point the way on a pathless path. That I am such a one is a wonder to me, and doubtless to others. Yet ultimately it has nothing to do with me. I can only express gratitude to my teachers, Robert Aitken and Willigis Jäger. These great teachers faithfully transmitted to me what was transmitted to them.

He described something of his path, the first call to religious life while he was a boy, the dark time as a seminarian, his discovery of the Zen path. He went on:

> Training in Contemplation or Zen is done face to face. One does the practice year after year, face to face with the Source, our true home. One comes face to face with one's teacher hundreds of times year after year. One personalizes the insight gained through practice in daily life year after year. How does one become a master of Contemplation or Zen? One earns the role by practice, insight, and personalization in life. A prospective teacher may be nominated by another recognized teacher but is confirmed in fact by those who come to him or her for guidance. There may be an official ceremony, as in the Zen tradition. It may be that, as in the Christian tradition, one's teacher simply says, "Now go, make your own soup." In each case what is transmitted is the one stream.[263]

This work of teaching for which Pat's life had prepared him, he pointed out, "is not to teach something, but to provide the opportunity for students to directly realize the Ultimate for themselves."

4

Early Years Post-Transmission

Pat and his confreres returned to an unusual amount of rain in Amarillo, relieving the previous winter and spring drought.[264] They added a Zen night to the weekly schedule at Bishop DeFalco Retreat Center. It was the same sitting in silence alternating with short periods of walking meditation, but the language was changed. For Zen nights the contemplation room was called the zendo, interviews were announced as dokusan, and the person assisting with interviews was called the jisha instead of the monitor. The bells and clappers were in Zen format, and instead of Evening Prayer, the period closed with the Zen tradition's Four Great Vows.

In addition to townspeople and out-of-town residents staying for extended periods of practice, there was increasing interest from complete strangers who heard of the practice through the *Blind Donkey* article or word of mouth and found their way to Amarillo. It was clear that a Zen sangha was forming at BDRC. Pat and Greg decided it was time to make it official. Pat wrote to Aitken:

> Dear Roshi,
>
> I've been pretty busy this summer with retreats in Los Angeles, Portland and here. All this summer there have been at least three trainees in residence. I have also received inquiries from five people in various parts of the mainland in regard to Zen practice. I responded positively to all of them, but it remains to be seen whether we will hook up face to face sometime in the future. All of these inquiries were a result of the publication of part of the transmission ceremony in *Blind Donkey*. No adverse reactions at all.
>
> I was unable to see Bernard McVeigh this summer. He is in California trying to overcome the immense pain he is suffering with his back. There was some talk in Portland that he may have to resign soon as Abbot of Our Lady of Guadalupe Abbey. I talked to him on the phone last night and he seemed in good spirits despite his affliction.

The number of Zen students here in Amarillo, and those who come from and are inquiring from other places, is such that we thought it would be a good idea to form a Sangha here. So we have provisionally chosen the name "Empty Sky Sangha" because it is one of Yamada Ko'un Roshi's favorite expressions and it also has the virtue of describing the sky in the Panhandle of Texas for most of the year. We have asked Fred Hill, a longtime student of mine who is a respected psychotherapist and non-Catholic, to be president and another longtime student to be secretary/treasurer.

We have set up weekly evening sittings exclusively for Zen practice and a schedule of zazenkai and sesshin. Once this is underway for a while we would then consider asking for affiliation with the Diamond Sangha. If you have any thoughts or suggestions about this, I would appreciate hearing them.

I'm getting ready to go to Korea. I leave on the 29th of this month. Also getting ready to lead sesshin at Koko An. I am enclosing one of the teisho I have prepared. Your criticism of it will be valued. Would you pass on to whoever would need to know that I will be arriving in Honolulu from Seoul on Korean Air Flight #60 on Tuesday, September 12th at 8:10 am.

I'm sure you are looking forward to your stay at Green Gulch.[265] May it be restful and enjoyable. Give my love to Anne.

Love,
Pat[266]

Pat and Greg traveled to Seoul, South Korea, that summer to conduct a five-day contemplative intensive retreat. The Irish Columban Fathers in Seoul ran an Enculturation Center, the mission of which was to adapt Catholicism to Korean culture. They had invited Willigis Jäger to lead a retreat. Willigis was too busy and referred them to Pat. Pat asked Greg to do it with him.

They stayed with the Columban fathers and did a little exploring of Seoul before and after the retreat. They had a map in English, but the street signs were in Korean, which neither of them could read. The Columbans said, "Oh, just get on the subway," so they headed out, interested in shopping at a famous Buddhist supply store in Seoul.

The weather was pleasant, but the subway was unairconditioned and stifling, crowded with the pungent odors of kimchee, garlic and sweat. They had figured out that the shop was five subway stops away. Stepping into the street, they were able to locate it, but when it was time to head back, they couldn't find the subway station. They were standing on the corner looking at the map and Greg said, "Pat, we are lost." Pat said, "No, we are not lost." Greg said, "Pat. We are lost!" A polite Korean came up and said, "Are you lost?" Greg said, Yes!" Pat said, "No." The Korean kindly pointed the way to the subway. They counted five stops and returned successfully to the Columban fathers' place.[267]

The retreat was held at the Passionist Monastery in the hills above Seoul, overlooking the city. Thirty-four people attended, mostly nuns, plus a few priests and Korean lay spiritual teachers. Language is not a barrier at a silent retreat except during personal interviews, the daily conference, and homily during daily Mass. For those, two bilingual Korean nuns were assigned as interpreters, one each to Greg and Pat.[268] The Vicar General of the Catholic diocese in Seoul, who happened to be one of the participants, commented at the end, "This is very Korean! It's very interesting that we had to get two Westerners to come over and teach us how to pray like Koreans." He expressed the hope that the contemplative intensive retreat would appeal to young Catholic Koreans searching for their cultural roots within the Church. As a follow-up to the retreat, Pat and Greg urged the priests and nuns to dialogue, and to practice meditation with and learn from the Korean Zen masters who, they suggested, are some of the most renowned and accomplished in Asia and the world.[269]

Greg returned from Seoul to Amarillo. Pat flew to Honolulu to lead sesshin at Koko An as a favor to Aitken, so that he and Anne could take some time off at Green Gulch Farm near Mill Valley, California. This was only the fourth sesshin Pat had attended in Diamond Sangha format. It was his first as the Zen master. He prepared carefully, sent teisho to Aitken for feedback, and kept the koan notes handy in the dokusan room. Beforehand Aitken sent him a synopsis of where students were in their practice. Pat made terse notes on each person's presentation during dokusan. Manfred Steger, the one who had most vocally opposed Pat's Jukai a few years earlier, was jisha. Perle Besserman, later to work with Pat for a time in Amarillo, was tanto.

Just as the sesshin started, word came from Japan that Yamada Ko'un Roshi, Abbot of Sanbo Kyodan, had died.[270] Some of the sesshin attendees had known Yamada from the years he traveled to Hawaii to teach Aitken and his sangha. Though Pat had never met Yamada Ko'un, in Aitken's absence, he led the memorial to which about 30 people came. This might have been a daunting task for a very green Zen master, but Pat was by that time 20 years a priest, with funerals part of his stock-in-trade. He was at home in the world of loss. His solemn, complete presence provided exactly what was needed. He received a letter of thanks when he got back to Amarillo:

> Dear Pat Hawk Roshi,
>
> Our sesshin with you last week was such a wonderful experience! The sense of unity and commitment have continued with us after your return to Texas. The progress we all made has confirmed us in our practice once again.
>
> It was important for the Sangha to have you present to conduct a memorial service for Yamada Roshi. That evening was a warm and moving

celebration of his life. We had a real sense of transmission having Yamada Roshi's "grandson in the Dharma" lead us in remembering him.

Since many of us have never worked with a Zen teacher other than Aitken Roshi it was especially important to have such a fine sesshin with one of his Dharma successors. We have already thanked Roshi for doing such a fine job of training you! We hope you will be back again for more sesshins with us.

Aloha and gassho,
Joan Rose, President
For the Diamond Sangha Board of Directors[271]

Zen Desert Sangha, December 1989

Following the transmission ceremony in May 1989, as news of Pat's talents and potential availability as a Zen teacher traveled the dharma grapevine, he began receiving requests from Zen groups, some of which developed into long-term relationships. Among these was Zen Desert Sangha in Tucson, Arizona. His Koko An experience having been an obvious success, Pat felt confident in accepting an invitation to lead sesshin for the Tucson group, thus beginning a close association that would last the rest of his life. Zen Desert Sangha at the time had grown from a core of eight dedicated people to a loosely associated group of seekers who shared a desire for silent sitting practice.

In the early 1980s, Tucson was home to several Zen groups with affiliations to various teachers, including Maezumi Roshi of the Zen Center of Los Angeles (ZCLA) and Joko Beck, at the time a senior student of Maezumi. Paul Markl was one of the Tucsonans interested in sitting, looking for like-minded others, and seeking out teachers. Paul was raised Catholic and as a young adult had come upon the Catholic mystics with whom he resonated. Tall, lean, soft-spoken, talkative in the right setting, he remembered, "I was a pretty devout person. I got into reading Thomas Merton at 18 or 19 years old, then through him, John of the Cross and Meister Eckhart. The mystics captivated me. The Catholic Church both captivated me and turned me off. The mystical side — yes; the authoritarian side — no." For a while Paul had a job at the Tucson Association for the Blind. While there he met a woman, a Quaker, who knew of Maezumi Roshi from the Zen Center of Los Angeles. Hearing that Maezumi would be in Tucson, she had invited him to give a talk at the Tucson Association for the Blind. Paul attended the talk, then attended a sesshin with Maezumi, then with Joko Beck.

A Maezumi-related group formed in Tucson and through it, Paul crossed paths with Bob Wallin. Bob recalled:

> I grew up Protestant, but just nominally, we weren't big churchgoers. Early in life I became disenchanted with organized religion. It seemed just pompous baloney. But at the same time, I had genuine spiritual aspiration. I was in high school during Vietnam — there were religious figures like Martin Luther King and Catholic priests like the Berrigans and Buddhist monks in Vietnam. Religious figures around the world were protesting the war and participating in the civil rights struggle. Priests and ministers who went arm in arm in civil rights demonstrations. That part of it was an inspiration. The established Christian churches at the time didn't attract me.

In college Bob became interested in Asian religion and philosophy, took classes, read a lot and experimented with psychedelics.

> After I graduated from college, I remember in my late 20s reading a book on Hinduism and yoga practice. But what this book was telling me was that I should stop reading this book and sit down and start meditating. So I did. Just by myself. Even had an all-day sit just on my own. I remember going out at the end of the day — it was after dark — going out and seeing the stars and having this wonderful experience; seeing the sky as fresh and new. And so I really early on understood the value of meditation as a practice. … So I looked around for different practices and different groups.[272]

Paul and Bob and a handful of the others sitting with the Maezumi group decided the group process — very much directed from the Zen Center of Los Angeles — was too authoritarian. They split off and began Zen Desert Sangha in 1982, sitting together in each other's homes following guidance from books or occasional contact with teachers passing through town. They were attracted by Robert Aitken's vision of a more egalitarian, democratic, decentralized model, as presented in *Taking the Path of Zen*.[273] Bob remembers reading an interview with Aitken in *Ten Directions*, the newsletter of ZCLA. "He talked a lot about consensus-based democratic group process. That became my inspiration for the way to organize a group. So that was our founding principle for our original sitting group — democratic and consensus-based."

They wrote to Aitken and found him most encouraging. Over the next few years, Aitken sent them letters and tapes of his talks. Some of the group attended sesshin led by Aitken at Ring of Bone Zendo in Northern California and/or in Hawaii. In 1984 Aitken suggested that they ask Nelson Foster, at the time one of his senior students, to come and lead sesshin for them. Two people from the Zen Desert Sangha group went to Hawaii to meet Nelson and invite him to teach in Tucson. He agreed, and for several years, two or three times a year, he swapped his student role with the sangha in Hawaii for the teaching role in Tucson. During this time, Zen Desert Sangha became officially affiliated with the Diamond

Sangha. When Nelson also started teaching at Ring of Bone, eventually becoming the official guiding teacher there, he stopped coming to Tucson, and for over a year Zen Desert Sangha was once again without a teacher.

Bob Wallin happened to be at Koko An when Nelson's transmission ceremony took place in July 1989. They spoke about what Zen Desert Sangha would do now that Nelson was taking over Ring of Bone and would be too busy to come to Tucson. Nelson suggested they approach Pat Hawk, which they did, with the result that he would come that winter to lead a weekend sesshin.[274] Bob met Pat at the airport, taking him to stay at the Benedictine Sisters' beautiful, Spanish-style monastery on Country Club Road, about a mile and a half from Bob's place where the sesshin was held.[275] Some of the Sisters were already tuned in to contemplative practice because of their co-religious, Sister Ludwigis Fabian, a German Benedictine nun. Sister Ludi was a dharma sibling of Robert Aitken, having trained with and been sanctioned to teach by Yamada Ko'un in Japan. She was based in Europe but had led contemplative retreats in Tucson for the Sisters and other interested people, some of them associated with Zen Desert Sangha.

More than 20 people attended that first sesshin with Pat,[276] including some of the original Zen Desert Sangha founders, a few of the Benedictine Sisters and various others. Pat led a full sesshin schedule and offered Mass at the monastery for anyone interested, a practice he later discontinued as he became more strict about not mixing Zen and Christian forms. Bob Wallin remembered:

> It was great. Everybody liked Pat. His style is different from Nelson's in that Nelson is a lot more gregarious. Nelson socialized with us and loved to go hiking. I remember every time Nelson came for a sesshin we'd all go out to dinner after and sit around a big table and tell stories. Nelson would be laughing — he has a really hearty laugh. Whereas when Pat came to town it would often be like he'd fly in the evening before and maybe we'd get together, although staying at the monastery he'd probably just have a quiet dinner over there. And often he would schedule a flight out early Sunday morning. Sometimes even before the sesshin ended somebody would take him to the airport. For those of us that were working with him and studying with him, it was okay. We got to work with him and listen to teisho and do dokusan, and some of us also went over to Amarillo.

"What a ragtag group," Pat wrote to Aitken after that first sesshin. "But they have great spirit. It is amazing to me that they have held together through the years."[277] Ragtag notwithstanding, he found them serious about practice and felt he'd done them some good. He accepted their invitation to come back at regular intervals.

A question of lineage

While Pat was thus getting established as a Zen teacher of the Diamond Sangha, the death of Yamada Ko'un, Abott of the Sanbo Kyodan, in September 1989 had thrown that organization into turmoil. Yamada had not named a person to succeed him as abbot nor made clear what he intended for the many teachers he'd appointed but had not made independent. Of more than 20 non-Japanese given permission to teach, only Robert Aitken in the United States and Brigitte D'Ortschy in Germany had been given *inka*,* making them fully independent Zen Masters. None of the others were officially sanctioned to verify kensho in their students nor to appoint their own successors in the lineage.

A major controversy arose regarding who could confer teaching authority within the Sanbo Kyodan. The problem had come to the fore in the several years prior to Yamada Ko'un's death, as his health was in decline. Aitken had pressed Yamada to clarify the succession, and the various teachers whose independence was at stake had expressed concern both among themselves and directly to Yamada.

As far back as Pat's year in Würzburg,[278] in letters between Jäger and Aitken about Pat's progress, there was discussion about the future of the Sanbo Kyodan lineage. It wasn't that one couldn't teach without transmission, nor that one's dharma eye would be any clearer with transmission, but there was the fundamental notion of authentic lineage. When Aitken was given dharma transmission by Yamada Ko'un back in early 1985, Willigis Jäger, who had heard about it from Joan Rieck, wrote to Aitken congratulating him. "To stay in a lineage gives much security and prevents us from falling into too individual versions of truth." Aitken replied, "I appreciate your kind congratulations about the *Sanmotsu*, the three documents certifying transmission or *Inka*. Indeed, these three pieces of paper are vitally important if anything is."

In August 1987, while Pat was having his busy first summer in Amarillo, Willigis Jäger had met with Yamada Ko'un — who in 1987 was still well enough to travel — at a Christian-Buddhist conference in Berkeley. At the time, Yamada promised him that he would clarify the succession. Jäger went to Japan that winter. His talks with Yamada yielded the impression that Kubota Akira[279] would receive a full authorization as teacher for the Japanese, and Yamada Masamichi,

---

* Inka Shomei: (Japanese) "legitimate seal of true attainment" — in practical terms inka is the certification of a Dharma heir as being a true link in the Zen lineage that originates with Shakyamuni Buddha, and thus is synonymous with dharma transmission. Robert Aitken received transmission from Yamada Ko'un in 1985. Both Yamada Ko'un himself and Brigitte D'Ortschy received transmission from Hakuun Yasutani (1885-1973), founder of the Sanbo Kyodan.

Yamada Ko'un's son, would receive authorization to teach the Western students.

A year later, Aitken wrote to Willigis Jäger that Pat had finished the koans — this was in 1988, during Pat's second resident training period in Hawaii. He told Jäger that he had authorized Pat informally to teach Zen, and that he was planning to give him dharma transmission as soon as he could work out an English version of the *Sanmotsu*. Jäger, seeing Aitken preparing to authorize dharma heirs, felt frustrated at his own lack of authority to do the same. He approached Aitken about sending a few of his senior students from Germany to Honolulu to be sanctioned in the Diamond Sangha. Aitken wrote to his four soon-to-be dharma heirs about Jäger's suggestion, explaining that it appeared there would be no more *Sanmotsu* from Yamada Ko'un,[280] who was having misgivings about some of the Europeans to whom he had given permission to teach.

While Aitken was thus exchanging letters with Jäger on the one hand and his prospective heirs on the other — still prior to Yamada Ko'un's death in September 1989 — he initiated a correspondence with Kubota Akira, his relative in the dharma from the days both worked with Yasutani Roshi.[281] Aitken's letter[282] was ostensibly to respond to an article by Kubota in *Kyosho*, newsletter of the Sanbo Kyodan, summarizing discussion from a meeting on the problems of the Sanbo Kyodan. It may also have been calculated to prepare for later communication with Kubota regarding Aitken's dharma transmissions to John Tarrant, Augusto Alcalde, Pat Hawk and Nelson Foster. Aitken, as dharma heir in the Sanbo Kyodan lineage himself, intended that his successors would be recognized in that lineage.

In his letter to Kubota, Aitken wrote about aspects of his thought and practice that had evolved since they were students together in Kamakura. One of Aitken's chief points was that he had shifted away from the notion of kensho as the be-all and end-all of Zen practice toward emphasis on *nen*, the mind of this moment. He had dropped the practice of *jahai* — public recognition of a student's kensho, usually at the end of sesshin — as encouraging too much orientation toward a goal. He was giving more recognition than he had previously to *shikantaza*, loosely translated as "just sitting," as a practice in addition to koan work. He finished with an appeal to their long association: "I offer these observations and examples to you as a colleague and as an old friend of thirty years and more, in the hope that we can establish a dialogue that will contribute in some measure to maintaining the Buddha Dharma of Dogen Zenji and Harada Roshi* through our troubled times and beyond."[283] The overall tone of his letter was tentative

* Harada Daiun Sogaku, (1871- 1961) Zen predecessor of Yasutani, founder of the Sanbo Kyodan.

and polite, perhaps to a fault, laying himself open to a harsh response from Kubota.

Yasutani's approach in teaching was strongly focused on kensho, and it's clear that Kubota had that bent. He replied to Aitken that although a student's initial opening may be weak, kensho is the beginning, the intermediate and the last goal of Zen. He hoped that Aitken continued to challenge and deepen his experience of enlightenment through continued practice and teaching. Aitken wrote back in agreement, but quoted Yasutani saying that kensho is like rubbing a clear place in a piece of frosted glass: "You peek through that aperture, and there is Buddha nature all right, but you need to clear up the whole piece, and possibly push it out." He cautioned that too glorious a promise about kensho can lead to disillusionment, even among very good students.

In all this, the focus of the exchange was entirely on practice and dharma views. Although Aitken was well aware that Kubota was the senior leader of the Sanbo Kyodan in Japan after Yamada Ko'un himself, he did not tell Kubota about the dharma transmissions, nor did he mention the issue of succession that so preoccupied the Western students of Yamada Ko'un. It was a period of intense activity among Aitken and his dharma heirs as they were preparing the four transmission ceremonies, yet Aitken said not a word about this. Only when the fourth transmission was complete — indeed, the very next day after Nelson Foster's transmission ceremony — Aitken wrote to Kubota with the news.

In his letter, Aitken expressed heaviness of heart at news that Yamada Ko'un was not responding to treatment, then said, "You are the successor of Yamada Roshi, so I want to share with you (and at your discretion with other leaders) some matters that are important to me at this crucial time in the life of the Sanbo Kyodan, and of the Diamond Sangha.

"Although the Sanbo Kyodan does not hear very much from us, we regard ourselves an intimate part of its organization and tradition. ... Our brochure and other publicity materials set forth this position clearly..." He goes on to introduce each of the four successors, saying among other things, that all four are unusually clear and of exemplary character. Of Pat, he explains that Pat studied with both himself and Willigis Jäger and that he is a Catholic priest. He says, "Patrick Hawk remains a Catholic priest and some of his retreats are contemplative and Catholic in name. However, the content of his teaching is consistently the Buddha Dharma, and many of his retreats are traditional sesshin."[284] It's not clear whether Aitken misunderstood Pat's limited experience to that point or whether he was deliberately downplaying it to Kubota. In fact, the Koko An sesshin of September 1989, still two months in the future, would be the first that Pat led.

Aitken was seeking an acknowledgment from Kubota of his new successors as being in the Sanbo Kyodan lineage, explaining that the transmissions recently made official were within the Diamond Sangha and not the Sanbo Kyodan, but that this was not because he lacked authority to give transmission within the Sanbo Kyodan lineage. As a documented "Authentic Zen Master" (*Shoshike*) holding the *Sanmotsu* with Yamada [Ko'un] Roshi's signature and seal, Aitken was authorized. He explained that he held back from declaring his successors to be in the Sanbo Kyodan lineage because he had not discussed the matter with Yamada Ko'un and because the three essential papers documenting transmission, the *Sanmotsu*, that he received from Yamada could not be replicated exactly since so far, Aitken had been unable to get them translated.

Aitken went on to express concern about European teachers who were mixing Zen and Christianity "in seemingly inappropriate ways," that this risked giving a bad name to others in Europe who were very good teachers. Among the latter, he included Willigis Jäger as well as Joan Rieck and AMA Samy — Jesuit priest and student of Willigis Jäger who was living at Haus St. Benedikt when Pat was there. Aitken closed with an aspiration toward mutual cooperation: "Diamond Sangha teachers too, are doing their best to live up to the high standards of the San'un Masters[285] and their ancestors. It is my hope that in this time of change we might all of us — in Japan and in the West — be looking for ways by which we can acknowledge one another and fulfill harmoniously the Dharma of our great teachers." The status of the Diamond Sangha in relation to the Sanbo Kyodan became a question wrestled with for the next five years.

Kubota replied with further news of Yamada Ko'un's health — he was a little better but still in no condition to discuss "such difficult matters as you raised" — and with a message about authority likely to have raised Aitken's blood pressure. He acknowledged that Aitken was an official successor of the Sanbo Kyodan and therefore qualified to name successors within the Diamond Sangha, but explained that they cannot be considered successors of the Sanbo Kyodan because "these four people are not acknowledged or sanctioned by Authentic Zen Master of Sanbo Kyodan." In the same letter, he went on to say rather confusingly, "By the way you are now *Shoshike* of the Sanbo Kyodan and qualified to give your disciples the sanction as your successor."[286] Aitken wrote for clarification:

> You say in your letter: "It is not appropriate to give [the four disciples] Dharma succession of the Sanbo Kyodan because these four people are not acknowledged or sanctioned by an Authentic Zen Master of the Sanbo Kyodan." … Now, as I say, for the reasons I outlined in my July 12 [1989] letter, I do not feel it proper to transmit the Dharma to these four new teachers

> under the name of the Sanbo Kyodan. However, my reasons do not include anything relating to my own status. If I am a *Shoshike* of the Sanbo Kyodan, then wouldn't it be correct to say in English that I am an Authentic Zen Master of the Sanbo Kyodan? Assuming that this is the correct translation, then I would suppose that if my status were the factor involved, then I might justifiably use the name.[287]

In this correspondence, Aitken was always conciliatory. He finished with, "It is my earnest wish to be in full and complete communication with you and other senior members so that we can have a complete understanding among us in our mutual task of fulfilling our dear teacher's vows. I am very grateful to you for your careful response to my letter. I hope very much we can be the best of friends as we carry our demanding work together." Kubota replied that although Aitken was a *Shoshike* and therefore Authentic Zen Master of the Sanbo Kyodan, Yamada Ko'un, before he became ill, had said he wished to set up a requirement that successors of overseas *Junshike*[288] and *Shoshike* be confirmed by Yamada himself before they can be sanctioned as Dharma successors of the Sanbo Kyodan. In other words, although Kubota and Aitken are technically equal as having been made *Shoshike*, Aitken as a non-Japanese is to be accorded lesser authority.

Aitken's next letter to Kubota, dated September 22, 1989, was one of condolence at Yamada Ko'un's death, quickly followed by a letter saying Aitken would be coming to a meeting of Sanbo Kyodan senior members in early October. He enclosed a letter from Willigis Jäger laying out the plight of the Northern European teachers. Aitken argued that the future of koan study in the west lay largely with the Sanbo Kyodan teachers, and as the only Western successor of the Sanbo Kyodan he, Aitken, felt a special responsibility. "I agree with Fr. Willigis that the continuation of our line will be difficult unless there is a clear unbroken line and a clear expression of trust from the Japanese Sanbo Kyodan to us in the West."[289]

A meeting of senior members of the Sanbo Kyodan was convened in Kamakura in early October 1989. Most of the attendees were Japanese, and much of the business was conducted in Japanese which Aitken could follow only with difficulty. He reported back to Jäger on what he had understood: that Kubota would be the new Abbot, that his term would be for five years, and — most disappointing for the European teachers — there would be no *Inka* or *Sanmotsu* forthcoming. Their future was to be left undecided while Kubota and Yamada Masamichi, Yamada Ko'un's son, gathered more information about them.

Jäger wrote back to Aitken:

> On the one hand, *Inka* and *Sanmotsu* mean very little to me; on the other hand, we shouldn't start a new Sangha without a direct succession. ... Did Yamada Roshi, have any kind of trouble with the Rinzai* or Soto† lines while he was still a layman? Is that why he became so cautious? If so, that would be one more good reason to break away from this dictatorial monks' den. Power struggles seem to be restricted not only to the Catholic Church![290]

As Willigis Jäger's letter traveled over the Pole from Germany to Honolulu, a letter from Aitken to Kubota made its way over the Pacific to Japan. Aitken had changed his mind about excluding any of the European teachers. For one thing, Joan Rieck, who had picked him up at the airport and brought him to Kamakura for the October meeting, corrected his impression that only a few of the European teachers were using koans. And more significantly, Aitken's work on a memorial appreciation of Yamada Ko'un recalled to him Yamada's great generosity of spirit in such matters.

Aitken expressed the importance of clear succession: "Sangha members need to feel that their new teacher is trusted by his master. Otherwise doubts will rise to their minds, and their practice will be impeded. The entire line of succession can be brought into question." He again acknowledged Yamada Ko'un's expressions of doubt in some teachers, as published in *Kyosho*, saying, "It is not clear to me why this came to his pen," and he suggested that, while recognizing that some of the foreign teachers might be better than others, they also accept that Yamada's empowerment of the teachers was an accomplished fact and that rather than try to reverse this they would do better to exert themselves in support of all the teachers, that they might reach their full potential. "We can do this by using the same *hoben*‡ that our Roshi used in his actual practice with his successors: to express full confidence in them at every turn." He reminded Kubota of the oft-quoted speculation of Yamada Ko'un, that Zen would become an important stream in the Catholic Church and, retracting his earlier suggestion that anyone mixing religions should be excluded, instead thought all should be supported. "If this effort is not 100% successful, well, the failures will die out naturally."[291]

Kubota's reply took a blunter tone. In response to Aitken's implied question about Yamada Ko'un's doubts, he said, "I know Yamada Roshi was very sad

---

* Rinzai Zen, one of the two major schools of Zen that have taken root in the West (the other is Soto Zen), characterized by strong focus on Kenshō and subsequent extended koan study to deepen realization.

† Soto Zen, one of the two major schools of Zen that have taken root in the West (the other is Rinzai Zen) emphasizes *shikantaza* or silent meditation with no thought object.

‡ Hoben: (Japanese) Skillful means; a device tailored to the particular individual to help attain understanding; in Sanskrit, *upaya*.

when he checked and found before his illness [that] the disciples who were allowed kensho by foreign Zen teachers had nothing to do with kensho at all. He deplored at that time that false Zen was prevailing all over the world."[292] Kubota made the rather sweeping statement that almost all foreign teachers think koan study is Zen itself and said that one's skill in handling koans has nothing to do with real Zen if you do not grasp your True Nature and live life without fear. He felt all people practicing Zen should continue 30 years more practice until even the consciousness of enlightenment is wiped out. He was not confident he could persuade all foreign teachers to do this and asked Aitken's help, then closed saying he would need another six months to decide what to do about the foreign teachers.

In his reply, Aitken described his own transmission from Yamada Ko'un and how important the event was to him and to his students:

> It was a rite of passage for me. It was an experience that differed from Jukai, when I simply acknowledged that I was the Buddha's disciple. Yamada Roshi himself felt the importance of the transmission ceremony. When he arrived from Japan on one occasion, I helped him carry his bags to his room at Koko An, and he asked me to wait a moment. Opening one of his bags, he took out a little document and handed it over to me, saying, "Here, this is for you." It was my *Shoshike* certificate. In other words, for the presentation of that certificate there was no ceremony at all, and there were no witnesses. However, the transmission ceremony, which he planned with me, was very different. It was a special meeting at the Koko An Zendo,* crowded with members and friends. It consisted of sutras, my teisho, a *hosen*† ceremony, and then finally words of approval from the Roshi and presentation of documents and gifts. It was a profoundly moving time for everyone. All members felt empowered. I felt empowered.[293]

Having shared the correspondence with his dharma heirs and gathered their responses, Aitken told Kubota:

> Three of my four successors declare that they are quite content that their lineage document simply shows that they are Diamond Sangha Masters. The fourth successor feels strongly that we should not break the line, and that he would want to have his document show that he is a Sanbo Kyodan master (*Shoshike*), with no break in the lineage between Sanbo Kyodan and Diamond Sangha. I tend to agree with him, though I have not said so in public.

---

* Koko An Zendo was the main home of the Honolulu Diamond Sangha at the time — 1985.

† Hosen: (Japanese) Dharma encounter testing insight.

> I feel that in the future it will be very important for the genuine Master also to have unquestionable documentation.
>
> I would hope that whatever procedures we decide to follow in the Sanbo Kyodan regarding the empowerment of teachers, that this will include *Sanmotsu* for the worthy ones. Once these worthy ones are in place, then our task will be to give them and their Sanghas support. This, it seems to me, is the way transmission has functioned down through the ages.
>
> I would hope you and Yamada Masamichi Roshi might reach European teachers soon so that they might have a sense of where they stand. I know that you and the other leaders of the Sanbo Kyodan are approaching this matter of foreign teachers conscientiously with Yamada [Ko'un] Roshi's deep concerns in the forefront of your minds. I join with you in this noble work and am grateful to be a part of it.[294]

Kubota replied: "Ko'un Roshi experienced lots of deeper enlightenments during his illness in bed and confessed to Mrs. Yamada that he would like to convey the world of his experience to all disciples, and in addition he would like to sit, sit and sit after the recovery of his health." From this, he makes a leap to, "I understand this means Ko'un Roshi would like to deny everything that he had done before his passing and would like to lead all disciples to the perfect realization equivalent to his own last experience."[295] Of course, if the authorizations given by Yamada Ko'un Roshi before his death were indeed treated as invalid after the fact, this would call into question the status of Sanbo Kyodan teachers generally, including Yamada Masamichi and possibly even Kubota, whose authorization from Yasutani was later affirmed by Yamada Ko'un.

Even as Kubota held back from giving transmission to the senior European teachers, he downplayed its significance: "The final aim of all disciples of Ko'un Roshi should find out their True Nature completely and become one with their daily life. Any papers are only tools to show if he has reached to this state of mind or not. If he has a complete enlightenment, he does not care of the existence of paper at all and any papers work well. If he is not confident in his enlightenment, any papers are useless." Therefore, he felt all disciples of Yamada Ko'un should restart their practice and become humble enough to have their *satori** confirmed.

Aitken was dharma brother of Kubota and senior to Yamada Masamichi (who, although sanctioned by his father, Yamada Ko'un, would not be elevated to *Shoshike* status until 1991) — how could he accept that they should set themselves as judge of his students over and against his own judgment?

---

* Satori: (Japanese) Awakening, realization, enlightenment; related in meaning to kensho, satori generally refers to a more profound and far-reaching experience.

As the Sanbo Kyodan story was gathering steam, Aitken and his newly transmitted teachers gathered[296] in the first of what would become regular meetings of Diamond Sangha teachers, to trade stories and provide mutual support. They met at the home of Blanche Hartmann in Marin County, north of San Francisco. It was a reasonably central location for them, except for Augusto Alcalde in Argentina. John Tarrant and Nelson Foster came from California, Aitken from Hawaii and Pat Hawk from Amarillo. The meeting was casual. Anne Aitken traveled with her husband as she often did and attended some of the discussions. In a photograph, she is sitting among the men, all four with beards, Aitken's well on the way to white.

They considered the Sanbo Kyodan situation, both their own status as transmitted teachers and the plight of the European teachers. Aitken shared his communications with Kubota Roshi and with Willigis Jäger. They settled on patience as an approach. "See what comes." An earlier suggestion to the Japanese teachers from Aitken that there be an English version of *Kyosho* morphed into the idea of a newsletter for the Western Zen students of Yamada Ko'un, including the Europeans and the Diamond Sangha teachers. They gave Pat the task of corresponding with the Europeans. For one, he'd met them during his year in Germany. And as a Catholic cleric himself, he seemed the logical choice.

In a letter to Aitken after the meeting, Pat expressed sympathy for Kubota's position, writing somewhat cryptically, "I appreciate Kubota Roshi's point of view in this matter. He seems to have taken the high road. If the Japanese elders can also appreciate that there is no high road without the low road, maybe we can all be on our way." Nonetheless, he made his personal opinion clear, saying, "...your USA successors feel no need for sanction from Japan. Your stature is such that the document you gave us is completely acceptable to our students and the Zen Sanghas in this country and Australia. There is quite a different situation in Europe where they are dependent on Sanbo Kyodan for sanction."[297] This was because there were no *Shoshike*/Authentic Zen masters in Europe — not counting Brigitte D'Ortschy, dharma heir of Yasutani, who had set herself apart and alienated the others.

As he had been delegated to do, Pat generated a proposal for a newsletter: "[It] would consist of a couple of lead articles by teachers from around the world that trace their line through Sanbo Kyodan and then news from all the groups. We would rotate the responsibility for compiling, editing, printing and distributing the letter among the Diamond Sangha masters to begin with. The purpose of this newsletter would be to give the Europeans and ourselves a sense that we are not isolated because all belong to a worldwide group and established line of Zen. Thus there would be support and encouragement while the Japanese elders try to figure out what they want to do." He sent the proposal to Willigis Jäger and Joan Rieck.

In his reply, Willigis invited Pat to attend the 1990 Easter meeting of European Sanbo Kyodan teachers to be held at Haus St. Benedikt in Würzburg. Pat had attended the meeting five years earlier while he was a student of Willigis, during his year in Germany. Thereafter it became an annual meeting of the Europeans whom the late Yamada Ko'un had authorized to teach. Pat decided to go. He took detailed notes for the folks back home.[298]

The meeting was attended by several of the European teachers appointed by Yamada Ko'un including Willigis Jäger, Joan Rieck, Niklaus Brantschen, Gundala Meyer, Johannes Kopp and Peter Lengsfeld. Yamada Masamichi presided. The stated purpose was for Yamada Masamichi to promote true Zen according to his father, Yamada Ko'un, to understand what the different leaders were doing, what problems they had, what kind of support was needed, and how to coordinate the European, American and Japanese teachers.

The Europeans raised many questions: Who actually has been given *Inka* by Yamada Ko'un? If someone asks to become a member of the Sanbo Kyodan, how is this done? Can the European students of these leaders participate in sesshin at Kamakura? Do the teachers need to do Jukai? Do people made teachers by the European leaders have to go to Japan for confirmation? What status do the European teachers have? Can we confirm kensho in our students? Lead people through koans?

Masamichi said that only teachers with *Junshike* and *Shoshike* status could confirm kensho.* Since none of the attending teachers had been given *Junshike* or *Shoshike* status, this raised more questions. Do all students have to go to Japan for confirmation of kensho? How are more teachers to be confirmed in Europe? What if they can't get to Japan? What about transmission for European teachers? Who is training and giving dokusan in Sanbo Kyodan at Kamakura? How can we improve contact with all groups who trace their line through Sanbo Kyodan? Masamichi said, "This is a big problem."[299]

There was speculation among the Europeans about the source of Yamada Ko'un's expressed doubts — that he had checked teachers and not been able to confirm kensho, that there was a lack of personalization of Zen, that there were quarrels among teachers, that teachers' egos were apparent. Some of Yamada Ko'un's impressions had been based on hearsay. Brigitte D'Ortschy, the only western teacher besides Aitken with full transmission in the Sanbo Kyodan line,

---

* Yamada Masamichi himself had only *Junshike* status at this point.

was critical of her fellow Europeans and had relayed her criticism to Yamada Ko'un. Although she had little contact with them and, they felt, didn't know what they were doing, he had taken the criticism seriously. Masamichi asked why there wasn't more communication between D'Ortschy Roshi and the other teachers. They said it was because she was rigid and uncompromising — a stance which perhaps weighed in D'Ortschy's favor with the Japanese leaders at the time.

Yamada Masamichi conveyed a message from Kubota with the same themes Kubota had written to Aitken: doubts about kensho, problems of false teachers, the mistaken idea that koans are everything when, in fact, they are simply a tool, enlightenment being central, the need for all students and teachers to do 30 more years of practice, lastly that they would need six months to settle matters. He proposed that in order to keep in touch and to preserve the quality of Zen teaching, once a year everyone should come to Kamakura and have a teacher sesshin. They would have dokusan, discuss problems, discuss how they treat students, and mutually improve each other's teaching. They asked if Kubota could come to Europe instead. Masamichi suggested that at least the first time all should come to Japan, then perhaps Kubota could come to Europe. He also expected that any student of the European teachers must come to Japan to have kensho confirmed. After more discussion, Masamichi yielded, saying since it wouldn't always be possible for students to go to Japan right away, the foreign teachers could confirm kensho provisionally, but at some point it must be checked by Kubota.

Among the European teachers, most of whom were clerics or former clerics of the Catholic Church, there were still the differences in approach that had thrown sparks when Pat had been with them five years earlier. Argument broke out about Christian Zen. Someone said bluntly that the idea of Christian Zen is nonsense, others made the point that Zen is profoundly religious, distinguishing religious from religion; still others argued for the value of integrating the Christian framework with Zen practice and worldview. Yamada Masamichi intervened, saying he was unconcerned about forms, that the essential was to be strict about real enlightenment. He came back to this point a few times. Pat wrote, "So Masamichi understands, but whether Kubota will remains to be seen."

Yamada Masamichi ended the meeting saying that there would be *Shike* in Europe who could approve kensho, but first everyone had to attend sesshin with Kubota. He said, "If you have some problem, we are flexible and happy to listen. You have been teaching a long time and want more independence. Please communicate with me." As Masamichi was getting ready to leave, he invited Pat — who was ironically the only confirmed Zen Master (*Shoshike*) present, having been given transmission by Aitken in 1989 — to join an international teachers' sesshin in Kamakura in November.

Following Yamada Masamichi's departure, the Europeans debriefed. Overall, they thought the meeting had gone well. The prospects seemed good that they would be recognized and have some independence in due course. They appreciated what they saw as young energy in Masamichi, that he listened, and that he was open to change. They felt that although old members were still in charge in Kamakura, something was emerging. There was a sense that perhaps Kubota was simply holding the Abbot position until Masamichi would be elevated to *Shoshike* and take over. They discussed a proposed newsletter and solicited articles, book reviews, etc., to be sent to Pat.

Once back in Japan, Kubota sent Aitken a personal invitation to the November Kamakura teachers' meeting. Aitken planned to attend but warned that his health was precarious. Noting that Masamichi had invited Pat, he wondered if an invitation would be forthcoming to his other three dharma heirs, and he sent Kubota their addresses.[300] To this Kubota replied that only teachers appointed by Yamada Ko'un were invited and that it would not be appropriate for Aitken's successors to come, including Pat. Aitken then begged off for health reasons. He told Kubota that Pat was planning to come based on a clear invitation from Masamichi and that Kubota should write to him directly and explain that he was not to come. Kubota relented, suggesting that Aitken come with Pat as his attendant, or failing that, that Pat come as his representative.

Diamond Sangha Teachers

The Diamond Sangha teachers decided to meet again within the year, on a weekend in June. Over that winter of 1989-90, Aitken had appointed Joe Bobrow, a clinical psychologist and longtime student, as apprentice teacher, hence he was also included. They went back to Marin County, this time to meet at Yvonne Rand and Bill Sterling's place. It was a long and expensive way from Argentina, and once again Augusto couldn't come. So it was Robert Aitken, Pat Hawk, Nelson Foster, John Tarrant and Joe Bobrow.

Themes on the agenda[301] would recur in future meetings: Sangha "Weather Reports," talk of how their senior students were doing, concern about students who have genuine experience but don't relate to koan work; organization, if any, for the greater Diamond Sangha, now disseminated widely beyond Honolulu; protocol for students going to other teachers; the transference in teacher-student relationships, both its value and how to handle it; and as an all-male group of teachers, how to relate to women students, women's ways of knowing and special needs that female students might have. Later, in preparation for the third teachers' meeting, Aitken would invite Joan Rieck saying, "Besides, we have a 100% male roster and need you to ameliorate our locker room atmosphere."[302]

Pat was recorder at the June meeting, his sometimes cryptic notes punctuated with elaborate doodles. Regarding transference, Aitken said, "When I see it, I poke fun at myself, tell stories that reveal my weakness, humanity. Try not to let them get away with it. Don't give me a face that is not my own." Someone suggested one should watch the moment when a student shows the transference, and not destroy it completely; that a good transference can carry a student right through. Another said he blocks the transference early on and wondered if that means he blocks a student's practice. Aitken replied that the transference goes through a natural cycle and that one does not have to do that much. He said to at least be light so that it is hardly even noticed. He liked the idea, apparently suggested earlier by Augusto, that there be something about it in the *shoken* agreement — this is what you're getting into.

Pat reported on the Easter meeting of the European Sanbo Kyodan teachers with Yamada Masamichi. Of immediate concern was the plight of Rolf Drosten, a student of Willigis Jäger who Willigis felt was ready for transmission. Since Willigis himself did not have full transmission, he could not give it to Drosten. He was exploring whether it was something Aitken would do. Aitken had examined Drosten and found him clear. However, at the time, Spring 1990, his sense was that he could not do it, partly because he had not worked extensively with Drosten, also because he, Aitken, was still hoping that the Sanbo Kyodan would recognize his four dharma heirs. did not want to disturb those waters any more than necessary.

Aitken was working both sides — continuing negotiations with the Japanese leaders of the Sanbo Kyodan for acknowledgment of his heirs within the lineage, at the same time supporting his heirs in their reluctance (or refusal) to be vetted by the Japanese leaders, even if it meant splitting off from the Sanbo Kyodan. Pat noted, "People at teachers' meeting don't care to go to Kamakura to get checked. RA [Robert Aitken] will accept proposal that DS [Diamond Sangha] will be independent school separate from SK [Sanbo Kyodan]."

During their three-day meeting, the Diamond Sangha teachers spent about an hour each afternoon doing koan review, taking turns facilitating. Proposed for review at that meeting were the *Mu* and the *Sound of One Hand* checking questions, the Introductory Koans, the *Mumonkan* koans, and the *Five Modes of Dongshan*.* As the meeting wore on Pat's notes got more and more sketchy, the doodles more

---

* The Five Modes (or Ranks) is a poem written by the Chinese Zen monk, Dongshan (Tozan), describing the stages of realization. Late in the Sanbo Kyodan koan curriculum, the modes are studied one by one as koans.

and more elaborate, at the end becoming a few words on a page chock full of random designs.

First visit to Japan

Pat prepared to go to the Kamakura meeting of Sanbo Kyodan teachers in November 1990. Aitken, in consideration of precarious health and feeling Pat could adequately represent him, decided he would not go. Kubota sent out an agenda for the meeting, which Aitken passed along to Pat:

> A. How to keep the purity of Zen and Zen Practice which Yamada Ko'un Roshi taught us and asked us to succeed.
> B. What is the process and conditions to acknowledge Zen Teachers as *Junshike* (Associate Zen Master) or *Shoshike* (Authentic Zen Master) of Sanbo Kyodan.
> C. How to find out the practical solution to the problem of confirming Kenshos by Zen Teachers in the world.
> D. How to deal with the people who have finished all Koans at the Zendo of Zen Teachers in the world.
> E. How to set up the financial foundation of Sanbo Kyodan (Until now most expenses have been supported by private donation by Yamada Roshi and his wife).[303]

Aitken began preparing Pat for the meeting, expecting him to push the case for having the Sanbo Kyodan leadership recognize Aitken's status as an independent master in the Sanbo Kyodan line, authorized to name his own successors in that line. Aitken sought the help of Jim Camp and Julian Gresser, both acknowledged experts on negotiations with the Japanese, although in the business realm. The latter had published an article on the subject,[304] which Aitken sent to Pat in September with a cover letter explaining: "I also enclose Julian Gresser's 'Mastering Negotiations with the Japanese.' I think we can learn from him. His main points are: (1) We should be clear about what we want. (2) We should place our friends at the Sanbo Kyodan in a position where they face the consequences of saying 'No.' They want to languish in a 'Maybe,' and that won't do. Specifically, they will need to visualize the consequences of cutting the transmission." The article and cover letter were copied to Joan Rieck, who was also attending the meeting.

There were two long conference calls during the week before Pat left for Kamakura. The agenda for these calls was to delineate Aitken's demands — not too strong a word given the tone of the conversations — and to establish a blow-by-blow plan for Pat's meeting with the Sanbo Kyodan elders. The professional negotiators stressed that without both these aspects being clearly articulated, the mission would fail. They helped Aitken produce a "critical list of five things for Father Hawk to accomplish in Japan:"

> 1. Have them become decent in their attitude toward me & others, not treat us like bums.
> 2. Acknowledge problems in objective way; [develop a] program and agenda for resolving them together
> 3. Accept their own responsibility as the center of a significant international movement.
> 4. Keep lines of communication open at all times.
> 5. Cultivate an attitude of trust in keeping with Yamada [Ko'un]'s spirit and mind.[305]

The negotiators gave some general tips:

> - People buy ideas because that idea or thought takes away their pain.
> - If you do not have a clear picture of what you want line for line, you will fail.
> - If they do not have a clear picture of the havoc they could create — They will make no decisions in your favor unless they have a clear picture of the pain they will inflict.
> - Make them so upset they can't sleep at night.[306]

Based on the first call, Aitken wrote out "What I Want from This Meeting." He read it over the phone during the second call. Pat's notes on the conference call reveal a language and stance that is remarkably aggressive given Aitken's usual diplomacy. It speaks to the visceral significance of lineage in Aitken's psyche, with all its implications of validation and empowerment. Aitken's list included:

> 1. I want the leaders of the Sanbo Kyodan to accept the fact that many Westerners were authorized by Yamada Ko'un Roshi to teach in his tradition and to make the very best of this fact with a broad and generous spirit.
> 2. I want the leaders of the Sanbo Kyodan to announce in Kyosho their unqualified support of my successors, and of me, as Authentic Masters of the Sanbo Kyodan. [307]

It went on to four more points with detailed suggestions about structure of the Sanbo Kyodan, programs to support teachers, and the offer that Aitken and his successors would help with these enterprises.

Negotiator Jim Camp advised Aitken that his list was too long and the tone too conciliatory. He further suggested all points be presented as questions. The result was seven questions, somewhat repetitive, more emotion-laden than Aitken's original points and stripped of practical suggestions:

1. Why do I, Robert Aitken, feel the spirit of Ko'un Yamada Roshi's dream is dying?
2. Why do I feel that the great tree which would shade all beings is losing its leaves and dying?
3. Why do I feel a dam is being built in the stream of Zen making it impossible to flow through to the Catholic Church?
4. Why do I feel that Ko'un Yamada Roshi's great compassion and tolerance of all beings is being lost here at Sanbo Kyodan?
5. Why do we feel you are so suddenly today destroying the teachings of the Three Clouds Dai'un Harada, Haku'un Yasutani, Ko'un Yamada?*
6. What is your understanding of Ko'un Yamada Roshi's dream and vision?
7. What do you want me to do?[308]

Some further questions raised in discussion that did not make the final cut were, "Is Kamakura racist? Would you dare challenge if I were Japanese? Why do you believe that a foreigner can't follow the path of Zen as well as a Japanese? Why do we feel that Yamada [Ko'un] Roshi's tolerance is completely lost?"

The negotiators gave some additional tips, including, "Ask the question three times, using the same tone of voice each time, no matter what the response." The discussion of strategy centered on the Julian Gresser article. Pat typed a summary from his notes, using the main points from the article as headings [capitalization Pat's]:

> WHAT IS OUR MISSION AND PURPOSE?
> Robert Aitken wishes to have a cordial acknowledgment that he is a qualified Master and can pass on the Sanbo Kyodan transmission.
>
> WHO ARE THE DECISION MAKERS?
>
> NO CHILD, NO EMOTIONS.
> It's nice to be liked, but it's more important that the American side is reliable, trustworthy and not a source of embarrassment. Focusing on the adversary's world requires intense concentration and a detachment of mind. No fear of failure.

---

* The Three Clouds refers to the three Zen ancestors in the Sanbo Kyodan lineage: Harada gave transmission to Yasutani who in turn gave transmission to Yamada Ko'un.

> PRODIGIOUS PREPARATION. NO ASSUMPTIONS.
>
> JAPANESE APPROACH IS GUIDED BY CONSENSUS. LOGJAM IF NO CONSENSUS.
>
> HELP THEM DISCOVER THE CONSEQUENCES OF THEIR ACTIONS.
> Put adversary in pain.
>
> JAPANESE PROTECT THEIR DECISION MAKER AND EXPOSE YOURS. REVERSE THIS PROCESS.
>
> QUALITY CONTROL. WHO DECIDES. BY WHAT CRITERIA.
>
> KEEP ASKING QUESTIONS:
> Is Yamada's life work valid?
> Is Zen valid, if so, why are we contradicting ourselves?
> If we don't do what we teach then are we not invalid?
> Why do we dismantle the work of Yamada and Aitken?
>
> STRESS DISCOVERY OF THEIR WORLD PICTURE.
> Where are they, what are they doing, who are they with?
>
> BE RESPECTFUL. NEVER LET YOUR GUARD DOWN.
> They are going to try to befuddle you.
>
> KEEP FOCUSED. VERY SOFTLY.
>
> With their PICTURE WILL APPEAR THEIR AGENDA.
>
> No Telling JUST ASKING.
> If their intentions are to dismantle, then Aitken will go on his own. Or they may discover they are making a mistake.
> Keep them talking then you are in control, if you're listening. They will try to get you to talk. Ask more questions. If they break off, then go away. Then come back.[309]

Pat's instructions were to ask Joan to arrange the meeting, explaining that she was to give nothing away regarding content of the meeting and show no emotion, simply call people together — Kubota, Masamichi and Yamada Ko'un's widow, Dr. Kazue Yamada — to a meeting with Aitken's representative. Pat wrote down this instruction. Next he wrote,

Quietly
Then WATCH

And next to this in small letters:

when shit hits fan

In case Joan was unavailable to bring the principals together, Pat was to call Aitken and ask him to send a telegram, the suggested text of which was to be, "My representative will arrive to discuss the future, please meet with him immediately." In case of difficulty, Pat was given complete contact information for negotiators Jim Camp and Julian Gresser.

The Gresser article was written for the business world. Both negotiators were business-oriented. In fact, Gresser admired the Japanese approach and wrote a book later with the theme of teaching Americans to approach business negotiating more like the Japanese.[310] However, translated into the world of Zen, it comes across as adversarial. It's hard to fathom how Pat, so given to conflict avoidance, could consent to be a player in this strategy. Bob Walker happened to be outside Pat's office when he emerged from one of these phone calls. Bob heard him say, "I am his equal."[311] Whose equal? Aitken's? Kubota's? Bob didn't ask.

Ironically, Pat's enmeshment in the conflict may have arisen from his conflict aversion. He could have tried harder to persuade Aitken away from struggling to preserve the lineage, but it was easier to let it go, and in any case, it was an impulse Pat surely respected. He could have argued against the strategies of the negotiation experts, their advice running so contrary to his natural instincts, but in the immediate present of the phone call, it was easier to acquiesce.

Pat arrived in Japan the same day as Joan Rieck, almost a week before the sesshin was to begin. It being Pat's first visit to that country and Joan having lived there for 18 years, they planned to do some sightseeing with Joan as tour guide. They went to Kyoto, visited temples, saw the Great Buddha of Kamakura. Pat took several film rolls of photos. Joan introduced him to friends of hers who, hearing it was Pat's birthday (his 48th), prepared a special meal and served them birthday cake, sitting on tatami.

Not surprisingly, Joan was appalled at the plan to meet with the Sanbo Kyodan leaders. She declined having anything to do with it. Thus, presumably Aitken sent the telegram. Somehow, the meeting was arranged. The report Pat sent Aitken afterward is lost, and when asked about it years later, he said he couldn't remember what happened.

Somehow Pat managed to present Aitken's concerns to the Sanbo Kyodan leaders with sufficient grace that there was no apparent rancor toward him at the teachers' sesshin. He attended with the others. The meeting was billed as, "The first foreign Zen Teachers Sesshin to commemorate one year after [Yamada] Ko'un Roshi passed away and to discuss the important matters on Zen Teaching of Sanbo Kyodan."[312] Topics included maintaining the purity of Zen; the process of confirming teachers; how to confirm kenshos that were confirmed by non-Japanese teachers; what to do with people who have finished the koan curriculum; how to set up a financial foundation for the Sanbo Kyodan.

Besides attending the discussion sessions, Pat worked happily on koans in dokusan with Kubota, who invited him back to Kamakura for the teachers' meeting two years later. There is no evident negative fallout toward Pat in the correspondence between Aitken and Kubota that followed.

It's clear that Pat conveyed the message to Kubota and Yamada Masamichi at least to some degree as planned, since Kubota wrote afterward to Aitken, quoting Aitken's first question — why does he think the spirit of Yamada Ko'un is dying. Kubota chided Aitken, asking in turn, "From when have you become so great a Zen Master in the world to judge and criticize the Zen spirit of Ko'un Roshi? Do you really understand the spirit of Ko'un Roshi?" He went on to say that no one, himself and Aitken included, is qualified to judge the spirit of Ko'un Roshi. Kubota reiterated his concern about maintaining the purity of Zen and concluded by saying he was confident that San'un Zendo was the most active and serious monastery in the world.[313]

The result of the meeting as far as the Diamond Sangha teachers were concerned was that, even though Aitken was *Shoshike* — Authentic Zen Master — of the Sanbo Kyodan, he could give transmission only within the Diamond Sangha. Only Kubota and Yamada Masamichi could give transmission within the Sanbo Kyodan.

Writing to Pat the following April (1991), Aitken said, "I hope you feel completed with your Kamakura excursion. I feel quite alright about the upshot as it continues to evolve. I'm very grateful to you for putting yourself on the line."[314] He reiterated this in a postcard handwritten and left for Pat on his arrival at the third Diamond Sangha Teachers' meeting the following month: "Just a note, Pat, to let you know how grateful I am for your work in Kamakura. We now have a clear picture of where they stand and they of us. Negotiations now can proceed. When you are settled, please call Nelson [Foster] and John [Tarrant] and give them your overview."[315]

Meanwhile, Willigis Jäger and others in Europe continued in limbo with regard to their authority to appoint teachers. Jäger wrote in frustration to Aitken that he had turned 66 and wanted to turn over teaching to senior students, but that the Japanese wouldn't allow it:

> When I was last in Hawaii you suggested that I return to get transmission from you to carry on the traditions of the Diamond Sangha in Germany in the Sanbo Kyodan. If you think this is okay, let me know. From the 1st October I could come to Hawaii for three or four weeks to study with you and to go over some koans and to talk to you about inculturation of Zen in the West. Maybe we can even have a meeting of some of your successors to talk over this matter. I think it is time to have our own thoughts about Zen in the West and not just to look to Japan.[316]

At the May teachers' meeting,[317] all four Aitken heirs once again agreed that they did not need sanction from Japan. John and Augusto both expressed strongly that they did not *want* approval from the Sanbo Kyodan teachers. Moreover, Augusto was emphatic about not approving any of the European teachers in the Diamond Sangha and thereby allowing entrée to Christian Zen. This in spite of the fact that he and Pat still shared a very cordial bond over cigarettes and good coffee.

Christian/Buddhist dynamics were a topic on the agenda, including the question of approving European teachers. Rolf Drosten and Pia Gyger, both students of Willigis Jäger, were being put forward to be approved as teachers in the Diamond Sangha, and Pia Gyger had begun coming over to work with Aitken with that in mind. Willigis and Joan Rieck were discussed as potential candidates for transmission within the Diamond Sangha, a move that would set aside the issue of Sanbo Kyodan transmission for those two European teachers. The name of Jack Duffy — a senior student in the Three Treasures Sangha, offshoot of the original Zen for Christians group — came up in the context of appointing new teachers, along with the usual topics: transference, sharing students and avoiding triangles when a student is working with two teachers, maintaining confidentiality, and a possible book of essays. Most topics were essentially a continuation of the discussion the previous year. There was some movement with regard to the European students of Willigis Jäger. Where previously, Aitken had been disinclined to consider Rolf and then Pia as Diamond Sangha teachers, he was now reconsidering, Augusto's position against Christian Zen teachers notwithstanding.

Manfred Steger was a new face at the meeting. He had been made an apprentice teacher by Aitken that January and was teaching at Koko An, not without conflict. He and his wife, Perle Besserman, both students of Aitken, were developing what they called a post-modernist Zen that did not include transmission as necessary for teaching authority. The approach was in their recently published book, *Crazy Clouds,*[318] which Aitken criticized. This and other friction with Aitken prompted Perle to leave and spend an extended period at Bishop DeFalco Retreat Center doing koans with Pat. She wrote about the BDRC experience in her book, *A New Zen for Women*:

> [Working with Manfred] opened me up to working with several different Diamond Sangha teachers, one of whom, Father Pat Hawk, a Catholic priest, became my main teacher for a while. I spent a month sitting with him at his retreat center in Texas working on koans with him in the morning and participating with the resident Catholic monks and nuns in some of their Buddhist/Christian services. That experience, too, offered an entirely new perspective on my Zen practice. I felt like I'd come out of a confined and stuffy closet into a vast open space and was at last breathing fresh air. The unfortunate side effect of the tonic these new teachers provided was that I no longer felt I could continue my koan practice with Aitken Roshi.[319]

On her return to Hawaii, Perle declined to have her koan work checked by Aitken. She told him Manfred would do the checking. There was heated exchange in person and in letters, and that summer Manfred resigned as a Diamond Sangha teacher. He and Perle left to establish their own Zen group in the Princeton, New Jersey area. The irony was surely not lost, that while the Kamakura leaders were struggling with Aitken to have him subject his transmissions to their approval, Manfred and Perle were declaring themselves free of any outside authority and striking out on their own.

Aitken's correspondence with the leaders of Sanbo Kyodan continued as before. Kubota insisted on having final approval of any teachers approved by Aitken — otherwise those teachers could not be considered Sanbo Kyodan. In a letter to Aitken, he claimed a precedent in tradition: "The relationship between Sanbo Kyodan and the Diamond Sangha … is equal to the relationship between *Honzan* (Main Temple) and the umbrella temples of any Buddhist school (Soto, Rinzai, etc.). … When his disciples get an enlightenment and wish to be affirmed as the successor of the sect, it is the common rule to come up to Honzan and get the Honzan's* confirmation as the successor of the sect (we call this *Zuise*)."[320] Aitken replied to Kubota:

> My one experience with Zuise in the Rinzai sect was when I accompanied Soen Roshi† to Kyoto for visits to Myoshinji and Myoshinji sub-temples, prior to his installation as Roshi of Ryutakuji in 1951. I was his attendant

---

* Abbot of the head temple.

† Nakagawa Soen (1907-1984), Zen master and abbot of Ryutaku-ji in Japan, as well as the New York Zendo and Dai Bosatsu Zendo in New York. One of the Japanese Zen teachers of Robert Aitken.

> and was with him at all times, and there was no *hosen*,* public or private; just an exchange of presents and tea ceremony wherever we went. I know also that Zuise in the Soto school is ceremonial, and nothing more. … At the recent meeting of Diamond Sangha teachers I offered the option to the teachers. The unanimous consensus was that it would be enjoyable to have *hosen* with you and others, but they did not feel comfortable about going to Kamakura if the purpose were an examination that they must pass in order to get a certificate. … They felt that this is a Japanese custom that cannot be found earlier in the Zen or Ch'an tradition. (Dogen Zenji's students did not go to China for confirmation — of course I am not Dogen!)[321]

Fresh from discussions with his Diamond Sangha dharma heirs at their meeting earlier in May, Aitken reported to Kubota that the teachers continued to feel they did not need approval from Kubota or anyone other than Aitken himself, a fully transmitted Zen Master. Aitken, like Kubota, was *Shoshike,* and as such Kubota had no greater authority. Aitken suggested that the one stream might split: "I confess that [the Diamond Sangha teachers'] decision disappoints me, for it seems that we are facing the option of becoming an independent school. I have always felt myself to be first and foremost a member of Sanbo Kyodan, and I still consider myself to be a member. I hope that we can work things out so that our two paths can be collegial and friendly. I am profoundly grateful to Yasutani Roshi and Yamada [Ko'un] Roshi, who saved my life, and to you and the other Sanbo Kyodan leaders who gave me encouragement over the years."

Aitken suggested in the same letter that the prize being dangled was not untainted: "Please understand that generally Japan has a mixed reputation among American Zen students. Although the Sanbo Kyodan has a pure name, and though two of my four successors themselves worked with Yamada [Ko'un] Roshi during his visits to the US, there is a distaste arising out of the outrageous scandals that have touched no fewer than six roshis from Japan. We all know that these scandals arise from the decadent state of Zen in Japan of which Yamada Roshi himself often spoke. Nonetheless there is a spillover of bad feeling that touches everything Japanese for the American Zen students. I deplore this, and recognize its illogicality, but there it is."

Aitken excused himself from the next Sanbo Kyodan meeting with the European teachers in Germany to attend a Buddhist Peace Fellowship meeting that was scheduled at the same time. He went on: "You see, I have close relations with a number of those teachers and feel that I should not be a factor in their thinking when they are working out transmission matters with you. I should stay out of

---

* Dharma encounter, dharma combat, testing the insight of a Zen teacher.

the way. Then your negotiations with them can be clean and unencumbered." Characteristically, Aitken was careful to leave the door ajar as he closed his letter: "This does not mean that I would not want to be part of such meetings in the future, after the negotiations are completed. I consider myself still to be very much a part of the Sanbo Kyodan, and to be loyal to you and to Yamada Ryo'un [Masamichi]."[322]

In case that was not clear, Aitken sent a short note to Kubota a few days later:

> On looking over the carbon of my letter to you of May 18 [1991], I am moved to clarify a couple of points. Though the present Diamond Sangha teachers and Junior Teachers have declined the opportunity to avail themselves of the Sanbo Kyodan succession under your terms, I want to leave open the option that they may at some future time change their minds and come to you for *hosen* and possible authorization, and also that any future Diamond Sangha teachers may do so. Also I hope that the Diamond Sangha itself will continue to be considered a part of the Sanbo Kyodan family, and that I will continue to receive invitations to the Sanbo Kyodan teachers' meetings.[323]

By August, Willigis Jäger had softened the suggestion made to Aitken in April that they consider a separate western stream of Zen that would include him and the other Europeans. He wrote to Aitken: "I think it was very wise of you not to confirm Drosten as a teacher of the Diamond Sangha. I would not do it in the near future with anyone from Europe. I think it is wise to leave Diamond Sangha in the US and to establish someday a European sangha. Mixing would surely produce troubles, misunderstanding and some kind of competition."[324] This change of heart may have been because at the August meeting of Sanbo Kyodan in Germany, Kubota and Yamada Masamichi had approved Drosten and Gyger (both students of Jäger) as assistant teachers in the Sanbo Kyodan, so it seemed that there was at last some movement on that front.

Willigis relayed the news that Masamichi had been elevated to *Shoshike* during the opening ceremony at Sonnenhof, Jäger and Rieck's new center for Zen and contemplative practice in the Black Forest region of Germany. At the same meeting, the Kamakura leaders presented what was to be the system of teacher authorization in Sanbo Kyodan: Assistant Teacher, *Sensei*, *Junshike*, *Shoshike*.* Willigis continued:

---

* In the Sanbo Kyodan these terms were delineated as follows: Sensei: Zen teacher; Junshike: Semi Zen master; Shoshike: Authentic Zen Master. Shoshike status implies full dharma transmission or *Inka*. A person with Shoshike status is recognized as an independent Zen master.

> As you know, they want to check all teachers of Sanbo Kyodan and grant them appropriate titles. The crucial point now is whether you should subject your teachers to this system. The danger is that we might get too much control and centralization — like in the Catholic Church where Rome wants to appoint and control every bishop. So, my recommendation is checking and transmission should be only on your side, but like in *Rinzai* and *Soto*, teachers may go to the main temple and get formal recognition by the head of, in this case, Sanbo Kyodan.[325]

In reply to a letter from Aitken, Kubota wrote the following January (1992), acknowledging with sympathy the need, because of age and health, for Aitken to name a successor. "If you proclaim the Diamond Sangha is in the stream of the Sanbo Kyodan, I think your successor should be granted at least as an Associate Zen Master of the Sanbo Kyodan itself just like you are granted as an Authentic Zen Master of the Kyodan by Yamada Ko'un Roshi." Kubota went on to invite the successors to the November 1992 teachers' sesshin in Kamakura, then said, "Yamada Ryo'un Roshi [Masamichi] and myself would like to check the depth of their enlightenment and discuss with you on the probabilities of appointing as your successor later on." He continued, "I do wish you appoint, as your formal successor of the Diamond Sangha, the man who would be agreed by Ryo'un Roshi and myself too."[326] Kubota wrote again a few weeks later, reiterating his position: the need to maintain the purity of Zen, the desire to check Aitken's successors, the impossibility of having them considered part of Sanbo Kyodan unless they are approved from Japan. To Aitken's citing Dogen for precedent, Kubota said, "I dare say we are not equivalent to Dogen Zenji and Dai-O Kokushi, so we are more and more modest and conservative to appoint our successors by cooperating with each other. If you or I misjudge on this point the fault exists on us but not on them. As my own responsibility as the Abbot of the Sanbo Kyodan, I would like to check and confirm at least the person who would be your successor in order to be faithful to Ko'un Roshi's will." To Aitken's suggestion that having been given full transmission by Yamada Ko'un in the Sanbo Kyodan, he is legally empowered to authorize teachers within the Sanbo Kyodan himself Kubota said, "As you mentioned, you are an 'Authentic Zen Master' approved by Ko'un Roshi, so you are quite free to appoint Zen Teachers of the Diamond Sangha and to decide the restructuring of the organization."[327]

Aitken thanked Kubota for the invitation to his successors to come to Japan for confirmation, and went on to explain:

> The four teachers, Foster, Tarrant, Patrick Hawk, and Augusto Alcalde, are my successors, masters in the lineage of the Diamond Sangha. They are

> teaching independently in their respective centers and have been doing so for several years. … There is the possibility that one of the three American teachers might move to Hawaii to take over that responsibility, but that would leave a vacancy at their own flourishing centers. I continue to work with students at Koko An, of course, but I don't see a potential teacher on the horizon at this time. I am hoping that a promising person might appear from our members, or somebody promising might show up, but the development of a teacher from such a point would be pretty far down the road.[328]

Aitken then reiterated the position of his dharma heirs — that he could legitimately give transmission within the Sanbo Kyodan — again referencing the historical precedent in Dogen:

> To be completely open with you, I must report that the teachers have expressed the feeling that since I am an 'Authentic Master of the Sanbo Kyodan,' I should be able to pass along the transmission to worthy successors. I have not done so, but legally, they suggest, I certainly can. After all, as I have heard it remarked, Dogen Zenji and Dai'o Kokushi did not send their successors back to China for confirmation. We will need to respond to this reasoning. … So, old friend, this is not an easy matter to deal with.[329]

Aitken relayed the invitation to the four teachers and encouraged them to accept. They continued to feel they did not need approval from Kubota or anyone other than Aitken himself, that Kubota had no greater authority than Aitken. Nonetheless, the idea of returning to Kamakura appealed to Pat. He wrote to Aitken, "If one or more of us does go to Japan for this Teachers' sesshin and by chance receives an approval as a Sanbo Kyodan Teacher — what does this say about your status in Sanbo Kyodan? I would not want to go if it brings more complications for you. Is there some cultural thing going on that I am missing?"[330] Aitken replied: "I think there is no problem about getting transmission from the Sanbo Kyodan via Kubota and Co. I am a Sanbo Kyodan master (*Shoshike*), after all. I am not bothered by these technical things."[331]

Above: Pat with his parents, Elnora (née Delmar) and Ed Hawk, circa 1943. The photo above was taken when Ed had a few days' leave while in the army.

Below left, Pat circa 1943. Below right: Pat with his sister Mary Ellen circa 1952. (Hawk family photo albums)

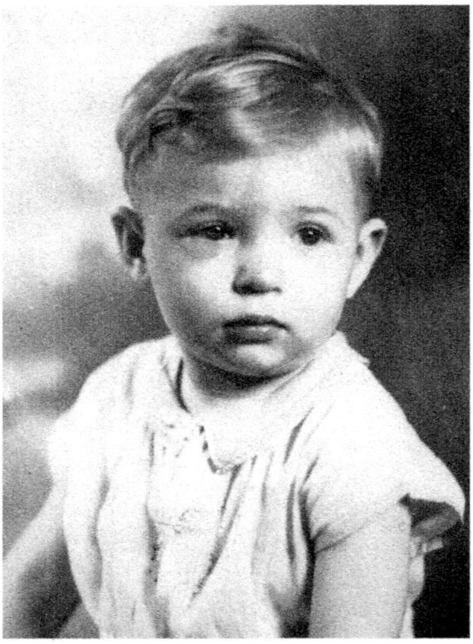

Pat, mid-1940s to early 1950s. Clockwise from above left: Pat, approximately 5th grade; with his cousin and best friend Nora Delmar. Altar boy. With his dog Rip.
(Hawk family photo albums)

Above: Sacred Heart School, Class of 1956; Pat is in the second row, second from right. (Hawk family albums)

Left: Eighth grade graduation dance; Pat is in the foreground with his back to the camera. (D. Betinec album)

Below: Sacred Heart School and Church. There were classrooms on either side of the central chapel.
(Photo by H. Amerongen of framed picture at Sacred Heart School)

Above L and R: Pat at St. Joseph's College Minor Seminary in Kirkwood, Missouri, 1957. (D. Betinec albums)

Left: Visiting home circa 1957. Elnora is sitting at Pat's right; Ed is in the background. (Hawk family albums)

Below: St. Joseph's College, Edgerton, Wisconsin, under construction. Lake Koshkonong is in the background. The minor seminary moved from Kirkwood, Missouri, to the new building in the Fall of 1957. (D. Betinec albums)

Above: The two Redemptorists who had the greatest influence on Pat's development. Left: Joe Bilsley. (Sant'Alfonso e dintorni website, July 2022.) Right: Kevin O'Shea. (*Redentoristi Scala*, May 2018.)

Below, left and right: At the end of the year of Novitiate, Pat professed temporary vows of poverty, chastity and obedience on August 2, 1963. (He professed perpetual vows in 1967.) (Left: Hawk family albums; Right: D. Betinec photo albums)

Patrick Hawk of Granite City to be ordained

The ordination of the Rev. Patrick Hawk, son of Mr. and Mrs. Edwin J. Hawk, 2620 Hodges Ave., Granite City, is scheduled at 9:30 a. m. next Friday at Holy Redeemer College in Waterford, Wis. The Most Rev. William E. Cousins, Archbishop of Milwaukee, will officiate.

Father Hawk will be ordained with 19 of his class to serve as a Redemptorist priest.

After attending Sacred Heart Elementary School in Granite City, Father Hawk entered the Redemptorist Seminary at Kirkwood, Mo., and later attended St. Joseph's College, Edgerton, Wis., before professing his vows on Aug. 2, 1962.

He received a bachelor of philosophy degree from Immaculate Conception Seminary, Oconomowoc, Wis., and a bachelor's degree in theology and a master degree in religious education from Mt. St. Alphonsus Seminary, Esopus, N. Y.

During the past three summers Father Hawk has worked in parishes in Chicago and Detroit. His first assignment will take him to St. Alphonsus (Rock) Church in St. Louis on July 13.

Father Hawk will concelebrate his first Solemn Mass at 3 p. m. June 29 at Sacred Heart Church, 2600 Washington Ave., Granite City.

Pat Hawk was ordained at Waterford, Wisconsin, June 27, 1969. Above: He said his first mass at his home parish of Sacred Heart in Granite City on June 29, 1969, concelebrating with eight of his confreres.

Below: With his parents, Ed, and Elnora and his sister, Mary Ellen following his first mass.
(Hawk family photo albums)

Above: First Zen Sesshin for Christians and other travelers. Robert Aitken is in the front row, slightly left of center, in a turtleneck. Abbot Bernard McVeigh is the leftmost person. Pat is the third person in a diagonal line to the right of and behind Bernard.
(Photo by H. Amerongen of framed picture at Bethany House, Our Lady of Guadalupe Abbey)

Below left: Abbot Bernard McVeigh with Robert Aitken. (Photo by H. Amerongen of framed picture at Bethany House, Our Lady of Guadalupe Abbey)

Below right: The sculpture of the shrouded Christ crucified. Aitken was very taken by the representation of a dead rather than a living Christ figure on the cross. (Pat Hawk photo albums)

Above: Pat at Guest House, 1979.

Above: Pat at Our Lady of Guadalupe Trappist Abbey during his residency there in 1981.
(Left and right: Pat Hawk photo albums)

Below: Palisades Retreat Center, overlooking Puget Sound. Pat was stationed at Palisades after his stay at Guest House, from September 1979 to December 1980.
(Photos by H. Amerongen)

(Pat Hawk photo albums.)

Pat in Germany August 1984 to August 1985.

Left: With Greg Mayers and Willigis Jäger at Haus St. Benedikt.

Middle: Out for a stroll with companions in the *Hausgemeinschaft* of Haus St. Benedikt.

Below: Postcard of St. Georgenberg Abbey on the edge of the Wolksklamm Gorge in the Tyrol.

Inset: The wooden footbridge that provides access to the monastery.

5

Branching Out

The Sanbo Kyodan drama was significant for Pat mainly in that it was important to so many he knew and cared about — Aitken of course, also Willigis Jäger, also friends among the European teachers, also Greg Mayers, who was at that time making regular trips from Amarillo to Germany to work with Jäger. However, it was far from the main focus of Pat's attention and energy even in the early 1990s when he was so closely involved.

Greg and Pat continued to grow the Contemplation program in Amarillo while also offering retreats in other parts of the country: the Pacific Northwest, California, Kansas, Ohio, Missouri. Greg was an important driving force for setting up retreats in Amarillo and elsewhere, and it's unlikely the program would have gotten off the ground without him. Unlike Pat, he was outgoing, easy to talk to in a social way, a natural conversationalist. He did the outreach and handling of requests for the two of them to lead retreats away from Amarillo. With Greg training intensively with Willigis, traveling to Germany for extended visits several times a year, he knew by personal experience the format, the language, the literature — the culture of practice — as well as Pat did, and for several years Pat and Greg ran most of the contemplative retreats together.

As 1990 began, Pat had committed to several retreats each for the Pacific Northwest group and for Zen Desert Sangha in Tucson, attendance at the Diamond Sangha teachers' meeting, a visit to his family, and visits with Aitken in Hawaii and with Jäger in Germany. Still, much of his effort was directed toward meeting obligations at Amarillo: offering retreats, being available for weekly sitting nights when he could, and sharing the regular pastoral duties that were the responsibility of the Redemptorists as the priests of Bishop DeFalco Retreat Center. But with dharma transmission, and as word spread of his talents, retreats at distant locations appeared on Pat's schedule with increasing frequency. Some of the remote locations became long term commitments for Pat, whose presence helped form a nucleus around which contemplative or Zen groups could strengthen.

Pacific Northwest — Seven Thunders

Even before he handed off to Willigis Jäger, Aitken had expressed frustration at the Pacific Northwest group, that since the first Zen sesshin in 1978, they had not established a structure and a space to continue a regular weekly sitting practice between retreats. One day in the mid-1980s, Abbot Bernard McVeigh sat with Leonard Marcel on lawn chairs looking at the pond on the grounds of Guadalupe Abbey. Bernard was the touchstone for a number of people who were on this path on their own without an identified teacher. He knew who was around and who was sitting and who was attending retreats. He said to Leonard, "You know there are a number of people sitting by themselves who would really like to sit with a group during the year in between these big retreats. I think you ought to get them together."

With a full private practice in psychiatry and the involvement in the medical world that went with it, Leonard was getting home at 9 and 10 at night. He told Bernard he was too busy. Leonard remembered:

> About a week or two later, I'm sitting at home Saturday night, doing zazen, and the thought comes to me during this sitting, when you get finished, you call so-and-so and so-and-so and so-and-so and so-and-so — I think there were nine names that came to mind. And here it is 9:00 on a Saturday night. When I get finished, I make nine phone calls. Nine people were at home, and everybody said, that's a great idea. We set up an organizational meeting. And Bernard had said if you get people together, I'll let you use a room in the monastery to sit in. So we had our first Saturday sitting in August of 1985.[332]

That group, which evolved into Seven Thunders, flourished, and has continued first Saturday sits at Guadalupe Abbey ever since. There was no flagging in participation after Willigis Jäger handed off to Pat. Attendance had to be capped at 50, both for space reasons and because one teacher couldn't reasonably attend to more than that number for the one-on-one interviews — ideally, at least one a day each throughout the retreat.

Many of the Washington retreats, one in spring and one in fall, were at Camp Indianola, a Methodist-run center in a beautiful patch of woods on a small peninsula accessible from the town of Indianola on Bainbridge Island by a one-way winding dirt road, about a two-hour drive from Sea-Tac airport. There were several rentable buildings, each self-contained with conference rooms, kitchen, sleeping accommodation and restrooms. The building they were in most often was a stone's throw from the beach and with room for a small, intimate group. On the opposite shore of Puget Sound from Palisades Retreat Center, Indianola shared similar mild air, shoreline, lush vegetation and stunning vistas that Pat loved at Palisades, and he relished the opportunities to spend time there.

The Oregon summer retreats, initially organized by Bernard McVeigh and the Trappists, were handed over to the Seven Thunders group. They took place at various locations around Portland, including the Franciscan retreat center at Mt. Angel, and Loyola Retreat House — venues that could house a large number of people comfortably. Pat continued retreats in the Northwest for large groups at least three times a year. Some of the attendees were among those who had been at the first sesshins for Christians offered by Aitken, then continued with Willigis when he took over, then stayed on with Pat when he took over from Willigis. Others heard about Pat from these originals and from the Trappists, who were sponsors of the summer retreat until 1995.[333] When they began hosting monthly Saturday sitting at the Abbey, the regular structure and schedule attracted people, many of who became Pat's students when he was in the Pacific Northwest. Some simply followed Pat as much as they could afford time-wise and money-wise, wherever he was teaching.

Melbourne, Australia — Melbourne Zen Group

Besides the request from Zen Desert Sangha in the wake of Pat's dharma transmission, he received additional invitations to teach Zen, including from Australia. Back in the 1970s, the Sydney Zen Centre had invited various teachers to lead sesshin for them. Only Aitken accepted. In 1979, he led a sesshin for the Sydney sangha, and for the next ten years he returned once a year. People came from other parts of Australia to Sydney Zen Centre for Aitken's visits. Various Australians traveled to Hawaii for more extended practice. Among them was a man from Melbourne, Ross Klinger, who happened to be at Koko An for Pat's transmission ceremony in May 1989. That summer he attended the first sesshin led by Pat when Pat subbed for Aitken at Koko An. When Ross went back to Australia, he reported to the Melbourne Zen Group that there was this newly transmitted, talented Zen master, and they should invite him to come to Australia. They worked to build up the financial commitment, and Pat agreed to a two-week visit.

Pat flew to Melbourne in August, winter in the land down under. They had planned a packed itinerary for him with a sesshin scheduled to begin very soon after he arrived. Years later Pat remembered being so jet-lagged that on the first day of sesshin he slept through until they came to wake him for teisho in the afternoon. The sesshin was at Greyfriars Monastery, a somewhat dilapidated retreat center in a beautiful setting near Melbourne looking out on the waters of Port Phillip Bay. About 20 attended, with the outcome that the group earnestly hoped Pat would return. After the sesshin, Pat stayed with Phil Pegler and Nicole Chavannes, major leaders of the group at the time, and at whose home the Melbourne Zen Group was meeting for regular sits. He returned to Melbourne every year for the next five, until there were Australian Diamond Sangha teachers to take over.

Several who met Pat on his first trip to Melbourne became his students, making the long trek to Amarillo as often as they could afford so as to spend more time with him. Some spent months in residence at Amarillo year after year. Gillian Jameson was one of these. She came to Amarillo often and for long periods.

A large woman, Gillian would build herself an elaborate nest of cushions in the contemplation room, folding herself onto them for the long periods of sitting. Sitting down and getting up took time, but when she got still, she was very still. In and out of the zendo, Gillian could be difficult. She had a tendency to be intimate, then in a moment of cozy trust, to turn cold and critical. Conflict followed her. There could be shouting in the reception area, cold wars in Meeting Room 4. She left in a huff more than once vowing never to return, only to be back a short time after. Then again, she could be very thoughtful. Lesley Hanks, another Australian who met Pat at that first Melbourne sesshin, remembered that when she was staying at BDRC, Gillian was "the only person who noticed that I was physically unable to carry a tray up the flight of stairs, and she always volunteered to take my meal up for me."[334]

Gillian was devoted to Pat, and although he too could be a target of her intrigues, he had great patience with her. She would have long interviews and dokusans, sometimes using up all the time in a period. She wasn't the only one with this particular sin, just the most conspicuous. Pat had control — for both interviews and dokusan, the teacher rang the bell to signal that you must make your bows and leave. Harsher Zen masters would ring people out ruthlessly, in mid-sentence even. Pat was not like that.

There is a story of Bernard of Clairvaux, founder of the Cistercian Order (aka Trappists) in late 11th century France. As the order grew and monasteries cropped up around the country, their Abbots would write to Bernard for advice. A common question was what to do with difficult monks. Bernard replied, saying that living with difficult monks was important for spiritual development, "and if you don't have enough difficult monks at your monastery, we have plenty at Clairvaux we can send you." Greg Mayers would tell a similar story about monks in a monastery, one of whom was driving everybody crazy. There was every possible kind of conflict when this monk was around. One day, finally the annoying monk was leaving. As soon as the Abbot got wind of the jubilation at his departure, he ran after him to bribe him to come back. The difficult monk is good for practice. Gillian filled that role at times, and indeed most people took their turn at it.

Besides Gillian there were other Australians who connected with Pat through the several Melbourne sesshins and became regular travelers to Amarillo in between what turned out to be annual retreats in Australia into the mid-'90s. Ross Klinger came several times for extended periods. Nicole Chavannes and Phil Pegler came several times, and they were there to help pack the U-Haul when it was time for Pat to leave Amarillo for good in 1998. Nicole was obviously very fond of Pat, managing to incite jealousy in some others with the attention she drew. Barbara Wooten's assessment was that Pat was fond of Nicole, and that his sometimes-apparent dismissiveness when her name came up in conversation was feigned, covering his tracks. Not that his behavior toward her was inappropriate. But, perhaps going back to his seminary days, he tended toward avoidance of anything that might look like particular friendship.

Santa Fe, New Mexico — Mountain Cloud Zen Center

Greg Mello was the person most instrumental in adding Santa Fe, New Mexico, to Pat's teaching roster. Greg had been a student of Philip Kapleau of Rochester Zen Center in New York. By the late 1970s, Kapleau was looking to establish a country Zen center to which he could retire. After investigating many locales, Kapleau moved to Santa Fe with some sangha members — eventually about 30, including Greg and his then wife, Franny Bishop (later ordained as Mitra). These people got jobs and established themselves in the town while they tried to buy land for a center. They fought strong opposition from locals, in the meantime practicing in a small zendo set up at Greg and Mitra's place. In 1983 sangha member Steve Hughes and his family[335] donated 43 acres on the outskirts of Santa Fe. Sale of almost half the land raised funds to build the center. Eventually overcoming continued strong opposition from the town, they broke ground in 1984, opening Mountain Cloud Zen Center (originally Great Cloud) in the fall of 1985.

Kapleau was a student of Harada, then of Yasutani, hence a dharma brother of Yamada Ko'un Roshi. Although ordained by Yasutani and given permission to teach, they disagreed over some personal and practice matters, with the result that Kapleau went independent even before he'd finished the koan curriculum. It was Harada Roshi that Kapleau most wished to emulate, and he set out to make

Rochester Zen Center into Harada Roshi's temple. This meant strict, rigorous practice. Greg remembered, "Everything was very tightly controlled at Rochester and very perfect. We were control freaks, the lords of discipline, *joriki** junkies. ... The Rochester Zen Center was a painful place, and it had lots of benefits but lots of problems. And Kapleau was wonderful but incomplete. And so the practice there was strong, violent, and cultish."

Among other things, Kapleau was rather doctrinaire about his methods, which meant others' methods were inadmissible. Greg continued, "There was not a single book by Robert Aitken in the library in Rochester. And that was just another sign that things were badly awry. And yeah, so no *Mind of Clover*[336] and no nothing. I was coordinating activities at Mountain Cloud Zen Center after it was built — I led discussions of the *Mind of Clover*."[337]

In time Greg Mello's interest in Aitken made him persona non grata with the Kapleau group, and in any case, he had become disenchanted. He had been the one standout voice against locating the Zen Center so far out of town — accessible only by car and therefore only able to be, as he put it, "a country club Zen locale rather than a city center that anyone could get to easily. And I was subscribing to the Diamond Sangha publication, *Blind Donkey*, at that point. That's how we learned about Pat, from *Blind Donkey*. So I just shot over there to Amarillo." He and Franny drove the four hours from Santa Fe to interview Pat and meet him face to face. "And I said okay, Roshi sanctioned him, he's gonna be fine. He's gonna be my guy." Greg started attending every retreat he could get to, contemplative or Zen, even moving to Amarillo for a time so he could be close to Pat and have regular dokusan.

> I worked with both Aitken and Pat whenever — it was a matter of money and schedule, so I went anywhere I could between those two. When my marriage ended [around that time] I had put off certain career things for a long time. And I was eager to be a person outside a Zen center. And I think that Father Pat certainly made that a lot easier.

After Kapleau, Pat's flexibility was a balm. Greg went on,

> At one of Pat's retreats, I was sitting up late at night and I decided I needed to visit my half-brother, who I had hardly any relationship with for some reason. So I shot off after the retreat and looked up parts of my family, which is an example of something that would never happen in Rochester.

---

* Joriki: (Japanese) Power of mind; the power of deep concentration that develops from extended zazen.

> There was a big hunk of me that needed to be brought in. And at Pat's retreats there was enough acceptance and broad lateral, spiritual experience, if you want, psychological sophistication, that would not just be thrown away as not my koan and therefore not worth thinking about.
>
> With Father Pat practice was more delightful and more interesting and less dangerous. Pat was not cultish, Pat had a very broad perspective and his Christianity helped with that, obviously. And I was very interested in uniting — bringing Pat to Santa Fe and healing the all-too-wounded Mountain Cloud Zen Center.

Greg Mello had come to Pat, the Zen master, but found the contemplative aspect of practice equally rich. "I thought that Pat, well, at the time — I hate to use this terminology; but I thought that he pretty much channeled Meister Eckhart and that I had a direct pipeline to the Middle Ages. And that it was a quite authentic Christian experience. I gradually grew not to distinguish too much between the [Zen and contemplative] retreats. It was kind of effortless."

After a year or so of coming to Amarillo for retreats, Greg persuaded the Kapleau remnant in Santa Fe that they should invite Pat to lead a sesshin at Mountain Cloud. After Mountain Cloud Zen Center was built, Kapleau lived there for about a year before he realized that the climate of New Mexico was not good for his health and he moved to Florida. The sangha remained, gradually dwindling. Though some Kapleau students remained in town, the place fell into disuse until a lone Rochester student, Sandy Anderson, was living by herself on the premises as a caretaker. With no teacher there, it was a natural thing to try to persuade Pat that he should come. He led his first sesshin at Mountain Cloud in May 1991.

Pat had so far led only four sesshin — the one in Hawaii in 1989 at the time of Yamada Ko'un's death, one again at Koko An a year later, both times to give Aitken a break, one in Tucson in December 1989, and one in Melbourne in 1990. For several years after his transmission, he continued to lead only contemplative retreats at Amarillo. It meant they weren't equipped with Zen accoutrements at BDRC. They had the cushions and benches they needed for sitting — those were the same on both sides of the Zen-Christian divide — but they needed instruments: *densho, shijo, kansho, inkin, mokugyo, han, umpan* — the various kinds of bells and drums. Pat ordered everything from a catalog. Then he taught the BDRC residents how to use the different instruments and perform the various rituals. He had them practice so they could serve as officers for the sesshin and look like they knew what they were doing. The day came, and they drove to Santa Fe in two cars, first loading all the paraphernalia. Pat checked off each item against a list as it was packed into the cars. When the last item was checked off, he said, "Now all we need is a roshi."[338]

They drove Route 66 across the Texas panhandle and into New Mexico, turning north into the foothills of the Sangre de Cristo Mountains to the outskirts of Santa Fe, almost missing the turn from Old Santa Fe Trail onto the narrow gravel road into Mountain Cloud. Driving in about a quarter of a mile, they came to a stop at a small parking lot, then got out to stretch their legs and have a look around before unloading the vehicles.

As they entered the main building, it was immediately apparent that the bells and other Zen paraphernalia brought from Amarillo could stay in the car. A huge *densho** hung in a small alcove just outside the zendo. A large *mokugyo*† was visible through open doors to the zendo. They entered the empty room in silence, bowing over the threshold toward the tall, chunky altar at the opposite end. They marveled at the massive vigas supporting a high ceiling and the elaborately carved corbels where the beams met the wall. Running the length of the room on either side was a silent row of empty cushions raised on a *tan*‡ under windows letting in afternoon sunlight. The bare mud-adobe walls held random bits of embedded straw that held the gaze of lowered eyes facing the wall during zazen. Bowing themselves out of the zendo, they went in the opposite direction down a hallway leading past men's and women's restrooms and a shower to the kitchen and dining room. Through a door at the far end of the dining room was the dokusan room, a small teacher's bedroom and a laundry room. A short distance from the main building among juniper trees were small cabins, each with three bunk beds, providing very basic sleeping accommodations for retreat participants.

Mary Riseley was among those from Santa Fe who became a student and friend of Pat's to the end of his life. She had discovered the Quakers when she was in boarding school. "I really liked the silence. And also, that meeting was very politically engaged. So when people did stand up and say things it was stuff I could relate to as a rebel against my Marine Corps General very conservative father. … When I went to college, I got atheized very quickly. I didn't even know anybody in college who thought seriously about God or spirituality." She had an affair with one of her professors at Stanford, for which she was pushed out by the Dean of Women, took a half year break spent in England then returned, this time to Berkeley. "That year, I really cut my political activist teeth and worked with the Congress of Racial Equality." She met some artists in the Bay area who

---

* Densho: (Japanese) A large bell or gong hanging from a frame, sounded with a striker. The densho sequence of rings calls practioners to the start of a period of zazen.

† Mokugyo: (Japanese) A carved wooden drum in the shape of a fish's head. The beating of the mokugyo keeps the regular rhythm of a chant.

‡ Tan: (Japanese) Platform, approximately knee-high, on which the *zabutons* and *zafus* (cushions for zazen) are placed.

were into mysticism and through them, came to Teilhard de Chardin and William Blake, reconnecting with a spiritual life. "I went to the Episcopal Church because there was no Quaker meeting there. But at that point it was a little hard to fit what I was feeling and experiencing into the liturgy. Now I don't have any problem, thanks to Pat."[339]

The sesshin at Mountain Cloud was Mary's first formal encounter with Zen, though not with Pat. She met him through Greg Mello who, for her birthday one year, gave her a week-long contemplative retreat at BDRC.

> And I have never been so tired in my life. I said to Pat I haven't felt this tired since I was in labor giving birth to my daughter, and he said you'll get a second wind. And I did. And I just took to it like a duck to water. I think because my personality is very gregarious and voluble, it was this balancing — the silence was this balancing that was very beautiful for me. … I went through all the stages of falling in love with Pat and imagining he would take over from Aitken when Aitken retired, we would get married, we would live in Hawaii. [Laughing] But I got over it. … But my impression of Pat when he spoke, when he gave the homilies at Mass and the conference talks, was I just saw how deeply intelligent he was and how he had so much to offer in terms of insight. It was just very rich for me. It was a really good match for me.[340]

Pancho (Frank) Burke was in Santa Fe at the time of that first sesshin at Mountain Cloud. He was from Illinois, not far from where Pat grew up, fifth of 13 children in an Irish-Catholic family. He had come out of high school intending to become a priest. He joined a diocesan seminary in Alton, Illinois, but it didn't take. In the late 1980s, Pancho was living in Santa Fe, married with two young children, and making a slim living as a carpenter. He was practicing Islam, praying five times a day, observing Ramadan. He said that somehow in this period of intense religious practice, he lost God — just completely lost him — but he kept up the practice anyway. At the end of a day during Ramadan — on the job with no cigarettes, no food, no water, he didn't want to go home crabby to his family, so he would hang out at the library and read until sundown. The books that attracted him were Zen books — D.T. Suzuki[341] was there, for example. One day he noticed Aitken's *Taking the Path of Zen.* That clicked, and he called Aitken to talk to him. Aitken told him about his four dharma heirs and that, as a matter of fact, there was going to be one of them in Santa Fe in a couple of weeks leading a sesshin at Mountain Cloud. By that happenstance, Pancho was another of the attendees at Pat's first Santa Fe sesshin. He arrived in time for the opening supper.

> And so I'm sitting here with all these good Catholics from Amarillo, and they're introducing themselves and whatnot. And it goes around to this little mousy guy, who's a little sunburnt and kind of shaky, and he mumbles under his breath I'm Bob Hawk and I'm from Amarillo. And I went, ah! This would be like a brother of the great — of the teacher — who is probably an alcoholic. I sussed this guy out. I reached the conclusion he was probably a family member ... maybe staying with his brother, the great teacher who was in the other room or back in the teacher's quarters or something like that.
>
> So I didn't get to meet this guy until the next day at 5 in the morning in the interview room, and let's just say we were both impressed. I had my coffee and cigarettes under the tree at 4 in the morning or whatever and prepared to meet the Zen teacher who had a right, as far as I could read in the literature, to scream at me or hit me or knock me to the wall or break my foot in the door like Unmon or whatever. So I'm ready for anything but I've got this strange wool blanket around me ... it looked like something you stole off a beggar in Bangladesh or something like that. So I've got it on, and I'm staying warm, and I get in there to the interview room, and I took a bow and sat in front of this man, and I remember he just — it's the biggest reaction I ever got out of Pat Hawk — one eyebrow just went up just a little bit.
>
> But we hit it off really well, and so I studied with him after that. Went to Amarillo some. I was raising little kids, and so quite often I couldn't do all that much in terms of retreats and things like that. But with Pat... I guess I just wanna say one thing about Pat Hawk, because anybody that you run into is gonna tell you how much they loved him and this, that and the other. ... The thing with Pat was that this guy is not going to drop a layer of assumptions over this situation and then start fixing things. Being good. Helping. I mean you could ask him for anything, you could tell him anything. He would help you with what you needed, but he wasn't gonna say, oh here let me fix your life for you. And it was so profoundly real, that lack of jumping in and assuming, that it could almost feel like a lack of caring. But it wasn't a lack of caring. It was a tremendous acceptance of what is.[342]

Twenty-five people attended that first sesshin at Mountain Cloud, ten of them from Amarillo. The group photos taken at the end, one in front of the altar, another outside on the front steps, show happy, smiling, laughing faces — even Pat looks joyful. The Amarillo contingent left that afternoon with promises to return, and thereafter, until 2006 when his health no longer allowed travel, Pat became an important teacher at Mountain Cloud. A half dozen or more of the Mountain Cloud group began making the drive east whenever they could for retreats and resident practice with him at Bishop DeFalco Retreat Center.

Bishop DeFalco as a Catholic retreat center and Mountain Cloud as a dedicated Zen center had a different ambience, the former very much reflecting the ethos of Greg Mayers and Pat, the latter established apart from either of them. Both were on the outskirts of town, both drew locals as well as people from a distance, and both were built as dedicated places of spiritual practice, MCZC for Buddhist practice and BDRC for Christian practice. BDRC was much bigger and afforded much more comfortable accommodation with its private rooms and baths, compared to MCZC's primitive shared cabins and bathrooms at a distance in the main building.

Yet for Pancho Burke and some others, Mountain Cloud, its rusticity aside, felt a bit like a club with an exclusive membership. MCZC at that time was haunted by the exactness, the strictness of form brought from Kapleau's Rochester Zen Center. There was a sense of having to follow rules down to the smallest detail: how to hold hands while walking, when to bow, how to dress, how strongly one should practice. Bishop DeFalco Retreat Center felt more inclusive. Despite a sometime cliquishness and friction between town and resident trainees, between the stricter Catholics and the contemplatives, between the various personalities of the long-term visitors, and increasingly, between Pat and Greg, there was a palpable ethic of mercy and tolerance. It made the place safer, looser, more comfortable for the downtrodden, so to speak, who were the bulk of people attracted to serious practice. Pancho reflected:

> Despite all of its horrible obvious faults, the Catholic Church has that vibe still of like, loser? Yeah. All of us are losers in some ways. That Christian doctrine of the equality of the soul that we're all Jesus, we're all just absolutely that great. And we're all in big trouble too. That sense. It's definitely in Islam. You know how they make the call to prayer and you get in there, the beggar. If they're filling up the rows if the beggar is standing next to the prime minister, they gotta get shoulder to shoulder and touch.
>
> For me, it's really about staying non-judgmental about people with nice cars and their bills paid and insurance and what not. Staying non-defensive over the fact that I gotta show up stinking because I don't have a shower, and I may have to take some heat for that. There may be misunderstandings, there may be a lot of things but, [at BDRC] I don't quite feel as much like I'm just going in there to steal the fire, the realization, you know, the nuts and bolts of Zen. And get the hell back out there to the penitentiary, to my family of origin. To my normal, alcoholic, drug-addicted, recovering family. Hahahaha. Yeah! In Amarillo, at least when Pat was there, there was this sense that — there was a great relief. You could see it on the faces of the captive people. You know the nuns like Sister Shirley that lived with him. There was this sense of great relief. You know, here's this one place where you don't have to pretend.[343]

Having acquired all the Zen accoutrements and with the demand obviously there, Pat started offering Zen sesshin at Bishop DeFalco Retreat Center in addition to the contemplative retreats. They had been granted affiliation with the Diamond Sangha as Empty Sky Sangha, a name bringing together the great spaciousness of Zen experience with the vast open sky of the Texas Panhandle. Sesshin and contemplative retreats often bookended resident practice periods, Zen at the beginning and contemplative at the end or vice versa. In non-retreat times there were sits at least two evenings a week, one in Zen format and one in contemplative format, with Pat offering dokusan and interviews when he was in town.

The formats for Zen and Contemplative retreats were not hugely different from each other since in either case most of the time was spent sitting in silence. For contemplative retreats, the daily presentation to the group was called a conference and was based on the Christian mystics or the Desert Fathers. For sesshin, the equivalent was teisho, given in the afternoon and usually based on a koan. Private meetings with the teacher were called interviews at contemplative retreats and dokusan at sesshin. There was more elaborate ritual around teisho, dokusan and other aspects of sesshin than around conference and interviews at contemplative retreats. But always, there was the silence, and many students of Pat's attended both types of retreats indiscriminately, based more on convenience of location and schedule than on confessional persuasion.

Harry Iwatsuki first began practicing with Pat at Mountain Cloud, then also worked with him at other locations. When he and his wife moved to the Northwest, he regretted to Pat that he had to travel so far for sesshin (for many years only contemplative retreats were offered in the Northwest). Pat encouraged him to try a contemplative retreat — after all, he could work on koans regardless, and most of the time was spent in silence anyway. At the first interview of his first contemplative retreat, Harry was surprised when he entered the little room and saw Pat sitting in one of two chairs facing each other instead of sitting on one of two cushions on the floor. He made a questioning gesture as if to say, what's with the chairs? Pat said dryly, "In Christianity, we have a merciful God."

Although there were priests, monks and nuns who practiced with Pat, the large majority of his students were lay, and of those, the large majority were not Catholic. There was both Buddhist and Christian practice but the two were kept separate, with Zen form or contemplative form in the regular weekly sitting schedule, and with sesshin or contemplative intensive offered as retreats, but never a blend of the two.

Bishop DeFalco Retreat Center, early 1990s

The program at BDRC quickly grew from a few students to a handful, and from a handful to a dozen, then outgrew the small contemplation room where they sat. They knocked out walls and did other renovations to accommodate ever-larger groups.

In the fiscal year July 1990 to June 1991, Bishop DeFalco Retreat Center welcomed over 3,000 guests for retreats, workshops and seminars, serving over 16,000 meals. The Contemplative Path Program led by Pat Hawk and Greg Mayers was one of the three main draws (the other two were the Methodist Walk to Emmaus group and the Thomas Keating-led Centering Prayer Retreats).[344] Running the place was a high-pressure job — all the activity, the widely diverse demands of different groups, and the finances. They weren't quite making ends meet. Pat took no interest in or responsibility for any of this practical side. He worked single-mindedly at offering what gift he had. Though both Pat and Greg Mayers were present as teachers, students coming to the contemplative program increasingly gravitated toward Pat.

In the summer of 1991, Bob Curry asked to be relieved of the BDRC directorship and Greg, already assistant director, took over. It added a heavy administrative burden to his already full schedule, which included participation in the contemplative program, offering regular Progoff Intensive Journaling workshops, and continued study with Willigis Jäger in Germany. Among other things, it meant he also became the Superior for the BDRC Redemptorists, including Pat. A tension grew between them, not apparent to most of the residents but enough that Pat spoke of it to Aitken. There began an unraveling of their long, constructive friendship.

Soon after he took over the directorship, in the late summer of 1991, Greg hired Angie Guerrero and Barbara Wooten as secretaries. They became part of the texture and flow of the place, remaining through all the years Pat and Greg were there and beyond, after a new bishop discontinued the Redemptorists' contract in 1998. Both women, smart and industrious, worked way beyond a secretary's job description.

Barbara Wooten was artistic, outspoken, blunt, witty, and by her own admission, socially clumsy. She and her husband Charlie lived about 20 miles south of Amarillo outside the small town of Canyon, Texas, from where she commuted to BDRC. Barbara recalled:

> I met Pat because I used to swim freestyle laps, and one of my neighbors dove in the pool and almost hit me. Afterwards, I was going to go up and chew her out in the locker room. Then we started talking, and she told me

> she was doing Zen at the retreat center. I went up there and met Greg. Pat was there. I went for Zen sittings for a little while then Greg asked me if I wanted to work there. I started in August 1991 as Greg's personal assistant and publicist for the Bishop DeFalco Retreat Center *Journal* and for brochures. I got to know Pat better and went to more of the sittings.
>
> But for some reason, I could not function within the contemplative group at all hardly — I don't know what it was. I just wasn't on board with the way everybody did things. I remember one night towards the end of the program there, they were all talking, and they said, we've decided to call it the Pathless Path. And I said, who decided? And they said, well, Pat decided. And I said you mean Pat's Pathless Path? Nobody laughed and I thought, uh oh, you made a mistake there. … They wanted to sit formally another time a week, and they were trying to decide as a group which night to sit. So they all decided to sit Friday night. And I said, "Friday night?! Friday night? Come on." I said, "That's the night I go home and get a beer and kick back in front of the TV and veg out." I think it's the time I used to watch *X-files*. And I just think the people there were really put off by my style. I don't think my aspiration was any less than theirs, but I think they were put off by my style.
>
> I started doing the Contemplative Path newsletter. I remember having a big argument with Bill Lawder. He's a nice guy. I really like Bill Lawder. Unusual for me to have an argument with him, but I did over the contemplative newsletter. I've lived in Amarillo most of my life. Since 1976. I've always had difficulty with the local people. People who are really Panhandle people. Because they're extremely hidebound people. I didn't want to be in more conflict with anybody than I already was. I tried to talk to Pat about it. Pat just didn't want to talk to me about my difficulties with the group. I think he thought I was trying to badmouth the sangha, and that was a big no-no. You know, Buddha, Dharma, Sangha.[345]

Angie Guerrero had high school and some business college training along with a native competence such that Greg gave her more and more responsibility for running the Center. She became business manager and more. She was Mexican American and Assembly of God Protestant — a combination not unusual in Amarillo — and although she never took any interest in Contemplative Path or Zen activities for herself, she was alert to their needs. This was critical. Her predecessor in the office was a strict Catholic, uncomfortable with Greg's casual management style and opposed to the contemplative approach. That person complained about many things and had written a letter to the bishop stirring up trouble. Bishop Matthiesen responded by relocating her to another part of the diocese. Angie's style complimented Greg's. Where he was laid back, she was organized and detail-oriented without being self-righteous or oppressive. She was very plugged into the activities in the town, liked to go dancing, and knew when and where to go for fun. She was cordial to all and a friend to some of the long-term residents who would drop into the office now and then to chat.

Angie worked with whoever was the Head Resident to organize the schedule of contemplative and Zen retreats. This was Shirley Morrissey at first. Soon after Greg took over directorship of the Center, without explanation or even much notice, Shirley was replaced by Bill Lawder. Bill did not have a great head for the job, and when he and Steve Daney started Edge City, Pat wrote to Aitken, "I'm thinking of making Paul Hughes head resident here now that Bill Lawder has moved on to the life of the Zen businessman."[346] When Paul decided to spend a summer living in a tent on Mount Hood, Glenna Pittock subbed for him, then when he did it again, she took over officially and was Head Resident for the remainder of Pat's time in Amarillo.

The Zen/contemplative program at BDRC had to be coordinated with other groups. They sometimes ran three retreats at a time at the center, making sure that more conservative groups — Christian Nazis, Barbara called them — were not there during contemplative or Zen retreats. The bookstore, run for years by Shirley Morrissey, looked a lot like any Catholic bookstore, albeit with more emphasis on contemplative practice and medieval mystics: Eckhart, John of the Cross, Teresa of Avila, etc. There was no sign of Zen unless Shirley was in there with you and knew of your interest, in which case she would discreetly open some big drawers under the main shelving and pull out title after title: Aitken's books, Shunryu Suzuki's *Zen Mind Beginner's Mind*, a selection of D.T. Suzuki, the koan collections of the standard Sanbo Kyodan/Diamond Sangha curriculum, various others — a pretty good selection.

Some spillover among groups was inevitable, which meant a simmering disapproval in the conservative quarter that would bubble up occasionally and reach Bishop Matthiesen. He was laissez-faire, even protective, a catholic Catholic, so to speak, open to all comers, happy with the vitality and obvious disciplined spirituality of the contemplative program. Mostly he followed the rules. Barbara Wooten and Charlie Kroeger had asked Matthiesen to officiate at their wedding, but since both were divorced, he wouldn't do it, and in the end they got married outside the Church. On the other hand, while he was attending a conference on the East Coast one time, there was a stir from a group of lesbians who wanted someone to say Mass for them. The local bishop opposed it and they couldn't find anyone to do it. Matthiesen got wind of the situation and said the Mass for them — a radical act that got written up in a Catholic newsletter and found its way back to Amarillo. He gave the hardcore plenty to complain about. But with the Contemplative Path mostly occupying the west wing and other groups situated in the south and east wings, and with creative scheduling to avoid overlap, overt conflict was generally avoided, and the program ran without interference and indeed thrived.

Paul Hughes was among those who came to Bishop DeFalco Retreat Center during this period, having met Pat in the Northwest. He had been doing a 13-week Ignatian retreat at Loyola in Portland, and during the last week of that retreat, in came Greg and Pat to get ready for a contemplative retreat. Paul decided to stay for it. Ignatian retreats center on practice of the spiritual exercises of St. Ignatius of Loyola, founder of the Jesuits. These involve prayer in the form of both directed meditation on scripture and the life of Christ as well as observation of the feelings that arise in conjunction with discursive meditations. Paul was primed for the contemplative retreat and loved it.

In one of Paul's interviews with Pat, he talked to him about the Ignatian experience, which culminated in the Divine Colloquy — what Paul described as a sort of back-and-forth inner conversation with Christ. He told Pat about it glowingly, saying it was the epitome. Pat brought him down to earth, "It's the pits."[347] Impossible to know what he had in mind. It may have been his instinctive resistance to what Merton had called sharing the fruits of contemplation. "Those who are too quick to think they must go out and share their contemplation with other men tend to ruin their own contemplation and give false notions of it to others, by trusting too much in words and language and discourse to do the work that can only be accomplished in the depths of man's soul by the infused light of God."[348] Certainly, Pat distrusted words and description when it came to mystical experience. Paul was taken aback but persevered.

At one point in another interview, Paul was puzzling over his understanding of God. Pat indicated a flower saying, "That's God." Paul said, "I was just fascinated with this widening of the boundaries of what Christianity was all about. Mystified and fascinated." He wanted to follow Pat to Amarillo but had just been accepted to the Capuchins and didn't want to derail a plan to become a friar. He spent two years with an excellent novice master who helped him recognize at the end of it that he needed a more contemplative approach and encouraged him to go to Amarillo after all. Paul sent an inquiry to Pat, who replied warmly and in beautiful calligraphy. Then when Paul phoned him with a question, Pat seemed curt and cold. It stung. "It was like he gave with one hand and took away with the other." Paul came to Amarillo anyway, becoming one of the long-term residents at BDRC, and for a time, Head Resident.

The west wing of Bishop DeFalco Retreat Center, very much home to long-term residents and regulars from town, was thoroughly inhabited and well cared for. Aromas of fresh baking wafted out of Meeting Room 4 along with conversation, sometimes lighthearted, sometimes intense, during free time. The courtyard flower bed flourished abundantly under Glenna's green thumb.

Bob Walker built things: a lectern that was the right height for a speaker sitting on a cushion, a hall cupboard for support cushions. He and Carmichael Peters, a theologian and former Jesuit, then a student of Pat's, built a bench nook for the meditation garden, and shoji screens that could slide across the doors from the garden into the zendo. A landscaper from town and student of the program, Mike Jager, designed and organized the construction of the meditation garden. For this and other large projects, they had extended work-practice periods to which townspeople were invited and which ended with a barbecue out in the main courtyard. Pat was a nearly invisible presence at such social gatherings, occasionally materializing apparently out of nowhere with a sidesplittingly funny zinger of an observation, all the more hilarious because of the usual quiet that was its source.

They often watched a movie on Friday nights or at the end of a retreat. Some movies came in through a video rental service to which Pat subscribed, or he would have Shirley Morrissey or Bill Lawder go to the video store to rent particular films. Then in the evening, they would all troop into the rectory living room. Pat would have popcorn or some other snack, along with teas and various other drinks, sometimes wine, for what was sometimes a double feature. The selection was often jarring after the silence of sitting. Pat liked anything Schwarzenegger no matter how violent, anything Monty Python, *Being There*, *Urban Cowboy*, *The Fisher King*, *Alien*. There were some directors he favored, including Ingmar Bergman. Recalling a resident training period Tracy McCallum said, "I remember we had a sesshin in the middle of it. Pat had this movie he wanted us to see at the end of sesshin, called *Mars Attacks*. It's just a wacky sci-fi movie." And, Tracy thought, "just the appropriate thing to release some energy after having a really intense sesshin."[349]

Once during a Zen sesshin, Richard Laue, attending from Tucson, was feeling restless. He asked Pat if it was okay to leave the retreat center grounds and go strolling toward town a bit. Pat looked at him with a raised eyebrow and said, "Sure, it's okay." Then after a pause. "But why would you want to?" The blocks of spare houses in bare yards with their derelict vehicles, fierce-looking dogs and chain-link fences drew Pat not at all. Richard said he was going to give it a try. Pat said, "You'll be back!"[350]

Another time at a sesshin officers' meeting, one of the officers was complaining about a particularly difficult and distracting participant. The others were nodding agreement with a certain amount of eye-rolling. Pat held ground for the person criticized, saying, "He's not heavy, he's our brother." He said it not as a persuasion to virtue, as if from the pulpit, but flatly, as a matter of fact. That shut it down. It was gentle but firm, and in an instant changed the tone of the meeting, a change reverberating out from the officers to the whole sesshin.[351] Years later, at Zen Desert Sangha in Tucson, Pat gave a similar response when one of the officers complained to him about a participant in the Saturday morning sits who, among other things, would rustle in late with a huge handbag containing a cell phone she sometimes forgot to turn off. She would sometimes whisper to herself audibly during zazen. Instead of the expected sympathy, Pat sided with the difficult one. He didn't quote, "He ain't heavy…" that time, but said neutrally, "She's fine." As so often with Pat, it was his manner that carried the message more than his words.

Kristen Larson

Kristen Larson first connected with Greg and Pat in the early 1990s. A few times a year, the two men led contemplative retreats in Palos Verdes, California. Kristen was attending 12-step programs for adult children of alcoholics, including an occasional retreat at the Daughters of Mary and Joseph Retreat Center. While she was looking for something to read in the bookstore there, one of the Sisters came over, and after chatting for a bit, recommended *The Cloud of Unknowing,* which Kristen devoured. The Sister told her of a little group doing contemplative prayer in the chapel. Seeing her interest, the same nun told her that a couple of priests would be coming in a few months and that they taught what *The Cloud* taught. Kristen signed up.

Greg Mayers seemed to be the leader of the retreat that first day, with Pat Hawk primarily simply keeping time. Kristen remembered, "The first time I saw Pat leading the line, walking, I knew he was my teacher. It was just absolutely clear. Wherever he was going I was following. That's all there was to it. He hadn't even said a word yet. He didn't have to. Greg was talking excellent talk. He talked beautifully. Pat just kept time. … I knew I wanted more, so that's what sent me to Amarillo."

She began looking for information about sitting on cushions — at Mary and Joseph, they'd been sitting in pews. The only book she could find with straightforward, practical advice about sitting was Robert Aitken's *Taking the Path of Zen.* At her first retreat in Amarillo, she took it to Pat and asked if he knew the author. "He said, 'I've heard of him.' I asked if this was a book that was okay to read. He said, 'It'll do fine.' Later in the retreat, I went upstairs to find out about the residency process. I kept prowling around, and I found a bulletin board in the laundry room. And on the bulletin board was a Diamond Sangha newsletter talking about

Pat's transmission. Next interview, I pranced in, plopped down and said, 'I have found out you are exactly who I thought you were!' He said, 'What is that?' I said, 'A Zen master!' He said, 'Does that change anything?' After a pause I said, 'No…' He said, 'Well, let's go on.' "

Years later Kristen said, "Finding Pat courtesy of Joanna Leahy radically changed my life. I started dedicating whatever spare time and spare money I could. I did my first residency in Amarillo in 1992. That was where I met Glenna [Pittock]. Everybody talked about Glenna. 'Glenna will be here in xyz days.' She sat down with me and said, 'So what brings you here?' I said, 'My husband has been given two years to live. He's taking early retirement. I've just been fired from what was supposed to be my career. I'm here to try and adjust and get some space between me and what's happening in my life before we move up to Seattle. I need some time to readjust my view as to what my life is going to be like'. Glenna said, 'You've been here for three weeks now — it doesn't matter anymore does it.' I said, '…No.' "

Kristen remembered her first residency period at Amarillo:

> During that time, looking through a sutra book, I found the Jukai ceremony. I said, this is for me. "Can I do this ceremony, Pat?" He said, "There's a lot of preparation." I said, "I really want to do this." I loved the way it was worded and the attitude. Most of the people I regard as the best Christians I know claim to be Buddhist. He gave me Aitken's *Mind of Clover* and started me on the path. It seemed every other day he had another gigantic pack of papers to study. Finally, he came out with directions to make a *rakusu*. I had no idea it was part of the bargain and that that was connected with Jukai. I really had to finagle to get a ride to a place so I could buy some cloth. Then studying and sewing and sewing and studying. Nothing else in my mind at all. Single focused on that for weeks.
>
> Pat said, "Well we're doing a sesshin next September, you can come and we'll do the ceremony." I said, "No, no, no. I want the ceremony before my bod is out of the place. I'm moving from California to Seattle — in fact I'll be able to go to one sesshin in Seattle." I vaguely understood what sesshin was. I told Pat I really want to do this right now and right here. He said, "Well, okay." We had one night of the week — Zen night, and they did the evening ceremony, "Kanzeon"* and "Great Vows."† I said, "Let's do it on

---

* A chant in honor of Kanzeon or Kannon, the *bodhisattva* of mercy (Chinese, Guan Yin).

† The four bodhisattva vows, also called the Great Vows, are often chanted after period of zazen, and several times during each day of sesshin.

> The many beings are numberless, I vow to save them.
> Greed, hatred, and ignorance rise endlessly, I vow to abandon them.

> our last Zen night." He said, "Okay, we'll do it." Carolyn Blasdel was Ino, a couple of people from Santa Fe, Greg Mello and Mary Riseley, came there because they heard this was gonna happen. Greg was probably beginning to consider redoing his [Jukai] with Pat. He had done it at Rochester [with Kapleau]. Glenna said to me, "What would you like to have at your reception afterwards?" Because there was always tea. I said, "I think the thing I would like most of all would be almond cookies." She combed the entire city to find almond cookies. There were none in all of Amarillo. So she bought some almonds and a cookbook and made me almond cookies for that reception.[352]

When Bill Larson, Kristen's husband, was told he had only a short time to live he and Kristen decided they would spend his remaining years sailing the San Juan Islands in the Pacific Northwest. They were already living aboard the 50-foot sloop, *Scrimshaw,* moored at Redondo Beach, California. They found a berth for her in the harbor at Port Angeles, Washington, as Bill prepared to take early retirement.

Bill, outliving his doctors' predictions by more than 20 years, also became a student of Pat. He joined Kristen at retreats some of the time, other times supporting her practice from a distance by looking after the home front. With one hiatus late in the Amarillo years, Kristen became a regular and devoted Pat student, spending a total of about four years at BDRC between 1991 and 1998, following Pat to Santa Fe and the Pacific Northwest and continuing practice with him after he left Amarillo and moved to Tucson. She was dedicated, and faithful in observance of the forms and the schedule. At the same time, she was creative, even flamboyant, in her presentations both in sesshin and in daily life. She was a strong presence in the program, her steadiness of practice a support to others.

Classes at Bishop DeFalco Retreat Center (BDRC) 1990s

At BDRC, Pat and occasionally Greg offered classes for residents of their growing program, including interested people from town.[353] A class called "What we do here" gave an orientation to Zen Buddhism. Speaking of the Four Noble Truths,* Pat said of *dukkha*, commonly translated as suffering:

Dharma-gates are countless, I vow to wake to them.
Buddha's Way is unsurpassed, I vow to embody it fully.

* The Four Noble Truths can be expressed as: 1) All life is dukkha. 2) The cause of dukkha is attachment (craving). 3) Dukkha can be relieved by letting go of attachment. 4) The means for release from attachment is the Eightfold Path (right view, intention, speech, action, livelihood, effort, mindfulness, concentration).

> I suggest we use the word anguish. It puts it in the human realm, which is where Buddhism belongs … Anguish is everywhere. We desire permanence for ourselves and our loved ones; these desires conflict with the way things are. Nothing abides. Release from anguish comes from personal acknowledgment and resolve. Let us accept reality fully and take care of one another while we can. … This acknowledgment and resolve is realized in the eightfold path of right views, right thinking, right speech, right conduct, right livelihood, right effort, right recollection and right meditation.

He explained that "right" here means correct, in keeping with the reality of impermanence. His tone carried no trace of Catholic moralism. He addressed the question of Buddhism as a religion:

> There is the argument whether Buddhism can be considered a religion, since it has no God. There is no worship in the Western sense. So is it just a philosophy? Well — this is where our two-pronged tradition begins to prick us. Yamada Roshi said his Christian students should not consider Zen a religion. Aitken Roshi says Zen is a religion because it is a path of liberation, salvation. Father AMA Samy says Zen is a religion. Willigis Jäger says, "I'm sorry, but it's not a religion!"[354]

Someone asked Pat, "What do you think?"

"Oh hell." Period. For Pat, these abstract questions were beside the point, and he rarely let himself be drawn into them. Pressed further for an opinion, Pat came out with, "Well, it's a religion but not in the usual way you think of religion." He steered back to the practical:

> This debate is still open, but there's no denying the depth of spiritual experience with practice. And it is definitely a path of liberation; it has been for centuries. The emphasis in Zen is on the personal experience of absolute freedom and realization of empty oneness. And the way it has been practiced, it is somewhat deficient in social work. The opposite is true of the way Christianity is practiced. The emphasis is social and not on personal liberation. So the encounter of these two great religions has much to offer, and it is not only a philosophical understanding of the way things are.

Pat gave a class on ritual and ceremony, beginning with Robert Aitken's essay from *Taking the Path of Zen*, then spoke of the interplay between Christian and Zen ritual. Regarding gassho or bowing he explained that bowing is not a bow *to* anything, just the action itself, likewise chanting, bells, incense; just this sound, just this breath. "The point I want to emphasize is to go beyond the literal. Become one with ritual. You'll find that it spills over into your daily life." Pat quoted a favorite phrase of Thich Nhat Hanh: " 'Any action done with attention and reverence is a ritual — eating, brushing teeth, talking with friends, relaxing.' One's whole life is an expression, an embodiment. Every place is the place of enlightenment." He talked about how Aitken, when he first practiced in Japan, hated bowing, then with repetition, came to understand. And how at Haus St. Benedikt in Germany, the Catholic and Zen ritual had been stripped down to where there was simply an abstract decoration behind the altar that served for both. And how at some point the Catholic Workers in the Pacific Northwest who split off into the Three Treasures Sangha led by Joan Rieck, at first reacted against the ritual they had been raised with as Catholics and threw everything out, then after a few months, brought back chanting, bowing, incense. Pat went on, "Here at BDRC, we do Zen [ritual] on Monday nights and Christian on other days of the week — my policy is that we do it separate: if Zen, Zen, if Christian, Christian." He added, "I would like to refute the charge that I'm inconsistent — I consistently do Zen as Zen, Christian as Christian."

He gave a class on the ten oxherding pictures, a well-known series of illustrations depicting the Zen journey. He pointed out that many of the ancestral teachers have presented stages or levels of the spiritual journey: Rinzai's four states of mind, Tozan's five stages of absolute and relative, Teresa of Avila's Interior Castle and her seven mansions or dwelling places.

Pat explained, "The ox as a metaphor was very important in China of this time; they depended on the ox to plow their fields, to give milk, to ride. So it is adopted as metaphor for essential nature, the *Tao*. It's like Jesus using everyday things — parables as metaphors for spiritual experience." Pat spoke of each stage, then summed up, quoting ninth century Qingyuan: "In the beginning mountains are mountains and rivers, rivers. Then as one penetrates, mountains are no longer mountains, rivers no longer rivers. And in the end, mountains are again mountains and rivers again rivers, but not like before. Before, they were perceived with discrimination. Now, there is no discrimination, no attachment; now, they are as they are."*

Pat said, "Some people practice Zen as an adjunct, like flower arranging. But our practice is not an adjunct to something else. Our Zen practice is directed to

---

* Qingyuan Xingsi was a Zen Buddhist monk during the Tang Dynasty. Three of the five traditionally recognized houses of Zen are commonly believed to have developed out of his lineage: the Caodong/Sōtō, Yunmen/Unmon, and Fayan/Hōgen schools. Ferguson, Andy. *Zen's Chinese Heritage: The Masters and their Teachers*, Wisdom Publications, Boston, 2000.

realizing essential nature, union with God, building of character." He was strict about keeping Zen and Christian practice distinct, and his contemplative intensive retreat conferences and Zen teishos rarely cross-referenced the traditions. But in his classes he was more inclined to indulge his students' interest in integrating the two paths by comparing and drawing parallels.

Pat gave more than a nod to the contributions of spiritual women of both traditions. Although most of the women contributors to the Zen lineage are unnamed, a women's Buddhist journal at the time, *Kahawai*,[355] set forth the stories of some of the few known women, and based on these Pat added the names of two women to the ancestors honored at every sutra service.* On the Christian side, he gave a class on the medieval Beguines — independent female spiritual seekers who were teachers and influencers of understanding. These women risked persecution and death because women's official role in the Church at the time (and since!) was one of subservience. He suggested that Eckhart and Tauler probably learned from the Beguines. "What most interests me about them is how these laypeople got together and lived a lay life as an alternative to established religion. They had no affiliation with any order. They picked and chose who they wanted to be their chaplains."

Discussion for this class went from the insight and power of these women to the reasons for their suppression, to sexism and the perceived dangers of female sexuality. Into this, he wove reference to a lecture by M. Scott Peck linking sexuality and spirituality — the sources lie so close together that you cannot arouse the one without the other. "In fact, [Peck] says he uses it as an indication of authentic spirituality. But," Pat goes on, "this is a reason for all the scandals lately in American Zen. That kind of face-to-face relationship is certainly authentic spirituality. But the sexual/spiritual connection is gonna be there. If you're not aware of it..." He didn't finish the sentence.

Pat gave a class on the Heart Sutra, another on the notion of Bodhisattva, another on reincarnation and karma.† Here he unpacked Buddhist constructs foreign to many of his Christian students. He spoke of the Buddhist image of reincarnation as the passing of a flame from candle to candle. Light is passed, but no substance is transferred. And related to this he explained karma not as punishment for things done in past lives — a notion he pointed out was akin to original

---

* Mahapajapati and Patacara were pioneering nuns at the time of the historical Buddha. Both became important teachers and can be considered Buddhist masters. Olivia, N. Women Buddhist Masters. *International Journal of Dharma Studies* (2017) 5:8.

† Karma: (Sanskrit) action, cause and effect. Pat understood the term in this sense. i.e. without the moral overtones it carries for some groups.

sin — rather, karma in its fundamental meaning as cause and effect. Our actions set in motion other actions. Our experience unfolds from actions that precede the experience. Simply because of the way life is lived, certain actions and events follow. But perhaps from his Catholic training in theology, or perhaps as an *upaya** or expedient (Pat sometimes made apparently contradictory statements to different audiences, as was the practice of Shakyamuni Buddha himself), Pat insisted on the existence of free will, implying that despite the inevitability of karma, we still can make choices.

Some of the BDRC classes were overtly comparative, for example, *Upaya* — skillful means — and *Gelassenheit*† — letting go; superficially very different ideas yet at bottom closely related. Another addressed Buddhist and Christian Enlightenment. He said that Yamada Ko'un, who had specialized in Zen training of Christians, especially priests and nuns, thought that the *satori* experience was qualitatively different for his Christian and his Japanese students and that for the former, there was a greater tendency toward experience of the personal. Pat said, "Spirituality, you know, does not like theology. I think both Western and Eastern forms of spirituality like the concrete. They look to the concrete. We want the thing, not the abstraction."

During his year in Germany as a student of Willigis Jäger, and again when he attended the Easter 1990 meeting of the European Sanbo Kyodan teachers, Pat had been exposed to a tremendous clash. At that first meeting in 1985, it had come to a shouting match, as some tried to synthesize a seamless whole from the doctrines of Catholicism and Buddhism, and others insisted on letting each be its own worldview. Pat expressed his view to the class:

> Some set out as a goal to integrate [the two religions]. I think this is dangerous. My way is to set forth the Christian contemplative way and the Zen Buddhist way. When one is truly immersed in silent practice, then they become integrated within the person, and then they are expressed in their unique ways. These expressions are the forms, the phenomena. The sense of personal presence, the sense of impersonal presence. These forms are exactly emptiness. Conflict arises when we get stuck on one form and think it's truth with a big "T."

---

* Upaya: (Sanskrit) Expedient or skillful means; a device tailored to the particular individual to help attain understanding.

† Gelassenheit: (German) Serenity. The term was used by Meister Eckhart to mean releasement, or letting go, and it continues to be used in that sense in the German mystical tradition. See e.g.: https://www.hermitary.com/solitude/eckhart.html

Paraphrasing the Diamond Sutra he said, "Is God the father personal or impersonal — s/he is neither; therefore we call God the Father. Does the Buddha have the 32 marks of the Buddha — no. Therefore, we say the Buddha has the 32 marks of the Buddha." He went on:

> For a teacher to set themselves out and say they are going to synthesize and integrate — No. But a person can integrate organically by practicing both. ... Yamada [Ko'un] Roshi thought that eventually there would be a Zen stream in Christianity. There are some who try to make the two ways equivalent — this causes a lot of consternation and difficulty. ... I'm not denigrating the excellent studies done in academia in comparative religion. And there are conferences on comparative religion, with lots of argument. What they find for the most part with these things is when they just go into the meditation hall and sit down, that's where they find common ground. And in compassionate action. Just leave the doctrines alone. They are fingers pointing at the moon.
>
> Buddha and Christ are archetypal — they are projections. There's nothing wrong with projections as long as you take them back. Once you take them back you have the realization that I and Abba* are one, I and the Buddha are not two.
>
> There is a way up the mountain. This is the equipment you have to take. This is the way you have to go. You get to the top — you have no way to describe it. If you go down to talk to people about it you have to use language. In Christian spirituality, there's the cataphatic,† the way of images, devotion; and the apophatic‡ — St. John of the Cross: *nada*, *nada*, nothing, no images, no thoughts.
>
> I am a cradle Christian — and was very devout to the point of entering the seminary at 13. I came to a point where it just worked as it should. The whole thing collapsed. I couldn't pray anymore. ... But there was no spiritual master to tell me that. So I just muddled along until I found a book called *Christian Yoga.* Then another book, *Zen Mind, Beginner's Mind.* Then more Zen books. And that got me going. Then I found a Zen master, Robert Aitken. Then I began to look into the Christian way, and found out what the Christian way could have been had I not found Zen. So I knew these were parallel paths. I studied for a long time with another Catholic priest who was a Zen master [Willigis Jäger]. Now I teach both paths. What I should have gotten in Christianity, I got in Zen.

---

* Abba: (Aramaic) Father; in this context, used as a reference to God.

† The cataphatic or positive theological approach uses language to describe what God *is.*

‡ The apophatic or negative approach uses language to say what God is not; it includes mystical practices of silent, wordless contemplation.

A few more questions and remarks, then he looked at the clock and abruptly adjourned: "Nine o'clock! Thank you very much."

Contemplative Intensive Retreat Conferences and Sesshin Teisho, 1990s

Unlike classes, in which he took pains to explain things, Pat's retreat talks, whether conferences in contemplative intensive retreats or teisho in sesshin, tended toward the presentational rather than the discursive. His words offered glimpses of the experiential, unmediated reality the sitters were seeking and exploring in the silence on their cushions. On the Zen side, talks were usually koan-based, a form he learned from Aitken. He generally began by reading a case from one of the koan collections, followed by historical details about the life of the master who featured in the case. He would thread together snippets from the ancient lore and from his own experience to bring the case from its origins in the past into the living, breathing reality of the participants in the zendo of that present moment.

Through teisho and through students' own work with koans, the old masters would become familiar, beloved companions, both staff and guide. Yunmen was a favorite of Pat's. So were Zhaozhou * and Dongshan,† among others. One or another would come up in dokusan, not only as the subject in a koan, but also because for those working on koans, the words and doings of the masters became part of the language of practice. The presentation of a koan long before might come back to a student as the expression of some new opening. More than once in such a situation, Pat would nod his head gently and say something like, "Old Zhaozhou …," in the manner of one fondly recalling an old dear friend.

On the contemplative side, conferences often included stories from the Desert Fathers‡ or the medieval mystics. Perhaps as a nod to his activist students of various stripes — so that they could feel they were not wasting time sitting in silence on their cushions instead of being out demonstrating and serving in soup kitchens — or perhaps simply because it fit so well with contemplative practice, Pat told the rainmaker story, learned from Willigis Jäger:

---

* Zhaozhou (778-897 CE), Chinese Ch'an master. (Japanese: Joshu)

† Dongshan Liangjie (807–869) Chinese Ch'an master (Japanese: Tozan Ryokai).

‡ The Desert Fathers and Mothers were early Christian hermits, ascetics, and monks who lived mainly in the desert of Egypt beginning around the third century CE. Mayers, Gregory. *Listen to the Desert: Secrets of Spiritual Maturity from the Desert Fathers and Mothers.* Chicago, Ill.: ACTA Publishers, 1996.

> The village had no rain for a long time. All the prayers and processions had been in vain. The skies remained shut tight. In the hour of its greatest need, the village turned to the great rainmaker. He came and asked for a hut on the edge of the village, and a five-day supply of bread and water. Then he sent the people off to their daily work. On the fourth day, it rained. The people gathered at the rainmaker's hut to ask about the mystery of rainmaking. He answered them, "I can't make it rain." "But it is raining," the people said. The rainmaker explained: "When I came to your village, I saw the inner and outer disorder. I went into the hut and got myself in order. When I was in order, you too got in order; and when you were in order, nature got in order; and when nature got in order, it rained."

For the anguish confided to Pat about all manner of perceived wrongs, one of the stories from Abba Macarius, a Desert Father, was a good one:

> A man who came to Abba Macarius asking, "Give me a word, that I may be saved." Macarius told him to go to the cemetery and abuse the dead. The man did so. Macarius asked, "Did they say anything?" "No." He told the man to go back, and this time praise the dead. The man did as he was told. Macarius again asked him if the dead had responded. The man said no. Macarius said, "Go and be like them."

Pat offered practical encouragement:

> Forget about some magnificent firework in your experience. Then we can relax into the simple present. Choosing colors, spices, places to walk, people to visit — all the very concrete decisions of everyday life that day by day either support or discourage. We are inseparable from our own selves and from the world. And both are found in all the many things. Zen is about the freedom and the pleasure of shaping our lives in the deepest intimacy with reality as it is. Zen begins with observance of how things are. Observance of breath, body, birds, trees, wind. Observance is a word from ritual and religion — it means to watch out for but also to keep, to honor, as in observance of a holiday. Observe, respect, honor whatever is the true fact of your life.[356]

Commonly after a retreat, there would be fervent requests for copies of the talks. As a result, classes, teisho and conferences were sometimes recorded and cassette tapes made available to the various groups that claimed Pat as their teacher, including Mountain Cloud in Santa Fe, Seven Thunders in the Pacific Northwest, Zen Desert Sangha in Tucson, and the Melbourne Zen Group in Australia.

Article on Role of the Teacher

Despite his great reluctance to have his words published, that winter of 1991-92 Pat agreed to write an article for *Studies in Formative Spirituality, a* "tri-yearly publication that studies and fosters the art and discipline of foundational human and Christian formation." It was published with the title, "Authority: The Role of the Teacher in Buddhist-Christian Formation."[357] In it he reflected on his experience as a teacher of both Christian contemplation and Zen Buddhism, what he called a bi-traditional person. He began with the question most often asked when people first learn he is both a Catholic priest and a Zen Master: "How does one integrate the two paths? And is it even possible to hold and practice two different religions?" Then there is the question, how does a bi-traditional person teach others? His point above all is that authority lies within the individual.

> There must be trust, but not blind faith, in the teacher. The point of this special pedagogy cannot be imitation or dependency. The teacher seeks to create those conditions in which the disciple realizes his or her own inner authority. The point is liberation. … The teachers of Zen and contemplation are not spiritual directors in the later Western sense, that is to say, they do not continually discuss spiritual states or levels. … The teacher presents his or her discernment of reality by word and action. What is sought by the disciple is not explanation, counseling, or any kind of dialogue arguing a point. The teacher is asked for, and is expected to give, what the Desert Fathers called "the Word of Life."[358]

Pat goes on to compare contemplative and Zen practice in terms of method. Modern contemplative practice has borrowed a basic framework from Zen, including retreats with blocks of silent sitting, one-on-one encounters with the teacher, a daily presentation from the teacher, and work practice. He points out that koans are a tool unique to Zen, at least traditionally, although someone like Aitken in his teaching of Christians, could offer koan-like sayings drawing from Christian sources such as, "In the beginning was the Word — What is that Word?" Here too, Pat makes the point about not mixing. "This author holds that Christianity should be taught from a Christian point of view and that Zen should be taught from a Zen point of view. To teach Zen from a Christian point of view and vice versa is to invite syncretism; it can at least be confusing and at worst distorting. … The real integration of traditions is not in doctrines or ecumenical meetings or action; it is something which takes place in the souls of individuals struggling on their own spiritual path."

Pat wrote beautifully. Like the article published in *The Catholic World* in 1990,[359] this one is cogent and helpful. Yet, not counting talks and reflections printed in newsletters from his various sanghas, these two articles are the only writings published by Pat Hawk. His reticence to put anything in print was partly out of a desire to fly under the radar of the Catholic Church. When he sent Aitken a draft of the article for *Studies in Formative Spirituality*, he said, "My paranoia really begins to boil and bubble when it comes to publishing."[360] And there were other deterrents. Around this time Greg Mayers was working on a book about the desert hermits — published in 1996 as *Listen to the Desert: Secrets of Spiritual Maturity from the Desert Fathers and Mothers*.[361] Seeing Greg labor dampened any inclination Pat may have had to contribute in writing himself. In any case, although he was an avid reader and very much current with whatever new came out in the vast and growing Zen Christian literature, he felt no need to add his own voice to the mix.

Many times over the years, his students pleaded with him to publish his talks. Once while recording a Q&A session, he mentioned something about possibly reviewing such discussions and using them as a basis for writing, but that came to naught. Various people volunteered to curate his talks for him and edit them into a book. He always declined. It wasn't just uneasiness at making waves in the Church and disinclination to invest his energy in that direction. He borrowed heavily from others, often without attribution, and had lost track of what was actually his.

While he was still in the major seminary, he developed a habit of photocopying books or sections of books that were important to him, cutting and pasting the parts he especially liked to make a more concentrated read. He did this with Aitken's *Gateless Barrier*,[362] in this case so that he could extract the cases and verses for handy reference without the commentary. He had several of these cut-and-paste efforts in his files. They must have taken hours to do. Digging some of these out one day in his office, he said with satisfaction, "This way, you can make your own book the way you want it."[363]

Perhaps from these roots, when preparing talks he would extract whole paragraphs, sometimes a chapter, cross out bits he didn't need, change a word here and there. Particularly with his talks for contemplative retreats, he had a knack for taking something from someone else, and with a few strokes, making it better than the original. He rarely kept track of sources, perhaps coming at it from his vow of poverty: he was unpossessive of his own words and did not trouble himself greatly about anyone else's copyright. What he offered in his talks — the tone of voice, the cadence, the penetrating look — made them more than what they were on the page. Whatever the source of the written words, they were made original in the presentation.

Diamond Sangha Teachers' Circle

Pat traveled to Hawaii for the Diamond Sangha teachers' meeting in May 1992. In advance of the meeting, Aitken had written to the teachers with updates and thoughts for discussion. Pat sent a handwritten note in reply, including Anne in his greeting:

> Dear Anne and Roshi,
>
> Of course I will be there for the May meeting. I am eagerly looking forward to it. I'm very happy to hear the news in your letter to the teachers. The news about Jack Duffy and Nelson is a particular relief to me — off the hook on those two. Two issues that is. I'm also happy about Rolf. I'm sure he will be a great teacher.
>
> Here's wishing you both a Happy Easter.
>
> Love,
>
> Pat[364]

With regard to Nelson, Pat's relief likely had to do with the fact that Nelson had agreed to organize the next teachers' meeting. With regard to Jack Duffy, Pat was probably referring to Aitken's intention to authorize Jack as an apprentice teacher. This was of particular interest to Pat since he was one of a few people being considered to replace Joan Rieck, who had been recruited as the teacher of the Three Treasures Sangha when they formed as a more Zen-focused offshoot of the original Pacific Northwest "Zen for Christians" group. Joan, who also had her own sangha at Sonnenhof in Germany, had announced her intention to give up teaching in Washington, and the group was looking for another teacher. Although Pat had an affection for many in the Three Treasures group and would not have wanted to let them down, his schedule was already more than full. Jack Duffy was part of the Three Treasures Sangha, and his appointment as a teacher would give the group a better choice in any case, since they wanted a resident teacher rather than someone who would come in a few times a year to offer sesshin.

At the May 1992 Diamond Sangha teachers' meeting, the lineage and authorization question involving Japan and the concerns about the relationship to Sanbo Kyodan, though still unresolved, were becoming secondary to the concerns about succession and authority within the Diamond Sangha itself. Three new apprentice teachers were invited, all from Australia, all John Tarrant students: Subhana Barzaghi, Ross Bolleter, and Geoff Dawson. John had given them permission to teach, with Aitken's rubber stamp only after the fact, a process that flew in the face of the caution Aitken had given at the time of transmission, apparently at John's suggestion, recommending a period of at least ten years before the new teachers themselves appoint teachers. Not only had John given permission to teach, some of the others didn't discover that this was in the works until they learned that the new teachers would be coming to their meeting. The result was a clash between John, who felt his new teachers were not being welcomed appropriately, and the others trying to catch up with the fact of these sudden additions to the group and the lack of collegial process in inviting them in.[365]

Tensions among the teachers lingered beyond the close of the meeting. John was difficult to reach afterward. He wrote an eloquent letter expressing dismay at the discord, the reception of his new teachers with rules rather than welcome, the attempt to reverse decisions.[366]

Meanwhile, Pat made plans for his second trip to Japan for the November 1992 meeting of the Sanbo Kyodan international teachers. He had hesitated out of concern for what it might mean for Aitken's standing with the Sanbo Kyodan — whether they would think Aitken was, after all, sending his dharma heir to be approved — and whether there would be implications for Nelson, John and Augusto. With no objections expressed by the others, Pat decided to go. He had enjoyed the koan work with Kubota during the previous visit, and he would enjoy seeing his European friends in Japan again.

The Aitkens visit Bishop DeFalco Retreat Center

In October 1992, the Aitkens came to Bishop DeFalco Retreat Center for some quiet time together, which included Aitken working on his *paramitas* book, *The Practice of Perfection*.[367] Pat's schedule was so full — in and out briefly between a sesshin in Melbourne, Australia, and a retreat for the Seven Thunders group in Oregon, he missed the Aitkens' visit. The Aitkens joined the group for daily zazen, and Aitken offered dokusan. He recorded a class on the *paramitas* that included discussion with the group, and it was those voices from Amarillo that were included as Q&As at the end of the chapters he worked on while he was there.

Aitken wrote from BDRC to the Diamond Sangha teachers with news of his various enterprises and a description of the place. "…an elegant retreat center, very large, it seems to me, though Pat says it is medium sized. There are 50 double rooms for retreatants, each with bath, some 16 single rooms with bath, a guest suite with two rooms and bath which we occupy. Plus a church-size sanctuary, three large assembly rooms, office, bookstore, commercial kitchen, two dining rooms, zendo, etc., etc. Zazen is just down the hall from us, meals are trotted out — ideal for our purposes, which was to have quiet time and space for writing and resting."

A personal message from Aitken to Pat runs to three pages, mostly impressions of individual students and how they're doing in their practice, with some further observations of the ambience:

> I begin this letter at noon, waiting for the lunch line to run down a bit before I step in. Anne and I have had a wonderful, memorable stay. Everyone has been very kind, and we have had everything we needed and wanted — and are most grateful. I finished the essays for the *Paramita* book, as you can see, and got a lot of letters written. Tomorrow I will finally get at the signing and sealing of the *kechimyaku* which you so kindly and diligently and artistically prepared for me. … The folks on the staff have been very kind and helpful. Barbara, Angie, Carol, Leroy, have been very friendly. You are fortunate to have such a supportive group. Greg too has been very friendly and very helpful. We have had many enjoyable suppers together.[368]

Aitken was pleased with Pat's sangha but not so fully satisfied that he could resist giving some detailed advice.

> I have certainly enjoyed zazen with the group in the evenings; having a zendo right down the hall with the folks there is conducive to regular practice. I felt right at home and was impressed with the diligence people show. There are little differences which help to give the practice individuality and are fine with me. I do have one suggestion, however. People seem to stand too quickly at the end of a period. They seem to flip the top leg down, stand on the mat, then walk around the *zafu* on the mat to the floor in front of the *zafu*. This risks injury to knees and ankles. I suggest that you advise them to take hold of ankle with one hand, knee with the other, and gently lift the foot to the mat. Then repeat with the other foot if necessary. Then swing around on the cushion and stand with both feet on the floor, not on the mat.[369]

There was little chance that Pat would relay this last advice to the group, he not being inclined to tinker with anyone's practice to that level of detail.

Anne wrote too, her letter dated over five days, handwritten in her rounded, upright script:

> We're having a restful, profitable and happy time here. Everyone has been so loving and helpful. Greg a most companionable host, loaning books, taking us to Palo Duro [Canyon] — always concerned about our comfort, which is total. But we do miss you — Your presence is always just around the corner.

> The special ambiance of those great skies and teasing thrusting winds and the infinitely flexible trees that thrash about and then are totally still — has grown on me — a quite new experience, and I revel in my walks.[370]

Anne had happily browsed Pat's library, dipping into lives of John of the Cross and Teresa of Avila. Not finishing either, she eventually settled on Victoria Lincoln's biography[371] of Teresa to borrow, "...my empathy with her holds me fast," though she left the life of St. John behind regretfully: "I would have reveled in being plunged into the astonishing complication of the social and political structure (and religious!) of the world he lived in, and explored the details of the way he held to his conviction and made his way through that tumultuous world."[372]

Pat began a reply to the Aitkens a few days later:

> Dear Anne and Roshi,
>
> Thanks for the letters you left for me to find on my return. I'm really happy your stay here has been restful and productive.
>
> Well, so much for that portion of the letter. It is now October 23rd. I started an eight-day Contemplative Retreat the night of the 15th, and I never got back to this until today. Your card arrived yesterday. So, I add my pleasure that your stop in Berkeley went well.
>
> I feel on the way back to normal. This has been a busy two months. Why am I not richer? Melbourne was cold, rainy; but all went extremely well — 33 participants, quite an increase from the first time. I also made contact again with my Redemptorist confreres from Singapore and we are negotiating a time I can go there to lead a retreat. I told the Melbourne Zen Group I would come to Australia only one more time, so get acquainted with the new Australian teachers, which they are doing. Portland was fine, and we had a full house for the last retreat here.
>
> Everyone here is in good health and spirits and still talking of how much your visit was appreciated, both of you. I have not had a chance to listen to the tape of the class but am looking forward to it.
>
> Take care of yourselves. Looking forward to seeing you in May.
>
> Love
>
> Pat[373]

There was nothing in these letters about the Sanbo Kyodan situation. Aitken was still angling for acknowledgment of his dharma heirs as masters within the Sanbo Kyodan. Pat had accepted Kubota's invitation to come to Japan. Less than a month after his return to Amarillo from Portland he would fly there — his second visit — for the sesshin and meeting of the Sanbo Kyodan teachers at San'un Zendo in Kamakura.

6

Further Adventures

Second trip to Japan, November 1992

All correspondence with Kubota Akira about Pat's visit to Kamakura was done through Robert Aitken. He wrote to Kubota in June explaining, "Pat Hawk will be traveling this fall with colleagues from his Empty Sky Sangha in Amarillo, Texas. He would like very much to arrange to attend the November sesshin for overseas teachers, and he asked me to sound you about this. He would be attending on his own and would not be representing me. He said that his purpose would be to deepen his understanding. He expressed appreciation for the help you gave him in dokusan during his last visit to Kamakura. He would be able to stay at the Redemptorist House [actually the Jesuit retreat house], so would not impose upon the San'un Zendo or Mrs. Yamada for accommodations." Kubota told Aitken that he would continue working on the Miscellaneous Koans[374] with Pat, and that Ryo'un Roshi [Yamada Masamichi] would like him to do *Hekiganroku*[375] Cases 6 and 55 and *Shoyoroku*[376] Cases 17, 46 and 64. "So please ask him to prepare them."[377]

Bill Lawder traveled with Pat to Japan. Years later, Bill remembered the train trip, rolling along between Tokyo and Kamakura. "We sat silently for quite some time: reading, looking out the window. After a while, Pat looked at me and paid me the highest compliment: 'You know, Bill, traveling with you is almost as good as traveling by myself.' "[378] Bill went off and did his own thing while Pat stayed at the Jesuits' place in Kamakura, getting up very early to go over to the sesshin.

The koan that came up first with Yamada Masamichi[379] was *Hekiganroku* Case 6:

> Unmon, giving instruction, said, "I don't ask you about before the fifteenth day; bring me a phrase about after the fifteenth day." Unmon himself answered in the monks' stead, "Every day is a good day."[380]

Pat rejected the obvious potential for denying the existence of pain and instead gave a presentation that included the wide breadth of human experience. Masamichi rejected it. They came to blows, figuratively, and Pat, sensing a power play on Masamichi's part and not wishing to indulge him, "shook out his sleeves and left."[381] It was a shock, not least to himself, also to the others present. For the remaining days of the sesshin, Pat stayed at the Jesuit retreat house, reading, sitting, and doing a lot of walking around Kamakura. He went back to San'un Zendo on the last day for the sesshin closing, then flew back to biting cold and snowy weather in Amarillo. He called Aitken first thing to tell him what had happened. Repercussions reverberated west to Europe and east to Hawaii and the Americas. This dharma heir of Robert Aitken had walked out on the leaders of the Sanbo Kyodan. What did it mean for the Diamond Sangha?

Father AMA Samy, one of those present at the Kamakura teachers' sesshin, wrote a diplomatic but pointed letter to Kubota and Yamada Masamichi expressing concern and pleading for greater trust. He was unhappy with the treatment of Willigis Jäger and of Pat Hawk, and through Pat, of the Diamond Sangha. He noted that the future of the Sanbo Kyodan will reside outside of Japan, and although he appreciated the efforts of the Japanese leaders toward maintaining authenticity, purity and depth of the organization, he objected to their approach. Regarding Jäger, he wrote:

> Fr. Willigis has been approved as Junshike. That means he has the right eye and that he can lead the students through koan training. Now if you go to check his students and confirm their kensho and competence, it will reduce Willigis in the eyes of his students to their own level and throw doubts on his right vision and competence. If you go as a friend, and let him do the work and only assist him, if and when he wants, then it will be different. To go almost as examiners of his students and issue certificates of pass-fail, over against the guidance and authority of Willigis, is to reduce his authority to a nonentity. No wonder he is feeling unhappy, and some of his senior students seem to be tired of this whole affair and want to go to Aitken Roshi.[382]

Samy acknowledged that he himself felt Willigis had too many students, but he thought this was unrelated to the issue of authority. He went on to express concern about the situation with Pat:

> The second point I would like to mention is the relationship between Sambokyodan and Aitken Roshi and Diamond Sangha. I do not know the exact status. Aitken Roshi and Diamond Sangha flow from Sambokyodan, and they have a great name and future in the USA, Australia, and elsewhere.

> Sambokyodan and Diamond Sangha are the future of Zen in the West. … [Aitken] has a good standing even with many Japanese Zen masters I have met. When Fr. Pat Hawk, who is accredited by Aitken as authentic Roshi, came for our sesshin, it was a fine gesture on the part of Fr. Hawk and of Aitken Roshi. I felt sad he left after the first day. … I do not know exactly what happened. Perhaps he was treated as an outsider and submitted to examination as an ordinary student.[383]

Samy gave a copy of the letter to Jäger, which Jäger then included in a letter he wrote to Pat, saying, "Thank you very much for your phone call. I understand Aitken Roshi very well. … You can share the letter of AMA Samy with him. I am definitely decided to go my own way, if nothing happens in August in Dietfurt. As you can see from the letter of AMA Samy, he is of the opinion, to appoint our own assistant teachers and form our own sanghas. Like AMA Samy I am very interested to integrate the Diamond-Sangha in Sanbo-Kyodan, without giving up their independence or right of self-determination."

Aitken didn't weigh in with Pat until mid-December, both of them having been occupied with *Rohatsu** sesshin earlier in the month:

> I appreciated your calling me the day you got back from Kamakura. I am not sure how supportive I was. You must have been feeling quite *je ne sais quoi* after the episode with Yamada Roshi. You have my full, unqualified support. You have standing there, and your action must have been a dash of cold water. I have a hunch that there was some self-searching afterwards on the other side. Ursula Baatz, who did a couple of training periods here a while back and is a student of Fr. Samy, wrote Jason from Japan that she heard there was a conflict between the Japanese and American contingents of the Sanbo Kyodan, but that it was patched up. That's the only feedback I've gotten. A card from Paul Shepherd said nothing about it.[384]

In the same letter to Pat, Aitken shifted to the continuing question of how to support Willigis Jäger in the face of Japanese refusal to give him independence. Still hoping to get formal acknowledgment of the Diamond Sangha within Sanbo Kyodan, he did not want to make waves.

> My response to Willigis's suggestion that I give him transmission just through me was off the top of my head. Augusto reminds me that we discussed such a possibility at the teachers' meeting before last. I have just a

* Rohatsu: (Japanese) The eighth day of the last month of the year; traditionally an 8-day sesshin commemorating Shakyamuni Buddha's enlightenment. Rohatsu usually takes place December 1-8.

> vague memory of that. It would be expedient if I felt that I could do it, but on careful thought I realize I cannot indeed consider it at this time. (1) It would be an exception that I can't be sure would be in keeping with my authority, and would establish a precedent for which I don't feel quite prepared. (2) It would mean a break with Kamakura, something I am not quite ready to do. (3) I meet too many students of Willigis who are further along on their koan study than their understanding would seem to justify. Thus I have questions about his own eye. (4) I am not sure where Willigis stands with regard to Buddhism. Could he do Jukai? (5) He should really approach me directly about the matter, and not try to negotiate through you.[385]

Pat replied to Aitken:

> First, there is no question of my feeling not supported by you. In fact I'm always amazed and grateful for your support and interest in me. … I'm beginning to realize my actions at the Kamakura sesshin have more karma flowing from them than for me personally. Willigis wrote to me and included a copy of AMA Samy's letter to Kubota and Yamada Masamichi. AMA Samy is expressing his own view in the matter. I did not expect to be treated differently than anyone else. Nevertheless, I agree that the confirmed teachers ought not have to go through this constant submission. I agree that Willigis ought to deal with you directly.[386]

In fact, although Willigis was dealing with Aitken directly, he had naturally also discussed his concerns with Pat when they were together in Japan and later over the phone, as Pat explained to Aitken. Pat wrote:

> And he [Willigis] told me he is going to write you [Aitken]. But, there are a couple of things I can still add. Willigis told me in Kamakura that he has no difficulty with taking Jukai. As to his Zen eye, I think it is quite clear. But his work in the dokusan room is often hurried and not much attention is paid to detail and clarity for the student. In Kamakura, the leaders often stress that koans are not important. They say the important thing is the experience of empty oneness and that freedom in handling the koans is the touchstone of the experience. I believe Willigis possesses much the same attitude.[387]

As did Pat.

Aitken did not communicate with Japan about the incident until January 1993, over a month after Pat had left Kamakura. He wrote to Kubota with his usual tact and diplomacy, still advocating for some of the European teachers. Regarding Pat's experience with Yamada Masamichi [Ryo'un Roshi], Aitken said in a letter to Kubota:

> Pat Hawk reported his unhappiness with the November *Kenshukai* (collective koan review). He had gone with the sincere purpose of koan review and was disappointed by what he perceived as a lack of give-and-take in Yamada Ryo'un Roshi's room. I am profoundly sorry about this falling out among people with whom I have deep personal and Dharma connections. It is good that Pat returned to the San'un Zendo after the meetings were over and effected a kind of reconciliation. My trust in him has not been disturbed in the least by this incident, but I can't be sure how it affects the broader relationships that are involved. I should like to carry his effort toward reconciliation even further and help to rectify any matters that might still need correcting.[388]

Aitken went on to discuss the situation for the European teachers:

> Pat wrote to me recently and enclosed a copy of Fr. Samy's letter to you and Yamada Roshi of November 27. I see in that letter mention of the relationship of the Sanbo Kyodan with me and with the Diamond Sangha, including the point that certain European teachers have begun turning to me for guidance and possible transmission. This gives me the opening I have been awaiting to take up these matters with you directly. I question the various European teachers and senior students who come here to sesshin and training periods to be sure that studying with me is all right with you. You and I discussed Sr. Pia's wish for transmission, but I should also mention that a significant number of others have inquired about it. I have simply told those people that I cannot sanction anyone as a teacher with whom I have worked very little and don't know very well. Actually, quite apart from knowing or not knowing the Europeans well, I want you and Yamada [Ryo'un] Roshi, as rightful successors of Yamada Ko'un Roshi, to have a clear field in training and acknowledging Sanbo Kyodan teachers.[389]

Having first rejected the idea, Aitken had changed his mind about authorizing Rolf Drosten. His letter to Kubota continued:

> Thus at present I am not considering any European as a teacher of the Diamond Sangha, except the Rev. Rolf Drosten. He is a disciple of Fr. Willigis, and as I recall did not have any contact with Ko'un Roshi. He has come to Hawaii three times for extended periods. I find that he has a good eye and that he is past any blocks on his path that would prevent him from becoming more and more clear. …
>
> I have taken my position about Drosten reluctantly, feeling that he is really Fr. Willigis's student and that it is Fr. Willigis who should be sanctioning him. This leads me to comment about Fr. Samy's plea for *Shoshike* status for Fr. Willigis. My impression is that Fr. Samy, like all Jesuits, has made a lifetime practice of obedience and patience. He may seem to be making his

> points quite gently but actually I find it a bit unusual that he should make them at all. I sense that he is voicing strong feelings that have probably been simmering for a long time. I also sense that he is a bellwether whose views are likely to be shared by others. Speaking to his points for myself: I view Fr. Willigis as the de facto leader of Zen Buddhism in Europe. If his position were also de jure, it would relieve me of some deep worries and, I feel, it would give him and the European Sangha the confirmation that they need at this difficult time.[390]

Aitken reiterated the point made earlier by Willigis Jäger about the importance of transmission:

> I remember a teacher from Japan who visited us on Maui around 1973. He asked me where I was in my koan study and I explained that I was in the final phases. He asked, "What will happen when you finish?" I said, "I don't know" (for Yamada [Ko'un] Roshi had not at that time talked to me about transmission) and then I added, "I suppose it doesn't matter." He replied, "Yes, you are right, it doesn't matter. It also matters very much." … I encourage the European teachers and senior students who come here to divert the energy of their anxiety to zazen and koan review, and they seem to find their stay productive. In other words, I try to prove that "it doesn't matter" with some success. But I know that "it also matters very much," and feel troubled.[391]

Aitken sent a copy of the letter to Pat Hawk with the handwritten note, "Thanks for your good letter. As you will see by this letter to Kubota, Samy's letter gives me the opening I was awaiting. … Of course your sense that I always trusted you is correct. But now my capacity to trust is deepened. My letter related to how I was by character. I will write soon."[392] Kubota's reply was much blunter than Aitken's careful diplomacy and bound to rankle. He pulled no punches with regard to Pat:

> As far as Fr. Hawk's problem is concerned, unfortunately I am obliged to confirm he had no real experience of enlightenment as he could not pass through koans in my Dokusan room. The real fact happened during the Sesshin was that he said abruptly he would leave Zendo on the 2nd day and never came back to challenge Koan study with me. As always mentioned, my responsibility is to keep the purity of Dharma transferred from Shakyamuni Buddha, all Patriarchs, Yasutani Roshi and Yamada Ko'un Roshi. So my advice is that he should restart his Koan study until he forget himself completely as Dogen Zenji mentioned.[393]

The censure of Pat, and by extension of Aitken's ability to confirm kensho in his students, was perhaps entirely based on Yamada Masamichi's rejection of Pat's presentation of the *Hekiganroku* case number 6 (Every day is a good day). Prior to that, Pat had worked fruitfully with Kubota in the dokusan room. It was not the only time Kubota was influenced to dismiss a presentation he might otherwise have affirmed. In the book, *A Straight Road with 99 Curves*, Greg Shepherd describes an experience where Kubota is swayed in his judgment, in this case influenced by Yamada Ko'un. Shepherd presents an experience to Kubota, who taking it at face value as kensho, takes him to see Yamada for confirmation. Shepherd writes, "I had been assigned to do dokusan with Kubota Sensei, a youthful fifty-two-year-old, who was rumored to be Yamada [Ko'un] Roshi's choice as successor. … Yamada Roshi looked probingly at me as I stood crying and laughing, and said something under his breath to Kubota Sensei. It must have been something along the lines of, "He does this kind of thing from time to time. Don't pay any attention to it,' because at my next dokusan later in the day, Kubota smiled sheepishly and said, 'You are a very good actor.'[394] "

Word was that Yamada Masamichi had recently experienced great *satori* and was living and seeing very much from the side of pure emptiness,* effectively feeling/seeing no pain. Some years later, Masamichi reconsidered. He sent multiple apologies to Pat via different emissaries, first Greg Mayers, who did not relay the message, then Nelson Foster who visited Kamakura in 2006, then again via a longtime student of Pat's who attended sesshin with Yamada Masamichi in Spring 2012.

It seems not surprising that Kubota and Yamada Masamichi, having insisted over and over again for several years that Aitken could not adequately recognize insight or authorize his own students and that only they could do this, would feel a strong incentive to vindicate their judgment by finding fault with Aitken's dharma heir. In the thick of this power struggle, Yamada Masamichi rejected Pat's presentation of Case 6 in the *Hekiganroku*, significantly widening the rift between the Diamond Sangha and the Sanbo Kyodan.

In his letter to Aitken, Kubota went on to argue against any authorization of Drosten as a teacher. Aitken put Kubota's letter in the mail to Pat then telephoned to let him know it was coming. In response, Pat wrote to Aitken:

---

* The experience of "emptiness" as referred to in Zen, relates to an aspect of the profound "seeing" that is the enlightenment or realization experience in which all separation falls away. "Body and mind drop away" as Dogen has said. *Record of Things Heard from the Treasury of the Eye of the True Teaching: The Shobogenzo-zuimonki, talks of Zen Master Dogen as recorded by Zen Master Ejo.* Translated by Thomas Cleary. Prajna Press, Boulder, 1980.

> Since our telephone conversation last month, I've been ruminating on Kubota Roshi's comment about my degree of insight. The most positive aspect is that it has me ruminating. Keeps the virtue of humility bright and the motivation for sitting and study strong. My negative feelings have to do with what they must think of your judgment in confirming me. I regret not giving a better showing for you. I still think, however, that the Sanbo Kyodan leaders do not grasp Western minds, and I certainly don't like what I've encountered of theirs — in the sense I have no wish to change my way or even temporarily adapt to their way. This is it.[395]

In fact, Pat's presentation to Yamada Masamichi of *Hekiganroku* Case 6 was widely agreed upon among the Western teachers. There was great consternation regarding the presentation Yamada Masamichi required, which was seen as antinomian — the Christian Anabaptist notion that true faith gives one freedom from morality, or as Aitken phrased the problem in a letter to the Diamond Sangha teachers, "It's all empty so what the hell."[396] Aitken appended a handwritten note to Pat at the end of a letter to the Diamond Sangha teachers: "Not to worry about Sanbo Kyodan. I admire your gumption and fortitude in taking them on."[397]

The tone in Aitken's next reply to Kubota was different. It's addressed to "Dear Ji'un Roshi," and is conciliatory — apologetic even. He wrote:

> I am sad that Fr. Hawk did not pass muster in your room and in the room of Ryo'un Roshi [Yamada Masamichi]. This is a bitter pill for me and I must swallow it like a man. He and I continue to work together in my room. I take your cautions very much to heart.[398]

Aitken was still trying to preserve the succession:

> You and I have known each other since 1957 and Ryo'un Roshi and I have known each other since 1960. 36 and 33 years — more than a generation! You and Ryo'un Roshi and I have a deep affinity through our practice together, our common Dharma heritage from Ko'un Roshi and Haku'un Roshi [Yasutani] and from our common loyalty to the San'un Zendo and its many members, particularly Mrs. Yamada [actually Dr. Yamada; wife of Yamada Ko'un, and mother of Masamichi]. I have not always honored this affinity, partly because of my character flaws and poor judgment, partly because of cultural and linguistic misunderstandings. It is, however, affinity I do wish to honor throughout my life as best I can, whatever happens.[399]

Kubota, for his part, was still fussing about Pat in June, explicitly disinviting him to future meetings. He sent Aitken a copy of the announcement for the fourth

European Zen Teachers' Sesshin to be held in Dietfurt from August 9-12, 1993. He understood that Aitken would not be able to come because of his health, but said, "I ask you not to allow Fr. Hawk to join it, to refrain from the same situation as the last year."

After the meeting in Dietfurt, Willigis sent Pat and Aitken a copy of the minutes. Once again, heated argument had broken out among the European teachers about Christian Zen, the exchange sufficiently charged that Yamada Masamichi, with great diplomacy, cut off the discussion and asked each of the teachers to express their views to him in dokusan. He presented a synthesis at the end of the meeting, with the upshot that "those who deem it important for Zen to grow and develop in its own as it is being transplanted into Western culture, and are careful not to let it be mixed with Christian concepts and imagery, you may continue in your approach. And for those who are looking for a way to integrate their Zen experience and their teaching with Christianity …you may also continue in your approach, seeking ways to deepen and purify your own experience and that of your disciples as you do so." He went on to caution: "The heart of Zen … is totally beyond all words and concepts. … As we continue indefatigably in our zazen practice, we deepen our realization and increase our inner freedom to be able to use all kinds of words and concepts, yet without the least reliance on any such words and concepts."[400]

There continued to be reverberations about *Hekiganroku* Case 6 and the fundamental difference between the Western and Japanese approaches. Roselyn Stone, who had been sanctioned to teach by Yamada Ko'un Roshi, had a sangha in Toronto and one in Brisbane, Australia. While traveling between Australia and Canada she stopped in for a visit to Palolo in Hawaii. Aitken wrote to Pat:

> Roselyn Stone was here for eight days. The members, particularly the residents, were stunned. Her account of dokusan with Ryo'un Roshi on Unmon's "Every Day Is a Good Day" was the same as I heard from you and from a cross-section of Europeans. However, this time the danger of the Roshi's preferred response finally sank in. I appreciated the more that you walked out. Well done![401]

The situation was not without humor. Aitken went on:

> Augusto told me about a comic strip somebody sent him. First frame: monk sees tree and says, "There is no tree." Second frame: monk sees river and says, "There is no river." Third frame: monk sees bear and says, "There is no bear." Fourth frame, bear is licking his chops and saying, "There is no monk."[402]

Mutual support, with friction

One of several outcomes from the 1992 Diamond Sangha teachers' meeting was that responsibility for setting the agenda would now rotate, Nelson Foster taking the baton first. He wrote to the group soliciting agenda items for the next meeting, acknowledging with concern the tensions at the previous meeting and pleading for communication and resolution of issues before the next one.[403]

Pat had set Nelson's letter aside as he prepared for his second trip to Japan in fall,1992. On his return he replied:

> Thanks for your letter of 9 November. Sorry for the late reply. I too was troubled by the discord of our last meeting. I was not expecting it, nor did I understand its source then or now. I find it hard to comprehend John [Tarrant]'s desire not to attend the next meeting. I think he makes a very desirable proposal on the pace of the meeting then says he will not come. What's going on? I have always felt somewhat of an outsider when it comes to the relations among the others — not a participant in some past history. So, for the sake of the group, perhaps the only agenda we should have is to work on our relationship. If we do that, then it would be best to have an outside facilitator. If we do that then John needs to be present. If John refuses to attend. Then we might as well go ahead as we have in the past. The only item of agenda I would like to add is *Kenshukai* [koan review]. I'm feeling a need to sharpen my meager skill in dealing with koans.[404]

Pat told Nelson about his clash with Yamada Masamichi: "I just returned from Japan where I attended part of the sesshin for the Sanbo Kyodan Teachers. It did not go well with me. Masamichi and I got quite angry and I left in the middle of it. The trip was not a total loss. I enjoyed seeing the European teachers."[405]

The discord among Diamond Sangha teachers set off some deep self-reflection in Robert Aitken. In December he wrote a long letter to each of the four transmitted teachers, a mixture of personal and boilerplate. The letter gives a perspective on the struggles and shifts in the Diamond Sangha Teachers' Circle identity, the love and respect Aitken had for his heirs, the deep humility he sometimes lived, the vulnerability he allowed in himself (Anne said to Pat once, "He has no carapace"), and his care about and sense of responsibility for the health and well-being of the Diamond Sangha:

> Here is some boilerplate, modified to relate to you, which I prepared for you, Augusto, John, and Nelson. Similar stuff will go to Joe [Bobrow, at that time an apprentice teacher] and to the Australians:

> Let me set forth what I have been going through lately with regard to our mutual concerns. I mentioned in our phone conversation that I was getting acquainted with my dark side. I have always acknowledged that like anyone else I have a shadow, and I knew that I projected it on others. With hard, painful work over the years, I came to understand the lineaments of the shadow, but I was not clear about its nature.

Aitken had begun working with René Tillich, a psychotherapist in Honolulu and son of the theologian Paul Tillich: "With René's help, I was able to use this crisis to understand something about my hidden nature. I am sure that I will get better and better acquainted with it as time goes on, but at least now I see more than its mere manifestations." He went on to describe in detail a dream that led him to reflect on the various people who had taught him.

> All my teachers had a shadow side. Senzaki[406] had a serious problem with authority. Yasutani[407] related inappropriately to women. Nakagawa[408] lived in a fantasy world. Yamada [Ko'un] was unable to be strict and exacting. I know that all of them were conscious of their shadows. Yamada confronted his the best of the four, but I feel that none of them really saw into the roots of their lifetime neuroses or discerned the lineaments clearly. The dark side was simply a part of their personalities and their projections on the world. While it colored their teaching, they were still marvelous roshis. I am their child in the dharma, for better or worse, and so are you, through me.[409]

After some soul-searching analysis in which Aitken blamed himself to some extent for the discord among his heirs he went on:

> I fully support your work and trust you from the bottom of my heart to live by the Buddha, Dharma, and Sangha, and to convey the Three Treasures to the world. I see clearly — and will practice continuing to see clearly — your various perspectives. But I don't know how to fix the present conflicts, and I suspect that I can't. My vision is that with my whole-hearted support, you and the other Diamond Sangha roshis will find compassionate means to cultivate the harmony of our family, while honoring its radically different constituents.

He continued with thoughts about a way forward for the teachers, news of various students and a comment about his health (he had chronic respiratory problems), then to books he knew would interest Pat, including Mircea Eliade's journals. "What a marvelous genius he was!… I will go on to read his autobiography, then some of his innumerable books."[410]

Pat replied to Aitken:

> I wrote to Nelson telling him I would be happy to have our May meeting work on our relationships, but that John would have to be there and an outside facilitator would be good in that case. If John decides to absent himself, then *kenshukai* would be high on my list of agenda items, but not exclusively.
>
> About our meeting last May. I felt that John and Nelson had other fish to fry while they were in Honolulu. I realize they used to live there and have many connections. But I felt their attention was divided. We didn't have time to sit together, every day felt pressured, tensions were building among us, but little room to call "time-out!" and deal with them. I hope in the future that our purpose for being in Honolulu in the first place is not short-changed. This is something that I have to communicate to John and Nelson myself of course. I have not written to John. I don't know what is blocking me, but surely it is my own shadow.[411]

Pat was largely peripheral to the disharmony among Aitken's other dharma heirs. This may have been partly because, unlike some of the Diamond Sangha teachers, he did not have the history of practicing side by side as students of one sangha. In the book based on conversations with Brother David Steindl-Rast, Aitken comments that "My most promising students have felt an imperative to power…"[412] Years later, reflecting on these Diamond Sangha Teachers' Circle troubles as well as various intrigues among students in his own sangha, Pat observed that not only do conflicts not necessarily diminish with longer practice, they are sometimes most marked in senior students and even in teachers. Speaking to me about this one day, Pat said, "I think I told you my first eye opening was when I was in Würzburg at a Sanbo Kyodan teachers' meeting during my year in Germany." Deeply conflict averse himself, Pat observed the flare-ups as one might watch a video game, engaged but mostly untroubled by implications for those involved.

In his reply to Aitken's long letter Pat easily slipped into the guide and counselor role to offer his old teacher words of support:

> I am in admiration of what you are now doing with your correspondence among us. It clarifies, invites unity and accepts diversity. But I especially admire what you are doing for yourself. You are truly a wonderful teacher and being willing to learn is a massive factor in that fact. No one learns who thinks he is complete.
>
> Your "ability to move and touch people" is demonstrated daily — even with your doubt. Even those who move away are touched. "Adequate human being?" It is rare to even be born a human being. Your being human is more than adequate for those who have realized their own adequacy in your

presence. We will all be pleased by your working with your doubts and becoming convinced. The Buddha is still sitting, confirming all incompleteness.

Your wrestling with your shadow and projections confronted me about mine own. It prompted me to do some re-reading of Hillman and others. Would that it were as easy to do as to know what to do. When Abraham wrestled with the angel all night, he received a wound and a blessing. Damn if they don't always come in pairs like that.

Although I haven't read Eliade's journals, I have enjoyed reading some of his other works. I met him once, back in the 60s. He gave a lecture at my seminary, but what I remember is his sitting on the hearth of the fireplace in our lounge, smoking his pipe and chatting away with us as equals. He was a gentle man.

It has been very cold and snowy here this month. Looks like we'll continue to get more of the same. I'm well, as is Greg and the others here. Hope you're over your cold and that Anne is well. My regards to all.

Love Pat[413]

Evident in this correspondence is Pat's evolution from callow, earnest young priest doing his first Zen retreat with Aitken in 1978 to the 1990s when he is as much counselor and encourager of Aitken as the reverse.

Looking ahead to the 1993 teachers' meeting, Joe Bobrow, one of five apprentice Diamond Sangha teachers (the others were Subhana Barzaghi, Ross Bolleter, Geoff Dawson and Jack Duffy, the latter recently appointed), responded to the group letters with a plea to devote the next meeting to their relationships. "I hope everyone will attend and that we will attend — to what is really before us."[414]

But as the meeting approached, Joe got cold feet and decided he wouldn't go. Ross Bolleter couldn't attend for other reasons. So without John, Joe and Ross, that meant eight teachers[415] including two new ones: Rolf Drosten and Jack Duffy. Rolf Drosten was in Honolulu in advance of the meeting to meet the other Diamond Sangha Teachers, and they began by voting to invite him to attend. Jack Duffy, having been made an apprentice teacher by Aitken in March, also came. Drosten was made apprentice teacher of the Diamond Sangha at this June 1993 meeting.[416]

They engaged René Tillich to facilitate. He set some ground rules to begin, paraphrased by Pat, who took minutes: "Be aware of language. Be aware of sibling stuff. Be aware of group/independence." They discussed distinctions between apprentice vs. transmitted teachers in their use of terms. They had agreed the year before that only teachers with dharma transmission would use the terms "dokusan" and "teisho" and carry the kotsu. Apprentice teachers who were not yet recognized with dharma transmission would use the terms "interview" and "dharma talk" respectively. The distinction in usage would serve as a reminder of a teacher's experience level. However, it became apparent that apprentice teachers appointed by John Tarrant were using the terms reserved for transmitted teachers, and at least one was also carrying a kotsu. They ratified the usages established previously, making an exception for Rolf Drosten — who, they decided, could continue usages set by Willigis Jäger. They decided to call themselves the Diamond Sangha Teachers' Circle to emphasize the egalitarian nature of the group, and that invitation to join the Circle would come from the members rather than from any individual, including Aitken.

Because of the expense both in time and money of meeting yearly with the whole group, they decided to alternate regional meetings and plenary/international meetings and to institute a "travel pool" to equalize expenses for members. They discussed gender balance among teachers and considered how to bring in a stronger female voice.

They discussed what their commitment as teachers encompassed, a question that included the conundrum of how many students is too many. There was the first of the four "Great Vows" recited regularly — to save the many beings. And it was enshrined in the Teacher Cautions given by Aitken at the transmission that they should take all comers. But how to serve all comers when they were coming in increasing numbers, not just in person but by phone, letter, tape (and soon to be by email and video chat)? The ancestors provided examples at both ends of the extreme — great masters with only one or a few students and others with thousands. What about among the Diamond Sangha teachers? In part, surely, it was a question of teacher support — more students meant more revenue, and for teachers not financially independent, this could be important. Based on Pat's notes from the meeting, that point was not prominent. Rather, the conversation focused on teaching styles and how much time each student takes.

One of the teachers expressed taking an interest in the lives of each of his students, not only as it relates directly to practice and what comes up in the dokusan room, but overall — their jobs, their relationships, their ways of coping with problems. He went so far as to say that if a student is in therapy, he sometimes asks for permission to speak with the therapist. Obviously, this approach would take a great deal of time and would necessarily limit the number of students a teacher could look after. This raised the question of selectivity. Should it be based on who is most promising? No one would want to consider that one student may be worth more or less than another, regardless of how unpromising they may appear at the outset. What about most committed? Both?

None of this troubled Pat. His style was spare. He did not get involved with his students' life struggles. Of course, their daily concerns came up in the dokusan room, but he felt no compulsion to solve anyone's problems. Life challenges were grist for the mill of practice, conditions to sit with, not necessarily to resolve. Although Pat said little at the teachers' meeting, he expressed his take on the subject at another time. It was at a contemplative intensive retreat in a conference titled "Curiosity" (later adapted as a sesshin teisho based on Case 55 of the *Hekiganroku*[417]). Pat talked about the ego's need to know as an impediment to realization; that the tendency to intellectualize, to step outside in order to objectify, separates and distracts from seeing what is. He cautioned, "Also, watch out for curious teachers. Nothing can lead a student more astray."

In the dokusan room, Pat evinced no curiosity about his students' lives, simply working with whatever they brought in, trusting that that was enough — "sufficient unto the day." With a problem presented in dokusan he would respond based on whatever the student revealed, not probing for more. He would pause in a silence of absolute attention, then offer his incisive two cents' worth. He kept it concrete and present, not indulging any student's tendency toward philosophical discussion, dredging up past experience, or ruminating.

Understanding in an intellectual sense held little sway for Pat as a tool in spiritual practice. He was there for seeing, for being, and for helping his students see and be. Although he was well-trained in counseling, and this helped sustain a mature presence in the face of students' psychological concerns, he did not provide psychotherapy. If he felt that was what a student needed, he expected that they would engage a psychotherapist.

At the same time, what Pat delivered could be profoundly therapeutic. A student came to him one day, troubled about a new relationship in her life with a man who was an avowed atheist and not interested in any sort of spiritual engagement beyond hiking in the woods. Although she cared very much for the man, as a spiritually-inclined person with a dedicated Zen practice she was doubtful about pursuing the relationship. She expressed this to Pat, saying, "So I guess I should break up with him," fully expecting that he would agree. To her surprise, he said, "Why would you do that?" He let the question hang in the air, then said quietly, "We are born alone, we live alone, and we die alone. You cannot expect anyone to carry your spiritual practice for you." His assertion of essential aloneness was akin to the assertion attributed in myth to the Buddha moments after his birth: "Above the heavens, below the earth, I alone am the world honored one." Reality is always here, in this very place, this very body. There is no other. The encounter in dokusan was brief and to the point, and it precipitated a life-changing shift for the student.

Pat's eschewing of intellectual discussion or psychological probing saved a lot of time in the dokusan room, such that the encounters with students were usually short — sometimes less than five minutes — which naturally meant that many more students could be seen each day. There were nonetheless some individuals who, for one reason or another, took longer. Although Pat's taciturnity — his great economy with words in dokusan — tended to discourage chattiness in most students, the naturally voluble could blow right past his signals. Unlike the masters of Zen lore, renowned for ringing students out of the room after an unsatisfactory presentation, even cutting off mid-sentence, Pat found it difficult to be ruthless. He would reach for the handbell — unarguable signal that the interview was over — but a determined student could keep talking and he would keep listening, leaning over with his hand on the bell but not ringing it.

During the discussion of student numbers at the 1993 teachers' meeting, Pat took sketchy notes, later modified when he prepared meeting minutes for the group.[418] Regarding the number of students he was teaching, he wrote:

> Numbers too many me
> Question of style - numbers tuff one
> Transference -
> Masamichi - few numbers
> Nelson's choice - real pastoral; numbers must be small
> Willigis style - huge zendo; huge numbers
> Bankei* style

Dokusan with a skilled teacher is like gold. With each ring of the roshi's bell from the dokusan room, the person at the front of the dokusan line rings the jisha's bell, the *kansho*, in response, then gets up and goes into the room as the person just rung out exits. There's a quiet shuffling in the line as everybody moves up one place. When the time for a dokusan period runs out, any remaining in line return to their places in the zendo. There's nothing quite like the disappointment of having something urgent to convey — a question, an insight, a presentation — and being turned away until the next time. And although dokusan with Pat was usually brief, with his reluctance to put his foot down, there would sometimes be a student who would stay in the dokusan room for 15, 20, even 30 minutes. From such moments and from the deep interpersonal relationship that develops with the teacher, competitions, envies, jealousies can arise within the context of the retreat itself and provide grist for practice.

With this kind of risk, the position in line is important. There are two main ways of determining this: with dokusan rush, at the sound of the jisha's bell announcing the beginning of dokusan, students leap to their feet and race to get in

---

* Bankei Yotaku (1622-1693) a Japanese Rinzai Zen Master.

line. Students allegedly demonstrate zeal for enlightenment by the degree of determination they show in getting to the line. At Philip Kapleau's Rochester Zen Center, the rush was energetic and ruthless. When dokusan was about to be announced, students would sit at acute attention, and the instant the bell sounded, leap to their feet and race to the line, elbowing each other out of the way in single-minded focus to get there first. Aitken's procedures also included dokusan rush, but it was gentler: "When the *kansho* rings, step to the dokusan line and take your place. If all places are filled, return to your seat and await a vacancy. Do not delay taking your turn; time will pass, and you may miss out." Aitken addressed the problem of sharing limited dokusan time in the guidelines (sesshin cautions) reviewed at the beginning of each sesshin: "Please be considerate of the rest of the group when pacing your dokusan. The younger members should be considerate of those who don't move quite so fast when the *kansho* rings. And the slower of us should pace our dokusan, especially when sesshin is very full and there may not be time for everyone to go." It was dokusan rush with less rush than Rochester, but still the same idea.

The method Pat used for regulating dokusan order eliminated the competitive aspect: All participants had a white index card tucked under their cushion in the zendo. When the jisha announced "Dokusan," anyone wishing to go would slide the white card out to make it visible, then the *jisha*, working clockwise around the room, would tap people on the shoulder to signal time to get up and join the dokusan line. People would then take positions in the line in the order they were tapped. This was the method used by Willigis Jäger, who learned it from the Sanbo Kyodan teachers. It fit well with both Zen and contemplative traditions. Pat had grown accustomed to it during his year in Germany and always used it.

Either way, at crowded retreats, getting in to see the teacher as often as wished was a factor to be reckoned with, and probably the most acute way in which students felt the question of how many students was too many. During the few years when Pat was doing extended residencies in the Northwest, Seven Thunders sent out a survey to its membership asking, among other things, how often they expected to have dokusan/interviews during a retreat. The average response, probably representative of students in other groups as well, was twice a day, definitely a limiting factor for the size of retreats.

It was not Pat's way to figure out how to manage this. He did not get involved in worrying about whether his students were getting enough of him. He gave the time he had, then left it to chance, students' determination, Head Residents and boards of directors to figure out how that time would be distributed. Pat's hands-off approach allowed for the possibility of serving more students.

Simply take them as they come. If they are there in front of you the time is there too, offer what you can. When they are not there, there is nothing to be done.

Vonna Smith, originally a Rochester student, later working with Nelson Foster, then for many years a Pat Hawk student, at one point during the Hawk period took a break from Zen practice. Vonna said, "This [approach of Pat's] made it very easy for me to disappear for seven years then just show up. I loved the fact that no explanation whatsoever was expected or wanted about my disappearance and subsequent return." The Rinzai teacher Sokei'an, one of the bringers of Zen to the West, hung a sign outside his New York zendo saying, "Those who come are received, those who go are not pursued."[419] Pat's approach was like that.

On the other hand, Pat did try to fit in as many retreats as he could for as many groups as asked for them. It gave him a grueling schedule. Except for January when he took most of the month off, he was generally offering two or more full retreats a month, making himself available for in-person and telephone (eventually video chat) dokusan, traveling to the different sanghas, to Diamond Sangha Teachers' Circle meetings, to visit family, to see Willigis, also giving talks, Q&A's and occasional classes relating to practice. Seeing Pat's schedule, Aitken once commented, "*Formidable*! As the French say."

Following the discussion of student numbers, the 1993 teachers' meeting proceeded to koan study, continuing where they'd left off the year before with the Miscellaneous Koans. They went on to further consider Diamond Sangha organization, ending with a decision about dates for the following year and an invitation to hold the 1994 teachers' meeting at Ring of Bone Zendo in the northern California foothills.

Meanwhile, Aitken was preparing to retire. He had spoken separately to his three North American dharma heirs about the possibility that they would take over in Honolulu. Pat explored with his Redemptorist superiors whether they would allow him to move to Hawaii and have that as his base of operations, while he continued to service the various retreat centers on his circuit. They said no. John also declined. Nelson accepted. Aitken announced to the teachers, "The members of the Koko An Zendo of the Sangha agreed by consensus at the annual meeting, held March 14, 1993, to welcome Nelson Foster as a visiting teacher, with the understanding that he is my choice to succeed me eventually on a full time basis."[420]

This brought a new altercation. Several of the teachers were accustomed to teaching at Koko An to cover for Aitken when he was away or simply as visiting teachers. Without consulting Nelson, Aitken invited Augusto Alcalde to lead an annual *Shingakudo** training at Koko An the following summer, and Augusto accepted. A tense exchange of letters between Nelson and Augusto followed. In time the disturbance died down, but it made shaky a relationship that was then further challenged by allegations of misconduct by Augusto with a student. It was the beginning of the end of Augusto Alcalde's participation in the Diamond Sangha.

Augusto's relationship with Pat remained warm throughout. It was expensive for him to travel from Argentina, and Aitken solicited financial help from the other Diamond Sangha teachers so he could attend meetings. Pat always contributed. In his thank-you note to Pat, Augusto appended a note about the resistance to his teaching at Koko An. He ended with, "Keep well, keep alive, a big hug."[421]

Given the tensions at the 1993 Teachers' Circle meeting, Nelson wrote to the Diamond Sangha teachers saying he'd recommended to the Ring of Bone Zendo board of directors that they decline the suggestion to host the 1994 Diamond Sangha Teachers' Circle so that the meeting could be held on neutral territory. He asked Pat to host in Amarillo instead. However, as the situation eased that was deemed unnecessary, and the 1994 meeting was held at Ring of Bone. It was Pat's second visit to ROBZ, having attended his first "real" Zen sesshin there back in 1987 as he was re-establishing his study with Aitken following the year in Germany.

Nelson wrote in advance to the teachers: "The accommodations at the zendo are rustic, [an understatement as far as Pat was concerned] with sleeping on *zabutons* or foam pads, enclosed outdoor showers (cold water only), and outhouses instead of flush toilets. … If you don't enjoy such rustic living or have a physical condition that would make it a hardship fear not! We're determined to make you comfortable, and several sangha members who live nearby have volunteered to take teachers into their homes."[422] Pat knew how rustic from his previous stay there. Describing the situation years later, he lingered with great eye-rolling on the lack of privacy, the encouragement to "water the trees," and other hints of what to Pat was well beyond the pale of civilized life. Although he had a deep and manifest love of the natural world, no one would describe Pat as outdoorsy. He opted for alternative accommodations.

Before the meeting, the teachers were encouraged to send around essays or position papers presenting whatever was on their minds teaching-wise, and a few did so. In the materials sent to Pat, the question was raised whether there is a bias

---

* Shingakudo: Taoist arts of movement, here practiced in the context of Zen.

in Zen toward an Asian sense of self, whether as teachers they should try to work with this or cater to a more Western sense of self, and whether one or the other could affect realization itself. Pat penciled in a question about how this would play out in koan practice.

The question of forms such as deep bowing — in some settings referred to as kowtowing — was raised vis-à-vis Western tropes of imperialism, racism, ethnocentrism, democracy, equality, dignity and courage, a rumination that led to a suggestion of the positive values of humility, submission and surrender. Here Pat, although — or perhaps because — schooled from his early teens in obedience, penciled in "*raihai* [full prostration] is body and mind fallen away, *NOT* submission."[423]

It's unlikely that Pat shared his opinions with the group — he would rather sit by in silence than argue. This was not timidity. It was more that, in a discussion, he held little stake in making a particular point. He was more like Hakuin with his famous, "Is that so."* Pat's notes for the 1994 Diamond Sangha Teachers' meeting are sketchy and scant. Photos show a very happy-looking Pat with Robert Aitken, Joe Bobrow, Ross Bolleter, Jack Duffy and Nelson Foster in the zendo, and later among the crowd at a large and congenial sangha picnic in pleasant, sunny weather.

Following the meeting, Aitken planned a full and complicated itinerary for a trip to Europe including: meet Pia Gyger in Basel, Switzerland; meet Ludwigis Fabian in Sachrang, Germany; present a paper at a Buddhist Christian conference at Lassalle House in Bad Schönbrunn, Switzerland; meet Pat's student Leonard Marcel — Pat had proposed Leonard as an apprentice teacher and wanted Aitken to meet him; visit Willigis Jäger at Haus St. Benedikt, Rolf Drosten in Leverkusen, Germany; Katarina and Paul Shepherd in Switzerland, and Joan Rieck in Germany; then fly back to California to preside at the wedding of Sean Shoemaker, son of Aitken's publisher.[424] All within six weeks.

The trip was canceled when Anne Aitken died on June 13, 1994. She and Robert Aitken were living in the teachers' quarters at Palolo when she became ill with what seemed like the flu. Two days later, she died of a massive myocardial infarction. Pat was in Amarillo at the time leading sesshin, unable to travel to Honolulu for the memorial. He placed Anne's photo on the altar and held a service in her memory for the Empty Sky Sangha. She was a woman whose support

---

* Hakuin Ekaku (1685-1769): This refers to a parable in which Hakuin is accused of impregnating a young woman. When he is given the newborn to raise he takes the child in and cares for it. When the woman confesses the real father and asks for the child back, Hakuin complies. At the initial accusation and again when he is exonerated his comment is, "Is that so."

Pat had felt unreservedly and whom he loved wholeheartedly. Her death darkened the clouds gathering around him.

Zen Desert Sangha at Indiana Nelson's 1993-1997

Although it meant heavy demands on Pat's time and energy, he was gratified to see the various sanghas he taught flourishing. Among others, the ragtag group that Pat had found in 1989 at Zen Desert Sangha (ZDS) in Tucson, Arizona, strengthened and grew despite having no fixed home in the city. ZDS, having kept up a weekly sitting schedule, at times in the homes of members, at times in a guest house on Justin Street, then in a place on Hedrick Street, then Timrod Street, holding sesshins where they could get space — often the Tucson Association for the Blind, sometimes the capacious meeting room in the basement of the Benedictine monastery, various other places — found themselves once again in 1993 without a place to sit. Some Tucson students were making the long drive to Amarillo to attend sesshin and resident practice periods with Pat at Bishop DeFalco Retreat Center. Tim Storer was one of them. So was Indiana Nelson.

Indiana, although from Tucson, had first connected with Pat in Amarillo. Flamboyant, artistic and warm, she regularly attended retreats at Bishop DeFalco with Father Thomas Keating, a Trappist from St. Benedict's Monastery in Snowmass, Colorado. Keating was one of the main architects of the Centering Prayer Movement, which began as a response to Vatican II's invitation to revive the contemplative practices of early Christianity known from writings of the Desert Fathers, Teresa of Avila, John of the Cross and the anonymous medieval work, *Cloud of Unknowing*. Keating conducted 10-day retreats to teach centering prayer to spiritual directors and other interested people several times a year at BDRC. Although not raised Catholic, Indiana was in a devout Catholic phase. Looking back years later on her journey with Keating and then with Pat, she remembered:

> Catholicism was just right for me in the '80s. I was all about being devotional. And not asking very many questions. Not being cerebral. But just experiencing my faith. And so that led me to Fr Thomas Keating .... I think in every journey there's a time when you need to get out. And Fr Thomas was having a long retreat at the Redemptorist Center in Amarillo, where Pat was. I didn't know Pat from Adam.[425]

A series of experiences involving encounters with hawks led Indiana to believe that Pat was a person she needed to know.

> I knocked on his door and I went in. And I can remember the interview. I will remember it to the end of my days. I introduced myself and said I was

with Fr. Thomas Keating's group, and he said, "Well, then that's where you need to be." And I said, "No. No. I know you're my teacher!" And he said, "No, I'm not." And I said, "Yes you are." And we kind of argued about it. Right there. And he said, "Why are you so sure?" and I told him… I said, "Do you have anything to tell me?" And he said, "Yes, go home and live your life." So that was the end of that interview.

As soon as I finished this interview, I went to the front desk and said when is the next retreat with Pat Hawk. I don't even remember if my first retreat with him was contemplative or Buddhist. But suddenly I was back in Amarillo, where I went for a couple of years and did as many retreats as I could possibly get. And I would say to him, "I just can't believe I'm doing this. I just can't believe I'm with a bunch of Zen Buddhists," because it didn't seem at all my métier. My way of coming forth. But neither did Catholicism. So, in that space of time, I gave up Catholicism, not in any formal angry resistant way but just gently laid it down. I realized it had been really good to me for seven or eight years, but I realized I no longer needed it. Pat said a really lovely thing. He said to me, "Religion is only a ladder to God. And when you no longer need the ladder, get off of it. But don't destroy it, leave it for others. It's a good ladder."

So my journey with Pat was to be released from Catholicism and from Zen. I think he recognized me and he recognized my way. I think he does this for most of us. … So that really is the source of my great gratitude to Pat. … I'll give you an example. We did koan practice together. And I loved it, it was really wonderful. I loved it. I was greedy for it. And then, at one point after some years, I don't remember how many years, I said to Pat, "Is this enough?" And he said, "What do you mean?" And I said, "Well, is there an end? I want to make sure I'm not quitting and giving up. I mean, if there's some wonderful plum around the next curve and I'm going to miss out." He said, "It's enough when you say it's enough." And that is an example of the whole journey I had with Pat.

You go as far as you need to go, and then you recognize the moment when to go one step further in this path in this journey with this teacher and this sangha is really not going to be the same as opening all your windows and doors and just jumping. Just jumping. Free fall. And that is the thing that I feel most grateful for. That Pat allowed me that. Without guilt. Without a tiny little word or whisper. Or a glance that would have said or even intimated — you're quitting? … He doesn't capture you with charm or personality or an agenda. He was a wonderful teacher for me. Pat was a huge, a huge liberator for me. It was almost like he was the parent who said, "Oh, just go home. Just go home. Forget all this stuff." I remember, at one point I told him I thought I was ready to take my vows. He said, "Oh for God sakes, Indiana."[426]

Tim Storer and Indiana Nelson bumped into each other one day in what was then Reay's Ranch Market in Tucson. Tim told Indiana that Pat Hawk was coming to town for sesshin and they were looking for a place to hold it. It happened that the Benedictine Monastery and the Tucson Association for the Blind were not available. Indiana said, "Oh, I have a place," then took off to India the next day. Immediately on her return, she called and offered the use of her small zendo and a dance studio in her home — a hacienda-style mansion on a large property in a well-to-do neighborhood in central Tucson.

The place was magical. They had the run of the kitchen and living space in the main house — large light-filled rooms with high ceilings and all manner of eye-catching artwork. As an artist, Indiana had trained in the Andrew Wyeth school, among others. There were bold colors, paintings and sculpture everywhere. The extensive gardens had a wild, beautiful unkemptness. There were only about ten people at that first sesshin at Indiana's,[427] but the group quickly grew. The ranks swelled with young, energetic seekers, not necessarily with a particular commitment to Zen, but drawn by the energy of the enchanted space around Indiana.

To accommodate the rapidly growing sangha, Indiana decided to enlarge the dance studio. There were wall-to-wall mirrors that had to come down, spackling to do, painting — lots of work. The ZDS newsletter reported, "… It was a group effort with people painting and plastering and bringing donations of a paintbrush or time or two bananas or bread, whatever they had. In truth, however, Indiana brought the space and the basic construction, which she paid for by trading to her friend the carpenter her turquoise blue jeep with the Virgin of Guadalupe painted on it and the big crystal ball at the end of the steering wheel and the rosaries and holy stuff hanging from the rearview mirror."[428]

Richard Laue, one of the newcomers to the group at that time, was there every spare moment helping to get the zendo ready.

> I was working there with everybody and I'd already heard there was this Zen Roshi that was coming from Amarillo to do sesshin. And I was already settling into the practice really well. I was clinging to it desperately. And I thought to myself, I'm ready to do a sesshin. I've never done one, but I'm ready. Then one day I'm in there doing whatever we're doing, and somebody says something about a Catholic priest. I don't even know in what context, and I said, What? "Yeah. Pat Hawk Roshi is also a Redemptorist Catholic priest." And I had issues with the Catholic Church in those days, and maybe it was just all this shit coming out.
>
> I threw a monumental temper tantrum. Just hysterical. Throwing things and ranting and raving. I stormed out of there. I was so furious. I don't know how I even made it home without killing somebody. That night I thought about it and said to myself, I am not going to let any goddamn Catholic priest drive me away from my sangha. I'm gonna do the sesshin. I'm signed

> up for it, I'm gonna do it. I'm just not gonna have anything to do with Pat Hawk. Fuck him. Then I find out that there's this thing called *sosan* [the first and last dokusan of a sesshin are called *sosan*, and they are required one-on-one meetings with the teacher]. Well, all right, that's fine. I'll go in, I'll sit down, I'll tell him my name, I'm gonna bow, and I'm gonna leave. Fuck him! Catholic priest! So Pat comes. Sesshin starts. I go in for my *sosan*. I do my bows, raise my eyes. And there's Pat looking at me. And I just started crying. And he's been my teacher ever since. Go figure. There was something in his eyes. Something so real there.[429]

Another student, Casey Hayden, wrote in the ZDS newsletter:

> We sat the sesshin in the new zendo. Father Patrick Hawk, from Amarillo, Texas, is our Roshi, a dharma heir of Robert Aitken Roshi, of whose Diamond Sangha we are a part. I was prepared not to like him because he is also a Roman Catholic priest and I am prejudiced in that direction, but I did like him, loved him even. How could I not, when there he was, presenting, embodying, enacting Buddha-mind with such precision, ingenuity, humor and courage, answering my deepest questions, my hungriest needs.[430]

Harry Iwatsuki, a student of Pat's from Mountain Cloud Zen Center in Santa Fe, wrote an article about the sesshin for the newsletter, including impressions of the place:

> [One] often saw people hugging, giving each other encouraging words, or just plain hanging out. Joyous. And the earthy feeling of living in someone's home. Comfortable. Nostalgic. The house a mixture of my mother-in-law's place and my old school days around art and architecture people. Works in progress, art everywhere, books, and even more books. The feeling of being a living part of an installation or theater piece. Very different from the impersonal austere Zen temple feeling that the Mountain Cloud buildings and grounds present.[431]

The lavish, generous artiness of the place, the warmth, the love, all reflected Indiana's personality. People gravitated toward her as a teacher as well as toward Pat, who after all, was only around for sesshin. Indiana's heart and playfulness flavored the whole group. For her part, she both enjoyed and rejected the guru role — enjoyed the love and didn't want the responsibility. With an eye for the whimsical, she would put odd things on the altar. One time she dug a pair of glittering gold high-heeled slingbacks out of her closet and put them in among the row of Birkenstocks and plain shoes by the door. Before and sometimes after sesshin, Pat and Indiana would share a meal, then sit together on the colorful, overstuffed couch facing the fireplace to sip wine and talk. The subject of Indiana's mother came up one time and Pat asked what she was like. Indiana said:

> Well, here's what she's like. She lives on popsicles and frozen lima beans and a couple of pieces of bacon every day. Because she's mad about being thin. And she's been drinking straight gin and straight vodka since she was 16 — she was then about 89 — and she's been smoking unfiltered cigarettes since she was 16, and she doesn't believe in exercise, and one day when we were driving down the street together in front of the Arizona Inn, she said, "Look at those good people." She said, "If there's one thing I hate, it's a good person." Hahaha! Pat just put his head back and said, "She sounds like my kind of woman."[432]

For sesshin, they often had a regular *tenzo** who was an amazing cook. Sometimes she was unavailable, and someone else would fill in. Once it was a minimalist cook who knew little of sauces, spices, or sweets. Indiana recalled:

> It was my duty to take the tray over [to Pat's room]. It was a little blob of brown rice and a piece of boiled zucchini or something. And I knew what Pat liked to eat. So I snuck into the refrigerator and pulled out a drumstick — haha — and stuck it on the side and some luscious piece of pie à la mode. And the cook looked at me and said, "This is an outrage! You've *sabotaged* the menu." And I said, "Look, I know exactly where you're coming from, and I know how you feel. It is insulting to have me doing this, but I'm thinking of our roshi, who is sitting over in his room starving to death." Hahahaha! "And who spent all morning in dokusan, and who will have to spend until nine tonight in dokusan." And I said, "I can't bear it." So I said, "I'll take the responsibility for doing this." So when I got back, we had a wonderful talk. This was a lovely man, the cook. And he said, "I can't believe I have a roshi that smokes and drinks and eats meat. And crams down these sweet things loaded with sugar." And I said to him, "You know this is exactly the roshi you need."

At Indiana's, they had regular sitting three times during the week and sesshin with Pat three or four times a year. They also had a steady trickle of visiting teachers. Robert Aitken, in Tucson for *The Nature of Reality - Buddhism as Transformation* conference,[433] came to the zendo and gave a teisho and a Q&A. Fitting with the leanings of the group at the time they talked about compassion. Another time, Bill Kwong† came. Yet another time, ZDS member Joe Montani brought in his

---

* Tenzo: (Japanese) Head cook.

† Jakusho Kwong, a Chinese-American Zen teacher in the lineage of Shunryu Suzuki.

teacher, Sheng Yen,* aka Shifu, a Ch'an master. He happened to be there when they had expanded into a new zendo, and they got him to preside over the opening, although Pat — the more appropriate person — was scheduled to arrive the next day. Indiana remembered, "So [Shifu] was standing at the altar wearing a long brown robe. He was lighting the first stick of incense to bless the new altar, the new group, the new zendo. And all of a sudden, he turned and he *screamed.* 'Get enlightened! Get enlightened quick!' Just like that."

Indiana picked Pat up at the airport and told him the story of Shifu. "Pat said, 'Well, I'm just gonna send my suitcase right back. I don't even need to come. You've had your sesshin. What more is needed?' " He must have felt odd at best that they'd let Shifu do the opening when he, their official teacher, was arriving the very next day.

The group at Indiana's grew to be about 60 people coming and going with about 30 regulars. Bob Wallin remembered, "We had a lot of new people who didn't have a lot of experience with meditation or with Zen." People were there for the whole scene. Pat was not necessarily the main attraction. Besides the thrice-weekly sitting, there were discussion groups, sangha meetings, a monthly zazenkai with recorded teisho from Pat or Aitken or some other teacher, baking cookies for Primavera homeless shelter, Full Moon Ceremonies, listening circles, potlucks. It was a joyous time of creative expression for many of them. One could be intimately engaged with the sangha and yet have little one-on-one encounter with Pat. Bob continued, "Pat would just come in for sesshin, arriving in the evening and sometimes even leaving before the retreat was done. Unless you were attending sesshin and working with Pat … you might not even have an opportunity to meet him or certainly to appreciate him as a teacher."[434]

Indiana recalled the early days at her place fondly:

> I think the thing I loved so about the group at that period was that it kind of matched the spirit of the house. Which was that — we were full of love. We were full of … experimental kind of Bohemian … silliness. Of course, it was serious in the sense that we were all devoted to what we were doing, but there was nobody there who was a professional. And then little by little, as time went by, some of the people became hardcore. And then we became divisive, and then there was all this discussing and group meetings about cookie crumbs on the zendo floor. And what people had to wear and how they had to behave.[435]

---

* Sheng Yen (1931-2009), teacher of Ch'an Buddhism in Taiwan and the United States.

Joe Montani was one of the people who was particular about protocol, and at one point he insisted that they shouldn't have coffee at sesshin. This occupied lengthy discussion at several sangha meetings as they considered it from all angles, finally deciding they would let Pat Hawk make the call. Richard Laue wrote Pat a long email explaining all the arguments for and against. Pat replied:[436]

> Dear Richard,
> No coffee, no Pat.

It was not so much that people became hardcore as that the many newcomers attracted to Indiana and her place knew little to nothing of Zen forms, while the original group of Zen Desert Sangha people wanted a more dedicated and stringent practice than Indiana's home and heart were suited for. They began to wonder about other options.

Sanbo Kyodan denouement 1993-1995

The Diamond Sangha's position with respect to the Sanbo Kyodan remained unresolved into the mid-1990s. Meanwhile, the Sanbo Kyodan was itself coming under attack from a different angle for espousing an inauthentic Zen. Kubota's opening comments for the fourth Sanbo Kyodan International teachers' sesshin were published in *Kyosho*[437] and drew the attention of a Rinzai Zen group in Berlin, Zen-Zentrum Mumon-Kai.* They surmised that the Sanbo Kyodan leaders who were appointing Catholic clerics to be Zen teachers were supporting a conspiracy of Catholics that would contaminate Zen Buddhism and essentially take it over for the Church. In a letter ironically reminiscent of Kubota's letter to Aitken championing Zen purity, the Berlin-based Mumon-Kai group wrote initially to ask for cooperation in stamping out any Christian infiltration. Identifying first their lineage credentials, noting in an echo of Kubota that their teacher had practiced for 30 years, the Mumon-Kai group complained that they had been hearing of Christian Zen for years and that this robbed Zen of its Buddhist basis and relationship:

> We are firmly determined to engage in the protection and to counter the abuse of original ZEN. We are neither anti-Christian nor do we maintain that ZEN is the only true way. We ask you who are our companions to be alert, to confront yourselves with Christian Zen, to clarify the situation for

---

* The name has since changed to the Rinzai community Mumon-Kai, Community Without Gates / Rinzai-Weggemeinschaft Mumon-Kai, Gemeinschaft ohne Tor.

> yourselves, and to show solidarity in the practice and preservation of ZEN for us and other searchers.[438]

There followed a scathing rebuke of Sanbo Kyodan stating that the lineage had no claim to succession from Dogen. They went on to say that the teacher ranks defined by Sanbo Kyodan were a corruption, "one of many deviations from authentic Zen," and that "to call the Koan method an inadequate training for a so-called 'Zen instructor' " as Kubota had done in the *Kyosho* article, "reflected a deep lack of understanding combined with extraordinary arrogance...." Further, the "Christian missionary mandate" was anathema to Buddhism, which, since Shakyamuni, was characterized by "unlimited self responsibility in the practice of ZEN." Asserting that Zen is diametrically opposed to Catholicism, the Mumon-Kai group accused the Sanbo Kyodan leaders of "a planned worldwide expansion" that "corresponds to the all-embracing, all-grasping claim to power of Catholicism."[439]

They rejected the Sanbo Kyodan claims to authenticity expressed by Kubota in the *Kyosho* article. The Mumon-Kai letter went on to say, "The large scale unification of present and planned Sanbo Kyodan centers is intended to create an illusion of legitimacy, an impressive institution to spread 'authentic ZEN'. We will counteract with a clarification campaign to inform searchers and companions worldwide about the plagative [sic] and ecclesiastically distorted propagation of original ZEN."[440] They sent the four-page diatribe to every sangha in the world whose contact information they could find. "We have informed 500 Zen centers" in 17 countries — to warn them away from Sanbo Kyodan.[441]

Regarding the status of the Diamond Sangha teachers, Aitken and the Sanbo Kyodan leaders, Kubota Akira and Yamada Masamichi, continued at an impasse. Aitken was invited to Japan to discuss the matter. He tried for several dates that fell through, then finally was able to book a flight for March 1995, tacked onto a trip to Bangkok. Preparing for the spring visit to Kamakura, Aitken asked Pat to ask the Kamakura Redemptorists to provide accommodation for him.

Pat was increasingly worn down from his grueling retreat schedule, as well as a gnawing, penetrating depression and a relapse into heavy drinking. He had stayed dry for years after his treatment at Guest House in 1980. By 1990, flying long distances to Germany, Australia, Korea, Japan, Hawaii, he used the accumulated frequent flyer miles to upgrade to first class. Without much thought, he accepted the complimentary drinks, and it started all over again. At Amarillo, he bought wine by the box. Some days he couldn't get himself out of bed for the early morning sit. In this fog, he first ignored Aitken's request to contact the Kamakura Redemptorists, then in reply to a further prompt, wrote to him:

Dear Roshi,

Sorry to have been out of contact for so long. Also accept my apology for letting you down about your visit to Kamakura. I have not contacted the Redemptorists. I'm sure Kubota Roshi will be able to find you a livable place.

Thanks for the letter and the article "Zen is not Buddhism." Willigis Jäger gave me a copy of it when I was in Europe this summer. I did not attach much importance to it at the time, but I will look into it again.

The Melbourne Zen Group has invited me back again next year. I have accepted. It seems that they are not going to settle on a permanent teacher but continue to invite various Diamond Sangha teachers to lead their sesshins.

I just returned from Tucson. We had a seven day sesshin with 28 participants. It was their first try at a seven day sesshin, and although they have come a long way from the days when I first met with them, they still have a long way to go. There were many with extreme emotional issues. All seemed to benefit, but what a struggle! We have no resident trainees at the moment but activity will pick up right after Thanksgiving. Looking forward to seeing Vicki Stoddard next week.

Both my parents are in bad shape. I expect either one or both to go at any moment. Right now they take turns spending a week in the hospital, on the brink then coming back.

I hope your journeys on the mainland did not wear you out. Again I'm sorry about the Kamakura accommodations.

Yours,
Pat[442]

Aitken's long-awaited meeting with the Sanbo Kyodan leaders finally did take place notwithstanding. He reported to the Diamond Sangha teachers in March 1995, on his return from Japan:

I met with Kubota Roshi in the living room of the Yamada home, with Dr. Kazue Yamada, (now 82) the widow of our old teacher, sitting in. Kubota Roshi was very cordial. We opened the meeting by my showing him photos of sesshins at Palolo. He had many questions about participants which led to explanations about the various other Diamond Sangha centers and their teachers.

We then discussed the relationship of the Diamond Sangha and the Sanbo Kyodan. He opened this part of the meeting by asking me how I viewed the relationship. I said that when he and Yamada Ryo'un Roshi indicated that they would not approve of my designating my successors teachers of the Sanbo Kyodan, they effectively cut the organizational tie between our two communities. Now, I said, I viewed our relationship as separate but cordial, with the Diamond Sangha part of the Sanbo Kyodan tradition. He

> agreed with this view, saying that we are like Nangaku and Seigen,* inheriting the same Dharma from the Sixth Ancestor, but founding separate lines.
>
> Kubota Roshi asked whether or not we have annual teachers' meetings. When I assured him that we do, he offered to come and exchange views about koan interpretations. I said that I do not check the koan understanding of students of my successors when I visit their centers. I suggested that with this precedent, his offer to come to our Teachers' Circle to discuss koans would probably not be well received. However, I said that he would be welcome to come and give teisho at the Palolo Zen Center. I said that his interpretation of specific cases from our formal study would undoubtedly enlarge the perspective of our students. I said further that some students from the centers of my successors come for sesshin to the Palolo Zen Center, and to centers of other successors, so this would form a kind of precedent for Diamond Sangha students voluntarily attending sesshin at the San'un Zendo [in Kamakura, Japan]. He expressed accord with all this.[443]

In the same letter, Aitken announced to the Diamond Sangha teachers that he had decided to give dharma transmission to Rolf Drosten and that the ceremony would take place in Germany the following year. His letter reporting on his visit with Kubota goes on:

> I told [Kubota] of my plan to extend transmission to Rolf Drosten. He remembered Rolf from Sanbo Kyodan teachers' meetings and questioned how a Christian minister could be independent as a Zen teacher. I tried to convey my view that belief is no longer a big issue with many modern Christians. Rolf can put himself in a ministerial role, conveying the teachings of the Christ, or in a Zen master role, conveying the teachings of the Buddha. I was not successful in conveying this view, and after some back-and-forth we agreed to disagree. I did not take up possible implications of his view for the European apprentice teachers of the Sanbo Kyodan.[444]

Pat relayed Kubota's question regarding how a Christian minister could teach Zen to Willigis Jäger. It was an odd thing for Kubota to say, given the history of the Sanbo Kyodan, and was perhaps a Hail Mary attempt to block Aitken's sanctioning of Drosten since the initial resistance on the grounds that it would undermine Willigis had failed. Or perhaps the criticisms by the Mumon-Kai group in Germany had given him pause. In any case, Kubota's doubting of Christian Zen teachers was enough to set off alarms among the European teachers, who were,

---

* Nangaku (Chinese: Nanyue) and Seigen (Chinese: Qingyuan), dharma heirs of the sixth Zen ancestor in China, Huineng, founded separate lineages.

as the Mumon-Kai group had accused, mostly Catholic clerics. Five of the European Sanbo Kyodan teachers, all with Christian backgrounds, sent a joint letter to Kubota, the text of which Willigis shared with Pat. In the letter, the teachers express gratitude for the openness to members of other religions expressed by Kubota in his "Opening Comments" in *Kyosho* No. 231 and which Yamada Masamichi reiterated at their meeting with him at Dietfurt in 1993. Based on these and other indications of support, they are puzzled by Kubota's questioning whether a Christian minister could also be a Zen teacher, especially since Yamada Ko'un had authorized them to teach Zen knowing full well that they are Christian clerics and Kubota had reaffirmed this. They pose three questions:

> 1) Do you see the clerical function of Rolf Drosten as endangering an authentic Zen teaching? In such a case, all of us who have similar functions within the Christian church as members of religious communities, priests or pastors would be affected.
> 2) Do you see formal membership in a Christian church as an obstacle to being an "independent" Zen teacher? In that case, all Christian laypeople would also be affected.
> 3) Are you basically of the opinion that full dharma succession can be given only to a person who is formally a Buddhist?

They go on to defend the validity of their roles as teachers of Zen:

> Through our Zen experience and our training in philosophy, theology, psychology, and anthropology, we feel in a position to make an important contribution to the integration of Zen in the West.
>
> From the perspective of Zen history, it seems to us that the present task of indigenizing Zen in western culture is comparable to the situation of Bodhidharma when he introduced Zen from India into Taoistic China.
>
> From the perspective of the evolution of humankind, it is also a matter of evolving a global consciousness to ensure the survival of life on earth and the further growth of human awareness. According to our understanding, this development of consciousness can only arise out of a trans-confessional and trans-religious spirituality.[445]

The letter was signed by Niklaus Brantschen, Willigis Jäger, Peter Lengsfeld, Gundala Meyer and Joan Rieck.

Thus, the growing pains continued in Europe. But for Diamond Sangha - Sanbo Kyodan relations, the matter was settled. Years later, looking back on his 1995 meeting with Kubota, Aitken said, "We agreed to a friendly divorce."[446] From that time onward, Diamond Sangha teachers acknowledged succession through Harada, Yasutani and Yamada Ko'un, and honored these ancestors in their sutra services, but beyond this there was no formal relationship between the two groups. Both continued to fan out into the world. The Diamond Sangha flourished as a loosely affiliated group of teachers and their sanghas with an egalitarian model of organization that Pat and others described as anarchic. The Sanbo Kyodan continued as a tightly controlled "benevolent dictatorship" overseen by the Japanese Abbot — at this writing, Yamada Ryo'un [Masamichi], son of Yamada Ko'un.

For the Diamond Sangha teachers, the dust quickly settled following the resolution of the Sanbo Kyodan situation. Their meeting in 1995, which was held at the San Francisco Zen Center on Page Street, focused on other matters. John Tarrant re-surfaced at this meeting at least for a day. Others included Pat Hawk, Robert Aitken, Pia Gyger, Joe Bobrow, and Nelson Foster. Pat's handwritten notes from the meeting are abundant. Some excerpts, scattered among the usual doodles, suggest his take on the discussion:

> Love? Walking together — transference.
> How do koans work, what about changing a person's life. N thinks they force one back on one's realization. What kind of person are we trying to produce? What kind of vision are we putting forth?

'Then, further down the page:

> I don't know — all things are possible. I don't want to produce anyone. Point of entry — absolute freedom.[447]

Regarding Aitken's retirement, Pat noted that on the one hand, they should consider what they needed to learn from Aitken before he is gone; on the other, they needed to make decisions without his involvement. With the latter was concern that Aitken may feel left out. They agreed that it would be valuable to schedule time without him at future meetings. Pat wrote: "How will it be when you are gone? Discussion took off and we found an expanded sense of identity."

There was the perennial discussion of what they wanted the Diamond Sangha to be, what they wanted the Teachers' Circle to be. Pat noted: "John being miffed at my support of Roshi." Later, in continued discussion of Diamond Sangha Teachers' Circle structure Pat wrote:

> John: Evolve in institutional level. Cooperate with each other without competition for Roshi's favor. Support each other in character formation, bringing new teachers along. Nelson: really independent centers, but with travel among them, trust, differences respected — be supportive in disaster, appreciative, not presume to understand one another, but check it out. What's

> precious about our tradition. Candid in questioning and criticizing one another in warmth.[448]

They considered what would be needed for Aitken Roshi's care. Pat agreed to organize the next meeting, to be in September 1996.

Elnora and Ed to 1995

Pat visited his family in Illinois at least once a year, often for major holidays like Christmas or Easter, sometimes in between. The visits became more frequent as his parents' health deteriorated. Especially his mother seemed to go from crisis to crisis in the early 1990s requiring bypass surgery and other interventions for longstanding and worsening coronary artery disease. He would fly in to say goodbye in case it came to that, to sit with his father in the waiting room until a surgeon came out and reported on how she was doing, then to sit by her hospital bed as she recovered, returning to her usual chattiness, at which point Pat would head back to Amarillo.

During one of his mother's episodes, sitting in the waiting room with his father, both men taciturn, never having really gotten to know each other, he learned for the first time what his father had done for a living. Of course, he had been aware that he worked for the railroad, then for Commonwealth Steel for many years, but he never knew what his father's employment entailed — repetitive tasks relating to quality control — until one of those late conversations in the 1990s.[449]

Paul Hughes was there when Pat got an urgent call about his mother. The Easter contemplative intensive retreat was just getting started, obviously a bad time for Pat to leave town, but he had no hesitation about what to do. Paul remembered, "It really opened up his emotions. His feelings for his family came through. His deep down connection with his family. I was Head Resident at the time and so he sort of opened up to me. Well, it was really quick. All he said was, 'I'm going.' And that said everything."[450]

The Hawks always assumed Elnora would go first, Ed being apparently much healthier. But in 1994, Ed was diagnosed with late-stage prostate cancer and he declined rapidly. He died in February 1995. Pat flew in to preside at the funeral Mass. His niece, Tina, remembers feeling moved at the long line of Pat's confreres processing in to concelebrate.[451] The Redemptorists did that for each other. When a family member died, whoever could, would come to support the bereaved confrere. Granite City being so close to Liguori — about 20 miles across the Mississippi River as the crow flies — a good number of them came. It meant a great deal to Pat.

Besides his father, two of Pat's uncles had prostate cancer. The youngest of these, Paul, a quiet man with no spouse or children, was diagnosed in the late 1990s. Having seen his brothers suffer through the painful death that was likely with prostate cancer in those days, he put his affairs in order, walked out to the abandoned cemetery at the end of Hodges Street, and shot himself. The family was devastated.[452]

Elnora died less than six months after Ed, in August 1995, second of the four Delmar sisters to go. Mona was the youngest, and she died first, of cancer, in 1976 and only in her late forties. She was buried at Calvary Cemetery, Glen Carbon, Illinois, to be joined later by many of the family. Marie was the oldest, and she died last. Three of the sisters — Elnora, Eileen (Bill), and Marie — all donated their bodies to medical schools.

7

Latter Years at Amarillo

Exhaustion and assistance

Aitken revived his canceled European itinerary for late May to late June 1996. He was accustomed to having Anne look after him, and with Anne gone he felt the prospect of travel alone daunting. Pat, planning to go to Europe that summer anyway, was persuaded to expand his itinerary and serve as Aitken's attendant. They met Leonard Marcel in London briefly, then flew to Germany. Aitken gave Rolf Drosten transmission in a ceremony with Drosten's sangha in Leverkusen. From there, they visited Willigis Jäger at Haus St. Benedikt. Then after a brief stop with Ludwigis Fabian in Sachrang, went on to Basel for a modified transmission ceremony for Pia Gyger — modified because the ceremony did not include Jukai. Pia Gyger — with Aitken's acquiescence — had opted to avoid stepping beyond what she saw as the bounds of her Christian affiliation. This was in contrast to Pat who, from his first encounter with Aitken, gave himself unreservedly to the Zen way while still retaining his Redemptorist community home and identity.

An aspect of the bond between Pat and Robert Aitken was a shared interest in the interleaved understandings of Buddhist and Christian seekers, regarding which, over the years, they carried on a continuing exchange in conversation and by letter, interrupted and resumed as opportunity and new books appeared. Hence it was picking up where they'd left off when, after their return from Europe in the summer of 1996, Aitken sent Pat an email saying:

> I am in the throes of my response to His Holiness [Pope John Paul II], a sixteen-page opus on Buddhist-Christian dialogue rather than a rebuttal of his points. In going over Batchelor's *The Awakening of the West*,[453] I found this quote from Hugo Lassalle: Kensho is "in itself neither Buddhist nor Chris-

> tian, not necessarily connected with any religious confession." Sound familiar? I suddenly realized Willigis' purpose. I don't have Willigis' book. Do you have it? Can you give me full bibliographical data? Can you find a place in it where he says that Zen is transconfessional? How many Sanbokyodan teachers do you suppose agree with Willigis about Zen being transconfessional? Batchelor is quoting from Lassalle's book, *Zen – Way to Enlightenment*, published in 1964, six years or so before he began work with Yamada [Ko'un] Roshi. Do you know if he changed his attitudes about the independence of Zen and its purpose a way to see God? Do you know the publisher of that book?[454]

At the same time, Aitken asked Pat if he would be coming to Honolulu for his retirement party in December, saying that even Kubota Roshi would appear. Pat replied the next day, also via email (sent at 3:57 AM!):

> I have collected most of the material to answer your questions. I will try to get it all to you later today. … I was in the hospital for five days last week with pneumonia and pleurisy. It was a severe case and the doctors tell me that it will not "resolve" (their word) for six weeks. For the past week I have been taking two kinds of mucho macho antibiotics and getting a lot of sleep. I have canceled all my retreats until Rohatsu. This thing started while I was leading a retreat here to end our training period and the students became alarmed and forced me into the emergency room the night of the first day of retreat. I never really got over that "flu" I had. The virus got into my lungs and chest.
>
> So, please accept my regrets about not attending your retirement ceremony in December. I have decided not to travel until after the first of the year. I have felt this coming for some time now. The last couple of months I have been dragging myself through the retreats and forcing myself just to do the daily things without doing much else. I just got too worn down. I suppose I was looking for a way to cut back without having to feel guilty about it. At least now everyone is on notice that I can't do it like I have in the past and I can make some adjustments with the understanding of my students.[455]

Later that same day Aitken replied with subject line, "Red light! Red light!":

> Dear Pat: I am quite overcome by the depth and breadth of your response. I look forward to the materials you are sending and will make good use of them I am sure. I'll get them back to you as soon as I can. Thanks also for your comments. … I am alarmed by the bad news about your health. I got sick with pneumonia and pleurisy in 1952, when I was 35 years old. I spent five days in a hospital, and seven months in convalescence. I suggest that you find a retreat from your retreat and stay there with your nicotine patches

> and your chocolate bars for the rest of the calendar year at the very least. Red light! red light! I am sorry that you won't be coming to the retirement ceremony, but I would be sorrier if you were dead. Love, Roshi.[456]

Pat canceled his obligations for much of October and November 1996. Zen Desert Sangha had a group of more than twenty signed up for a November six-day sesshin, and they decided to go ahead anyway. They missed Pat of course, but the group had developed sufficient maturity that no one canceled, and they were able to sustain a full sesshin schedule for the week. Contrary to indications in advance, Pat was back in the saddle by mid-November and though still exhausted, paid an unscheduled visit to Mountain Cloud Zen Center in Santa Fe. The Mountain Cloud newsletter reported:

> We changed our half-day sitting in November from Sunday to Saturday to accommodate a surprise visit from Pat Hawk Roshi. The sangha demonstrated its appreciation by a great show of attendance. Twenty-two members participated in the sitting and stayed for Pat's birthday lunch immediately afterwards.
>
> Our teacher's tremendous effort, especially in light of his very recent bout with pneumonia, was an inspiration to all. Judging by the comments, his teisho touched many of us, with words that lasted well beyond their utterance.
>
> Excitement about Pat's visit peaked even before his arrival. In his presence, the *dojo* filled with a heightened attentiveness to practice and centered sitting. The sangha experienced feelings of gratitude, ease and warmth from the shared effort.[457]

In November, feeling unable to keep up his teaching obligations, Pat wrote to Aitken saying he was considering asking Leonard, Carmichael Peters and Bob Walker for help. Aitken wrote back[458] expressing concern about appointing new teachers, the unspoken caution perhaps being about making new teachers without his (Aitken's) approval, an echo of the Sanbo Kyodan's handling of Aitken's own appointments. Pat replied, "Thank you very much for your personal letter of Oct 22nd — I treasure your legacy and will treat it as an equal of all the Buddhist Jewels." Undeterred by Aitken's reluctance regarding authorizing new teachers, Pat went on, "Another favor you could do for me is send a copy of your teisho for the Handing-On Ceremony."[459]

Pat had approached Bob Walker that summer and asked him if he would teach. In Pat's deferent manner, he didn't make it clear how much he needed help. Rather he offered the role to Bob as a natural progression of Bob's own path, given that he seemed obviously able. At that time, Summer 1996, Bob felt unprepared to take that major step.

Bob was serious, bright, methodical, and skilled with his hands both in woodworking and in nursing, for which he had trained at University of Ohio and University of Georgia. From the first residency period in the late 1980s and through the 1990s, he had come often for extended stays in Amarillo. His handiwork was evident all around the place. He was a steadying presence for others, and years of intense practice opened his own eye. Pat recognized Bob's potential as a teacher early on, and often called on him to be sesshin tanto and contemplative retreat monitor.

Bob and Pat spent a lot of time together, now and then going into town for a burger or an errand, both comfortable with long silences. Bob was sometimes given accommodations within the rectory rather than upstairs with the other residents. Regardless of where he was staying, he was often invited into the rectory common room to watch TV, have supper or just hang out. Bob Walker and Glenna Pittock, themselves close friends, were Pat's closest companions in Amarillo or probably anywhere at the time. They regularly sat in the rectory of an evening and watched *The Simpsons*. They made a good threesome, Glenna's light humor, easy conversation and always-ready laughter lifting the two quiet men into sociability.

Others who were regulars in the Empty Sky program were aware from early on that Bob was seen somewhat as the gifted child, though Bob himself was oblivious to this when Pat approached him in the spring of 1996 to ask if he would be willing to teach. Congenitally modest, reticent, and most comfortable in the background, Bob demurred. He questioned Pat's judgment in putting him forward. Lack of confidence in his own insight, reluctance to be in the limelight, and a deep natural shyness all contributed. While Bob was thus taking his time, Pat was increasingly exhausted and depressed. That he needed help was brought home sharply when he was hospitalized with pneumonia that October. Bob wasn't Pat's only option.

Ever since 1987, when Willigis Jäger had turned over responsibility for the Pacific Northwest "Zen for Christians" group to Pat, Leonard Marcel had taken Pat as his teacher. In late 1992, Leonard had moved to Saudi Arabia after deliberating for some time about whether to take a position there. "I said to Pat, 'You know I've got this possibility, I'm not sure what to do about it.' I was agonizing. And he just looked at me the way he could sometimes and said, 'They need you.' And that settled it." Leonard began his own sitting group in Saudi Arabia while he continued his training with Pat, having dokusan over the phone twice a week and visits to Amarillo for retreats once or twice a year. With Pat's encouragement, he also worked with Rolf Drosten in Germany.[460]

Pat had indicated to Leonard as early as 1993 that he was considering him as teacher material.[461] In 1994, he wrote to Aitken expressing the thought, and they planned for Aitken to meet Leonard in Europe that summer. The trip was canceled after the death of Anne in June, and it was then arranged for Leonard to meet Aitken at Rohatsu in Honolulu that same year. They met a second time in 1996 in London, where Pat and Aitken stopped on their way to Germany for the transmissions of Rolf Drosten and Pia Gyger. In those first meetings, Leonard found Aitken unspontaneous, reserved and even somewhat judgmental — for example, in comments about people passing on the street. He felt himself scrutinized, and indeed he was scrutinized, with Aitken afterward expressing reservations to Pat about the appointment, including a concern that Leonard was too Catholic.[462]

Unlike Bob Walker, Leonard felt ready and willing to take on the teaching role. Though reserved himself, far from being shy, he was accustomed through his profession as a psychiatrist to hearing the most intimate details of his patients' lives. His clinical training meant that, whatever a student brought into dokusan, he could triage the psychological and hone in on the spiritual. Two years after Pat had first broached the subject, he told Leonard that he'd like to go ahead with the appointment, and it was scheduled for the Rohatsu sesshin at Bishop DeFalco Retreat Center in December of 1996. Pat announced the appointment to the sangha at the time of the event, prefacing his remarks with a convincing because feeble-voiced, "I need help," though it was clear, given that Leonard still lived in Saudi Arabia, it wouldn't be possible for him to provide substantial help for some years.[463]

Leonard gave an authoritative dharma talk, after which two cushions were placed for the traditional *shosan*. The first person to take the seat facing Leonard was Cäcilia von Schöning, attending Rohatsu during one of her extended visits from Germany to work with Pat. She settled on the cushion then reached up to her own head. Taking hold of a tuft of hair, she said, "Lion Cloud turning silver," indicating Leonard's hair. He acknowledged her with a bow and she returned to her place. There was a long silence, and when no one else came up, Pat said to Leonard, "You might want to work a little on the intimidation factor." Everyone laughed.[464] The ceremony proceeded, and Leonard was duly authorized as apprentice teacher. He began teaching students in the group he'd organized in Saudi Arabia, and leading some retreats for Rolf Drosten's sangha in Germany.

Guest House II

Besides the Rohatsu sesshin at Bishop DeFalco Retreat Center in December 1996, Pat led the annual Contemplative Intensive Retreat during the week after Christmas. He was by then in a fog of exhaustion, depression and alcohol addiction, with most retreat participants oblivious to the personal struggles that would soon surface, just grateful to have him there. The January 1997 *Empty Sky/Contemplative Path* newsletter carried this letter from Pat:

> In the excellent book *The Roaring Stream* edited by Nelson Foster,[465] there is a poem by Po Chu-I with which I have been resonating of late:
>
> Sick Leave
> Propped
> on pillows, not attending to business;
> For two days I've lain behind locked doors.
> I begin to think that those who hold office
> Get no rest, except by falling ill!
> But the clouds that hover on its far distant peak
> Bring shame to a face that is buried in the world's dust.
>
> The shame on my face is that I've not attended to business for far more than two days. I want to thank all those who sent me get well wishes and held my health in good thoughts. My physical health is restored, but I had a hard time reclaiming energy.
>
> In the future I'm resolved to seek some help with my retreat schedule. I intend to do almost all of my 1997 schedule with a couple of exceptions. I will call on the help of Dr. Carmichael Peters and Dr. Leonard Marcel to help me. I believe that almost all of you know or know of these two wonderful people and will take advantage of the teaching they are most competent to offer.
>
> Greetings to one and all in the New Year. May your practice carry you on.[466]

What he was able to hide from most of his students, Pat could not hide from his confreres, and especially from Greg Mayers, who was the day-to-day witness and whose patience with Pat's great popularity on the one hand and lack of responsibility on the other had worn out. The situation came to a head. In between Pat's submitting the letter saying he planned to keep up his 1997 obligations and before the actual newsletter appeared in print, his confreres, led by Greg Mayers, organized a second intervention. They handed him a plane ticket, and 18 years after his first stay, Pat found himself once again at Guest House, now in Rochester, Minnesota.

Since Pat's first treatment in January 1979, the Catholic Church had recognized that not only male clerics have problems with substance abuse. They designated the original Guest House in the old Scripps mansion in Lake Orion, Michigan, for women and built a second facility for men in Rochester. So it was to the new facility that he went in January 1997. He found the same excellent care as before. Pat always spoke highly of the program at Guest House — how they honored the individual in so many ways; how it was fully understood that addiction is an illness and there was no shame in it, simply the need to get well. It was particularly important to Pat that they had an all lay staff, not necessarily even Catholic. There was no burdensome overlay of guilt or of divine rejection in their way of looking at things.

Part of the program was art therapy. During his first stay at Guest House, Pat had hooked a rug — it hung in his room at Amarillo. This time he chose sketching and painting. Most of his artwork during that time and later does not survive, but there is a charcoal sketch, a self-portrait, done at Guest House that he had framed and that hung in his bedroom thereafter. The image is of a skinny, naked man/boy mouth open wide in a scream reminiscent of Edvard Munch's painting. He sketched the anguished face after an image in an ad for a horror movie called *The Relic* which was showing at the time in Rochester, Minnesota. The arms reach down and together, the body disappearing out of view such that the hands are not visible. Behind him, like a ghost or a shadow, is the faint outline of a cross.

He did a color version of this work, the expression like that in the charcoal but with more of the body showing. The view extends to just above the knees in the color image, revealing the hands brought together to cover the genitals. The shadowy cross in the background is a little more obvious than in the charcoal. The color image especially is one of stark vulnerability, linking the anguished expression to sexuality and shame.

A photo of the color version was squirreled away for years in a shoebox stuffed with loose photos. One day in about 2008, Pat took the box out from the back of the closet in his office in Tucson, blew the dust off, and handed the whole box to me to scan as part of a project I had undertaken digitizing his photos. Going through the piles of disorganized photos, I came across the one of the painting. It's likely he had forgotten about it, or he would have removed it before giving me the box. For this project, I arranged all the scanned photos into digital "albums," which we went through systematically so Pat could identify faces and recall whatever events the photos brought forth. When the photo of the painting came up, he tightened slightly. There was a silent moment before he composed himself, then said simply that he had painted it while at Guest House, photographed it and destroyed the original. We continued with the other photos.

Leonard Marcel remembered an occasion in Amarillo when Pat showed him the framed charcoal version: "He had this two-room apartment. The one room he used for dokusan and the back room was his bedroom. There was one occasion where he took me into his bedroom and showed me some of his paintings and he showed me that one, and I saw that as an opening to — maybe he wanted to talk about something, so I asked him if he could say some more about the painting or about how it touched him, but he shut down."[467]

At Guest House, as before, there was considerable attention given to physical health, recognizing that a person in the throes of alcohol or other substance abuse tends to neglect themselves. During the physical exam, his doctors discovered a nodule on his prostate. The biopsy showed malignancy. Further tests suggested the cancer had not spread beyond the prostate. At the end of April, he had a radical prostatectomy. They let him stay on at Guest House beyond the time his treatment program ended so he could rest and recover from the surgery before returning to work. Pat sent a handwritten letter to his students, relayed by Glenna to the various sanghas at Pat's request.

> Dear Friends,
>
> You have not heard from me in a couple of months. I apologize for any distress my abrupt departure and disappearance may have caused any of you.
>
> The truth of the matter is that I was sick, exhausted and depressed. I was in a condition in which I refused to recognize or accept what was happening. My religious brothers decided to act, since I would or perhaps could not, to remedy the situation. In true clerical fashion, they told me of their plans at the same moment they handed me my plane ticket. I am grateful to them.
>
> I am at a facility that is run exclusively for priests to help them regain their health and sense of well being. I am being well taken care of. In the nine weeks I have been here I have made great strides in regaining strength and equilibrium.
>
> However, a difficulty has surfaced that will delay my return to practicing with you. The treatment here is wholistic, and of course part of it is a thoroughgoing physical examination. Last week a series of tests revealed the presence of cancer in my prostate gland. As I write, I am awaiting further tests to see if the cancer has spread to my hip.
>
> I had hoped to be back at work in the middle of April. Now all is on hold again. If all goes well (and I confidently think it will) I may be able to resume some activities in early summer. Also I will be revising my schedule for the second half of 1997.

In the meantime, do keep up your practice and take advantage of the wonderful teachers that are helping to cover some of our retreats and sesshins. Be as good (better) to them as you have always been to me.

Again, I deeply regret not being able to fulfill the commitments I made to you all. Please remember me with good energy. Be mindful of one another's needs, gentle and welcoming.

With love for you all, Pat Hawk[468]

The surgeon was confident that he'd gotten all of the cancer but further tests revealed this was unlikely. In May, Pat wrote another letter, again distributed to the various sanghas.

Dear Friends

I thank you all from my heart for the outpouring of love and support you have shown to me in the past couple of months. I'm touched to the point of being overwhelmed. I wish to reply to each of you. Please be patient as I do so. I accept and cherish all the letters, cards and gifts. I especially am grateful for all the strong energy, prayers and sutras dedicated for my well-being.

I am writing to you from Guest House in Minnesota where I have been residing since January 13. I am returning to Amarillo on May 22. I have done all I can here to get back in shape. The experience has been tremendously renewing.

As you may know, I underwent surgery to remove a cancerous prostate. The procedure went smoothly, and the surgeons were quite pleased and confident of a cure. I have been recovering very well with little discomfort.

However, all our optimism about a cure may have been premature. On May 10 I had the staples over the incision removed and was told the surgeon wished to speak with me. In his hand was a revised pathology report. The further examination of the lymph nodes also removed during surgery showed cancer cells. This means I still need further treatment.

I will simply go on. I don't know how I will be affected by the treatments, but I don't expect to be slowed down too much. Although I don't know how long I will survive with this disease, my time could well be quite extended.

Thank you for your compassionate concern. Keep sending that energy. So—

Will be around a while
Pat[469]

The retreats he was missing while at Guest House were led by other teachers. Joan Rieck, who was transitioning back to the States from Europe and was living part of the year in Belen, New Mexico, came in February to visit and give a class. Greg Mayers tried to take up some slack in Amarillo by offering interviews during regular weekly sitting. It was not the same thing at all for Pat's students, and most simply went without. Carmichael Peters led the Easter contemplative intensive retreat at Bishop DeFalco. Formerly a Jesuit priest, trained in philosophy and theology, and by many accounts brilliant, Carmichael had lost both legs in an accident as a young man, but with upper body strength and adept use of prostheses or a wheelchair, he was agile and anything but disabled. He was good with his hands and could build things. Although he left the priesthood, he continued his contemplative practice. He was a deep, silent, steady sitter and a charismatic individual. Richard Laue remembered sitting with him: "Oh my God. Just his presence. Just him being in a room."[470]

Pat suggested to the Northwest group that Carmichael could lead the March contemplative intensive retreat, but they balked. Alice Ray, a core member of that group, had been involved with Carmichael some years before, until "I found out that I was just one bead on his rosary."[471] Word got around, though apparently not to Pat, until they let him know that Carmichael wasn't going to work out for them. All Pat's groups ran democratically, and although they sought his counsel and often followed it, he did not have a deciding say in anything except his own participation. They looked for someone else, with the result that Jack Duffy led the March and May retreats for Seven Thunders in Pat's place.

Pat asked John Tarrant to help with the sesshins scheduled for February in Santa Fe and March in Tucson. John invited Joan Sutherland, whom he had recently made an apprentice teacher, to lead the Tucson retreat with him and the Santa Fe retreat on her own.

Ripples at Zen Desert Sangha

John and Joan came to Tucson in March 1997 to lead the sesshin at Indiana Nelson's in Pat's place. Zen Desert Sangha, now in its fourth year at Indiana's home, was no longer the happy, *gemütlich* environment that had fostered such growth in the early years. In a discord that predated Pat's illness and absence, devoted sangha members, serious about Zen practice as they understood it, worked toward a more regulated form and a more carefully kept silence than was offered at Indiana's. Indiana herself held to a more whimsical, light-hearted version of practice. Besides, she felt increasing resentment and exhaustion at what came to seem like imposition of the sangha in her home.

Although a core group of committed, responsible folks pitched in to take care of the space, there were many times when everybody went home and left Indiana with the cleaning up. They paid a small monthly stipend for use of the place and developed a pretty large sense of entitlement. There were sangha meetings in which people complained about Indiana's unorthodoxy and disregard for tried-and-true Zen form. They saw her as disruptive, needy, claiming the role of spiritual leader on the one hand and shunning it on the other. She came to feel as an outsider in her own home. At one point after a listening circle, a sangha member approached Indiana and said that some people are asking whether she is even a Buddhist — with the implication that she didn't belong if she wasn't. Stunned, she responded in a letter, the crux of which was, take it or leave it:

> You are guests in my house. To me it does not matter if the guest or the caretaker of this house is Muslim, Hindu, Jewish. What does matter is how we treat one another. If you do not like it here then it is up to you to move on. I remember once during a particularly hideous sesshin (for me!) in Amarillo when Pat Hawk was driven to ask me to go—or choose to stay. I was blathering loudly and making an ass out of myself. I think he gave me an hour to pack my bags. I chose to stay. It need not matter to you if I am a Zen Buddhist or not—if you honor me as a human being and as your host.[472]

Pat was aware of the struggles. One day in his terse way he offered the dictum, "As far as *samu* goes, you don't contribute, you don't eat. You don't come. It's very simple." But for the most part, he did not get involved. He left discussion and decisions to sangha members. The stake he held in the day-to-day was not strong enough to overcome his natural aversion to conflict. People brought their concerns into dokusan and he listened, which could be healing in itself, but he rarely offered an opinion or advice. He was only in Tucson for sesshin, and in any case, it was simply not his nature to take part in sangha struggles. For that and many other reasons, the situation was deteriorating.

It was this situation of growing disharmony that Pat left when he went to Guest House in January 1997. To this scene at Indiana's, John and Joan arrived for the March sesshin as a terrific gust of fresh air.

John Tarrant was the first person given transmission by Robert Aitken. Although that was partly an accident of scheduling — the transmissions of Augusto Alcalde, Nelson Foster, Pat Hawk and John Tarrant were all announced at the same time, and it was then a matter of doing the ceremonies for each at workable times — it was the case that John stood out among Aitken's students as his white knight. He came forth as charismatic, flamboyant and creative, with a breathtaking facility for expressing the dharma in poetic, evocative language. He was also roguishly handsome, warm, lighthearted, jovial. Given permission to teach by Aitken, John established his own Zen center, the California Diamond Sangha in Santa Rosa, California. Joan Sutherland was his equally inspired student, who he had recently appointed as an apprentice teacher.

People loved Joan and John. It was perfectly natural that some found a deeper affinity with them than with Pat and wanted to continue working with them as well as Pat, or even instead of Pat, once he returned from Guest House. But somehow a rift formed between the Pat loyalists and the Joan and John contingent, not only at Zen Desert Sangha where the situation was somewhat troubled to begin with, but also at Mountain Cloud Zen Center in Santa Fe.

Where Pat was incisive and spare in the dokusan room and largely invisible outside of it, John and Joan were friendly and accessible, chatty, sympathetic, involved. For each person in the dokusan room, Pat responded to whatever was brought before him but evinced no curiosity beyond what was offered. Whatever came forth, he received without editorial comment. There was rarely anything like, "that's really difficult, isn't it," or "how wonderful," or "good for you" — nothing overlaid on whatever the student brought in, just a complete, unfiltered reception. Then he would sit with the person for a bottomless instant of deep silence, and as if it were coming through him rather than from him, he would offer a few pithy words to further a person's practice. Far from being unsympathetic, it was a rarefied sort of sympathy that reached beyond day-to-day cares.

Such brief interventions continued rather than interrupted the building silence of sesshin and were well-suited to those wholeheartedly cultivating that silence. For anyone in need of feedback and encouragement in life's more quotidian challenges — that is, everyone some of the time — Pat's offerings simply cast one back on the bare fact. John and Joan, on the other hand, conversed, explored nuance, drew a person out, and provided an embrace of emotional support. One felt appreciated, understood, and personally, individually loved. Besides, they were more fun than Pat could ever be. Many people, especially those who had joined Zen Desert Sangha during their time at Indiana's and who were drawn to the richness, the voluptuous, artistic aspect of practice that had flourished at her place, felt themselves more at home with John and Joan than with Pat.

To the growing fault lines between Indiana and the sangha, John and Joan brought concern and practical attention. Indiana remembered that they had her sit at the front of the group:

> ...and they said, "Indiana has an issue that needs to be talked about in the sangha. She feels that you are transferring onto her this role as the mother and she doesn't want that role." And I had just read something wonderful that an Indian teacher had said to her followers. She said don't treat me as your mother, because people are rude to their mothers. Treat me as your child. And I said that to the group. I said I don't see myself as the mother. I don't want that responsibility. And John and Joan backed me up in that. They gave me huge support in that. But things went right on.[473]

Leaving Indiana Nelson's 1997

The strain wore on everyone, especially Indiana, who became seriously ill with valley fever, eventually needing surgery to remove part of her lung. Richard Wahl, a physician and sangha member, saw the toll on her. She recalled: "Finally, Richard Wahl came up to me and he said, 'Kick us out. We're killing you.' Just those few words. … So it was very sad. Because it was the end of something fun and joyous and very sweet."[474] With reluctance, Indiana gave notice that they had to leave, then quickly changed her mind, then changed back again. She wrote a long letter to Zen Desert Sangha, getting to the heart of a struggle faced in some degree perhaps by all sanghas:

> In this moment the sangha is seeking a home. And in this moment the doves are nesting in the tree outside my window. The bird, of course, knows exactly what is required for her survival; attentive, she finds the balance with all her surrounding world: sun, cloud, worm, earth, water, tree, predator. To each of these she establishes her own relationship. In this way she offers shelter, as the tree shelters her, and the cloud shelters the tree. It is a beautiful task.
>
> Our task is also one of survival. Perhaps, though, not always in the way we imagine. The surrounding in which we place ourselves forms us, it influences how or even if we will survive. But the survival I speak of has less to do with buildings and groups than with our one heart. I am thinking now of this spirit of love which funds and fuels and inspires our sangha. This is where we live. If we can pierce through to this once again, we will survive…
>
> When we "practice" kindness it often carries us away from our hearts. These long business meetings imprison us in our brains. Do they feel good? Look around at the faces. Am I frowning, does my own face feel tight? Does this feel kind, does it feel loving? Even a bird knows if the sunlight on his branch feels good. So then, how can we serve one another? We can listen, certainly, and pay attention to our own nerve endings. We can ask ourselves how and in what way we each want to contribute to the heart life of sangha. In this way we live together in deep respect. We offer shelter in the most profound sense: as the bird, the tree, the cloud, effortlessly, and simply by being ourselves. It is a beautiful task.[475]

As Indiana vacillated between asking the sangha to leave and wanting them to stay, this note appeared in the Zen Desert Sangha newsletter:

> As most of you know by now, Zen Desert Sangha will be moving from its present location to a new site in June. We are very grateful to Indiana Nelson for her gracious and open-hearted generosity in housing us for the last four years. Those of us who have shared her space will never forget its nurturing beauty, its impish unpredictability, and most of all, its sustaining aura of love.

> For many of us, Indiana's home — and Indiana's heart — was a sanctuary and a place of healing. For others it was a playground, or a nursery, or a "home base." For ALL of us, it will forever be a cherished memory, held with gratitude and a grin![476]

In May 1997, just after John Tarrant and Joan Sutherland had led a second sesshin in Pat's place, the sangha moved out. There followed a year of "wandering in the desert" for Zen Desert Sangha, sitting at members' homes or at the Quaker House on 4th Avenue, or the Unitarian Universalist Church in southeast Tucson, holding sesshin where space could be had that included overnight accommodation.

Despite the rift that began to appear in the sangha between those who continued to identify Pat as their teacher and those who gravitated more toward John and Joan, all put effort into finding a home following the move from Indiana's. Most continued to participate in sangha social events, though the events decreased in frequency. The sangha incorporated, and a board of directors was formed, an important step toward having a solid organization that could purchase and administer their own property. The democratic spirit that had informed Zen Desert Sangha organization from the beginning was carried into the procedure for selecting the six-member board: any full member willing to serve put their name in a hat from which the six names were drawn, with particular positions — president, vice-president, treasurer, secretary and two members at large — worked out casually.

In May 1998, after intense fundraising and generous contributions from some sangha members, they took possession of a property on Martin Avenue in central Tucson.

Joan Sutherland and Pat Hawk, Mountain Cloud Zen Center

While Pat was at Guest House during the first quarter of 1997, Joan Sutherland subbed for him at Mountain Cloud Zen Center by herself, John Tarrant having other commitments. If there was ever any question about whether she could stand on her own as a teacher independent of John, there was none after these retreats. It was clear in the voices of participants that appeared in *Cicada,* Mountain Cloud's newsletter, following her first sesshin with them:

> Joan Sutherland Sensei,* dharma heir to John Tarrant Roshi, was kind enough to come to Santa Fe from Sonoma County, Calif., to run our retreat.

---

* Sensei: In this context, apprentice or associate teacher.

> Joan's presence was universally appreciated and everyone is delighted at the prospect of her returning." "[Sesshin] is Joan Sutherland Sensei floating into the *dojo*, her robes rustling her dark hair cascading in waves down her back as she makes her final appearance of the evening. Holding her wooden staff aloft and calling us "dear ones" in a tinkling, beneficent voice, she is our very own Glinda the Good.[477]

Another wrote in the same issue of *Cicada*, perhaps with some foreshadowing of the struggle that was to come:

> We have a strong, loving and energetic sangha. There are a number of unknowns in our future. As time goes by, we will have more answers and the way will become clear to us. We can all rest easy in the sincerity and devotion of our sangha. In the meantime, as we sit with our uncertainties, let's try reminding ourselves, "What a great opportunity to practice."[478]

Joan was brilliant, beautiful and accessible. People took to her readily. Women felt they had found the closest of dharma sisters. One person remembered, "She was just lovely in dokusan and she was kind and welcoming and very compassionate. She's beautiful, sweet, gives lovely teishos. You go into dokusan and she greets you like she's just been waiting for YOU to come. And Pat looks scary and solemn and doesn't talk that much. Joan was much more user-friendly."

Not everyone was enthralled. One student remembers her warm welcoming presence in dokusan extending to saying, "You should come around more often. We should get to know each other better," in a way that made him uncomfortable. It was not that there was any sense of impropriety of a sexual nature, but that there was no acknowledgment of the fact that he was already committed to a teacher: Pat Hawk. A Sutherland student reflecting back years later commented that Joan seemed aggressive in developing a program at Mountain Cloud. Joan was overheard to say when the issue of sharing of students between teachers or transfer from one to another came up, that she couldn't help it if people wanted to work with her, which of course, was true. But in retrospect it seemed to some who witnessed the drama that followed, that from the beginning, Joan may have seen this as a potential opportunity to establish herself with her own sangha in disregard of Pat's position at Mountain Cloud. No doubt, she was also simply responding to the very obvious desire for her frequent presence with the sangha.

Many students who had been working with Pat — perhaps as many as half the Mountain Cloud sangha — took to Joan wholeheartedly, and by the end of that spring, had embraced her as their teacher. They worked toward bringing her back for sesshin as often as possible, and the Mountain Cloud schedule for years thereafter included some events with Joan and others with Pat. For a time, students now working with Joan set up phone dokusan sessions dubbed "dial-a-roshi," for which she charged $75 per hour, the cost to be shared among whoever participated.[479] This financial side, which also touched the teacher's fee for sesshin, was new to people who had worked with Pat. As a Redemptorist priest, though he most certainly wanted to — and did — contribute financially to his community, he felt no pressing need. His food, clothing and shelter were guaranteed. John and Joan, as laypeople, had to provide for their own subsistence. Both had to make a living, which meant that for either of them to spend substantial amounts of time teaching Zen, it had to pay. Perhaps this need to have sufficient numbers to support Joan's visits contributed to the conflict.

For many people, the strength and depth of the bond that forms between teacher and student in the intimacy and long-term sharing of dokusan rivals — and even surpasses — the intensity of the parent-child bond or the bond between lovers. It surely contributes to many of the transgressions of teachers with their students, subject of frequent scandal in the larger Zen community. Despite all the hours of silent Zen practice and the cultivation of equanimity, and not unlike a mother bear when her cub is threatened, a student deeply attached to a teacher can rise up viscerally against any threat to the relationship. The rift that formed in Tucson between devotees of Pat and those of John and Joan appeared more intensely at Mountain Cloud.

Ever since Philip Kapleau had left Santa Fe in 1986, the question of who would be the teacher for Mountain Cloud was floated from time to time at sangha meetings. With the discovery of Pat and his willingness to come from Amarillo, that was resolved in some measure, although having someone living in the vicinity and available for more regular encounters would have been preferable. Joan's students leaped to the hope that Joan would become principal teacher at Mountain Cloud, maybe even resident teacher, while Pat's students wanted to continue arrangements with him. At meeting after meeting for several years, there was contention between the Sutherland and Hawk camps. Some of Joan's students openly declared that Joan felt Pat was no good as a teacher. It surfaced that Joan and John had gone so far as to write a letter to Robert Aitken saying that they thought Pat was not a good teacher. One Pat student recalled, "I'd walk out [of sangha meetings] feeling like I'd been stabbed in the heart."

It was announced by one of Joan's students that Pat had given his students in Tucson an ultimatum that they must choose him or John Tarrant, and Joan wanted people at Mountain Cloud to do the same. This sounds unlike Pat, and when the question was raised with some of the longtime students from Tucson they could not recall that he gave any ultimatum. It may have been a misunderstanding arising upon Pat's return from Guest House and discovery of the tremendous sway of support toward John and Joan. He wondered whether the sangha still wanted him to come and teach. Pat raised the point at the August sesshin that year, addressing the group matter-of-factly, saying, "They think I shouldn't be teaching. Maybe they're right. But here I am." He shrugged, indicating, it's up to you. It wasn't an either-or ultimatum so much as an offering to the sangha to discontinue inviting him if they wished. One of Pat's students remembered,

> The final straw was when somebody came to a sangha meeting — again the age old search for a teacher. And one of Joan's students said, Joan will be the teacher. And I said, well good she can teach and Pat can teach. She said no, Joan would be the only teacher. She just wants to be the only teacher at Mountain Cloud and Pat's students will have to leave. It was like throwing up flame in the middle of the sangha meeting.

Without verifying the rumor with Joan, the Pat loyalists wrote a letter to the sangha in which they accused her of saying they should leave. Her students then denied Joan had said this. Tracy McCallum wrote an apology that was published in *Cicada*.[480] Sometime after this, Joan wrote the sangha asking them to write a letter stating that she had not said Pat's students should leave. Emotions were raw. Many people — whether Joan's, Pat's or uncommitted students — left the sangha. Attendance at regular sits dropped. Many times, Lucie and Will Brennan, Mountain Cloud members from Kapleau days, could expect to be the only ones who showed up. The sangha president resigned and the vice president became president, with great reluctance.

Feeling herself under attack, she called Pat in distress. When he picked up the phone all she could do was sob. He held on. At last she managed to choke out her name and explain why she called. "Should I just resign? Should I just let go and leave Mountain Cloud?" Surprising her with his strength and decisiveness, Pat said, "Stand your ground." It was not about holding firm against whatever threat to himself there may have seemed to be from Joan and her students, nor expecting someone else to defend his territory. He had no territory he cared to defend. To enter into any sort of conflict on his own behalf was not his way. It was about throwing a lifesaver to someone floundering in rough water. Every once in a while, he would stand up like that.

Struggling to get along and finding nothing they could discuss without hard feelings, the remnant, including both Pat and Joan students, at one point decided they would simply sit together in silence. There at least was common ground.

The bitterness of those struggles in both Santa Fe and Tucson was perhaps a testament to the wisdom of the Diamond Sangha Teachers' Circle in setting up a specified protocol for students who wished to work with other teachers, whether for something like a single visit while traveling or for a more extended period that might result in a complete transfer from one teacher to another. The protocol was developed over several years' worth of discussions in Diamond Sangha teachers' meetings, and by 1997 it included mutual communication between the *home* teacher and the *visited* teacher. There was to be exchange regarding where the student was in their practice, such as was demonstrated to Pat by Aitken. When Pat was to lead a sesshin for him in Hawaii, and likewise after Aitken saw Pat's students in dokusan during his visit to Bishop DeFalco Retreat Center, he sent Pat detailed notes about each student's practice. It was up to the teachers themselves to inform students about expectations in this regard.

Notwithstanding, Pat himself was disinclined to follow the protocol when students came to him from other teachers, instead simply trusting, not unlike Joan Sutherland, that they knew what they needed. Students from various teachers — many from Rochester —switched to Pat over the years, without any communication from Pat to the formerly primary teacher. Part of this was perhaps his seminary training and the deeply ingrained seal of the confessional. Besides, Pat was by nature so private himself. Unless he was particularly close to another teacher, and even then at times, he could easily excuse himself from the effort to reach out for anything of this sort. Nonetheless, in looking back some years later on the messy situation that followed Joan and John's incursion into two of his sanghas, Pat invoked the protocol as something they could have followed to effect a smoother transition and subsequent relationship. He experienced the defection of students and what some called Joan and John's takeover, to the extent that it occurred, as a betrayal.

Last year in Amarillo

As confreres and longtime associates, Greg Mayers and Pat Hawk had some of the relationship of siblings, including the familiarity, the sense of home, the support, the inevitability, and the friction. Having known each other since they were young teenagers, they had the shared history of the seminary environment of Kirkwood, Edgerton, De Soto, Oconomowoc. They got to know each other as friends after ordination, both participating in "talk groups," as Pat called them, run by Joe Bilsley. Every priest was required to do eight weeks of personal retreat every year, which could take many forms. Joe Bilsley ran his Rogerian-style counseling circles during summer breaks in the 1960s and '70s, and both Greg and Pat participated. The groups provided an opportunity to share among themselves, build trust, cultivate psychological wholeness, and at the same time learn to be better counselors.

From the friendship that developed out of the talk groups, Pat and Greg discovered a mutual interest in meditation. Comparing notes and sharing books on the subject, they encountered the works of Alan Watts, great popularizer of Zen in the 1960s, and the seminal book, *Zen Mind, Beginner's Mind*,[481] a collection of talks by Shunryu Suzuki, founder of the San Francisco Zen Center. Pat followed Greg to Palisades, Greg followed Pat to Germany, they traveled around Europe together, went to Korea together, had friends in common, established the program at Amarillo, offered retreats all over the country. Developing along contemplative/Zen lines in parallel, they were an in-group for each other within the larger and largely indifferent Redemptorist community.

At the same time, they were a study in contrasts. Outside the interview room and the tight format of contemplative retreat or sesshin and the occasional class, Pat was barely noticeable to many people — like the wallflower at a dance, hanging back with a sort of mousy reticence, all the more separate in counterbalance to Greg's sociability. It was not shyness. Pat was one of those rare people who was completely comfortable being the silent one at a party. He felt no obligation to assist a conversation, and while others might fidget and shuffle and cast about for something to say, Pat was comfortable offering nothing. Greg was blond, blue-eyed, half a head taller than Pat, well-proportioned, nicely dressed and good-looking. He talked more, smiled more, and took more interest than Pat did in the day-to-day intrigues of the retreat center inhabitants. Certainly, that was part of Greg's job, and it also fit his personality. You could walk into his office and just chat for a while. Except for a few people — Glenna Pittock was one — that wasn't possible with Pat. Trying to engage him in social chitchat or light gossip could be like talking to a black hole; one's remarks were swallowed up into vast emptiness.

Greg was both more open and more self-defended than Pat. He was easier to know at a social level. He talked easily, including sometimes about himself, both in and out of the interview room. With Pat, in the interview room often it was as if there was no Pat — just the transparency of complete attention, so that whatever one brought was reflected back. There was no social commentary, no judgment. There was nothing that could not be revealed, no matter how odd or ugly, nothing that in that space was not perfectly accepted and real, such that the encounter was extraordinary. With Greg, at least for some, there was less presence, less revelation of depths. There was more conversation *about* what the student brought forth rather than the simple reception of, and terse response to, whatever was presented.

So there was more of Greg showing, so to speak. The sexually repressed world of the seminary that Greg and Pat entered as young teenagers arrested to a degree the maturation of sexuality so that there was a greater mana around sexual subjects, sexual jokes and physical contact than for the average non-celibate adult where sexuality was more integrated. For both, sexuality still perhaps carried the exaggerated attraction of the forbidden. With Pat, this was under the surface. With Greg, it was more overt, appearing in off-color jokes and insinuations. Pat enjoyed as much prurient interest as the next person, but other than with those who lived in close proximity, his confreres, for example, it didn't show. Greg would bring in sexual innuendo to a talk to raise a laugh. Pat mostly left the whole area alone.

There were asymmetries in their trajectories from early on: Although Greg stood out as social and urbane while Pat was reticent and all but invisible, at the first Zen sesshin for Christians in October 1978, it was Pat who caught Aitken's attention as being the promising one among all participants, Greg not connecting with him at all. Thenceforth, though it was Greg who had been first to take an interest in Zen and who had been instrumental in organizing that first sesshin, it was Pat who came out of it with a Zen teacher with whom to correspond and be guided. And again, when Willigis Jäger came onto the scene, it was Pat he noticed and invited to spend a year in Würzburg — Greg only coming at the end of that year to visit and to work toward his own relationship with Willigis. Following on these attentions, opportunities and resultant experiences, it was Pat to whom Aitken gave full transmission in the Diamond Sangha. It was Greg who took the lead in establishing a contemplative program at Amarillo but it was around Pat that the program grew and thrived, attracting as he did by far the greater number of students. It was Greg who was assigned the directorship of Bishop DeFalco Retreat Center — something Pat would have had no interest in or aptitude for. And as director, Greg became Pat's Superior within the congregation, therefore the one to whom Pat's vow of obedience was most directly subject. As director of the retreat center, Greg had a laid-back hand on the tiller that could be both maddening and generous. The generosity suited them both, but Pat preferred order to laxity in administration, his dissatisfactions with Greg's style expressed with passive aggression rather than any sort of constructive assistance. Greg had an unruliness that extended to at least one intimate relationship with a female student, whereas Pat tended to be careful to a fault about maintaining boundaries. While both Pat and Greg enjoyed a drink and Greg had experimented mildly with psychedelics,[482] Pat was increasingly abusing alcohol, which in their close association put Greg in the position of increasingly frustrated enabler. The differences in temperament and circumstance eroded the tight friendship they had enjoyed in their early years of spiritual exploration and working together.

Pat had mentioned difficulties with Greg to Aitken even in the early 1990s, for which Aitken was sympathetic. Paul Hughes remembered that around that time, while Paul was Head Resident for the program, there was an administrative meeting during the whole of which Pat and Greg wouldn't speak to each other. From these beginnings, the trouble grew.

Pat descended more and more into alcohol and depression. While he was away for his second treatment at Guest House, open conflict erupted between Pat's closest allies in Amarillo and Greg. Some of the longtime contemplative/Zen participants were critical and unsupportive of Greg's management decisions and unwelcoming of his overtures to step in for Pat as a teacher. Greg, for his part, exhausted from the demands of managing the retreat center, fed up with the adulation of Pat who it seemed could do no wrong in the eyes of his students, and enraged by the alcoholism he in some degree enabled, refused to countenance any communication between Pat and his friends at Bishop DeFalco. He insisted that no one be told where Pat was. Greg tried to intercept a letter from Pat addressed to Glenna, which she narrowly succeeded in claiming.

The situation deteriorated to the point that when Pat returned from Guest House, Father Tom Picton, Vice-Provincial Superior of the Redemptorist New Orleans Vice-Province at the time, came in to do three days of mediation with Pat, Greg and Glenna in an attempt to restore a working relationship. Though they continued to function side by side for the year remaining at Bishop DeFalco, the friendship was irreparably damaged.

Pat was back in Amarillo from Guest House in late May 1997. The sobriety he embraced in the supportive milieu of Guest House was more difficult in the tense atmosphere of the Bishop DeFalco Retreat Center rectory. Nevertheless, he resumed his schedule, students populating his retreats with enthusiasm, most of them unaware of his struggles, though for Pat a mist of depression still lingered. He hit another low when Abbot Bernard McVeigh died in early June at Guadalupe Abbey.[483] Bernard was one of a few father figures in Pat's life. First, there was Joe Bilsley from his seminary days. Pat had admired Bilsley from the beginning when, as Prefect of Students at Oconomowoc, he supported Pat through the crisis that almost had him dismissed from the seminary before final vows. Then they'd worked together at the seminary high school in Edgerton, Wisconsin. In those years Pat had been able to breach the father-son, teacher-student distance and find in Bilsley a friend and colleague. Although Bilsley had been involved in the intervention that sent Pat to Guest House the first time, it was as colleague rather than authority figure.

Aitken was another important father figure for Pat, a transference Pat was able to work out in the long years they knew each other, in the shelter of Aitken's unwavering support, and with Pat's own maturation as a teacher.

With Bernard McVeigh, it was different. Pat admired Bernard from when they met at the first Zen retreat for Christians. There was Bernard's apparent complete ease in the monastic life, his urbanity, his sense of humor, his ability to keep the monastery on an even keel, and his service as spiritual guide for a far-flung flock of clerics and laypeople. When Pat tried out the Trappist life for three months in the early 1980s, he was under Bernard's authority, subject to his evaluation. There was a sense for Pat of something held back, that somehow he did not have Bernard's wholehearted support. And Bernard, so at ease with so many different kinds of people, wasn't quite at ease with Pat. Over the years of Bernard's organizing the Northwest retreats, first with Robert Aitken, then with Willigis Jäger, he didn't go out of his way to include Pat in pre- or post-retreat social events like going out for dinner. Bernard expressed reservations when Willigis handed Pat responsibility for the Northwest group. Many others, at first doubtful that anyone could adequately take over from Willigis, were reassured of Pat's ability once they had worked through a retreat with him. Bernard was not so sure. It's possible that not having the encouragement of deep realization experiences himself, the support of Willigis Jäger's charisma was necessary to Bernard, and that Pat, with insight present — an insight Bernard could not see — but energetic charisma lacking, seemed to fall short.

Although Bernard nonetheless attended all the Northwest retreats taught by Pat that he could and although he went to interviews with him, Pat always felt a lingering sense of something missing in this relationship, something he must strive for. With Bernard's death, the possibility of earning Bernard's unconditional approval was gone. Coming as it did at a time of vulnerability as Pat struggled to re-enter life upon return from Guest House, the loss of Bernard hit him hard. Sitting with some of his students in the zendo for a Q&A not long after hearing the news, Pat seemed terribly downhearted.

Besides this loss and the continuing conflict with Greg, there were institutional changes afoot at Bishop DeFalco Retreat Center that left the Redemptorists unsettled. In January 1997, not long after Pat was sent to Guest House, Bishop John Yanta was appointed to replace Bishop Leroy Matthiesen who was retiring. The handing over took place in March. BDRC belonged to the Diocese of Amarillo and therefore was under the bishop's jurisdiction. The Redemptorists, directors of the center since it opened in 1982, had enjoyed a cordial and tolerant relationship with Matthiesen. They had been given tremendous leeway in offering whatever programs they saw fit, including the program of Zen practice opportunities.

Bishop Yanta was a different beast. Where Matthiesen had been among the most progressive Catholic bishops of that era, Yanta was deeply conservative. Matthiesen was tolerant of diversity in many dimensions. Yanta leaned more toward an orthodoxy that, in many ways, rejected the tenets of Vatican II. Both had a pro-life stance, which for Matthiesen meant opposing the death penalty and nuclear armament, encouraging parishioners who worked at Pantex — the final assembly place for all US nuclear missiles — to find other kinds of employment. For Yanta it meant being anti-abortion, demonstrating outside Planned Parenthood and urging parishioners who worked there to seek jobs elsewhere.

Some conservative Catholics among the faithful welcomed Yanta as a breath of fresh air, appreciating his support of their causes, but by and large his effect was divisive and strife-generating. He was a micromanager with a strong need for control. An article in the *National Catholic Reporter* written not long after Yanta took over contrasts the two bishops:

> [Matthiesen's] biggest fault was that he sometimes listened too much. People would sometimes joke, especially toward the end of his tenure, that his decisions would be swayed by the last person in his office. But he was well liked by most priests, and the atmosphere in the diocese was congenial. Priests used to meet and talk about their ministries, their parishes, tell jokes. Now the whole atmosphere in the diocese is one of mistrust.
>
> Matthiesen was widely regarded as a "Vatican II bishop" in the progressive sense. Seven priests who spoke [to the *National Catholic Reporter*] under the condition of anonymity, five of them in leadership positions in the diocese, and more than a dozen lay leaders and activists, described Yanta as personable in public, well-liked by "pew people," but rigid, controlling and suspicious in his dealings with priests, authoritarian and confrontational in his administrative style, pietistic in speech and manner, and a poor listener who makes up his mind before he consults. One priest said, "Yanta talks incessantly about unity while thriving on — even generating — division."[484]

Privately, Pat took to calling Yanta a troglodyte.

The Redemptorists felt the change of tone coming from the chancery office even before Yanta officially took up his position. By the time Pat got back from Guest House, Yanta had let them know he planned to have the retreat center run by the diocese, giving them about a year's notice. In the meantime, all programs continued. For Pat, this meant offering resident training periods in the summers of 1997 and '98, regular sitting two evenings a week with interviews or dokusan, the usual schedule shared by all priests for saying Masses, and a heavy travel schedule to serve the distant sanghas.

Although Pat recovered well from prostate surgery, lab tests indicated that he was not cured. He wrote to Aitken in June, one year after leaving Guest House, speaking frankly within that trusted relationship:

> I must apologize for my silence in the past month. To tell the truth I don't know why I am reluctant to call. I can think of all kinds of reasons that are not at all reasonable. Sometimes I feel that I'm breaking in on you. Sometimes I feel like I am a rank beginner with no clue and reluctant to advertise it. Sometimes I say to myself that I am busy, which I am, but not that busy. And underneath all, at some half conscious level, the cancer is weighing me down. In the past two months my PSA has begun to rise and there is definite progression of the disease. The doctors are talking about hormone treatments again but not pushing. On the surface, I really don't think about it much and certainly don't talk about it, but recently I have come to believe that it must be affecting me anyway.

He finished with, "Looking forward to Damme [the upcoming teachers' meeting to be hosted by Rolf Drosten in Germany]."[485]

Concerns about his health notwithstanding, the darkness that seemed to hover over Pat around the time of Bernard McVeigh's death the year before was lifting. The uncertainties that had greeted him on his return from Guest House — where he would live and work, the rankling conflict with Greg — were resolved. During the year leading up to the Redemptorists' dismissal from Bishop DeFalco Retreat Center, he had variously considered moving to Oregon, Santa Fe or Tucson. In the end he decided to join his confreres at the Redemptorist facility on the northwest outskirts of Tucson and continue his work from there. Greg Mayers would remain in Amarillo, taking up work as a fundraiser for Food for the Poor.

Just before the Redemptorists were to leave Bishop DeFalco, Pat offered a last resident training period, which was attended by many of his longtime students. It began in the middle of June and continued until the end of July, in time for Empty Sky to pick up stakes and leave. Much of the *samu* during the training period was directed at packing. There were 20 registered — not a large number for sesshin or contemplative retreats but a remarkable number for the extended period that resident training entails.

Tracy McCallum, a student of Pat's from Santa Fe, was among those who attended. Years later, he reflected on his encounter with Pat:

> I grew up a Methodist — that barely qualifies as Christian ... And I was supposed to become a Catholic when I got married. My first wife was a Catholic. But when it came right down to it, I couldn't do it. I couldn't connect with the message. So Pat was a real enigma for me because of the way he was able to balance the two. I first started sitting in 1965 with [Shunryu] Suzuki in San Francisco. I was only there for about a year, then I stopped sitting for about five years. In New Mexico I sat with a Korean teacher — I took vows with him — then different ones here and there for a while. Finally, I heard about Mountain Cloud. Somebody told me about this little Zen master that looks like an accountant. And in the fall of '94 I sat a sesshin with him and decided that this was the guy that I really wanted to study with. Just the way he expressed himself and carried himself. It was the kind of teaching that was accessible to me. He made it really accessible to me. I was very taken by him. I felt I was really able to enter the dharma through him in a way that I hadn't done before. We've just had this ongoing wonderful rapport. It has been a major influence in my whole life. In 72 years the last 17 or 18 working with Pat have been the most powerful and moving time of my life.[486]

Tracy remembered that last resident training period at Bishop DeFalco:

> They laughingly called it the last dance at Amarillo. It was really, really fantastic. The people there were really something. Paul Sanders and this other Australian guy who was a forest ranger and his opera-singing wife. Sue [Weimer was there. Kristen [Larson] had just signed on to be there for a year, she was going to spend a whole year with Pat. Karen [Johnson] and Richard Laue were there. And everybody just became really close. It was a tight group. And that goes into my memory as one of the most profound times I've ever spent.[487]

During the training period, representatives from Pat's main sanghas got together. Besides reviewing and agreeing upon a common ritual, sesshin cautions, and officer guidelines, they discussed the future of Pat's programs and how they would support him after he left Bishop DeFalco Retreat Center. The idea was floated that he could divide his time among periods in residence with his three main constituencies: the Seven Thunders group in Oregon, the Mountain Cloud group in Santa Fe and Zen Desert Sangha in Tucson. The proposal had to include financial support, to be prorated according to the amount of time Pat would spend with each group. A post-Amarillo itinerary began to emerge, and with plans taking shape, Pat seemed to relax.

The following note was published in the July 1998 edition of the *Seven Thunders Newsletter*:

> Jane Huyer has just returned from Amarillo where she met with members of the Zen Desert Sangha from Tucson and the Mountain Cloud Zen Center from Santa Fe. The three meditation groups are communicating with one another and with Fr. Pat to successfully meet the needs and goals of all concerned. As there are many unanswered questions, it has been agreed that 1999 will be approached as an experiment with many creative adjustments along the way. We anticipate a growing interest and involvement on the part of the membership to share ideas, energy and resources.[488]

Already in the preceding April, Jane, a longtime student of Pat from Corvallis, had sent out a survey to the Seven Thunders mailing list with the heading, "A UNIQUE OPPORTUNITY. Do we have your support?" The survey read:

> As of now, Pat is willing to spend several months of the coming year in each of the three places (Tucson, Santa Fe, and Oregon) where he has been leading Contemplative Retreats and Zen Sesshins for several years. …
>
> [This] provides us with a unique opportunity to strengthen our local practice community and to open ourselves to the wider Contemplative and Zen communities While in residence here, Pat would be able to attend evening and weekend sittings, give weekly conferences, be available for interviews 2-3 times per week, and in addition to retreats, offer weekend (Saturday) all day sits or zazenkai. We might be able to entice him here for 6 to 8 weeks this fall, if we hurry. If this fall is too early to suit his plans then surely by next summer.
>
> To take advantage of this opportunity will require financial resources: Pat would need at least a simple apartment, and we will likely need to rent facilities for sitting and visitors. The board is beginning to consider details, but we can't make many plans without knowing the level of your support. I therefore ask for your input: Do you agree that it is important to take advantage of this opportunity? Do we have your moral support? How much financial support could you contribute, on a regular, irregular or one-time basis? Do you have other resources (time, materials, talent) that you could contribute? Do you know of other resources/facilities that might be available?[489]

They received pledges from 27 people totaling over $10,000, and the offer of a house sit for Pat during part of his stay, all of which meant they could easily cover expenses and a modest stipend.

The situation was more complex for the Santa Fe sangha. Sandy Anderson and Tracy McCallum came back to Mountain Cloud Zen Center from the summer resident training in Amarillo with a proposed schedule of events for 1999. The prospect of having Pat in residence for an extended period gave the membership some lively meetings. Deliberations and decisions were made while the overall teacher situation at Mountain Cloud remained uncertain. A committed group of members, many of whom had been around for years, and who reliably took care of the many jobs needed to keep the place in reasonable running order, including Sandy Anderson who had been temple keeper since before Pat appeared on the scene, considered Pat to be their only teacher and Mountain Cloud's main teacher. At the same time, the strong and largely more recent group who had bonded with Joan Sutherland during her two visits filling in for Pat continued to work with Joan and sought ways to increase their practice opportunities with her at Mountain Cloud.

The membership nonetheless came together to approve a schedule of extended stays by Pat, which had been "...by no means a foregone conclusion. Some spoke eloquently in favor of it; others raised difficult questions that brought the goals and purposes of the sangha into the discussion. Some changed their minds and others reaffirmed their position. In the end, mixed sentiment shifted around to total commitment."[490] This was in the September/October 1998 issue of *Cicada* newsletter, which also noted that they would engage a facilitator to guide the discussion at the next sangha meeting.[491] The November/December newsletter[492] reported that the sangha had agreed in principle that they wanted a resident roshi, that they would begin a search by asking Joan Sutherland, and that Joan had agreed to begin the process of becoming Mountain Cloud's resident teacher. At the same time, they firmed up plans to have Pat reside at MCZC for three months in 1999, divided between an extended visit in March and one in September/October. He would offer a sesshin and zazenkai at both visits and an additional sesshin in June. At the November meeting, those present voted unanimously to approve the proposed residency program for Pat and agreed to pay one quarter of his yearly stipend to cover the three months in Santa Fe. The sesshin schedule took shape as four per year to be led by Pat and an additional three to be led by Joan, with some wondering whether Mountain Cloud could support that many major events.

For Zen Desert Sangha (ZDS), the fact that Pat would be moving to Tucson and residing with his Redemptorist community meant that there wouldn't be the financial commitment faced by Seven Thunders and Mountain Cloud since they would not have to cover living expenses. It became simply a matter of figuring out a schedule of activities since, in addition to his availability to ZDS, Pat would be added to the roster of priests offering daily and weekend Masses at the Redemptorist Renewal Center and at parishes in town serviced by the Redemptorists. Still, those ZDS students of Pat that had for years made the long drive and incurred the expense of working with Pat in Amarillo were in the enviable position of knowing that he would be much more accessible to them.

Farewell Amarillo

Pat, Greg, Glenna and Bob left Bishop DeFalco Retreat Center (BDRC) at the beginning of August, 1998.

At the time of their leaving, Barbara Wooten wrote an article for the BDRC newsletter, *Journal,* eulogizing the Redemptorist years, closing with, "And finally I want to say that the Redemptorists were good friends and excellent co-workers. They were involved in the community and made this area their home for a generation. I will miss them and their special brand of kindness and their flawless integrity. They took very little and gave a lot. Fr. Greg gave me a job, Fr. Pat was my Zen teacher, Br. Mike helped my husband and son put on our roof and Fr. Elmer always made me feel like I was a child of God. Thank you."[493] Barbara's mention of Pat as her Zen teacher was the only reference to Zen in the BDRC newsletter, *Journal,* for all the years that Pat and Greg were there.

At the end of each issue, the *Journal* included a selection of letters from guests. The summer 1998 issue included this note to Glenna: "Thanks for always being there when you were really needed. Your kind and patient attention got me through many difficult times during my stay at the retreat center. Your humor and insight will be greatly missed; and your leaving will remain one of those vast and fathomless mysteries." The remaining retreats scheduled for 1998 at BDRC were canceled or moved elsewhere. Years later, Barbara Wooten, who stayed on as staff of the retreat center, still remembered the abrupt change in ambience when the Redemptorists left:

> A lot of those people never turned up again at the retreat center after the Redemptorists left. I was the only one that stayed on at BDRC, and it was hard. I liked the Redemptorists — they were a real free and easy kind of bunch. Pat, Mike, Elmer. They didn't have an agenda and ideology like the new people did. It was a lot more fun up there. There was Glenna, Gillian, Nicole. And Angie and Shirley. ...when I look back on things, the people who stand out as making everything much more fun were Shirley and Glenna and the cooks and Mary and Cindy [the housekeepers]. It was just a combination of personalities and Pat and Greg's total refusal to try to control everything. That made it just frustrating and a lot of trouble but also a lot of fun. Because there was always something exciting going on. The cooks would make so much food when Greg was there. And there was always food for all the staff and the office. Once the Redemptorists left, you had to tell the cook you were eating or there wouldn't be anything left over. With Greg, you could hang out in the kitchen; hang out and talk and eat. You couldn't do any hanging out and enjoying yourself after they left. People out there were like family. People in the contemplative group, Pat, Greg, people who worked there. While the Redemptorists were there we were like family. We

> were a scrappy family, but we were like family. The life went out of the place when the Redemptorists left.[494]

The newsletter for the contemplative/Zen program went with Pat to Tucson and was named *Pathless Path.* They kept Empty Sky as the name for the Zen program in Amarillo, which would be continued by the locals at a new venue, yet to be found. Many people sent farewells with mixed sadness and gratitude. Pat wrote in the last issue of the Empty Sky newsletter: " 'Do not dwell in a famous place. Do not lay any foundation when you build yourself a cell. Do not become the disciple of someone with a great name.' Abba Zeno's[495] advice is on a yellowing piece of paper on a bulletin board in my office. I do not remember how long it has been there. Somehow I knew that advice would come in handy one day and now is the day." Regarding Pathless Path, he wrote, "That is an appropriate name for what the future looks like right now."[496]

Angie Guerrero, never a participant in the program but indispensable to it in her capacity as administrator, wrote:

> As Secretary for the Bishop DeFalco Retreat Center for the last seven years, my heart is saddened by the closing of the Contemplative Program here at the center. … I want to express my love to all of you. I have become close to most of you through the years here. Several of you I know by name only because of the work I do on the accounting books. Fr. Pat and Glenna, who are the greatest part of this group, will most definitely leave a void here at the center and in my heart. Fr. Greg and Brother Mike will also leave a great void. I claim God's promises to all of you that he will give you the desires of your heart.[497]

Sandy Anderson wrote about what she would miss:

> The sound of the relentless wind rattling the tree leaves, and the symphony of train whistles and church bells. The air conditioner blowing from behind and the hot air blasting me frontally as I sit in the chair in front of the window of my room ... listening. The most unexciting empty looking flat field with its equally unexciting and pretentious bumps and its annoying holes which keep me alert, its trees ...its only hope. The summer light, different every morning, playing in the air's moisture and dust at the field. The dark field's hopping frogs at night.[498]

Paul Sanders was one of those who met Pat in Melbourne, then made the long journey to Amarillo when Pat stopped going to Australia. About Amarillo he wrote:

> Pat would often drop a comment, "It is no place to holiday, there's nothing there" and of course the notion of no-thing was exactly what was being sought. So, it was paradox and irony that brought us all to Amarillo. … If I might be so bold to speak for those others who have crossed distant shores, risking long nights without sleep to come to the Bishop DeFalco Retreat Center and lose more nights without sleep, we applaud you all. We will miss your friendliness, warmth of hospitality and kind care. Finally, has this place not been a macrocosm of possible inter-faith, ecumenical and inter-race relations, that a Protestant minister (not much protest left in me!) could link with a Catholic center, find a teacher and enjoy the riches of eastern and western spirituality? This is and has been a special setting for us all.[499]

Bob Walker gave a nod to the Amarilloans who also came:

> Those of us who are used to coming and going from this place, for whom packing and unpacking has always been a part of our time here, are especially grateful to the local town residents who come here regularly to sit. You have become adepts at flowing with the inconvenience of being regularly displaced. We know this is your place, your home, your ground of practice, and we know that it has often been disrupted by our arrival. Your manner of quietly accommodating us has not gone unnoticed. Thanks for joining with us in making these training sessions and retreats possible. It is reassuring to know that such a solid group of people will remain here [in Amarillo, not at BDRC] and continue to gather for regular group practice.[500]

Both Pat and Bob spoke of place. Pat wrote:

> In one way place is important. It is important because we make it so with our practice and dedication to the ground upon which we sit. The contemplation room/zendo here at the DeFalco Retreat Center may never be used explicitly as such again. Nevertheless, it has been charged with the practice of many people over the years. The vibrations will surely enhance whatever activity goes on.[501]

Bob took this further:

> The importance of place is a key aspect of our practice and it is no wonder that many of the old teachers came to be known simply by the names of the places where they taught. I have long sensed a sort of perfection here in Amarillo. Of course, the facility is comfortable, and the staff is always genuinely gracious. But the town itself is a constant reminder of the gift of being human. In practical matters it provides for our needs — its clerks, the cashiers, the gas station attendants, folks who help with groceries or photocopies seem to have an uncommon sense of lightness and their good humor flows

> smoothly and seamlessly with the rest of the activities here. The town itself, lacking in so many modern enticements, keeps its beauty well hidden, and has gently taught us the power of not preferring to be elsewhere.[502]

Cushions, sitting benches, gongs, drums, statues, boxes and boxes of books, files — all were packed into a U-haul truck that Nicole Chavannes and Phil Pegler, Australians who had made the trek to Amarillo as often as they could afford, drove to Arizona. After the vehicles pulled away, Glenna Pittock and Bob Walker lingered to tidy up loose ends, then headed out themselves, Glenna back home to Oregon and Bob to Georgia.

The first issue of *Pathless Path*, August 1998, included the announcement that effective immediately, Pat's new address was the Desert House of Prayer in Tucson.

8

Home Base Tucson

New quarters in the desert southwest

The Redemptorists had a large property with two retreat centers across the road from each other, situated along the northwest outskirts of Tucson, Arizona, in the foothills of the Tucson Mountains, bordering on the richly vegetated Sonoran Desert wilderness of Saguaro National Park. On the south side of Picture Rocks Road, the 120-acre Redemptorist Renewal Center offers views to the city below and to the red-brown rocks of the Tucson Mountains. The mountains rise on the other side of an arroyo that traverses one corner of the property, their lower slopes carrying forests of the tall, improbably branched saguaros and all manner of other cacti and arid-land vegetation. The place had initially been named Picture Rocks Retreat House for the petroglyphs on a massive rock formation facing the arroyo — a name that stuck for many who had come to know and love the place.

Desert House of Prayer, nestled into equally stunning landscape on the north side of the road, is an offshoot of the main retreat center but designed to provide a place for people to live in silence for extended periods. It had its own chapel, office and kitchen, and several hermitages spread out from each other, conducive to solitude in a changing community that came together for daily Mass and silent meals. With its emphasis on silence and contemplation, Desert House seemed like the more appropriate location for Pat, and his appointment was officially moved from Bishop DeFalco Retreat Center to Desert House of Prayer on August 1, 1998. His new quarters included a small room, no office of his own, no private phone, no internet, and no kitchen service, the residents sharing kitchen responsibilities. His room had no air conditioner, only evaporative cooling, and in the humid days of the monsoon season which was upon them when he arrived, it was marginally comfortable at best. He lasted there one month before persuading his Superior at the time — no longer Greg Mayers as soon as they left Amarillo — that the main retreat center would be more appropriate for his needs.

He moved into the rectory at the Renewal Center, a building whose independent apartments opened to a walled oasis courtyard with a fountain, lounge chairs and fruit-bearing trees. He had a spacious bedroom/sitting room with a large walk-in closet and private bath. The rectory included a comfortable common room with a TV and sound system, a well-equipped kitchen and a dining room with meals usually provided by the retreat center kitchen staff. There was also a wet bar, which to the end of his life, Pat found difficult to walk past without pouring himself a drink. His personal living quarters were a stone's throw from the main administration building that opened to the same courtyard from a side door. It included individual offices for all the priests opening off a reception area for retreat center guests. Pat's office, besides having its own bathroom, had two entrances — one to the retreat center front desk and reception area, and one directly to the outdoors, very convenient for stepping outside for a smoke.

The administration building and the large chapel nearby were built of rough-hewn stone. Further out were freestanding buildings with meeting rooms of various sizes for the variety of retreats that the center hosted, as well as three long buildings with guest accommodations — private rooms with bath — each opening directly to the outside. The center's buildings occupied only a fraction of the property, the rest covered with native vegetation through which footpaths meandered for intrepid wanderers willing to keep an eye out for rattlesnakes and other desert wildlife.

The timing of his arrival in Tucson coincided with Zen Desert Sangha purchasing and moving into their own space at last. They had left Indiana Nelson's in April 1997. A year later, with a dedicated sangha and financial contributions that included some substantial chunks from core members and/or well-heeled donors, they managed to put a down payment on a house on Martin Avenue at the edge of a residential neighborhood a few miles north of the University of Arizona. The one-story, double-brick construction house had been converted to a beauty parlor sometime in its history with addition of a large, adobe brick great room perfect for a *dojo*. There were two and a half bathrooms, the half bath attached to a bedroom that could work for teacher's quarters, a large living room with a fireplace, and miscellaneous small rooms that could be adapted for dokusan, library, and storage. The front door opened to a somewhat ragged parking lot with partial shade from a mature mesquite tree and a huge Aleppo pine. The back had a shaded patio, several large citrus trees, a large mesquite, a few small outbuildings and a good amount of open ground for an outdoor *kinhin* path.

The new building was about a half-hour drive into town from the Redemptorist Renewal Center. When Pat was in residence at the Renewal Center, he would come to ZDS three times a week — Monday and Wednesday evenings and

Saturday mornings — to sit with the group and offer dokusan. His first major event in Tucson was a sesshin at ZDS's newly acquired home. Both the Pat Hawk-leaning and John Tarrant-leaning students participated, and all went well. Richard Laue reported for the Zen Desert Sangha newsletter:

> Twenty-four people, including five of Pat Hawk's old students from out of town — a full house! The energy was wonderful, the sitting deep and solid. Bob Wallin did a great job as *tenzo* (head cook) and kept everybody fed with imaginative and appealing meals, which we ate "*oryoki*" style in the zendo. The officers — several of them new to their jobs — kept everything on track and navigated through the inevitable confusions of a first-time sesshin with grace and dexterity.
>
> After the sesshin, everybody remarked about how well the house had worked with us and for us. We all agreed that the house itself seemed to welcome us, and to be glad that it was being used, appreciated, and cared for by loving people. It truly felt like "home!"
>
> Speaking personally, this sesshin reminded me again of everything I love about this sangha. The cooperation; the willingness to pitch in and help; the depth and sincerity of the practice; most of all, the very REAL sense of mutual support and encouragement....[503]

Richard recalled later:

> I spoke to Pat Hawk Roshi a few days after the sesshin and mentioned that while he seemed tired — don't forget, he had just moved from Amarillo! — he also seemed in very good spirits. I asked him how the sesshin had been for him. He told me that it was one of the most satisfying and rewarding retreats he's done in years, and he was deeply moved by the wonderful spirit that flowed through this sesshin from its opening moment.[504]

Both Pat Hawk students and those who shifted to John Tarrant had contributed to finding and purchasing the Martin Avenue property. There was ambiguity and argument about who should be the guiding teacher. Discussions finally came to a vote, and in a meeting of the full sangha held not long after that first sesshin, the group decided in favor of Pat, easily obtaining the minimum 75% supermajority required by the bylaws to pass the motion. At the time, Pat was in Germany for a visit to Willigis Jäger in Würzburg, followed by the Diamond Sangha Teachers' Circle meeting in Damme. On his return to Tucson in mid-September, Pat was presented with a formal invitation from ZDS, which he accepted.[505]

There then arose the question of whether John Tarrant would be invited to teach at ZDS at all. The situation was complicated by allegations of ethical violations that had surfaced from various quarters over several years in regard to John.

Friction developed, exacerbated by the joint stake in the property of Tarrant and Hawk students. Relationships were sufficiently strained within the sangha that it was difficult to fill ZDS Board positions.

Diamond Sangha Teachers' Circle ethics

The ethical questions raised around John Tarrant were a focus of the Diamond Sangha Teachers' Circle meeting in Damme, Germany, in September 1998, which Pat attended. The teachers were concerned about allegations that John had become involved sexually with Joan Sutherland and possibly others of his students, and that he was encouraging some students to enter psychotherapy with him. The latter, if true, was deemed a conflict of interest. The concern regarding a teacher engaging sexually with a student was not without ambiguity, since more of the Diamond Sangha teachers than not were acting as teachers for their spouses or partners. Perhaps in part for this reason, and perhaps also out of reluctance to dress down a colleague, the situation with John was left to ride until the news of it spread beyond the Diamond Sangha to the larger international Zen community, and there came to be increasing pressure from the outside to act.

As Pat was adjusting to his new home base and heavy teaching schedule, the Diamond Sangha Teachers' Circle became preoccupied with the allegations against John Tarrant, with the Damme meeting only the first of several dominated by discussion of how to respond. They decided to address the matter initially by sending a joint letter to John, and to work on a more comprehensive and longer-term solution by developing an ethics code and grievance procedures. The letter to John, to which Pat contributed, explained their intentions and requested a meeting. John, Joan and three others from the California Diamond Sangha sent a polite reply declining the invitation and expressing doubts about the utility of a grievance procedure given a process that "has thus far served to initiate and perpetuate rather than to resolve a long series of internal conflicts," and the difficulty of even finding a process for making decisions, let alone handling matters as delicate as grievances. The letter ignored the suggestion of impropriety and offered an alternative invitation: "We realize that there is much we don't know about what many of you are doing in your own work, and we are interested in sharing information about our various projects, obsessions, dreams, failures, and successes. We warmly welcome this kind of dialogue."[506] There was tremendous dynamism and activity in John's growing enterprise, and they didn't have time for or interest in the expressed Diamond Sangha concerns.

The Diamond Sangha teachers began work on a draft ethics code based on the San Francisco Zen Center Ethics and Grievance guidelines, the former based on the sixteen Buddhist precepts. Leonard Marcel, being a psychiatrist familiar with the American Medical Association's *Principles of Medical Ethics,* took the lead in revising the SFZC documents and sent his revisions to the group. Others weighed in, but Pat was silent. He had participated in the initial decisions at Damme but then got cold feet.

The whole project went against the grain for Pat. Although there was still the vague sense of betrayal from John and Joan having recruited his students without due process and their apparent undermining of his position as a teacher, there was also a deep humility about his own faults that countered any interest he might have in accusing anyone. Plus, whether from his seminary training or by nature, he held a sense of sin as inseparable from redemption. "Everyone is completely all right down to the very bottom," he would say. He had no inclination toward self-righteousness. If anything, he tended to enjoy rather than shun the company of tax collectors and prostitutes or their modern-day equivalents. He once repeated a quote attributed to Mark Twain regarding the desirability of "heaven for the climate and hell for the company." At the same time he, like the others, acknowledged a responsibility to do something in this situation for the sake of vulnerable students.

Pat dropped out of the ethics conversation for months despite emails from Leonard Marcel and from Nelson Foster inviting his input. Others, mainly Leonard, Nelson, Robert Aitken and Joe Bobrow honed the document. They agreed that they could leave out things already covered by the law related to weapons and to sex with minors. They ran into difficulty drawing the line between John's involvement with his student, which they disapproved of, and their own involvement with spouses and partners. Joe Bobrow proposed a very clear boundary. In a letter to the teachers, he wrote:

> I do not think any Diamond Sangha teacher, or for that matter, any Zen teacher, should teach Zen to his or her lover, partner, or spouse. If a teaching "couple" wants to become an amorous couple, that is their business, but they should cease the teacher-student relationship, period. If a member of a loving couple [the other member of which happens, incidentally, to be a Zen teacher], wants to study Zen, s/he should find a teacher elsewhere. …
>
> I am well aware that this has become almost THE modus operandi of DS teachers. … I submit that what we have here is a major group blind spot, and a dangerous one at that, despite the fact that, somehow, certain couples seem to pull it off.[507]

He got no traction. Nelson protested — most of the Diamond Sangha teachers would be under sanction from that strict a rule, including himself, and he couldn't subscribe.[508] The difficulty of preserving permission for one's own situation while condemning John's could look like hairsplitting to an uninvolved observer, but they continued, generating a line to walk between the permissible and the proscribed.

Pat was busy. Moving between centers, from Tucson to Santa Fe to Oregon and back, offering sesshin and contemplative retreats, dokusan via phone, email, Skype and in person. The number of days actually in retreat added up to over 100,[509] and among the various centers he was caring for, about that many students. Nelson was alarmed at the number of students and even suggested that the Diamond Sangha teachers consider enshrining in the new ethics guidelines that it be considered a violation if a teacher had more students than they could look after.

After a long silence from Pat as the ethics situation was discussed via email, he resurfaced for the next Diamond Sangha Teachers' Circle meeting in December 1999 in Honolulu. Bob Walker, having been made an apprentice teacher that May[510] accepted an invitation to the meeting, his first. He was dismayed at the zeal with which some sought to apply grievance procedures to the Tarrant situation. He watched as an open letter was edited and approved by the group.

Although officially retired at the end of 1996, Aitken continued to attend Diamond Sangha Teachers' Circle meetings and continued to have a strong voice in steering individuals within the Circle, albeit more often from behind. There was pressure to sign the letter from the group as a whole and from Aitken in particular directed at any holdouts. Augusto thought better of signing, then caved to Aitken's pressure, later regretting his participation and sending a letter of apology to John. Bob Walker did not sign, nor did Rolf Drosten.

Dated December 16, 1999, and signed by eleven of the Diamond Sangha teachers including Pat, the letter was circulated to the relevant sanghas with the heading "Diamond Sangha Teachers' Circle Open Letter to John Tarrant." It was published in the *Sydney Zen Centre Newsletter* along with the Ethics Code. It stated that there were serious and plausible allegations against John, that numbers of his colleagues had reached out to discuss these with him, and that respected leaders from the larger North American Zen community were urging action. The text finished with:

> We submit this letter to you not as judges or superiors but as your peers, who feel the great stress you must be under and are concerned for your well-being now and in the long term. At the same time, we cannot in good conscience go on without voicing our deep concern for the anguish others have suffered and continue to suffer to this day. We urge you to take clearly visible steps to deal with the backlog of grief former students and also colleagues feel, so that all involved can be released from pain.[511]

The letter reflected the long and careful deliberations of the teachers, nonetheless carrying an element of stone-throwing that made Pat uncomfortable. Regardless, he returned to Tucson and summarized the proceedings at a well-attended meeting of Zen Desert Sangha called for the purpose. Years later, reflecting back on the Diamond Sangha Teachers Circle process and letter, Pat said, "That was a bad business," then shaking his head, "I *like* John." The unsurprising outcome of the whole process — apparent before the formal letter was sent — was a splitting off of Tarrant's California Diamond Sangha as an independent entity.

Aitken, with his characteristic building and maintaining of bridges, wrote to the California Diamond Sangha — soon to be re-named Pacific Zen Institute — comparing their split from the Diamond Sangha to the latter's split from the Sanbo Kyodan, asserting that in both cases, the separation was amicable. He added, "I want to maintain the friendly ties with old-time CDS students and teachers which I enjoyed in the past, and to keep communication in general completely open. I cannot deny the deep sadness and regret that I continue to feel about the events and differences that occasioned the separation, but I'm sure it is a necessary step. I send my warmest wishes to you all for fulfillment on your path."

Circuit riding

As the ethics discussions took place across several Diamond Sangha teachers' meetings, Pat was focused on adjusting to a changed schedule of retreat offerings following his departure from Amarillo. After the Damme meeting in September 1998, he returned to Tucson for ten days — enough time to do laundry and get over jet lag — then drove to Santa Fe for a public talk and five-day sesshin at Mountain Cloud. In October, he flew to Portland to offer a seven-day Contemplative Intensive Retreat for the Seven Thunders group at St. Benedict's Lodge in McKenzie Bridge, Oregon. Bob Walker came too, and helped Pat with interviews for the first time.

Pat stayed on a little extra time in Oregon and joined Seven Thunders' first-Saturday-of-the-month sit in Bethany House at Our Lady of Guadalupe Trappist Abbey. They had not had anyone regular to say Mass for them at those sits since Bernard McVeigh's last illness, and were grateful to have Pat for both interviews and Masses. Always, when Pat said Mass, the wine used for communion was de-alcoholized. He had asked Willigis about this once — whether he thought the small amount of wine used for communion would be okay. Willigis was firm. "No Pat, not even that." He got it, and for all that onlookers could tell, stuck to it.

Back in Tucson, Pat resumed a weekly schedule, plus led a sesshin at Zen Desert Sangha in November and another — the eight-day Rohatsu sesshin — in

December 1998, also at ZDS. He stayed in town for Christmas then went back to Amarillo for the end-of-December contemplative retreat held at Bishop De-Falco Retreat Center, the relationship with Bishop Yanta notwithstanding.

It had become the custom for Pat to take the month of January off and he did that in 1999, spending most of the time in Kaimu, Hawaii, with Robert Aitken, who had built a retirement home there on top of the lava and across the road from his son Tom.

The experiment with extended residency began in the Pacific Northwest in late January with a slightly longer than one-month stay in Oregon. It included dokusan four evenings a week — two in Portland and two in Corvallis at the Friends Meeting House, two daylong sittings at the Trappist Abbey's Bethany House and one in Corvallis, and a five-day Contemplative Intensive Retreat at McKenzie Bridge. Reporting on Pat's extended stay for the *Seven Thunders Newsletter,* Jane Huyer commented, "I continue to be impressed by the many new faces that come into our midst, somehow already familiar with our procedures, somehow from the larger sangha."[512]

In addition to the formal practice opportunities, which were numerous, outside of retreat times Pat offered office hours for people wanting to meet with him informally, and he attended a few social evenings. These personal encounters outside dokusan that Pat's extended residency made possible gave people who had previously known him only within formal practice settings a glimpse of the man behind the curtain, so to speak.

The contemplative intensive retreat toward the end of the month, at St. Benedict Lodge, McKenzie Bridge, Oregon, was filled to capacity. Situated on the scenic McKenzie River and surrounded by wooded hills, for Pat, the lodge was a welcome change from the dry, cactus-rich Sonoran Desert that was his new home. The lodge's deck overlooked river rapids, the murmur of flowing water ever-present in the sitting room.[513] During the retreat, the place was blessed with a thick blanket of snow, up to foot-high cones topping boulders in the river rapids just beyond the lodge deck.[514] The quiet snowfall amidst the river sounds was still on Pat's mind when he went for his extended stay at Mountain Cloud the next month. It appeared in his first teisho there, magically coinciding with the weather in Santa Fe.

Ramon Melcon wrote in the Mountain Cloud newsletter:

> Late winter retreat at Mountain Cloud took off with a powerful blizzard. Raising our eyes a little higher than permitted by strict sesshin observations, we all gazed in disbelief as the thick, fluffy snowflakes blanketed the whole body of the earth. Time froze. Blinds froze. In the ephemeral beauty of the falling snow, we could experience the totality of the present moment. There

> was absolutely nothing else. Pat Hawk's teisho that afternoon had dealt with no other koan but... "Layman P'ang's beautiful snowflakes." Coincidental? Deliberate? We couldn't say. But I do remember him, our peerless, snow intoxicated lecturer, standing still in the middle of the dining floor, while we were circumambulating around him during long *kinhin*, completely absorbed in the view beyond the windows, his wide open eyes full of white clouds and trees and dancing snowflakes. I had never seen him that happy. He had become a perfect snowman.[515]

Pat's accommodation at Mountain Cloud Zen Center was more primitive than in Oregon. Although the Mountain Cloud sangha had made plans to sell five acres of their land to finance the building of teacher's quarters, the construction was not yet underway. They had spiffed up the teacher's room for him and moved the dokusan room across the hall — formerly it had been in his sleeping quarters — but he still shared the common men's bathroom and had to use the single shower that served for everyone. He would come shuffling out very early in the morning before the wake-up bell at 4:00 AM, half asleep and disheveled, looking like a homeless waif, humbly stifling his deeply felt inclination toward personal privacy.

During Pat's residency at Mountain Cloud, the temple keeper, Sandy Anderson, was alone on the property with him except when there was a scheduled event. She cooked one meal a day for him, and other than that, hardly saw him. He was elusive, moving quietly in the building, stepping out for a cigarette, always keeping to himself. Some days she insisted that he help with the dishes, which he would do obediently. Someone wandering into the kitchen from the zendo after a sit would see him there at the sink and exclaim, "Pat! Doing dishes! I can do that for you." He would drop the scrubber without a word and head out for a smoke. Once a week, Sandy persuaded him it was his turn to provide a meal, and he would take her out to dinner. They'd go in her truck, mostly quiet on the way in, still quiet at dinner, quiet again on the way back. Waitresses fussed over him — he had a little-boy quality that would surface with female strangers.[516]

The value of the extended residency to Pat's students at Mountain Cloud was profound. They were accustomed to keeping a regular weekly sitting schedule without a teacher. With Pat in residence, the regular evening sitting was transformed.

> Sitting quietly in the *dojo* on a weekday evening, just a few of us, the teacher on his cushion before the altar. He stirs softly and pauses before leaving, saying, "If any of you would like to have dokusan, I'll be in the dokusan room." One by one, the three people slip out for this rare, unscheduled op-

> portunity for an interview with Pat Hawk. It was a moment of intimacy between teacher and students that could only have happened during the settled long-term presence of the teacher. And it happened more than once during Pat Hawk's residencies...[517]

Having Pat living at Mountain Cloud offered a whole new level of relationship. Now they could come across him by himself in the dining room and sit with him for a quiet cup of coffee, ask a question, or watch birds flitting in trees just outside the window or sipping from the fountain. While Pat was in residence, some of his students from Tucson and Amarillo extended their stays beyond sesshin, solidifying bonds among the greater sangha in addition to those between teacher and student.

Between the spring and fall residencies at Mountain Cloud the March program was evaluated. Tracy McCallum reported in *Cicada*: "Specific program elements were added for the fall residency, and a number of previously reticent members were emboldened to a deeper involvement. Not long after Pat arrived in September, the sangha met with him twice and some touchy subjects were brought forth. His responses to our questions and the discussions we had with him really cleared the air and made everyone feel more comfortable."[518]

Pat was uninvested in any conflict with Joan Sutherland, uninterested in staking territory, and acquiescent to peaceful co-existence. A new ease developed, evident in lighthearted talk at meals and better attended weekday sits. "Towards the end of Pat's stay, there was an almost festive atmosphere. Some special things had happened. Teacher and Sangha had come together and come through it together. They had gotten to know each other in new and different ways. They sat together, ate together, and communed with one another. And they eagerly agreed to do it again next year."[519]

The waxing paschal moon dominated the night sky in the latter part of Pat's stay, and he made it back to Tucson in time for the Triduum of an April 4th Easter. Tucson rarely gets any snow in any year, but that year saw huge wet flakes falling on and off for a couple of hours Easter morning. Pat stood out in the rectory courtyard, watching the flakes melt as they touched the fountain, looking beyond the garden wall to the mountains as they received a light dusting of white. A snowman indeed. Such offerings from nature touched him at least as deeply as any human offering.

He led another sesshin in April at Zen Desert Sangha, then flew back to Oregon for a sesshin in May at McKenzie Bridge, the first Zen offering to the Pacific Northwest group. Having formed from the original group that gathered for the Zen retreat for Christians led by Robert Aitken back in 1978, when the "Zennies" had split off as the Three Treasures Sangha from the original "Zen for

Christians" group, the more Christian-format branch had become Seven Thunders. Many in the latter group were following Pat wherever they could regardless of retreat flavor. When the group decided to widen their offerings to include Zen, some who were still exclusively following a Christian contemplative path felt uneasiness. For these latter folk, there was anxiety about introduction of the alien form and uncertain interest in participating. Glenna Pittock addressed this with information and lighthearted reassurances in the newsletter.

> There is always an adequate introduction and explanation the first night, with clarifications and demonstrations and time for questions and answers. No need to worry about it, everyone seems to catch on easily by the second day and no one expects anyone to come to her first sesshin knowing what to do. Old timers occasionally forget what to do next, mess up; this can be a wonderful beginner's experience for them. The form of our ritual comes from the Hawaiian Diamond Sangha tradition. It developed over a period of years at the Honolulu Diamond Sangha and has coalesced into the style we use at Pat's sesshin. During last summer's training period in Amarillo, representatives from each of Pat's Sanghas (Seven Thunders, Mountain Cloud Zen Center, & Zen Desert Sangha) met, reviewed, practiced, and agreed upon a common ritual, sesshin cautions, and officer guidelines to use at all the locations.
>
> So, Zen Sesshin is sort of a jazzed up version of what you may be used to on our Contemplative Retreats. Noisier: gongs, bongs, whacks, claps, tanto's encouraging words, the up and down of bowing, longer periods of sitting, never any time to get away from the practice, intense. Which do I like best? Other than the occasional thought when my knees are really hurting in sesshin wishing it were a contemplative retreat instead, I'd say I really appreciate the differences and like them both for just what they are. I'm grateful that Seven Thunders is now offering these two approaches to religious practice.[520]

After the sesshin, Pat flew from Oregon back to Tucson, dusted himself off, then drove to Amarillo to offer a contemplative intensive retreat at his old home base, where they still kept two of Pat's retreats a year on the schedule, one in the late spring/early summer and one during the week after Christmas. There were no Zen sesshins of course — Zen events at Bishop DeFalco Retreat Center were discontinued when Bishop Yanta took over.

Pathless Path

Pat went from Amarillo to Santa Fe for a residency there, concluding with a sesshin that he left before the final lunch so that he could get back to Tucson in time to offer a contemplative intensive retreat at the Redemptorist Renewal Center —

the first at his new home. The retreat was held in the St. Alphonsus building, a moderate-sized, one-story structure at the southeast corner of the Renewal Center property. The building was originally constructed to house the nuns who had lived on site to care for the Redemptorist fathers in earlier days. It had about seven bedrooms, each with private bath. At one end of the single, long hallway was a small chapel with a large picture window looking out to the west over a vista of saguaro and other green, cactus-studded desert covering the slopes of the Tucson Mountains. At the other end was a kitchen/dining room. Both the kitchen and the chapel opened to a neglected walled courtyard that stretched most of the length of the building.

None of it was set up appropriately, and when they first started sitting, it was in what was essentially an oversized utility closet. Nonetheless, the retreat was attended by a strong (and crowded) group, including several from out of town. Sandy Anderson came early from Santa Fe and helped get things organized. Meals prepared by the retreat center staff were served cafeteria-style to all at the center in the main dining room a short walk from St. Al's. Pat's group sat in a small side room so they could eat in silence. Work practice — considered an important aspect of any retreat and necessitating finding jobs for everyone — included helping the retreat center staff with the industrial-sized dishwashing operation, keeping the contemplation room tidy and dusted, watering the few living trees in the forgotten courtyard and removing accumulated debris as a first step toward building a Zen garden. Producing meals that were vegetarian and working alongside the dark-clothed, silent retreatants was a new experience for the retreat center staff, all of whom were gracious. During the retreat, a long dry spell broke dramatically and auspiciously with two soaking rains, a visceral relief in the breathtaking heat of Tucson in early summer.[521]

Following this retreat, Pat went back up to the northwest for a period of residency, then back again to Tucson to lead Sesshin for Zen Desert Sangha, then to Santa Fe, again for an extended residency, then back to Tucson, then to Oregon. Needless to say, the constant travel and long periods of sleeping in different beds, adjusting to different routines were exhausting.

In November 1999, Father Tom Santa was appointed Director at the Renewal Center and superior of the Redemptorist community there. Santa, seeing that Pat was offering retreats scattered across the western US and spending at least as much time away from Tucson as on his new home turf, decided they should open a program at the Renewal Center, and had the St. Alphonsus building remodeled to be better suited for the purpose. Construction included sacrificing one of the sleeping rooms to enlarge the chapel into a zendo/contemplation room that could accommodate about 30 sitters comfortably, and moving the wall between two other sleeping rooms to make a largish library and a smaller dokusan/interview room. Pat called the new program the Pathless Path. The name, already in use for the newsletter that followed him from Amarillo, was derived from the article Pat wrote for the *Catholic Worker* back in 1990. It was a name that encompassed the Christian and Zen approaches under one umbrella.

Pat's extended stays in the Northwest and in Santa Fe continued for a time — one more each in 1999 and two each in 2000, with additional visits to both locations for shorter stays including sesshin and contemplative intensive retreats (the latter only in the Northwest), and a full schedule of events in Tucson when he was in town. As the Pathless Path program took root and flourished at the Renewal Center, he discontinued the long residencies elsewhere. He thanked the Oregon and Santa Fe sanghas heartily for keeping him employed during a period of transition and let it be known that he would no longer be doing extended stays away from his home base. However, he continued to travel to Santa Fe and Oregon to offer retreats several times a year.

Susan Weimer

Susan Weimer became a student of Pat's during the last year at Bishop DeFalco Retreat Center and followed him to Tucson when he moved. Her parents lived in Tucson, and when her father died, leaving her mother on her own with significant rheumatoid arthritis, Susan decided to move there to help her mother and continue work with Pat. She played an important role in getting the program established at the Redemptorist Renewal Center.

She'd been in Amarillo for about a year prior, having accepted a faculty position at West Texas A&M University. Her spiritual home before coming to Amarillo had been the Catholic Workers on the East Coast. Under five feet tall and with legs bowed and of uneven lengths from a congenital condition, the initial distraction of her physical stature was quickly redirected by a personality articulate, witty and wise. She was raised in a loving family, but her atypical phenotype attracted ridicule and bullying in grade school. That background contributed to a vague mistrust of people and a strong spiritual bent. The Church — she was raised Episcopal — provided a sanctuary of sorts. She became involved with the Catholic Workers in New York, and for a time shared a bedroom with Dorothy Day. It was from her that Susan first heard of Robert Aitken, Dorothy having taken part in Bangor Summer on the West Coast in 1977. Susan recalled, "Having Mass at these broken-down tables was always wonderful; with people in their cups, people with dementia. Down the basement, Lyle Young, who was this wonderful priest from Australia, would hear confessions down with the potatoes and onions and carrots. It was just a wonderful, funky atmosphere. It immediately struck a chord."[522]

The Little Brothers of the Gospel were good friends with the Catholic Workers in New York City, and a few of them became good friends of Susan. They had a chapel with bare walls and cushions to sit on, much like a zendo, and she began silent sitting there alone, sometimes for hours. She worked variously as a musician, then teaching German and French, eventually doing a master's degree, then a Ph.D. in social work. Teaching positions were few and far between, and when one came up at West Texas A&M in Amarillo, she applied, got the job, and moved west in 1997.

Susan sought community at St. Andrew's Episcopal Church, where one of the priests told her, "You should go out to Bishop DeFalco Retreat Center. There's a guy there who's a contemplative master and a Zen master." She called and arranged for a private retreat. "The way they used to do it, the question was, 'Why are you here?' And I said, 'I'm here because this is here.' I'd already seen the room — the zendo — and it was like Brothers of the Gospel. Forget all the words, it's the same damn thing. Pat said, 'Finally, a mature student.' " When she sat her first contemplative retreat, she realized this was home. It was like the Little Brothers, only now with a structure and a community. Susan recalled:

> There was Pat and his overall demeanor. There was Pat's presentation for the evening words the first night, "Be wide, be open," that kind of thing. And he would say little droll things that would make everyone laugh. The first teishos were a little Greek-like until I started on koans. This thing started happening, this great effusion of light. And I told him, you have this great light. And he said, "No, it's you not me." … At one point, chatting with Carolyn Blasdel up in Meeting Room 4, Carolyn said to me, "You know Pat has cancer. You know he's an alcoholic." It was like it should have pushed me away. And I thought, well, that's pretty much who I would end up with.[523]

Upon moving to Tucson, she was given a room at the Renewal Center as a volunteer.

> I'd go back and forth between Mom's house and Picture Rocks. The first renovation happened in 2000, but we did have a contemplative retreat in 1999. I would go over for dokusan every day, pretty much, to see Pat. And one day — this was in January of 1999 — he handed me something and I said, "What's this?" And he said, "That's a retreat schedule." And I said, "Should I do this [take care of retreat administration]?" And he said, "Well, somebody has to." So that was the beginning. Then the summer of 2000, I became an employee up there.[524]

Susan was hired by then-director Tom Santa, with a job description that included organizing and administering contemplative intensive retreats, Zen sesshins, resident practice periods, individual retreats/residencies, public sittings and any other Pathless Path events. It meant correspondence, phone and e-mail contact, bookkeeping and deposits, scheduling dates for Pat at Picture Rocks as well as coordinating dates for him elsewhere, producing a quarterly newsletter, being aware of maintenance needs in St. Al's, and working with the Renewal Center administrator and other staff. For this, she received room and board, a small stipend and health insurance.

Her living quarters were in the St. Alphonsus building where the Pathless Path physical space was being established and included a small bedroom, a living room/office, private bath, one entrance directly to the outside and another into the contemplation room/zendo. She kept it in a comfortable shambles, with papers and other odds and ends scattered on bookcases and on the floor. She remembered, "It was pretty good in the beginning although pretty isolated." The isolation motivated her to encourage social events such as going out for dinner after retreats. It meant a small group often got together the evening a retreat ended, which was a wonderful way to wind down and "re-enter." The social angle that Susan fostered contributed to some deep bonds forming among students from in and out of town who came regularly for Pathless Path events. With her interest in people and tendency toward light gossip, she was a good foil to Pat and helped keep people in touch across his various programs.

Rohatsu at Nestucca

In December 2001, the St. Alphonsus renovation wasn't yet ready for a large group, and the Rohatsu sesshin — always the most well-attended retreat of the year — was held at the Jesuit-owned Nestucca Sanctuary[525] on the northern coast of Oregon. The retreat center there included a large woodstove-heated yurt that served as zendo, with kitchen and accommodations in separate buildings on the property. Sesshin was hosted by Seven Thunders and co-led by Pat Hawk and Leonard Marcel with Bob Walker as tanto. Kristen Larson provided a description and photos for a scrapbook his students produced in celebration of Pat's 65th birthday:

> The first night we all gathered for the cautions and guidelines in the yurt. It was raining and beginning to get cold. The fire was burning, but not heating very noticeably and a very cold wind began to rise during the first sit. The tent-like roof was billowing by the time Pat made his entrance from the very

> small covered entryway to say his welcome words. He quickly left. … As the wind grew and the rain increased, [Bob Walker] had to move to the center of the room in order to be heard. Finally, when the heavy hail began to pound down on the canvas roof, the noise was cacophonous, Bob just stopped trying to talk. When it was time for us to return to our rooms, it was raining lightly again, but the pea-sized hail remained on the ground rolling around underfoot as we tried to negotiate the pitch black, muddy walkways down the hill and over large tree roots.
>
> We were all trying to make the best of it, remembering that Rohatsu is supposed to be the "toughest" of all sesshins. The cold kept increasing, and the yurt gave little barrier to the wind that came up through the floor. But by morning (4:30 AM) the rain had stopped. Good thing, the dokusan line was set up on the approach path in plastic chairs with cups taped to them to hold flashlights because the dokusan rooms were two paths and many raised tree roots away. People worked hard to build a bigger fire, bring in as many small space heaters as the electrical system could support and close up the sides of the yurt as tightly as they could.
>
> One night, in a screaming, pouring gale, a helicopter was clearly flying as low as possible along the coast and investigating the complex estuary. Bill Larson broke silence to remind us all that they were the Coast Guard called out to search for lost mariners. Pat and Leonard were gallantly carrying on their assigned tasks, however Leonard was wearing a radiant glow with broad smiles from under many layers of clothing under his robes, while Pat was seeming to glare out from under his layers of coverings, including a wool blanket and a multicolored stocking cap. Pat was not holding back his opinion of this cold, muddy, frozen, wind howling place with only a tent to sit in! However, the teishos on both Roshis' parts were as crisp and clear as the weather was cold and cutting. Pat especially would incorporate the moment's natural happenings into whatever he was saying, as though it was just part of the program.
>
> The nights got colder each day of the sesshin. Once Bill Jackson cried out in the middle of zazen, "I'm fucking cold!" For once, one of his outbursts did not seem at all out of place.[526]

As tanto, it was Bob Walker's job to rein in anything untoward happening in the zendo, but he — uncharacteristically for any tanto and especially for Bob — had stepped out to make a cup of tea and warm up. Kristen's account continued:

> On the third or fourth day, while there was no rain falling, the chimney flue completely stopped up during zazen. The chemically tinted smoke from the fire began to fill the yurt and gradually each one of us was compelled to get up and leave. The one priest and caretaker of the place had to get up on the framework at the chimney in order to clear it. (Insurance liability prevented his allowing any of the agile, strong, young men from doing it, though they

> did volunteer.) Jane Huyer who was *karmadana* (work coordinator) rousted people to help open up the yurt to air it out and then have it all closed down again with the fire and heaters going in time for the next block of zazen.
>
> The dokusan line, completely outside on a path, became more unmanageable with each new type of storm, and eventually, Glenna Pittock, jisha, cleared just enough space for the two lines to sit shoulder to shoulder inside the small, fiberglass covered entryway. Umbrellas and raincoats and jackets filled the area, and juggling them and flashlights (for 5 AM and 7 PM dokusan) made for quite a show for us all to pretend we weren't watching. Pat worked hard at training each of us to forgo the ceremony of bowing in his dokusan room's open doorway. He eventually moved himself into a position where he could reach the edge of the sliding door when it was open, so as to close it himself as quickly as possible. He sat right beside the one small heater. He told many of us that he never wanted to come back to this ____ place again. And indeed, he has not. While his show of misery in the cold was openly presented the whole time, the consensus was evident that Pat had never been sharper.[527]

Jim Maher did Jukai at the end, the ritual serving as closing ceremony for the whole retreat as was the custom when there was a Jukai. At the moment in the ceremony where Pat — the presiding teacher — presented the *kechimyaku* document showing the unbroken succession of names, the "bloodline" transmission, there was the customary statement, "I am the '*n*' in line from Shakyamuni Buddha and you are the '*n+1*' ", Pat suddenly couldn't remember the number. He asked Leonard, "What number am I in the transmission?" A photo snapped at that instant shows them leaning into each other, both grinning, the relief and mirth in the yurt at the end of that memorable sesshin evident in their expressions.

Bob Walker, Leonard Marcel

As Pat established a new home base in Tucson, Bob Walker set aside his reluctance to take on a wider role and began giving talks, offering interviews and helping with retreats. It was gratifying to Pat having this most promising student take on the new role, and a great relief. Pat's schedule was heavy as ever, and Bob's help was needed and appreciated. But there gradually arose a disconnect between the two of them. Bob very much wanted Pat's guidance as he navigated this uncharted territory. Pat — weary of guiding, and wanting only to hand off some of the load — somehow expected that Bob would assume the teaching mantle fully-fledged. As Bob reached out to him for help, Pat pulled back coldly. After the many years of quiet rapport and easy understanding, after the careful, still tentative decision to teach, it was discouraging to Bob.

Nonetheless, he held steady. Whatever Bob's own uncertainty, students found him helpful, gravitating to him in increasing numbers. At the May 1999 sesshin at McKenzie Bridge in Oregon, Pat had held a formal ceremony appointing Bob as an apprentice teacher in the Diamond Sangha. Almost immediately, Bob found himself in demand to offer retreats independently. Invitations came in from Mountain Cloud in Santa Fe, from the Augustine Contemplative Community and the Melbourne Zen Group in Australia, and from Seven Thunders in the Northwest. He covered for Pat in 2001 when Pat was given radiation treatments to try to knock back the prostate cancer, which was progressing. Bob accepted all invitations and all comers, though with a lurking sense of doubt about whether he wanted the job. He reached out strongly to Pat for help, seeking coaching, feedback, moral support.

Possibly Pat was forgetting that he himself had had years of formation in the seminary before he was called on to teach, that most teachers do not spring forth readymade but are cultivated, straddling for a time the dual roles of student and teacher. Possibly Pat was too inwardly preoccupied with his own struggles at that time to see that Bob needed more of a guiding hand. Several men had served as father figures supporting Pat's immature vulnerability. Perhaps in some deep place, he himself was still the boy needing a father figure. In any case, he was unable to support that vulnerability in Bob, who felt not only that he was left to fend for himself but that his overtures seeking support were actively ignored.

When Bob accepted an invitation to teach at Mountain Cloud Zen Center. the situation there was still volatile, the sangha in factions with Sutherland students seeming to claim the Center for their own teacher and Hawk students striving to maintain a foothold for Pat to come and teach. Pat gave Bob no history and no warning. Bob was stunned and sickened by the discord between the Hawk students, some of whom were his close friends from Amarillo days, and the Sutherland students. He felt not at all cut out for handling the situation. It was another weight tipping the scale in favor of not teaching. He continued nonetheless and quickly developed a full schedule leading retreats in the US and Australia, ostensibly doing well but experiencing increasing difficulty.[528] He found teaching independently a great deal more challenging than teaching alongside Pat. Even though there was not much interchange, nonetheless, in retrospect he had felt himself under Pat's wing. As he reached for that wing when he was on his own, Pat shut down, shrugged him off. Unresolved anger seethed in Bob and bubbled up against Pat. Pat, for his part, was mostly oblivious to Bob's anguish, seeing only his clear eye and his obvious talent as a teacher, ready and waiting for Bob himself to be ready for dharma transmission.

In December 1999, Bob went to Honolulu for his first Diamond Sangha Teachers' Circle meeting, stepping into another messy situation as the teachers wrestled with the ethics code. Bob found the discussions focused on John Tarrant baffling. In the end, he refused to sign the condemnatory letter against Tarrant in spite of feeling pressure from Robert Aitken to do so. The tension with Aitken reappeared at the teachers' meeting the following year, with John Tarrant still a major topic. Bob recalled, "I got very crosswise with Aitken, who cornered me during a break and grew quite aggressive with his posture and tone. … Next day in an attempt to put things back on track I offered my services chairing the DSTC. I … worked diligently in the coming year and was able to clear up some financial matters … and arrange schedules and locations for DSTC meetings for the next few years."[529]

While Bob was thus finding his way, Leonard Marcel, apprentice teacher since 1996, had been guiding the sangha that formed around him in Saudi Arabia and assisting when he could with sesshin for Rolf Drosten's sangha in Germany and Pathless Path in Tucson and Oregon. He grew steadily in the teacher role while continuing to deepen his understanding, working as co-teacher and student with both Rolf Drosten and Pat Hawk. As the twentieth century turned into the twenty-first, Pat decided it was time to give Leonard dharma transmission.

The ceremony took place in October 2001 in Damme, Germany, in the presence of Rolf Drosten's Wolken und Mond Sangha,* as well as some who came from a distance, including Jane Huyer and Bob Smith from Oregon. Jane wrote a report for the Seven Thunders newsletter:

> Our friend and founding member Leonard Marcel received full Transmission of the Dharma from Fr. Pat Hawk Roshi in Damme, Germany on October 21, 2002. As usual in the Diamond Sangha, the ceremony took place at the end of a sesshin, which had been led jointly by Leonard Marcel and Rolf Drosten Roshi (in German and English). Attendees included four of Leonard's students from Saudi Arabia and two old friends from Oregon.
>
> During the ceremony, Leonard gave a Teisho (in English) on Case 39 of the Hekigan-roku, "Yun-men's (Unmon's) Flowering Hedge", presenting us with both the Flowering Hedge and the Golden-Haired Lion. Afterwards Leonard renewed his Jukai vows in English, with the assembly responding in German. After successful completion of shosan, Pat Hawk presented Leonard with a lineage chart, a brocade rakusu, and a teacher's stick. Leonard's Dharma Lineage stretches back through 88 generations to Shakyamuni Buddha. The teacher's stick (kotsu) was carved by Bill Larson

* Clouds and Moon Sangha

> of zebrawood from Africa, especially appropriate for one whose teaching name is Lion Cloud. The ceremony ended with the presentation of gifts from friends near and far. One of these was a gift of violin music, which culminated in a Swedish line dance for the entire assembly led by Rolf, Leonard and Pat (believe it or not!).[530]

Bob Walker was in Germany at the time. Having interacted with Rolf Drosten at the teachers' meetings and having enjoyed his common sense, warm affability and dharma clarity, Bob accepted an invitation to visit Rolf and had been in Germany for about a month before Leonard's transmission ceremony. Throughout Bob's stay in Leverkusen, the town where Rolf and his wife Christa lived, he and Rolf did koan work together, meeting three times a day for dokusan. Questions Bob had brought up with Pat only to get terse, dismissive answers, he could bring up with Rolf and have conversations about. It was tremendously validating and underscored Pat's weakness as a mentor for Bob.

In August 2002, the Diamond Sangha Teachers' Circle meeting was at the Redemptorist Renewal Center in Tucson. At this point, Tarrant had split off and the wagons were circling around another Diamond Sangha teacher, again for alleged sexual violations. Notwithstanding the inherently divisive situation, a letter was sent out by one of the teachers in advance suggesting they think of the meeting as a sort of family reunion, something Bob found disingenuous considering the ethics wrangling and internal censure that had occupied so much time at the previous two meetings. Although more at ease with the group this time, Bob refused to participate in the discussions censuring the other teacher, and continued to feel that the Teachers' Circle was not where he belonged, in part because of continued ambivalence about his own role. He communicated his doubts to Pat, who responded with an email:

> Thanks for the message. The last time you were here in Tucson [at the teachers' meeting], it seemed to me you were preoccupied. And we have not been doing very much communicating.
>
> The doubts about yourself have been around for some time. As far as I'm concerned, I have been waiting to see which way you wish to go. I'm ready at any time to give you the transmission. Some time ago I remember you recounting a dream and your comments indicated to me that you did not want transmission, at that time anyway. I want to wait until you are ready in your own mind and soul.
>
> I have confidence in your realization and ability to teach, and there are many people who appreciate your work. I also know what it can take out of a person and the tiredness that comes with it. Disillusionment goes with the territory.

> I say to you what I say to so many people, What does your soul want? What do your dreams image to you? I want you to do what you really want to do. I have no intention to push you into anything. You don't have to do anything with the Diamond Sangha teachers. I apologize if I have contributed to your disillusionment.
>
> It looks as if I will be around indefinitely. My check up Tuesday revealed that the PSA level is the same as last time. No further action to be taken. Next check up in three months. So, take your time.[531]

Bob replied with two long emails a few days apart. Pat printed the emails and marked up the paper copies with yellow highlighter, noting Bob's remarks about frustration with the Diamond Sangha teachers, his recognition that he must come forth with his own dharma, not some facsimile of Pat's, and especially Bob's statement: "I also understand at a very fundamental level what I am doing as a teacher — the very real and sublime work that is quite undivided by name and preference and sect. Regardless of sectarian trappings and insignia I will continue to practice this."[532]

Pat wrote back saying he and Bob would talk when Bob came to Tucson — they were slated to co-lead Rohatsu at the Redemptorist Renewal Center. Bob planned to remain in Tucson for a week afterwards, staying in the teacher's room at Zen Desert Sangha. At the end of Rohatsu, Pat drove Bob to ZDS, and they attempted to talk things out along the way, in the distracting setting of Tucson traffic. There was no one around when they got to ZDS, and Bob asked if they could sit down and talk but Pat said no and left.

Bob continued to teach, and was leading retreats in Tucson, Amarillo, Santa Fe, Flagstaff and Australia, as well as co-leading a few retreats with Pat. He bought a house in Corvallis, Oregon, which positioned him to serve as a resident teacher for the Seven Thunders group, some of whom were old close friends from Amarillo. Then in early 2003 while sitting, he had a realization that opened the way for him to accept the transmission. He contacted Pat and the event was announced in August.[533]

That summer, Leonard Marcel moved back to Oregon from Saudi Arabia. At the annual Seven Thunders meeting and social, held at Glenna Pittock's place in Corvallis, Leonard — having received transmission from Pat a few years before — asserted himself as leader of the Seven Thunders group, perhaps not fully appreciating Bob's by then established presence as a teacher as well. The frustration with Pat's passivity, Bob's own ambivalence about teaching, his disenchantment with what seemed like a focus on form more than substance in some sangha members, and now some further rough water to navigate — a simmering inner turmoil bubbled over one evening among a small group at the local Corvallis sangha. He let the sangha know he was canceling the transmission, then told Pat.

Pat wrote, accepting the decision, leaving the door open for Bob to change his mind. Bob wrote an angry email back, acknowledging deep love for Pat and their long and fruitful relationship, yet recalling Pat's cold rejection, his failure to be present in Bob's time of need. "And let there be no mistake whatsoever that it was your inability to respond to me with simple human concern that I so flatly refused to inherit." There followed angry words, eloquently expressed, then, "I see the irony. I realize that in throwing [the hook] off I have taken hold of it most firmly and that I have finally honestly and to my own satisfaction received your teaching. And I hope that you are able to receive this email with some wry sense of satisfaction in a job well done." Pat replied:

> Dear Bob,
>
> "...some Pharisees who were present said to him, 'So we are blind are we?' Jesus replied: 'If you were blind, you would not be guilty, but since you say, "We can see," your guilt remains.' John 9:40-41.
>
> I am sorry for not seeing. I knew you were in pain. I was blind to what is. I do not see clearly now. But thank you for your candor. I am very sorry for not responding and turning my back.
>
> Without irony I say you are a good man, Robert Walker. I have been privileged to be in your company these many years. I am grateful for your support, financially, the hours you spent driving me, the moral encouragement, your loyalty to your practice.
>
> I was waiting. I wait no more. It may be more blindness, but I see no ball in my court, nor in yours.
>
> May you always live in freedom. You won it by your own courage.
>
> Pat Hawk[534]

Avoiding alcohol

In November 2003, Susan Weimer organized a potluck dinner party for Pat's 61st birthday, inviting about a dozen of Pat's closest local students as well as his confreres. Responding to a request from me about what to bring, she first suggested wine. Later she had second thoughts and sent a note saying, "In fact, it's probably best just to leave the wine at home. ... I'm a bit worried (that is my trademark) that bottles of de-alcoholized wine might get mixed up with regular wine. It wouldn't hurt you or me, but it could cause harm to some for whom alcohol is quite toxic." At that point, I had worked intensively with Pat for three years, and in that time it had never occurred to me that he might be alcoholic. Although it was obvious from Susan's email that someone coming to the party must be, it did not dawn on me that it was Pat. The event, which proceeded with food, drink and merriment but no alcohol, was a wonderful, warm encounter of the Redemptorists and the Pathless Path students coming together to celebrate Pat with good humor and laughter. He seemed relaxed and happy.

A few months later, I happened to have three extra tickets to a production of *A Streetcar Named Desire* and sent an invitation to Susan, Pat and any interested confrere of his to attend the play. Pat declined with thanks. Hamish Swanston, eminent St. Alphonsus scholar, was in residence for a time at the Renewal Center, visiting from Britain. Susan accepted for herself and Hamish (he preferred to be called Hamish rather than Father Swanston, or even Father Hamish), and the three of us attended the play. I had brought along a handful of liqueur-filled chocolates leftover from the holiday season that we enjoyed at intermission. By this time, I was accustomed to warmth and cordiality when I saw Pat in dokusan. Seeing him in dokusan a few days after the play, I encountered instead a breathtaking, icy coldness such as I had never met before. Something in the exchange suggested that the reversal was linked with the alcohol treat which, had he come, would have been put before him as a temptation. It took a few weeks for him to thaw out.

Some months after that, I saw Pat react with a similar abrupt hostility when a risk of alcohol was put before him. It was at Zen Desert Sangha and Shelly Dorsey was making soup for a zazenkai. Shelly stood out among sangha members as warm and lighthearted, with a ready laugh. She and Pat had an easy, jovial relationship. They had some exchange as she stood stirring the soup and he suddenly turned that startling cold shoulder on her and walked away. She was visibly shocked. Tasting the soup at supper, it was obvious that there was a considerable amount of white wine in the recipe. In this case, as with the liqueur-filled chocolates earlier, it seemed that he was reacting to the horror of being put in harm's way by a casual, inadvertent offer.

Another time, having made the long drive to Santa Fe for a sesshin, Pat and I were looking for a place to have supper the evening before the retreat was to begin. We pulled into the parking lot of what looked like a congenial restaurant and went in. It was apparent on stepping in the door that it was a bar. Without a word, Pat turned abruptly and walked back to the car. I followed, by this time surmising the cause, and we drove away. Ever since his second stay at Guest House, knowing too well his own vulnerability, he had that kind of brittleness about alcohol at times. It was the one comestible that he denied himself assiduously.

The next morning, we met a few of Pat's longtime students from the Mountain Cloud sangha for breakfast at Harry's Roadhouse, a popular eatery near the zendo. Pat ordered a loaded omelet, and before it arrived, Joel Carp, one of Pat's students, himself a vegetarian, warned in a serious tone, "You know, I think that'll have bacon in it." Pat said, "Oh good." Although retreat fare was always vegetarian, and he always made a point of serving himself salad and vegetables with whatever was the entree, Pat was a meat and potatoes man by inclination. His favorite retreat food was cheese enchiladas, but his favorite food of all was a bacon cheeseburger.

Lenten Morning of Prayer

Come spring of 2004, the Redemptorists took turns each Wednesday morning of Lent to offer a reflective prayer service followed by Stations of the Cross. The beautiful outdoor Stations were distributed around a quarter-mile walking path on a more or less level area on the far side of an arroyo that ran through the west end of the retreat center. Susan sent an email to Pat's local contemplative students — some of whom happened to be mainly practicing Zen — to say that it would be Pat leading the morning of prayer that week and to invite them to come. A few of us took her up on the invitation. The Lenten Morning of Prayer events were mostly attended by a handful of the more devout Catholics who frequented the retreat center services in the chapel. When Pat entered the chapel that morning, he looked slightly surprised and a little discomfited to see some of his students there. He was a master of skillful means, coming forth for each person individually from his large storehouse of possible offerings. For a Zen student, Zen language. For a Christian student, Christian language. For the secular, the unaffiliated, even the atheist averse to religious language of any sort — perhaps especially for these people, genuinely seeking though they knew not what — he offered the language of naked faith.

Here he was faced with the devout Catholics, for whom the language of the prayer service was well-suited, and a handful of his students who were varying degrees of heathen. Pat read the short readings and then, scrapping any prepared remarks he might have had, invited the dozen and or so that were assembled to ask questions. One woman from among the devout spoke, saying that her husband had died recently. Slowly, and fighting back tears, she asked Pat if he believed that there was life after death and if she could know that her husband was in heaven. Having recently heard Pat speak of life and death in a sesshin teisho, his Zen students wondered how he would respond.

Pat had included in his teisho a story about one of his annual visits to Aitken in Kaimu. As they were out on one of their long, often silent, walks along the beach, the subject of life after death came up, whether there might be some manner of existence after one's physical death. Some years before she died, Anne Aitken, speaking of death, had said she thought it was like getting on a bus. "You just get on the bus and go" — somehow with the implication that nothing remains. Pat asked Aitken if he thought nothing remains, and Aitken said he had a sense there might be something. Pat, asked years later what he himself thought, said he thought nothing remains. At another time he said, "I make a big distinction between belief and faith. Faith is something quite different from belief. As one's conceptualizations begin to change, confession of beliefs is not literal anymore. But the faith is always — faith has been something I suppose I've always had. How one describes that 'something' really changed through the years. And it's trying to describe the indescribable, express the inexpressible. Faith is more experience, it's not a head thing, not an intellectual thing." Whether there is life after death as it is conceived in the Abrahamic religions is an intellectual thing. It is necessarily not an experiential thing. For Pat, the nothing that remains after death is the emptiness that is exactly form,[535] impossible to explain. But here he was, faced with this devout, grieving woman, a handful of his Zen students looking on.

He looked at the woman with the full acceptance that was his particular gift, and in answer to her question — was her husband in heaven — in his great mercy he nodded his head, yes. She could rest assured, her husband was in heaven. He added a few remarks — something to the effect that hell was something she needn't worry about. Though the literal truth was not the same for the woman and for Pat and she would understand his words differently than he did — yet at some level it was the same truth. It was a beautiful presentation by Pat of *upaya*, skillful means.

Following the brief service in the chapel, a smaller group continued on to walk the Stations of the Cross, after which everyone dispersed except Pat, Susan and myself. We went to the cafeteria for lunch and conversation that wandered variously from retreat miscellany to movies and books. A title came up — maybe something like *Lolita* — that in my naiveté at the time I thought might be embarrassing for a Catholic priest. Susan said, "He likes raunchy. The raunchier the better." Pat gave a slight shrug. Notwithstanding the personal temptation of alcohol addiction and treatment which he carefully avoided, and his responsibility to students and vows, his mind, at least, harbored no great taboo. He enjoyed the freedom of the full range.

Construction at Redemptorist Renewal Center

In 2003 the Redemptorists undertook a $4.2 million capital campaign to fund renovation and expansion at the Renewal Center.[536] It included adding two large buildings — a new rectory and a two-story building with meeting rooms, restrooms and library; adding a swimming pool; expanding the main kitchen and adding a new, larger kitchen and two public bathrooms to the St. Alphonsus building. It would mean major disruption of all programs during the construction period — originally hoped to be about six months but in the end stretching to almost two years.

Susan's position was an enviable one from the perspective of students who worked with Pat and wanted more time with him. It could generate friction. Susan said she and Glenna had talked about how a lot of that went on in Amarillo. Now Head Resident herself, she felt Pat put her in a difficult middle position, not only between him and his students but even at times between him and his confreres. "And that is not right. And a lot of time I was between him and other students. He always asked me to screen people first." It led to jealousies.

As she gained familiarity and confidence with her administrative tasks, Susan proposed new offerings for the program, some of which she intended to teach herself. She emailed Tom Santa a list of suggestions for events she would lead at St. Al's, addressing him as Dear Tom. Replying with veiled opposition, he said he understood her role to be administrative and temporary, not ministerial or permanent, deflecting her familiar "Dear Tom" and beginning his email with "Susan," signing off with "Fr. Santa." Santa had been a student at the minor seminary in Edgerton, Wisconsin, when Pat was principal there. Though he was now in the role of Pat's Superior he seemed to retain some of the adolescent's need for Pat's approval, at the same time exercising a strong tendency to control. Pat navigated apparent obstacles with his usual passive, grudging acquiescence while Susan came to see Santa as enemy.

On edge with Santa, she became relentlessly critical of the building project, cultivating a discontent that increasingly attempted to engage the sympathy of people coming for retreats: the cost of the project would be astronomical, the debt impossible, the construction disruptive, the sheer ambition obscene. Hamish Swanston, a visitor at the Renewal Center as construction plans were being discussed, happily encouraged her. He commented that priests need to undertake big construction projects for the sake of their mothers since they wouldn't be producing grandchildren for them. It was true that the cost would be astronomical, and at a time when the retreat center was having difficulty operating in the black. In fact, a recognition of the need to improve retreat center facilities to appeal to more and larger retreat groups was a significant motivation for the project. Pat indulged in a grumble now and again but was mostly noncommittal. He was schooled from early adolescence in the vow of obedience, which could be understood not only as doing as one's superiors dictated, but also as an excuse to eschew responsibility for thinking about things beyond one's immediate job description, in Pat's case that of retreat master. Pat could not be accused of saintly docility — rather he tended toward grudging acquiescence or sometimes passive resistance — but he did fully inhabit the "not taking responsibility" implication of his vow.

Susan's predictions of disruption came true. By late spring 2004, construction was expected to begin in earnest in the St. Alphonsus building. After the June contemplative intensive retreat, participants helped move cushions, benches, instruments, statuary and other *objets* into storage. There were many treasures housed in St. Al's — gifts and purchases accumulated over Pat's long years of practice and teaching. Pat's inclination was to leave everything where it was — the library and contemplation room/zendo were not to be touched by the construction. At Susan's insistence, however, everything was moved out other than the books, a small number of cushions and two fountains in the courtyard.

The old St. Al's kitchen was destined to be torn out, and that area remodeled into public bathrooms, a new entrance area and a hall closet. The ramada in the courtyard was taken away and the wall between the kitchen and hallway was torn out that summer, turning the building very much into a construction site. Susan's quarters became unavailable, and no place was offered elsewhere at the Center. The August and September retreats were canceled, then the work stalled for months as the project waited for permits. To the construction update sent out that summer Susan appended an optimistic, "Pat and I are eager to get back to work in St. Alphonsus. An announcement will also be forthcoming once we are ready to resume public sitting."

By September things were still dragging, and Susan wrote, "It's as destructive and discouraging as I thought it would be." With no end in sight, space was made available elsewhere on the property so that the October contemplative intensive retreat, November sesshin, Rohatsu sesshin and a December resident training period could go ahead. With the main kitchen and the St. Al's kitchen both out of commission, they hired a catering service.

Construction at last began in earnest on December 6 — day six of the Rohatsu sesshin, "…but in no way marred a particularly wonderful event. The project is well underway now, and the whole place is filled with the sound of musical beeping from backhoes, etc. Serious work begins on the new addition to the St. Alphonsus building next week."[537] The heaviest and noisiest part of the work was expected to be done in the following six weeks, which prompted cancellation of the December contemplative intensive retreat — unnecessarily, as it turned out, because of further delays. In February 2005, Susan wrote darkly, "Nothing has been done on St. Alphonsus in the construction department. We canceled the December CIR for no reason. They don't seem to be following the schedule at all, but they've gone ahead and knocked down the courtyard wall. Prepare yourself."

By January, construction was projected to be complete in August. They planned to offer the full schedule of retreats and resident practice periods regardless, and the twice weekly public sittings, interrupted when St. Al's was dismantled the previous June, were resumed. Susan wrote, "Things will continue to be stirred up for a while and we will enter the gate there."[538] Nothing to be done except go on.

With the main kitchen and the St. Al's kitchen both torn up, the retreat center again hired caterers for meals. That necessitated following the same meal schedule as the main dining room, which meant rising at 5:00 instead of 4:00 AM during sesshin to allow for breakfast at 8:00 instead of 7:00. The milder schedule suited Pat, given health concerns, and it stuck even after construction was finally complete.

Through the spring and early summer of 2005, St. Al's came back into use despite the state of the building. It turned out that South Mountain, the rocky elevation at the edge of the property, extended invisibly under the site of the new kitchen wing, and during one retreat there was relentless jackhammering to chip away at solid rock. St. Al's kitchen was removed while at the opposite end of the building in the zendo the steady rounds of *zazen* and *kinhin* continued. The customary outdoor *kinhin* path was inaccessible, so other trails were pressed into service. These led deeper into the desert and were favored thereafter.

Besides keeping up the schedule at Picture Rocks (construction permitting) and at Zen Desert Sangha, Pat was still offering three retreats a year in the Northwest and three in Santa Fe. He would fly to and from the Northwest retreats, but Santa Fe was just close enough that he would drive, leaving early in the morning and arriving in time for supper. Riding with Pat provided an opportunity for a few people to spend time with him outside the teacher/student environment, with easy, long silences and occasional talk about anything at all.

The most direct route takes I-10 East out of Tucson, connects by a short jog to Hatch, New Mexico, "Chile Capital of the World," then goes up I-25 North to Albuquerque, with a short last leg to Santa Fe. Much of the landscape crossed is open, arid rangeland extending to hazy blue peaks at the horizon. One time after a long silence, somewhere north of the town of Truth or Consequences, New Mexico, Pat pointed across to a tiny farmhouse nestled at the foot of the distant mountains. He said, "Sometimes I think I'd like to live out there and be a hermit."[539] In fact, he was probably too fond of creature comforts to live in much rusticity, but the desire for solitude was genuine.

As it became clear that renovations at the Renewal Center would not be completed by midsummer, the August sesshin was canceled in the interest of avoiding further delays. The end of summer brought continued construction and cancellation of the fall retreats. The mood at the retreat center was edgy. There began to be complaints from Pathless Path students about Susan — including that she interfered with getting in to see Pat, sometimes even though he himself had suggested the meeting. She was in the difficult position of shielding him from too much attention and overstepping into too much shielding. She exhibited a territoriality over him that annoyed him. This, and friction between Susan and Tom Santa (not helped by the endless construction), led to her being asked to leave the Center. She held on. That summer while Pat was in Oregon for the sesshin at McKenzie Bridge, he told a few friends that the Renewal Center staff were having difficulty getting Susan to leave, a behind-the-back move that Susan herself heard about from these same friends. She made plans to take a month and a half leave from the Renewal Center and work with Rolf Drosten in Germany.

While Susan was away, the main dining room was finally completed, slated to be back in operation in October. Days before the official opening, the Redemptorists woke in the early hours of October 7 to flames engulfing the new kitchen. They rose from sleep and watched the place burn in the night, wondering for a time if the fire could leap to the chapel, office and rectory. No one was hurt, and firefighters prevented spread beyond the kitchen and dining room building, but that structure burned to the ground. Pat was unfazed. As people woke to the news, his inbox chirped with expressions of concern and offers of help. He was reassuring:

> We are all doing fine. We will do meals for ourselves, there is a kitchen in the rectory, and we are retaining our cook. As for volunteer help, we may need some toward the end of November. The plan seems to be that all effort will be directed to finish the St. Alphonsus building, so we may need help to get ready for Rohatsu. There is a big meeting here today with the architects, contractors, Redemptorist big wigs, etc. to plan how to recover. The mood is optimistic and we're taking it all with good humor. It was only material after all and great excitement. More pictures on desertrenewal.org.
>
> Thanks again and be well.
>
> Pat[540]

A sign was posted outside the blackened ruin where the remains of charred metal lawn furniture, melted in varying degrees, lay helter-skelter along the former patio: "Look beyond and see not the pile of burned out bricks but rather that which will emerge from the ashes. In Him there is plentiful redemption for all." Santa told reporters, "We are getting donations from people who don't even know us. A neighbor to the center just brought in a check for $1,000. Another donor had been here for a funeral 15 years ago. I'm actually overwhelmed by the support."[541]

It was quickly apparent that they would not be able to reopen before the New Year, and all events were canceled at the retreat center through December. At least a few dozen people had sent registrations, some with deposits for the canceled retreats. With Susan away, Pat was left as the contact person, an administrative responsibility pretty much completely beyond his ken other than to simply forward correspondence to the retreat center office staff.

Susan returned from Europe in late October and took things in hand, with resistance from the Renewal Center administration, still pressuring her to leave. Finally, in January she sent out a regretful message to the Pathless Path email list announcing with deep sadness her departure as a staff member of the Renewal Center and administrator of the Pathless Path program, closing with Case 37 of the *Shoyoroku*:

> Isan asked Kyozan, "Suppose someone asks you, 'How about one who says all sentient beings are in a disorderly karmic consciousness and have no base to rely upon?' " Kyozan said, "If someone appears, I call to him. When he turns his head, instantly I say, 'What is that?' " I wait while he hesitates, and then I say to him, "There is not only disorderly karmic consciousness, but there is no base to rely upon." Isan said, "Oh good."[542]

Carmen Patterson of the Retreat Center staff was assigned to administer Pathless Path thereafter, thus beginning a more straightforward arrangement that separated administration of the program from any particular teacher/student relationship. Although there was a steep learning curve for Carmen, she rose to the task. This despite some initial interference from Susan, including refusal to share the Pathless Path mailing lists, another contentious area from which Pat distanced himself.

Pat Hawk, new health concerns

In about 2002 or 2003, Pat's prostate specific antigen (PSA) level started creeping up again, an ominous confirmation that the surgery of 1997 had indeed not removed all the tumor. His oncologist recommended radiation treatment telling him it would give him "a few more years." The treatment wreaked havoc with his pelvic viscera, giving him intermittent rectal bleeding for the rest of his life. A few times over the course of several years, he was taken to the Emergency Department with an alarming urinary tract infection and hematuria. He also needed regular monitoring of his blood pressure, which tended toward high, likely related to his smoking habit. All of this meant frequent doctor visits, tests and medications.

As follow-up to one of the bleeding episodes, he went in for a cystoscopy during which the urologist biopsied some areas of concern, and for a brief period Pat thought he might have bladder cancer as well as prostate cancer. One of his students happened to see him walking down the main corridor of the university hospital immediately following this revelation. He looked visibly shaken.

Pat was always very clear that the prospect of death did not trouble him. He said at least once, "I'm just waiting for my Jesus to come and get me." It was the getting there that bothered him. The illness, the physical pain, the nuisance: after the radiation treatment he sometimes needed to wear adult diapers, what he called his paper underwear. He contributed a short article to the *Pathless Path* newsletter sharing his frame of mind:

> These days I find myself waiting. Waiting for construction to begin. Waiting to see if construction will ever continue. Waiting for appointments for medical tests. Waiting for results. Waiting to see if the tests will ever produce results. Sitting and waiting. T.S. Eliot has famously written in his poem "East Coker:"
>
> I said to my soul, be still, and wait without hope
> For hope would be hope for the wrong thing; wait without love
> For love would be love of the wrong thing; there is yet faith
> But the faith and the love and the hope are all in the waiting.
> Wait without thought, for you are not ready for thought:
> So the darkness shall be the light, and the stillness the dancing.
>
> A basic contemplative attitude, indeed. The practice itself is waiting, watching, awake, responsive. "Watch then, for you do not know what day your master will come" (Mt 24:42). Jesus uses various comparisons and parables, which are the source of contemplative waiting. The coming of the Son of Man will be as unexpected as that of a thief in the night (Mt 24:43), or of a master returning in the late hours without warning (Mk 13:35).
> We do not know what to wait for: we do not know how long we are to wait. It is just watching, waiting, awake.[543]

In April 2006, as construction at the Redemptorist Renewal Center continued, Pat had another episode of urinary tract bleeding, this time accompanied by severe flank pain. He was diagnosed with a kidney stone. Imaging revealed it was no ordinary stone that would pass of its own accord, albeit with excruciating pain. It was a large, infected concretion occupying the funnel-shaped origin of the ureter from the kidney. It was also discovered that on the side with the stone he had a double ureter, both tubes narrower than a normal single ureter would be. Such anatomical variations are not uncommon, and often don't come to attention except incidentally when imaging is done for some other reason. In Pat's case, the unorthodox anatomy conspired with other factors to produce a problem needing treatment. He was subjected to multiple episodes of shockwave lithotripsy attempting to break up the stone. A stent was placed to hold the ureter open enough to allow the passage of the resulting fragments, and it was left in place for about nine months. It caused a constant dull discomfort in his flank on the one side, rising at times to sharp, breathtaking pain when he moved.

The 2006 Easter Triduum contemplative intensive retreat was canceled, a weekend sesshin at Zen Desert Sangha went on without Pat, and the May sesshin at the Renewal Center was run with participation from Pat to the extent he was able. He felt tired and surly. In dokusan a sharp, cold, dismissive side sometimes appeared. For the late June sesshin in Santa Fe, uncharacteristically, he couldn't face the long drive, so he flew to Albuquerque where he was picked up at the airport and brought to Mountain Cloud. One of those who had driven from Tucson for the sesshin remembered, "He was just not himself. I kept wondering what had happened, if it was something in my presentation. He was just not there in the way he usually was."

Pat was back in Tucson for a few weeks, then flew to Oregon for the summer contemplative intensive retreat at McKenzie Bridge, with — as was his pattern — a little extra time in the Northwest tacked on so he could relax and get some relief from the summer heat in Tucson. He and Bob Walker met for lunch in Corvallis, and the question of transmission came up again. Pat was mildly dismissive, and Bob erupted at him, old wounds resurfacing. As Bob dropped Pat off where he was staying, Pat seemed visibly shaken. A few days later, still in Oregon, Pat was taken to the Emergency Department with an episode of hemorrhagic cystitis — another urinary tract infection with severe bleeding. Regretting how he'd left things, Bob followed Pat back to Tucson. "I booked a flight over and arrived late. Pat was standing out front waiting for me. At the end of the time we talked again about transmission and he was amenable to going ahead with it in time, though no date was set."

Despite the bleeding episode in Oregon and the relentless, ache-inducing stent in his flank, Pat resolved to carry on teaching in Tucson but announced he would make no more trips to sanghas at a distance. His students could come to him. They did come from all over and regularly, especially from Australia, Washington, Oregon, Texas, California and New Mexico. Though he sometimes resorted to sitting in a chair — he would normally sit in lotus position on a cushion — he kept up the retreats, resident practice periods and other events in Tucson, both at the Renewal Center and at Zen Desert Sangha.

Cyber-roshi

When Pat was studying with Aitken in the early 1980s following their initial meeting at the sesshin for Christians, he did so mostly through the mail. When Pat himself became a teacher, he too offered long-distance availability to dedicated students who couldn't get to Tucson for regular dokusan. At first, it was over the phone or via cassette tapes sent back and forth through the mail. With Pat's decision to no longer offer sesshin away from Tucson, the possibility of communication across distance became all the more important for students in his remote sanghas.

Though not particularly facile with computers, in 2008 Pat was persuaded to get a Macintosh laptop with built-in camera so he could offer face-to-face dokusan via internet for distant students. Once the Mac was set up for him, he tried the camera in preparation for getting the video conferencing working. It got stuck in the "On" mode. He couldn't get his own live image off the screen. He complained about it at the lunch table after one sesshin, which recruited a few moderately tech-savvy volunteers to help. It turned out that, as soon as he had turned on the Mac camera for the first time and had suddenly seen himself looking back out of the computer screen in the ghoulish light that computer cameras of that vintage would so often produce, he hit buttons — any buttons — on the keyboard to get the thing turned off, which ironically froze the camera. Even restarting the computer would not unlock it. He was comically livid.

The solution ended up being to remove the battery from the laptop — a maneuver that made him dubiously nervous about losing saved data but did the trick. From there it was a simple matter to get him set up for video chatting. He learned to position the laptop to avoid the most unflattering angles, and from then on could see his students in their local backgrounds in Port Angeles, Corvallis, Portland, Melbourne, Denton — and in the case of Katherine Holmsen, various places in Africa — while they saw him in his office or at the rectory.

The number of students from away increased after Pat himself stopped traveling to Santa Fe, Amarillo and the Northwest, and by 2008 there were around 20 with whom he worked at a distance.* He received students via phone, email, Skype, FaceTime or some combination. Pat responded to whatever and whoever came to him. One of his students called one day in great distress saying, "I have a desperate need to be forgiven for my affairs with married men." Pat said without irony, "I have that authority. You are forgiven." And there was the time a student

---

* These included Stephen Slottow, Katherine Holmsen, Karen Johnson, Kristen and Bill Larson, Glenna Pittock, Jane Huyer, Emma Stone, Leonard Marcel, Marsha Linehan and others.

called in tears at the height of the controversy at Mountain Cloud. And countless other calls, mostly the scheduled weekly dokusans, but always in between, the random voices from out of nowhere. He took them in stride.

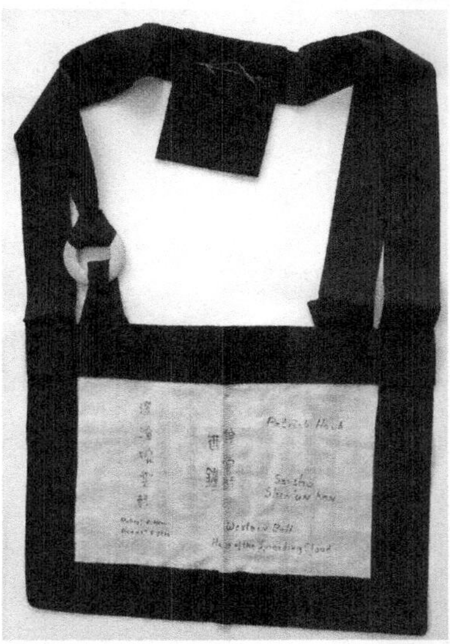

Above left: Pat with confrere, Bob Curry, in Hawaii for Pat's transmission ceremony.
Above right: With Robert Aitken, following Pat's transmission ceremony on May 24, 1989. Pat is wearing his newly bestowed ceremonial rakusu.

Left: The back side of Pat's Jukai rakusu. sewn by Shirley Morrissey, inscribed by Robert Aitken for the Jukai ceremony, August 5, 1988.

Below: Sanbo Kyodan Teachers' Sesshin, at San'Un Zendo in Kamakura, Japan, November 1992. Pat Hawk is in the front row, first on the right.
(Rakusu photo by H. Amerongen; all others: Pat Hawk photo albums)

Top: Pat's calligraphy of a Rumi poem was framed and hung outside the dokusan room at Amarillo and later in the dokusan room at the Redemptorist Renewal Center in Tucson.

Middle: Robert Aitken wrote numerous gathas, which he asked Pat to render in calligraphy with the idea of producing a book of gathas. The project was never finished.

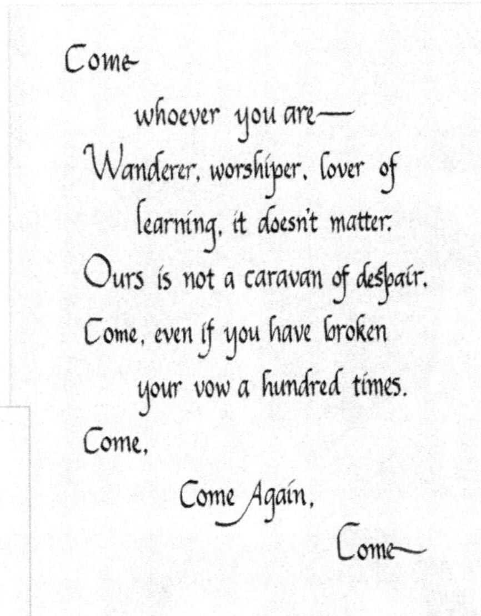

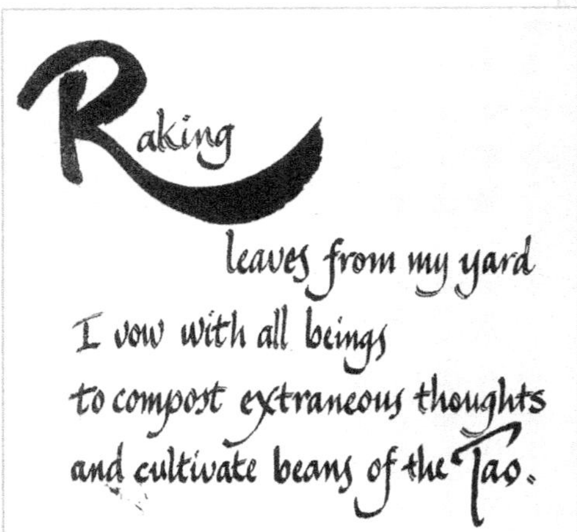

Bottom: Pat Hawk's notes toward the end of a Diamond Sangha Teachers' Meeting. His many pages of notes from each meeting would start out as mainly notes, then drift to mainly doodles.

(Pat Hawk papers)

Top: Photo taken after sesshin, at Mountain Cloud Zen Center, Santa Fe, New Mexico, 1991.
(Pat Hawk photo albums)

Below, clockwise from upper left: At Bishop DeFalco Retreat Center: Bob Halter, Greg Mayers and Pat Hawk. Pat with his parents, Elnora and Ed Hawk, early 1990s. Glenna Pittock. Pat with Rev. Bernard McVeigh, Abbot of Our Lady of Guadalupe Abbey.
(Pat Hawk photo albums)

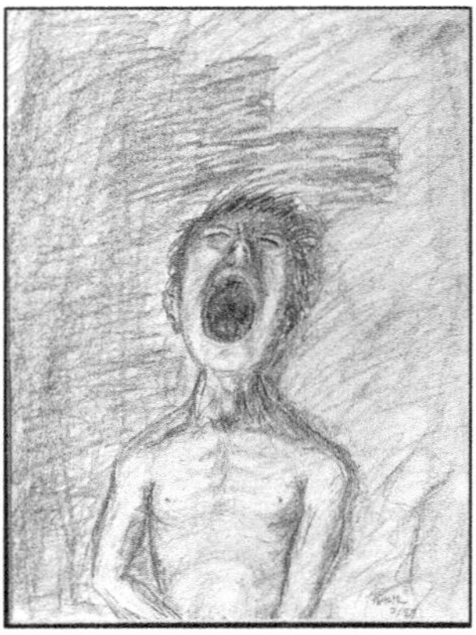

Above left: Bishop DeFalco Retreat Center, Amarillo, Texas. (Pat Hawk photo album) Above right: Pat Hawk self-portrait while at Guest House in Rochester, Minnesota; February 1997. Pat framed the image and it hung it in his quarters at BDRC, then at the Redemptorist Renewal Center in Tucson, Arizona. (Photo by H. Amerongen)

Middle: Dokusan room (left), and zendo/contemplation room altar (right) at the Redemptorist Renewal Center. Below: View looking west from the Redemptorist Renewal Center. (Photos by H. Amerongen)

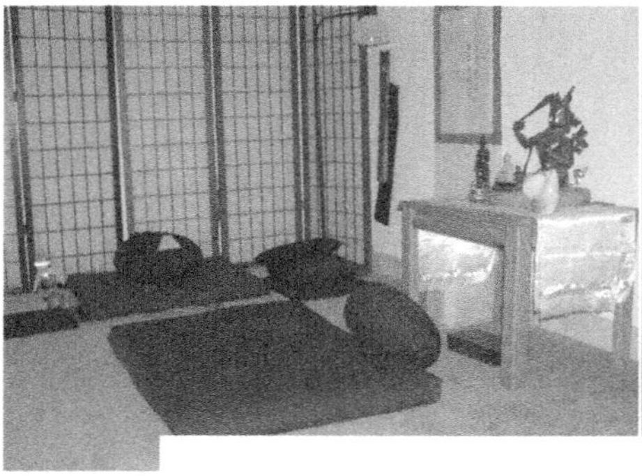

Top: Celebration of Pat Hawk's 65th birthday, November 2007. Left: Pat browses the Festschrift Scrapbook produced from contributions of friends, students and colleagues from all over the world.
Right: Birthday cake – Zen Desert Sangha, Tucson, Arizona.

Middle: Anniversaries celebrated at the Redemptorist Renewal Center in July 2009; 100 years of service: Pat Hawk's 40th year of ordination, Brother Mike Rhodes 40th year of profession, and Brother Steve Fruge's 20th year of profession.

Left: Pat with his sister Mary Ellen Pope, who traveled to Tucson to attend the celebration of Pat's 40th year of ordination.

(Photos by H. Amerongen)

Above: The last Rohatsu sesshin; Redemptorist Renewal Center, Tucson Arizona, December 2011.

Below left: Pat Hawk, December 8, 2011, last day of Rohatsu.
Below right: Barbecue at Zen Desert Sangha, March 23, 2012. Students and friends came to celebrate and thank Pat for his many contributions. Some failed to recognize him at first because of the pronounced fluid retention that had developed since December. Bob Wallin is seated to Pat's right. (Photos by H. Amerongen)

Pat gave dharma transmission to Leonard Marcel in October 2001 (Top photo; L-R Rolf Drosten, Leonard Marcel, Pat Hawk), and to Bob Walker in April 2008. (Middle photo).

Bottom: In late March 2012, in a ceremony conducted by Leonard Marcel on behalf of Pat Hawk who was too sick to attend, four others were given transmission. L-R: Dan Dorsey, Leonard Marcel, Susan Weimer, Marsha Linehan, Kristen Larson.

(Top: from Pat Hawk photo albums; middle and bottom: Photos by H. Amerongen)

Pat Hawk funeral, May 10, 2012, at St. Clement Health Care Center, Liguori.

Top, L-R: Pat Hawk's confreres John Schmidt, Harry Grile and Bob Halter concelebrate the funeral mass.

Middle: The wooden urn sits above a photo of Pat. To the left of the photo is Pat's Redemptorist rosary, bestowed at the time of his first profession of vows, August 1963.

Bottom: Bob Walker carries the urn from the chapel to the burial site. Walking with him are Bob Halter, John Schmidt and Harry Grile.

Photos by H. Amerongen

9

Recollecting, Handing Over

Pat recollecting

The evening after the end of Rohatsu in 2006, about ten of the participants went out for supper in town, as was customary at the time. Conversation was lively and light with post-sesshin effervescence. A few around the table, including Bill Jackson from Redway, California, and Neale Povey from McMinnville, Oregon, who had been practicing contemplation and Zen for decades, were exchanging stories of the early years at Guadalupe Abbey, Portland and Palisades.

Over the Thanksgiving weekend, I had read *Crooked Cucumber*, David Chadwick's biography of Shunryu Suzuki.[544] There were anecdotes in that story that came up during sesshin in ways that I found supportive to practice. Hearing the many stories around the table that night after Rohatsu, it occurred to me that somebody should gather the stories of Pat's various sanghas through the years. I mentioned this to him when I saw him a few days later, fully expecting him to dismiss the idea. Instead he said, "Well there's a project!" I thought Neale Povey would be a good option to take on such an endeavor since he was not only retired and articulate, he had a long history with Pat and with some of the sanghas. I asked Pat if it would be okay with him if I were to propose it to Neale and if it would be true to say that he, Pat, supported the idea. He said sure, and was sincere enough to add a few comments about how it would need to be done, in particular, that one would need to do recorded interviews, not just assemble casual recollections.

Neale responded to the proposal with enthusiasm, copying in his email reply about a half dozen others in the Seven Thunders group. But he added, "...as Bob Dylan says '….it ain't me babe.' "[545] Comments from the others trickled in over the next few days, mostly supportive of the idea but with no immediate takers. On December 25th I went to the Renewal Center to wish Pat a Merry Christmas and filled him in on the responses. At that point, it was not at all clear what form such a project could take if it were to take off at all. There was a vague idea of following the stories of the various sanghas and the main characters within them. I said to Pat, "You know, whatever form this story would take, you would have to be interviewed about your own life," quite sure this would put an end to the whole thing as far as he was concerned. Pat, surely the most private person I had ever met, would never consent to anything focused on himself. Instead he said, "You could interview me."

In early January he came to my office at the Arizona Health Sciences Center to meet and discuss how we would proceed. We'd met for coffee a few times before when he'd come to see his oncologist, always in the hospital cafeteria, which was near the Cancer Center. This time he asked for directions to my office, located at the other side of the Health Sciences complex through a maze of corridors running through and between buildings. Not expecting him to make the trek, I sent him directions anyway and told him to call when he was out of his appointment and I'd meet him in the cafeteria. The morning of the appointment, expecting his call any minute, I was startled by a cheery hello as he poked his head through my office doorway looking pleased as punch with himself.

We devised a simple plan: I would get a digital voice recorder, and we would meet in his office a few times a month to talk about his life, beginning with parentage. At first, it was simply an oral history, something that could be used as a resource for anyone who might take on the larger story of the various practice communities of which Pat was the center. At some point much later, in a conversation about Bob Wallin writing a history of Zen Desert Sangha and how that would interact with the work we were doing together, Pat said, "This biography of me, this is your project." That is what it became from then on.

A few months into the work with Pat, the opportunity arose for me to go to a medical education meeting in Honolulu, and I tacked on an extra week to visit Palolo Zen Center and spend a little time in the place Pat had helped build, also to meet Robert Aitken. Aitken was suffering from one of his frequent respiratory infections but nevertheless met with me twice, consenting to have our conversations recorded. To my surprise he seemed a rather spare conversationalist — without much thought, I somehow expected the widely acknowledged Dean of American Zen to be more communicative. In fact, he was a bit stilted and difficult to draw out. His mind was sharp, and though he apologized for a faulty memory, his recall of dates and events was remarkable.

Aitken's recollections of Pat were warm and energetic, including his first impressions at Palisades back in 1978, Pat's growth afterward, his warm friendship with Anne, and his great help to Aitken with Aitken's students. Perhaps in part because of Pat's being a priest, never mind that he was a Catholic priest, people sought him out for counsel, a role he could slip into naturally.

Aitken said, "I'll tell you a funny story about Pat: I'm terrible as a correspondent, and my letters just stack up. One time when he was visiting in Kaimu, I took him a stack and said, "Here, you asked me if you could help out. Well, here's what you could help me with. I need to send at least a perfunctory answer to all these people…" And I left him alone. The next day I went back, and the letters were gone. No sign of the letters. I said, "Did you answer all those letters already?" He said, "No, I threw them away. If there's anything I can't stand, it's a messy desk." Aitken laughed, "So, that took care of a whole generation of Zen students I think."[546] Hearing this story later, Pat corrected it to something much more Pat-like:

> Well, the funny story about the correspondence. Yes, he loaded this huge stack on me, and some of them I answered for him. A lot of them were just like emails you get. You read 'em and there's no reason to respond. I filed them. I didn't throw them away, I filed everything. When I got there, he had these cardboard boxes with all his correspondence from way back when. And there was also a cardboard box with his finances in it. And they were in this little office between the zendo and his office and the bedroom. I was working in there and sorted all this stuff. And there was an old file cabinet in the garage that was rusting. I sanded it, I spray-painted it, and I put all his correspondence in alphabetical order in this cabinet. But it's true that I didn't answer everything. That would have taken *years*. At any rate, I answered those things that I thought should be answered. And I told him, I filed the rest of it.[547]

Aitken told the story of Pat's clash with Yamada Masamichi, something Pat had thus far said nothing about. "Yamada Ryo'un [Masamichi] Roshi checked Pat with this koan [*Hekiganroku* Case 6], and Pat gave the response that we usually give, which he knew very well and was very clear about. And Ryo'un Roshi said, 'No, that's not right'." Aitken gave details of Yamada's response, then went on, "That kind of response of emptiness didn't go over with Pat, and he bowed and left the room, and he left the koan review seminar and took a plane and went home." Aitken chuckled at the recollection. "Which action endeared him to my heart. It's something that I'll never forget. It's wonderful. Somebody else might have said, 'No, I don't agree' and would have tried to argue, or somebody would have said, 'Oh, is that so.' But not catching a plane and going home. That was a pretty strong statement. And I think it was a statement that was justified. And Ryo'un Roshi said to me a few years later, 'I want to talk to Pat, and I want to apologize to him.' So Pat had a very strong influence on that man, I think. Very important." Aitken ended our interview with, "Anyway, we all of us sure enjoyed his visits. And he was very helpful in his quiet way to me as I had to deal with a lot of ups and downs in establishing a new center there in Kaimu."

With Aitken's permission, I gave Pat a copy of the transcript from our conversations, and when he'd had a chance to read it, asked him what he thought. "I was very moved," Pat said, "I didn't think he was that impressed with my actions. I always used to talk about it as my failure in Kamakura. … I didn't think he had such a good opinion of me."[548]

With approximately twice-monthly meetings, the first pass through Pat's life from birth to the present took about six months. The story was spare, Pat not ever chatty, least of all about himself. When we came to the end of the first series of interviews, it seemed a good idea to put a little more flesh on the bones, so we continued from various angles. Pat had pulled out his photo albums from time to time to illustrate some place or person or event. As a next step, he agreed to have the albums digitized so we could then go through photo by photo, again with the recorder running, while he recalled events, names and dates.

Pat's office was a good-sized room off the reception area at the Redemptorist Renewal Center. There was comfortable seating with two love seats at right angles sharing a coffee table in front. The end table in the corner between them held a modest sound system and behind it were shelves with CDs of classical music, opera, some Philip Glass, some Beatles, miscellaneous others. A wainscot of faux brick came halfway up two of the walls, mostly hidden by one of the loveseats and several full-height bookcases. A large L-shaped desk jutting into the room from the corner opposite the couches held a computer, a telephone, a small lectern, whatever papers Pat was using at the time, and some low shelves with data CDs and DVDs carrying photos people gave him, computer back-ups, various games — many of them different versions of mahjong, his favorite among games of solitaire.

A floor-to-ceiling cupboard behind the desk had sliding wooden doors that held a bulletin board with the usual bulletin board paraphernalia: a calendar, a page of phone numbers of Renewal Center personnel; a red bumper sticker with "Born Okay the First Time," given to him by Mary Riseley; a small poster, probably a gift from some other student, saying, "What part of NO didn't you understand," presumably a pun on the Mu koan; and a small plain poster, "ABSOLUTE ZERO", from the jazz-rock band — not necessarily because he was a fan.

A door opened to a private bathroom, the tub and shower now with loaded storage shelves. Pleasant sunlight came in through a south-facing window above one of the couches, heating the office beyond the building's cooling capacity in summer. The space was over-warm in summer and chilly in winter. When that was pointed out to him one day, he said with mock self-pity, "Yeah, no wonder they gave it to me."

Along the same wall as the window, a metal door opened directly to the outside — handy for Pat, who never smoked indoors. From time to time, he'd be standing outside on the stoop having a cigarette. One time as he was stepping out for a smoke break, there was something dark at the edge of the stoop.

Looking at it I asked, "Is that a lizard?"

"Yeah, it looks like the cold got it." It was late November and there had already been a few frosty nights.

"Is it dead?"

"Well, it's not moving very fast. Let's put it that way."

"That's for sure."

"Part of the natural cycle. Everything always in flux and change." He delivered this clichéd bit of wisdom with exaggerated gravity.

Another time as I approached the office building, a hawk was busy with something around the stoop of Pat's office door. The bird seemed unusually tame, especially for a raptor, flying up into a nearby tree only as I got quite close. Generally, Pat himself was the only one hanging around that stoop, so the obvious connection popped to mind.

Speaking to Pat in his office, I said, "There was a hawk out there, hanging around the stoop. Of course, I thought it was you."

He said, "Oh it was."

Dropping the whimsical I said, "There was probably some prey it was after."

Not missing a beat, Pat said, "Yum, yum!"

Although we mostly met in his office, occasionally if he was in town for an appointment with his oncologist, we met at my office, in a building in the same complex as the Cancer Center. There was an espresso bar in the hospital cafeteria, and he surprised me the first time we went there for coffee by ordering a latté. So fervent was he about coffee, I assumed he'd be strictly a black-coffee man. Early on in our regular meetings for this project, remembering this, I called from the road to see if he'd like a latté from the Starbucks at the bottom of the hill leading to the retreat center. There was a fair chance he would react indifferently, even gruffly, one never knew. But he accepted the offer with happy enthusiasm, like a weary boy perked up by a treat. "That would be *lovely*!" he said. Thereafter that became part of the routine — arrive for interviews with laptop, recorder and latté.

In about February 2007, unbeknownst to Pat, his students, colleagues and friends were invited to contribute photos and anecdotes toward a *Festschrift* — to be a scrapbook of memories that could be presented to him for his 65th birthday, coming up in November of that year. Part of the motivation behind the scrapbook was the sense that time was short. Pat was still struggling with urinary tract complications, still had the ureteral stent. At one point, he said he used to think he would die of prostate cancer; now it seemed to him he would die of these urinary system afflictions. Some people thought it was doubtful Pat would even be alive by the time of his 65th birthday and wondered darkly whether the project was worth attempting. The invitation to participate was signed by at least one representative from each of the sanghas, so that the recipients would recognize that the project was widely supported. It was not a foregone conclusion, given Pat's natural reserve and the risk that such an undertaking might make him feel exposed and therefore cause displeasure. A few people expressed concern about this, and at least one declined to contribute for that reason.

The great kidney stone episode at last receded, the stent was removed, and by August Pat was feeling much better. In the fall, he was approached about whether he'd consent to a birthday celebration at Zen Desert Sangha — he usually wanted no fuss. He said yes. For years he had dutifully come to ZDS's twice annual sangha dinners, held on a Saturday evening, which for Pat meant driving down Saturday morning for the regular sit and dokusan, then coming back in the evening for the dinner. Still weary from the long bout of health issues, he was too tired to come into town at the end of the day, so the party was organized as a midday barbecue, with lots of vegetarian fare, all the fixings for bacon cheeseburgers, and an enormous cake carved in the shape of a sitting buddha.

About 50 people came, many with gifts. Then came the moment of truth — would he hate the scrapbook? He took off the wrapper and with a puzzled expression, opened the cover to a large map of the world with arrows pointing to the many different locations from which contributions had been sent — about 130 in all, from 22 of the United States and four continents. He was grinning as he leafed through and people huddled around him to see. On his return to the Renewal Center afterward, Carmen Patterson, seeing him coming through the office, asked how it went. He said, "It was ecstatic!" A slight sardonic edge to his voice couldn't hide that he was beaming, genuinely pleased.

Bob Walker transmission

In the years following the exchange between Bob Walker and Pat over whether he would accept the transmission, Bob continued to work with a few students, one from the East Coast, one from Australia, one from Tucson, a few others here and there, in this limited way growing into the teacher role on his own account rather than as offspring of Pat. Those he worked with found him true in his presentation and guidance. After several tense discussions with Pat over several years, in December 2007, Pat and Bob agreed to go ahead with transmission. Bob remembered:

> By the end of 2007 I was feeling some urgency to go one way or the other with the teaching and I continued to sense that the transmission was an important step even if I was not planning to reassert myself in the conventional ways. I arrived in Tucson Christmas Day 2007 and spoke with Pat the next day. We had a nice exchange... I told him that I was wanting to go one way or another with the teaching, that I was leaving transmission up to him, though I did express a slight bias to just ending it altogether and winding up my remaining teaching duties in my own time. We discussed structures, etc. — I think he was trying to respect my distance from Diamond Sangha — and I said no let's go all the way and just do a Diamond Sangha transmission. He was clearly delighted.[549]

A date was set. The transmission was quietly announced. Several people came from a distance, including Kristen Larson from Port Angeles and Jane Huyer from the Seven Thunders group, effecting a measure of reconciliation after Bob's abrupt breaking off from most teaching in 2003. Will Brennan was there from Santa Fe. People working with Bob came, including Paul Sanders and Pauline Yule from Australia, and longtime friend and student Marianne Roche from New York.

The dharma talk, based on *Hekiganroku* Case 74 (Kingyu's Rice Pail), interwoven with Toni Morrison's *Beloved*, was lengthy — about an hour. By the end, Pat looked tense and drawn. Bob said afterward, "I considered ditching the talk right up to the end. But working through that story of Toni Morrison had been so instrumental in helping me to accept my own heart that I felt, inappropriate or not, it was a necessary offering." *Shosan* (the opportunity for anyone present to challenge the person about to be transmitted) proceeded without a hitch, and Bob was duly transmitted at the end of the spring sesshin on April 27, 2008.

Kristen Larson appointment

From the time they first met in 1990, Kristen Larson was among the most faithful and diligent of Pat Hawk's students. She had at one point aspired to be a minister in the Episcopal Church but they turned her down. Early encounters with Pat and Zen training redirected her toward a strong sense that she could and should be a Zen teacher. In 1994 she and her husband Bill started a sangha in Port Angeles, Washington, where they were living on the sailboat *Scrimshaw*. As Bill got less able-bodied, they sold the boat and moved to a house in town overlooking the harbor. They named it Murre Cottage, setting up one of the rooms as a small zendo where they continued regular Saturday morning sitting followed by tea, followed by brunch at Rick's, a favorite eatery in downtown Port Angeles.[550]

As early as 1996, that sangha of dedicated practitioners sent a letter to Pat with 16 signatures asking him to give Kristen permission to teach. He was startled and angry, saying the suggestion was inappropriate.[551] Kristen and her sangha continued undeterred and Kristen continued working with Pat year after year. Years later, while she was in Tucson in March 2009,[552] at the regular Saturday morning sit at Zen Desert Sangha, Pat announced that instead of the usual sutra service, there would be a simple ceremony to mark the fact that he was giving Kristen Larson permission to teach. There was no advertising of the event beforehand, no dharma talk and no *shosan*, just the simple renewal of Jukai, handing over of koan notes and assertion of lineage. There was no celebration afterward because no advance notice, however there were photographs. The night before, Kristen had sent me an email saying, "If you would be so kind to bring your digital camera to the zendo at ZDS tomorrow, I'd much appreciate it. I really want to show Bill what the place looks like now and we could email pix from your camera to him."[553] She said later that even at that moment, she wasn't positive Pat was going to go through with it, but she wanted the camera there just in case.

There was speculation afterward that Pat had made the appointment in the inconspicuous way that he did because he anticipated resistance from some in the sangha. Neither Dan Dorsey nor Susan Weimer, later to be appointed as teachers themselves, happened to be present in the zendo that morning. Both expressed concern afterward. Susan arrived at the zendo for a board of directors meeting, learning what had happened as she arrived, having just missed the ceremony. Shortly after, out in the parking lot as Pat was getting in his car to leave, she vehemently took him to task, an odd ripple in the usual Saturday morning quiet. The next morning there was a small celebratory brunch up at the Renewal Center on the patio outside the St. Alphonsus kitchen before Kristen headed back up to Washington to celebrate with her rejoicing sangha.

The timing of this permission to teach meant that Kristen, now a *de facto* member of the Diamond Sangha Teachers' Circle, was invited to attend the 2009 teachers' meeting held at Palolo Zen Center in conjunction with a celebration of the Diamond Sangha's 50th anniversary.

Celebrating anniversaries, summer 2009

The Diamond Sangha 50th anniversary celebration was a grand event that drew members and friends of the Diamond Sangha — hundreds —from Australia, New Zealand, Europe, North America and Hawaii. Montages of memorabilia sent from sanghas around the world were displayed as colorful reminders of the rich personalities, varied places and many diverse encounters that had filled the fifty years since Robert and Anne Aitken established the Diamond Sangha in 1959. A scrapbook of this history was compiled from photos going back to the beginning and including a bright collection from the celebration itself. In one of these the teachers are lined up outside the zendo along the lanai in order of transmission, Aitken leading in his wheelchair, Pat immediately behind him in robes, kotsu in hand, with an expression of suitable gravitas. With Augusto Alcalde and John Tarrant no longer associated with the Diamond Sangha, Pat was first in line behind Aitken, Nelson Foster right behind him.

Besides the great gala, there was the Diamond Sangha Teachers' Circle meeting, colored by an acute awareness that this would likely be the last gathering of Diamond Sangha teachers in which Aitken could participate. Even at this meeting, his lucidity came and went, though he was remarkably able to recognize and remember old friends. Frail, cared for from head to toe by his angels, as he called his round-the-clock Tonga caregivers, he tired easily and couldn't stay long at any of the sessions. With that fragile situation, there was acute consciousness of the need to wrap up some unfinished business that loomed over the three teachers to whom Aitken had given permission to teach but not transmission: Don Stoddard, Marian Morgan and Danan Henry, the latter a full dharma heir in Philip Kapleau's line but not in the Diamond Sangha. In the case of Danan, Aitken had expressed his intention to go ahead with transmission, but he had not followed through.[554] Although these three teachers had permission to teach, without full transmission they were not independent masters authorized to themselves appoint new teachers in the lineage. It meant that for them and their students, the line of transmission would be a dead end.

The subject had been on the Diamond Sangha Teachers' Circle agenda again and again with no resolution. At the 2009 meeting there was a strong sense of, "Let's fix this thing"[555] — although there were one or two holdouts who felt that Aitken had not given the three transmission because he felt transmission was inappropriate. In 2005, Aitken had sent an email to the Teachers' Circle regretting the proliferation of teachers in the Diamond Sangha. He singled out Australia, doubting that there could be so many enlightened teachers there."[556] On the other hand, many of the teachers at the 2009 meeting were in sympathy with the plight of the untransmitted and were interested in finding a way to make them independent. At one point in a side conversation, Pat offered to give Danan Henry transmission himself — something that would have been expedient and perhaps kind, though not appropriate, as Danan himself said when he learned of Pat's idea after the fact.[557] The meeting ended with the matter unresolved, a limbo that was to influence Pat's decision late in his life to give transmission to his own apprentice teachers.

Pat returned to Tucson invigorated as he often was by contact with his Diamond Sangha peers. These were his people in a way that his confreres could never be. Though the confreres were brethren to him, they could not fathom the deep mutual understanding shared with these others who saw as he saw, which for Pat was so much more than the narrower vision he'd learned at De Soto, Oconomowoc and Esopus. And though his confreres had also evolved since their seminary days, they still largely held that earlier vision.

There was another major anniversary for Pat to celebrate that summer of 2009. He was ordained on June 27, 1969, the day before his sister Mary Ellen Pope's 20th birthday. Two of his confreres at the Redemptorist Renewal Center, Brother Mike Rhodes and Brother Stephen Fruge, were celebrating anniversaries of Profession of vows — 40 years for Brother Mike and 20 years for Brother Steve. The Redemptorists planned a big event in July to honor all three. Pat invited Mary Ellen to the celebration, sending her the plane ticket for her 60th birthday present. He told me about it during one of our meetings in June.

I offered to announce the event at Zen Desert Sangha and he seemed to agree, but the morning the announcement was to be made, he took me aside and asked that I not mention it. No explanation. It wasn't that it was to be an intimate gathering — it was announced at all the Masses in the Renewal Center's St. Gerard Chapel. Perhaps he felt that since the celebration was also for his confreres, Brother Mike and Brother Steve, he shouldn't be inviting a bunch of Zen heathens.

A few days before Mary Ellen was due to arrive in Tucson, I offered to help with her visit. Pat replied with surprisingly sociable acquiescence: "Thanks for your offer. I surely will take you up on it, as I am hopeless as a host. I don't know what kind of schedule we can set up. Mary Ellen arrives tomorrow afternoon and I suppose that she will want to rest. She will be here until the 29th, Wednesday. Anything you can suggest will be a big help."

We met in Pat's office the morning after Mary Ellen's arrival. He was in high spirits and affable, almost chatty. So uncharacteristic, it was a case of, "Who are you and what have you done with Pat Hawk?" He and Mary Ellen did not know each other well — she was seven when he entered the seminary and he took little interest in his family thereafter — but there was an obvious deep affection between them. The family resemblance was subtle. She was heavier than he and with a fuller mouth. Both had blue eyes, Mary Ellen's without the reserve of Pat's. A patch of reddish skin on her neck was very like the skin that stood out on the palms of Pat's hands, something he said he'd had all his life. Mary Ellen had a sweet, pretty smile, trusting and open. Pat introduced us with a cordial smile of his own, and they made small talk about her trip and what she'd like to do during her stay in Tucson. When she took out a cigarette, he leapt to his feet to light it, then produced a little tin box for her to use as an ashtray. He himself did not smoke indoors.

We visited for a bit, looking at photos from their childhood that Mary Ellen's grandson had scanned and sent. She and Pat reminisced. Among the "must see" tourist attractions in the area, Mary Ellen chose San Xavier del Bac Mission, begun in 1692, the late 18th-century church now a National Historic Landmark, sometimes called the Sistine Chapel of the West. It was a blazing hot day (there's an excellent chance that any day in Tucson from June through August will be blazing hot), and there were fewer than a dozen other tourists at the mission in the stark heat. We wandered through the dim, unairconditioned main chapel, then out into bright sun and back to Tucson, to El Charro's for a late lunch downtown. Mary Ellen talked about family in Granite City and about her impending heart surgery. She had had bypass surgery eight years earlier and needed to have it again. Her doctor had been encouraging her to do it for about a year. She'd stalled then agreed, and it was scheduled for that August, two weeks after her return from Tucson.

The celebration the next morning began with Mass in a packed chapel, Pat and his priest confreres concelebrating. Pat saying Mass in this auspicious, well-dressed gathering and in front of so many was the same as Pat saying Mass at a contemplative retreat for the dozen or so participants sitting silently on cushions in a circle completed by a low altar. There was never any sense that this was a play put on for an audience, nor that it was routine and that his mind might wander to what was happening in any other place. His words and gestures were empty of anything but the moment, and his utter presence anchored the attention of the faithful.

Pat gave the homily, providing a view of his outlook at that time regarding vocation, both his own and in general:

> Good morning.
>
> I am deeply grateful to my Redemptorist brothers for arranging this celebration and to all of you for being here and participating. I'm also grateful to my sister, Mary Ellen Pope, who came from the St. Louis area to be with me on this day.
>
> I'm going to read you a story that has been an inspiration to me for many years. St. Paul in the reading we have this morning, in the letter to the Ephesians says, "Live in a manner worthy of the call you have received."

This is a challenge to not only Brothers Mike, Steve and myself, but to all of us.

The story goes like this:

> There was a disenchanted rabbi who was weary of threatening sinners with the wrath of God and of comforting the meek with God's goodness. And so he deserted his synagogue. He set off on his wanderings in disguise. He came to an old woman who lay dying in her drafty hovel. "Why was I born, asked the old woman, when as long as I can remember nothing but misfortune has been my lot." The disguised rabbi replied, "That you should bear it." And that set the dying woman's mind at rest. As he drew the sheet over her face he decided that from then on he would be mute.
>
> On the third day of his wandering he encountered a young beggar girl carrying her dead child on her back. The rabbi laid it in the ground, covered it up, broke bread and to the beggar girl's every word he answered with gestures. "The poor thing got nothing neither pleasure nor pain. Do you think it was worth him being born?" At first, the rabbi in disguise made no move but when the girl insisted, he nodded, yes. Thereupon he decided to be deaf as well as dumb.
>
> He hid away from the world in a cave. There he met no one, only a ferret. Its foot was hurt so the rabbi bound it with herbs, whereupon the ferret brought tasty seeds. The hermit prayed, the tiny beast wiggled its nose and the two grew fond of one another. One afternoon a condor plummeted from a great height, and as the ferret was basking in the sun at the mouth of the cave it carried it off before the rabbi's eyes. At that, the rabbi thought to himself that it would be better if he closed his eyes too.
>
> But since, blind, mute and deaf he could do nothing but wait for death, which he felt it was not seemly to hasten, he girded his loins and returned to his congregation. Once again, he preached to them on the subject of good and evil according to God's law. He did what he had done before. But now he waxed strong in his shame.

The challenge facing anyone called to the service of the kingdom of God can be discouraging. One can be tempted to flee like Jonah from God's call. Easier to be blind, deaf and mute, easier but not better. How can a vocation be carried out in the face of the evil and indifference that is met along the way? Certainly not by one's own strength. Only with the strength that is given by grace.

And I think the rabbi of our story was shamed because he thought he could rely on his own strength, and he missed the opportunities for grace that came to him from the people and the animals that he met. No matter

> what vocation in life we follow, we need grace, and the faith to see grace right in the middle of it all. Grace lifts and brings to joy. And what, as we age, do we cherish and value more? The reading from Ephesians says, "You were also called to the one hope of your call; one Lord, one faith, one baptism, one God and Father of all, who is over all and through all and in all."
>
> "Over all and through all and in all." No exceptions, no exclusions. Grace is granted to all women, all men, all children, all faiths, all nations, whether or not they have the Word of God in their mouths and hearts. The Church has always said this, no controversies and wrestling matches and murders done over this issue — a miracle.
>
> Each person experiences grace as he or she does human and divine love — that is uniquely, all in your own way, ways different from all others. So the call is not so much connected to what we do in life as how we respond. The doing is important because it is the environment in which you learn something deeper than doing. The call, the vocation of all, is to see, listen and hear, to discover and respond.
>
> What we celebrate and give thanks for today is not just the years Brothers Mike and Steve and myself have given, but what we *all* have given, and ask for the grace to keep on giving, a life lived in a manner worthy of the call we have all received, with all humility and gentleness, with patience, bearing with one another through love, striving to preserve the unity of the spirit through the bond of peace.[558]

The confreres wore Redemptorist robes under their vestments, and most changed to civvies after the Mass, but Pat kept his robe on for the brunch. In major seminary at Oconomowoc and Esopus, and later as a teacher at the high school seminary, the robes were the daily uniform, but since Pat left Edgerton in 1979, occasions for wearing them seldom arose. Being a Redemptorist was integral to his self-identification, and he made the most of this rare opportunity to dress the part.

On Mary Ellen's last full day in town, we planned a driving tour of Tucson up into the foothills of the Santa Catalina Mountains, with a stop at Tohono Chul Teahouse for lunch, then to Sabino Canyon and back through the university area, thence through downtown and back to the Renewal Center. In the event, Pat was not feeling well, so Mary Ellen and I went without him. Over lunch, with Pat not there, she was freed to tell stories, now oft-repeated family lore, of Pat's irreverence as a boy. There was the time they were walking home from church and Pat was swinging his rosary, and as his mother glared at him, he called out, "Hang on Jesus! You're going for a ride!." And the time he called a loud "Aaaaamen!" during Mass when the homily went on for too long.

On the driving tour with Mary Ellen, we stopped in at Zen Desert Sangha so she could get another glimpse of the Zen side of Pat's life (her first glimpse was Pat's 65th birthday scrapbook, a copy of which she had received a few years earlier).[559] We toured the building, then stood outside for a few minutes while she had a cigarette, smoking not like a habitual smoker, but delicately, as if it were something new. She spoke of how proud their parents had been that Pat had become a Zen roshi — Mary Ellen pronounced it rawshi, then giggled when she heard the more usual pronunciation — though no one in the family had much idea of what it was.

On our way back to the Renewal Center, Mary Ellen asked to see the petroglyphs, about a five minute walk from Pat's office door, but then decided she was too tired to go. As we said goodbye, we made plans that she would come back in cooler weather, none of us registering just how serious was the condition of her heart.

I had recorded Pat's anniversary Mass and sent Mary Ellen a copy. A few weeks later, the day before she went in for heart surgery, she sent an email saying the CD had arrived and they would listen to it as a family that evening. The next day, Pat sent news: "The surgery did not go well. My last word was that Mary Ellen is in intensive care, and her heart has stopped three times. The doctors say they have done all they can and she is not expected to live through the night. Right now I am arranging to go to Granite City. I will not be at the zazenkai [planned for that weekend]. Go ahead with it. Play a tape or just sit the day." The next morning he wrote: "It's 6:20 AM Friday. I just got a call that Mary Ellen has no brain activity and they will proceed to take her off life support. I will be leaving this morning. Thanks for your support."[560]

There was an outpouring of sympathy from Pat's students at Zen Desert Sangha and a great desire to express support to Pat and his family. It was decided to hold the zazenkai as a memorial to Mary Ellen. A photo of her and Pat taken at the 40th-anniversary celebration brunch in July was placed on the altar. The sutra service expanded to include 108 recitations of the "Kanzeon" chant of boundless compassion, 108 being the usual number of beads on a Buddhist or Hindu *mala*[*] and an important symbolic number in Asian mythology. A hat was passed collecting a donation to the American Heart Association, the family's designated charity, in the name of Mary Ellen Pope, and participants at the zazenkai signed the card. A few dissenting voices, doubting the appropriateness of a Zen group sending a condolence card to this very Catholic family, were overruled by the majority.

---

[*] Mala: (Sanskrit) A string of beads commonly used in Hinduism, Jainism, Sikhism, Buddhism and Shintō for the spiritual practice known in Sanskrit as *japa*. The main body of a mala is usually 108 beads, though other numbers are also used.

When Pat resurfaced after his return from Mary Ellen's funeral in Granite City, he expressed warm gratitude to ZDS. He was touched by the rare moment of coming together of his rather traditional Catholic family and his Zen sangha. The zazenkai was held without him though he was back in Tucson when it took place. And he was sufficiently recovered that he agreed to go ahead with a Q&A that was on the schedule for the following Saturday at ZDS. The good spirits with which he had returned from Hawaii and which were prominent during Mary Ellen's visit in late July seemed not greatly dampened after her death a few weeks later. Something of the depression that had weighed Pat down on and off since his seminary years seemed to have lifted that summer and never came back.

Susan Weimer, Marsha Linehan appointments

The teaching role that Susan Weimer had described to Tom Santa in 2004 as part of her Head Resident duties grew beyond the Redemptorist Renewal Center as she began leading occasional zazenkais in Amarillo and serving a small group in Sierra Vista near Tucson. After she moved out of the Renewal Center, Pat quietly gave her permission to lead and conduct interviews for these groups, although without any public elevation to teacher status. At the October 2009 sesshin at the Renewal Center, in the sesshin officers' meeting, Pat said incidentally that he would be appointing Susan Weimer as an apprentice teacher instead of the usual sesshin closing ceremony.

It had been Pat's plan at the end of this sesshin to appoint both Susan Weimer and Marsha Linehan, a longtime student of Willigis Jäger and more recently of Pat, but Susan insisted that the ceremony be for her alone. Pat relented and told Marsha he would make her official appointment at a later date. It happened that the sesshin at which Susan was to be appointed had an unusual number of cancellations as well as several people who for various reasons had to leave early, making it a small remnant that would be present for the ceremony. Realizing this, Susan suggested to Pat that the event be delayed. He put his foot down telling her it was now or never. A few people arrived from Zen Desert Sangha for the ceremony — Susan had advertised to friends in advance — but as with the Kristen Larson appointment, there was no general announcement and the event was conducted without fanfare.

The immediate response was mixed, with some longtime Pat Hawk students expressing strong objections. The number of people opposed surprised Pat, who may have had in his mind that Susan could assist him with teaching at Zen Desert Sangha and perhaps take over when he retired.

The following Saturday was the Zen Desert Sangha annual sangha meeting and gala dinner. Pat attended, and as was his wont, mostly sat quietly, occasionally making a bland expression if his name came up, occasionally chuckling at something funny. Then just before the election of new officers, he made an announcement, saying he was feeling his mortality and he wanted to know who he should appoint as a successor. He said that this year he had appointed Kristen Larson and Susan Weimer as apprentice teachers and that he would appoint Marsha Linehan at the end of Rohatsu. "This is a year for appointing teachers, and I would like you to form a committee to discuss who among the ZDS people you would like to have as a teacher."

Some confused conversation ensued. Partway into it Pat said, "The nearest one would be Susan Weimer, but she's a divisive person." One of the senior ZDS members said, "She is?" Pat, perhaps smarting a little from the recent feedback about Susan's appointment, said vehemently, "Come on!" He explained that when Aitken Roshi appointed Manfred Steger as a teacher, some people were opposed to it and they left the sangha. He wanted the sangha to choose someone they felt they could get behind. The question was raised, "What about the dharma eye?" He said, "I'm just asking for suggestions. An appointment wouldn't necessarily follow directly." At one point, tilting his hand back and forth in a characteristic way, he said, "You know, this is a democracy. I don't want to impose someone that people don't feel they can work with." Shelly Dorsey commented that a prophet is never appreciated in his own land — that we know too much about each other — and could our feedback to Pat be that we think it should be someone from the outside. He nodded. Bob Wallin said he didn't think anyone at ZDS was ready to be a teacher.

There was buzz about this at the annual gala that evening continuing into the days and weeks that followed. The point was raised that it wasn't up to Pat to appoint a successor teacher for the sangha. He could make teachers as he saw fit, but Zen Desert Sangha would decide on its own teachers and might choose from among his appointees or not. Bob Walker's name came up as a possibility. Some wondered about considering teachers beyond the Diamond Sangha, perhaps from the Sanbo Kyodan. There was the need expressed to have someone on a regular basis, not just three or four times a year for sesshin, and then on the other hand, that it would be better to have a really good teacher from time to time rather than a mediocre one who could be around all the time. The conversation continued in the following weeks and months and became contentious.

Not long after the annual meeting, Susan sought permission to offer interviews at Zen Desert Sangha, and the item was put on the agenda for the January board of directors' meeting. She and Bob Wallin spoke on the phone the night before. Susan was interested in securing a teaching foothold at ZDS, and Bob was expressing that she not offer events such as zazenkais in case it would give

Pat a reason to cut back on his own offerings. The conversation became heated. Susan hung up, calling back later to smooth things over.[561] The next morning she left a note for Pat in his room justifying her position. She closed with, "I am in no rush to enter the ZDS theatre, and yet…"[562]

That morning before the board of directors meeting began, Bob suggested to Pat that he should recuse himself from the agenda item addressing whether or not to give Susan teaching privileges at ZDS since his presence would stifle discussion. Pat attended anyway — he had already promised Susan that he would. So although she wisely stayed away, he did not. When the item came up for discussion no one spoke for or against, and the ZDS Board voted in favor. It was an unfortunate beginning to Susan's teaching role at Zen Desert Sangha, one for which Pat took flak. The evident opposition to Susan may have contributed to his motivation to appoint Dan Dorsey as a second teacher associated with ZDS the following year.

The appointment of Marsha Linehan as an apprentice teacher was less controversial, likely because few among Pat's various sanghas knew her or even knew of her. Not long after he moved to Tucson, Pat connected with Marsha, a psychologist, psychotherapist and professor at the University of Washington, known internationally for her development of a mindfulness-based treatment for borderline personality disorder. She worked with Pat both as his student and as co-leader of an annual mindfulness retreat for mental health professionals. The health professionals came to learn from Marsha and quickly discovered that Pat Hawk could make a profound contribution to their understanding and practice. For his part, Pat was impressed with the quality of practice that the health professionals brought into interviews with him. He found a real depth. The mindfulness retreats were always filled to capacity and had a waiting list.

Marsha studied psychology in part to understand her own psyche — she was hospitalized in her teens for severe self-destructive behaviors including attempted suicide. During her hospitalization she vowed if she ever got out, she would come back to help others. A committed Catholic with a strong prayer life, she recounted how, "One night I was kneeling in [the chapel], looking up at the cross, and the whole place became gold — and suddenly I felt something coming toward me. It was this shimmering experience, and I just ran back to my room and said, 'I love myself.' It was the first time I remember talking to myself in the first person. I felt transformed."[563]

Though she was not necessarily delivered to a happily ever after, from then on, emotional storms no longer sent her into a self-destructive tailspin. She sought to understand what had changed and to develop a treatment that could bring about the change for others.

> I was a treatment researcher and I was a behavior therapist to the core. I got a grant to apply behavior therapy to suicidal behavior. I had asked to treat extremely suicidal people because I wanted to be able to show my treatment worked. So I walked right into a group of people who later came to be called Borderline Personality Disordered. Nor did I expect what happened. The treatment was catastrophic. … The problem is… you've never heard of tragedy until you hear the lives of these people. … It became clear to me that (a) I needed to teach them — you have to accept your childhood; if you don't have a home to go to for Christmas, you can't make one. I had to teach them to tolerate suffering until they could change. And (b) the therapist had to accept the patient and not just walk in with the technology of change.[564]

It came down to the need to develop what Marsha called radical acceptance — acceptance of what was fundamentally unacceptable simply because it *is*. There would be no way to move forward without that starting point. "Radical acceptance means completely and totally accepting something from the depths of your soul, with your heart and your mind. You stop fighting reality. When you stop fighting you suffer less."[565] Marsha described:

> Because I had had a totally transforming spiritual experience earlier that I had lost, I myself couldn't accept, and if I couldn't, how was I going to teach the patients and the therapists? That made me think I had to learn this myself so I could teach it. The question was how? So I wrote all these people I knew. I wanted the best teacher in the world. It was very cut and dried in my mind. Two names came in more than once: Willigis Jäger and [Jiyu Kennett at] Shasta Abbey. I looked them up. Willigis a Benedictine priest, Kennett[566] in Zen. I read her book[567] and liked her right away — anybody who could go into the situation she went into and survive. I asked my Chair — can I take time off without a sabbatical? He said is it work? Yes. Ok you can go.
>
> I thought, am I a woman or a Catholic, and decided on Shasta Abbey for three months then one month to the Benedictine priest. Shasta Abbey said — no, you can't come for three months. You can come for a weekend. If you like it and it's right… I thought, I don't care if I like it, this is irrelevant. So I packed up for three months and went down. The only thing I remember, I was terrified. I ate lunch with a person who did a lot of meditation. She said — listen, Marsha, not every single moment is going to be terrible. I knew within a couple of days that I had absolutely found what I was looking for.[568]

From Shasta Abbey, Marsha went to the first retreat Willigis Jäger led for the Northwest group in Portland, Oregon.[569] From there, she arranged a long-term stay at Haus St. Benedikt in Würzburg — originally planning a month but then taking a further leave from the University of Washington and staying for three months. She returned regularly thereafter for years. She was at Haus St. Benedikt when Pat arrived in August 1984 for his year with Willigis.

> Willigis was more hierarchical than he is now, or than Pat is now. The first in line [for dokusan] were people on koans. The second group were people who were his students, not on koans. The third group were non-students. I was a non-student, so I was always at the end of the line. Everything was fine with me. I loved being there. It was so beautiful. Willigis, and certainly the people working with him, had an unbelievable sense of beautiful. You could take dance class, which is how I got so into spiritual dance and put it in a lot of the stuff I do now. I went twice a year back over, then dropped to once a year. And except for one year, I've gone back every year.[570]

Although she met Pat in Germany, "…we never talked. For some reason, we never talked. I knew him from the Palisades retreat, and that's where I heard he was an alcoholic. And I remember that because I remember him sitting more in the back, and he looked like this little nobody from nowhere … and I was told by someone, over there that's Pat Hawk and he's an alcoholic. And I didn't talk to him there either."

Marsha attended a few retreats in the Northwest after Willigis had handed off to Pat. Although she went to interviews with Pat, she was focused on Willigis as her teacher, and Pat made no great impression.

> But other people would talk to me about Pat and say how wonderful he was. The reason I came [to work with Pat, approximately a decade later] is that Willigis sent me to him. Willigis was always trying to send me to Pat. He would say, "You should see Pat," or, "Ask Pat."
>
> I went to Pat — the thing about Pat, I was just talking to him before lunch, we were analyzing the difference between him and Willigis and why people come to him. I was telling him my opinion. … The difference is Willigis is beyond charismatic in every way. He is a person who is charismatic. Pat is not charismatic. If you go to dokusan with Willigis, it would be impossible to feel more understood and validated than with Willigis. He'll sit there and tell you he's never suffered in his life — so how he understands others so well is beyond me. You feel totally understood. On the other side, he talks nonsense-science and no matter how much you tell him that, he doesn't quit because he believes it all: evolution, we're moving into this new world; we're all going to be conscious; it drives me nuts. You've got to ignore that part. [Willigis] has a deep understanding and an intense love of everyone who comes in the door.

> Pat, on the other hand … here's how I describe Pat to Pat: "[You're] like a comedian on the radio. They talk in a monotone voice, then they say something hysterical, then back to monotone. You're like a radio comedian, very entertaining not in the same way as Willigis. Plus — you might have written your talks out, but you don't read them. [You are] able to talk about very deep things in ordinary language that you can listen to." So you don't get in a battle with him about what he's saying. He doesn't say esoteric things or outlandish things. He can talk about ultimate reality without using that word.[571]

Marsha and Pat began offering an annual mindfulness retreat for mental health professionals in 2000, the first one held in Santa Fe at Mountain Cloud Zen Center, thereafter moved to the Redemptorist Renewal Center except for one year when the Center could not accommodate a large group because of construction. Marsha remembered:

> For the mindfulness retreat talks, I said to him, "Ok Pat, I need you to give talks, but you can't use the words Jesus, Buddha or God." He crossed them out and substituted mindfulness language. That makes him just like Willigis. He can cross them all out and still give the exact same talk. The way he is in interview is very much like Willigis except — with Willigis you feel he'll start crying with you at any moment. Pat is not like that, but he is so radically accepting of anything you say or do. He has this ability to listen to what a person says and find something to give back to them that they need in that moment.
>
> I've said to many — it used to be I remembered every single thing Pat ever said to me because every single thing he said was life changing. … He has a capacity where — with Willigis, a lot is his emotional connection — with Pat, it's a lot more what he actually says to you, which is incisive and to the point, and somehow he's capable of saying exactly what someone needs at the moment.[572]

The 2009 Rohatsu sesshin at which Pat appointed Marsha Linehan as a Zen teacher in the Diamond Sangha was one of the only Zen sesshins she attended other than those at Haus St. Benedikt where the format was very much neutral, neither Zen nor Christian. Marsha explained that she sought the appointment, not because she wanted to be made a teacher — she was already a teacher. She had brought her mindfulness approach to thousands, either through in-person work with mental health professionals and her own patients, or indirectly through her well-known published works. Marsha's method not only improved quality of life for countless people, including the therapists who sought to practice it themselves in order to teach it to their patients, it literally saved lives among many who were otherwise suicidal.

Recognizing that her therapy had an important spiritual dimension, she said, "You have to not mix psychotherapy and spirituality. I'm trying to find a path where I can be on this path over here [psychotherapy], and that path over there with those looking for a spiritual path." She felt it would be most effective to develop this more spiritual approach as a credentialed spiritual teacher. It was also a means for her to build a community of Zen practice herself, something that was simply not on the table with psychotherapy.

The treatment Marsha developed, Dialectical Behavior Therapy — dialectical because it sought to integrate the contradictory elements of radical acceptance on the one hand and change on the other — was informed by her own practice. DBT has four stages, the first two being directed especially at the borderline personality disorder cohort the therapy was initially designed to treat. The third and fourth stages are understood to be powerful and important tools in the lives of any person. The first two stages seek to move the individual beyond catastrophic interference of self-destructive behaviors that prevent normative behavioral functioning, and the third stage develops the capacity of living life with ordinary happiness and unhappiness. The fourth stage is directed at questions like, "What now?" and, "Is this all there is?" There is no mental disorder, but the person is looking for more. With this in mind, Marsha developed the goal of joy as the fourth stage.

> So I'm in dokusan one day with Pat and he said, "I don't know what you're talking about Marsha when you say all this stuff about joy." And I said, "What are you talking about, don't you feel joy? I mean you're a Zen Master." He said, "Wouldn't you rather have freedom, so you can have anything? You don't have to have joy." I thought wow, that's better than joy. You don't have to have joy, you can have freedom. Freedom is a whole lot better than joy — you're ok with everything. But they said, we want joy. So I said how about freedom and joy. So it has now permeated my new book, it's in there all over the place. And if you listen to Pat it's in everything that he talks about. Willigis says you'll be happy. Pat says you'll be free of needing to be happy.[573]

After years of co-leading the mindfulness retreats with Marsha, as well as regular telephone then Skype dokusan, and with Willigis's blessing, Pat decided he would give her permission to teach Zen. The ceremony was like that for Susan and Kristen in that there was no dharma talk and no *shosan*. There was Jukai, although in Susan's case it was a renewal of Jukai. For Marsha, it was Jukai for the first time.

Pat gave Marsha the dharma name "Skillful Means." She said, "It's amazing he gave me the name Skillful Means. I autograph books a lot. I always write one of two things: 'When a book and a bird disagree, follow the bird.' In the other book I always write 'I wish you skillful means.,' It's uncanny [that he gave me that name] in that it fits so many aspects of my life."

Marsha's exuberant mixing of methods, though perhaps as true as could be to the fundamental Buddhist doctrine of *upaya*, was to cause ripples within the more orthodox Zen world in which Pat himself was a recognized Zen Master. He was untroubled by this. After that Rohatsu, with the teacher appointment accomplished, he said to her, "I think I've done something really dangerous putting you out there, Marsha."[574] It was as much a compliment to her energy and brilliance as it was a caution.

Other voices

Approximately eight years after the radiation treatment that he'd been told could give him a few more years, Pat's PSA levels were climbing alarmingly, and he consented to androgen deprivation therapy. His oncologist had been recommending the therapy for several years before Pat finally agreed to it. He googled his options thoroughly, deciding on intermittent rather than continuous therapy. The treatment was effective in a medical sense, in that six months after the first injection, his PSA had dropped from 350 to 12. But he hated it. Although the twinges of bone pain he had begun to experience were completely gone, hot flashes woke him at night and his energy level plummeted. He felt like an old man. He said, "I hear Gary Snyder is in the same situation, and he's going around saying 'Sisterhood is sweet.' "

He went on: "I thought Jesus was coming for me, but now I have to wait."

"And you're disappointed?"

"Yes I am!"

"Why did you do it?" Pat had said several times earlier that he was not interested in any further therapy.

"He threatened me with paralysis below the waist and loss of control of elimination function." Fate worse than death — or even than life as a weakened old man — for this always fastidious person.

Around this time — late 2009 — what had begun as a simple oral record of his recollections broadened to include additional voices. Other than the serendipitous opportunity to speak with Robert Aitken early on, I had not reached out to others for their stories, although when the project began to be referred to as biography I knew that would have to come. I pointed this out to Pat and asked how he would feel about me interviewing others — students, colleagues, friends —

who had their own stories and were part of his story. He agreed to it with mixed feelings, first resisting with a squinty, sour look. With the next breath, he looked quizzical and said, "It'll be interesting to hear what people have to say."

There was a resident practice period going on at the Redemptorist Renewal Center from late November to early January, and I took the opportunity to speak to some of the participants. Marsha Linehan was there, and we agreed to meet after lunch on her last day in town. The resident practice participants and Pat attended lunch together, and as was typical, Pat got up to leave before anyone else. Walking past Marsha's chair to say goodbye he made an amused comment, wondering what she might say about him. His smile was relaxed and genial. Marsha's own charm and charisma brought out the handsome in him.

Not everyone was as reflective and forthcoming as Marsha, and in early January, I met with Pat to discuss interview questions that could draw out people's recollections. In his manner of blowing hot and cold, on that day he was feeling edgy about the project. The week before, I'd had a conversation with his confrere and good friend Bob Halter. Bob had been rector at St Joseph's College seminary in Edgerton while Pat was principal there, and they'd been friends ever since. Bob, now these many years later having become a contemplation student of Pat's, was at the Christmas contemplative intensive retreat. I met him at the lunch afterward and mentioned the work on Pat's biography. Bob was raised in rural South Dakota, as straightforward and down to earth a person as one could hope to meet. He offered recollections of Pat, in a short time touching on their work together in the seminary, the intervention that sent Pat to Guest House for the first time, various of Pat's achievements. He mentioned it to Pat afterward. Although there was no subject in Bob's recollections that Pat had not touched on himself, something in the situation — possibly the extra attention back at the rectory — had left Pat feeling exposed. As we were discussing interview questions a few days later, at one point he stopped and said, "I'm embarrassed. All my life, I've played my cards close to my chest." Then relaxing, thinking disgruntledly of the effects of the androgen deprivation therapy he said, "I don't know the difference between embarrassed and a hot flash."

One of the people who came up as an obvious person to speak with was Greg Mayers. By the time they left Bishop DeFalco Retreat Center in 1998, the long, fruitful friendship of Pat and Greg was at an end. They no longer had news of each other except through confreres. Having heard dark rumors of their difficulties during the latter Amarillo years but no details, I asked Pat directly if he would talk about what happened. He said, "Nothing happened. Just, he went his way and I went mine." Later, when I was able to study the Aitken-Hawk correspondence, I came across a letter from Aitken to Pat saying, "… and I join you,

Pat, in your tribulations with Greg, and the situation there at Bishop DeFalco."[575] I thought, hmm — Exhibit A, and brought it up at our next meeting. Pat said, "Have you ever seen the movie, *The Lion in Winter*, starring Peter O'Toole and Katherine Hepburn? There's a scene in the movie where Henry and Eleanor have just had a knock-down, drag-out fight. He has left the room, and she is picking herself up. She sighs and says, 'Every family has its problems.' "[576] Pat gave a low chuckle.

Greg Mayers lived in Burlingame, California, having taken over in 2004 as teacher for the East-West Meditation group begun by Father Thomas Hand at Mercy Center. It was a former convent, now retreat center, set on beautiful grounds. Greg graciously agreed to a visit, and I spent about a week at the center, during which he gave generously of his time, including several long conversations. Although Greg's official community was at the Redemptorist Renewal Center in Tucson and the Director of RRC was the Superior to whom he reported, he lived as a hermit in an apartment near Mercy Center. The program for which he was director occupied a carpeted zendo/contemplation room, an office, part of which was set off as a dokusan/interview space, and a meeting room with well-stocked library mostly assembled by Thomas Hand. Scrolls, sculptures and other works of art, many from the East, looked out from walls and alcoves. The rooms were around an L-shaped corridor that opened by a side door to a well-tended Zen garden. Along one wall of the corridor was a striking set of the oxherding pictures, purchased years before by Greg, as by many people including Pat, from the gift shop at Haus St. Benedikt. Pat had framed his set and put them up in Amarillo, but since he'd moved to Tucson, they hadn't been taken out of the box they were packed in.

Greg was informal and unassuming. Conversation was easy. His group had a regular Wednesday evening sit preceded by social time and an opportunity to sign out books from the library. When I arrived for the social time, Greg saw me across the room and immediately came over like a good host, ushering me in and introducing me to the group. He seemed as different from Pat as could be.

About 15 had gathered for the Wednesday evening sit, and most went to dokusan. Greg gave a brief talk, extemporaneous, referring to a photo of Willigis Jäger he had recently placed on the shelves behind the teacher's seat in the zendo, and talking about his Zen/contemplative heritage, which, he pointed out, was the heritage of everyone there. We went for lunch together one day, to a restaurant with some good vegan options on the menu. Greg had been diagnosed with hepatocellular carcinoma in the early 2000s, at that time given a few years to live. At one point he had metastases to the brain, and there was talk of moving him into hospice. A longtime friend pleaded with him to go on a vegan diet and he eventually did, to please his friend. The tumors receded. At the time of our meeting, tumor markers were negative and a recent scan had found no cancer.

Back in Tucson after the visit to Greg, the first time I saw Pat was in dokusan. He greeted me with a slightly raised eyebrow evincing a rare curiosity. He was interested in all the details, which made a much longer dokusan than usual. In a pregnant silence after the main story was told, I said, "There are no bad guys in this story. Every person fully understood is completely justified." He said, "That's why I gave you this project." This was revisionist — the project came about by happenstance — but nonetheless, the sentiment was sincere. He was not interested in reviving old battles nor fanning any flames.

We sat down together a few days later to look at photos of Mercy Center inside and out, including a few of Greg. In those years of working together on his life story, I took lots of photos on any trip away from Tucson, since Pat obviously enjoyed looking at them. He seemed particularly interested in those from Greg's life. He tut-tutted at a photo of Greg looking heavy and unfit, examined photos of the library, the carpeted zendo, the Zen garden and the oxherding pictures on the wall with little comment. But not more than a week later, along the hallway in the St. Alphonsus building at the Renewal Center, Pat's own set of framed oxherding pictures appeared — finally taken out of their packing box twelve years after the move from Amarillo to Tucson.

Bodies... the exhibition

Bodies... the exhibition came to Tucson that summer of 2010, a display of human cadavers preserved by plastination, posed in lifelike positions and intricately dissected to reveal body systems. A private company put on the controversial exhibit for profit and had first opened in Florida some years earlier. It was still traveling the world in spite of ethical concerns about use of human remains for commercial purposes, the manner of procuring bodies, and the effect that viewing cadaveric material might have, especially on children. Because of my involvement with medical student education, I was interested in viewing the exhibit to determine whether it would be a good resource for our students' study of anatomy. It was July, and Pat was taking a month off from teaching. His mother had donated her body to the medical school at Washington University in St. Louis, and two of his aunts had done the same, so he was no stranger to the idea of human dissection. In fact, for a few years when I was teaching medical students in the gross anatomy lab, he had threatened to donate his body to the program in Tucson. On a long shot, I sent him an email inviting him to come to the exhibit. His reply came back in minutes. He would like to go.

He'd been holed up in the air-conditioned rectory for weeks, stepping out now and again for a smoke, otherwise taking shelter from Tucson's excruciating July heat. We headed into town on the early side, in time to be there when the exhibit opened. Entering dimly lit rooms with spotlights on bodies and body parts, each with some explanatory text, we shuffled in for a closer look. Pat paused often at the various displays. He was particularly interested in the male pelvis dissection. We stopped there, and I did my best to answer his questions about the anatomical relationships of the prostate, including which nerves and other structures were at risk when he had had his surgery. He nodded gravely, mentioning in a significant tone something he had alluded to earlier regarding the prostate cancer surgery he'd had while at Guest House — that he'd had a really good surgeon. Some displays were deliberately aimed at health education, including juxtaposition of obese and normal weight bodies, and dissection of a blackened smoker's lung, at which Pat raised a rueful, maybe even apologetic eyebrow.

We were just coming around to the last displays when a horde of students on a field trip arrived with loud remarks and erratic to-ing and fro-ing, suddenly chasing the dark museum-quiet, and driving us out into the hot bright sun to look for a place for lunch. When dropped off at the rectory that afternoon Pat seemed pretty pleased with the whole expedition, saying thanks for relieving the monotony of his time off.

Robert Aitken RIP

On Thursday, August 5, 2010, Robert Aitken died of pneumonia at Straub Hospital in Honolulu. Word came to Pat in the middle of the August sesshin at the Redemptorist Renewal Center. In time for the next day's sutra service, he added Aitken's dharma name, Gyo'un Chotan, to the line of ancestors, as well as the dedication, "…to you Robert Aitken Roshi, whose life, teaching, and writing have guided us through many years of the Diamond Sangha." Aitken was 93. There were no regrets or unfinished business in Pat's relationship with his old teacher. He had seen him in 2009 knowing it would almost certainly be the last time, and his equanimity was undisturbed by the loss.

Pat's teisho the next day took up Case 55 from the *Hekiganroku* in which Dogo and Zengen are making a condolence call.

> Zengen rapping on the coffin, says, "Alive or dead?" Dogo says, "I won't say alive, and I won't say dead." Zengen threatens to hit Dogo if he won't say. Dogo says, "You may hit me, but I won't say." After Dogo has died, Zengen goes to another teacher, Sekiso, tells him the story and asks again, "Alive or dead?" Sekiso says, "I won't say alive, and I won't say dead."

Zengen says, "Why won't you say?" Sekiso says, "I won't say, I won't say." Whereupon Zengen has an insight.[577]

Pat juxtaposed this story with the last chapter of Aitken's book, *Zen Master Raven*:

> Raven took his perch on the Assembly Oak and addressed a special meeting of the Tall spruce community saying, "It's time for me to be moving on."
> Porcupine asked, "Where will you be going?"
> Raven said, "Where cedar roots stand bare in the creek."
> A hush fell over the circle. Grouse could be heard sniffling. At last Porcupine asked, "Do you have any last words for us?"
> Raven said, "Trust."[578]

Pat closed the book, paused a long moment, then repeated, "Trust."

He continued with a recollection of going up to Hawaii's Punchbowl Cemetery with Aitken not long after Anne's death, wandering among the graves, Aitken now and again commenting on old friends buried there.

> Aitken said, "Anne always thought that when you died that's it, nothing left. Poof, it's all gone."
> Pat asked, "What about you, Roshi?"
> "Well you know I've attended some deaths and I've always felt something was lingering. Something was hanging around. What about you?"
> Pat said, "I agree with Anne."

Pat went on to recount a conversation with Aitken years after Anne had died. Pat was visiting Aitken at his retirement home at Kaimu on the Big Island, as he did every January for some years. "We were strolling along the beach, and Aitken asked, 'Where do you see yourself in five years?' I said, 'Dead.' " Pat's oncologist, monitoring his PSA levels regularly, was recommending another radiation treatment. "Aitken wasn't in very good shape himself and hadn't been for years. We were all expecting him to drop off and he just kept going. And he said, 'Yes, I see myself dead also. It will be a relief.' " Telling the story in his teisho, Pat said, "This just goes to prove that any prediction made by a Zen master is liable not to come true. I'm still here. And he was here until last week." Pat ended the teisho where he'd begun, reflecting on Zengen's words to Dogo:

> Only parts face death, not the whole. This is where the trust comes in. Like all opposites, being and nonbeing, form and non-form are an inseparable unity, and behind their apparent difference they ARE each other. Living and dying, birth and death are simply two different ways of viewing this moment. Every moment is the last moment, every moment is the first moment. The

> eternal and the timeless now is an awareness which knows neither past nor future. No boundary, no tomorrow, nothing in front of it, nothing behind it. And that's the very condition of death. To accept death is to be totally comfortable living without a future. Living in this present beyond time. So I can't say. The fact is, I won't.[579]

As soon as the memorial date was announced — August 22 — Pat made plans to attend. I went too, knowing it would be the only chance to see him in that place and milieu that had been so important in his growth as a Catholic priest to a Zen master. Pat stayed at the five-star Pacific Beach Hotel in Waikiki, using his sabbatical fund to cover airfare and accommodation. Saturday morning, the day before the memorial, I picked him up from his hotel to drive across the island to Kaneohe, where Aitken's son Tom lived. As a favor to those organizing the memorial, we were to pick up a box of Aitken's ashes that had been left at the funeral home inadvertently, the agent at first not realizing there were two boxes.

We drove across the island, Pat tentatively giving directions. As prearranged, Pat called Tom Aitken when we got close and he came down to the main road to meet us. Tom shook hands with Pat and gave him the ashes. He told us about an interesting temple at a nearby cemetery that he thought we might like to see. We were in no hurry to get back and set off to do a little sightseeing, but Pat, his gastrointestinal system unpredictable ever since the radiation treatment some years before, suddenly needed a restroom, and since we couldn't easily find one, decided he wanted to go straight back to his hotel.

I dropped him off and arrived back at Palolo with the box of ashes, running first into the administrator, Roland Sugimoto, at the door to the kitchen. Indicating the box, I explained that here were Aitken's ashes. He said, "No we already have the ashes." It took a few tries — both gravity and humor in the exchange — to convey that there'd been a mistake at the funeral home, but that now we had both boxes. Ginger Ikenberry, then templekeeper, organized an impromptu ceremony to combine the ashes. She and I had gone shopping the night before to find a suitable container in which the ashes could be placed for the memorial, after which they were to be divided into four portions and sent to destinations Aitken himself had specified, including Sydney Zen Centre in Australia, Ring of Bone in California, and of course Palolo's columbarium. Ginger had selected a few large tea towels in solid colors with "Mu" — by happenstance the name of the tea towel company — embossed on them. Eido Frances Carney, an old friend of Aitken who had come from Olympia, Washington, for the memorial, sewed the towels into a sac using thread from Anne Aitken's sewing box. The sac was lined with a plastic bag to keep the ashes out of the fabric.

A small group including Ginger, Carolyn Glass, a longtime caregiver of Aitken, and Nelson Foster, gathered in the zendo of the teacher's quarters. After some brief planning, Eido Frances and Ginger poured the ashes from each box into the single sac, puffs of fine ash rising in the air, while all chanted the "Heart Sutra," then "Great Vows." The sac with combined ashes was covered completely and decoratively with large tea leaves, then placed on the main altar.

Aitken had specified that his memorial should begin solemnly and end joyously, a wish that was carried out. An overflow crowd bulged out of the Zendo. After preliminary chanting, Michael Kieran gave a brief dharma talk and all who wished were invited to approach the altar and offer incense and words to Aitken directly. Many took the opportunity. Pat was among the first to rise, with remarks characteristically brief, not without humor. He began by saying, "You took in a sinister papist…" finishing with words of gratitude. Nelson spoke of love and friction, sympathizing with Aitken for how difficult it must have been when Nelson didn't do things his way. Perle Besserman performed a dance.

Many came from around the world despite very short notice: Gilly Coote from Australia; Marian Morgan from Britain; David Loy, dharma brother of Aitken; Alan Senauke, Joe Bobrow, David Weinstein, and many others. Among the locals were some who had been students alongside Pat and who had attended his first sesshin in September 1989, including Vicki and Don Stoddard, Doug Codiga, Perle Besserman and Manfred Steger. A crowded lunch on the lanai followed the formal memorial and segued to an informal sharing of recollections in the afternoon. Pat stayed until 4:30, then began looking tired and uncomfortable, gratefully accepting the offer of a ride back to his hotel.

The next day I had arranged to work with Hawk-related correspondence in the Aitken Papers at the University of Hawaii, after which Pat and I were to have supper together. He called to say he was still having GI troubles and would have to beg off. Instead, I joined a small group at Kaimana Beach for a picnic of leftover peanut butter and jelly sandwiches and other odds and ends from the memorial lunch, enjoying the sunset while we drank a few bottles of wine so that there would be corks of the right size to plug the urns containing Aitken's ashes. Walking back along the beach under a setting sun, Vicki Stoddard spoke of her love for Pat, saying he's a real ace in the hole, perhaps the best teacher from Aitken Roshi. She told of how in her first dokusan with Pat he finished by saying, "Is there anything else?" She said this was a revelation. That he could care for her in this way, somehow in contrast to Aitken. Aitken's dark side had come up in the sharing circle that afternoon — that he could be unapproachable, distant. I relayed Vicki's comments to Pat, and he said Bob Walker told him that the phrase, "Is there anything else," was the most useful thing Pat had given him.

"Useful how?"

"Useful for ending the conversation!"

Tuesday, Pat was to fly back to Tucson. He had to be out of his hotel by 11:00 AM, and his flight wasn't until 7:00 in the evening. He asked if I would entertain him in the meantime and we planned a little sightseeing. In the event, Pat looked so weary when I picked him up, we had lunch at a Thai restaurant, then went back to Palolo. The restaurant had a bar and Pat ordered a coconut drink. When it arrived looking suspiciously like a cocktail, he suddenly worried that it might have alcohol in it. I asked if I should taste it and he pushed it over to me without a word. The report was, terribly sweet but with no suggestion of alcohol. He drank it.

Back at Palolo, Pat was given the teachers' quarters to rest in until time to go to the airport. Before settling down, he showed off the wood frame of a doorway he had spent hours working on more than 20 years before as one of the students on the construction crews building Palolo. When it was time to leave, I came out to find him deep in reflection leaning against the lanai railing, looking across to the *hojo* (a small freestanding building used for dokusan).

We crawled to the airport in Honolulu rush hour traffic. After a time in silence, looking out to the green hills beyond the city, Pat said, "It's a long, slow goodbye." He spoke it slowly, thoughtfully.

"Do you feel nostalgic?"

"No."

"Do you ever feel nostalgic?"

"No."

Pat had a horrible flight, his guts relentless. Safely back in his office in Tucson he said, "I could barely keep my dignity." From that time forward, he swore off travel, canceling plans to attend his niece's wedding in October in Granite City.

Steps toward succession

Zen Desert Sangha (ZDS) held a memorial service for Aitken on August 14 in Tucson, and somehow during the refreshments and socializing that followed, without any formal announcement, it came to be generally known that Pat had offered Dan Dorsey permission to teach and Dan had accepted. Ever since Pat had appointed Susan Weimer, he'd been under pressure from various quarters to provide ZDS with an alternative. His request for suggestions back in October 2009 had yielded about a half dozen names and no clear front runner. Dan had recently finished the koan curriculum, and he had been a strong presence for years, teaching a class on Buddhism at the local college and giving talks on Buddhism at ZDS. He had lots of tanto experience, a steady, low-key manner, and importantly, he was willing.

Dan Dorsey had started sitting during his freshman year at college and had joined Zen Desert Sangha before Pat offered sesshin there for the first time. Looking back, he said:

> I read a book that a lot of people read who come to Zen — Kapleau's *Three Pillars [of Zen]*.[580] Of course, there wasn't much support at Stephen F. Austin State University in Nacogdoches, Texas. [He chuckled.] We were raised, my brother and I, in the Disciples of Christ Church, which was closely attached to Texas Christian University, where my grandfather was the history department head for many years. He had a degree in divinity and went to TCU himself right after WWI. So we had this close association. And we were made to go to Sunday school every week until we were 16. At that point, my mother told us we could decide for ourselves whether we wanted to go or not. And I stopped going the day I turned 16. I just wasn't attracted to Christianity the way it was taught there. Of course, there was no contemplative aspect there at all, in most mainstream branches of Christianity.
>
> So I bought some incense and started sitting. There was this empty apartment and I started sitting in this bathroom of this empty apartment next to mine. I would slip in there at night and light incense and try to sit. I'm one of those people that just always for some reason took to it early. Karma or whatever. I made myself a sitting bench out of two concrete blocks and a piece of wood. Course I didn't know what I was doing, just followed along with the book. ... After I graduated from college, I went to Japan for two years and worked for the National Security Administration, intercepting Chinese and Soviet communications in far northern Japan. Then I still had two years left on my commitment, and I was stationed here at Fort Huachuca [Arizona]. When I got out of the army, I had the GI Bill so I came here to Tucson in late 1985 and enrolled in the landscape architecture program.
>
> I found ZDS shortly after. There were only five of us at the time. Bob Wallin, myself, Paul Markl, Anne Murray and one or two other people who would come regularly. We sat in a trailer, in a mobile home park on Hedrick Street. I asked my teacher, Nishijima Roshi* from Japan if he would come over and do a tour of the US and stop in Tucson and give a talk. That was in about 1988. He came over and stayed with me and gave a talk — it was just a one-day thing with everyone. He was part of what was called the Japanese Men's Bamboo Society and they had tons of money. He was Soto.†

---

* Gudo Wafu Nishijima (1919-2014), Japanese Zen Buddhist priest and teacher.

† Soto Zen: one of the two major Zen schools in the United States.

> His teacher was Kodo Sawaki Roshi. Nishijima wrote an entire translation of Dogen's *Shobogenzo*.[581] So I started out in the Soto tradition in Japan.[582]

Dan attended a talk Pat gave at the University of Arizona in about 1990. "I remember Pat got physically up on the table to demonstrate zazen. Somebody asked him, what is the essence of Zen, and he got up on the table in front of the class and demonstrated the lotus posture. Stuck a couple of books under him. He said, 'This is the way we sit.' "

Like many others, Dan recognized Pat as his teacher not from any public appearance but as soon as he met with him in dokusan. He was untroubled by the fact that here was a Catholic priest.

> I think I would have been more disturbed by it if Pat had tried to put those together into some new thing. But he — especially as he went on — got more and more, "When we're doing a Zen retreat, we'll do a Zen retreat and when doing a CIR [contemplative intensive retreat] we're doing a Christian thing." And I liked that he didn't encourage anyone to do anything else. No pressure. He accepted everyone. I liked the way Pat accepted everyone no matter what background you were from.

Years later, shortly after Pat had appointed him as an apprentice teacher, Dan reflected:

> Of all the Zen teachers and Roshis I've met, I've found Pat to be absolutely unique. He is someone who I believe has truly realized emptiness. I mean, that's been a big part of his teaching. And he really lives that out. What I admire a lot about Pat — very attracted to him as a teacher — is he does not exude any neediness. Oftentimes Zen teachers, even subtly, exude that they need something from the student. Pat exudes none of that. And I believe Pat, in his deep realization of emptiness, also has this incredible acceptance. When you're in his presence — it's not an embrace or anything. It's just, he's like a mirror.[583]

Pat decided Dan's appointment as apprentice teacher would take place at the end of the zazenkai, September 9, 2010. He emphasized to the sesshin coordinator that he wanted it advertised widely so that as many ZDS people as possible would attend. He was making it clear that when he himself had to relinquish the torch, there would be options to choose from. During the reception after the appointment, Pat was asked in a side conversation who he thought would become the teacher at ZDS, Dan or Susan. Chuckling, he said he didn't know, Susan and Dan could fight it out.

The ceremony followed the same simple format Pat had used for Kristen (March 2009), Susan (October 2009) and Marsha (December 2009): chanting, renewal of Jukai, presentation of the koan book to the new teacher, and a few words spoken by Pat. Unlike with the appointments of Leonard Marcel (December 1996) and Bob Walker (October 1999), there was no dharma talk and no *shosan.*

Pat seemed pleased and confident in taking this step with Dan. As he finished his brief remarks, he said to him, "Upright," like a closing statement. He trusted that with Dan there would be no intrigue, no scandals, no drama, just the steady effort that was Dan's signature. Dan was a steadying influence for Zen Desert Sangha from his early days there, skilled at practical tasks, with an interest in the characters, lineages, doctrines and lore of Buddhism, and with a solid practice.

Dan, Susan Weimer and Kristen Larson — three of Pat's four new teachers — attended the October sesshin that fall. Although Pat was the main teacher for the sesshin, the three apprentices gave him a break in the evenings by offering interviews during the last period of each day. It created a wild time for the jisha, who had to keep track of three different colors of cards to manage three lines for the three teachers, but it gave the participants a chance to work with the new teachers, and released Pat to get some rest.

The sesshin ended with a Jukai ceremony for Lee Zurcher, a student of Kristen's who came with her to Tucson from the northwest, since Kristen herself, as an apprentice, could not preside over Jukai. Lee gave a strong presentation, a reminder that regardless of Kristen's rather recent official appointment as a teacher, she had been teaching for years.

That December, Leonard Marcel came from Oregon to help Pat with Rohatsu. Instead of having his newer appointees in teaching roles, Pat had them serve as officers, Dan as tanto, Susan as ino, and Kristen as jisha. Pat and Leonard took turns offering teisho, their styles a contrast. They both began in the traditional way with a koan or case. Both situated the main players of the koan in their time and lineage, spun off tangents to related cases, told anecdotes — whatever worked to present the kernel, the nature of the message more in the open space around words than in didactic argument. Their differences came through partly in the occasional "you should" in Leonard's talks, the more direct exhortation to practice, sometimes with a slight edge of scolding. Pat could not scold to save his life. He tended more toward the passive aggressive if he really wanted to shift a person's behavior, but much more often, and certainly in the context of teisho, he simply accepted his hearers as they were.

Another divergence in approach was that after Pat formally delivered the text of the case and before he began the main presentation, he would always say,

"Sit comfortably." Leonard, in contrast, expected people to sit in formal zazen posture. Absent the option to look at the teacher's face as he spoke, words and intonation had to carry the entire message. Pat's "sit comfortably" came from Aitken. It was the custom in the Diamond Sangha, and before that in the Sanbo Kyodan, to invite participants to relax their posture and face the speaker. At the signal to sit comfortably, there was a shuffling as people unfolded their legs, turned on their cushions, leaned on a wall if one was nearby. For many, it was not so much abandoning the discipline of attentive sitting as it was allowing full attention to the presenter, including gesture and facial expression as well as voice.

Pat would take advantage of his listeners facing him to make piercing eye contact, gesture, raise a dubious eyebrow, or pause and form a subtle grin. His listeners were right with him. The slightest humor drew a ripple of chuckling. Though he could be beautifully fluent with language, it was not his main medium. The message came through sheer presence, a presence that registered most strongly face to face.

At the closing lunch after sesshin, a participant accustomed to Pat's more informal approach suggested to Leonard that requiring the formal posture for teisho excludes some of the richness of the presentation and "makes for a weaker tea." Leonard said, "Oh no! It makes for a stronger tea." Pat, sitting at Leonard's elbow, said, "Good luck. I've been trying to tell him that for years." The teacher has little reach over the later direction of his heirs. Such is the fecundity of the dharma.

Working on Colin, 2010

In the interviews of Pat about his life he tended toward the circumspect, so that on the first pass through any subject or period, I picked up the skeleton of events but very little detail and even less reflection. Coming at events at different times and from different angles helped put flesh on the bones of his stories. In this vein, we sometimes talked about books he'd read at different times, or movies, or travel — some topic to cut across eras.

One day, talking about books he'd studied in the seminary, he suddenly got up, saying, "Come with me." He led me outside, across the parking lot and down to the Renewal Center library, to a wall of shelves at the back that held Redemptorist books. There were the multi-volume works of Alphonsus of Liguori, books about other Redemptorist saints, histories of the congregation, contemporary books by and about Redemptorists, works about theology and Vatican II, various editions of *Constitutions and Statutes* — the Redemptorist Rule, several copies of the pocket-sized *Monthly Virtues*, and some rather dated-looking volumes with worn dust jackets that Pat began pulling off the shelf.

"We read these in my novitiate," he said. Most that he indicated were by Louis Colin, a French Redemptorist who published in the 1950s, and whose works translated into English were used extensively in Redemptorist formation back in Pat's day. The books served as the main reminder for Pat of the training he'd had in his novitiate. Going through them together, he was both interested and detached — whatever it may have meant during his novitiate, Colin's world was not his world now.

Looking for Pat's impressions, I read several of these books and noted passages to ask him about. I read him a short excerpt that included the word "distraint": "…this complete 'distraint' of God upon the consecrated soul necessarily implies the idea of separation. Because Jesus is the great Consecrated, He is also the great Separated." The word distraint was unknown to either of us and Pat leapt up to get the dictionary. "How do you spell that word? 'Distraining, distrainable, distrain: to press, compress or grasp tightly. To squeeze. Obsolete. To hold captive or in constraint; to control by force, subdue.' So the distraint of God upon the consecrated soul that separates the religious from the rest of the world. Yeah. Being grasped by God, eh?" After a pause, he said, "It's got an extreme ring to it now." He granted there may be a certain appeal to the view, but he was more struck by the dualism, which to him, characterized the Christian path.

Pat did not place his experience as a young boy, the experience that drew him to the priesthood, "something in the candles and the incense," in the same box as Colin's sanctity. Pat said, "This is what was presented to us. And I didn't have the vocabulary to talk about those experiential kinds of things. You were given all this conceptual framework."

"Did you buy it?"

"At that time, yes."

"Was it any sort of disconnect with that other realm?"

"No, no. That experiential realm has always been the same, untouched. However, I tell different stories about it now. It's kind of inexhaustible in the ways of expressing it. It took a while, more experience to work out that this is all metaphorical."

"But out in the general faithful … there is still very much the notion that it's all in the afterlife."

"Yeah, some people still take it all literally."

Considering the vow of poverty in the context of life in a well-appointed rectory with dazzling views, state-of-the-art sound system and wide-screen TV, Pat shrugged. "I think generally not just with us but with all groups we just kept pace with the general culture. As economics improved for everybody, it improved for us too."

Browsing Colin's chapter on chastity, Pat raised an eyebrow and gave a somber chuckle at the obvious inadequacy of the presentation, so evident from the ever-worsening scandal of sex abuse by clergy. In that context, Colin goes so far as to say, "Pleasure, even when it is legitimate — and notice that the word appears nowhere in the Gospels — is a poison." This reminded Pat of a comment of one of his confreres. "The other night Tom Santa, he was president and publisher of the Redemptorist magazine, *Liguorian*, told of one of the times they got the biggest number of protest letters was when they put a picture of the laughing Christ on the front of the *Liguorian*." However contemporary Catholics were actually living, the ideal of renunciation was alive and well in the third millennium CE.

The chapters on obedience recalled for Pat the crisis at Oconomowoc in the 1960s. A fellow seminarian from those days had just visited Tucson. "You know the guy I took to the airport yesterday? HD, we always called him. He is one of the ones who got the ax. Extremely intelligent man. He was the one who argued Karl Rahner with the professor of dogmatic theology… That was a prelude to being kicked out. He wasn't kicked out, because he was in final vows, but they told him they would not ordain him. We're great friends. He came to make a retreat at Desert House but I picked him up at the airport, took him to San Xavier. Yak yak yak. It's like he never left. It's really too bad. It should not have happened. There was another guy in his class in final vows — they told him they were not going to ordain him. But he stuck with us. Lived in the novitiate, did farmwork then they finally realized their mistake and he got ordained."

He paused, then, "How did I get off on that. What was my point? What were we talking about?" I reminded him: "The notion of submission of the intellect."

> Well at any rate. I don't know — just the ferment. We just — some guys did not submit. Others did. I was in temporary vows. And they were gonna kick me out. But I went around to the faculty and got support and they allowed me to renew my temporary vows for one more year before they allowed me to be perpetually professed. So I knuckled down and shut up. But I'm trying to contrast something here. Trying to give you a feel for what it was like there at that time.[584]

We talked about the great emphasis on death and the afterlife — that the sacrifice inherent in the vows will only be perfect after death. "Do you think that enters into any desire you may have to die?" He had made it clear on occasion that he would welcome death, that it was the getting there he found arduous. "No, no, that's something different. I'm tired. Just tired. The obedience now is just to draw the next breath."

In Colin's reflections on the discernment of vocation, there is a passage that resonates with the story Pat tells of his own boyhood:

> Some appear to have known their undeviating path from the earliest years, and thanks to an extraordinary concomitance of providential circumstances. At the age of six or seven, they were ready, saying, very seriously: 'Mommy, I'm going to be a priest; Daddy, I'm going to be a nun.' Their course is like a river flowing from its source to the ocean between flowery banks, through a broad plain, slowly and majestically, without encountering a single obstacle.[585]

I asked him, "Does that sound like you?" He said, "Yeah. But there were obstacles. Very poetic and flowery, but yes, right."

Colin again: "To this must be added the fact, that those in authority have not only the right, but the duty to see that their charges acquire solid virtues, and to try out their powers of resistance." Pat looked skeptical.

I said, "Like Zen masters with their sticks. I wonder if in your teaching as a Zen master, you do that to people."

"What, test them? No. If I make errors, it's in the opposite direction. I think. Compared to other masters."

"I've heard you say that, of course. But I think also you sometimes do push powers of resistance."

"Well, I try not to falsify. I try not to give the impression that this practice is pie-in-the-sky-by-and-by, and if you keep going it'll be wonderful."

It was November 2010, and Colin's pre-Vatican II orthodoxy was suddenly brought closer. In the middle of the month, the American Conference of Catholic Bishops elected Archbishop Dolan of New York to be their president. Not only was he a very conservative choice, it was a departure from the tradition of electing the vice president, who at the time was Bishop Gerald Kicanas of Tucson, representing a more liberal, social justice-oriented stance.[586]

The Redemptorists as a congregation, unlike diocesan priests, are independent of the bishop. Rather, they are under the direct authority of Rome. Nonetheless, Kicanas had been approached more than once by local conservative Catholics disturbed that there was a Catholic priest doubling as a Zen Master operating within the diocese. Kicanas handled the situation diplomatically, asking only that Pat keep a low profile. Pat had mixed feelings about the passing over of Kicanas for the highest office. "It's best to keep him local, and now he'll probably be here till he retires. But it just shows how most of the bishops in the country are locked into the past. Ultra, ultra conservative. Abortion, gay marriage. That's all they can think of. You know — what are they there for! They're there to preach the gospel.

The Church has a long history of social teaching. Where are they? Nowhere! That's the bad side. Even, one of the bishops described it as disgraceful. A real slap in the face."

As Pat finished this comment, I warned him that the digital recorder was running in case he'd rather not say anything radical. "What me? Radical? You don't know what you're talking about." He was a Zen Master offering sesshin and the like well within the range of any standard Zen practice, if there can be said to be such a thing — his was not a watered-down Zen — but he was careful to stay under the radar of the Catholic Church hierarchy as much as he could.

Colin speaks of observing the rule of the congregation in a way reminiscent of what is often heard in Zen circles, that all one needs is to practice diligently and the opening will come. For Colin, "No one can keep [the rule] scrupulously, faithfully and lovingly, without making immense progress on the road of perfection…" A message that Pat spoke commonly to his Zen students was that the realization experience was open to everyone, it was simply a matter of adhering to the practice. As we considered this, he clarified that the road to perfection Colin speaks of is not to be understood as a path toward mystical experience. "That was always set in front of us as an extraordinary grace that you should not look for. That's not for you, sort of thing. Well, who was it for? Not for you! As Willigis said, and I suppose it kind of applied to religious superiors too — Willigis always used to say, 'Nothing is more upsetting for a bishop than the rumor that there might be a saint in his diocese.' "

"Because saints are trouble?"

"Yeah. They're free."

I said, "Colin writes, 'His freedom from captivity dates from his profession: on that day, one of the finest of his life, of which he cannot think without joy and an immense gratitude to God, the net was broken and the bird flew away.' "

Pat chuckled. "Purple passage."

"I thought of your homily [on grace] on your 40th anniversary," I said.

"Was it that bad?"

"No, it wasn't bad. But just that notion of grace. This sounds very flowery now. At the time, would you have identified with that?"

"At the time we would have all bent over and vomited. I mean, even in those days, we didn't go in for that kind of language. Used to be quite a bit of mockery of some of the stuff we had to read."

Regarding the fourth vow, of perseverance, unique to Redemptorists, much of the exhortation to persevere as discussed in Colin's *The Practice of the Vows* is related to gratitude. Was Pat grateful for the life the Redemptorists have given him?

"Oh yeah."

"Then and now?"

"Sure. I probably would be in jail if it weren't for the Redemptorists.

"In jail for what?"

"Being stupid. I don't know. Something." His tone was not casual, and there was a silence before we picked up on another subject.

There is nothing in any of the rich stories and materials gathered from all stages of Pat's life that would suggest that he ever did anything illegal. But in knowing Pat, one sometimes had a sense that there was something dark in him that he kept from the world. Certainly, a darkness developed in him during his years in the seminary and dogged him in varying degrees afterward.

Though Colin speaks of all sorts of temptations that challenge the vows, there was nothing about addiction, and Pat recalled no mention of addiction during his seminary years.

> Probably more denial than anything. There was never any cover-up that drinking was a bad thing. But it was controlled. Nobody was supposed to have their own supply. Everything, as usual, was in common. And it was locked up, unlocked for special occasions. For a cocktail before supper, let's say. Or in the evenings it was opened up and people sat around talking. I remember some great talking sessions when groups got together. Like those times we got together for those talking sessions we used to do in the summer. Twenty guys and the evenings were spent yakking, yakking, yakking then go to bed. But it was all still done out in the open. It's when people started sneaking their own, drinking out of view of everybody, that it got bad. And it was always something that was taken care of on the QT.

In fact, Guest House had been founded in 1956, the year Pat entered the seminary, but he didn't become aware of its existence until he was sent there.

> And instead of sending alcoholics to what we used to call ecclesiastical prisons — which is what they were, they just locked you up — there was Guest House. And it was all run by laypeople, the clergy didn't have anything to do with it. It was supported by religious orders and diocese but there was no clergy involved in the running of it whatsoever. Which I thought was one of its important features. Because of the hangover from the past of treating alcoholics as moral failures. Failure of will, etc. They started treating it as a condition that needs to be treated. ... Attitudes changed. But you know what the big problem is now? Gambling. Addiction to gambling. And the people who do the treatment say it's the hardest thing to eradicate. To relieve someone of the burden of that addiction. It's almost impossible.

I asked, "How does it arise?"

"Casinos! That's how it arises."

"Have you ever been to a casino?"

"Never. Never set foot in one. I'm such a penny pincher I can't imagine spending a dime that wouldn't come back to me in some way. I've got my own problems and that's not one of them."

When we were through with considering passages in *Practice of the Vows*, I asked Pat, "Do you think reading Colin during your novitiate was useful?"

"Gee it was so long ago. It's hard to remember how it was. Sometimes I wonder how I got through with all the stuff that was thrown at us. I suppose it had some positive effect. But how much of that sticks I don't know."

Intimacy, transference

Whatever cautions and repressions Pat encountered in his seminary training, to many he seemed an asexual being, and though always fastidiously groomed, he could seem willfully plain. Yet in the depths of intimacy that filled Pat's interview room he was transformed, and for some, what had been unremarkable became handsome.

Several of the women I spoke with acknowledged falling in love with Pat. One had the sense to distance herself until the feeling passed. Another, during a time when there was discussion about Pat taking over the sangha in Honolulu, fantasized about marrying him and moving to Hawaii. During the Amarillo years, a student travelled faithfully to retreats, leaving her husband and young children at home, intent on spending every minute she could with Pat. Passionate by nature, during one Rohatsu sesshin she stormed out from dokusan before Pat could ring the bell, packed her car and left in a huff never to come back, allegedly because Pat had rejected a proposal of marriage. Yet another woman sent a formal marriage proposal in a long letter detailing how he could transition out of the priesthood and into lay life, what their finances would be, where they would live.

Another student remembered, "There was clearly a time when I thought Pat walked on water. I absolutely had the whole, 'Take me, take me wherever, whatever; you say jump, I say how high' or probably even start jumping before he even asks. No questions, no hesitancy. At one point Pat knew it was time to cut that off. Pat took aim and shot one arrow and then took the tremendous beating I gave him in response to it. And just took it, and took it, and took it and never said a word."

It wasn't just the women. There was a deep fulfillment in the personal encounters with Pat in dokusan and interview, with the sense that he saw you completely and accepted you completely. It brought a moment of salvation from whatever angst, whatever suffering one carried. It is a rare experience, one that many people coming to Pat had only with Pat. In that experience, the small, quiet, unobtrusive man could easily become the white knight, the wise, the all-good, the handsome prince. People wanted simply to be near him. For some, it was intoxicating and aphrodisiac.

Pancho Burke told this story about how he dodged the inclination to elevate Pat above the human:

> At one point, Pat asked me if I'd seen the movie *Clerks* when it first came out. So I just rented it on my way home. We were living in a little trailer just over the hill, and I rented *Clerks* and went home and watched that and laughed my ass off. I was doing the laundry a while later and hanging up clothes and I asked myself, okay what is it that keeps somebody human in your mind. You know, allows them to retain their full humanity no matter how great they are or how many awards they've won. Keep their feet of clay. What can you think about a person that keeps them human? And from *Clerks* I sort of got this image of how pitifully human we are in our sexuality. ... And there was that dimension in Pat. It was actually very humble and very human.[587]

Pat was aware of transference as a phenomenon in counseling relationships: the psychological sleight of hand where significant relationships from the early life of the student are re-constellated in the teacher-student relationship, and the student imposes on the teacher the unfulfilled expectations from the earlier relationship. The third of five cautions given by Aitken to Pat and the other three dharma heirs as part of their transmission ceremony stated, "Respect transference from your students and turn it back with support of their practice." Transference became a regular topic for discussion in Diamond Sangha Teachers' Circle meetings. There were important possibilities for growth of the student if the emotionally-laden transference relationship could be carried by the teacher, rather than deflected, exploited or rejected. The student could integrate the wound from childhood, then grow up and take back to themselves the power temporarily bestowed on the teacher, and in this way, become whole.

Of course, it was not just students who were subject to the heady intensity of the transference. A teacher had to be aware of their own tendency to buy into the student's adoration, to enjoy the feeling of being super-parent or super-lover and worst of all, to take advantage of the student's total offering of self and let it devolve into a sexual relationship. This was happening in the Zen world beyond Amarillo, with stories of teacher impropriety — Chögyam Trungpa, Taizan Maezumi, Eido Shimano, Richard Baker, and soon to be many others rumored or exposed — becoming very much part of Western Zen lore.

One could sometimes see in the adoring looks, the desire to be near, the sweet glances and the jealousies, that a sexual dimension was constellated around Pat. Once during a discussion at a Diamond Sangha Teachers' Circle meeting, Aitken said, "I get the impression that Pat runs from transference." Pat said, "Yes, as fast as my little legs will take me." In fact, he was gentle with the childlike, vulnerable love he was offered when a transference was first blossoming.

One student with training in counseling herself, expressed it this way: "That [teacher-student] relationship seems almost designed to encourage transference. And you just hope that the teacher can handle it and that it will end up for the best. I guess Aitken means just be aware of it and hold it until it's over, to avoid the countertransference where you are playing into that story or using it to inflate your own ego. If you really come back to that concept of what is being transferred from what. Sometimes it's easier to speak of projection in the sense of what we project is what we can't own, whether positive or negative — our true nature. You can kind of project that wholeness onto someone. It seems kind of important to have a chance to do that."

Reflecting on her work with Pat she said, "Retrospectively, I'm tempted to say it's been very useful for me. And I'm glad I encountered someone who was so able to hold it and also give it back. Be able to recognize it with some kind of objectivity in order to see it and accept and not try to mess with it, but also not buy into it. Rightly or wrongly, I've always seen that as a really fortunate thing, and Pat as having some kind of maturity in the way that he's been able to do that."

But when the deep neediness and abject love in the transference shifted to manipulation and a student's struggle for power, Pat would lose patience. All of a sudden, he could withdraw coldly and ruthlessly, and the hapless, needy student would be left to pick up the pieces. For the student who persisted, Pat remained present, it was just a very different kind of presence. He never turned a student away, but for one who clung too hard, there was no warmth.

Unlike so many who are made heroes in peoples' estimation, Pat was mostly undistracted by the adoration of his students. And as for the temptations and opportunities, he avoided them. He generally shrank from physical contact. For the most part, he didn't touch anyone beyond a handshake nor suffer himself to be touched if he could help it. Barbara Wooten said once, "On the few occasions that I hugged him he felt so insubstantial and light that I felt like a dark, howling tornado." It was as if he either loathed the contact, or sometimes perhaps, that he craved it, like alcohol, and could not trust himself to take even a sip. A few examples illustrate that he was not impervious to temptation from this realm.

For some of our work together on the biography, Pat and I sat side by side on the small couch in his office looking at a laptop screen displaying photos, the recorder on the cushion between us. It happened sometimes that he would move over imperceptibly until his shoulder brushed my shoulder. One time as we sat together, his hand rested lightly against my thigh. I glanced sideways at him and he withdrew, looking a bit sheepish. Other similar instances occurred occasionally in or out of his office. There was something almost compulsive about these restrained gestures, the right hand not knowing what the left hand was doing. It seemed adolescent, even child-like.

Another instance occurred when a Zen Desert Sangha member who was acting in a play, *The Vagina Monologues*, came directly from a performance to the teisho of a zazenkai.* She was dressed in full costume, complete with flowing, passion-red skirt, low-cut blouse and dramatic make-up, a startling apparition among the zazenkai participants dressed in plain, dark clothing, sitting on their black cushions. The tanto tried to seat her in an inconspicuous place in the zendo so she wouldn't be a distraction, not least to Pat as he gave his teisho. When the talk was over, visitors were invited to leave as usual. Pat left in a hurry as soon as the clappers sounded, and went here and there in the building, apparently looking for her. She came back from her car with some homemade bread that he raved about. Again in this situation, he was like a boy reaching toward a mother, with a sexual dimension in the mix but secondary. I caught his eye while he was in full thrall. When I saw him a few days later, he looked embarrassed. I raised a questioning eyebrow, and he said, "I'm just a dirty old man."

While Susan Weimer was Head Resident at the Redemptorist Renewal Center, Pat said of an elderly Redemptorist who visited for a time that when he, Pat, was principal at Edgerton, he had to keep an eye on this man. Wringing his hands in an exaggerated way he said in a drawn-out Gollumesque lisping voice, "He likes young boys." Pat had hinted to Glenna at some point that he had experienced abuse as a boy in the seminary. During one of the tense times between Pat and Greg Mayers at Bishop DeFalco Retreat Center, Greg mentioned that Pat was attracted to adolescent boys. It may have been a dark joke. If indeed Pat had any such inclination, it would not be surprising given the seminary experience that was standard in his day — taking boys at 13 and 14, such vulnerable and malleable years in terms of sexuality, and answering the strong drives of burgeon-

---

* Whether they occurred during zazenkai or sesshin, teishos were open to the public, as were contemplative retreat conferences.

ing hormones with repression. Once, commenting to me on psychosexual development in the seminary, Pat got very thoughtful. Sounding regretful, even apologetic, he said, "It leaves an immature sexuality."

Pat knew his own foibles as a man, and whatever his inclinations, the idea that he would take advantage of the mana inherent in his position either as a priest or a roshi was deeply abhorrent to him. It was the 1980s, the 1990s, the early 2000s. He watched colleagues on both sides of the aisle — Zen and Catholic — succumb to the temptation, some even cultivating opportunity. Though I sought information in this realm, I found no evidence or rumor that Pat succumbed. Rather, his few awkward missteps in this direction attest to his holding back from the territory. Far from cultivating opportunity, he ran from it. The slight traces left here and there speak only to his being human.

Reviewing correspondence, 2011

Over the course of the following year, the archivist at the University of Hawaii, Manoa, sent requested materials from the Aitken Papers including mainly Aitken's correspondence with Kubota Akira, Willigis Jäger, and Pat Hawk. The correspondence provided an important source at various points in Pat's story, and reviewing the letters with Pat provided another thread to trace across years.

In the letters from Pat to Robert Aitken up until about 1987, Pat addressed Aitken as Dear Bob. After that, he shifted to Dear Roshi. Was it that Pat mirrored back to Aitken whatever level of familiarity Aitken was using in his signature? The Aitken side of the correspondence in the Aitken Papers was all carbon copies from which Aitken's signature was absent. When I pointed this out to Pat he jumped up, stepped to a cabinet, pulled out a folder, and started flipping through papers. When I had asked him previously if he had correspondence he'd be willing to share he had said no, he didn't save letters, he'd thrown them all away. So it was with a slightly sheepish grin that he looked up from the folder containing letters Aitken had written to him. "Hmmm… It was in '85 that he actually became Roshi. But maybe he took a little time to sort of step into that… '89, signed Roshi. … Roshi. …Ah! '79! Dear Bob… Dear Pat… Steadfastly, Bob… Isn't this interesting. Dear Pat… gassho Bob, '86. '88 Roshi! Fascinating! '89 March 8, love Roshi. … It looks like whatever he signed, that's what I wrote. How about that. These have been sitting there for years and years, and I haven't looked at them." He looked in my direction. "Do I see lust in your eyes for these?" Chuckling, he handed over the folder.

Working with Pat on his life story went like that: questions would be answered sparely if at all, relevant materials withheld, cards played close to the chest. Then bit by bit, he would loosen up. He would say when something first came up that he hadn't saved the relevant materials or perhaps that he didn't know where they were. Then a topic would resurface, and he'd pull out a file folder and give it to me to examine. Again and again, he took time to get used to the idea that something would be revealed.

When he did come around to sharing a folder, he would sometimes flip through it first, pulling out things he didn't want seen or wasn't ready to share. He did this, for example, with a folder of correspondence from Guest House. Other times he handed things over willy nilly, allowing surprising revelations. For example, a three-page, handwritten letter from a student of his in Amarillo proposing marriage was tucked into the folder containing his mother's death certificate, his father's obituary, records of Pat's priestly faculties (permissions to perform the sacraments) and other personal records. In a box containing mainly Pat's practice calligraphy, there were several letters and cards from a woman obviously in love with Pat.

I presumed these lapses in confidentiality were accidental since if he realized he'd given me something sensitive he would sometimes apologize. Living with his own strong preference, he generally also extended the courtesy of privacy to his students, and if anything, erred on the side of non-disclosure. In contrast, Aitken exposed vulnerabilities freely, his own and other people's. In an age when mental/emotional dysfunction was considered shameful by many, Aitken was open about his need for counseling. Once he even invited Pat to join him for lunch with his psychotherapist. That stance — so open in the one person and so shielded in the other — extended to students' confidences as well. Once Pat had been given permission to teach, Aitken's letters to him included detailed revelations about students and teachers they knew in common. Pat accepted this but did not reciprocate. He ignored the Diamond Sangha teachers' policy that when sharing a student, they should share details of the student's situation and progress. The seal of the confessional aligned perfectly with his own reticence.

In Aitken's long letter of December 1992 to his four dharma heirs, part boilerplate and part individual, he spoke of how each of the four of them carried some aspect of himself.

> I chose my successors because they were qualified, but also because in my heart I felt they were me, conveying my talents and traits in their own ways. Each of them is just as complex as I am. They are not my clones for I did not look for clones. Each has one or two of my traits, transmuted in a unique personality that includes other personal qualities and tendencies. So when these folks come together they do not necessarily harmonize as they might if each had all of me, but sometimes fight with a bitterness that is, after all,

> not surprising among people with such different personae who are linked by strong family ties...[588]

As we reviewed this particular letter, it was March 2011, and Pat had appointed six teachers, four of them still apprentice, all with very different personalities. I asked him, "Is this how you feel about your successors — that they carry your traits?"

"No."

"Do you have a sense of qualified?"

"Oh yeah." Long pause. "You know there's a strain — that you're supposed to find successors even if they have only one eye." Pat was perhaps thinking of Robert Aitken's reference to Soen Nakagawa. In his book, *Original Dwelling Place: Zen Buddhist Essays*, there is a chapter called "Remembering Soen Roshi," in which Aitken says, "At the same time, he [SN] often said to me that it was the first duty of a roshi to find a successor with clear eyes. 'If he does not have two clear eyes, at least he should have one clear eye. If not one eye, at least half an eye.' I believe that he, in his great modesty, considered that he might have half an eye and that it was his karma and his responsibility to accept his position as wholeheartedly as possible and to maintain and pass on the teaching that he had received from the Buddha through Bodhidharma, Hakuin, and Gempo."[589]

Taking the responsibility to provide dharma successors seriously himself, Pat had by this time appointed six teachers, two of whom had been given dharma transmission.

That May of 2011, the Diamond Sangha Teachers' Circle meeting was in Damme, Germany again. For the first time, Pat was unable to attend. His strong identification as a teacher within the Diamond Sangha and his hitherto strong inclination to participate had waned since the 2009 meeting in Honolulu from which he had come back in high spirits. He had mixed feelings about going, but in any case, was simply incapable of making the journey. All of Pat's newly appointed teachers were eligible to attend but only Kristen Larson went. Marsha Linehan had very little identification with the Diamond Sangha — her Zen formation was mainly through Willigis Jäger and only latterly through Pat — and Dan Dorsey and Susan Weimer had neither funds nor inclination to go.

The teachers' meeting was sufficiently unsatisfactory that year that Rolf Drosten resolved it was the last he would attend.[590] Kristen, on the other hand, who came back from Germany directly to Tucson to the May sesshin at the Redemptorist Renewal Center — still led by Pat — was excited about the possibility of holding an American Diamond Sangha Teachers' meeting in Tucson. If Pat couldn't come to the meeting, perhaps the meeting would come to him. Pat agreed to this, and a date was tentatively set for January 2012. Kristen took charge and set about spreading the word among the Diamond Sangha teachers. Dan and Susan, who, as local Tucson teachers would be expected to co-host the event, at first showed only mild interest in response to Kristen's enthusiasm, then felt shut out from the planning. Pat wearily tried to mediate. There was a lukewarm response from other teachers to the invitation Kristen sent out, and the idea was dropped. Pat felt simultaneously relieved not to be involved in a big event and hurt that his longtime colleagues did not express more interest in coming to Tucson to see him as his health waned.

The May 2011 teachers' meeting in Germany had been the first since Aitken's death, and the future of the Diamond Sangha was high on the agenda. Following the meeting, a letter soliciting input into a vision for the Diamond Sangha going forward was sent to the teachers to be shared with and discussed in their sanghas. Susan responded to the letter somewhat dismissively without soliciting input from the Tucson sangha. There came to be a sense from both of Pat's new Tucson teachers that the Diamond Sangha as an organization no longer held its former value for them. This was to some extent reinforced by Pat himself, perhaps in part because of his disappointment at his colleagues' response to the invitation to Tucson.

10

Winding Down

Last retreats

In the fall of 2011, Pat began having intractable skeletal pain, and it was determined that his cancer had spread to at least one rib on the left side. In early November, he wrote to Leonard Marcel, Dan Dorsey, Susan Weimer, Marsha Linehan and me:

> Dear People,
>
> Here is the deal. My recent pain is being caused by an active area of cancer in my rib bones. This pain may be reduced by radiation therapy. This therapy is in the process of being scheduled. Don't know when, don't know how long. In the meantime I have been encouraged to take the prescription pain medicine I have been taking. You are all authorized to tell others what is happening.
>
> I plan on being at ZDS tomorrow, Saturday, and to do the zazenkai on the 17th, God, or Buddha, or whoever willing.
>
> Pat Hawk[591]

Pat's oncologist explained that the tumor seemed no longer to be hormone dependent — an expected eventual outcome of the treatment — and therefore there would be no point doing another course of androgen deprivation therapy, something Pat had resolved to turn down in any case. He was offered chemotherapy — a relatively recent option for prostate cancer, with seriously unpleasant side effects and the promise of maybe a few more months of life. He declined. He submitted to a series of radiation treatments that made very little difference. He began low-dose morphine. He continued to show up at Zen Desert Sangha most Saturdays to offer dokusan but had to bow out of the November zazenkai and have Dan Dorsey run it.

Pat went ahead with Rohatsu sesshin in spite of everything and presented opening comments in good humor to a room filled to capacity:

> Welcome to the great O-sesshin* of Rohatsu. People all over the world are sitting for these eight days that celebrate the awakening of Shakyamuni, when on the eighth day he said, "Now I see. All beings have Buddha nature, but they do not see it because of their delusions." ... I'm going to say a word about my health, so I don't have to repeat it 35 times: For the last 2-3 months I've been having pain in my back and finally I gave up and went to the doctor. They did some tests and there is an active site of cancer in my ribs that is causing the pain. They have treated this with five bouts of radiation. Takes about two weeks to get to the full effect. In the meantime, my doctor says, 'Take your pill.' One pill makes you small, one pill does nothing at all... It means I won't be here with you all the time. Luckily, I have help...

He went on to explain that Kristen, Dan and Susan would each give a dharma talk so that he would have a break on alternate days, and that all three would offer interviews during the evening period.

Rohatsu — the most arduous and the most well-attended sesshin of the year — is a rite of passage of sorts. The sesshin was eight days, longer than the usual five, and the forms were adhered to most carefully. If you sat Rohatsu you were serious. More people would come from sanghas at a distance to Rohatsu than to other sesshins during the year, and this could make for some variability in expectations regarding the format of sutras and other ritual. For example, people who sat regularly with Leonard Marcel's sangha were accustomed to bowing after every chant or recitation, whereas the local sangha was more minimalist, which was Pat's preference. He would not have volunteered his opinion, except that the question of when to bow during sutras was brought up at the first officers' meeting. He explained. Then on the first morning, he surprised everyone by coming to sutras. Whether to demonstrate the bowing or to encourage or simply to be with this strong group one more time, chanting the familiar words, he was there in full voice, albeit sitting *seiza*† rather than his usual lotus. More than one person, knowing what it cost him in physical effort to be there, fought back tears at his presence. And in more than one heart-mind around the room, with the full week of sitting stretched out ahead and the realization that almost certainly this was the last Rohatsu with Pat, there was an overflowing gratitude in being there.

---

* O-sesshin refers to a particularly significant sesshin, for example, rohatsu or in some centers, the long summer sesshin.

† A sitting posture in which the legs are folded under the thighs with the buttocks supported on the heels or on a cushion (*zafu*).

For every sesshin, there is a daily sutra recitation, teisho, dokusan, and occasional, brief encouraging words. Otherwise, the days pass wordlessly except for here and there a whispered exchange between officers dealing with some logistical issue or during the *samu* (work practice) period as people get their jobs done. There were other sounds of course — the cheerful gurgle of a fountain near the open window, the guttural call of a cactus wren at the fountain, bells and clappers in the zendo signaling starting or stopping of zazen, the clatter of dishes in the kitchen during meals. Sounds take on a new depth and richness during sesshin. In the wordless space, the usual prattle that fills most waking minds quiets. In that prolonged inner quiet the thoughts that do come up carry more punch, such that small joys are bigger and small annoyances are amplified.

Seasoned practitioners accustomed to particular ways of doing things can suddenly flare up into irritation at some little thing not done right. For this Rohatsu, there was the battle of the blinds. The St. Alphonsus building is perched on one bank of an arroyo that winds between the building and the mountains rising on the far side. At the far end of the zendo is a large picture window facing west, requiring that blinds be closed to keep out the intense afternoon sun. Some people felt strongly about leaving the blinds open to the view of the desert and the changing light except during the afternoon. Paul Hughes as tanto, was technically the only person who should be adjusting the blinds and the thermostat, but old-timers in particular would feel they could ignore that rule and adjust conditions to what they thought was appropriate. As far as the blinds went, there were several constituencies — those who had trouble with glare and wanted daylight kept out, those affected by seasonal affective disorder who wanted as much light as possible, and those who simply wanted to enjoy the view. The blinds were vertical slat blinds, so there was great variation in how they could be positioned — fully closed, fully open, or partially opened and closed with slats arranged to let in varying amounts of light.

Paul's method was to close the blinds at lunchtime, then open them again once the sun was off the window late in the day, leaving them that way until the following lunchtime. But there would be someone who would come into the empty zendo before the afternoon sit and turn the slats to let in some light, or someone else in the early morning who would close the blinds completely. Sometimes one person's action on the blinds would be altered by another person coming in a little later, still before the room filled for the next sitting period. Then there was the time when, after the bell had rung to begin the sit, with the room completely silent, someone suddenly got up in a swish of robes, stepped over to the cords and noisily closed the blinds. Not a word was spoken, but her overflowing exasperation and Paul's big-eyed, "What the heck?!" were palpable. Such were the small preoccupations that caught the still mind unaware.

In the evening block each day, with people sore-kneed and weary, Paul would offer tanto's words, sometimes wise, sometimes funny. "That cactus wren, that's it. All the evil karma and the dharma gates we haven't awakened to, that's not it." "It's never too late for a happy childhood. To do that, let go of ideas of right and wrong and wondering whether your meditation is going well." "Emptiness can also be boring." And toward the end: "This is the last full day. When Shakyamuni sat, he didn't know it was the last day; he was just cold — it was cold at that time of year where he was — no expectations. Let's sit like that."

Although Pat did not show up for sutras after the first day and did not sit with the group, he managed to offer dokusan every day for a few hours. He was in fine form, attested by chuckling or sometimes a loud laugh filtering through the closed door of the dokusan room. He gave a teisho every other day, even managing the full prostrations of *raihai* before and after. Except for a few meals, he ate with the group.

The December zazenkai was held at Zen Desert Sangha with the house fuller than usual. There being a strong sense of opportunity running out, all effort was made to fit everyone in. All who attended were given one dokusan with Pat. He kept up good spirits and good energy except, he said, for a short period in the afternoon when, as his morning dose of morphine was wearing off and before it was time for his afternoon dose, he thought he might have to withdraw.

At the end of Rohatsu, Pat had been asked if a retreat schedule should be drafted for him for 2012 and he said yes, emphatically. A few days after the zazenkai he met with the sesshin coordinator and approved a schedule. It was initially given very limited circulation given his precarious condition. A few days later he did not make his usual appearance at Christmas Mass. The next day Emma Stone, a longtime student on an extended visit from Australia, met with him briefly — they had had an appointment for lunch — but he was in such pain he excused himself and went to find his confrere, Father Paul Coury, to take him to Emergency. They gave him stronger pain meds than he could give himself, which helped a little.

An email was sent to everyone registered for the Christmas contemplative retreat, due to begin December 27th, letting them know that Pat could not be there. There was a flurry of email and questions — whether the retreat would go forward, what would be the format without Pat — whether silent retreat with no talks and no interviews or something else. It was too late to cancel completely, especially since about half the participants were coming from out of town and were on their way or already there. Pat relayed via Carmen Patterson that he would like the retreat to go forward without him and that he wanted Emma Stone to lead it in his stead. Susan Weimer offered to provide the daily talks as well as interviews. Registrants sent in their preferences by email, some happy to have Susan assisting, most preferring a teacherless retreat.

It was decided to use recordings of previous talks by Pat for the daily conference. Paul Hughes (at Pat's suggestion) and Susan made themselves available for interviews, and the retreat went forward with no cancellations. The weather was glorious and the sitting solid, though solemn with concern for Pat's condition. He showed up for the closing lunch, looking ghastly pale and weak. Mary Riseley saw him as he was heading from his office to the St. Alphonsus building before lunch and gave him a last hug, thinking he could not survive more than a week or two. But at the lunch, when he was asked again about his 2012 teaching schedule, he said very firmly that it should be sent out.

Pat retirement

Pat took the month of January off as usual, letting it be known through the grapevine that not only his regular local sits with dokusan but also his dokusan appointments — he was still working by phone or video call with about 20 regular long-distance students — were canceled for the month. The first event on his 2012 schedule was a beginner's Zen retreat in early February, and with Pat's encouragement, an email was duly sent out to the various email lists announcing that registration was open. On January 18, Pat sent an email to the Diamond Sangha Teachers' e-tree abruptly announcing his resignation. He had just had a full-body bone scan which showed tumor foci throughout his skeleton. His oncologist repeated the offer of chemotherapy made the previous November. Pat again declined. He said that after meeting with his oncologist he knew he could finally make the decision to retire. He seemed untroubled at his prognosis, relieved even, that there was a definitive prediction and that the long journey with cancer was nearing an end. He sent an email to ZDS the next day:

> I wish to announce to you that I am retiring from teaching as of the 18th of January 2012. As a result I herewith submit my resignation as the guiding teacher of the Zen Desert Sangha. I apologize for the abrupt announcement. However, this past month has seen a precipitous decline in my health and level of energy. My oncologist suggests that in my present condition statistically I have perhaps 8 to 10 months to live with no prospect of improvement ahead. I am sure that the associate teachers recently appointed will hold up the teaching of the Dharma until your search reveals a new guiding teacher.

My deep, deep thanks for the support you have given me these past years.
Gassho
Pat Hawk[592]

That same day he met with Paul Coury, Director, and Peter Tran, Business Manager of the Redemptorist Renewal Center to talk about the future of the Pathless Path program. They were committed to fulfilling the retreat schedule for 2012 and to continuing the program indefinitely. They set about finding leaders for the RRC events on Pat's 2012 schedule. It was further decided that all the Zen and contemplative paraphernalia — robes, bells, scrolls, icons, gifts — everything would belong to the Redemptorists of Arizona. Pat made it clear that this was to avoid divisiveness in figuring who gets what or what goes where.[593]

Letters, emails, cards, calls, flooded in from friends, other teachers, current and former students. They expressed concern, questions about the future and most of all, appreciation. One example conveys the tone: "First and most important, as you take this major step, I want to thank you for all you have done over all these years for me and for so many. Your work and this practice have made me real. Had it not been for you, I might have missed my life in large measure. Most profound gratitude to you — words cannot convey."

Susan Weimer took over as teacher for the February beginner's sesshin, which drew an uncharacteristic number of old-timers from afar, hoping to have a last opportunity to see Pat. In the event, he was unable to put in any appearance, and he declined to have anyone come to him in the rectory. In the zendo, Susan herself opted to sit along the wall with the participants rather than take the teacher's seat in front of the altar, so Pat's cushion stood fittingly empty. She no doubt was missing him as acutely as anyone.

Asked if he would still be seeing any of his students individually or communicating with them in any other way after stepping down as guiding teacher for Zen Desert Sangha, Pat's answer was an emphatic No. Dan Dorsey asked if Pat could offer any directions in the search for another guiding teacher. Pat told him the candidates could be any roshi or associate teacher in the Diamond Sangha, or any roshi or associate teacher in the broader Harada-Yasutani lineage. Beyond that, Pat asked to be left alone unless he asked for help. He said he would stay in Tucson for as long as he could look after himself, then move to the Redemptorists' care facility near St. Louis.[594]

Shirley Morrissey, Pat's longtime friend, spiritual companion at Glenview, assistant and student at Amarillo, came to Tucson and was able to visit with him. He expressed to her a concern about leaving his apprentice teachers dangling.

Shirley, feeling that giving dharma transmission to the new teachers would be inappropriate, expressed alarm that Pat might be considering it.[595]

I met with Pat shortly after Shirley's departure (he had indicated on the day he officially retired that I should keep working with him on the biography, and I was seeing him periodically). He was in evident distress — he seemed near tears — that he felt pressured to "make teachers," indicating a letter on his desk that he had printed from an email. It was from Kristen Larson, written after Pat sent his resignation to the Diamond Sangha teachers. It addressed what for the apprentice teachers was most pressing: "The complexities and potential problems of your leaving teachers without full transmission are vast. As is the implication of quickly moving transmission onto too many at once." She reminded Pat of the situation with the three apprentice teachers appointed by Aitken but left without transmission at the time of his death.

Later the same day, Pat received an email from a senior student concerned that he might consider hasty transmissions:

> My thought about [authorizing teachers] is that it ought not to be about the fulfillment of any individual's desire to be a teacher or get transmission — when a teacher becomes a teacher it's not about that person and their personal goals. It's about service to others.
>
> Don Stoddard and Marian Morgan were left dangling by Aitken, and both are functioning teachers nonetheless. The only thing they can't do is give transmission. I have no idea of their insight or lack of it. In a case where someone doesn't get it very well ... it seems just as well if they can't give transmission. These associate teachers may deepen their insight over the years, but that itself is less likely if their development is cut off by graduating too soon.
>
> The thread by which your associate teachers dangle could be a lifeline that saves them from misplaced self-confidence and drives them to seek deeper understanding by working as students with another teacher. Giving transmission could cut that lifeline. No one wants to be left dangling, but that may be best for the teachers (and their students) besides being least effort for you.
>
> I hope you will find the strength to resist whatever pressure is being brought to bear on you (including this note if it is off base), and to discern and do what is best. Whatever you do I support.

At about the same time this message was sent to Pat, I received an email from Kristen Larson making clear that Pat had made his decision: "I suppose that you know by now ... our beloved teacher will give all four of his [apprentice teachers] Full Dharma Transmission at once! It's his way of doing the right thing." A few dates were considered, and they settled on March 31st.

In retrospect, Pat's drama when he spoke with me of being pressured to make teachers seemed partly just that. He could bring forth a performance when he needed to, and in this case, he surely knew there would be opposition to the transmissions. Conflict averse as he was, he could deflect criticism away from himself by claiming pressure from the outside. Despite protest from many, including a few of his colleagues among the Diamond Sangha teachers, he was resolute about going forward. He gave various reasons for his decision, sometimes different reasons to different people. He told several, including Marsha Linehan when she was in town to lead the annual mindfulness retreat in February, that if he weren't dying, he wouldn't be doing the transmissions at this time.[596]

One week before the ceremony was to take place, I visited Pat in his office. The retreat center was mostly deserted, with chairs out of the chapel and meeting rooms, and a strong smell of bleach in all the public spaces. A norovirus epidemic had forced cancellation of events and fumigation of the premises, including sleeping rooms of anyone who had reported symptoms. Pat's office was unaffected. I found him listening to Handel on his boombox and playing mahjong. He was getting around with a cane, and his body had puffed up tremendously over the course of a few weeks, mostly due to impaired fluid regulation, with perhaps a contribution from his diet. He had been gaining weight since he'd quit smoking a few years before. Since the final diagnosis, he had abandoned any semblance of eating healthily, asking his confreres to pick up all manner of junk food for him.[597] The radiation treatments destroyed his sense of taste, though he said he could still enjoy Dove Bars and Drumsticks. All things considered, Pat seemed in good spirits. He talked about the epidemic:

> We had to cancel all this week; we're losing money hand over fist. Be careful when you go out. It's been terrible here, just terrible. Epidemic. Health department has been here 3-4 times just this last week. It's very contagious. I've stayed at the rectory or in this room and don't touch anything outside of this. I come in my private door. So far so good. [Father] Charley got it but everybody else is okay so far. It's a disaster. Called up the insurance company — they won't cover the loss of business. We thought we had insurance for loss of business because of fire, whatever, but they won't cover it. If you go two days without anybody getting symptoms, then you're out of the woods.

The subject came back around to the upcoming transmissions. I asked him, "For the sake of posterity and not to give you any flak, I'm trying to understand what your mind is around the transmissions..." He looked blank and was silent. I suggested, "Let me tell you what I see, and you can tell me if I have a correct impression." He nodded. I went on:

> So you retire, somebody points out that it would not be good if you were to leave people in the lurch and gives the example of what Aitken did with his teachers. Kristen spoke to me about what she called the tragic situation with Danan Henry [What with various delays, Aitken did not give him transmission in the Diamond Sangha despite an expressed intention to do so.] Plus, the Diamond Sangha Teachers' Circle has talked about this and never come to a resolution, and that's been frustrating to you I gather. So you have a choice between two risks — one is the risk of not giving transmission and therefore teachers that perhaps sometime in the future ought to get transmission don't get it. And the other risk is giving transmission to teachers for whom it's premature, and you can't know whether sometime in the future it will be appropriate to give them transmission. Either way, it's a risk and you're choosing the risk of making them [fully transmitted] teachers and see if they sink or swim.

Pat nodded, "Yeah."

"Is that it?"

"That's right. Pretty fair."

I went on. "So then is the transmission here about making teachers more than it is about confirming some kind of mind to mind recognition, would you say?"

Pat said, "Yes. ... There's nothing special about teachers as far as I'm concerned." There was a long pause, then he said, "I don't know how this happened. I have no — I am so... oblivious to how people perceive me. I don't get it."

"Why people see you as a great teacher?"

"A great teacher... what's that? I don't get it. Never got it."

"You don't see people's growth under your influence?"

"I don't get it. The connection."

"Between what you do and people's growth."

Like the peach blossoms that cleared Lingyun's doubts, Pat did not know his own strength.* Fundamentally, he trusted the practice — that a person persistent in the practice of intense silence would open to realization; that diligent practice, usually for a long time, could ripen a person to the point where the clear sound

---

* The village peach blossoms didn't know
 their own crimson
but still they freed Lingyun
 from all his doubts.

of a pebble, the wafting scent of a flower, the turning word of a teacher — anything could throw open the gateless gate. He trusted the practice, and he trusted these teachers to faithfully provide a field of practice for others.

But as he bore his late-stage illness and faced his imminent death while also suffering objections and encouragements — strong on both sides — from all and sundry, Pat was beyond frustrated. "Yeah. So what happens? So here I am in this circumstance, not one I wanted to be in, not one anybody would want to be in. I'm making some teachers. Maybe something like what happened with me will happen with them. I don't know. It all seems chaos to me. Just a bunch of chaos. ... I'm throwing some more in just to keep it going..." There was a pause. I said, "There's been a fair bit of talk about the word *roshi*. Some ambiguity about what it means, whether these teachers will become roshis." Pat said, " 'Old Master'. Don't have to use it. Nothing special about it. I'm not conferring any title of roshi on anybody. Just giving people their independence." His voice was impatient and suddenly flared into anger. "It's a dilemma. It's not easy. This big fuck-up here. Everybody's telling me big fuck-up, big scandal. Big-shit deal. Doesn't matter. Completely empty." The room went quiet. I raised an eyebrow. He caught his breath, said, "I'm sorry," looking slightly sheepish. Calm returned.

At Zen Desert Sangha, at least as early as fall 2011 and perhaps going back to the year before, when Dan had been made associate teacher, there began to be serious conversations about what would happen when Pat could no longer teach. He had been guiding teacher at ZDS for more than 20 years. He had weathered with them the years of offering retreats wherever they could book a place, the exuberance then the crash at Indiana's, the split over John Tarrant and Joan Sutherland, the search for a permanent home, and the purchase and settling into the zendo on Martin Avenue.

Opinion was divided between those who were ready to accept Dan and Susan as teachers and those who felt they could work with neither of them and wanted an outside search. Among the latter group was a sense that the new teachers were not sufficiently mature. Pat himself acknowledged this. The expectation he conveyed to several people at the time of his retirement was that Dan and Susan could cover until ZDS found a guiding teacher. The division in the sangha was partly — though not completely — between old-timers who had worked with Pat for many years, and relative newcomers who didn't know him well and so had little basis for comparison. Pat had a solid and devoted following at ZDS. He had had a profound effect on the lives of so many of his students. The question of who would step into the teacher role felt vital. Discussion was heated.

The news that Dan Dorsey and Susan Weimer would be given transmission burst into the already turbulent discussions taking place. For some, it shattered whatever weight and reverence the terms "transmission" and "roshi" had carried when the reference point had been Pat himself. For others, it strengthened the case in favor of having the local teachers take over at ZDS. Paul Buckwalter and Casey Hayden were old-timers who came down stridently on the side of the new teachers. Casey was a longtime Zen practitioner who joined Zen Desert Sangha during the years they were at Indiana's, and who first opposed having Pat at ZDS because he was a Catholic priest, then became his dedicated student. Paul, who had come to Zen through Casey, was a retired Episcopal minister. Pat had presided at their wedding years earlier. When Pat's intention to give the new teachers transmission was announced, Paul especially asserted that once Dan and Susan were made roshis, they would no longer be as ordinary people, and they must, by the fact of their position, be accorded authority — an idea anathema in Zen but familiar in Christianity.

People from both sides pleaded with Pat to provide a clear direction. On the one hand, "Tell them you expect Susan and Dan will be the teachers." And on the other, "Make it clear that you expect there to be a search, that there is no obligation to have Susan or Dan as the teachers." Pat refused to get involved. "This is something for people to decide themselves. It has nothing to do with me anymore."

Shortly after Pat announced his retirement, the Zen Desert Sangha board of directors wondered at the possibility of a social event to celebrate and thank him. With the precariousness of his condition, it was variously considered that they could have a barbecue at ZDS, or a simple tea up at St. Al's, or a card that everyone could sign. He agreed to a lunchtime barbecue at ZDS if he could make it. A date was set for one week before the transmission ceremony. Pat did make it. Longtime student Greg Anderson brought him back and forth from the Renewal Center since he was in no shape to drive himself at that point. About 50 people came. The weather was good — both the meteorological and the social kind. The sangha was bruised from some of the strident arguments around successors, and the event with Pat brought everyone together. There was the usual barbecue fare and a Cheesecake Factory vanilla bean cheesecake for Pat, one of the few things he could still enjoy. He was so puffed up from fluid retention, some who had not seen him for those months since retirement walked past without recognizing him. Nonetheless, he held his own and even chatted about old times. People were terribly grateful for the chance to see him.

Transmission to all

The following Wednesday evening, Pat collapsed in his room at the rectory. He moaned for help and no one heard. He managed to reach his cell phone and call Glenna, who was visiting the Renewal Center from Oregon, having come at Pat's request to help prepare the articles of transmission. She hurried to the rectory and alerted his confreres, who found him in his chair shivering, in desperate pain. An ambulance took him to Emergency at Northwest Hospital, where he was wheeled here and there for imaging and other tests, then finally admitted. A cancer-riddled rib had fractured spontaneously. There was little doubt that he would not be able to attend the transmission ceremony that Saturday, let alone preside, and Leonard Marcel was summoned from Oregon. Leonard had earlier indicated that he would do the transmission on Pat's behalf if Pat was alive, not otherwise. He was able to visit Pat at the hospital that Friday, by which time they'd gotten the pain under control and Pat's spirits had risen weakly.

On Saturday, March 31st, St. Al's zendo was filled with rows of chairs for the ceremony. Each transmittee was allowed to invite five guests, and the remaining seats were given first come, first served to people registering in advance. People arrived from all over, assembling with quiet greetings, sharing bits of news, concern for Pat, and a jumble of feelings about the transmission, until the ringing of a *densho* sequence called people to find their places in silence. Leonard conducted the ceremony with grace:

> This is a bittersweet day for us here, a day of sadness but also a day of joy and gladness. The sadness is due to the fact that the man who has been primary Zen teacher for many of us for many years is not able to be with us today. As some of you may know, he has been hospitalized for several medical problems, and although he has improved, it is not nearly to the point where he could be here. Although he cannot be with us in body, he is certainly with us in spirit. I would like for all of us to honor that spirit by a minute of silence. …
>
> Pat has asked me to act in his stead and with full authority to confirm the candidates we wish to honor today. That is the joy and gladness of the day. For almost 25 years, Shin'un Seisho Pat Hawk Roshi has labored in the dharma field and spread his dharma seed. And today, that work bears fruit with the four candidates who sit before you.

Leonard continued with brief biographical details about each candidate, followed by a joint renewal of Jukai. He called out the precepts one by one, and the candidates responded in turn with a brief comment to personalize each vow. Then speaking for Pat with the customary words, Leonard went on:

> Transmission comes from two directions: from the old teacher and from the sangha. Your acceptance as teacher by the many students who come to you, and by the many others who now invite you to lead them in their practice,

> clearly indicates your acceptance by your sangha. Your presence to these people has been instructive and convincing for everyone.
>
> Shinun Seisho, Pat Hawk Roshi, has found that you verified his confidence in you at each step in your work together, to the final step today. He confirms you as worthy to teach as master in the Diamond Sangha lineage, which extends back through the Sanbo Kyodan through the Soto Zen stream through the Chinese and Indian ancestors to Shakyamuni Buddha.
>
> With that, I am happy to present to you your *rakusus*, the lineage chart and your kotsu [ceremonial stick]. The lineage chart is the *kechimyaku*. It traces the bloodline transmission directly from Shakyamuni Buddha through 88 generations to the new Diamond Sangha masters sitting here before us. Each chart was written by hand by each recipient. And Pat Hawk has inscribed them with his dharma and master name and theirs. These dharma masters are now part of the 89th generation.

Pat gave each of the transmitted teachers a cloud or teaching name, which he had inscribed on a formal rakusu for each, and which Leonard duly called out: Kristen Larson, Purple Cloud;[598] Susan Weimer, Temple of Endurance Cloud; Marsha Linehan, Temple of Mercy Cloud; Dan Dorsey, House of the Guardian Cloud.

Leonard continued:

> Now one more ceremonial token and perhaps the most important. The cautions for the new teachers. There are five of them, signed by Pat Hawk Roshi and presented to each of the new teachers with their dharma names and dates.
>
> 1. Your practice begins now. You will probably mature as a teacher after ten more years.
> 2. Remember that guidance is a matter of encouragement.
> 3. Respect transference from your students and turn it back in support of their practice.
> 4. Let the word go forth that your sangha and yourself are open and friendly.
> 5. Countless buddhas have sweat blood for this transmission. Be faithful. Be faithful.
>
> Please take these cautions to heart.

Leonard led the four transmitted teachers in the verse of the rakusu, then said, "Ladies and gentlemen, I give you new masters of the Diamond Sangha." Each of the new teachers offered brief words. Kristen spoke of the precepts, Susan of beginner's mind; Marsha of compassion; Dan of dedication to practice. There were gifts, first from Pat — a kotsu and bowl for each; then from Leonard and Theresa Marcel — incense from Dogen's Eiheiji Temple; then from a procession of guests, the room shifting to lightheartedness as people moved from the zendo to St. Al's dining area for light refreshments.

Casa de la Luz

Pat was discharged from Northwest Hospital to Casa de la Luz Hospice, it being determined that the rectory at the Renewal Center was not set up to give him the care he needed. He was given a large light-filled room with a hospital bed, a comfortable reclining chair and a few homey pieces of furniture. The day he arrived, he was incoherent — possibly too much morphine — but by his second day there, he thought he would soon be on his feet again and going back to the rectory. "Everybody says I've been looking so much better. I'm feeling so much better. Maybe I'll get around again. They're getting the pain under control, no higher and no lower than 2. Once they establish that, they can work on getting me to stand up. And walk. Then I can leave and experience minimal help from home. Then they'll send Home Hospice three times a week. And once we're there and I'm home and stable, we can see about travel to St. Clement."

In the fall of 2011, while the need for care that he knew would come was still at an undetermined distance, Pat said to several people that he planned to stay in Tucson to the end of his life. He wanted to be among his people, and that was not only his confreres. His active life was with his Zen and contemplative students and friends at least as much as with the Redemptorists.

Since January, however, with his decreasing capacity to be independent, he increasingly considered that he should "go out the Redemptorist way," which would mean moving to St Clement, the Redemptorist care facility at Liguori, Missouri. They were set up there for all levels of care, he would know people there, including some of his old teachers from the seminary, and the caregivers would have a better sense of who they were dealing with. At the hospital and at Casa de la Luz they were perfectly kind and competent, but they called him honey, sweetheart, dearie. Although he cringed at that, he expressed gentle, sincere thanks at each thing done for him, and the caregivers became fond of him. He was well enough to enjoy a trickle of visitors. At least one confrere came to see him every day, and there were a few longtime students who had been told where he was.

Pat was eager to see photos from the transmission ceremony, and obviously pleased at the whole thing. He spoke warmly of some who had come from a distance, expressing regret that he hadn't had a chance to see people. As he looked at the photos, he was interested in news — someone's new haircut, a move to Vermont, a widow's coping after loss of her husband, gifts that were given to the new teachers — he wanted all the details. In a photo of one couple, he recognized only the husband, his longtime student Philip Boatright. Of Philip's wife, he said,

"I don't think I've met her." I reminded him, "Yes, you've met her — she doesn't sit at ZDS, but she comes to the parties." He said, "Sounds like a great Zen practice to me."

Bob Halter led the Easter contemplative intensive retreat. There was a long break in the afternoon of Good Friday so participants could attend the service, and I took the opportunity to visit Pat. He wanted to know how the retreat was going. "Going smoothly, though quite different. Bob's talks are quite Christian theological." "Yeah. He's very connected to all those ideas. … He's about as close as I could get to what I do. People come to me because of how I see things, I guess, and I don't know if anybody else can do that. … Anyway, he's a skilled presenter. … We've gone through a lot together. I don't know how it happened, but we did." He paused a bit then said, "So you're pretty much done for the day." "Except this evening." "Oh yeah, that's right. Lose track of the time." I said, "I'm not going to the Good Friday service." "No, I don't blame you." Bob Halter's comment when he came to visit Pat after the retreat was, "Well, we got through the retreat without doing too much damage. It was small, so not terribly taxing." Pat said, "Thank you. You saved a countless number of souls."

Pat's confreres kept tabs on how he was doing, brought anything he needed, and entertained him with local news, comings and goings from the rectory, the wider congregation. On Easter Sunday afternoon Pat, Paul Coury and Bob Halter whiled away a few hours reminiscing about the seminary. Old familiar names surfaced: Turk Rooney, Joe Powers, Joe Bilsley, Gerry Pecht, Bill Cosgrove, Benny Guthrie, the Schwartzes, Forbes, Bockwinkel, …

Pat, looking round and puffy, turned to me and said, "Paul was just telling me how I looked like one of our old, one of the big characters of our congregation, Turk Rooney. He was a teacher in the major seminary. That was his actual family nickname. His real name was Bernard. Everything was a crisis for Turk. We made up the Stations of the Cross for Turk. Let's see if I can remember. Turk is stripped of his credit cards. Turk falls on his face for the third time. Turk crucifies your ass to the cross. Old time stuff."

Earlier, Bob Halter had been trying to give a sense of what the novitiate was like, and now he asked Pat: "Helen kept asking questions, so I think she doesn't understand. But you were there, you're usually pretty good at putting things succinctly."

Pat: What do you want me to put succinctly?

Bob: What it was.

Helen: A year of deep spiritual formation.

Paul Coury: That's beautiful.

Pat: It was a year of deep spiritual survival.

This segued into reminiscences of the novitiate year, which they'd each done at different times. Pat told of his first novice master, Forbes, dying in his sleep after the first month, being replaced by Powers who thought they were spoiled. Paul Coury was two years after Pat at De Soto, and one month into his novitiate, the old building burned to the ground. They spoke of how from Pat in '62 to Paul Coury in '64 the sixties happened. There were more guitars and freewheeling in 1964. The conversation wandered back to the present and Easter Sunday Masses, then to Pat's visitors. Pat said, "I had a nice visit from [Greg Wiest] the other day. We sat here laughing like crazy. It's always good to have somebody to laugh at your punchlines."

Bob told the story of Pat Hawk when they were both teaching at Edgerton, Pat coming into the staff lounge one morning, looking out at the endless winter and cursing Wisconsin. Pat said, "I do remember that." Then back to major seminary. All three had seen different stages of the rebellion against scholastic philosophy as the one true vision. All had experienced the old guard digging in heels — Pat especially, having been ahead of the other two, his classmates the upstarts who pushed for change. They still held vivid memories of the characters and the crisis in the mid-sixties. Then in counterpoint to speaking of philosophy, Bob Halter brought up the experiential, bringing the conversation back to the present and contemplative practice. "I think that has validity. My experience, my observations. That's something about the practice I saw from the beginning. I saw it as a way to come to freedom for all. A gentle way to know yourself or something."

Now and again during visits, Pat would ask for ice chips, or for his feet to be rubbed, or a blanket to be adjusted. When the afternoon sun streamed in, the room heated up sometimes uncomfortably. One day, sitting in the recliner, he asked me to switch a blanket draped over him for a lighter sheet. Having seen a nurse do this while still preserving the patient's modesty I was about to lay the sheet over the blanket then pull the blanket out from underneath. But saying, "No, take this off," this usually so modest man whipped the blanket off and was suddenly there naked but for his diaper, his hospital gown wide open as I lay the sheet over him. He was getting used to the intimate attentions of nurses.

By Easter Sunday, Pat had been at Casa de la Luz hospice for a week. He was struggling with breathing and with constipation — the latter a side effect of the morphine. The breathing difficulty kept him awake at night and he was on oxygen to help him sleep, with limited effectiveness. He was making no progress in regaining the ability to walk. He felt exhausted getting from the chair to the bathroom or the chair to the bed. The attending physician thought he was not in good enough shape to get on a plane — that the airline would not allow it. She suggested he work on building up his strength over the next several days, and if that turned out not to be possible, they should move him to a hospice in town where he could receive more individualized care, to build up his strength there. A problem with that was there was no space for him at the designated hospice. Pat said he felt pretty good except for the exhaustion and the inability to move his legs. "If I could move, I could do all kinds of things for myself."

Several weeks earlier, even before Pat landed in the hospital with a broken rib, Bob Walker — himself an experienced nurse — had offered to take a leave of absence from his job at an Athens, Georgia, hospital and look after Pat for as long as necessary. Bob called the Redemptorists with the offer but did not tell it to Pat directly, perhaps not wanting to put him on the spot. Later, when Pat was in the hospital the message was relayed to Glenna who was concerned that Pat might be upset by it. Having learned of Bob's intention, as the situation seemed at an impasse, I conveyed the message to Pat.

"I don't know if you've heard this already: Bob Walker said he'd take a leave of absence to come and look after you." Pat said, "No, I haven't heard." There was a pause before he went on. "I'm very sad that I haven't responded to him. You know we've got a history, and I would like to respond to him in a positive way and listen to what he has to say and accept what he has to offer." Pat paused again. "But I don't know how that can work. Maybe in this medevac flight, we can hire him as the nurse; he's certified. Perhaps you could communicate with him?" "Sure. He works weekends. But he said he was ready to drop everything if you need him." "Yes. So yes, it's very real."

In the decision about what to do, there was apparent the long habit of obedience, which in Pat tended toward learned helplessness and an avoidance of responsibility for his own decisions. "I don't know yet. That's the thing. I wish Paul Coury [Pat's Superior at the time] had not gone out of town, but he has. So I'm out of the loop. He's in communication with the doctor, Dr. Kligman… Kligman's and Paul Coury's thinking may be different. We need somebody to coordinate this thing. But I am definitely in favor of doing this medevac thing. It's the easiest, most straightforward. I don't give a damn about money. The Redemptorists can come up with $10,000 if I can come up with $1000 [from his Sabbatical Fund]."

Within less than a day, it was arranged. American Airlines would accept Pat with a certified nurse providing care, he and Bob traveling as first class passengers. They would expedite his getting through security at the airport, bring the wheelchair onto the plane, and set up a continuous oxygen feed from the airline's supply so he wouldn't be carrying a tank.

Bob drove through the night from his home in Athens, Georgia, to St. Louis airport, then flew to Tucson, arriving the morning of April 16th. He went straight from the airport to the hospice where Pat was being prepared to travel.

The door to Pat's room was closed and carried a sign, not there the day before, that said, "Do Not Disturb." After he was discharged from the hospital to hospice care, the Renewal Center office staff had been instructed not to disclose Pat's whereabouts except to a designated few, so that he would not be overwhelmed with visitors. But the news had gradually leaked out along with the knowledge that Pat would soon be leaving Tucson for good, and in the last few days, there had been an exhausting stream of people coming to say goodbye to their beloved teacher.

Pat's normally fastidious grooming had been neglected, his hair beginning to curl at the neck until Greg Wiest gave him a brush cut the day before he was to leave for St. Clement. The nurses dressed him for travel in a black sweatsuit brought by his confreres, very different from anything he would have picked for himself, but comfortable and becoming. Pat said, "Very good choice in clothes. I approve." Paul Coury was there checking last-minute items: where things needed for the journey were packed, sound system and headphones, warm wrap, medical supplies, paperwork, and a fat bundle of cash for Bob in case of any expense. Paul relayed a message from Mercy Center: "Greg Mayers called last night to say blessings on your trip and everything." "Then it's assured," Pat said. His mind drifting, he went on, "There'll be an empty room for the Chapter [Redemptorists of the Denver Province were gathering later that week at RRC], you might want to use it."

Paul Coury said they would not be touching Pat's room or his office for a while, and if there was anything he needed, they would bring it to him. In fact, although it's customary for all papers of a deceased confrere to go to the Redemptorist archive for processing and controlled access, as early as that same week Paul Coury and Tom Santa were seen going in and removing boxes containing Pat's typed talks and other materials from his office. Although Pat was adamant about not wanting his talks published, they were apparently considering the possibility.

At the nurses' station outside Pat's hospice room, Bob Walker was briefed on Pat's condition, and a healthcare power of attorney was signed over to him in case decisions had to be made en route. The handoff was worked out for every step of the way — hospice to airport by non-emergency ambulance (as it happened, with the same kind and competent driver who had brought Pat from the hospital to Casa de la Luz), help at the gate in Tucson, help at the gate in St. Louis, nurses at St. Clement in communication with nurses at Casa — everything prepared in detail so that the transfer was seamless.

Susan Weimer and Patty Kelley, another longtime student of Pat, greeted him at the airport entrance in Tucson and waved him on as he was wheeled straight through to the boarding area. Susan sent an email to the Amarillo folks so they could wave as the plane went over.

St. Clement Health Care Center, Liguori, Missouri

Liguori, Missouri, is an 80-acre tract of land about 25 miles south of downtown St. Louis, purchased by the Redemptorists in 1947, wooded on the periphery, and with a road winding roughly down the middle. Liguori Publishing House and a large priests' residence are at the far end of the property. They were the first two buildings to be constructed there. In 1960, a residence was built for Redemptoristine Sisters. It sits between the publishing house at one end and St. Clement Health Care Center, added in 1988 nearer to the entrance to the property. The buildings are well separated in a park of tall shade trees and mown grass. Between the publishing house and the Redemptoristine monastery is a cemetery where Redemptorists are interred, some of whose deaths long precede the date the property was purchased. As Redemptorist houses in the St. Louis Province have closed down, generations of Redemptorists have been exhumed and their graves and gravestones moved to Liguori. One can see at a glance which rows of gravestones come from elsewhere by their different cuts and colors — red granite from Oconomowoc, grey with a particular cut from De Soto, others from Kirkwood, and so on.

St. Clement, home to retired and infirm Redemptorist priests and brothers, provides a range of care from mildly assisted living to hospice. Father Ted Lawson, then Director, took one look at Pat on arrival and thought he would not survive the week. He called Pat's niece and nephew, children of his sister Mary Ellen, who came out from Granite City to see him. Then after a few days Pat perked up, taking an interest in life and the people around him. We spoke on the phone. He was deeply relieved to be there, happy with the care and happy with the trip that brought him there. Asked how things were, he said, "Very, very good. First class. They know how to treat you here and some of your background. And some of my old professors … we chat and everything."

About the traveling, he said, "I'm very happy about my trip with Bob Walker too. A very good trip. Both he and I were exhausted. The miracle of miracles, the airlines were very cooperative. I was really pleased. And it was just like old days — instead of having something between the two, we were just companions. It was really pleasant. … I'm grateful he offered." He went on, "It's very nice here.

The springtime, the grass is greened up, trees putting out the new green leaves. Really lush. Pretty warm. Flowers… real nice. I get out about maybe an hour, sit in the sun in the afternoons." We had arranged before Pat left Tucson that I would visit once he was settled, and he asked when I was coming, with uncharacteristic impatience for company from Tucson.

I arrived a week later and was surprised again by Pat's enthusiastic welcome. He seemed sweetly grateful for having a visitor, very much a turnaround from his latter days in Tucson, as he drew on what patience he could muster to put up with the ever-increasing numbers who had discovered where he was. Unlike the crush of visitors during those last few days, things suddenly had gotten very quiet — too quiet — and he was feeling forgotten. He was upbeat but a bit disappointed. "The only one I've heard from was, I got a call from Nelson [Foster]. That was pretty good." Then another day he said, "Nobody's visited yet. I haven't heard from anybody. Nobody's called from the Chapter. I don't know what to think. I did too good a job of putting people off — told people not to come or call so they didn't." Asked if we should continue not giving his phone number to people who asked for it, he said, "No, go ahead." He said, "Tina, Jimmy and Michael [Pat's niece, nephew and great nephew], the three of them came out. I think they were shocked to see me, but nevertheless they came." That was important to him.

The residents of St. Clement gather every day for Mass in the chapel, some walking in unaided, some with walkers, others wheeled in by the nurses. Chairs rather than pews left lots of space for the wheelchairs and other conveyances that are brought in. As they gathered for Mass, one could tell the priests from the brothers by who gets draped by the nurses with a priestly stole, necessary vestment for celebrating the Mass. So draped, the priests concelebrated from wherever they sat, raising their hands at the consecration together with the priest at the altar.

In marked contrast to the average parish church, the singing at every Mass was full and hearty, the enfeebled men's voices confident in the message and stronger than they could ever be again outside the chapel. During a homily, one of the brothers, sitting toward the back in a wheelchair, started up a discordant chant which rose to a distracting volume, and Ted Lawson eventually got up to ask him to be quiet — a request that was successful only for a time. Another day this brother's chant was so loud he was wheeled out partway through the Mass. Everyone remained seated throughout — the custom at St. Clement, so no one blocks the view of anyone unable to stand. When the Mass ended, caregivers arrived to wheel out those needing that assistance, while the others shuffled out under their own power, all to return later in the day for the rosary.

Any of the fathers still mentally capable could give the homily. One day Father Frank Novak was brought to the pulpit in his wheelchair to deliver a well-crafted, fiercely conservative message including sharp criticism of the American nuns — specifically mentioning Joan Chittister — whose voices were being suppressed by then Pope Benedict XVI and his episcopate. It was sufficiently offensive to Ted Lawson that he spoke up loudly at the Prayer of the Faithful, asking that we appreciate the contribution of women religious and pray for an end to divisiveness within the Church.

Frank Novak and his brother Henry, also at St. Clement, had been among those who, years earlier at Glenview, had scorned Pat for his dedicated contemplative practice, a rejection that stung at the time. Henry Novak had a reputation — dating back to his time at St. Alphonsus Church in Chicago in the late '60s and early '70s — for being the meanest of Redemptorist superiors. Between the one brother's rather strident homily and the other's reputation, confided to me by one of the confreres earlier, I was much surprised when, after the Mass, Frank Novak was wheeled up to me to introduce himself, expressly to say that in those days back at Glenview, Pat Hawk had taught him to pray. He was moving in his sincerity, and perhaps there was a touch of repentance. I relayed this to Pat, who nodded solemnly.

Unable to walk since before he left Tucson, Pat opted to stay in his room rather than be shuffled back and forth to the chapel. At this point, he was well beyond the wounds of Glenview, and disinterested in anyone's understanding, whether toward assent or disapproval. Nor was he interested in hearing the dogma-bound spirituality of some of his confreres. Near his bed, a portable oxygen pump was groaning away, the tube to his nose a constant fixture. As over the phone earlier, he enthused about the place. "The care here is terrific. They actually have two people helping. They always have two people. They know everybody's name. They don't call you sweetheart, they call you Father. It's all very respectful." But, "Legs don't work. If I could get up and do little things for myself, it would be a lot better, but I can't move." He could still feed himself. I wondered if he'd like a supply of Dove bars. He declined, "I don't want to make a fuss. This is not an individual place; it's a group place. I don't want to make myself too far out of the group."

I was to have supper one night with Pat's niece Tina and her son, and lunch another day with Dave and Barb, cousins on the Hawk side, children of Pat's Uncle Bob. Dave Hawk was a regular at Jerry's Cafeteria, whose proprietor, Jerry Roderick, was an elementary school classmate of Pat's. Dave put me in touch with Jerry, who put me in touch with other classmates. One of these, Kitty Reither, a natural social organizer, graciously arranged a lunch at Jerry's Cafeteria, so that I could meet as many of Pat's former elementary school classmates as could come in person. Pat encouraged my visits to Granite City and environs, then took an interest in the stories and photos of the people and places from his life before entering the seminary.

I met Dave and Barb at Jerry's for lunch. While working on Pat's life story with him, and through the wonders of Ancestry.com, I had uncovered his family tree going back a long way, especially on the Hawk side. The Hawks appear in the new world in 1765, in Virginia, and an unbroken line of seven generations connects to Pat. His great, great, great grandfather was one of the early white settlers of Illinois. Among records from his life is a copy of the deed for his initial purchase of 80 acres near present-day Winchester, Illinois, complete with the legal description and signature of John Quincy Adams. It seemed possible that this farm was the one Pat remembered visiting on Sunday drives with his family when he was a boy. Dave, and Barb pored over these materials at lunch. Their father was alcoholic — a condition that appears with some frequency in the Hawk men going back several generations. They remembered a rough and unstable childhood without ties beyond their immediate family. Hungry for roots, they joined in a plan to go up to Winchester and look for the old farmstead.

The three of us headed up one wet day, driving the 40 miles past green, well-managed farms to the town of Winchester, where we went into the assessor's office to get a plat map, without which we could not translate the coordinates from the 1820 deed to a location we could drive to. A helpful clerk pulled up the map with the parcel described as "County, Scott; Meridian 3; Range 12W; Township 14N; Section number 10; Lot W2SW" and — amazing to us — still marked "Hawk."

Many of the roads in the area around Winchester were unmarked. Despite having GPS we got lost a few times, but eventually came to the right road and driving along it, were satisfied that we'd reached the destination and that we must be looking at the old Hawk farm on our left. The land was fenced and cultivated, but there was no farmhouse in sight.

Passing a break in the fence, to our astonishment, we noticed a small handwritten sign partially hidden in weeds that said "Bob Hawk", confirming that this was indeed the Hawk property. The opening in the fence was to an almost invisible road, overgrown with tall grass, wet from the on-and-off drizzle. We drove in about 200 yards and came to a smaller enclosure with massive trees, some derelict lawn furniture and vehicles, an antique rusted plow and the ruin of a farmhouse. It would have been a lovely place in its day — a modest home made glorious by the huge, silent trees in the fenced yard. Only a chimney, rising from the crumbling brick foundation, remained of the actual house. Outside the house perimeter was a nearby water pump that still worked. Dave immediately collected a few lichen-covered bricks from the ruin to take as a souvenir, and I did the same for Pat. We drove back to the public road and continued up it looking for a Hawk Cemetery, indicated on a crude map of the area found from a Google search. No luck.

We returned to the "Bob Hawk" sign, which had a phone number on it. Dave called the number, and to our thrilled amazement, a Bob Hawk answered. He was in Florida — still owned the land but leased it to a local farmer. They talked briefly about parentage, figuring how they were related. Bob explained that the farmhouse had burned down several decades earlier, and the cemetery was actually along the same unused track that the farmhouse was on. We should continue up the track past the crumbling remains of the house. Not far past the ruined homestead, we had to abandon the car for fear of its getting stuck in the wet ground. The path ahead looked to be a difficult slog, and I wondered if Barb might opt to wait in the car. Definitely not. The three of us tramped on foot through wet growth and dripping overhead branches until we saw a few stones at odd angles showing through dense bushes and saplings on a small rectangle of land. The graveyard was long abandoned — the most recent burial was 1959 and most graves were much earlier. Robert Hawk, purchaser of the land in 1820, died at age 46 and was the first buried there, in 1836, later joined by others whose names we'd seen on the family tree. There were some large, very prominent stones suggesting prosperity. Others were flat slabs at ground level that required clawing away of overgrowth to be seen. All were unkempt, hidden in varying degrees by exuberant greenery. The inscriptions were a revelation in terms of what Pat had assumed regarding his background. Nowhere was there anything the least bit Catholic. In fact, except for the most recently placed stone, which bore the Protestant-sounding inscription "Let me die the death of the righteous, and my last end be like His", there was not a shred of religion anywhere. Pat — who had learned remarkably little about his family history — had always assumed they'd been Catholic from the beginning. This discovery made it unlikely on the Hawk side.

We spent a long time among the wet growth looking in vain for the stone of James Elbert Hawk, the grandfather of Dave, Barb and Pat, who had died in 1941. Eventually, we decided to try St. Mark's Catholic Cemetery in town, Dave and Barb coming away reluctantly from that old, earthy place that felt so much like roots. Stopping first at the Winchester Cemetery on the way to St. Mark's, the three of us spread out to read all the headstones. There were a few more Hawk ancestors, not many, and the grave of James Elbert was not there. Both the Winchester Cemetery and St. Mark's Catholic Cemetery were immaculately kept, very different from the abandoned Hawk Cemetery, where the overgrown, cracked, tilting, sinking stones spoke of forgotten history. Spreading out again at St. Mark's, this time we found it — a large stone marking the grave of James Elbert Hawk and Nora Hawk, née Quinn. James Elbert must have converted to Catholicism to marry Nora. They were buried in the Quinn family plot. Quiet, alcoholic James, and sad, long-suffering Nora — first he, then eight years later she, had died in Granite City and been brought to Winchester to be buried. Right next to their stone was a tiny one with the simple inscription "Baby" — an aunt or uncle neither Pat, Dave nor Barb had ever heard of.

Pat took great interest in the photos from this adventure — the cemeteries, the drive, the old homestead. He examined thoughtfully the fragment of lichen-covered brick from the crumbling foundation of the farmhouse he remembered visiting as a child. The next day he told the story to Jane Huyer — she had called from Oregon — and suggested lightly that she should do a painting of a gravestone for him. She had taken up painting in retirement and was becoming quite accomplished. Jane requested the photos and chose a small area in the Hawk cemetery where two stones faced each other as the model for *Dokusan in the Woods*, completed a few weeks later.

Another day I met Pat's niece Tina and his great-nephew Michael at Ravanelli's Italian restaurant. Tina had an attractive expression, vulnerable and saucy, that recalled her mother, Mary Ellen. Michael had handsome features I didn't recognize. They lived in a house just a few blocks from where Pat grew up, overlooking part of the abandoned cemetery where he had played as a boy. Tina had a stack of old family photo albums inherited from her mother that she allowed me to copy for Pat, and that he and I later went through in some detail. Through Tina's reminiscences, it became apparent that Pat's cousin and closest childhood friend, Nora, was still living in Granite City.

I visited Nora the next day in her immaculate, pleasant home on a quiet street of well-kept gardens and modest houses. Her dog, a terrier of some sort, was shy but welcoming, a little like Nora herself, a self-confessed shrinking violet and the sort of person one trusts immediately. The conversation about Pat was poignant. She was interested to hear about his influence as a teacher of Zen and contemplative practice. She talked about their early friendship, how they played at priest. "He was always the priest. We kneeled and we prayed..." I asked her, "Was it fun?" "Everything we did was fun." She said it wistfully and tearing up slightly said, "I have missed him all my life." After Pat entered the seminary, he relinquished family ties, including their friendship, and Nora only ever saw him again occasionally when he visited with family. She asked if Mary Ellen's children Tina and Jimmy kept in touch with Pat. "Not much," I said, "They're busy, and he's not very good at keeping in touch." She nodded, and one felt a history of sadness in the nod.

Back at St Clement, Pat listened to the story and looked for a long time at the photo I took of Nora, a wistful expression on his face. I let him know what I'd said to Nora about him — how fortunate we all felt to work with him, how skilled he was as a spiritual guide. With a sweet smile, he nodded his head gently at each point. It was as if he were outside himself and we were talking about someone we both loved very much. Looking again at the photo of Nora, this time impishly, he said, "We were going to get married. We told our parents we were going to get married and they said, 'You can't, you're Catholic. Catholics can't marry first cousins.' So we said we would go to Mexico and get married." I told Pat what Nora had told me, adding, "She has loved you all her life." He nodded.

Lunch at Jerry's Cafeteria, with Pat's elementary-school classmates was a rollicking good time, boisterous with memories and laughter. The restaurant was a longstanding eatery in Granite City. It was opened in 1945 in a different location by Jerry's parents, Oliver and Theresa Roderick, and it had been a favorite dining spot for Pat's parents. The Rodericks were good friends of the Hawks — Ollie and Theresa were in the wedding party when Ed and Elnora married. The original Roderick's restaurant was sold, and Jerry opened the cafeteria on Edison Street downtown. In 2012 it was a bit rundown but pleasant, the food plentiful American fare, rib-sticking and good. We were given the event room off the main dining room for the gathering of Pat's classmates.

Photo albums from the parish archive spread out on some of the tables served as catalyst for recalling old familiar names of students and nuns, sketching personalities and catching up. These people obviously enjoyed each other's company. Memories were fond, and there was both pride and wonder at the strictness, the antics, the devotions, and the characters that filled those late 1940's early 1950's Catholic school years. The 59 students in the Class of '56 eighth-grade photo had been together since first grade —give or take a handful. Pat was in the give and take, having spent second grade in the one-room schoolhouse in Collinsville.

They remembered Pat: "Quiet." "Very quiet." "He was always quiet." "Very pious, very quiet." "And Pat was so quiet." It came up again and again. "But his father was very quiet." "He always had beautiful hair when we were children."

Snapshots of their school days flashed from voices around the room. "Sister pulled Jimmy Predinger's hair and got a handful. Took his hair and pulled him up out of the seat, and his hair came with it. If you did that today, you'd be behind bars." "Somebody turned a big spider loose in the room one day." "Who put the frog in Sister Ackland's desk?" Boys supposed to be watering some plants outdoors, "took the hose and aimed it at the window. ... Punishment was to kneel in the church. They knelt on the communion rail. Sister said, 'No, no, on the floor!' " "Sister Thomas More. I remember one thing she taught me: "'Patience is a virtue," ...the others joined in chanting, "...possess it if you can, it's seldom in a woman, and never in a man!" Remembering Father Costello coming into the classroom and quizzing them from the catechism in first and second grade, they could still come forth with the rote answers all these years later.

They recalled the religiosity that permeated the school day. Kitty reminisced, "I brought a sack breakfast every day because I went to communion every day." Pat did the same. Someone remembered getting up in the middle of the night and drinking water. "Couldn't go to communion the next day, and I felt so bad." That sparked another recollection: "Talk about being afraid — for my first confession, in first grade? ... Because you were scared of what you might have forgotten." The name of their seventh-grade teacher came up and someone said, "Pardon me, the nun from hell." "Yeah, she was a little bitty sharp." They talked about their children — divorce, broken families, health issues, diets, grandchildren, travel. Even the heavier stories were told lightheartedly. One felt their spunk and resilience.

They asked many questions about Pat's ministry: "Helen, exactly what is Zen? Is it meditation?" "Do you have to study Buddhism to do Zen? Do you have to be a Buddhist?" "How did Pat get started with this?" "How does he fund all these travels?" At that point, we were looking at photos from Pat's retreats in various settings. They listened to answers with an interest that included sympathy when his dark times in the seminary and his times at Guest House came into the conversation. If there was resistance or disapproval in these dyed-in-the-wool Catholics, it didn't show. The only concern expressed was for Pat's health and whether he was well cared for now, in his final illness. "Please tell him we remember him fondly." They all signed a card for him.

Ed Ruder had died since they had gotten together for a reunion the previous October. It was Ed, Dan Betinec and Pat who went together toward the end of eighth grade to check out the Redemptorist seminary at Kirkwood, driven there by Dan Betinec's mother. All three entered together. Only Pat went through to ordination. Dan was among those attending the lunch, and he had brought several albums from seminary days. We stayed to look at them after the rest had gone, happy anyway to wait out the rain that had begun hitting the windows of Jerry's Cafeteria.

Just as we were putting the albums away there were suddenly knocking, cracking sounds, so loud that at first it was hard to tell that they were coming from the roof. Tennis ball-sized hail was falling. Dan's car and my rental car happened to be parked side by side, noses under a tree. It meant the front ends were relatively spared, but the rear windshields were shattered, and the car bodies looked beyond repair. The Hawk family photo albums, still on loan from Tina, were safe in the trunk, put there as an afterthought instead of on the back seat, which was now covered with leaves, hailstones and broken glass. Dan had asked earlier if he could join me in a visit to Pat, and Pat had agreed, but plans to go that afternoon had to be shelved as we dealt with the damaged vehicles.

We went to St. Clement the next day, stopping at a gas station partway to Liguori to add more duct tape to hold the plastic covering the place where the rear windshield should have been on Dan's car. Pat was alert when we came in. "Hi Dan, my God, how long has it been?" "Well, probably about 45 years." Pat said, "Do you remember Al Babbin? Cosgrove? Novak? They're all here now. … So is Gerry Pecht." Dan brought his photo albums and we helped Pat get propped up on the bed so he could look at them comfortably. The two of them were quickly absorbed in names and faces from the old days.

"Skating on the pond at Kirkwood." "Here's Babbin. He taught us Latin." "He's down the road now [at Liguori Mission House]." Looking at a photo of a chess game, Dan said, "I think you got him checkmated there, Pat. You've got that big grin on your face." They remembered how cold it was at Kirkwood in the winter, cracks in the walls, ice on a water bucket indoors. Coming across a group photo from Edgerton with over a hundred young men, all wearing the same light-colored polo shirt, standing casually looking up at a camera, they picked out familiar faces. "There's Otterbacher. Colgan. LeBlanc…" and many more. Frequently, a name was followed by the observation, "He left." "He dropped out." "Yeah, he left us in the novitiate." "He dropped out at Oconomowoc."

I left them to their reminiscences and headed down the hall to visit George Rassley, librarian from Oconomowoc much admired by Pat, to whom I had already spoken several times over the phone. For each of our conversations I brought questions, but he had more. He was engaged, interested in people — an inquisitor, Ted Lawson said of him — well-loved by his confreres. He wanted to see photos of Pat's life, interrogating me all the while. "And how have you been? How did you find Pat?" Rassley had been in the hospital when Pat arrived and had not yet had a chance to see Pat himself, though he hoped to. I explained Pat's condition.

He asked: "He's not dying, is he?"

"He is dying."

"But not right way."

"They told him in January eight to ten months, but at that time he was still driving, walking…"

Rassley changed the subject with, "Did you find what I told you useful?" and we shifted to recollections of Oconomowoc and Esopus until he was ready for his nap. "I can't stay up much longer. Anything else you want to know, you ask me."

When I visited Pat the next day he was still sitting up and cheerful. His laptop had arrived from Tucson, and he was thinking maybe he would start offering Skype dokusan again. I gathered my things to leave, promising I would return in June. He nodded. As I looked back from the door of his room, he called out, "You be careful out there," the slight, unmistakable Pat Hawk grin discernible despite his terribly swollen face.

I left Missouri the following day and got a call later the same day from Ted Lawson saying Pat had breakthrough pain again. He reported that as the nurses were getting ready to increase the dose of morphine, Pat said, "Give me as much as you can." Ted began sending email updates to a handful of people to forward to all who were following Pat's situation with concern. May 3, he wrote, "Pain control is the major issue right now and it has become a daily challenge, but the pain meds are still effective and there continue to be options to keep him comfortable. If you'd ask me how much time does he have? My answer would be that I simply do not know. Through the course of the day it can look close and then again not, later on the same day."

The annual North American Sanbo Kyodan sesshin led by Yamada Ryo'un Roshi (Masamichi) was in progress at Mercy Center in Burlingame, California, at the time, and one of Pat's longtime students from Santa Fe was in attendance. She broke silence during the sesshin to send an email recounting a long conversation with Yamada regarding his encounter with Pat in dokusan at the international teachers' sesshin in Kamakura in 1992 — 20 years earlier. Yamada described himself as being young and arrogant at the time, expressing regret at the way he had behaved toward Pat. He said he admired Pat for continuing to teach for so long after being diagnosed with prostate cancer and that he would pray for him. I forwarded the email to Ted Lawson, who read it to Pat. It's difficult to know what he heard, since he was not showing much response to anything. Ted conveyed that Pat was composed and at rest.

On May 5, Ted sent this update:

> Pat's condition has deteriorated considerably. I just came from his room and his responses are minimal. You know Pat. It's hard to tell if he is unresponsive (he can't) or not responding because he has found a place within himself to maintain the peace that he radiates. Radiate is the only term I can use.

> Entering his room is an experience of peace. Don't get me wrong, this is tough, and yet it's a privilege to experience such holiness.

On May 6 Ted wrote:

> Pat's condition has leveled a bit. He took some food later in the day yesterday and was trying to talk. His struggle to speak continues to drain him and it is very difficult to understand the one or two words he tries to speak. The effects of the stronger medication are showing, and the breakthrough pain has subsided. He is quieter. He was enjoying visits but now he seems to appreciate them being brief. He was enjoying listening to his music but asked to have it turned off. I'm going to check with him a little later to see if he'd like it back.
>
> As you know full well, Pat is an unusual man; not odd but unusual. He is not showing the classic signs of being close to the end. Rather than simply being unresponsive, it appears very often that he is meditating when we enter the room. Several of us have come to that idea/theory before discussing it with each other about 20 minutes ago. Regardless of our accuracy, he certainly embodies peace whatever the state may be.

Father Joe Butz, a confrere Pat had not seen in years, dropped in from the Mission House and said to Pat in a loud voice, "Well, Pat, you were a tough nut to crack but you finally opened up some." It was perhaps a succinct representation of his more conservative confreres' view. Whether Pat heard it or not, he was surely unruffled by it.

The next day, May 7, he was resting peacefully, not responsive. The morning of May 8, Ted called to say Pat had had a quiet night. As we chatted, he excused himself from the call when a nurse looked into his office and signaled meaningfully. Minutes later, Ted called back to say that Pat was gone. He had stopped breathing at about 9:50 AM Missouri time. George Rassley died later that same day.

Memorials

Redemptorists, friends and family crowded St. Clement chapel the evening of May 15 for rosary and vigil, including informal recollections, and again the next morning for the funeral Mass. The Mass was concelebrated according to Pat's request by the three leaders of the Denver Province at the time — Reverends Harry Grile, Provincial Superior, Bob Halter, Consultor, and John Schmidt, Vicar. Harry Grile and Bob Halter especially were dear friends of Pat's with a long shared history, so the timing was good that way.

Ashley Large, archivist for the Denver Province, arrived with — as was customary — a photo board illustrating the many stages of Pat's life with the Redemptorists. At Ted Lawson's request, a board with photos of Pat as Zen master and contemplative teacher was also produced, the two displayed side by side in the hallway outside the chapel. Also on the table were traditional prayer cards with, on one face, Our Lady of Perpetual Help, patroness of the Congregation of the Most Holy Redeemer, and on the other, dates of profession, ordination and death. Instead of including a photo of Pat on this flip side as was customary, Ted asked that we provide a Zen saying. Words were chosen from the Heart Sutra, chanted by and with Pat over the many years of his teaching: "...with no hindrance in the mind, no hindrance and therefore no fear."

Many years prior, Pat had made it known that he wished to be cremated. He commissioned an urn from a woodworking confrere, Paddy Power, who produced a beautiful handmade box for the purpose. Pat had kept the box in his room in Tucson, ready for whenever the time came. Now put to its intended use, it was on display at the front of the chapel, draped with the long wooden rosary and crucifix that a Redemptorist receives at the time of his profession and wears with his robes. The box did not contain all the ashes. Pat had asked Ted Lawson that some be set aside "for the Zen community," and this request was carried out.

Four of Pat's students came to the services: Bob Walker from Georgia, Susan Weimer, who had been driving across country to visit Pat when the news came of his death, Mary Riseley, and me. After the funeral Mass, Bob Walker, flanked by Harry Grile, Bob Halter and John Schmidt, carried the ashes from the chapel to the cemetery for the graveside service. A tall cedar stands in the cemetery, its gnarled, raised roots interrupting the regular row on row of gravestones. There was just the right amount of space under it to bury an urn. A headstone added later marks the spot. Pat's ashes rest there in the shade of the wide branches.

Pat's various sanghas held memorials of their own. Instructions from Pat to Ted Lawson about his funeral had included, as near as could be gathered from Pat's faint and muffled words, that he would like to have the old, tender love song, *Luna Rossa,* sung in French by Lucienne Delyle, played. This was not done at St. Clement for the funeral — it surely would have been beyond the pale for the confreres — but it was included in the memorial at Zen Desert Sangha. The poignant romantic strains of this song to a lover and to the moon, together with other music Pat loved, not necessarily spiritual, alongside the old familiar chants of the sutra service, harmonized beautifully with the tender mood in the zendo, the graceful, solemn service then giving way to refreshments and shared recollections.

Thoughts drifted back to Rohatsu, the last sesshin with Pat. At suppertime of the last evening, the warmly lit kitchen held the muted sounds of food service amidst the deep quiet. Some retreatants took their places at indoor tables, others at tables on the lighted patio. One longtime student stood outside leaning against a brick pillar of the covered patio, looking out toward the desert and the shadowy mountains. Her silent gaze into the star-filled night recalled all the years of sitting with Pat Hawk — at Palisades, Indianola, Portland, Amarillo, Melbourne, Santa Fe, Tucson — all were held in that silence.

Across the Empty Sky

Acknowledgements

Perhaps more than any other genre, a biography requires the input of scores of people who in some way knew the subject. The biographer is at the mercy of their generosity. In addition to Pat Hawk's liberal sharing of recollections and resources during the five years before his death, numerous people contributed recollections for this project, many at length and some over multiple meetings.

Many thanks to a host of fellow travelers who shared memories and reflections, including: Josh Abrams, Robert Aitken, Augusto Alcalde, Greg Anderson, Sandy Anderson, Dale Armstrong, Dan Betinec, Joe Bobrow, John Bormanis, Lucie Brennan, Bill Broker, Bill Bruce, Pancho Burke, Paul Coury, Steve Daney, Jim D'Elia, Dan Dorsey, Shelly Dorsey, Rolf Drosten, Christa Drosten, Frances Duos, Millicent Easter, Mark Filut, Nelson Foster, Jim Green, Harry Grile, Bob Halter, Lesley Hanks, Dave Hawk, Barbara Copeland (née Hawk), Danan Henry, Katherine Holmsen, Vivian Hsu, Paul Hughes, Jane Huyer, Bill Jackson, Jill Jameson, Pamela King, Bill Larson, Kristen Larson, Richard Laue, Ted Lawson, Marsha Linehan, Leonard Marcel, Paul Markl, Greg Mayers, Tracy McCallum, Greg Mello, Dan Mintie, Jim Mish'alani, Shirley Morrissey, Indiana Nelson, Henry Novak, Nancy O'Connor, Kevin O'Shea, John Otterbacher, Ilya Perez, Glenna Pittock, Mary Ellen Pope, Tina Pope, George Rassley, Neale Povey, Alice Ray, Kitty Reither, Joan Rieck, Mary Burton Riseley, Karen Robinson, Jerry Roderick, Joan Saalfeld, Paul Sanders, Peter Schavitz, Tom Schiltz, Bill Scott, Stephen Slottow, Bob Smith, Vonna Smith, Barbara Spalding, Vicki Stoddard, Emma Stone, Tim Storer, Kristine Stremel, Hamish Swanston, Tony Tackitt, Nora Thomas, Rich Wahl, Bob Walker, Bob Wallin, Susan Weimer, Greg Wiest, Barbara Wooten and Pauline Yule. I am deeply grateful to all who shared their stories, employing both tact and candor to contribute to a portrait that I hope is balanced and true.

Tracy McCallum, Dave Piper, Vonna Smith and Stephen Slottow read full drafts of the manuscript and gave substantial and detailed feedback, including fact-checking, requests for clarification, thoughtful reflection, and corrections of grammar and spelling. Bob Halter, Nancy O'Connor and Paul Sanders also read full drafts and gave useful input. They read with an eye toward gentleness in handling sensitive subjects which I very much appreciate.

Members of the Hawk family were welcoming and generous with stories and photos, especially Mary Ellen Pope (née Hawk), Tina Patrick (née Pope), Dave

Hawk, Barbara Copeland (née Hawk), and Nora Thomas (née Delmar). Dave, Barb and I went on a wonderful adventure exploring Hawk roots, driving north of Granite City to visit the old Hawk farmstead and cemeteries near Winchester, Illinois.

Kitty Reither applied her buoyant spirit to organizing a luncheon with Pat's elementary school classmates at Jerry's Cafeteria in Granite City. Jerry Roderick provided the contact information for the Sacred Heart School Class of 1956, as well as the space for us to gather for lunch. Many thanks to Kitty, Jerry and the other classmates who shared stories and photographs from Pat's elementary school days. Among those people, Dan Betinec and I, being the last to leave the luncheon, found our cars totaled (my rental car) or near totaled (Dan's car) by the pounding hail that fell while we were inside Jerry's browsing photo albums.

Thanks to Ginger Ikenberry and Carolyn Glass for making me welcome at Palolo Zen center during my visits there to meet Robert Aitken and to explore Pat's experience in Hawaii. Lynn Davis, archivist at the University of Hawaii Manoa, introduced me to the Robert Baker Aitken Papers after Aitken himself encouraged me to delve into those materials. Lynn kindly replied to my multiple emails with the materials requested. Others including Carolyn Blaisdel, Jane Huyer, Pamela King, Kristen Larson, Richard Laue, Tracy McCallum, Carol Neese, Barbara Spalding and Barbara Wooten provided newsletters and other print materials and/or audio recordings. Brother Mark Filut and Jane Huyer provided detailed records of the early sesshins for Christians in the Pacific Northwest. Brother Mark and other Trappists were cordial and helpful when I visited Our Lady of Guadalupe Abbey. Ashley Large, archivist for the Redemptorist Denver Province, responded to my requests by sending several bundles of papers on different occasions. During my visit to the Redemptorist archive in February 2013, in Ashley's absence the assistant archivist, Kathy Joda, was a great help, as was staff member Kristine Stremel. Carmen Patterson, a lead staff member at the Redemptorist Renewal Center in Tucson, was an always warm and steadying presence and helped in many ways, including facilitating access to some Hawk-related materials and making me welcome during many hours spent at the Renewal Center working on the biography.

The Redemptorists have been generous with their time and resources throughout the project. Several warrant special mention. Kevin O'Shea responded to queries and provided his unpublished article on the proceedings and results of Vatican II. In addition to giving feedback on the manuscript, Bob Halter helped facilitate my visit to the Redemptorist Denver Province Archive including arranging for comfortable living quarters, meals with the resident Redemptorists and access to the archive. Greg Mayers graciously consented to have me visit him at Mercy Center in Burlingame for a week during which he welcomed me as a participant in his sangha and gave generously of his time to answer my questions and recollect seminary and Amarillo days. Ted Lawson kept me and others informed of Pat's condition during his last week and provided accommodation at St. Clement Healthcare Center while I was visiting Liguori. George Rassley conversed at length over the phone several times giving useful information and recommending references. He then met with me at St. Clement in May 2012, still fully engaged and engaging just one week before he died.

Many thanks to Bob Walker for sharing recollections and for stalwart support of my practice over many years. Nelson Foster provided moral support in the months of Pat's final illness and after his death, in several long phone calls and then in person when he came to Tucson to lead a zazenkai. I'm grateful for his kindness and interest.

Rolf Drosten and his wife Christa provided a delicious lunch and an afternoon of helpful conversation when I visited them in Leverkusen, Germany. Also in Germany, the staff at Benediktushof in Holzkirchen provided gracious hospitality while I was there for several days to meet Willigis Jäger.

I spent many happy hours in conversation with Katherine Holmsen, mulling over events, recollecting characters and encouraging each other in our respective projects. Tracy McCallum, besides contributing his recollections and providing feedback on the manuscript, was always willing to ponder whatever information or idea I was wrangling with. Vonna Smith has been an enthusiastic, indefatigable source of encouragement, advice, and indispensable input through all stages of writing. I am deeply grateful to these dear friends.

Lastly, I thank Julia Amerongen Maddison for thoughtful advice and encouragement even as she had her own projects to tend to, and Dave Piper, partner extraordinaire, who besides providing abundant helpful feedback on the manuscript and applying his considerable librarian skills to various aspects of the project, gave unwavering support throughout, including innumerable instances of cheerful assistance on the home front.

Abbreviations

BDRC	Bishop DeFalco Retreat Center, Amarillo, Texas
CIR	Contemplative Intensive Retreat
CSsR	*Congregatio Sanctissimi Redemptoris* — Congregation of the Most Holy Redeemer. The Redemptorist Congregation
DBT	Dialectical Behavior Therapy
DSTC	Diamond Sangha Teachers' Circle
FSPA	Franciscan Sisters of Perpetual Adoration
MCZC	Mountain Cloud Zen Center, Santa Fe, New Mexico
OCSO	The Order of Cistercians of the Strict Observance (Trappists)
OSB	The Order of St. Benedict (Benedictines)
RRC	Redemptorist Renewal Center, Tucson, Arizona
ZDS	Zen Desert Sangha, Tucson, Arizona

Glossary

Note: Non-English terms are Japanese unless otherwise indicated.

Apostolate The assigned ministry of each priest.

Awakening The experience of seeing the essential nature of reality, the core Zen experience. Also referred to as kensho, satori, realization, enlightenment.

Benediction In the Roman Catholic Church, a rite involving prayers to the Blessed Sacrament exposed in a monstrance and blessing of the faithful.

Blessed Sacrament In the Roman Catholic Church this refers to the consecrated host, believed to be the body and blood of Christ.

Bodhisattva (Sanskrit) enlightened being. A person committed to the awakening/enlightenment of all beings.

Canon Law In the Catholic Church, the body of ecclesiastical laws and regulations that govern procedures and conduct.

Ch'an (Chinese) transliteration of the Sanskrit word dhyana — concentration, meditation. The Japanese word, "Zen" derives from "Ch'an."

Charism Within the context of a congregation of religious, charism refers to the special virtue or mission of the congregation.

Cloud name A person given authorization to teach Zen is given a teaching name that includes " 'un" or in English, "Cloud", e.g. Pat Hawk: Shin'un Ken (House of the Spreading Cloud).

Congregation A religious congregation is a type of Catholic institute of priests or nuns. Members of religious congregations take vows of poverty, chastity and obedience; in the case of Redemptorists, they also take a vow of perseverance. Congregations of religious operate outside the diocesan structure and are subject directly to Rome rather than to a bishop.

Densho A large bell or gong hanging from a frame, sounded with a striker. The densho sequence of rings calls practitioners to the start of a period of zazen.

Dharma (Sanskrit) Universal law, universal truth. Dharma brother, dharma sister, dharma sibling: students of the same teacher. Dharma eye: refers to a person's seeing into the nature of reality. Dharma heir: designated successor of a Zen master. Dharma name: name given by a Zen master to the student at Jukai. See also dharma transmission.

Dharma transmission Zen dharma transmission originated with Ch'an Buddhism in China, as a formal acknowledgement from a Zen Master to a disciple of a "mind to mind" recognition of essential nature. The essence of dharma transmission is the acknowledgement of a wordless understanding of dharma between master and disciple. In practical terms, dharma transmission carries with it a permission to teach Zen; it goes beyond a simple permission to teach, however, certifying the individual as an independent Zen master, themselves authorized to give transmission.

Diocese, Diocesan A diocese is a district under the jurisdiction of a bishop, typically including multiple parishes. A diocesan priest serves one or more of the parishes within the diocese and is subject to the bishop's authority.

Dojo Meditation or practice hall. See also zendo.

Dokusan Personal interview between Zen student and teacher; also called sanzen.

Enlightenment See realization, kensho.

Eucharist The ritual commemorating the Last Supper of Jesus of Nazareth with his disciples. The term is often used interchangeably with Mass. The Eucharist also refers to the sacrament of communion.

Frater Title bestowed on men preparing for the priesthood, from the time of their first profession of vows until ordination.

Gassho A simple bow, hands held with palms together.

Inka, Inka Shomei "Legitimate seal of true attainment" — in practical terms inka is the certification of a dharma heir as being a true link in the Zen lineage that originates with Shakyamuni Buddha.

Ino Chant leader.

Jiki, Jikijitsu Timekeeper.

Jisha Teacher's attendant.

Jukai Ceremony in which a student formally accepts the Buddhist precepts.

Junshike In the Sanbo Kyodan lineage this refers to "Semi Zen Master" a teacher one step below Shoshike, "Authentic Zen Master."

Kansho Jisha's bell, rung outside the dokusan room to signal to the teacher inside the room.

Karma (Sanskrit) action, deed; cause and effect.

Kechimyaku Blood line/lineage chart documenting the line of masters beginning with the Buddha and connecting in unbroken succession to the person now receiving transmission. From: Nelson Foster article reprinted in *Pathless Path*, Volume 4:4, July August 2001.

Kensho Ken = seeing; sho = essence or nature; the experience of seeing into essential nature; kensho often refers to an initial experience of this insight, expected to deepen with practice.

Kenshukai Collective koan review.

Kinhin Meditative walking, usually led by a Jiki (timekeeper).

Koan A story, question or statement, engagement with which can help a student break through the bounds of conventional thought to a deeper perception of reality. Many koans in current use are stories of master student interactions from Tang dynasty Chinese Buddhism (Ch'an).

Kotsu Curved wooden stick, said to be shaped like a human spine, used ceremonially by a Zen master as a symbol of transmission; sometimes used to bang loudly or otherwise make a point during teisho or dokusan.

Major Seminary The last six years of the thirteen-year seminary training program, including the final two years of college and four years of post-graduate study.

Minor Seminary The first six years of the thirteen-year seminary training program, including four years of high school and the first two years of college. The high school years are distinguished as "first academic," "second Students in the first three years of high school comprise the juniors. Those in their last year of high school (fourth academic) plus the college freshmen and sophomores comprise the seniors.

Novitiate The seventh year of the thirteen-year seminary training program. During the novitiate year, academic study is suspended and the focus is on personal spiritual development.

Raihai Full prostration, done as part of Zen ritual.

Rakusu A bib-like garment worn around the neck. The rakusu is sewed with pieces of cloth in a rice-field pattern, said to symbolize the fecundity of the dharma.

Realization See awakening, kensho.

Religious, co-religious A person who has taken religious vows, i.e. of poverty, chastity and obedience. A co-religious is a person in the same congregation or order.

Rinzai One of the two major schools of Zen that have taken root in the West (the other is Soto Zen) characterized by strong focus on kensho and subsequent extended koan study to deepen realization.

Rohatsu The eighth day of the last month of the year; traditionally an eight-day sesshin commemorating Shakyamuni Buddha's enlightenment. Rohatsu usually takes place December 1-8.

Roshi Venerable teacher; an honorific given to a Zen master.

Samu Work practice, mindful work; considered an important aspect of Zen training.

Sanbo Kyodan Order of the Three Treasures. A Zen lineage founded in 1954 by the Zen monk, Haku'un Yasutani. It is a lay Zen organization that includes elements of both Soto and Rinzai Zen traditions. Also referred to as Sanbokyodan or Sambokyodan. The name was changed to Sanbo Zen International in 2014.

Sangha (Sanskrit) Fellowship; community.

Sanmotsu Three documents certifying transmission: the *shisho* (inheritance certificate), *odaiji* (the great matter), and the *kechimyaku* (bloodline of the authentic transmission).

Satori Understanding, enlightenment, awakening, realization; the state of realization, enlightenment. See also, kensho.

Sensei Apprentice or associate teacher.

Sesshin "To touch the mind" A multi-day Zen retreat. The main element is usually zazen, silent sitting. In addition, there is teisho, dokusan, and chanting or recitation of sutras at specific times each day.

Shoken An exchange, usually at the first dokusan with a teacher, formally acknowledging a teacher-student relationship. It may include a token gift of "incense money" from the student to the teacher.

Shosan A public exchange between student and teacher in the setting of sesshin. At a dharma transmission ceremony, it is an opportunity for all present to ask questions or otherwise challenge the person about to receive dharma transmission, to probe that person's dharma eye.

Shoshike "Authentic Zen Master" of the Sanbo Kyodan. A person with Shoshike status is empowered to certify the kensho of others.

Sutra A Buddhist scripture or canon. Sutras are often recited or chanted, for example in the context of sesshin.

Soto One of the two major schools of Zen that have taken root in the West (the other is Rinzai). Emphasizes shikantaza or silent meditation with no thought object.

Tanto Head of practice. A senior practitioner who is responsible for procedures and conduct of a sesshin or zazenkai.

Teisho Presentation of the shout. Presentation by a Zen master in the context of a sesshin or zazenkai; it is a presentation of dharma insight rather than a discursive exposition.

Transmission See dharma transmission.

Upaya (Sanskrit) Expedient or skillful means. A teaching device tailored to the particular individual to help attain understanding. The Japanese term is *hoben*.

Zabuton Padded mat placed under the zafu, used for zazen.

Zafu Cushion used for zazen.

Zazen Seated meditation.

Zazenkai Short Zen retreat, often a day or half day in length.

Zen Derived from the Chinese word "*Ch'an*," which is a transliteration of the Sanskrit, "*dhyana*," meaning concentration or meditation.

Zendo Meditation hall. The term can refer to the building in which the meditation hall is a room, or to the room itself, also called dojo.

Selected Bibliography

Aitken, Robert, D Steindl-Rast. *The Ground We Share: Everyday Practice, Buddhist and Christian.* Boston: Shambhala, New York: Distributed in the United States by Random House, 1996.

Aitken, Robert. *Taking the Path of Zen*, North Point Press, San Francisco, 1982.

Aitken, Robert. *The Gateless Barrier: the Wu-men kuan (Mumonkan).* San Francisco: North Point Press, 1990.

Aitken, Robert. *The Mind of Clover Essays in Zen Buddhist Ethics.* New York North Point Press, Farrar, Straus and Giroux, 2000.

Aitken, Robert. *The Practice of Perfection: The Pāramitās From a Zen Buddhist Perspective.* New York: Pantheon Books, 1994.

Aitken, Robert. *Zen Master Raven: Sayings and Doings of a Wise Bird.* Boston: Tuttle Pub., 2002.

Alphonsus of Liguori (Saint). *Guide for Confessors from the Praxis Confessarii of St. Alphonsus Liguori.* [Edited by R. Schiblin. Oconomowoc, Wisconsin. N.d.]

Anderson, J and Schwartz, Steven Z. *Zen Odyssey: The Story of Sokei-an, Ruth Fuller Sasaki, and the Birth of Zen in America.* Wisdom Publications, Somerville, Massachusetts, 2018.

Batchelor, Stephen. *The Awakening of the West: The Encounter of Buddhism and Western Culture: 542 BCE - 1992.* San Francisco: Thorsons, 1995.

Besserman, Perle. *A New Zen for Women.* New York: Palgrave Macmillan, 2007.

Besserman, Perle. Steger, Manfred. *Crazy Clouds: Zen Radicals, Rebels, and Reformers.* Boston, Mass.: Shambhala Publications, 1991.

Blyth, Reginald Horace. *Zen Buddhism in English Literature and Oriental Classics*, Hokuseido Press, Tokyo, 1942.

Busenbaum, Hermann. *Medulla Theologiae Moralis, Facili ac Perspicua Methodo Resolvens Casus Conscientiae,* France Huré, Sébastien 1657, translated into English by the Redemptorists.

A Century of Blessings 1907-2007, Mount St. Alphonsus, Esopus New York, Centennial Jubilee, 2007.

Chadwick, David. *Crooked Cucumber: The Life and Zen Teaching of Shunryu Suzuki.* New York: Broadway Books 1999.

Cleary JC and Thomas Cleary (Transl.). *The Blue Cliff Record.* Shambala Publications, 2005. An English translation of the Ch'an koan collection *Pi-yen lu* (Chinese), *Hekiganroku* (Japanese).

Cleary, Thomas (Transl.). *Book of Serenity: One Hundred Zen Dialogues*. Shambala, Boston and London, 2005. An English translation of the Ch'an koan collection *Congrong lu* (Chinese), *Shoyoroku* (Japanese).

Colin, Louis, CSsR. *The Practice of the Vows* The Mercier Press, 1961.

Congar, Yves. *Mon Journal du Concile,* Les Éditions du Cerf, 2002. Excerpts translated by Father Kevin O'Shea.

Déchanet, Jean. *Christian Yoga*, Harper and Brothers,1960. Originally published under the pseudonym, Yogin du Christ, La Voie du Silence; L'expérience d'un Moine. [Bruges] Desclée de Brouwer 1956.

Enomiya-Lassalle, Hugo Makibi. *Zen: Way to Enlightenment.* London: Burns & Oates, 1967.

Ferguson, Andrew. *Zen's Chinese Heritage: The Masters and Their Teachings.* Wisdom Publications, Boston, 2000.

Foster, Nelson and Jack Shoemaker. *The Roaring Stream: A New Zen Reader*, Ecco Press, 1996.

Gresser, Julian. *Mastering Negotiations with the Japanese*, Palo Alto, California, 1990.

Howard, Robert P. *Illinois: A History of the Prairie State*, William B Eerdman's, Grand Rapids, Michigan, 1972.

Kapleau, Philip. *Three Pillars of Zen: Teaching, Practice and Enlightenment*, Harper and Row, 1966.

Kennett, Jiyu. *Selling Water by the River: A Manual of Zen Training*, Vintage Books, 1972.

Lincoln, Victoria. *Teresa, a Woman: A Biography of Teresa of Avila.* SUNY Press, 1985.

Matthiesen, Leroy. T*he Life and Times of a Cottonpicking Texas Bishop*, Self-Published. Printed by Custom Printing Company, 2005.

Mayers, Gregory. *Listen to the Desert: Secrets of Spiritual Maturity from the Desert Fathers and Mothers.* Chicago, Ill.: ACTA Publishers, 2014 [First edition: 1996]

Merton, Thomas. *Seeds of Contemplation.* Dell Publishing, 1949.

Mojtabai, A.G. *Blessed Assurance: At Home with the Bomb in Amarillo, Texas,* Houghton Mifflin Harcourt, 1986.

Shepherd, Gregory. *A Straight Road with 99 Curves: Coming of Age on the Path of Zen.* Berkeley, California: Stone Bridge Press, 2013.

Suzuki, Shunryu. *Zen Mind, Beginner's Mind: Informal Talks on Zen Meditation and Practice.* New York, Weatherhill, 1973.

Williams, Harley. *Don Quixote of the Microscope: An Interpretation of Santiago Ramón Y Cajal* (1852-1934) Published by Jonathan Cape, London, 1954.

Notes

Preface

[1] Chadwick, David. *Crooked Cucumber: The Life and Zen Teaching of Shunryu Suzuki*. New York: Broadway Books 1999.

[2] Aitken, Robert, D Steindl-Rast. *The Ground We Share: Everyday Practice, Buddhist and Christian*. Boston: Shambhala, New York: Distributed in the United States by Random House, 1996.

[3] E.G. When the Saints Go Marching In: Modern Day Zen Hagiography, Stuart Lachs. Published online March 2011.
https://terebess.hu/english/WhenTheSaintsGoMarching.pdf
Accessed August 2020.

[4] Gurus, Death, Drugs and Other Puzzles, Chapter 5 in *Waking Up*, Sam Harris, Published by Simon & Schuster, 2014.

[5] Williams, Harley, *Don Quixote of the Microscope: An Interpretation of Santiago Ramón Y Cajal (1852-1934)* Published by Jonathan Cape, London (1954) p.146.

Chapter 1 – Early Years

[6] Howard, Robert P, *Illinois: A History of the Prairie State*, Eerdman's, 1986, p 526

[7] "Sold American" was a song performed by Glenn Miller; reissued by Biltmore Records as 1108 (B22974-1) in the 1949-1951 period.

[8] Dates from Holy Family Church website accessed March 2017.

[9] Pat Hawk, The Pathless Path, *Catholic World*,129-131, May/June 1990.

Chapter 2 – Seminary Years

[10] *Catholic Encyclopedia* entry on Redemptorists.
https://en.wikisource.org/wiki/Page:Catholic_Encyclopedia,_volume_12.djvu/765 Accessed August 2020.

[11] Greg Wiest, Pat Hawk: Man of Influence, article in St. Joseph's College Edgerton student newsletter [*The Mirror?*] March 16, 1979.

[12] *The Mirror*, 1957-62.

[13] *Student Rule of St. Joseph's College, Edgerton*. [Note that the edition of the Student Rule I consulted, kindly provided in pdf form by the Redemptorist archivist Ashley Large, was reprinted in 1964, two years after Pat Hawk left minor seminary.]

[14] *The Mirror*, 1960-62.

[15] Pat Hawk interviews, 2007-2012.

[16] Conversation with Tom Schiltz, March 20, 2012.

[17] *The Mirror*, 1960-62.

[18] *The Mirror*, 1960-62.

[19] *Student Rule*, 13.

[20] *Student Rule*, 14. A virtue is assigned for each month.

[21] *Student Rule*, 10.

[22] *Student Rule*, 16.
[23] Pat Hawk interviews, 2007-2012.
[24] Pat Hawk interviews, 2007-2012.
[25] Pat Hawk interviews, 2007-2012.
[26] Pat Hawk interviews, 2007-2012.
[27] *Student Rule*, 20.
[28] Miscellaneous materials from Tom Schiltz, including St. Joseph's College playbills.
[29] *The Mirror*, 1957-62.
[30] *The Mirror*, 1957-62.
[31] *The Mirror*, 1957-62.
[32] *Student Rule*, 18.
[33] *Student Rule*, 22.
[34] Conversation with Greg Mayers, January 2010.
[35] *The Mirror*, 1957-62.
[36] *The Mirror*, 1957-62.
[37] Pat Hawk interviews, 2007-2012.
[38] *Student Rule*, 36.
[39] *Student Rule*, 37.
[40] *Student Rule*, 35.
[41] Pat Hawk interviews, 2007-2012.
[42] *The Mirror* 1957-58.
[43] *The Mirror* 1957-58.
[44] Pat Hawk interviews, 2007-2012.
[45] *The Mirror* 1959-60.
[46] *The Mirror* 1959-60.
[47] *The Mirror* 1959-60.
[48] *The Mirror* 1958-59.
[49] *The Mirror* 1958-59.
[50] *The Mirror* 1958-59.
[51] *The Mirror* 1960-61.
[52] *The Mirror* 1962.
[53] *The Mirror* 1962.
[54] *The Mirror* 1962.
[55] Conversations with Father Bob Halter and Tom Schiltz, 2012.
[56] Colin, Louis, CSsR, *The Practice of the Vows*. The Mercier Press, 1961, 41.
[57] Beattie, T, Scruples and Sainthood: Overcoming Scrupulosity with the help of the Saints, Loreto Publications, 2011.
[58] Colin, Louis, CSsR, *The Practice of the Vows*. The Mercier Press, 1961, 38.
[59] *The Rule of St. Benedict*, Chapter LVIII.
http://www.liturgialatina.org/benedictine/holyrule.htm Accessed July 2022.
[60] Assistant to the novice master.
[61] Colin, Louis, CSsR, *The Practice of the Vows*. The Mercier Press, 1961, 37.
[62] *Practice of the Vows*, 26.
[63] *Practice of the Vows*, 10.

[64] *Practice of the Vows*, 5.
[65] *Practice of the Vows*, 48.
[66] *Practice of the Vows,* 89.
[67] *Practice of the Vows*, 138.
[68] *Practice of the Vows*, 174.
[69] *Practice of the Vows*, 83.
[70] *Practice of the Vows*, 187.
[71] *Practice of the Vows*, 198.
[72] Conversation with Greg Mayers, CSsR, Easter 2013.
[73] Conversation with Greg Mayers, CSsR, February, 2010
[74] *Practice of the Vows*, 222.
[75] *Practice of the Vows*, 195.
[76] *Practice of the Vows*, 242.
[77] *Practice of the Vows*, 248.
[78] *Practice of the Vows*, 206.
[79] *Practice of the Vows*, 255.
[80] *Practice of the Vows*, 268.
[81] *Practice of the Vows,* 276; …and will possess eternal life.
[82] Pat Hawk interviews, 2007-2012.
[83] Conversation with Bob Walker, Nov 18, 2013.
[84] Patrick Hawk, May 26th, 1963. Hawk papers, Redemptorist Archive of the Denver Province (since 2018, housed with the Redemptorist's Baltimore Province Archive).
[85] Colin, Louis, CSsR, *The Practice of the Vows*. The Mercier Press, 1961, 50.
[86] Conversation with Bob Halter, April 2012.
[87] Conversation with Harry Grile, Feb 2013.
[88] O'Shea, Kevin, CSsR, Retrospect: The Past Fifty Years, a series of lectures on Vatican II given at Australian Catholic University, Sydney, Fall 2012. Written notes on which these talks were based kindly provided by Father Kevin O'Shea, October 2012.
[89] Encyclical of Pope Pius X on the Doctrines of the Modernists, 1907, http://www.vatican.va/content/pius-x/en/encyclicals/documents/hf_p-x_enc_19070908_pascendi-dominici-gregis.html
[90] Pomerleau, Wayne P., Immanuel Kant, *Encyclopedia of Philosophy: A Peer reviewed Academic Resource.* https://iep.utm.edu/kant-rel/ accessed August 2020.
[91] 1920, *Éléments de Philosophie I: Introduction générale à la philosophie*, Téqui. [*An Introduction to Philosophy*, E. I. Watkin (trans.), London: Sheed and Ward, 1944.]
1923, *Éléments de philosophie II: L'ordre des concepts*, I — Petite logique (Logique formelle). Téqui. [*An Introduction to Logic*, New York: Sheed and Ward, 1937a; Formal Logic, Imelda Choquette (trans.), New York: Sheed and Ward, 1937b.]
[92] O'Shea, Kevin, CSsR, Retrospect: The Past Fifty Years, October 2012.
[93] O'Shea, Kevin, CSsR, Retrospect: The Past Fifty Years, October 2012.
[94] Congar, Yves, *Mon Journal du Concile,* Les Éditions du Cerf, 2002. As quoted in O'Shea, Kevin, CSsR, Retrospect: The Past Fifty Years, October 2012.
[95] Conversation with Pat Hawk and Bob Halter, April 2012.
[96] Neuhaus, RJ. What Really Happened at Vatican II 2008.

https://www.firstthings.com/article/2008/10/what-really-happened-at-vatican-ii Accessed August 2020.

97 Cardinal George Pell, quoted in Neuhaus, RJ, What Really Happened at Vatican II. https://www.firstthings.com/article/2008/10/what-really-happened-at-vatican-ii Accessed August 2020.

98 Pat Hawk interviews, 2007-2012.

99 Pat Hawk, The Pathless Path, *Catholic World*,129-131, May/June 1990.

100 Colin, Louis, CSsR, *The Practice of the Vows.* The Mercier Press, 1961.

101 Déchanet, Jean, *Christian Yoga*, Harper and Brothers,1960. Originally published under the pseudonym, *Yogin du Christ, La Voie du Silence; L'expérience d'un Moine.* [Bruges] Desclée de Brouwer 1956.

102 Conversation with Bob Halter, Paul Coury and Pat Hawk, April 8, 2012.

103 Basilica and National Shrine of Mary Help of Christians at Holy Hill, Hubertus, Wisconsin

104 Pat Hawk interviews 2007-12.

105 Encyclicals of Vatican II.

106 O'Shea, Kevin, CSsR, Retrospect: The Past Fifty Years, a series of lectures on Vatican II given at Australian Catholic University, Sydney, Fall 2012; Written notes on which these talks were based kindly provided by Father Kevin O'Shea, October 2012.

107 Pat Hawk interviews 2007-12.

108 Pat Hawk interviews 2007-12.

109 Pat Hawk interviews 2007-12.

110 Conversation with George Rassley, April 2012.

111 *A Century of Blessings 1907-2007,* Mount St. Alphonsus, Esopus New York, Centennial Jubilee, 2007, 32.

112 *A Century of Blessings*, 26.

113 *A Century of Blessings*, 42.

114 Sanks, T. Howland, Education for ministry since Vatican II, *Theological Studies* 45: 1984.

115 Pat Hawk interviews 2007-12.

116 *Unitatis redintegratio* 3 *(Documents* 345-46); *Lumen gentium* 15 *(Documents* 33-34 as quoted in T. Howland Sanks, Education for ministry since Vatican II, *Theological Studies* 45: 1984.

117 Sanks, T. Howland, Education for ministry since Vatican II, *Theological Studies* 45: 1984.

118 Conversation with Harry Grile, CSsR, February 2013.

119 Busenbaum, Hermann, *Medulla Theologiae Moralis, Facili ac Perspicua Methodo Resolvens Casus Conscientiae*, France Huré, Sébastien 1657, translated into English by the Redemptorists.

120 Alphonsus of Liguori. *Guide for Confessors from the Praxis Confessarii of St. Alphonsus Liguori.* [Edited by R. Schiblin. Oconomowoc, Wisconsin. N.d.]

121 Alphonsus of Liguori. *Praxis Confessarii* (Transl) p.7.

122 Alphonsus of Liguori. *Praxis Confessarii* (Transl) p.123.

123 According to Pat Hawk, the arrangement was by Charles McKitrick (b.1913, d.1976), himself a Redemptorist.

124 Greg Wiest interview of Pat Hawk, St. Joseph's College, Edgerton, newsletter, March 1979 [from a photocopy of the article — full reference not available].

125 Conversation with Al Weinert, February 2013.

126 Conversation with Greg Wiest, circa December 2011.

[127] Patrick Hawk papers, Redemptorist Archive.
[128] Article by Greg Wiest in the student newspaper, St. Joseph's College, Edgerton, March 1979.
[129] Conversation with Pete Schavitz, April 2012.
[130] Conversation with Bob Halter, April 2012.
[131] February 10, 1978, Patrick Hawk papers, Redemptorist Archive.
[132] June 16, 1978, Patrick Hawk papers, Redemptorist Archive.

Chapter 3 – Zen and Contemplative Training

[133] Matt Dundas, *Founding a non-violent community at Bangor, Antiwar and Radical History Project*, University of Washington, 2008.
http://depts.washington.edu/antiwar/nukes_dundas1.shtml accessed August 2020.
[134] Conversation with Dan Mintie, 2012.
[135] Conversation with Dan Mintie, 2012.
[136] Robert Aitken, Willy Nilly Zen, In: *Taking the Path of Zen*, North Point Press, San Francisco, 1982.
[137] Blyth, Reginald Horace. *Zen Buddhism in English Literature and Oriental Classics*, Hokuseido Press, Tokyo, 1942.
[138] Robert Aitken, Remembering Blyth Sensei, In: *Blind Donkey* 8,1984. *Blind Donkey* was the title of the Honolulu Diamond Sangha newsletter (now called *Honolulu Diamond Sangha)*.
[139] The Sanbo Kyodan is a Zen organization founded in 1954 by the Zen monk, Haku'un Yasutani. It is a lay organization that includes elements of both Soto (Caodong) and Rinzai (Linji) Zen traditions. The name was changed to Sanbo Zen in 2014.
[140] Matt Dundas, Founding a non-violent community at Bangor, Antiwar and Radical History Project, University of Washington, 2008. https://depts.washington.edu/antiwar/nukes_dundas1.shtml accessed August 2020.
[141] Shelly Douglass quoted in Matt Dundas, Founding a non-violent community at Bangor.
http://depts.washington.edu/antiwar/nukes_dundas1.shtml accessed August 2020.
[142] Conversation with Greg Mayers, February 2010.
[143] Robert Aitken letter to Bernard McVeigh, June 13, 1978, papers kindly provided to the author by Mark Filut, OCSO (Order of Cistercians of the Strict Observance, aka the Trappists, founded in 1098 CE as a branch of the Benedictines).
[144] Alice Ray, June 13, 1978, papers provided by Mark Filut, OSCO.
[145] Angelus Silesius (1624-1677) German Catholic priest and physician, also a mystic poet.
[146] Hakuin Ekaku (1686-1769) aka Hakuin Zenji (Zenji is an honorific) highly influential Zen monk and teacher.
[147] Conversation with Dan Mintie, December 2012.
[148] Conversation with Dan Mintie, December 2012.
[149] There are numerous English translations of this koan collection with commentary, including: Robert Aitken, *The Gateless Barrier,* North Point Press, New York, 1990.
[150] Robert Aitken, October 1978, transcribed from cassette tape recording provided by Pat Hawk, a digitized version of which is in possession of the author.
[151] Conversation with Robert Aitken, April 2007.
[152] Conversation with Joan Saalfeld, SNJ, November 2012.
[153] The Pathless Path, E. Patrick Hawk, *Catholic World*, 129-131, May/June 1990.

[154] https://guesthouse.org/about-us/our-history/ accessed April 2022.

[155] Pat Hawk interviews 2007-12.

[156] Pat Hawk letter to Very Rev Edmund Langton, June 10, 1979; Redemptorist Archive.

[157] Letter of Very Reverend Edmund Langton to Very Reverend James Stratton, July 17, 1979; Redemptorist Archive.

[158] Langton letter to Jo Holladay, Guest House, July 17, 1979; Redemptorist Archive.

[159] Thomas Merton, OCSO (1915-1968): American Trappist monk whose personal explorations and writings helped bring contemplative and Zen practice into the Christian sphere.

[160] November 14, 1979.

[161] November 25, 1979.

[162] This letter of Pat's is undated but is clearly following Aitken's of November 1979.

[163] May 15, 1980.

[164] This postcard is dated May 5, 1980, however it seems evident from the context that it must fall between Pat's letters of May 15 and August 11, 1980. I've understood it in that sequence, guessing that Aitken mistook the date.

[165] Guigo II https://www.urban-monk.org/images/PDFS/Guigo%20II%20and%20the%20Development%20of%20Lectio%20Divina%20for%20Web%20Site%20Article.pdf [accessed July 2022].

[166] The letter is undated; a reply from Aitken refers to it as the letter of August 11th [1980].

[167] September 18, 1980, Hawk papers.

[168] Brigitte D'Ortschy (1921-1990) was the first authorized Zen Master outside of Japan in the Sanbo Kyodan lineage.

[169] Jäger letter to Aitken, February 15, 1980, Robert Baker Aitken Papers, University of Hawaii at Manoa.

[170] Pat Hawk interviews, 2007-2012.

[171] August 12, 1981 Hawk papers, Redemptorist Archive.

[172] Ordinary Provincial Council (of the St. Louis Province of Redemptorists).

[173] August 20, 1981 Hawk papers, Redemptorist Archive.

[174] September 7, 1981, Redemptorist Archive.

[175] September 29, 1981 Hawk papers, Redemptorist Archive.

[176] Pat Hawk interviews, 2007-2012.

[177] December 4, 1981 Hawk papers, Redemptorist Archive.

[178] Conversation with Shirley Morrissey FSPA December 2009.

[179] Undated Aitken letter to Willigis Jäger, Spring 1982, Robert Baker Aitken papers, University of Hawaii at Manoa.

[180] Undated Aitken letter to Willigis Jäger, Spring 1982, Aitken papers.

[181] Conversation with Robert Aitken April 2007.

[182] Willigis Jäger, as quoted in an undated newspaper article by Dan Mintie spring or early summer, 1982.

[183] "The sound of one hand" is the same koan Aitken had given Pat at the Palisades retreat in May 1980.

[184] October 1, 1983, Aitken papers.

[185] November 8, 1983, Aitken papers.

[186] Conversation with Greg Mayers, January 2010.

[187] Pat is referencing the *Constitutions and Statutes*, the Redemptorist Rule.

[188] Joseph Pfab, then Superior General of the Redemptorists.
[189] Early May 1984 (undated), Hawk papers, Redemptorist Archive.
[190] Early May 1984 (undated), Hawk papers, Redemptorist Archive.
[191] Early May 1984 (undated), Hawk papers, Redemptorist Archive.
[192] May 5, 1984 Hawk papers, Redemptorist Archive. *Liguorian* is a monthly Redemptorist magazine.
[193] Steve - surname not known.
[194] Henry Novak was then treasurer of the St. Louis Province of the Redemptorists.
[195] October 2, 1984 Hawk papers, Redemptorist Archive.
[196] Conversation with Joan Rieck, December 2012.
[197] And later authorized by Yamada Ko'un to teach Zen.
[198] Hawk interviews 2007-2012.
[199] Hawk interviews 2007-2012.
[200] Assistant to Willigis Jäger, 1980-84, later a teacher of contemplation.
[201] Hawk interviews 2007-2012.
[202] Conversation with Dan Mintie, December 2012.
[203] Drosten contribution to Hawk 65th birthday scrapbook, compiled by Helen Amerongen, November 2007; Redemptorist Archive.
[204] Surname unknown.
[205] December 7, 1984, Hawk papers, Redemptorist Archive.
[206] Drafts were not found among Pat Hawk's papers.
[207] Aitken, Robert. *The Mind of Clover: Essays in Zen Buddhist Ethics.* New York North Point Press, Farrar, Straus and Giroux, 2000.
[208] March 18, 1985, Robert Baker Aitken papers, University of Hawaii at Manoa.
[209] Pat Hawk, The Pathless Path, *Catholic World,* May/June 1990.
[210] Pat Hawk papers, Redemptorist Archive.
[211] Pat Hawk, The Pathless Path, *Catholic World,* May/June 1990.
[212] Conversation with Henry Novak, May 2012, at St. Clement, Liguori MO.
[213] Pat Hawk interviews 2007-2012.
[214] January 17, 1986, Robert Baker Aitken papers, University of Hawaii at Manoa.
[215] January 24, 1986, Aitken papers.
[216] Conversation with Greg Mayers, February 2010.
[217] Conversation with Greg Mayers, February 2010.
[218] Conversation with Greg Mayers, February 2010.
[219] In the Catholic Church, the chancery is the administrative office of a diocese.
[220] Mojtabai, A.G., *Blessed Assurance: At Home with the Bomb in Amarillo, Texas*, Houghton Mifflin Harcourt, 1986.
[221] *Blessed Assurance*, 79.
[222] *Blessed Assurance*, 146.
[223] Matthiesen, Leroy, T*he Life and Times of a Cottonpicking Texas Bishop*, Self-Published. Printed by Custom Printing Company, 2005.
[224] *National Catholic Reporter* March 26, 2010.
[225] Notes from Bob Walker, 2010.
[226] The carbon copy of this letter is dark at the top, obscuring the date. Aitken's reply refers to this letter and gives a date of March 30. Robert Baker Aitken papers, University of Hawaii at Manoa.

[227] Pat Hawk interviews 2007-2012.
[228] Conversation with Leonard Marcel, January 2013.
[229] Conversation with Leonard Marcel, January 2013.
[230] Conversation with Joan Saalfeld, SNJ, November 2012.
[231] Conversation with Dan Mintie, December 2012.
[232] Pat Hawk interviews 2007-2012.
[233] Pat Hawk photo album, Redemptorist Archive.
[234] Robert Aitken letter to Pat Hawk, April 29, 1987, Robert Baker Aitken papers, University of Hawaii at Manoa.
[235] Pat Hawk interviews 2007-2012.
[236] Pat Hawk papers, Redemptorist Archive.
[237] Pat Hawk interviews 2007-2012.
[238] [Undated] Robert Baker Aitken papers, University of Hawaii at Manoa.
[239] May 13, 1988, Robert Baker Aitken papers.
[240] From Mark Filut, OCSO materials provided to the author, page 23.
[241] Conversation with Stephen Daney, December 2013.
[242] Conversation with Stephen Daney, December 2013.
[243] Conversation with Barbara Wooten, August 2012.
[244] Conversation with Glenna Pittock, February 2011
[245] Robert Curry, CSsR, August 9, 1988, Pat Hawk papers.
[246] Pat Hawk papers.
[247] Thanks to Nelson Foster for pointing this out; email May 2012.
[248] From the Flower Sermon, as quoted in *Buddha World*: http://www.tamqui.com/buddhaworld/Flower_Sermon Accessed July 2022.
[249] Aitken, Robert. *Original Dwelling Place: Zen Buddhist Essays*. Washington, D.C.: Counterpoint Press, 1996.
[250] Foster, Nelson, Bloodline, quoted in *Pathless Path* July-August 2001.
[251] Robert Aitken letter to Augusto Alcalde, Nelson Foster, Pat Hawk and John Tarrant, October 22, 1988, Robert Baker Aitken papers, University of Hawaii at Manoa.
[252] Robert Aitken letter to Pat Hawk, March 8, 1989, Robert Baker Aitken papers, University of Hawaii at Manoa.
[253] Robert Aitken, *Pacific World* New Series 4, 1988
[254] Pat Hawk letter to Robert Aitken, April 25, 1989, Aitken papers.
[255] Pat Hawk interviews 2007-2012
[256] Pat is quoting the verse from *Mumonkan* Case 35. In: Robert Aitken, *The Gateless Barrier,* North Point Press, New York, 1990.
[257] From *Blind Donkey*, Summer 1989.
[258] Seisho (Western Bell) is Pat's dharma name. Shin-un Ken (House of the Spreading Cloud) is Pat's teaching name. Both names were bestowed by Aitken at the time of Pat's *Jukai.*
[259] Transcribed from cassette tape recording provided by Pat Hawk, a digitized version of which is in possession of the author.
[260] Pat Hawk interviews 2007-2012.
[261] Pat Hawk interviews 2007-2012.
[262] May 31, 1989, Pat Hawk papers.

[263] Pat Hawk, The Pathless Path, *Catholic World*, 129-131, May/June 1990.

Chapter 4 – Early Years Post-transmission

[264] *Southern Accent* October 1989.

[265] Green Gulch Farm, a Zen practice center associated with San Francisco Zen Center, founded by Shunryu Suzuki.

[266] August 15, 1989, Robert Baker Aitken papers, University of Hawaii at Manoa.

[267] Conversation with Greg Mayers, January 2010.

[268] *Southern Accent* October 1989.

[269] *Southern Accent* October 1989.

[270] Yamada Ko'un died September 13, 1989.

[271] September 26, 1989 Hawk papers, Redemptorist Archive.

[272] Conversation with Bob Wallin, November, 2010

[273] Aitken, Robert. *Taking the Path of Zen.* New York, NY: North Point Press: Farrar, Straus and Giroux, 2000, 1982.

[274] Thomas Harter, The History of the Sangha, *Zen Desert Sangha* Summer 10th Anniversary Edition, 1992.

[275] Benedictine Sisters of Perpetual Adoration, a Catholic contemplative monastic community, located in Tucson, Arizona until 2019.

[276] *Zen Desert Sangha*, November December 1989.

[277] December 23, 1989, Robert Baker Aitken papers, University of Hawaii at Manoa.

[278] August 1984 - August 1985.

[279] Kubota Akira Ji'un-Ken: Akira is Kubota's given name, written by Japanese convention following the surname; Ji'un-Ken is the 'Cloud' name given at the time of Kubota's dharma transmission and full authorization as a Zen master in 1983.

[280] October 22, 1988, Robert Baker Aitken papers, University of Hawaii at Manoa.

[281] Hakuun Yasutani (1885-1973), founder of the Sanbo Kyodan Zen sect. Yasutani taught Yamada Ko'un, Kubota Akira and Robert Aitken. He gave dharma transmission to Yamada Ko'un and Kubota Akira.

[282] April 4, 1988, Robert Baker Aitken papers, University of Hawaii at Manoa.

[283] April 4, 1988, Robert Baker Aitken papers, University of Hawaii at Manoa.

[284] July 12, 1989, Aitken papers.

[285] San'un Zendo in Kamakura, Japan, built adjacent to the home of Yamada Ko'un and his wife, Dr. Kazue Yamada, is the dharma home of the Sanbo Kyodan Zen lineage.

[286] July 25, 1989, Robert Baker Aitken papers, University of Hawaii at Manoa.

[287] August 7, 1989, Aitken papers.

[288] In the Sanbo Kyodan lineage this refers to "Semi Zen Master" – a senior teacher one step below Shoshike, "Authentic Zen Master."

[289] September 22, 1989, Aitken papers.

[290] October 30, 1989, Aitken papers.

[291] October 31, 1989, Aitken papers.

[292] November 20, 1989, Aitken papers.

[293] December 13, 1989, Aitken papers.

[294] December 13, 1989, Aitken papers.

[295] January 9, 1990, Aitken papers.

[296] November 1989 [letter from Aitken to Jäger of October 18, 1989, says that the Diamond Sangha teachers will be meeting "next month."

[297] December 23, 1989, Aitken papers.

[298] The account of the Easter 1990 meeting of the European Sanbo Kyodan teachers is based on Pat Hawk's notes, in: Pat Hawk papers.

[299] Pat Hawk papers.

[300] May 23, 1990, Aitken papers.

[301] From Pat Hawk notes written during this and subsequent meetings, Pat Hawk papers.

[302] September 9, 1990, Aitken papers.

[303] Pat Hawk papers.

[304] Gresser, Julian. *Mastering Negotiations with the Japanese*, Palo Alto, California,1990. https://alliancesfordiscovery.org/guide/laughing-heart/julian-gresser-cv/

[305] Pat Hawk papers.

[306] Pat Hawk papers.

[307] Pat Hawk papers.

[308] Pat Hawk papers.

[309] From Pat Hawk notes following conference call November 13, 1990 with Pat Hawk, Robert Aitken, Julian Gresser and Jim Camp; there is a handwritten draft of these points and a more polished, typed version which is quoted here. Hawk papers.

[310] Gresser, Julian. Who will control your Japanese negotiations: you or your adversaries. New York, NY.: Practising Law Institute, 1992.

[311] Conversation with Bob Walker circa 2013.

[312] May 15, 1990, sent by Kubota to Jäger who then sent it to Robert Aitken, Robert Baker Aitken papers, University of Hawaii at Manoa.

[313] December 25, 1990, Aitken papers.

[314] April 19, 1991, Aitken papers.

[315] Undated postcard, Pat Hawk papers.

[316] April 26, 1991, Pat Hawk papers.

[317] Summarized based on Pat Hawk notes taken at the time, Hawk papers.

[318] Besserman, Perle; Steger, Manfred. *Crazy Clouds: Zen Radicals, Rebels, and Reformers*. Boston, Mass.: Shambhala Publications, 1991.

[319] Besserman, Perle. *A New Zen for Women*. New York: Palgrave Macmillan, 2007.

[320] April 22, 1991, Robert Baker Aitken papers, University of Hawaii at Manoa.

[321] May 18, 1991, Aitken papers.

[322] May 18, 1991, Aitken papers.

[323] May 23, 1991, Aitken papers.

[324] August 22, 1991, Aitken papers.

[325] August 22, 1991, Aitken papers.

[326] January 27, 1992, Aitken papers.

[327] February 2, 1992, Aitken papers.

[328] February 15, 1992, Aitken papers.

[329] February 15, 1992, Aitken papers.

[330] March 7, 1992, Aitken papers.

[331] March 18, 1992, Aitken papers.

Chapter 5 – Branching Out

[332] Conversation with Leonard Marcel, January 2013.

[333] Brief history of Seven Thunders, compiled by Jane Huyer, August 2000, with occasional subsequent corrections.

[334] Emma Stone interview of Lesley Hanks, November 2012.

[335] Brennan, Lucie. History of Mountain Cloud Zen Center, October, 1997.

[336] Aitken, Robert. *The Mind of Clover Essays in Zen Buddhist Ethics.* New York North Point Press, Farrar, Straus and Giroux, 2000.

[337] Conversation with Greg Mello, December 2012.

[338] Conversation with Paul Hughes, February 2013.

[339] Conversation with Mary Burton Riseley, February 2012.

[340] Conversation with Mary Burton Riseley, February 2012.

[341] Daisetsu Teitaro Suzuki (1870-1966), Japanese author on Buddhism whose books provided an introduction to many Western students.

[342] Conversation with Pancho Burke, December 2012.

[343] Conversation with Pancho Burke, December 2012.

[344] BDRC *Journal* Fall 1991.

[345] Conversation with Barbara Wooten, August 2012.

[346] December 19, 1992, Robert Baker Aitken papers, University of Hawaii at Manoa.

[347] Conversation with Paul Hughes, February 2013.

[348] Thomas Merton, On Sharing the Fruits of Contemplation, in: Merton, Thomas. *Seeds of Contemplation.* Dell Publishing, 1949.

[349] Conversation with Tracy McCallum, February 2012.

[350] Conversation with Richard Laue, December, 2011.

[351] Conversation with Tracy McCallum, February 2012. This particular instance happened at Mountain Cloud Zen Center.

[352] Conversation with Kristen Larson, January 2010.

[353] Recording of Pat Hawk class, Bishop DeFalco Retreat Center circa 1991, Pat Hawk cassette tape collection.

[354] This and other excerpts from Pat Hawk classes were transcribed by the author from cassette tapes provided by Pat Hawk.

[355] *Kahawai.* Diamond Sangha. [Honolulu, Hawaii] 1979-.

[356] Recording of Pat Hawk class, Bishop DeFalco Retreat Center circa 1991, Pat Hawk cassette tape collection.

[357] Hawk, Patrick. Authority (1): The Role of the Teacher in Buddhist/Christian Formation. *Studies in Formative Spirituality* 14 (1993): 23-9.

[358] *Studies in Formative Spirituality* 14 (1993): 23-9.

[359] Hawk, Patrick, The Pathless Path, *Catholic World*,129-131, May/June 1990.

[360] March 17, 1992, Robert Baker Aitken papers, University of Hawaii at Manoa.

[361] Mayers, Gregory, *Listen to the Desert: Secrets of Spiritual Maturity from the Desert Fathers and Mothers.* Chicago, Ill.: ACTA Publishers, 2014 [First edition: 1996].

[362] Aitken, Robert. *The Gateless Barrier: The Wu-men Kuan (Mumonkan)*. San Francisco: North Point Press, 1990.

[363] Pat Hawk interviews 2007-2012.

[364] April 2, 1992, Robert Baker Aitken papers, University of Hawaii at Manoa.

[365] Pat Hawk notes from Diamond Sangha Teachers' Circle meeting, 1992, Hawk papers.

[366] John Tarrant letter to Diamond Sangha teachers, November 1, 1992, Pat Hawk papers.

[367] Aitken, Robert. *The Practice of Perfection: The Pāramitās from a Zen Buddhist Perspective*. New York: Pantheon Books, 1994.

[368] October 9, 1992, Robert Baker Aitken papers, University of Hawaii at Manoa.

[369] October 9, 1992, Aitken papers.

[370] October 8, 9 and 12, 1992, Hawk papers. Redemptorist Archive.

[371] Lincoln, Victoria. *Teresa, a Woman: A Biography of Teresa of Avila*. SUNY Press, 1985.

[372] October 8, 9 and 12, 1992, Hawk papers.

[373] Dated October 15, 1992, Robert Baker Aitken papers, University of Hawaii at Manoa.

[374] Miscellaneous Koans: an unpublished collection.

Chapter 6 – Further Adventures

[375] *Hekiganroku* (Chinese: *Pi-yen lu*; English: *The Blue Cliff Record*) is a collection of 100 Ch'an Buddhist koans initially compiled then expanded and annotated in 12th century Song Dynasty China. The collection is part of the Sanbo Kyodan koan curriculum.

[376] *Shoyoroku* (Chinese: *Congrong lu;* English: *The Book of Equanimity* or *Book of Serenity)* is a collection of 100 koans written by Ch'an Buddhist master Hongzhi Zhengjue, published with added commentary in the 13th century. This collection follows the *Hekiganroku* in the Sanbo Kyodan koan curriculum.

[377] June 19, 1992, Robert Baker Aitken papers, University of Hawaii at Manoa.

[378] Lawder contribution to Hawk 65th birthday scrapbook, compiled by Helen Amerongen, November 2007; Redemptorist Archives.

[379] Now Yamada Ryoun Roshi since being given dharma transmission by Kubota Akira in August 1991. Son of Yamada Ko'un.

[380] From Cleary JC and T Cleary. *The Blue Cliff Record*. Shambala Publications, 2005. An English translation of the Ch'an koan collection *Pi-yen lu* (Chinese) or *Hekiganroku* (Japanese).

[381] Pat Hawk interviews, 2007-2012.

[382] Letter from AMA Samy to Akira Kubota and Masamichi Yamada, November 27, 1992; copy sent to Willigis Jäger who then sent it to Pat Hawk who sent it to Robert Aitken.

[383] Letter from AMA Samy to Akira Kubota and Masamichi Yamada, November 27, 1992.

[384] December 11, 1992, Robert Baker Aitken papers, University of Hawaii at Manoa.

[385] December 11, 1992, Aitken papers.

[386] December 19, 1992, Aitken papers.

[387] December 19, 1992, Aitken papers.

[388] January 4, 1993, Aitken papers.

[389] January 4, 1993, Aitken papers.

[390] January 4, 1993, Aitken papers.

[391] January 4, 1993, Aitken papers.

[392] January 4, 1993, Aitken papers.

[393] January 25, 1993, Aitken papers.
[394] Shepherd, Gregory. *A Straight Road with 99 Curves: Coming of Age on the Path of Zen.* Berkeley, California: Stone Bridge Press, 2013.
[395] March 17, 1992, Aitken papers.
[396] Early January 1994 [*sic*], Pat Hawk papers.
[397] March 23, 1993, Pat Hawk papers.
[398] April 5, 1993, Aitken papers.
[399] April 5, 1993, Aitken papers.
[400] March 27, 1993, Aitken papers.
[401] June 14, 1993, Aitken papers.
[402] June 14, 1993, Aitken papers.
[403] November 9, 1992, Pat Hawk papers.
[404] November 30, 1992, Pat Hawk papers.
[405] November 30, 1992, Pat Hawk papers.
[406] Nyogen Senzaki (1876-1958).
[407] Hakuun Yasutani (1885-1973).
[408] Soen Nakagawa (1907-1984).
[409] December 11, 1992, Aitken papers.
[410] December 11, 1992, Aitken papers.
[411] December 19, 1992, Aitken papers.
[412] Aitken, Robert, D Steindl-Rast. *The Ground We Share: Everyday Practice, Buddhist and Christian.* Boston: Shambhala, New York: Distributed in the United States by Random House, 1996.
[413] December 19, 1992, Aitken papers.
[414] Joe Bobrow letter to Diamond Sangha teachers, December 18, 1992, Pat Hawk papers.
[415] Robert Aitken, Pat Hawk, Nelson Foster, Augusto Alcalde, Subhana Barzhagi, Geoff Dawson, Jack Duffy, Rolf Drosten. Pat Hawk papers.
[416] The following account of events at the meeting is based on minutes taken by Pat Hawk. Pat Hawk papers.
[417] Case 55 of the *Hekiganroku* is based on the story of a monk who, attending a funeral with his teacher, knocks on the casket and asks, "Alive or dead?" Both the talk on Curiosity and the teisho were recorded on cassette tape.
[418] Pat Hawk papers.
[419] Anderson, J and Schwartz, Steven Z, *Zen Odyssey: The Story of Sokei-an, Ruth Fuller Sasaki, and the Birth of Zen in America.* Wisdom Publications, Somerville, Massachusetts, 2018.
[420] Aitken letter to Diamond Sangha teachers, March 27, 1993 Pat Hawk papers.
[421] Undated letter from Augusto Alcalde to Pat Hawk, circa summer of 1993, Pat Hawk papers.
[422] March 16, 1994, Pat Hawk papers.
[423] Diamond Sangha teacher's meeting, June 1994, Pat Hawk papers.
[424] Aitken itinerary sent to various, May 1994, Robert Baker Aitken papers, University of Hawaii at Manoa.
[425] Conversation with Indiana Nelson, August 2011.
[426] Conversation with Indiana Nelson, August 2011.
[427] In February 1993.
[428] *Zen Desert Sangha*, Spring 94.

[429] Conversation with Richard Laue February 20, 2012.
[430] *Zen Desert Sangha*, Spring 1994 — Casey is reporting after the second sesshin at Indiana's, which took place in December 1993.
[431] *Zen Desert Sangha* Winter 1994.
[432] Conversation with Indiana Nelson, August 2011.
[433] October 1994.
[434] Conversation with Bob Wallin, November 29, 2010.
[435] Conversation with Indiana Nelson, August 2011.
[436] Conversation with Richard Laue, December 2011.
[437] Fall 1993, pp 38-39; undated photocopy from Pat's notes.
[438] Mumon-Kai letter: "We have informed 500 Zen centers" in 17 countries. January 1, 1994 Pat Hawk papers.
[439] Mumon-Kai letter, January 1, 1994.
[440] Mumon-Kai letter, January 1, 1994.
[441] Pat Hawk papers.
[442] November 21, 1994, Pat Hawk papers.
[443] March 15, 1995, Pat Hawk papers.
[444] March 15, 1995, Pat Hawk papers.
[445] April 24, 1995, Pat Hawk papers.
[446] Conversation with Aitken, April 2007.
[447] Pat Hawk papers.
[448] Pat Hawk papers.
[449] Pat Hawk interviews 2007-2012.
[450] Conversation with Paul Hughes, February 2013.
[451] Conversation with Tina Patrick, April 2012.
[452] Pat Hawk interviews 2007-2012.

Chapter 7 – Latter years at Amarillo

[453] Batchelor, Stephen. *The Awakening of the West: The Encounter of Buddhism and Western Culture: 542 BCE - 1992*. San Francisco: Thorsons, 1995.
[454] October 14, 1996, Robert Baker Aitken papers, University of Hawaii at Manoa.
[455] October 15, 1996, Aitken papers.
[456] October 15, 1996, Aitken papers.
[457] *Cicada* January February 1997.
[458] Aitken's letter is missing. Based on Pat's reply, the date of Aitken's letter is October 22, 1996. Hawk papers.
[459] November 6, 1996, email, Aitken papers. Pat is referring to the ceremony for appointing an apprentice teacher.
[460] Conversation with Leonard Marcel, January 2013.
[461] Conversation with Leonard Marcel, January 2013.
[462] Conversation with Robert Aitken, April 2007.
[463] Conversation with Kristen Larson, January 2010.
[464] Conversation with Tracy McCallum, spring 2022.
[465] Foster, Nelson and Jack Shoemaker. *The Roaring Stream: A New Zen Reader*, Ecco Press, 1996.

[466] Pat Hawk, *Empty Sky/Contemplative Path,* January 1997.
[467] Conversation with Leonard Marcel, January 13, 2013.
[468] March 13, 1997, in *Seven Thunders Newsletter*, April 1997.
[469] May 14, 1997; in *Empty Sky/Contemplative Path* newsletter, June 1997, reprinted in the *Seven Thunders Newsletter.*
[470] Conversation with Richard Laue, December 2011.
[471] Conversation with Alice Ray, January 2010.
[472] April 1997 letter from Indiana Nelson to Zen Desert Sangha. Among loose papers provided to the author by Pamela King.
[473] Conversation with Indiana Nelson, August 2011.
[474] Conversation with Indiana Nelson, August 2011.
[475] *Zen Desert Sangha* March 1997.
[476] Unattributed; *Zen Desert Sangha* February 1997.
[477] *Cicada* March April 1997 Vol II No II.
[478] *Cicada* March April 1997 Vol II No II.
[479] *Cicada* May June 1997 Vol II No III.
[480] *Cicada* May June 2002 Vol VIII No III.
[481] Suzuki, Shunryu, *Zen Mind, Beginner's Mind: Informal Talks on Zen Meditation and Practice.* New York, Weatherhill, 1973.
[482] Conversation with Barbara Wooten, August 2012
[483] June 3, 1997, at Our Lady of Guadalupe Abbey Lafayette, Oregon.
[484] Pamela Schaeffer, Tale of Two Bishops *National Catholic Reporter*, April 2, 1999 http://www.natcath.org/NCR_Online/archives2/1999b/040299/040299d.htm
[485] June 25, 1998, Robert Baker Aitken papers, University of Hawaii at Manoa.
[486] Conversation with Tracy McCallum, February 2012.
[487] Conversation with Tracy McCallum, February 2012.
[488] *Seven Thunders Newsletter*, July 1998.
[489] *Seven Thunders Newsletter*, April 1998.
[490] Tracy McCallum, *Pathless Path* November December 1998.
[491] *Cicada*, September October 1998.
[492] *Cicada* November December 1998.
[493] Barbara Wooten, *Journal*, Summer 1998.
[494] Conversation with Barbara Wooten, August 2012.
[495] Abba Zeno (died 451 CE), one of the early Christian Desert Fathers.
[496] *Empty Sky* July 98.
[497] *Empty Sky* July 98.
[498] *Empty Sky* July 98.
[499] *Empty Sky* July 98.
[500] *Empty Sky* July 98.
[501] *Empty Sky* July 98.
[502] *Empty Sky* July 98.

Chapter 8 – Home Base Tucson

[503] Zen Desert Sangha, September 1998.

504 Conversation with Richard Laue, February 2012.

505 Zen Desert Sangha, September 1998.

506 Letter signed by Matthew Stevens, Joan Sutherland, John Tarrant, Daniel Terragno, David Weinstein, December 14, 1998. Pat Hawk papers.

507 Email, April 23, 1999, Pat Hawk papers.

508 Email, April 30, 1999, Pat Hawk papers.

509 110 in 1999, including zazenkais, sesshins and contemplative retreats, based on *Pathless Path* newsletters.

510 May 1999, at the end of sesshin at McKenzie Bridge, Oregon.

511 Sydney Zen Centre Newsletter, February-March 2000.

512 Seven Thunders Newsletter, March 1999.

513 Modified from Jane Huyer, *Pathless Path,* January-February 1999.

514 Jane Huyer, *Pathless Path*, March 1999.

515 Ramon Melcon *Cicada*, May June 1999.

516 Conversation with Sandy Anderson, March 2016.

517 Tracy McCallum, *Cicada,* November-December 1999.

518 Tracy McCallum, *Cicada,* November-December 1999.

519 Tracy McCallum, *Cicada,* November-December 1999.

520 Glenna Pittock, *Seven Thunders Newsletter* March 1999.

521 Susan Weimer, *Pathless Path*, June-July 1999.

522 Conversation with Susan Weimer, May 2015.

523 Conversation with Susan Weimer, May 2015.

524 Conversation with Susan Weimer, May 2015.

525 As of 2013, part of Nestucca Bay National Wildlife Refuge.

526 Kristen Larson entry Hawk 65th birthday scrapbook, compiled by Helen Amerongen, November 2007; Redemptorist Archive.

527 Kristen Larson entry Hawk 65th birthday scrapbook.

528 Notes from Bob Walker, 2012.

529 Notes from Bob Walker, 2012.

530 Seven Thunders Newsletter, Fall, 2001.

531 November 7, 2002; Pat Hawk papers.

532 November 19, 2002; Pat Hawk papers.

533 Conversation with Bob Walker, November 2014.

534 December 15, 2003, Pat Hawk papers.

535 From *The Heart Sutra*: "Form is exactly emptiness, emptiness exactly form."

536 *Arizona Daily Star*, Rise from the Ashes, October 7, 2005.

537 Susan Weimer, email to Pathless Path list, December 2004.

538 Susan Weimer, email to Pathless Path list, December 2004.

539 Conversation with Pat Hawk, July 2005.

540 Pat Hawk email to author, October 7, 2005.

541 *Arizona Daily Star*, Rise from the Ashes, October 7, 2005.

542 Susan Weimer, email to Pathless Path list, January 10, 2006.

543 Pat Hawk, *Pathless Path*, Spring 2005.

Chapter 9 – Recollecting, Handing Over

[544] Chadwick, David. Crooked Cucumber: The Life and Zen Teaching of Shunryu Suzuki. New York: Broadway Books 1999.

[545] Neale Povey email, December 20, 2006.

[546] Conversation with Robert Aitken, April 2007.

[547] Pat Hawk interviews, 2007-2012.

[548] Pat Hawk interviews 2007-2012.

[549] Bob Walker, November 2014.

[550] Later relocated to the waterfront, renamed Smuggler's Landing.

[551] Pat Hawk interviews 2007-2012.

[552] March 14, 2009.

[553] Kristen Larson email, March 13, 2009.

[554] Conversation with Danan Henry, February 2013.

[555] Conversation with Danan Henry, February 2013.

[556] Aitken email to Diamond Sangha teachers, May 2005, Pat Hawk papers.

[557] Conversation with Danan Henry, February 2013.

[558] Transcribed from a recording by the author.

[559] Hawk 65th birthday scrapbook, compiled by Helen Amerongen, November 2007; Redemptorist Archives; a smaller printed version was produced for the Hawk family from an electronic copy.

[560] Emails to the author, August 2009.

[561] Conversation with Bob Wallin, January 9, 2010.

[562] Susan Weimer, handwritten note, January 8, 2010, Pat Hawk papers.

[563] Carey, Benedict. Expert on Mental Illness Reveals Her Own Fight. The New York Times, June 23, 2011.

[564] Conversation with Marsha Linehan, December 2009.

[565] Hall, Karyn. Three blocks to radical acceptance, *Psychology Today* 2013 https://www.psychologytoday.com/us/blog/pieces-mind/201312/three-blocks-radical-acceptance

[566] Foundress and Abbot of Shasta Abbey, California.

[567] Kennett, Jiku. Selling Water by the River: A Manual of Zen Training, Vintage Books, 1972.

[568] Conversation with Marsha Linehan, December 2009.

[569] In October 1983; conversation with Marsha Linehan, December 2009.

[570] Conversation with Marsha Linehan, December 2009.

[571] Conversation with Marsha Linehan, December 2009.

[572] Conversation with Marsha Linehan, December 2009.

[573] Conversation with Marsha Linehan, December 2009.

[574] Conversation with Marsha Linehan, April 2012.

[575] December 11, 1992, Robert Baker Aitken papers, University of Hawaii at Manoa.

[576] Pat Hawk interviews 2007-2012.

[577] Case 55, *Hekiganroku* (*The Blue Cliff Record*). There are many translations available.

[578] Aitken, Robert. Zen Master Raven: Sayings and Doings of a Wise Bird. Boston: Tuttle Pub., 2002.

[579] Pat Hawk sesshin teisho, August 6, 2010.

[580] Kapleau, Philip. Three Pillars of Zen: Teaching, Practice and Enlightenment, Harper and Row, 1966.

[581] The *Shobogenzo* is a collection of works written in the 13th century by Eihei Dogen Zenji, founder of the Japanese Soto Zen school.

[582] Conversation with Dan Dorsey, October 2010.

[583] Conversation with Dan Dorsey, October 2010.

[584] Pat Hawk interviews 2007-2012.

[585] Colin, Louis, CSsR, *The Practice of the Vows.* The Mercier Press, 1961.

[586] Goodstein, Laurie. Dolan Chosen as President of U.S. Bishops' Group. *The New York Times*, November 16, 2010. https://www.nytimes.com/2010/11/17/us/17bishops.html?smid=url-share Accessed April 2022.

[587] Conversation with Pancho Burke, December 2012.

[588] December 11, 1992, Robert Baker Aitken papers, University of Hawaii at Manoa.

[589] Aitken, Robert. *Original Dwelling Place: Zen Buddhist Essays.* Washington, D.C.: Counterpoint Press, 1996.

[590] Conversation with Rolf Drosten, June 2016.

Chapter 10 – Winding Down

[591] Email, November 18, 2011.

[592] Email to Zen Desert Sangha Board of Directors president, Evan Long Casler, forwarded to the ZDS e-tree, January 19, 2012.

[593] Conversation with Pat Hawk, January 2012.

[594] Conversation with Dan Dorsey, January 2012.

[595] Conversation with Shirley Morrissey, FSPA, February 2012.

[596] Conversations with Bob Wallin, Marsha Linehan, February 2012; conversation with Path Hawk, March 2012.

[597] Conversation with Paul Coury, March 2012.

[598] Kristen Larson had made her own rakusu, of purple silk years earlier and Pat had presented it to her inscribed with the name Purple Cloud at the time of her appointment as apprentice teacher in 2009.

Index

C

D

E

F

G

H

I

J

K

L

S

T

U

V

Printed in Great Britain
by Amazon

41998479R00270